PERSPECTIVES ON SELF-DECEPTION

TOPICS IN PHILOSOPHY

PERSPECTIVES ON SELF-DECEPTION

Edited by
BRIAN P. McLAUGHLIN
AND
AMÉLIE OKSENBERG RORTY

UNIVERSITY OF CALIFORNIA PRESS
Berkeley   Los Angeles   London

University of California Press
Berkeley and Los Angeles, California

University of California Press, Ltd.
London, England

Copyright © 1988 by The Regents of the University of California

Library of Congress Cataloging-in-Publication Data

Perspectives on self-deception / edited by Brian P. McLaughlin and
   Amélie Oksenberg Rorty.
      p.   cm.—(Topics in philosophy: 6)
   Bibliography: p.
   1. Self-deception.   I. McLaughlin, Brian P.   II. Rorty, Amélie.
III. Series
BD439.P47   1988   128'.3—dc19   87–27471
ISBN 0-520-05208-0 (alk. paper)
ISBN 0-520-06123-3 (pbk: alk. paper)

Printed in the United States of America

1 2 3 4 5 6 7 8 9

CONTENTS

Part IV
THE SOCIAL DIMENSION OF SELF-DECEPTION

Part V
THE MORAL DIMENSION OF SELF-DECEPTION

Part VI
SELF-DECEPTION IN LITERATURE

INTRODUCTION

BRIAN P. MCLAUGHLIN AND AMÉLIE OKSENBERG RORTY

Are we ever self-deceived? If so, how and why do we become so? For once, philosophical questions capture the force of the concerns that beset us in our reflective moments. But there is more controversy than consensus on the philosophical issues that surround self-deception. Indeed there is no agreement on whether there *are* bona fide cases of self-deception; nor is there a received view concerning the necessary and sufficient conditions for self-deception or its relation to rationalization, to wishful thinking, or to other self-manipulative psychological strategies. The debates about self-deception—including the bad jokes about whether those who deny self-deception are more self-deceived than those who affirm its possibility—appear to take place "on a darkling plain, swept with confused alarms of struggle and flight where ignorant armies clash by night." But there are good reasons for this confusion: explaining, or explaining away, the phenomena of self-deception raises many of the central problems in the philosophy of mind.

We have used self-deception as a microcosmic case study that bears on a range of issues dividing contemporary philosophical psychology. The discussion of the issues surrounding self-deception gives us a red-dye tracer for tracking what is at stake in a variety of debates central to the philosophy of mind. Disagreements about the existence and analysis of self-deception express disagreements about the unity of consciousness, homuncularism in psychological explanation, the criteria for the attribution of belief, the conditions for intentionality and rationality, the primacy of cognition in psychological processes, the viability of functionalist and computational accounts of psychological states and processes, the relation between motivational and epistemic attitudes, the social formation and malformation of belief and self-deception, and moral constraints on responsible belief.

The broad concerns of the volume's six parts and the topics of the papers included in each are summarized below.

PART I. THE ANALYSIS OF SELF-DECEPTION

What are the conditions for self-deception? What kind of self is capable of self-deception? What psychological and intellectual processes are engaged in deceiving oneself? These issues and others concerning the analysis of self-deception are addressed by the papers in this part.

1. Amélie Oksenberg Rorty, "The Deceptive Self: Liars, Layers, and Lairs." Rorty asks, "What must a person be like, to be capable of self-deception?" She examines two models of persons, the unified panoptical model of a rational scanner with access to all its operations, and the model of a set of relatively independent, loosely integrated subsystems. Self-deception is incoherent according to the first model, which is required to explain the possibility of rational, critical evaluation of knowledge and action; it is reclassified as a failure of integration on the second model, which best explains a wide range of psychological and physical processes. The phenomena of self-deception arise from the superimposition of the two models: only those who interpret the relatively independent activity of their sub-systems in the light of the unified panoptical model recognize the possibility of self-deception. Rorty defends such a superimposition, arguing that self-deception is a tangential by-product of otherwise adaptive and functional cognitive and psychological processes.

2. Brian P. McLaughlin, "Exploring the Possibility of Self-Deception in Belief." McLaughlin pursues the question of how self-deception is possible in order to explore a variety of related ways in which desire can influence belief by biasing thought. He compares and contrasts self-deception with wishful thinking and with self-induced deception, which involves intentionally deceiving oneself. He then explains how it is possible simultaneously to hold contradictory beliefs, and he employs this explanation to show how a certain prima facie problematic kind of self-deception in belief is causally possible.

3. Mark Johnston, "Self-Deception and the Nature of Mind." Having raised a host of difficulties for the view that in self-deception a subsystem of the self-deceiver intentionally deceives the main system, Johnston proposes an alternative account that does not require that self-deception involve intentional deception. Self-deception is, he maintains, a species of wishful thinking, motivated belief in the face of contrary evidence. He develops the notion of a "mental tropism"—a purpose-serving but nonintentional mental mechanism—to argue that typical cases of wishful thinking and self-deception involve subintentional rather than intentional deflection of belief by desire. Arguing more generally that the interpretative view of the mind mistakenly overrationalizes mental processes, he claims that "mental tropisms are not peripheral pathologies but are the causal bases of rational and irrational connections alike."

4. Robert Audi, "Self-Deception, Rationalization, and Reasons for Acting." Audi proposes an analysis of self-deception, and then examines the relation between self-deception and rationalization, offering a rich and de-

tailed account of how rationalization promotes and sustains self-deception, and of how both are related to rational action.

PART II. THE EPISTEMIC DIMENSION OF SELF-DECEPTION

The possibility of self-deception presents difficulties for claims of privilege in self-knowledge, and it raises issues concerning the effects of desire on the evaluation of evidence.

5. Bas C. van Fraassen, "The Peculiar Effects of Love and Desire." A rich range of examples presented by van Fraassen show how the phenomena of self-deception appear to undermine the possibility of certain sorts of self-knowledge. His response to thoroughgoing skepticism about self-knowledge draws on St. Paul, St. Augustine, Pascal, and William James. Preserving the phenomena of self-deception, he argues that it is not irrational to allow faith to go beyond evidence in determining belief. Capitulation to skepticism is, van Fraassen maintains, a failure of will, of courage, of faith. "Yes, the facts are ambiguous, and confidence may ebb; alternative interpretations may leap like leopards from every tree, every step of the way. But no, there is no failure of rationality in the very phenomena of trust, confidence, and affirmation."

6. David H. Sanford, "Self-Deception as Rationalization." Sanford argues that the self-deceived misapprehend the structure of their psychological attitudes, mistaking in particular the sources and explanations of those attitudes. He claims that although genuine self-deception requires rationalization, it does not require holding contradictory beliefs or intentionally deceiving oneself.

7. Adam Morton, "Partisanship." Morton argues that acquiring valuable knowledge requires our willingness to risk being irrational as well as wrong. He shows that desire can, in some cases, legitimately influence belief in ways that are integral to rational scientific practice. He compares scientific partisanship—a commitment to a scientific program—with other sorts of partisanship, e.g., commitment to a friend or to a political cause.

8. Frederick F. Schmitt, "Epistemic Dimensions of Self-Deception." Schmitt examines and evaluates the epistemic conditions necessary for deception and self-deception, and analyzes the ways in which both deception and self-deception are epistemically objectionable.

PART III. THE PSYCHOLOGY OF SELF-DECEPTION

The philosophical interest of self-deception extends to the interplay of self-deception with a variety of psychological phenomena. How is self-deception related to bad faith? To repression and denial? To the conflict between avowals and centrally functioning attitudes? Are there unconscious or self-deceptive emotions? Is self-deception always motivated? What are the psychological strategies exercised in self-deception?

9. Allen W. Wood, "Self-Deception and Bad Faith." According to Wood, Sartre claims that (1) a self-deceiver must be victim and liar, believing (as a victim) what (as a liar) he disbelieves; (2) the belief and disbelief must be simultaneous; and (3) the self-deceiver must deny either his belief or his disbelief. Explaining self-deception, Wood maintains, requires showing that (1)–(3) are compatible. In examining Sartre's attempt to do this, Wood critically assesses Sartre's reasons for rejecting the Freudian appeal to the unconscious. He discusses the relationship between Sartre's theory of human freedom—in particular the theory of facticity and transcendence—and evaluates Sartre's proposed account of bad faith.

10. Edward Erwin, "Psychoanalysis and Self-Deception." Erwin argues that psychoanalytic discussions of self-deception are relevant to philosophical problems of self-deception. He claims that if psychoanalytic examples of self-deception are explained by psychoanalytic theory, standard philosophical analyses of self-deception are wrong. Self-deception does not require holding contradictory beliefs, nor does it require that someone who self-deceptively believes *p* have adequate evidence that not-*p*. Erwin points out that psychoanalytic cases might defeat certain philosophical analyses of self-deception without psychoanalytic theory's being true, since philosophical analyses purport to state logically necessary and sufficient conditions for self-deception. While he expresses skepticism concerning the truth of psychoanalytic theory, he also allows that psychoanalytic therapy may cure particular cases of self-deception.

11. Leila Tov-Ruach, "Freud on Unconscious Affects, Mourning, and the Erotic Mind." Tov-Ruach argues that Freud's view that there are no unconscious affects rests on his distinction between the ideational content of an idea and its psychological energy. She applies this distinction to expand Freud's account of denial and to extend his account of the submersion of affects associated with intellectual development. Charting some of the problems in Freud's account of unconscious processes, she proposes a functionalist solution to resolve some of his apparent inconsistencies.

12. Georges Rey, "Toward a Computational Account of *Akrasia* and Self-Deception." Rey claims that *akrasia* is a failure to act on one's highest preference, while self-deception is a failure to act in accordance with sincerely avowed belief. Both involve a discrepancy between what people do and what they say. Rey shows how the computational theory of mind can explain these discrepancies by distinguishing avowed attitudes from central attitudes. The computational relation constitutive of central belief differs from that constitutive of avowed belief. Reports of central attitudes are, he holds, more reliable

than reports of avowed attitudes. If one is self-deceived in believing that *p,* one avowedly believes that *p* and centrally believes that not-*p*. If one performs an akratic act, then one acts against one's highest avowed preference but not against one's highest central preference.

13. Adrian M. S. Piper, "Pseudorationality." Placing the problems of self-deception within the framework of a Kantian theory of rationality, Piper argues that self-deception is a species of "pseudorationality." She distinguishes three pseudorational strategies—denial, dissociation, and rationalization—and traces their respective roles in self-deception.

14. Ronald B. de Sousa, "Emotion and Self-Deception." Three kinds of rationality are distinguished by de Sousa: strategic, cognitive, and axiological. He argues that self-deception in emotion involves a person's being taken in by his or her own pretense: it bears the same relation to self-feigning that self-deception in belief bears to deceit.

PART IV. THE SOCIAL DIMENSION OF SELF-DECEPTION

Social and political structures affect and are affected by the capacity for self-deception. What is the nature of that influence? What roles do others play in promoting and sustaining self-deception? How are we socialized into the practices of deception and self-deception?

15. Allen W. Wood, "Ideology, False Consciousness, and Social Illusion." Wood analyzes Marx's account of the relation between ideology and false consciousness, and argues that "the notion that ideology operates through self-deception is itself a piece of ideology."

16. Rom Harré, "The Social Context of Self-Deception." Harré attempts to provide what he calls "a social constructionist" theory of the self in self-deception. He examines the force of such self-commenting speech acts as 'I have been fooling myself about X', and argues that self-deception does not require interactions between "two self-like components" or "two psychological centers around which knowledge and belief cluster."

17. William Ruddick, "Social Self-Deceptions." Ruddick investigates the ways we elicit the unwitting cooperation of others in inducing and sustaining self-deception. His account connects the analysis of self-deception with the social conditions for belief and with the interactive and dynamic character of psychological and cognitive activity.

18. Bruce Wilshire, "Mimetic Engulfment and Self-Deception." Wilshire uses the notion of 'mimetic engulfment'—the natural tendency of humans to imitate one another without recognizing that they are doing so—to provide a phenomenological analysis of self-deception. He suggests that in self-deception "we voluntarily and intentionally keep ourselves from fully recognizing our own intentions, and we do this by voluntarily and intention-

ally keeping ourselves from fully recognizing how we become mimetically engulfed in others."

PART V. THE MORAL DIMENSION OF SELF-DECEPTION

What, if anything, is morally wrong with self-deception? In what sense can people be held responsible for constructing their conceptions of themselves? In what sense can they be responsible for deceiving themselves?

19. Stephen L. Darwall, "Self-Deception, Autonomy, and Moral Constitution." Darwall asks, "Why is it that self-deception has seemed a matter of fundamental concern to some moral philosophers while others have given it only scant attention?" He distinguishes three different types of ethical theories: value- or end-state-based, duty- or conduct-based, and character- or moral-worth-based. Each offers a different account of the relationship between the right and the morally good. Darwall explains why self-deception is a fundamental concern to moral theorists who embrace a character- or moral-worth-based ethics.

20. Marcia Baron, "What Is Wrong with Self-Deception?" Baron characterizes the immorality of the actions that induce or sustain self-deception and distinguishes the wrongs of self-deception from those of deception.

21. Stephen L. White, "Self-Deception and Responsibility for the Self." White argues that the standard puzzles about self-deception—how one can believe both p and not-p and how one can succeed in deceiving oneself—can be resolved by a homuncular theory. According to such a theory, we are constituted by subsystems with their own beliefs, goals, plans, and strategies. Self-deception involves one subsystem's intentionally deceiving another. On this view, self-deception is a special form of other-deception. According to White, the central problem for the homuncular theory is that of explaining why we hold a self-deceiver morally responsible for his or her self-deception, despite the fact that the deceiving and deceived subsystems are distinct. He offers a theory of moral responsibility according to which the self-deceiver could be held morally responsible.

PART VI. SELF-DECEPTION IN LITERATURE

Examples of the phenomena of biased and deflected thought found in literature provide a rich source of material for the study of self-deception. How do Proust, Goethe, and Henry James distinguish the onset of self-deception from a mere change of attitude? How do they describe the difference between self-deception and wishful thinking, error, or confusion?

22. Martha Nussbaum, "Love's Knowledge." Nussbaum examines

Proust's account of self-knowledge, self-discovery, and self-deception as represented in Marcel's recognition of his love of Albertine in *Remembrance of Things Past*. She also analyzes a short story by Ann Beattie, which depicts the effects of self-deception on a person's knowledge of her emotions. She argues that the model of intellectual self-scrutiny—and its purely cognitive successes and failures—is inadequate to account for our complex self-awareness and self-disguising.

23. Margret Kohlenbach, "A Case Study: Error or Self-Deception?" Kohlenbach examines the case of Eduard in Goethe's novel *Elective Affinities,* arguing that Eduard is mistaken in seeing himself as a self-deceiver. She shows how Eduard has unintentionally rather than intentionally misled himself into believing in fate. Cases of self-deception are, she suggests, cases of evasion.

24. Rüdiger Bittner, "Understanding a Self-Deceiver." Using the case of Verena in James's *The Bostonian,* Bittner suggests that putative examples of self-deception are complex actions of evasion or manipulation. He argues against a number of standard analyses of self-deception and presents an alternative account of intentional action that does not require the agent to have a reflexive understanding of his or her own psychological or cognitive states.

Part I

THE ANALYSIS OF SELF-DECEPTION

1

THE DECEPTIVE SELF: LIARS, LAYERS, AND LAIRS

Amélie Oksenberg Rorty

Self-deception is the best cure for melancholia.

If anyone is ever self-deceived, Dr. Laetitia Androvna is that person. A specialist in the diagnosis of cancer, whose fascination for the obscure does not usually blind her to the obvious, she has begun to misdescribe and ignore symptoms that the most junior premedical student would recognize as the unmistakable symptoms of the late stages of a currently incurable form of cancer. Normally introspective, given to consulting friends on important matters, she now uncharacteristically deflects their questions and attempts to discuss her condition. Nevertheless, also uncharacteristically, she is bringing her practical and financial affairs into order: though young and by no means affluent, she is drawing up a detailed will. Never a serious correspondent, reticent about matters of affection, she has taken to writing effusive letters to distant friends and relatives, intimating farewells, and urging them to visit her soon. Let us suppose that none of this uncharacteristic behavior is deliberately deceptive: she has not adopted a policy of stoic silence to spare her friends. On the surface of it, as far as she knows, she is hiding nothing. Of course her critical condition may explain the surfacing of submerged aspects of her personality. Self-deception is not always the best explanation of cases of this sort: sometimes people do undergo dramatic changes, changes whose details have complex but nevertheless straightforward explanations. But let's suppose that Laetitia Androvna's case is not like that. The best explanations of the specific changes in her behavior require supposing that she has, on some level and in some sense, recognized her condition.

To deceive herself, Laetitia need not be lying to herself, need not assert what she believes to be false. Without focusing on what she is doing, she can mislead herself, blind herself, distort or misrepresent her actions, attitudes, perceptions, moods, and tastes. Most effectively, she can direct her attention in ways that subvert what she takes to be her primary attitudes. Such deflections can bear all the hallmarks of intentionality: they are often finely discriminating and patterned; they can be sensitive to the norms of inference and the subtleties of a person's characteristic symbolic codes. In systematically, persistently, and uncharacteristically avoiding paying attention to what is obvious, Laetitia must recognize and scan the domain in order to determine not to look further. Although the phenomena are much richer, I shall focus on cases of straight-out denials of attributable beliefs: these are the hardest cases of self-deception, in which the phenomena are most difficult to preserve and to explain.[1]

As is the way with other forms of deception, self-deception multiplies. Not only is Laetitia deceiving herself about her cancer: to maintain this deception she is also deceiving herself about her self-deceptive moves, the significance of her uncharacteristic focusing, deflections, and denials. If self-deception involves more than being mistaken or conflicted, it seems (on the face of it) to require some second-order attitudes as well: some recognition of the conflicts among her beliefs, and some ad hoc strategies to reconcile those conflicts. If the charge of self-deception is to hold, these second-order attitudes should not themselves be mistaken or conflicted: as tailor-made, trumped-up, ad hoc rationalizing maneuvers, they are themselves deceitful.[2]

The phenomena of self-deception seem, on the face of it, paradoxical. How can a rational person deliberately lie to her present self? Of course she can unintentionally contradict herself; and she can also intentionally and even deliberately initiate a process whose predictable outcome is that she comes to believe what she initially disbelieves. But if that process succeeds, she will no longer hold her initial belief. Those who deny self-deception argue that its attribution is incoherent: a person cannot deliberately believe what she takes to be false; nor can she be simultaneously aware and not aware of her beliefs. The phenomena of deflected focusing, inconsequent beliefs and actions, and problematic lack of self-knowledge cannot best be described as involving the strict numerical identity of the deceiver and the deceived, and the intentional affirmation of what is recognized as a contradiction or misrepresentation. If the self is rationally integrated, automatically scanning and correcting its beliefs, self-deception is incoherent.

By contrast, a self that is a loosely organized system composed of relatively autonomous subsystems seems hospitable to the possibility of self-deception. Self deception is demystified and naturalized, and even to some extent explained, if the self is a complexly divided entity for whom rational integration is a task and an ideal rather than a starting point. Yet despite its initial hospitality, the second picture of the self also undermines the possibility of strict self-deception. Where there is no presumption of systematic unity, nonintegration is not a flaw or failure. After examining the grounds for interpreting the self as a rationally integrated system, and those for interpreting it as composed of relatively autonomous subsystems, I want to save the phenomena of self-deception. Our ordinary practices presuppose that the self is both a rational integrator and that it is composed of relatively independent subsystems. The classical description of strict self-deception arises from the superimposition of two ineliminable and irreducible conceptions of the self. Despite its evaporation under the close scrutiny of each of the two reigning pictures of the self, strict self-deception does nevertheless exist . . . for some sorts of selves.

I

A true self cannot deceive itself.

If the self is essentially unified or at least strongly integrated, capable of critical, truth-oriented reflection, with its various functions in principle accessible to, and corrigible by, one another, it cannot deceive itself. According to the classical picture, the self is oriented to truth, or at least directed by principles of corrigibility that do not intentionally preserve error. The self is of course engaged in many other activities besides those of amassing or attending to truths or even minimizing the possibility of error. We are busy avoiding or creating trouble; worrying about and enjoying our friends and relations; running for office or at least keeping the scoundrels out of office; being dazzled by the seasons and by paintings of the seasons; enhancing and ornamenting our world and ourselves; wooing; engaging in, and trying to avoid, hierarchical squabbles; despairing of our lives. But the successful exercise of all these activities is made possible by our capacities for critical reflective rationality, which dominate capacities directed to other intellectual and psychological goods such as richness of associational consequences, the joys of amazement, reverence, irony, and intensity.

But a dominantly truth-oriented self need not be incapable of ignorance or error, careless and unregulated judgment, failures of attention, illogical inferences, erratic belief, or unrecognized conflict. A complex unified self can suffer all these debilities: but it is in principle capable of being aware of its disorders, and under normal circumstances, their correction requires no additional motivation. Nothing structural stands in the way of integration and everything is actively directed toward it.

Ad hoc irrationality—putative cases of self-deception included—can be given ad hoc explanations, by the intervention of deflecting, interfering psychological causes. When such causes are not reasons, the unity of the rational self is not jeopardized by them. Under conditions of opacity, there is nothing mysterious about unintentionally suffering from failures of attention, particularly when—as might happen when a person is tired or ill—it would take unusual acuity to recognize relevant material. Nor is there anything mysterious or illicit about a person's finding herself unable to free herself from a particular piece of irrationality. As long as she acknowledges it, she need not be self-deceived, particularly if she follows some sort of principled strategy for attempting to suspend or reconcile her conflicts. It would be enough for her to confess, helplessly, that she is unable to dispel the conflict or correct the failure. (But she could be self-deceived in this very confession.)

But patterned and persistent forms of irrationality, especially those that involve monitoring material to be ignored, and those that uncharacteristically resist obvious, readily available correction, require more than ad hoc explanations or apologies. Laetitia needs entrenched, finely attuned discriminative monitoring—monitoring that standardly conforms to canons of rationality—to distinguish the symptoms she wants to suppress from those bodily conditions she normally notices. Explaining the phenomena of systematic, discriminative, entrenched irrationality requires postulating interfering systems that, while falling outside the system of supportive reasons, nevertheless also function within the system of rational beliefs and attitudes.[3] Interfering causes appear in a system of double-entry bookkeeping, within the system of rational beliefs and attitudes on the one hand, and as part of an interfering causal system on the other. Distinguishing the belief that rationalizes from the belief that causes without rationalizing assures the independence of functions in the double-entry bookkeeping. But that solution generates problems of its own, problems of determining criteria for the identity of beliefs, under distinctive functions.

Of course responsible believers can sometimes justify regionalized or contextually distinctive criteria for validity, without thereby automatically demoting themselves to erratic believers. It is not necessarily irrational or self-deceptive for thoughts to be guided by fears and wishes: a person might have a justified principle defining acceptable conditions and contexts for such maneuvers. Aware of her tendency to hypochondria, and knowing diagnostic physicians are susceptible to fears of illness, Laetitia might have adopted a general policy of attempting to ignore, or at any rate avoid, monitoring her physical condition. Her denial of her cancer need not be an unprincipled, ad hoc maneuver: it might be rationalized by a justified policy of avoiding occasions for hypochondria. If it brings strong benefits, a policy that allows self-deception as an unintended but predictable consequence can sometimes be the most reasonable policy, all things considered. The self-deception is irrational; the policy that tangentially accords it hospitality, not.

Yet sometimes—and this is what is at issue in determining whether there is bona fide self-deception—the motives or policies that rationalize self-deception and other persistent patterned forms of irrationality are not principled: they become themselves increasingly ad hoc and specialized. In blatantly unacknowledged or denied ways, they conflict with the person's most fundamental epistemic policies. To explain such cases of unprincipled irrationality, the picture of the self that best explains epistemic and practical integrative responsibility gradually drifts from strong to increasingly weakened conditions of unity, transparency, truthfulness, reflexivity.

The simple version of the first picture of active, effective, critical rationality requires that the self be: (1) a simple *unity* dominated by rationality; (2) *transparent,* in that its states are accessible to one another or to a central panoptical scanner; (3) oriented to *truthfulness,* in such a way that its transparency is organized to maximize truths or at least minimize error; (4) *reflexive* in that the criteria for rationality can themselves be subject to critical evaluation. Attempts to explain patterned irrationality—particularly that kind of irrationality produced by the intervention of functions that unite nonrational and rationalizing psychological causes—weaken these requirements: *integration* replaces *unity*; *systematic connectedness* replaces *transparency*; *rationalizing principles* replace *truthfulness*; and the condition of *reflexivity* becomes a regulative ideal.

(1) The *unity requirement* has increasingly weakened conditions for unification:

(a) The self is a simple unity, with access to all its psychological states. The panoptical center is also a judicial and to some extent a legislative center, capable of evaluating beliefs and forming its judgments accordingly.

(b) In the absence of a central scanner, the self is hierarchically organized, so that its mutually accessible, mutually supportive psychological states form a conflict-free system that maximizes truth.

(c) In the absence of a hierarchical organization, subsystems are cooperatively related; there is a procedure for resolving apparent conflicts between independent functions.

(d) In the absence of a central procedure for resolving conflicts, subsystems are designed so that localized conflict-resolving procedures automatically go into operation when conflict arises.

(e) In the absence of such localized conflict-resolving mechanisms, the system is so constructed that it is not destroyed by conflict: it can operate and survive at lower levels of efficiency and energy, because its various functions are either replaceable or substitutable when the integrative processes are damaged or depleted.

(2) The *transparency requirement* has increasingly weakened conditions for accessibility:

(a) There is a central panoptical scanner with direct and immediate access to all psychological states.

(b) There is a central panoptical scanner that can in principle initiate a process to access any psychological state. But sometimes this method is (i) mediated (an intervening process is required for access) and (ii) indirect (the content and character of at least some psychological states can only be inferred).

(c) In the absence of a panoptical scanner, mutually relevant and appropriate psychological states are automatically accessible to one another.

(d) The system can continue its basic operations at a diminished level even if its psychological states do not automatically have appropriate relevant access to one another.

(3) The *truth orientation requirement* has increasingly weakened conditions for truthfulness:

(a) All psychological functions are cognitive, and operate in their propositionalized forms. It is as propositionally formulated reasons that they operate as causes.

(b) Though not all psychological operations are truth oriented, their independent functions coincide with, and are supported by, the formation of true beliefs in propositional form.

(c) Although they need not function in their propositional forms, psychological operations can in principle be propositionalized in such a way that they can be assessed for their rationality.

(4) The *reflexivity requirement* has increasingly weakened conditions for reflexivity:

(a) The content and sequence of thought has a reason that rationalizes it, according to the person's principles in the light of her other attitudes. All general strategies can be rationally justified and corrected. Every critical self-assessment is in principle sufficient to produce an appropriate modification in thought.

(b) Every thought can be critically assessed for its truth and for the appropriateness of the categorical assumptions implicit in its formation.

In attempting to deal with the phenomena of intractable patterns of irrationality, the first picture gradually drifts toward the second: unity moves to integration, and compartmentalization becomes a strategy of integration. It might seem as if that drift could be checked by relativizing and regionalizing integration. But the problems for self-deception remain unaffected. The possibility of self-deception remains exactly coordinate with variations in degree and region: Laetitia could be self-deceived only in those regions where, and to the extent that, she is integrated, truth bound, and reflexive.

It might also seem as if the drift to the second picture could be blocked by making the first picture purely regulative. But the descriptive problem would remain: only if and to the extent that the capacities for critical rationality are in working order can self-deception be charged. If those capacities are not actualized, putative cases of self-deception reduce to ignorance, conflict, or error. Where there is no presumption of, or capacity for, rationality, there are no failures of rationality.

II

Nothing is as brilliantly adaptive as selective stupidity.

We would not have survived as the creatures we are if our sole capacities were those of unified, transparent, critical inquirers; we would not even have survived if critical rationality were our central regulative ideal, dominant over all others. The second picture of the self—the complex survival picture—

is generally constructed to explain our adaptive strategies rather than our capacities as responsible believers and agents. On this picture, the mind is not a unified system but rather "a problematically yoked-together bundle of partly autonomous systems. Not all parts of the mind are equally accessible to each other at all times."[4] The loosening of the integrative bonds of the self moves to its psychological conclusion: it is to our benefit that relatively independent but integrable subsystems sometimes fail to communicate. Some integrative strategies are local, others generalized and centralized. When there is overlap and replication of functions, there can be tension among the various integrative strategies.

Fragile creatures who survive in highly differentiated, changing environments must be able to discriminate between subtly different sorts of dangers and opportunities without being too sensitive to adaptationally irrelevant changes.[5] Though for some purposes a central panoptical monitor is adaptive, we are also well served by autonomous and automatically triggered subsystems. Survival is served by psychological and physical plasticity, as well as by replication and specialized differentiation. Plasticity and replication allow substitutability of functions in cases of damage; diversification and differentiation allow for relatively automatic, unmonitored, highly specific responses. Compartmentalization, self-manipulated focusing, selective insensitivity, blind persistence, canny unresponsiveness—capacities and habits that undermine integration—have enormous benefits. The more sensitive the creature, the more high-mindedly rational, the more vulnerable it is to disorientation and debility by attack at one central point.[6] A creature whose critical rationality is impaired by lack of sleep, let alone by the flu, is well served by regionally specific, automatically activated habits.

What are the attractions of being capable of self-deception? The structures and capacities that enable us to manipulate ourselves in situations of indeterminacy allow self-deception as an unintended, tangential consequence.[7] In the interests of generating a self-fulfilling prophecy, we intentionally shift our epistemic policies. We can speak to ourselves as the friendly neighborhood demagogue, cannily conning ourselves into believing that we can do things that are only distantly or marginally within our repertoire. Self-deception is an effective, if irrational, cure for melancholia. Devoting energies to many of our projects often involves carefully shifting perspective, refusing to see matters *sub specie aeternitatis,* ignoring the relative unimportance of our various enterprises and projects, shelving doubts and hesitations, setting aside the large corrective perspective. Effective focusing enlarges what is directly present and blurs what is on the periphery: what is blurred falls out of sight and becomes irrelevant. Writing philosophy papers, devoting ourselves to political causes, taking the minutiae of our friends' tribulations seriously, and believing in the futures of our students do not, of course, require self-deceptive manipulation. But it helps.

Trading on the fact that declarative sentences normally assert beliefs, we use them to induce beliefs: on one reading, such sentences express vague intentions, perform non-truth-functional rituals. On another reading, they assert presumptively true beliefs. It is by playing on the ambiguity of these two readings that we can induce the beliefs that serve us well. If we were careful to avoid deceptive manipulative strategies, we would be restricted, unable to act energetically and loyally beyond our initial means. (Yet the capacity to be one's own rhetorician also allows the hypocritical immoralist to congratulate herself on her nobility.)

Just as there are patterns of dominance in visual attention (e.g., red over gray, irregularly moving over stationary objects), so too psychological salience follows strongly entrenched patterns that do not always reflect a person's beliefs and priorities. There is a *general* correlation between a person's considered priorities about what is important and the patterns of her attention. Magnetizing attitudes—fear, aggression, erotic bonding, bonding to children, actions and reactions to power—are connected with what is important to us and to our well-being. But the strength of those generalized habits of attention can override considerations that are appropriate to particular situations and events. When that happens, a person may not be able to use the material at the periphery of her attention, material of which she is, as we say, marginally aware, to correct magnetized attention. *Being aware of something* does not occur at a single glance, at an instant. It takes place over time; it integrates distinctive actions of focusing, scanning, refocusing, and reconstructing a series of interpretations derived from shifting the foreground and the background of attention. Standardly, marginal information corrects the distortions of attention that arise from intensive focusing.

But when a person is afraid or absorbed in love or grief, or concentrated on some form of hierarchical combat, she can fail to integrate the relevant material that is at the periphery of her strong, attentive focusing. Sometimes patterns of tunnel vision and salience are constitutionally based; sometimes their origin lies in the person's individual history. Sometimes their import is direct and obvious; sometimes it is indirect, encoded by idiosyncratic associations. Sometimes it is directly motivated; sometimes it is a by-product of functional but unmotivated psychological structures or habits. When attention is strongly riveted, the periphery or background of the perceptual field is not closely attended. Still, a person knows in a general way what is there, and may even know that it provides a corrective to her strongly focused salient beliefs and attitudes. Even in normal, nonpathological cases, when someone is aware that her magnetized attention does not reflect her general all-things-considered attitudes, what is not salient can seem subjectively unimportant. Though salience and importance (particularly importance for corrigibility) are strongly correlated, they can vary independently. It is this feature of psychological structures that makes both self-deception and *akrasia* possible.

Another psychological and intellectual strategy that is hospitable to self-deception is the inertia of belief in the face of counterevidence.[8] The utility of conservation does not lie in the particular case but in the general practice of resisting oversensitive criteria for revision and modification of beliefs. Latitudinarian believers develop strongly entrenched habits that work best when they operate relatively automatically and unreflectively. Susceptibility to self-deception is the unintended but predictable cost of the benefits of such psychological strategies. Of course in principle, decently grounded rules for self-manipulative focusing, compartmentalization, and latitudinarian policies of belief are distinguishable from indecent ad hoc policies of convenient blurring. But when the cost of constant, alert scanning is greater than the benefits of the unmonitored application of latitudinarian policies, there is a natural slide from sensible strategies to dangerous self-deception. The habits of compartmentalization and selective focusing are (to our general benefit) usually stronger and more deeply entrenched than the principles that guide, correct, and check them. Even when the occasion makes them inappropriate, we follow entrenched habits of thoughts, hiding the behavioral traces that reveal the carefully preserved myopia, the consistent, canny, averted gaze. Of course the local irrationality that is the fallout of a globally beneficial epistemic policy has a double evaluation. In particular cases, self-deception and irrationality are undesirable, to be identified and eliminated. But the policy of eliminating occasional local irrationality is, for latitudinarian believers, outweighed by the more general policy that allows such irrationality initial hospitality. The problem is both theoretical and practical: how can we distinguish a well-grounded from a suspiciously convenient ad hoc policy? How can we avoid the natural slide that occurs when we follow a policy that endorses not monitoring attention?

We've described some of the attractions and operations of creatures composed of relatively independent subsystems. But we have not yet characterized this second picture of the self in any detail. On one version of the picture, the self is divided into homuncular subsystems that are themselves composed of increasingly simple, independent subsystems, eventually reaching a level of relatively mechanical, subpersonic, specialized proto-intentional functions.[9] On this picture, the self includes subsystems that fix patterns of visual and psychological attention, whose weighted salience (e.g., fear, eroticism, bonding, competition and combat, hierarchy and domination) may serve long-range survival, even though they do not always express or reflect individual commitments, priorities, or even welfare.[10] Intentionality begins with relatively simple preconscious discrimination, and ranges through increasingly complex forms to self-consciously and systematically justified clusters of propositionalized beliefs. Since these routines of intentional activity can occur relatively independently of one another, intentionality can be a matter of degree.

We can distinguish:

(a) pre-intentional, physiologically based discrimination (e.g., discrimination between light and dark, sensitivity to heat).[11] While such discriminative responses are integrated within a person's articulated system of beliefs, they also simultaneously continue to function pre-intentionally, i.e., relatively automatically;

(b) prelogical categorial discrimination, which, while itself too vague to be propositionalizable, can be specified by general descriptions (e.g., mood responses to colors or to weather). Such discriminations can be integrated within an articulated system of beliefs, where they often affect patterns of inference. But they are usually not cognitively corrigible by counterevidence or argument;

(c) propositionalizable interpretive descriptions of events (e.g., seeing a situation as dangerous);

(d) propositionalized interpretations of situations and events ("This is a cumulus storm cloud");

(e) critically evaluated propositionalized interpretations of situations and events ("In these climatic conditions, a cumulus storm cloud gives a 76 percent probability of rain"); and

(f) reflexively and critically evaluated propositionalized interpretations of situations and events (e.g., critical evaluations of the statistical laws predicting weather conditions).

Some psychological states can function as carriers of information without performing any functions that require their 'having the information they bear': though such proto-logical weather vane states conform to some conditions of intentionality, they do not fully conform to conditions of rationality.[12] But those states, and the information they bear, can also be functionally connected with propositionalized intentional states. They are, so to say, two-faced: under some descriptions they function within the system of rationally corrigible beliefs; under others, they function as causes to modify perception and behavior. While by some standards of rationality, the functions of such subsystems preserve the intentionality of the mental, they are defective by other standards. Similarly, pre-intentional states that also function in an intentionalized form (e.g., reactions to color, light, and weather) can be arational by some standards, irrational by others. For the explanation of self-deception, it does not matter whether the phenomena of pre- and proto-intentionality reveal that some intentional activity is subconscious or that some conscious intentional activity is subdoxastic. What matters is that some psychological states fuse a number of different functions with intentions whose rationality is measured by quite different standards. Relations among the various intentional subsystems affect the relations between the nonrational and the rationalizing functions of intentional actions or inference. On this version of the second picture, there is nothing unusual about possible conflicts among the various grades of intentional "takes" on the same event or situation. At least some types of self-deception involve a conflict between two independent intentional "takes" on an event or situation, when there is a presumption that the two processes should be coordinated.

On this picture of the self, a person's activities—including intentional, voluntary, and even purposive inferences and actions—need not arise from any particular set of motives: they can arise directly from constitutional structures without motivational intervention. Selective focusing and compartmentalization occur whenever the conditions for triggering the operations of the relevant subsystems obtain. A particular irrational inference or action might have several distinctive etiological sources: overdetermination allows a psychological state or an action to be (nonmotivatedly) constitutional along one etiological line, while being motivated along another. In principle, constitutionally based and motivationally generated activities might sometimes conflict. There is no particular difficulty in explaining the frequency and persistence of what is, on the first picture, simply classified as irrationality. On the first picture a good deal of thought and behavior is simply classified as erroneous, irrational, conflicted, and ignorant. But when irrationality is patterned, and when purportedly rational beings show unexpected resistance to correction, we need an explanation. We want to know not only how it occurs but why it is such a fashionable indoor sport. Why it is often so highly patterned? And does the pattern explain the attractions it has for us? The first picture does not help us answer these questions.

On the second picture of the self, self-deception is readily assimilated with failures of integration among systems that are standardly coordinated: it is a natural by-product of functional structures and strategies. Because there is no assumption that the system is constantly either self-informed or even informed about its condition, no defensive regression into deception about the first-level strategies is required. Even the capacities for critical, rational reflection are subdivided into subsystems. Rule-bound patterns of inference, calculation, "stepping back to evaluate evidence" are analyzed as themselves arising from a variety of relatively independent constitutional, psychological, and cognitive habits. Because psychological and intellectual activities are performed by loosely conjoined subsystems, there is no difficulty in explaining how a person can believe contradictions, can be aware and not aware of herself as holding contradictory views, and can adopt conflicting policies and strategies. The phenomena of self-deception are naturalized and demystified on all varieties of the second picture. Since Laetitia need not be aware of the etiology of her beliefs, she might well have persistent, patterned, unfounded or malformed beliefs without being implicitly aware of her condition.

But it now seems as if this second picture of the naturalized self as a strategic survivor has demystified self-deception so thoroughly that it has evaporated. Starting out by saving the phenomena, we seem again to have lost them. The picture of the self as a loosely confederated system of subsystems, which includes the various activities of critical rationality without giving them any dominant centrality, loses self-deception: it has abandoned the identity of the deceiver and the deceived. The left hand is misguiding the right hand, the neck is averting the gaze of the eyes. But the eyes do not both see and not see exactly the same things in the same way at the same time. If self-deception is incoherent and impossible on the first picture, it is lost on the second. The phenomena of self-deception again turn out to be nothing more than ignorance, conflict, nonintegration, or compartmentalization.

III

Self-deception is a disease only the presumptuous can suffer.

Have all our attempts to preserve self-deception failed after all? I think not. Despite the elusiveness of its various forms, self-deception resists evaporation and reduction. We certainly think we can recognize self-deception in others, and we strongly suspect it in ourselves, even retrospectively attributing it to our past selves. If this is illusory, why is the illusion so persistent? Why are the many varieties of self-deception so recognizably and subtly chronicled in biographies, novels, and case studies? Why is it the subject of such passionate indignation—and sometimes envy—among friends and enemies?

The reason we are convinced that there is self-deception is that we cannot renounce either of the two pictures of the self. The classical picture of the integrative, rational self is the picture that makes sense of systematizing beliefs and attitudes, and integrating (even) independent subsystems. Even the weakest form of that picture, taken as an active regulative ideal, is essential to thinking of ourselves as responsible agents and responsible believers. Those committed to and actively capable of rational integration attempt to avoid false beliefs, correct them where possible, and suspend judgment when necessary. Responsible agents, like responsible believers, must be able to carry out a rationally structured, complex plan of action, by giving the capacities for critical rationality not only the authority but also the effective force that reflects the normative power of their rational justification. The requirements of responsibility and rationality are not satisfied by assigning the subsystem of critical rationality the weight it would have on a principle of "one subsystem, one vote," or even "weight each subsystem according to its psychological strength." Even those who take epistemic and moral responsibility to be regionally a matter of degree must treat the capacities of critical rationality as *prima inter pares,* with centrality and dominance in the areas, and to the degree, that responsibility is assigned.

We can't imagine what it would be like to give up this picture of the self.

Who would be the *we* who would consider whether, in the interests of truth and accuracy, we should renounce the pretentions of an actively regulative principle of rationality? Even characterizing the self as a set of subsystems seems to introduce a system, distinct from other systems-of-subsystems. After all, there are all sorts of subsystems: which do, and which do not, fall into the rough area of the self? In any case the self is, after all, a biological organism, a body that lives and dies, thrives or fails as one entity. Even when the subsystems do not always work together, even when they actually conflict, still at a minimal level, they are all either alive together or dead together. Organic interdependence provides a presumptive basis for psychological integration.

But from the point of view of the second picture, the claims of the first picture of the self are empty: what is at issue is not the existence but the character and structure of organic interdependence. Any serious version of the first picture must introduce other capacities besides those of critical rationality: a creature whose only beliefs and motives are derived from the principles of critical rationality would be a very boring and short-lived creature. On the second picture, some of the component subsystems of an organism can be effectively dead while the whole survives. Relying on the details of modular theories of all kinds, the second picture explains our hospitality to self-deception and other forms of irrationality.

Each picture claims to represent the important features of the other, and to save the phenomena neglected by the other. From the point of view of the first picture, the picture of the self as a complex survivor fails to account for the dominant centrality of critical rationality in integrative processes. Even the division of labor among subsystems sets a presumption of their integration. But from the point of view of the picture of the self as a complex, naturalized survivor, the first picture suffers from delusions of grandeur. Rational subsystems and their modes of integration may well claim centrality. That is their function and that is their business. Such regulative principles are meant to (attempt to) establish the dominance of rational strategies. But a subsystem, even a centrally important subsystem, claiming dominance by no means thereby establishes the validity of such a claim. From the point of view of the second picture, the first picture is unnecessary: whatever benefits it can genuinely bring can be captured within the second picture. Any other benefits it might claim are illusory.

A modified version of the second picture—one that accords special status to the range of capacities exercised in critical reflection—might seem to save the phenomena of self-deception. But it is a version that effectively superimposes the first picture onto the second, superimposes the capacities for critical rationality onto the system of subsystems, according it legislative as well as panoptical powers. The capacities for critical rationality are allotted independent and dominant status. Themselves causally independent of other subsystems, they can nevertheless modify and correct them. They have not only judicial but legislative and executive power that enables them to scan and effectively integrate all other systems.

Justifying beliefs and attitudes requires a process of integration whose normative power is not reducible to the system of subsystems that, according to the second picture, compose the self. If the effective normative power of the capacities central to critical rationality had no independent status, the justificatory strength of any rational argument could only be a function of the effective causal strength of the subsystems that formed it. In order to make sense of the self as actively having the power to initiate integration and to evaluate and correct persistent perspectival distortions, the power of the capacities for rational integration cannot merely be a function of their causal (psychological) strength in relation to other subsystems that compose the self. The first picture of the self cannot be absorbed into the second; the self of critical rationality cannot just be one among the system of subsystems.[13] Its power must be a direct function of its rational authority, rather than of the vicissitudes of its psychological and physical history. (But the second picture moves us to ask, "What kind of *must* is this? The *must* of a desperate and presumptuously imperious wish?")

Though each of the two pictures claims to represent the other—claims to give an account of what seems right about the other—they remain stubbornly opposed. Both are required; neither is eliminable; neither is reducible to the other. They cannot be reconciled by making one a part of the other. Nor can they be reconciled by characterizing the first as presenting a regulative ideal for rational inquirers and responsible agents and the second as a descriptive account of the self. The rational have, by definition, actualized that ideal: it *is* the way they function. Those committed to the first picture must take it to describe the deep structure of their actual functioning, and not merely a projected ideal for which they might strive in an irrational way. The process of striving must itself conform the canons of rationality.

Nor can the two pictures be reconciled by classifying the first as the subjective or first-person perspective of the self and treating the second as representing the objective or third-person point of view. It is not necessary to rehearse the familiar arguments that thought and action presuppose a community of inquirers engaged in common enterprises and practices, requiring the principle of charity in interpreting one another. The first picture gives an objective account of the intellectual and psychological structures that anyone capable of epistemic and practical integrative responsibility must have, whether or not she is experientially aware of herself as having or applying those structures. On the other hand, the second picture can also represent the first-person perspective: as virtually all of Dostoyevski's novels vividly show, psychological dissociation and disintegration can be phenomenologically experienced.

The apparent intractibility of self-deception comes from the *superimposition,* rather than the *subsumption* or *complementarity* of the two pictures, the two selves. When the first picture is projected onto the second, the self is deceived by itself when its subsystems uncharacteristically, persistently, and systematically resist the correction and integration that is readily available to them. When the two pictures are superimposed, what is (on the second picture) a failure of integration is interpreted (by the first picture) as a piece of irreducible irrationality.

Only those who, despite their effective, actual commitment to the first picture, are actually composed of relatively autonomous subsystems can fail to integrate what they believe. So only a presumptively integrated person who interprets her system-of-relatively-independent-subsystems through the first *picture of the self,* only a person who treats the independence of her constituent subsystems as failures of integration, is capable of self-deception. Not everyone has the special talents and capacities for self-deception. It is a disease only the presumptively strong minded can suffer. Only to the extent that Laetitia Androvna superimposes the first on the second picture of the self, only to the extent that she interprets the activity of her subsystems in terms of the structures of critical rationality, can she be self-deceived.[14]

NOTES

1. A first rough characterization of self-deception, as it applies to that subclass of propositional beliefs, meets the following conditions:

(1) The person believes that p.
(2) Either (a) The person believes not-p. Standardly this involves the person believing q, which (given her beliefs and her strongly entrenched habits of inference) she ought to recognize as equivalent to not-p.
    Or (b) The person denies that she believes p.
(3) If self-deception does not reduce to error, the person must on some level recognize that she has conflicting beliefs. Standardly, attributing such recognition is an inference to the best explanation of the person's behavior or inferences.
(4) If self-deception does not reduce to conflict, the person must on some level deny that her beliefs conflict. Sometimes this is achieved by an ad hoc strategy for reconciling the apparent conflict. The self-deceiver usually makes no attempt to suspend judgment, or to determine which of her beliefs are defective.
(5) The attribution of self-deception presupposes an account of what the person would normally believe, perceive, notice, infer; it presupposes that she accepts canons of rationality and that she is alert to the sort of evidence that weighs against her belief.

Philosophers in England and the United States have largely focused on cases of self-deception, cases in which an individual adopts a complex strategy in the face of a conflict of specific belief of which she is presumptively aware. While such cases have not been neglected in France and Germany, philosophers there have focused primarily on *mauvaise foi* as a general condition in which consciousness denies its condition as nothing-but-the-reflection-of-some-arbitrary-content-before-it. Or they have focused on false consciousness as a condition of a class of people whose beliefs and desires have been manipulated and directed in such a way as to violate their natural latent awareness of their real condition.

2. Straightway, then, self-deception seems problematic. For a start, its attribution seems to require a suspicious regression. Because I want to concentrate on other issues, I shall set aside at least some of the familiar puzzles about the attribution of self-deception. Certainly the general difficulties of identifying and attributing beliefs in opaque contexts make it difficult to demonstrate that there are bona fide cases of strict self-deception that do not reduce to error or to conflict. But since these difficulties attend *any* attribution of belief—let alone the attribution of conflict of belief—they should not by themselves cast doubt on the existence of cases of strict, bona fide self-deception.

3. Donald Davidson, "Deception and Division," in *The Multiple Self,* ed. Jon Elster (Cambridge: Cambridge Univ. Press, 1986).

4. Daniel Dennett, "The Self as the Center of Narrative Gravity," in *Consciousness and Self,* ed. T. Cole, D. Johnson, and F. Kessel (New York, 1987). Dennett is referring to the work of M. S. Gazzaniga and Joseph Le Doux, *The Integrated Mind* (New York: Plenum, 1978). See also Howard Gardner, *The Shattered Mind: The Person After Brain Damage* (New York: Knopf, 1975), and E. R. Hilgard, *Divided Consciousness* (New York: Wiley, 1977).

5. Cf. Ronald de Sousa, "What Computers Will Need to Feel: Emotion and Cognitive Science" (unpublished manuscript).

6. Cf. Gilbert Harman, "Coherence and Foundations: Positive vs. Negative Undermining," in *Change in View* (Cambridge: MIT Press, 1985).

7. Cf. David Pears, *Motivated Irrationality* (Oxford: Oxford Univ. Press, 1984); M. R. Haight, *A Study of Self-Deception* (Sussex, 1980); Herbert Fingarette, *Self-Deception* (New York: Humanities Press, 1969); Amélie Rorty, *Mind in Action* (Boston: Beacon Press, 1988); Shelley Taylor and Jonathan Brown, "Illusion and Well-Being: A Social Psychological Perspective on Mental Health," *Psychological Bulletin,* 1988.

8. Adam Morton, *Frames of Mind* (Oxford: Oxford Univ. Press, 1980). See also Morton's article in this volume (chap. 7) and Harman, op. cit.

9. The second picture of the mind is a schema that is realized in distinctive ways by a larger variety of theories:

(a) For evolutionary accounts of the structure of the brain; see P. D. MacLean, *A Triune Concept of Brain and Behavior: The Hincks Memorial Lectures,* ed. T. Boag and D. Cambell (Toronto, 1973), and Eliot Sober, "Evolution of Rationality," *Synthese* 46 (1981):95–120.

(b) For psychological studies of the compartmentalization and confabulations of inference, see R. Nisbett and T. Wilson, "Telling More than We Can Know: Verbal Reports on Mental Processes," *Psychological Review* 84 (1977):321–359; R. Nisbett and L. Ross, *Human Inference: Strategies and Shortcomings of Social Judgment* (Englewood Cliffs, N.J.: Prentice-Hall, 1980); L. Ross, M. R. Leper, and M. Hubbard, "Perseverance in Self Perception and Social Perception," *Journal of Personality and Social Psychology* 32 (1975):880–892; A. Tversky, D. Kahneman, and P. Slovic, eds., *Judgement Under Uncertainty* (Cambridge: Cambridge Univ. Press, 1982); Ulric Neisser, *Cognition and Reality* (New York: W. H. Freeman, 1976); Alvin Goldman, "Varieties of Cognitive Appraisal," *Nous* 13:22–38.

(c) For neuroanatomy and brain physiology, see G. E. Schwartz and D. Shapiro, eds., *Consciousness and Self-Regulation* (New York: Plenum, 1976). See especially A. R. Luria, *The Nature of Human Conflicts,* trans. W. H. Grant (New York, 1932); Patricia Churchland, "A Perspective on Mind-Brain Research," *Journal of Philosophy* 77 (1980):185–207; A. R. Luria, *The Working Brain* (New York: Basic Books, 1973); Patricia Churchland, *Neurophilosophy* (Cambridge: MIT Press, 1986).

(d) For cognitive and functionalist theories in philosophical psychology, see Daniel Dennett, *Brainstorms* (Montgomery, Vt.: Bradford Books, 1978); Daniel Dennett, "Making Sense of Ourselves," *Philosophical Topics: Functionalism and the Philosophy of Mind* 12 (1):63–81; Daniel Dennett, "Three Kinds of Intentional Psychology," in *Reduction, Time and Reality,* ed. Richard Healy (Cambridge, 1981); Daniel Dennett, "Consciousness," in *Oxford Companion to the Mind,* ed. Richard Gregory (Oxford, 1987); Daniel Dennett, *Elbow Room* (Cambridge: MIT Press, 1985); William Lycan, *Consciousness* (Cambridge: MIT Press, 1987); Hilary Kornblith, ed., *Naturalizing Epistemology* (Cambridge: MIT Press, 1985) (see especially the articles by Nisbett and Ross, Stich, and Harman); Stephen Stich, "Dennett on Intentional Systems," *Philosophical Topics: Functionalism and the Philosophy of Mind* 12 (1):39–62; Stephen Stich, "On the Ascription of Content," in *Thought and Object,* ed. Andrew Woodfield (Oxford: Oxford Univ. Press, 1982); Stephen Stich, "Beliefs and Subdoxastic States," *Philosophy of Science* 45 (1978): 499–518; Stephen Stich, *From Folk Psychology to Cognitive Science* (Cambridge, 1983); Stephen Stich, "On Genetic Engineering, the Epistemology of Risk, and the Valuation of Life," in *Logic Methodology, and the Philosophy of Science VI,* ed. J. L. Cohen et al. (New York: North Holland, 1983).

(e) For Freudian theory on internalization and introjection, see H. Kohut and Ernest S. Wolf, "The Disorders of the Self and Their Treatment: An Outline," *International Journal of Psychoanalysis* 59 (1978):413–425; H. Kohut, *The Restoration of the Self* (New York: International Univ. Press, 1977); Roy Schafer, "Concepts of Self and Identity and the Experience of Separation-Individuation in Adolescence," *Psychoanalytic Quarterly* 42 (1973):42–59.

(f) For social psychology and the internalization of social norms and models, see J. Aaronfreed, *Conduct and Conscious: The Socialization of Internalized Control Over Behavior* (New York: Academic Press, 1968); the selections by Durkheim, Weber, Freud, Mead, Cooley, and Schutz in *Theories of Society,* vol. 2, ed. Talcott Parsons, Edward Shils, Kaspar Naegele, and Jesse Pitts (Glencoe, Ill.: Free Press of Glencoe, 1961).

(g) Last, and by no means least, see the history developed by Julian Jaynes, *The Origin of Consciousness in the Breakdown of the Bicameral Mind* (Boston: Houghton Mifflin, 1976).

10. Cf. de Sousa, "What Computers Will Need to Feel," and A. O. Rorty, "Moving Magnets of the Mind" (unpublished papers read at a meeting of the Boston Colloquium for the Philosophy of Science, 1986).

11. Eleanor Rosch, "Principles of Categorization" in *Cognition and Categorization,* cd. Rosch and B. Lloyd (New York: John Wiley, 1978)

12. Cf. Stich, "Beliefs and Subdoxastic States," loc. cit., and Robert van Gulick, "Mental Representations: A Functionalist View," *Pacific Philosophical Quarterly* 63 (1982):3–19.

13. This is of course the view developed by the philosophic tradition that runs from Descartes to Kant; it is recently represented by Harry Frankfurt in "Freedom of the Will and the Concept of the Person," *Journal of Philosophy* 68 (1971):5–20.

14. I am grateful to Rüdiger Bittner, Martin Bunzl, Owen Flanagan, Jens Kulen-kampff, Brian McLaughlin, Michael Martin, and Richard Schmitt for their constructive criticisms of earlier drafts. Discussions of this paper at colloquia at CUNY-Brooklyn and SUNY-Albany were also illuminating and helpful.

An earlier version of this paper was published in *Analyse und Kritik,* 1985.

2

EXPLORING THE POSSIBILITY OF SELF-DECEPTION IN BELIEF

Brian P. McLaughlin

It seems not uncommon for a person to be self-deceived. Here are some garden variety examples: the alcoholic who is self-deceived in believing that his drinking is under control, the cuckold who is self-deceived in believing that his wife is not having an affair, the jealous colleague who is self-deceived in believing that her colleague's greater professional success is due to ruthless ambition, and the AIDS victim who is self-deceived in believing that he has a fifty-fifty chance of surviving the disease. As, perhaps, this last illustrates, self-deception need not be disadvantageous to the self-deceiver: for it can relieve the person of some of the burdens of a sad situation beyond the person's control. Not the harms and benefits of self-deception, however, but rather the very possibility of self-deception is my immediate concern.

In addressing it, I will address issues bearing on deception, the nature of belief, intentional action, wishful thinking, and positive thinking. My focus will, obviously, have to be on only those issues concerning these matters that bear on the possibility of self-deception. However, exploring the possibility of self-deception sometimes has the benefit of presenting these matters from a perspective that makes salient some of their more neglected features. Here, I find, is part of the fun in exploring the possibility of self-deception.

THE PROBLEMATIC

1. The guiding question of this paper is: how is self-deception possible? The question presupposes that it is possible. This presupposition has been challenged. Self-deception has been called "paradoxical."[1] Skeptics claim that while self-deception seems not uncommon, it can, upon reflection, be seen to be impossible.[2] They allege that there are conditions that (i) are required for self-deception and that (ii) are impossible. Such conditions would be *excluders* of self-deception.[3] In what follows, I hope to explain how self-deception is *causally* possible, so I shall be concerned with whether there are excluders of its *causal* possibility.[4]

Self-deception *in belief* is the sort whose causal possibility is considered most problematic,[5] so I shall try to explain how it is causally possible to be self-deceived in *believing* something.[6] I shall do so by stating conditions that are (i) jointly causally possible (i.e., that co-obtain in some causally possible world) and (ii) jointly metaphysically sufficient for a state of self-deception in belief (in any metaphysically possible world in which they obtain, a state of self-deception in belief obtains).[7] Such conditions must jointly imply every causally necessary condition for self-deception in belief. Let us, then, turn to a condition that the leading skeptical arguments presuppose is metaphysically (and so also causally) necessary for it. (Hereafter, to avoid prolixity, I shall drop 'in belief' and speak simply of self-deception, drop 'causally' when speaking of necessary conditions,[8] and of possibility and impossibility.)

1

A SKEPTICAL ASSUMPTION

2. It is fairly common ground among skeptics that a state of self-deception is *ipso facto* a state of intentionally self-induced deception. One is in a state of *intentionally self-induced deception* in believing that *p* just in case (a) one is deceived in believing that *p* and (b) one has intentionally deceived oneself into believing *or* into continuing to believe that *p*.[9] (Hereafter, I shall abbreviate 'intentionally self-induced deception' by 'self-induced deception'.) There are acts of deception and there are states of deception. Condition (a) concerns states of deception: one is in a *state* of deception if one is deceived *in* believing something. Condition (b) concerns acts of deception: if one intentionally deceives oneself *into* believing or *into* continuing to believe something, one performs an *act* of deception, and one is both agent and victim of the act. When one deceives oneself into believing something, one acts in a way that contributes to the belief's being *induced* in oneself. When one deceives oneself into *continuing* to believe something, one acts in a way that contributes to the belief's being *sustained* in oneself.

According to the skeptic, then, being self-deceived in believing that *p* requires being deceived in believing that *p*: a state of self-deception is a state of deception. Moreover, being self-deceived in believing that *p* requires having intentionally deceived oneself. Whether one must have intentionally deceived oneself into believing that *p* or into continuing to believe that *p* depends on how one became self-deceived. To have become self-deceived in believing that *p* by coming to believe that *p,* one must have intentionally deceived oneself into believing that *p*. However, many exemplars of self-deception are of a person self-deceived in believing something he or she already believed prior to becoming self-deceived in believing it: for example, an alcoholic may have believed that he was not an alcoholic before becoming self-deceived in believing it. Such cases do not require that one have intentionally deceived oneself into believing that *p*. The skeptic holds that in such cases, one must have intentionally deceived oneself into *continuing* to believe that *p*.

The claim that a state of self-deception is *ipso facto* a state of self-induced deception is controversial. It is typically a point of dispute between skeptics and nonskeptics. Some nonskeptics hold that self-deception does not require *intentionally* deceiving oneself,[10] and some hold that self-deception does not require deceiving oneself at all.[11] However, *some non*skeptics hold, along with skeptics, that a state of self-deception is *ipso facto* a state of self-induced deception.[12] Before entering this controversy, let us first ask an obvious question.

IS SELF-INDUCED DECEPTION AN EXCLUDER
OF SELF-DECEPTION?

3. Given the assumption that self-deception requires self-induced deception, whether self-induced deception is itself an excluder of self-deception turns on whether self-induced deception is possible. Is it? That depends on whether one can intentionally deceive oneself.

There is a certain worry about the possibility of one's intentionally deceiving oneself. Roughly, to deceive oneself, one must get oneself to believe something that one disbelieves. (One disbelieves that *p* just in case one believes that not-*p*.) The worry is that one's relevant disbeliefs and one's knowledge of one's deceitful stratagem would forestall one's coming to hold the intended belief.

The source of this worry is an oversimplified conception of what a deceitful stratagem can involve. It has been noted, in answer to the worry, that part of one's deceitful stratagem can be that one will *forget* the stratagem and lose the relevant disbeliefs by the time one is to be taken in by the deceitful act.[13] Let us label such a stratagem 'a memory-exploiting stratagem'. One can intentionally deceive oneself by means of such a stratagem. To see this, let us consider a case in which a person intentionally deceives herself into believing something, and then a case in which a person intentionally deceives herself into continuing to believe something.

Consider the following example, which I shall label 'the appointment example'.[14] In order to miss an unpleasant meeting three months ahead, Mary deliberately writes the wrong date for the meeting in her appointment book, a date later than the actual date of the meeting. She does this so that three months later when she consults the book, she will come mistakenly to believe the meeting is on that date and, as a result, miss the meeting.[15] Mary knows that she has a poor memory and a very busy schedule. And she justifiably counts on the fact that when she consults the book around the date in question, she will have forgotten the actual date of the meeting and that she wrote the wrong date. Sure enough, three months later, having forgotten the actual date of the meeting and the deceitful deed, she innocently acquires the intended mistaken belief by consulting her appointment book. Her deceitful stratagem succeeds. Mary thus deceives herself into believing that the appointment is on a certain date. Moreover, she is deceived in believing that it is. This is a possible case of self-induced deception.

It is likewise unproblematic that one could be deceived in believing something one intentionally deceived oneself into *continuing* to believe. To see this, consider the following example, the supplemented appointment example, which I shall just briefly sketch. Let the situation be as in the appointment example with the following additional features: Mary knows that she will come to be deceived by at least a certain date by consulting her appointment book. And she does something to ensure that she will continue to hold the mistaken belief at some point after that time.[16] She arranges for a weekly appointment sheet, which she will receive sometime after having already become deceived by reading her appointment book, to list the date of the meeting as the same day that she has written in the book. As before, she knows she will have forgotten the stratagem by the time she receives the weekly appointment sheet. (Recall how busy her schedule is and how bad her memory.) Things go as planned: her mistaken belief is sustained by her reading the weekly appointment sheet. She thereby succeeds in intentionally deceiving herself into continuing to believe that the meeting is on the date in question. And she is deceived in believing that it is on that date. This is a possible case of self-induced deception.

To sum up, the condition of being in a state of self-induced deception is not itself an excluder of self-deception. For it is possible for the condition to obtain. One can intentionally deceive oneself into believing something and into continuing to believe something via a memory-exploiting stratagem.

I do not mean to suggest that this is the only way one could do this. Deceitful stratagems can be quite elaborate, involving various ongoing projects and activities that exploit other people and rely on various nonevidential, belief-influencing factors. How elaborate a deceitful stratagem can be and yet be one by which one intentionally deceives oneself is uncertain. Tom, a nonbeliever, studies Pascal's Wager and becomes convinced by it that it is in his best interest to believe that God exists. So, taking Pascal's advice, he embarks on a program for inducing belief: he takes holy water, has masses said, associates with believers and avoids nonbelievers, and so on. When he embarks on the belief-fixing strategy, he views it as one by which he will mislead himself into falsely believing that God exists: he views himself as embarking on an attempt to carry out an elaborate deceitful stratagem. However, it may be possible for the program to succeed without Tom's ever having forgotten his stratagem. If, after a period of vacillation and confusion, Tom becomes a believer, he will view the program from a changed perspective. From the new perspective, the stratagem will reflect the desperate attempt of a lost soul with the *hubris* to think he could manufacture belief, when all that was required was that he open his eyes to see how God makes his presence known. From Tom's new perspective, he once was lost but now is found, once was blind but now can see. Whether this would count as Tom's having intentionally deceived himself into believing that God exists, however, is uncertain (even if God does not exist).[17]

In any case, we have seen that self-induced deception is possible. A skeptic, however, would maintain that we have yet to see whether self-deception is possible, since self-induced deception does not suffice for it. A skeptic would argue that self-deception is a certain species of self-induced deception, differentiated from the genus by the context in which or the way in which one must intentionally deceive oneself, and that that species is impossible.

I agree with the skeptic that self-induced deception does not suffice for self-deception. (The appointment example, the supplemented appointment example, and even the Pascal example could, for instance, be fleshed out in ways that reveal that they do not count as examples of self-deception.) I say why in section 7. Unlike the skeptic, however, I do *not* think that self-deception requires self-induced deception; I explain why in section 9. Self-induced deception is neither necessary nor sufficient for self-deception.

In what remains of Part I, I shall examine several skeptical arguments without challenging the assumption that self-deception requires self-induced deception and so requires intentionally deceiving oneself. I shall close Part I by noting a kind of self-induced deception that has at least *apparent* excluders, conditions that, at least at first blush, *seem* necessary for it and *seem* impossible. My aim is to answer some wrong-headed skeptical concerns. In Part II and Part III, I shall try to develop an explanation of how self-deception is possible.

DECEIVING ONESELF INTO CONTINUING TO BELIEVE WHAT ONE ALREADY BELIEVES

4. In this section, I present a skeptical argument against the possibility of a certain kind of case of self-deception and then reply to the argument.

Consider cases of self-deception in which one becomes self-deceived in believing something one already believed prior to becoming self-deceived. Let us label such cases 'continued-belief cases'. The skeptic maintains that in continued-belief cases, one intentionally deceives oneself into *continuing* to believe something. The supplemented appointment example shows that it is possible to do that. Nevertheless, there is an important difference between what happens in the supplemented appointment example and what would have to happen in continued-belief cases if they required self-induced deception. In the supplemented appointment example, Mary intentionally deceived herself into continuing to believe something. However, she did not deceive herself into continuing to believe something she already believed when she initiated the deceitful act. In contrast, suppose continued-belief cases of self-deception required intentionally deceiving oneself into continuing to believe something. In that case, they would require that one intentionally deceive oneself into continuing to believe something *one already believed when one initiated the deceitful act in question.* Could one do that? If not, and if this feat is required for continued-belief cases, such cases are impossible.

Suppose that one intentionally deceived oneself into continuing to believe something one already believed when initiating the act in question. It might be claimed that in order to do that, one would have had to simultaneously hold contradictory beliefs when one initiated the act. This claim follows from the following fairly widely held assumption about acts of deception: (A) for any *x* and for any *y,* if *x* intentionally deceived *y* into believing or continuing to believe that *p,* then *x* must have disbelieved that *p* when *x* *initiated* the act of deception in question. Suppose that (i) one intentionally deceived oneself into continuing to believe that *p* and that (ii) one already believed that *p* when one initiated the act. Then, given (A), when one initiated the act, one believed that *p* and disbelieved that *p.* A skeptic might claim that it is impossible to believe and disbelieve that *p* at the same time. If it is, then such an act of deception could not be initiated and so could not be performed. So if continued-belief cases of self-deception required performing such an act, such cases would be impossible.

If they were indeed impossible, that would be a serious blow for the non-skeptical position. As I have already mentioned, many of our exemplars of self-deception are continued-belief cases. Moreover, regardless of how a self-deceiver initially became self-deceived, it is characteristic of a self-deceiver to engage in such activities as rationalization, evasion, and overcompensation, by means of which the relevant belief is sustained. *If,* as a skeptic might maintain, such activities are ones by which the self-deceiver *intentionally* deceives himself, then cases of self-deception involving such activities are continued-belief cases.

The argument in question, however, fails. For one thing, it is possible to hold contradictory beliefs simultaneously. I shall sketch an explanation of how this is possible in section 11; however, I need not do so for present purposes. Another reply to the skeptical argument is available: namely, that (A) is false. One can intentionally deceive someone, oneself or another, into believing or continuing to believe that *p* *without* having disbelieved that *p* when one initiated the act.

To see this, note, to begin with, that one can intentionally deceive someone into believing something that, when one initiates the deceitful act, one believes is true. Take any Tom, Dick, and Harry. Let Tom be the deceiver, Dick be the one the deception is about, and Harry be the victim. Tom believes that Dick is innocent of a certain wrong-doing. Harry believes Dick is guilty. Tom is unable to produce evidence that will change Harry's mind. So, diabolical as he is, Tom attempts by deceitful means to get Harry to believe that Dick is innocent. Tom tries to convince Harry by lying about some particularly pertinent matter, Dick's whereabouts on a certain night. Tom thus performs an act of deception by means of which he intends to get Harry to believe that Dick is innocent. Suppose that Tom succeeds: Harry believes the lie and infers that Dick is innocent. Then, Tom will have succeeded in intentionally deceiving Harry into believing that Dick is innocent. Yet Tom himself believed that Dick was innocent when he initiated the deceitful act. So, one can intentionally deceive someone into believing something one believes is true when one initiates the act in question.

Moreover, one can intentionally deceive someone into *continuing* to believe something that, when one initiates the act, one believes is true. Tom believes Dick is innocent of a certain wrong-doing. Harry does too. Tom encounters damaging evidence against Dick. It does not shake his confidence that Dick is innocent, but Tom recognizes that it would overturn Harry's belief. Tom wants to prevent this, so he lies to Harry about the evidence. Suppose Harry is taken in by the lie and as a result continues to believe that Dick is innocent. Then, Tom has succeeded in deceiving Harry into continuing to believe that Dick is innocent, yet Tom believed that Dick was innocent when Tom initiated the deceitful act. Likewise, one can intentionally deceive oneself into continuing to believe that p, something one already believed when one initiated the act, without having disbelieved that p when one initiated the act.

In the last Tom-Dick-and-Harry example, Tom acts with the intention of deceiving Harry into continuing to believe something he takes Harry to believe already prior to the deceitful act. It is worth noting that Tom's acting with this intention does not require his believing that Harry falsely believes the something in question. Tom acts with the intention of deceiving Harry into continuing to believe that Dick is innocent, but Tom does *not* believe that Harry falsely believes this. Rather, Tom believes that Harry truly believes that Dick is innocent.

Likewise, one can act with the intention of deceiving oneself into continuing to believe something—say, that p—that one takes oneself to believe already prior to the deceitful act, without believing that one falsely believes that p. On the contrary, one can believe that one truly believes that p, while acting with the intention to deceive oneself into continuing to believe that p. That is all to the good, since it is, to be sure, problematic how one could believe that one falsely believes something.

It is also worth noting that both Tom-Dick-and-Harry examples can be used to illustrate that one can intentionally deceive someone *into* believing or continuing to believe something the person is not deceived *in* believing. A common assumption, mine too, is that one can be deceived in believing that *p* only if *p* is false.[18] However, one can be deceived into believing or continuing to believe something that is true. This happens to Harry if Dick is innocent.[19]

Nevertheless, on any occasion on which one intentionally deceives someone, one gets or allows the person to believe or to continue to believe *something* the person is deceived *in* believing and so something that is false. Moreover, I do *not* deny that: (B) for any *x* and for any *y*, if *x* intentionally deceives *y* into believing or continuing to believe something, *p*, then there is something, *q*, (*p* or something else) that (i) is false, that (ii) *x* disbelieves when initiating the deceitful act, and that (iii) *x* intentionally gets or allows *y* to come or to continue to believe.[20]

Suppose, then, that one intentionally deceived oneself into continuing to believe something that one already believed, and believed one believed, prior to initiating the act. Given (B), this would require that one have gotten or allowed oneself to believe something that (I) is false and that (II) one disbelieved when one initiated the deceitful act in question. We have already seen how that is possible. It would not require holding contradictory beliefs simultaneously. In the appointment example, for instance, when Mary initiated her deceitful act, she disbelieved that her appointment was on a certain date. When she came to be deceived, she came to believe, mistakenly, that it was on that date. But by the time she came to believe that the meeting was on the date in question, she had already forgotten her deceitful deed and lost her earlier relevant disbeliefs. Recall that she employed a memory-exploiting stratagem. Such a stratagem could be employed successfully in the sort of case in question now.[21] One would not have to hold contradictory beliefs simultaneously in order to intentionally deceive oneself into continuing to believe something one already believed when one initiated the deceitful act. The condition of having so intentionally deceived oneself is not *itself* an excluder of any case of self-deception, for the condition can obtain.

DECEIVING ONE'S CONTEMPORARY SELF

5. It is time now to address a certain issue. Some might count the appointment example as one of a person intentionally deceiving her "future self" into believing something, and the supplemented appointment example as of a person intentionally deceiving her "future self" into continuing to believe something. And some might claim that while one can intentionally deceive oneself by means of a memory-exploiting stratagem into continuing to believe something one already believes prior to the deceitful act, this is just a way one can deceive one's "future self" into continuing to believe something that one

currently believes. Indeed, a skeptic might allow that one can intentionally deceive one's "future self" yet take that to be irrelevant to whether self-deception is possible. For a skeptic might hold that (I) being self-deceived requires having intentionally deceived one's "contemporary self" and that (II) it is impossible to do that. If such a skeptic were right on both counts, then self-deception would be impossible: the condition of having intentionally deceived one's "contemporary self" would be an excluder of self-deception. Let us, then, address this skeptical argument.

The first question to ask is: what is it to deceive one's "contemporary self" rather than one's "future self"? The idea might be this: a person can be divided into temporal parts, and a person deceives his or her "contemporary self" just in case a temporal part of the person that initiates the deceitful act is a contemporary of a part that is deceived by it. And one might count temporal parts with the same temporal extension only as contemporary.

In any case, I find the notion of a person's having temporal parts deeply puzzling.[22] But it would be a digression for me to voice my worries here, for the skeptic's main claim can be recast without appeal to temporal parts. The skeptic might just point out that in self-induced deception, one initiates a deceitful act at a certain time, and one comes to be deceived by it at a later time (leaving open what this consists in).[23] Let us label the time period between and including the time of the initiation of a deceitful act and the time the person is taken in by the deceitful act 'the temporal span of the act', and label the appropriate temporal span for deceiving one's "contemporary self" rather than one's "future self" 'S'.[24] The skeptic's claim, then, is this: self-deception requires that one have intentionally deceived oneself within S, and it is impossible to deceive oneself intentionally within S.[25]

The question to ask, then, is this: what is the *appropriate* temporal span for intentionally deceiving one's "contemporary self" rather than one's "future self"? Until this is answered, it is hard to assess the claim that intentionally deceiving one's "contemporary self" is impossible.

What counts as contemporary can, of course, vary with interest. This makes it hard to see what is to count as the appropriate temporal span. Recall that in the appointment example, three months passed between Mary's initiating her act of deception by writing the wrong date for a certain meeting in her appointment book and her coming to be deceived about the date of the meeting by consulting the book. If the appropriate temporal span can, for instance, be three months, then the appointment example is of a person's intentionally deceiving her "contemporary self." Presumably, three months is too long a temporal span to count as appropriate. However, examples could be provided in which the temporal span of the deceitful act is considerably shorter than in the appointment example.[26] If, for instance, the appropriate temporal span can last long enough for one to lose one's relevant disbeliefs and to forget one's deceitful deed, there is no problem about how one could intentionally deceive one's "contemporary self."

There are, to be sure, temporal spans so short that it would be causally impossible to deceive oneself within them. But there are, likewise, temporal spans so short that it would be causally impossible to deceive someone else within them. No act of deception can achieve its aim instantaneously. The skeptic in question would have to show that self-deception required intentionally deceiving oneself within a temporal span so short that it would be impossible to do so. Otherwise, someone, for instance, who thought that self-deception just consists in self-induced deception might respond that the skeptic has shown at most only that certain *limiting* cases of self-deception are impossible. And the obvious response is that certain *limiting* cases of "other-deception" are likewise impossible: limit the required temporal span enough and one cannot intentionally deceive anyone else's "contemporary self."

Nevertheless, it is easy to see that there are a variety of understandable worries behind the skeptical argument just considered. But the length of the temporal span is irrelevant to some of them. If Mary regained her relevant disbeliefs and recalled her deceitful stratagem after three months (or if she never forgot them), it would be just as problematic how she could have been taken in by her stratagem as it would be a half hour after she wrote the wrong date in her appointment book.

The skeptic might, of course, claim that when a self-deceiver becomes deceived in believing that *p,* the self-deceiver must retain the relevant disbeliefs and not have forgotten his deceitful stratagem. Even if this claim could be justified, however, that would not suffice to show that self-deception is impossible. Perhaps it is possible for the relevant disbeliefs and knowledge of the stratagem to be rendered inoperative, so that they will not forestall one's acquiring the intended belief. A mechanism such as *suppression* or *repression,* for example, might be invoked in an attempt to explain how they could be rendered inoperative in this way.[27]

The skeptic might object that this would nevertheless require that the self-deceiver simultaneously hold contradictory beliefs when he comes to be deceived and that that is impossible. But, to repeat myself, I maintain that it is possible to hold contradictory beliefs simultaneously.

INSINCERE THOUGHT

6. Turn now to a kind of self-induced deception that has at least *apparent* excluders: conditions that, at first blush, *seem* required for it and *seem* impossible.

It is sometimes claimed that the self-deceiver deceives himself by *lying* to himself. One can deceive oneself by lying to oneself. In the appointment example, Mary would, I think, count as lying to herself when she writes the wrong date in her appointment book.[28] However, the self-deceiver might be thought to lie to himself in a way different from the way Mary lies to herself.

It might be claimed that the self-deceiver lies to himself *in thought,* that the self-deceiver engages in *insincere thought* and is taken in by it.

It is, to be sure, *hard to see* how one could lie to oneself in thought and be taken in by the lie. There is no received view about what it is to lie. However, the following conditions, if unnecessary for lying, are at least characteristic of it. If *x* lies to *y* about *p,* then, characteristically, (a) *x* intentionally presents himself to *y* as believing that *p* (typically, though not invariably, by telling *y* that *p*), (b) *x* takes himself thereby to be presenting himself as believing something he does not, namely that *p,* and (c) *x* intentionally attempts to conceal from *y* the fact mentioned in (b). Lying thus, at least characteristically, involves insincerity with respect to the representation of at least one of one's beliefs. It is not required that a liar *succeed* in hiding from his intended victim the fact that he takes himself to be misrepresenting himself as believing that *p.* Some people are bad liars. However, if the liar fails in his attempt to conceal, the victim will not be taken in and so the liar will fail to deceive. It is *hard to see* how one could insincerely represent one's beliefs to oneself in thought and be taken in. To mention one reason, it is hard to see how one could succeed in the attempt mentioned in (c) while so engaged. And if one could not, then one would not be taken in.[29]

There are, to be sure, kinds of self-induced deception that are impossible. But if they are not required for self-deception, they are not excluders of it. While it would be interesting to pursue whether the kind in question is possible, that is beyond the scope of this paper. Whether it is possible has no bearing on whether self-deception is possible. For one can be self-deceived in believing that *p* without ever having lied to oneself in thought about anything. Nevertheless, a person who is self-deceived in believing that *p* characteristically *misleads* himself by the way he *thinks* about *p* and matters he takes to bear on the truth of *p.* Moreover, in extreme cases, a self-deceiver misleads himself in thought into continuing to believe something he also disbelieves. However, it is a gross *overintellectualization* to characterize him as engaged in *insincere* thought, as *lying* to himself in thought.

I shall recur to these points in Parts II and III, and discuss them in detail in the final section. However, I want first to begin to sketch a partial picture of what self-deception consists in by comparing and contrasting it with self-induced deception and wishful thinking. This will help set the stage for what follows.

II

SELF-DECEPTION, SELF-INDUCED DECEPTION, AND
WISHFUL THINKING

7. It has been claimed that self-deception is a species of wishful thinking. If it were, then self-induced deception would not suffice for self-deception. For

self-induced deception does not suffice for wishful thinking: there are conditions that are necessary for the latter and unnecessary for the former. One is this: if believing that p is wishful thinking on one's part, then one desires that p. In contrast, one can be in a state of self-induced deception yet not desire that p. In the appointment example, Mary is in a state of self-induced deception in believing that her appointment is on a certain date, yet she does not desire that her appointment be on that date.

However, while self-deception often involves wishful thinking, it is not a species of wishful thinking. To note one reason briefly: one can be self-deceived in believing that p without desiring that p.[30] Paranoia, for instance, can involve self-deception (though, of course, it need not). A paranoid might be self-deceived in believing that he is constantly being gossiped about. To be so self-deceived, the paranoid need not want to be gossiped about. It is, in part, because he wants not to be gossiped about that he suffers deeply in believing that he is being gossiped about.[31] He is not a wishful thinker, yet he is a self-deceiver.

Despite their differences, self-deception and wishful thinking share the following feature, among others: each involves a belief that is causally sustained, in part, by a desire.[32] The shared condition is a *synchronic* causal condition: the sustaining desire must be cotemporaneous with the belief. In wishful thinking, the wishful belief that p must be causally sustained by a desire that p. In self-deception, the relevant belief must be causally sustained by *some* desire. But, as we saw above, it need not be sustained by a desire that p. It can, for instance, be sustained by a desire to believe that p. One can desire to believe that p without desiring that p. In the appointment example, when Mary initiated her deceitful act, she desired to believe that her appointment was on a certain date, but she did not desire that it be on that date.

Moreover, self-deception and wishful thinking share essential features not shared by self-induced deception. So, self-induced deception does indeed not suffice for self-deception. Let us note one such feature.

If one is self-deceived in believing that p, or if believing that p is wishful thinking on one's part, then one's belief that p is epistemically unwarranted.[33] I mean here that the belief-state token is epistemically unwarranted insofar as it is a belief that p. One way this can happen is for the belief not to be appropriately *based* on evidence.[34] One way it can fail to be so based is for one not to possess *adequate* evidence for p.[35] But even if one possesses adequate evidence for p, the belief that p will still fail to be so based if, for instance, one arrives at it by faulty reasoning. Typically, the self-deceiver and wishful thinker lack adequate evidence for the relevant belief. But in those atypical cases in which they possess adequate evidence for it, the belief will fail to be appropriately based on that evidence and so fail to be warranted.[36]

In contrast, self-induced deception does not require an epistemically unwarranted belief. One can be in a state of self-induced deception in believing that p while one's belief that p is epistemically warranted.

To see this, notice to begin with that an effective way of trying to deceive someone into believing that p is to ensure that the person will come to possess adequate evidence for p in a situation in which (1) the person will likely be epistemically warranted in believing the evidence and in which (2) the person will likely acquire the belief that p in an epistemically appropriate way on the basis of the evidence, for example, by sound inductive reasoning from the evidence. Here is an example. Tom wants to frame Dick for the murder (and Dick is in fact innocent). So, Tom tries to deceive Harry, the sleuth on the case, into mistakenly believing that Dick is the murderer. The most effective way for Tom to do that in the circumstances is for him to ensure that Harry will come to believe, warrantedly, evidence that confers warrant on the belief that Dick is the murderer. Given Harry's interest in finding the murderer and his skills as a sleuth, Tom can count on Harry's drawing the intended inductive inference. Tom might succeed by these means in deceiving Harry into falsely believing that Dick is the murderer, yet Harry may well be epistemically warranted in holding the belief.

Likewise, one can intentionally deceive oneself in this way via a memory-exploiting stratagem. One might, that is, deceitfully arrange to come to be in a situation in which (i) one will be warranted in believing adequate evidence for p and in which (ii) one will come, in an epistemically appropriate way, to have a false belief that p on the basis of that evidence. If things go as planned, one will come to be in a state of self-induced deception in believing that p, yet one will be epistemically warranted in believing that p. Such a stratagem could succeed.

We see, then, that self-induced deception does not suffice for self-deception. For self-deception requires that one's relevant belief be epistemically unwarranted, while self-induced deception does not.

Turn again to wishful thinking. It is generally acknowledged to be possible, indeed to be not uncommon. However, it is also thought to fail to suffice for self-deception, though there is no general agreement as to why.

One reason why the skeptic would deny that wishful thinking suffices for self-deception is, of course, just this: wishful thinking does not suffice for self-induced deception.[37] Wishful thinking does indeed not suffice for self-induced deception. Believing that I will go to Europe this summer can, for instance, be wishful thinking on my part without my having intentionally deceived myself into believing or continuing to believe that I will. However, since I do not think that self-deception requires self-induced deception either, I take this to be no reason to deny that wishful thinking suffices for self-deception. But before saying whether it does, let us explore the notion of wishful thinking in more detail.

8. To begin, recall that if believing that p is wishful thinking on one's part, then one's belief that p is (I) epistemically unwarranted and (II) causally sustained by one's desire that p. Conditions (I) and (II), however, do not jointly suffice for wishful thinking.

Consider the following scenario. I arise, go to my stationary bike, set its timer for twenty minutes, and then start pedaling. I plan to stop when the timer goes off. I believe that the timer is set for twenty minutes and that it is functioning properly; on this basis I believe I will stop pedaling in twenty minutes. My belief is sustained, in part, by my desire to stop pedaling in twenty minutes. If I ceased to so desire, I would cease to so believe: for I would then change my mind about stopping at that time and, as a result, cease to believe that I will. Moreover, my belief that I will stop in twenty minutes is epistemically unwarranted. For the belief is based, in part, on my belief that the timer is functioning properly, and this belief is epistemically unwarranted. The bike's timer is actually malfunctioning: it runs too slowly. Although the alarm is set for twenty minutes, it will not go off for twenty-five. Moreover, given the evidence in my possession, I should realize that the alarm is slow. However, I do not realize this. I am preoccupied with the day ahead and so do not pause to think about whether the timer is functioning properly. The point to note is that my desire to stop pedaling in twenty minutes plays no role at all in my failure to realize that the timer is malfunctioning. Rather, my preoccupation with what I will be doing in the day ahead is what results in this failure. This is not, I think, a case of wishful thinking. For while (I) and (II) both obtain, they are not suitably related for wishful thinking.

The following is a necessary condition for wishful thinking that is absent in the case just described.[38] When believing that p is wishful thinking on one's part, *one's desire that p renders one biased in favor of evidence for p.* Wishful thinking is a species of biased thinking.

Thus in wishful thinking, one believes that p, in part because the desire that p renders one inappropriately responsive, from the epistemic point of view, to the evidence in one's possession. Here is a typical scenario: one's belief that p is epistemically unwarranted because one lacks adequate evidence for it. One "jumped" beyond the evidence to the conclusion that p, prompted by one's desire that p, and the desire that p bolstered the belief despite the absence of adequate evidence.[39] This is not what is going on in the pedaling example. My desire to stop pedaling in twenty minutes does not figure in the explanation of why I failed to be appropriately responsive to the evidence in my possession that bore on the truth of p.

What might happen in a typical case of wishful thinking is this. One's desire that p affects one's interest and attention in such a way as to bolster one's belief that p in the absence of adequate evidence, or even in the face of disconfirming evidence. This might happen as follows. The desire affects one's interest so as to make what one perceives as evidence for p psychologically salient: such evidence "captures" and "absorbs" one's attention, while what one perceives as evidence against p "deflects" one's attention.[40] In this way, the desire works to accentuate the positive and eliminate the negative from consideration. An example will help.

Consider a case of charitable wishful thinking: one likes a person and wants the person to succeed in a certain endeavor. The evidence one possesses indicates that it is more likely than not that the person will fail. But one does not realize this. For, as a result of one's charitable attitude, what one perceives as evidence in favor of the person's eventual success captures and absorbs one's attention, while what one perceives as evidence against this deflects it. An *un*charitable attitude toward someone might have the effect that what one perceives as evidence in favor of the person's eventual success deflects one's attention, while what one perceives as evidence against it captures and absorbs one's attention. In neither case does the desire that p result in the inaccessibility of the evidence against p; rather, the desire just pushes such evidence into the background by bringing evidence for p into the foreground. An unbalanced diet of attention to evidence in favor of p results in one's continuing to believe that p, even though a cool, careful weighing of the evidence in one's possession would result in one's seeing otherwise.

The desire does not work alone. A complex motivational structure is involved. *Habits of mind* such as optimism can play a role too. Take an optimist who wishfully and charitably believes his friend will succeed. It would not be uncharacteristic of the optimist, when he thinks of the person's succeeding, immediately to think of a reason for the person's succeeding. And not uncharacteristically, he will be satisfied by the reason, whether or not it is an epistemically good one, and he will turn his mind to other matters. For such an optimist, pursuing lines of thought that favor the person's eventual success is pleasant and enjoyable, and something he easily slips into doing. Pursuing lines of thought indicating the opposite would require his enduring frustration or anxiety. His attention is deflected from them.

While a wishful thinker's attention to evidence may appear selective, the person may do little by way of directing his attention where evidence that bears on p is concerned. The wishful thinker accentuates the positive and eliminates the negative more out of habit and interest than design. Desire affects interest, and interest, in turn, affects attention, even perceptual attention. (The amplifying and filteration effects of interest on perceptual attention are well-known: when one attends a boring lecture, one's mind can drift, and this can result in "a deaf ear" to the speaker; but if the speaker mentions one's name, the signal may come in loud and clear.)

The wishful thinker need not be engaged in any belief-fixing strategy, deceitful or otherwise. Nevertheless, in wishful thinking, it is not atypical for a desire that p to bias the wishful thinker in such a way that he misleads himself, albeit unintentionally, into believing or continuing to believe that p. A wishful thinker is not atypically "an unintentional self-misleader."[41] And even if *mere* wishful thinking does not suffice for self-deception, the question arises whether wishful thinking involving unintentional self-misleading does.

FROM MERE WISHFUL THINKING TO SELF-DECEPTION

9. Following Bertrand Russell, George Graham has recently claimed that there is a continuum of cases from mere wishful thinking to self-deception.[42] I think there is indeed such a continuum: while self-deception does not require wishful thinking, there is no sharp difference between the two. Intuitions will vary as to where along the continuum we reach self-deception. For some, wishful thinking involving self-misleading may seem far enough along the continuum to count as self-deception. If it is, then plainly self-deception is possible.

Self-deception, I maintain, typically involves unintentional self-misleading *rather than* self-induced deception. Typically, a self-deceiver is (a) misled in believing that p and (b) has unintentionally misled himself into believing or continuing to believe that p. The skeptic is mistaken in thinking that a self-deceiver *must intentionally* deceive himself. However, I won't rest my antiskeptical case here. One reason is that I do *not* think that wishful thinking involving unintentional misleading suffices for self-deception, at least not for clear-cut self-deception.[43] My antiskeptical case will not be complete until section 12, where I shall recur to the point that self-deception typically involves *un*intentional self-misleading.

In this section and the next, I shall discuss some of the ingredients of clear-cut cases of self-deception; then in section 12 I shall attempt to say how the ingredients can be combined with others to make a clear-cut case. However, I shall not pause to defend the claim that these ingredients are required for clear-cut cases. Those, for instance, who think we have already seen how self-deception is possible by seeing how wishful thinking involving self-misleading is possible can take me to be characterizing a prima facie problematic kind of self-deception whose possibility I wish to explore. In so doing, I hope to learn something about how desire can influence belief by biasing thought.

To begin, then, a wishful thinker typically believes that p while lacking adequate evidence for p. However, a self-deceiver typically believes that p "in the teeth" of strong evidence against p. Typically, the totality of evidence the self-deceiver possesses makes not-p much more likely true than p. Here, then, is one dimension along which the continuum from mere wishful thinking to self-deception runs: as we move toward self-deception, the evidence against the relevant belief mounts.

Moreover, typically, or at least not atypically, the self-deceiver appreciates, at least at some level, the import of the evidence. If one is self-deceived in believing that p, then one has at least some inclination, based on evidence, to believe that not-p. In contrast, in the appointment example, for instance, Mary might not have had, at any level, the slightest suspicion that her appointment was not on the date recorded in her appointment book. Likewise, our charitable wishful thinker might not have had, at any level, the slightest suspicion that his friend would not succeed.

Here, then, is yet another dimension along which the continuum of cases from mere wishful thinking to self-deception runs: as we move in the direction of self-deception, the person in question moves from slight inclination to believe that not-p toward actual belief that not-p. (There is a second continuum here, one from cases of slight inclination to believe to firm conviction.)[44] In *extreme* cases of self-deception, the self-deceiver simultaneously holds contradictory beliefs: he believes that p and believes that not-p at the same time.

The inclination to believe, or actual belief that not-p, combined with a strong desire p, characteristically leads the self-deceiver, at least at some level, to have a negative emotion toward not-p, for instance, to fear that not-p.[45] The fear that not-p might prompt acts that cause the belief that p to be sustained. *Both* the belief that not-p and the desire that p might contribute to sustaining his belief that p (more about this in section 12).

The following, then, are some of the ingredients for the kind of self-deception in believing that p that interests me: adequate evidence for not-p, an emotional stake in whether p involving a strong desire that p, and a belief that not-p. I want to close Part II by discussing one more ingredient.

MOTIVATED BELIEF

10. Let us say that one is in *a state of motivated belief* in believing that p just in case one believes that p and the belief that p is causally sustained (in part) by a motive for believing that p. The skeptic might hold that self-deception is a species of motivated belief. I need not decide whether it is. Suffice it to note that in what follows, I shall focus on a type of self-deception that is a species of motivated belief. In this section, I shall discuss the notion of motivated belief in detail, perhaps more detail than the purposes at hand require. My excuse is that the notion is of interest in its own right.

By 'a motive for something' I mean, roughly, a complex mental state consisting of an appropriate belief and desire. A belief and a desire count as a motive for being something or doing something if they provide the subject of the state with at least *some* rationale, from his or her own point of view, for being or doing that something. The desire fixes an end and the belief is a belief that one can achieve the end by being or doing that something, in the case in question, by being a *that-p* believer.[46] Thus, in the appointment example, Mary had a motive for believing that her appointment was on a certain date: she wanted to miss the appointment and believed that she would if she believed that it was on that date.

Self-induced deception involves a motive for belief. But self-induced deception is not a species of motivated belief. For while self-induced deception requires that the relevant belief have a motive in its causal ancestry, it does not require that there be a cotemporaneous motive that sustains the belief. For instance, when Mary came to believe that her appointment was on the date written in her appointment book, there was no motive sustaining the belief.

It is worth noting that positive thinking is a species of motivated belief. If a belief that *p* is an instance of positive thinking, it is sustained, in part, by a certain sort of motive for so believing. In positive thinking, one desires that *p* and believes that believing that *p* will significantly increase the chances of *p*'s being true; and one's belief that *p* is sustained, in part, by such a motive. The powers of positive thinking are legendary. Kellye Cash, Miss America of 1986, attributed her success in part to positive thinking: "I thought I was going to win, because I don't think you can win if you don't think you can."[47] Right or wrong, she had a motive for believing that she would win.

In contrast, wishful thinking is not a species of motivated belief. Our charitable wishful thinker, for example, need not be engaged in positive thinking: he need *not* believe that his believing his friend will succeed will increase the chances that his friend will, and need not promote the belief in himself by acting on this motive. Mere wishful thinking does not even characteristically involve a sustaining motive.[48]

Motives for believing something can count as *prudential* reasons for believing that something. Prudential reasons are different from *evidential* reasons.[49] A reason *R* for believing that *p* is an evidential reason for believing that *p* just in case *R* is evidence for *p*. However, a prudential reason for believing that *p* is a rationale for being a *that-p* believer. One can have prudential reasons for being a *that-p* believer just as one can have prudential reasons for being a doctor, lawyer, or Indian chief. Recall that Pascal's Wager was intended to show that we all have a conclusive prudential reason for believing that God exists. However, the Wager was not intended to provide evidential reason to believe that God exists, that is, evidence for God's existence. But it was intended to show that we all have conclusive prudential reason for promoting or sustaining the belief. *R* is a prudential reason for one to be a *that-p* believer if and only if *R* is a prudential reason for acting to promote or sustain the belief in oneself, if necessary, to acquire or retain it.

Prudential reasons for belief affect belief differently from the way evidential reasons do. If one sees strong evidential reasons for believing that *p*, it is hard to resist believing. In contrast, contemplating even conclusive prudential reasons for being a *that-p* believer will, *by itself*, do no more to make one a *that-p* believer than contemplating conclusive prudential reasons for losing weight will make one lose weight. For such reasons to be effective, one must start doing something to promote the desired state. And one way of promoting the desired belief state is, of course, to seek and to emphasize evidential reasons for so believing. Prudential reasons and evidential reasons have intrinsic appeal to different sides of the mind, evidential reasons to the cognitive side, prudential reasons to the willing side. Contemplating conclusive prudential reasons for being a *that-p* believer may well prompt one to promote the belief in oneself.

Finally, it is worth noting that it has been claimed that self-deception involves motivated irrationality.[50] The kind of self-deception that now concerns us is a species of motivated belief. Moreover, the motivated belief it involves must be epistemically unwarranted. However, it is, I think, controversial whether holding an epistemically unwarranted motivated belief counts as irrational. One might, of course, stipulate that a person is *epistemically irrational* in believing that *p* if and only if the person's belief that *p* is epistemically unwarranted. If so, then, of course, the self-deceiver is epistemically irrational in believing that *p*. However, *prudential rationality* is different from epistemic rationality. It is by no means obvious that self-deception must involve prudential irrationality. As I noted at the outset of the paper, self-deception need not be disadvantageous to the self-deceiver. Beliefs are states with effects that can further or frustrate one's ends. Motivated beliefs can be prudentially rational, and they can, I think, be so even when they are epistemically irrational.[51] However, the question of the prudential rationality of self-deception and the broad issue of the relationship between epistemic and prudential rationality—are they independent, or is epistemic rationality a species of prudential rationality?—are beyond the scope of this essay.

In Part III of this paper I shall attempt to explain of how the prima facie problematic kind of self-deception that I have partially characterized is possible. The kind in question requires, by stipulation, simultaneously holding contradictory beliefs. So I begin with a discussion of how it is possible to do that. For the condition of simultaneously holding contradictory beliefs might be thought to be an excluder of the kind of self-deception in question. I should note at the outset, however, that I do not expect that I will say enough about how one can simultaneously hold contradictory beliefs to *convince* someone who is *skeptical* about whether this is possible. But my purpose will be served if I say enough at least to hit the ball into such a skeptic's court. A more detailed explanation must await another occasion.

III

THE ACCESSIBLE/INACCESSIBLE BELIEF DISTINCTION

11. Consider the following claims:

(1) At time t, x believes that he himself is overweight.
(2) At time t, x disbelieves that he himself is overweight.
(3) It is not the case that at time t, x believes that he himself is overweight.
(4) At time t, x believes that he himself is overweight and that it is not the case that he himself is overweight.

Claims (1) and (2) attribute simultaneously held contradictory beliefs to x. (Recall that one *dis*believes that p if and only if one believes that not-p.) The question is whether (1) and (2) could both be true. They could not be if they jointly implied (4), since (4) could not be true. However, they do not jointly imply (4): one's beliefs are not closed under logical consequence. What is at issue, then, is whether (2) implies (3). For (1) and (3) could not both be true: we contradict ourselves if we assert (1) and (3).[52] I maintain that (2) does not imply (3). Claims (1) and (2) are compatible. Indeed, it is causally possible for (1) and (2) to be true.

To begin, Jeffery Foss has argued at length that the actions to which a belief-that-p state could give rise are so many and varied that contradictory beliefs may fail "to clash" in a vast range of circumstances in which they are manifested.[53] This is because what actions, if any, a belief-that-p state will give rise to in a given circumstance will depend on what other psychological states the person is in. The point is that one could hold contradictory beliefs without that becoming apparent to one (or to anyone else for that matter).

I basically agree with Foss, but more needs to be said. For it is hard to see how the beliefs in question could fail to clash if the topic of his being overweight comes to x's mind. Suppose that x were to think of his being overweight. Then, if (1) and (2) were true, would he think that he is overweight, or that he is not overweight, or would he just not know what to think? What he *cannot* do is think that he is overweight and that he is not overweight. So, it would seem that if the topic of his being overweight came to x's mind, x would either lose one of the two beliefs or lose both. And the self-deceiver may well think about what he is self-deceived about; indeed, he may defend the belief.

I shall use the expression 'think of p'[54] in a technical sense to cover just those mental occurrences that consist in consciously thinking that p, consciously thinking that not-p, or being consciously uncertain as to what to think about whether p. (Hereafter, I shall drop the qualifier 'consciously' when speaking of thought, thinking of, and thinking that.)

One can, of course, believe that p at t without thinking that p at t. What relation does thinking that p bear to believing that p? Thinking that p is a mental event. Beliefs, recall, are states. Beliefs have *characteristic* manifestations in thought and speech. The characteristic manifestation in thought of the belief that p is thinking that p. The characteristic manifestation in speech of the belief that p is sincerely saying that p. These characteristic manifestations, unlike other manifestations, *express* the belief.[55] Thinking that p is a manifestation of the belief that p, and so is a causal consequence of the belief. But it also expresses the belief. One thing that makes the possibility of contradictory beliefs problematic is that it seems that they will clash in situations that prompt their *expression*. Thus if one believes that p and, at the same time, that not-p, then were one to think of p, the beliefs would, it seems, clash. While perhaps the belief that p and the belief that not-p can be manifested in thought at the same time, they cannot be *expressed* in thought at the same time. For, as I remarked above, one could not think that p and that not-p at the same time.

A standard response is to argue that one can believe that p while believing that not-p, if one of the beliefs is *unconscious*. Indeed, even some leading proponents of the view that simultaneous contradictory beliefs are impossible allow this case as a special exception.[56] I hesitate, however, to appeal to the notion of an unconscious belief.[57] Instead, I shall appeal shortly to a notion of my own that will do the relevant work.

There are belief-that-p states that would not receive expression in thought in circumstances appropriate for such expression—for example, when the believer considers whether p. Whether a belief that p will be manifested by the believer's thinking that p, even in appropriate circumstances for the belief's expression, will depend on other psychological factors. Let us note some that are relevant for present purposes. Short-lived self-consciousness about what one ought to think and emotional stress can, for instance, affect whether the belief state receives expression in such circumstances. Such factors can forestall the believer's thinking that p *without overturning* his belief that p. It may be that a person believes that p at time t, yet, because of extreme emotional stress or heightened self-consciousness about what he thinks he ought to think, the person is at t (consciously) uncertain what to think about whether p. Perhaps in his highly emotional state, he thinks that he does not know what to think about p. But this is compatible with his believing that p.

We can draw a useful distinction here between two kinds of beliefs. Let us say that:

x's state B is an accessible belief that p at t if and only if (i) B is a belief that p at t, (ii) x can think of p at t, and (iii) were x to think of p at t, x would do so by means of B's being manifested by x's thinking that p at t.[58]

And let us say that x's state B is a *consciously inaccessible* belief that p at t if and only if (a) B is a belief that p at t and (b) at t, B is not an accessible belief that p. (I shall abbreviate 'consciously inaccessible' by 'inaccessible'.) It follows that if B is an inaccessible belief that p at t, then either x cannot think of p at t or else it is *not* the case that were x to think of p at t, x would do so by means of B's being manifested by x's thinking that p at t (that is not how x would think of p). In the second alternative, condition (i) obtains but (iii) does not.[59]

It should be noted that I include (ii) to handle cases, if there are such, in which (iii) is *vacuously* true because x cannot think of p. It may be the case, for instance, that a nonverbal animal (e.g., a dog) can have a belief that p even though it cannot (consciously) think that p, think that not-p, or be uncertain as to what to think about whether p. If so, it could have a belief that p and vacuously satisfy (iii). However, I would not want to count such a belief as accessible. If there are such beliefs, they are inaccessible. In any case, I leave open whether (i) implies (ii). If it does, then (ii) is at worst redundant.

A variety of points should be noted about the distinction between accessible and inaccessible beliefs. First, in saying that there are two kinds of beliefs, I do not mean to suggest that 'belief' is ambiguous. There are at least two kinds of typewriters, electric and nonelectric, but 'typewriter' is not, thereby, ambiguous. Second, I do not claim to find this distinction in ordinary speech. The above definitions are *purely stipulative* and as such should be judged in terms of their theoretical fruits. Third, I do *not* offer this distinction as an explication of, or as a replacement for, the distinction between conscious and unconscious beliefs.[60] Fourth, a belief can be accessible at one time, inaccessible at another. Accessible beliefs can become inaccessible and inaccessible beliefs can become accessible. Fifth, and finally, every belief that p is either an accessible or an inaccessible belief that p, and no belief that p is both.

It is impossible to hold accessible contradictory beliefs simultaneously. For it cannot be the case that were one to think of p, one would think that p and think that not-p. However, it is possible, I maintain, simultaneously to hold contradictory beliefs if at least one of the beliefs is inaccessible. One can in this case believe that p and at the same time believe that not-p, without the beliefs' clashing in conscious thought when one thinks of p. For if one has an accessible belief that p and an inaccessible belief that not-p, then were one to think of p, one would do so by thinking that p.

Someone who is self-deceived in believing that p may well think that p, sincerely say that p, and even defend the belief that p. The question naturally arises as to whether, when the belief that p is expressed, that would eradicate the belief that not-p. I maintain that it *need not*. A person's thinking that p, for example, will, to be sure, forestall his thinking that not-p even when he disbelieves that p. But it can do so without eradicating the disbelief. What it can do instead is render, or contribute to keeping, the belief that not-*p* *inaccessible*. One can inaccessibly believe that not-*p* even though one is (consciously) thinking that *p*. This sort of situation is, as I remarked, extreme. Such discrepancies *must,* I believe, be the exception rather than the rule (but I cannot pause to argue that here). However, this extreme falls within the realm of (causal) possibility.

The sorts of cases in which we are inclined to attribute contradictory beliefs are those in which the person seems to sincerely say that *p,* perhaps even defends *p,* yet, this aside, the best explanation of the person's behavior includes the fact that the person disbelieves that *p.* Things can be as they seem: a person might sincerely say that *p,* thereby expressing an accessible belief that *p,* while also believing, albeit inaccessibly, that not-*p.*[61]

Indeed, as we shall see later, the belief that not-*p* can join with other psychological states to contribute to the expression of the belief that *p* in circumstances that are appropriate for such expression, for example, when the person thinks of whether *p.* Thus, an inaccessible belief that not-*p* might even bolster an accessible belief that *p.* It might do so by sustaining a motive for believing that *p* that prompts acts that result in the person's thinking that *p* in the circumstances in question. I have presented these points briskly, but I shall say more in section 12.

ONE WAY TO BE SELF-DECEIVED

12. The following is an explicit characterization of *one* way of being self-deceived:

x is self-deceived in believing that *p* at *t* if

(1) *x* has an accessible belief that *p* at *t*;
(2) *x* has an inaccessible belief that not-*p* at *t*;
(3) *x* is misled in believing that *p* at *t*;
(4) *x*'s belief that *p* is epistemically unwarranted at *t*;
(5) *x* desires that *p* far more than that not-*p* (or desires that *p* and does not desire that not-*p* at all);
(6) *x*'s desire that *p* and *x*'s belief that not-*p* contribute to sustaining a motive for believing that *p* that, in turn, contributes to sustaining *x*'s belief that *p*;
(7) the motive sustains the belief that *p* by disposing *x* to act and to think in ways that bias him in favor of evidence for *p*;
(8) moreover, some motive sustained by *x*'s desire that *p* and *x*'s belief that not-*p* (perhaps the same motive as in (6) or perhaps another motive) has prompted *x* to act and think in ways that have (I) misled

him into believing or into continuing to believe that p and (II) made
the belief that not-p become or remain inaccessible;
(9) the acts and mental activities in question in (8) have included x's
rationalizing, evading, or overcompensating in a biased way when x
was confronted with what he perceived as evidence against p.

I do *not* claim that *any* of these conditions is *necessary* for being self-deceived
in believing that p. However, each is either characteristic of self-deception
or at least not uncharacteristic of it. As I remarked earlier, intuitions vary as
to where along the continuum from mere wishful thinking to self-deception
we reach self-deception. Joint satisfaction of $(1) - (9)$, however, occurs far
enough along the continuum to count as self-deception. The conditions are
also jointly (causally) possible. Thus self-deception is (causally) possible.

Let us see, to begin with, how someone might come to satisfy condition
(6). Here, in very broad strokes, is *one* possible scenario. A person wishfully
believes that p. Evidence against p begins to mount, however, with the result
that the person has a growing inclination to believe that not-p. As the person
comes gradually to believe that not-p, he gradually comes to fear or regret
or be disappointed or be ashamed or just to be embarrassed that not-p. Growing fear or regret, etc., that not-p engenders a motive for believing that p.
The upshot is that the desire that p, the belief that not-p, and the negative
emotion sustain a motive that sustains the belief that p.

The motive disposes the person to try to act and think in ways that result
in his thinking that p on appropriate occasions for the expression of the belief
that p. The motive might prompt activities that result in x's avoiding thinking
that not-p by thinking that p and, thereby, result in x's not *feeling* or *experiencing* a negative emotion. This can happen without eradicating x's belief that
not-p or preventing x from actually coming to believe that not-p. Instead,
such activities might keep or render the belief inaccessible. This sort of
situation involves a delicate balance of factors. It is, as I remarked earlier,
an extreme sort of case. A more common situation would be that the activities
keep x, who has a growing inclination to believe that not-p, from actually
coming to believe that not-p. (However, if the activities significantly weaken
the inclination to believe that not-p to the point where the negative emotion
departs, the person may well lose the motive for believing that p. And that,
in turn, might result in the belief's being overturned by counterevidence.) In
any case, the extreme sort of case falls within the realm of (causal) possibility.

As noted in (7), in the sort of case of self-deception in question, a motive
will sustain the belief that p by disposing x to act and think in ways that result
in x's being biased in favor of evidence for p. When the person is confronted
with what he perceives as evidence against p, the motive might prompt him
to engage in rationalization: he might offer evidential reasons for believing
that p in order to sustain the belief. The motive might prompt him to engage

in evasion: he might try to avoid thinking about the evidence or thinking about p altogether. And the motive might prompt him to overcompensate in any of a variety of ways for his conflict-ridden state of mind about p: he might tell himself that p or rehearse evidential reasons for p or frequently imagine enjoyable consequences of p or seek the council of people who re- inforce his belief that p or operate with higher epistemic standards for the acceptance of not-p than for the acceptance of p; when the topic of p arises, he might immediately think of evidential reasons for p, and so on. The acts and activities, in the circumstances in question, (i) bias x's acquisition of evidence and (ii) bias his use of the evidence he already possesses. In this way, the activities serve to protect the belief that p from reality and memory.

Conditions (1)–(9) jointly imply that x is in a state of wishful thinking in believing that p. However, they do not jointly imply that x is in a state of self-induced deception in believing that p. For (8) and (9) can hold without x's having intentionally deceived himself into believing that p, since they do not require that the misleading be intentional.

I could add that the misleading must be intentional. However, intentional misleading would have to involve a memory-exploiting stratagem or activities by which x's knowledge of the stratagem and his belief that not-p were gradually *suppressed* and thus rendered *inaccessible*. But I won't add this, for *intentional* misleading is *uncharacteristic* of self-deception: to think other- wise is to overintellectualize what typically goes on in self-deception.

It might be insisted that a self-deceiver must have deceived himself. But one might claim in response that unintentional misleading *ipso facto* counts as unintentional deceiving and so as deceiving. Thus, when a self-deceiver unintentionally misleads himself, he deceives himself. However, preanalytic intuitions, I find, vary about whether unintentional misleading *ipso facto* counts as unintentional deceiving.[62] So I won't maintain that unintentional misleading counts as unintentional deceiving in defending my position; I shall leave open whether it does. The issue need not be settled here. For *the way* in which a self-deceiver unintentionally misleads himself counts as deceiving himself.

To begin with, consider being self-taught.[63] If one is self-taught in French, then in some sense one taught oneself French. However, the way one will have taught oneself French will be interestingly different from the way one person teaches another French in paradigm cases. For example, in such cases, the first imparts her knowledge of the language to the second. In contrast, one does not, of course, impart one's knowledge of the language to oneself when one teaches oneself French. The point generalizes: *the way* one relies on oneself when one is self-reliant is, for example, interestingly different from the way one relies on someone else in paradigm cases. Likewise, the way a self-deceiver must deceive himself is interestingly different from paradigmatic acts of deception. For example, paradigmatic acts of deception involve a deceitful intention. But, I claim, a self-deceiver characteristically misleads himself by means of rationalization, overcompensation, and evasion in a context in which he thereby counts as deceiving himself, even though he lacks a deceitful intention.

The skeptic might insist that the self-deceiver *must* intentionally try to make himself believe or continue believing something that he disbelieves. This, however, I deny. The self-deceiver need not, indeed characteristically does not, do this. The self-deceiver may well intentionally try to make himself believe or continue believing that *p*. And, since he disbelieves that *p*, it follows that *what* he is intentionally trying to make himself believe or continue believing is something that he disbelieves. However, it does *not* follow that he intentionally tries to make himself believe or continue believing something that he disbelieves.

Notice that one can try to *A* without intentionally trying to *A*. Oedipus intentionally tries to push an old man out of the way. The old man is his father, so, in a sense, Oedipus tries to push his father out of the way. But Oedipus does not intentionally try to push his father out of the way. For Oedipus does not realize that the old man is his father. Rather, Oedipus *un*intentionally tries to push his father out of the way. In the tough sort of cases of self-deception in question, the self-deceiver tries to make himself continue believing something he disbelieves. But he does *not* intentionally try to make himself continue believing something he disbelieves. For he does not realize that *p* is something he disbelieves; the belief is inaccessible. When he thinks of *p,* he does not think that *p*.

Nevertheless, as I remarked, the self-deceiver might well *intentionally* try to make himself continue believing that *p*. To be sure, the self-deceiver does not typically take himself to be trying to make himself continue believing that *p*. However, one need not believe one is trying to make oneself continue to believe that *p* in order for one to be intentionally doing so.[64] One typically tries to do many things at once. It need not be the case that for each of the things one is intentionally trying to do, one believes one is trying to do it. At a department colloquium, one offers an objection to something a speaker said in her paper. One believes one is doing this in order to point out a mistake. Indeed, one is. But one is also trying to impress one's colleagues. However, one may not believe one is trying to do that. One can intentionally *A* (e.g., try to impress one's colleagues) without believing that one is.[65] What motives one *takes* oneself to be acting on can depend, for example, on one's conception of one's character and what other psychological states one takes oneself to be in.[66] And one can be mistaken about such matters, with the result that one is blind to certain of one's motives.

If one intentionally *A-ed,* then in *A-ing,* one was acting on a motive one had for *A-ing*. If one intentionally acts on a motive, one must believe that one has the motive. However, one can act on a motive without intentionally acting on that motive. Indeed, one might often act on motives that one would *not* intentionally act on. There is a distinction between (a) intentionally acting and so doing on the basis of a motive *M* and (b) intentionally acting on *M*. If one intentionally acts on a *M*, then one believes that one is, or at least that one is trying, to act on *M*. But one can act on a motive without intentionally acting on that motive. If this were not possible, there would be an unacceptable infinite regress: to act intentionally, one would have to act intentionally on a certain motive, and to act on that motive, one would have to act intentionally on another motive, and so on *ad infinitum*.[67] This is wildly implausible and is surely not required for acting on motives. A child wants attention and believes he can get it by complaining.[68] This want and belief prompt the child to complain. The child intentionally tries to get attention, but the child need not intentionally act on his motive for getting attention. And the child need not believe that he is trying to get attention. Likewise, fear that not-*p* may, for instance, engender a motive for continuing to believe that *p* and this motive may, in turn, be one the self-deceiver acts on, albeit unintentionally.

In rationalizing, a self-deceiver might take himself to be offering reasons to believe that *p*. Indeed, he is. But he is also by trying to convince himself that *p*, yet he does not realize he is trying to do that. In evading a certain issue, he might, for instance, take himself to be turning his attention to matters that interest him more at the time. And he is. But he is also trying to avoid thinking about *p*, or about what he perceives as evidence against *p*, without realizing he is. In overcompensating by seeking advice from someone who will say what he wants to hear, he might, for example, take himself to be seeking advice from someone he trusts. And he is. But he is also seeking to be told what he wants to hear, without realizing this. In each of these cases he might be acting on a motive for believing that *p*, yet not be intentionally acting on that motive.

When a person is engaged in rationalization, evasion, and overcompensation *in such circumstances,* the person counts as "kidding himself" or "fooling himself." Moreover, when a person, who disbelieves that *p*, intentionally tries to make himself believe or continue believing that *p* by engaging in such activities, and, as a result unintentionally misleads himself into believing or continuing to believe that *p* via biased thinking, he *deceives* himself in a way appropriate for self-deception. No deceitful intention is required for this. The sort of unintentional misleading in question counts as (unintentional) deceiving in the sense appropriate for self-deception. And if the belief he misleads himself into holding or continuing to hold is false, he counts as *deceived* in holding it.[69]

NOTES

1. For a discussion of the so-called "paradoxes" of self-deception, see also Herbert Fingarette's *Self-Deception* (London: Routledge and Kegan Paul, 1969), chap. 1. For

an excellent recent discussion of the literature on "the paradoxes," see Alfred Mele's "Recent Work on Self-Deception," *American Philosophical Quarterly* 34 (1987):1–17.

2. For a defense of the skeptical position, see S. Paluch, "Self-Deception," *Inquiry* 10 (1967):268–278; David Kipp, "On Self-Deception," *Philosophical Quarterly* 30 (1980):305–317; and M. R. Haight, *A Study of Self-Deception* (Sussex: Harvester Press, 1980). The skeptical arguments in this paper, however, are, for the most part, of my own making.

3. I borrow the notion of an 'excluder' from Robert Nozick. See his *Philosophical Explanations* (Harvard, 1981), p. 9.

4. Skeptics typically allege that there are excluders of the *metaphysical* possibility of self-deception. Of course, excluders of its metaphysical possibility are *ipso facto* excluders of its causal possibility.

5. Some leading nonskeptics have *not* attempted to explain how self-deception *in belief* is possible. For example, see Robert Audi, "Self-Deception, Action and Will," *Erkenntnis* 18 (1982):133–158, and Kent Bach, "An Analysis of Self-Deception," *Philosophy and Phenomenological Research* 41 (1981):351–370.

6. I follow the common philosophical practice here of using 'belief' in a broad sense that includes fleeting and superficial opinions as well as, for instance, enduring and deeply held convictions. It should also be noted that being self-deceived in *expecting* something does not raise any interesting issues not raised by being self-deceived in believing something. (Indeed, expecting that *p may* just consist in believing that *p* will be the case.) Whether self-deception in *emotion* requires self-deception in belief is a question that I must leave open. (See Ronald de Sousa's paper in this volume [chap. 14] for a discussion of self-deception in emotion.) Indeed, whether all self-deception is or involves self-deception in belief, even in this broad sense, is a question I leave open.

7. It should be noted at the outset that there is no received view as to what self-deception consists in. Indeed, there is no leading contender for general acceptance, nor even a dominant trend. See, for instance, the papers in this volume and the ones in *Self-Deception and Self-Understanding,* ed. Michael Martin (Lawrence: Univ. Press of Kansas, 1985). I shall *not* attempt to state noncircular necessary and sufficient conditions for self-deception. I doubt that that could be done.

8. By a 'causally necessary condition for something' I mean a condition required for that something in every causally possible world. Every condition is causally necessary for itself, and metaphysically necessary conditions are causally necessary conditions. When I speak of what is 'required' for self-deception, I mean 'at least causally required' in the sense in question.

9. Each disjunct of condition (b) is intended to require that one intentionally deceives oneself in a *de se* sense and not merely a *de re* sense: one must conceive of oneself by means of the first-person indexical concept as an intended or potential victim of the act. Condition (b) should be stated using Hector Castaneda's quasi-indicator 'oneself*', which attributes a use of the first-person indexical concept. (See his *Thinking and Doing* [Dordrect, 1975].) But for stylistic reasons, I use 'oneself' rather than 'oneself*'.

10. See, for example, Alfred Mele's "Self-Deception, Action and Will: Comments," *Erkenntnis* 18 (1982):159–164, and his "Self-Deception," *Philosophical Quarterly* 33 (1983):365–377.

11. See, for example, Frederick Siegler's "An Analysis of Self-Deception," *Nous* 2 (1968):147–164; Patrick Gardiner's "Error, Faith and Self-Deception," *Proceedings of the Aristotelian Society* 70 (1970):221–243; Béla Szabados's "Wishful Thinking and Self-Deception," *Analysis* 33 (1973):201–205, and his "Self-Deception," *Canadian Journal of Philosophy* 4 (1974):51–68.

12. See John King-Farlow's "Self-Deceivers and Sartrian Seducers," *Analysis* 23 (1963):131–136; David Pears's *Motivated Irrationality* (Oxford: Oxford University Press, 1984); Donald Davidson's "Deception and Division," in *Actions and Events: Perspectives on the Philosophy of Donald Davidson,* ed. Ernie LePore and Brian P. McLaughlin (Oxford: Blackwell, 1985), pp. 138–148; and Stephen White's paper in this volume (chap. 21). King-Farlow, Pears, and White hold that the self-deception involves deceitful interaction between autonomous agents that somehow contribute to constituting the self-deceiver. Mark Johnston, in his contribution to this volume (chap. 3), criticizes attempts to explain how self-deception is possible by appeal to such homunculi. (His criticisms do *not* involve denying that there are homunculi.) I am in great sympathy with his criticisms (and, as should be apparent, with his positive view as well). Space is not available to me here to discuss homuncularist approaches to self-deception.

13. See R. Sorensen's "Self-Deception and Scattered Events," *Mind* 94 (1985):64–69.

14. Cf. Davidson's "Deception and Division," p. 145.

15. I won't speculate on her motive for getting herself to miss the meeting in this way since it does not matter what it is. One could be described.

16. As before, her motive does not matter.

17. Given my purposes in Part I, it is best hereafter to stick with examples of self-induced deception involving a single act of deception (if a unifier view of act individuation is correct), or of acts of deception on a single action-tree (if a multiplier view of act individuation is correct).

18. I do not defend this assumption since (i) it is common and (ii) nothing in what follows turns on whether it is true.

19. A point worth noting here about self-induced deception and self-deception is this. Suppose it were shown that to be self-deceived in believing that *p,* one must have intentionally deceived oneself into believing or continuing to believe that *p.* That would not suffice to show that being self-deceived in believing that *p* requires being deceived in believing that *p.* For, as we have just seen, one can be intentionally deceived *into* believing or continuing to believe something one is not deceived *in* believing. Of course, if being self-deceived in believing that *p* requires having intentionally deceived oneself into believing or continuing to believe that *p,* then being self-deceived requires being or having been in some state of self-induced deception. But it would remain to be shown that in order to be self-deceived in believing that *p,* one must be deceived in believing that *p.* For perhaps one can be self-deceived in believing something that is true, and so in believing something one is not deceived in believing. Maintaining this would not require denying that being self-deceived in believing that *p* requires having intentionally deceived oneself into believing or continuing to believe that *p.* But nothing turns on this in what follows.

20. Roderick Chisholm and Thomas Feehan discuss cases of intentional deception involving *allowing* someone to continue to believe something, in their "The Intent to

Deceive," *Journal of Philosophy* 74 (1977):143–159.

21. To avoid an excessive detailing of particulars, I pass on describing a case; but this could easily be done.

22. My worries center on the fact that noninstantaneous, partially overlapping temporal parts will have minds of their own. I worry about how their minds are related and how their mental state tokens relate to physical state tokens. But a footnote is not the place to pursue these worries either.

23. The skeptic need not commit herself to the view that persons are three-dimensional entities persisting through time either. Such deep metaphysical issues are best skirted in the present context.

24. Some might take the temporal span of a deceitful act to be the time the deceitful act is performed; some might take the *initial* time of the temporal span of the deceitful act to be the time the deceitful act is performed; and perhaps there are other possibilities. This issue can be left open. Whatever one's theory concerning the time of an action, one can allow that acts of deception have a temporal span.

25. The parallel claim in terms of temporal parts is this: self-deception requires that a temporal part of a person have intentionally deceived another temporal part with the same temporal extension, and it is (at least causally) impossible for a temporal part to last long enough to do that.

26. It may well be possible, for instance, for a person to take a pill that makes her forget what happened in the last half hour. On the spur of the moment, Mary decides, as a prank, to deceive herself about something. She quickly constructs a deceptive setup to this end, and then takes a pill of the sort in question. The pill takes effect: Mary forgets what happened in the last half hour. She encounters the deceptive setup and is taken in by it, thereby becoming deceived. To be sure, the example is quite farfetched. Nevertheless, it seems possible. (Mark Johnston has a similar example; see chap. 3 in this volume.)

27. Pears can be viewed as attempting to explain how this is possible in *Motivated Irrationality,* and also in his "Motivated Irrationality," in *Philosophical Essays on Freud,* ed. Richard Wollheim and James Hopkins (Cambridge: Cambridge University Press, 1982).

28. In writing the date in her appointment book for her future reference, she asserts to herself (or to her "future self") that the appointment is on the date in question, with the intention of lying to herself (or to her "future self").

29. Cf. Davidson, "Deception and Division," pp. 144–145.

30. Raphael Demos makes this point in "Lying to Oneself," *Journal of Philosophy* 57 (1960):589. Davidson develops the point at length in "Deception and Division," p. 144. I do not defend the point at length since nothing turns on it in what follows.

31. To be sure, the paranoid may, for instance, want to suffer. Further, the paranoid may to some extent want to be gossiped about. But this last want, for instance, is not required for him to be self-deceived in believing that he is being gossiped about. It is possible for one to want *p* and to want not-*p* if, for instance, one wants one of them more. Believing that *p* can be wishful thinking on one's part even if one wants not-*p* to some extent, provided that one wants *p* much more. But even if our paranoid wants to some extent to be gossiped about, he (by stipulation) wants far more not to be gossiped about.

32. Two points will avert misunderstanding. First, it may seem more appropriate for me to speak here of wishes rather than of desires. The differences between wishes and desires are, however, irrelevant for present purposes. 'Desire' is the broader notion. Second, the desire will only partially sustain the belief: no desire has the causal power to sustain a belief by itself. Hereafter, I generally follow common practice and use 'sustain' to mean at least partially sustain, as we use 'cause' to mean at least partially cause.

33. This common feature of self-deception and wishful thinking is not implied by the first: a belief can be sustained (in part) by a desire without being epistemically unwarranted. I might be epistemically warranted in believing that I will leave the room in two minutes, even though my belief is sustained (in part) by my desire to leave the room in two minutes. To take a different sort of case, a desire to remember that *p*—say that a person's phone number is such-and-such—might sustain one's belief that *p* and yet the belief be epistemically warranted.

34. There is a large literature on *the basing relation*. For excellent recent discussion, see Robert Audi's "Belief, Reason, and Inference," *Philosophical Topics* 14 (1986):27–65.

35. Whether one possesses *adequate* evidence for *p* depends, of course, on the *totality* of evidence one possesses bearing on *p*.

36. Of course, I need not *insist* that self-induced deception does not suffice for self-deception since my main task is to explain how self-deception is possible. This task does not require that I argue that certain conditions are necessary for self-deception. So I need not insist that there is some necessary condition for self-deception that fails to be necessary for self-induced deception. If you continue to think self-induced deception suffices for self-deception, then take me to be focusing exclusively on cases of self-deception that involve a belief that is epistemically unwarranted and causally sustained by a desire.

37. It is worth noting that the reason wishful thinking fails to suffice for self-deception cannot be *just that* it fails to suffice for self-induced deception, *if* the possibility of self-deception is indeed problematic. Let us say that one is in a state of *self-induced wishful deception* in believing that *p* just in case (1) believing that *p* is wishful thinking on one's part and (2) one is in a state of self-induced deception in believing that *p*. Self-induced wishful deception is (causally) possible: one could intentionally deceive oneself by ensuring that one will encounter a situation in which one will, unwarrantedly and mistakenly, come to believe that *p* prompted by one's desire that *p*, having forgotten one's stratagem. A deceiver can exploit his own biases to deceive himself.

38. I leave open whether the condition combined with (I) and (II) yields a sufficient condition for wishful thinking.

39. Bela Szabados deserves credit here for his pioneering work on the relationship between wishful thinking and self-deception. See especially his "Wishful Thinking and Self-Deception." See also his recent paper "The Self, Its Passions, and Self-Deception," in Martin's *Self-Deception and Self-Understanding*, pp. 143–168.

40. Alfred Mele discusses the effects of desire on attention in this context in *Irrationality: An Essay on Akrasia, Self-Deception, and Self-Control* (Oxford, 1987), chap. 10. I am deeply indebted to him here.

41. I borrow the apt term "self-misleader" from Mark Johnston (chap. 3 in this

volume). He too thinks that a self-deceiver can be an unintentional self-misleader. (Scc my discussion below) Mele makes essentially the same point in each of his pieces cited above.

42. George Graham, "Russell's Deceptive Desires," *Philosophical Quarterly* 36 (1986):223–229.

43. The distinction between clear-cut cases of self-deception and non-clear-cut cases is, of course, itself vague in application.

44. There is no sharp distinction between inclination to believe and actual belief.

45. The self-deceiver might take *p* to reflect on his character, and the fact that not-*p* might conflict with his favored self-image. Of course, this is not required.

46. The end is the content of a desire. The desire need not be *endorsed*; one need not, for example, desire to have that desire.

47. *Time,* September 1986, p. 51.

48. Thus wishful thinking does not require positive thinking. Positive thinking does not require wishful thinking either: for it is *possible* for believing that *p* to be positive thinking on one's part and yet for the belief to be epistemically warranted. Consider William James's well-known example of a man trapped at the edge of a deep gorge. The only chance for the man to survive is to leap across the gorge. But it is uncertain whether he can make the jump. The man wants to leap across the gorge, however, and believes that if he believes he can, that will greatly increase his chances. It is *possible* that, given the evidence available to him, he is epistemically warranted in believing that he can make the jump *if* he believes he can. Suppose that it is and that his belief that he can make the jump is sustained (in part) by this motive for believing and is also appropriately based upon the evidence in question. Then, this is positive thinking and not wishful thinking.

49. The distinction between prudential and evidential reasons is essentially the same as Davidson's distinction between evaluative and cognitive reasons in "Deception and Division," p. 143. The distinction is *not* exhaustive. Nor is the distinction, drawn below, between epistemic and prudential rationality exhaustive of types of rationality.

50. See, for example, David Pugmire's "Motivated Irrationality," *Proceedings of the Aristotelian Society* 56 (1982):179–196, and David Pears's discussion of self-deception in his *Motivated Irrationality*.

51. Consider, for example, a case in which one lacks adequate evidence for *p* but knows that one must believe that *p* or die.

52. Cf. Davidson's "Deception and Division," p. 138.

53. Jeffrey Foss, "Rethinking Self-Deception," *American Philosophical Quarterly* 17 (1980):237–243.

54. In a sense, it would have been more appropriate to use 'think of *p*-ing' rather than 'think of *p*' to indicate that I am using a place-holder for a gerundive nominalization. But in another sense it seemed inappropriate.

55. This does *not* imply that, nor do I think that, thinking that *p* is a matter of silently saying that *p* to oneself in thought.

56. See, for example, Richard Foley's "Is It Possible to Have Contradictory Beliefs?" in *Midwest Studies in Philosophy X,* ed. French, Uehling, and Wettstein (Minneapolis: Univ. of Minnesota Press, 1986), pp. 327–356.

57. I do so for a wide variety of reasons, two of which I shall rather bluntly list.

First, the distinction carries a lot of heavy theoretical baggage with it which I do not wish to carry. Second, as the notion of an unconscious belief is sometimes understood, it seems inappropriate for present purposes. For an unconscious belief may be "too deeply buried" to explain the sort of "tension" that seems present in the minds of some self-deceivers. The typical self-deceiver is more conflict-ridden than he would be if one of his contradictory beliefs were unconscious in the sense in question. Unconscious beliefs in this sense are manifested only in a restricted range of ways, for example, in dreams or in slips of the tongue. Unconscious beliefs in this sense might well not even count as evidence *in the person's possession* since they may not be suitably available to the person.

58. Two points should be noted. First, I cannot pursue such matters as the nature of content in this paper. Suffice it to say that the definition could be formulated in terms of believing that p under a mode of presentation and thinking of p under a mode of presentation. Such definitions could be employed should the contents of beliefs and thoughts prove to be propositions, where these are understood to be functions from possible worlds to truth values. Second, a *related* notion of inaccessibility could be defined for other sorts of propositional attitudes. But here I make use only of the notion of an inaccessible belief.

59. Two unrelated points: first, I here allow myself the simplifying assumption that x will have only one belief-that-p state. However, it is, I believe, causally possible to have more than one belief that p. This raises the issue whether one could be accessible and the other not. But nothing turns on this in what follows. Second, I should note that the distinction between accessible and inaccessible beliefs is different from Georges Rey's distinction between avowed and central beliefs in his contribution to this volume (chap. 12). However, I cannot pause to discuss the differences here.

60. I am inclined to think that unconscious beliefs are inaccessible beliefs, though not conversely. But nothing turns on this. The point to note is that *inaccessible beliefs* can be manifested in any way that does not involve consciously thinking that p. They can generate "the tension" mentioned above in note 57 when they are accompanied by contradictory *accessible* beliefs.

61. Audi has attempted to show how many cases in which a person sincerely says that p but disbelieves that p can be explained without attributing contradictory beliefs. (See his contribution to this volume [chap. 4].) We can attribute to someone a disposition to sincerely say that p without attributing a belief that p. However, as the sincerity condition is typically understood, sincerely saying that p requires believing that p. So if the disposition is activated, the person would, on this understanding, believe that p. Thus Audi's account would not provide another option to what I am suggesting. Audi holds that a related notion of 'sincerity' can be explicated that does not have the belief requirement. But, in any case, in some circumstances of the sort that interest us, the self-deceiver sincerely defends the claim that p. Even in a weakened sense of 'sincerity' it would seem that the person thus is at least of the opinion that p, even if, perhaps, the opinion is superficial and fleeting. And that counts as believing that p in the broad sense of 'belief' that I am employing here (see note 5). Perhaps Audi is using 'belief' in some more restricted sense. In any case, Audi uses the notion of an 'unconscious belief' in a sense that allows a wide variety of manifestations. He may have nothing stronger in mind than the notion of an inaccessible belief. It may be that the disagreements between us are, at bottom, verbal. But I cannot pursue this here.

62. Intentional misleading *ipso facto* counts as intentional deceiving. But the issue is whether unintentional misleading *ipso facto* counts as unintentional deceiving. One can unintentionally mislead someone without performing *any* intentional act of misleading. However, some types of action are such that on any occasion on which they are tokened, some intentional action of that type is tokened. Lying is one such. One might unintentionally lie to Tom, for one might have intended to lie to Harry and have mistaken Tom for Harry. But on any occasion on which one lies, one performs some intentional act of lying. On the occasion in question, for instance, one intentionally lied to the person one was addressing. (One can, of course, deceive without lying.) Intuitions vary on whether deceiving is like lying or like misleading in the respect in question. Paradigmatic acts of deception seem, to me at least, to involve intentional deceiving. But see the discussion below of 'self-X' terms.

63. Thanks are due here to William Ruddick for helping me appreciate this point. See his paper in this volume (chap. 17).

64. For a complementary but different view as to why, see Mele, *Irrationality: An Essay on Akrasia, Self-Deception, and Self-Control,* chap. 10.

65. If one continues to think that intentionally *A*-ing requires believing that one is *A*-ing or that one may well be *A*-ing, the point can, for present purposes, be put in terms of *motivated action*. The point, then, is that the self-deceiver's attempt to make himself believe or continue to believe that *p* is motivated.

66. See Sanford's and Audi's discussions of rationalization in this volume (respectively, chap. 6 and chap. 4).

67. I owe this argument to Mark Johnston (see chap. 3 in this volume).

68. Bach uses this very example to make a related point in "An Analysis of Self-Deception," p. 368.

69. In addition to acknowledgements in earlier notes, I wish to thank the following people for helpful discussions: George Graham, Anne Jacobson, Robert Kraut, Ernie LePore, Tim Maudlin, Howard McGary, Georges Rey, and especially Amélie Rorty (who sparked my interest in self-deception). I am indebted to the following for comments on an earlier draft: Jonathan Adler, Robert Audi, Gary Gleb, Peter Klein, and Alfred Mele.

3

SELF-DECEPTION AND THE NATURE OF MIND*

MARK JOHNSTON

When paradox dominates the description of a widespread phenomenon, dubious presuppositions usually lurk. Paradox dominates the philosophical treatment of bad faith or self-deception.[1] Part of the explanation is that the descriptive content of any claim that someone has deceived himself can be made to seem paradoxical. Such paradox mongering is not a fetish found only among analytic philosophers. Here is J. P. Sartre:

> One does not undergo one's bad faith; one is not infected with it . . . but consciousness affects itself with bad faith. There must be an original intention and a project of bad faith: this project implies a comprehension of bad faith as such and a pre-reflective apprehension of consciousness as affecting itself with bad faith. It follows first that the one to whom the lie is told and the one who lies are one and the same person, which means that I must know in my capacity as deceiver the truth which is hidden from me in my capacity as the one deceived.[2]

This suggests *the surface paradox of self-deception*. If bad faith or self-deception is lying to oneself then a self-deceiver must stand to himself as liar to liar's victim. As liar he knew or strongly suspected that, as it might be, he was too drunk to drive home safely; as victim of the lie he did not know or strongly suspect this. If the same subject of belief or knowledge is both liar and liar's victim, we have a simple contradiction in *our* description of his condition: he both knew and did not know that he was too drunk to drive home safely.

There is a natural homuncularist response to this surface paradox of self-deception.[3] Distinct subsystems that play the distinct roles of deceiver and deceived are located within the self-deceiver. So no single subject of belief is required to both believe (know) a proposition and not believe (know) it.

The homuncularist picture has some independent appeal. For there is another sort of epistemic duality in self-deception which the homuncularist

---

*In writing this paper I have been helped by John Cooper, Raymond Guess, Gilbert Harman, Richard Jeffrey, David Lewis, Alison McIntyre, Michael Smith, and Bas van Fraassen.

picture can capture. There is a sense in which the self-deceiving drunkard who believes and claims he will make it home safely also knows he may very well not, but this latter knowledge is suppressed, unacknowledged, or inoperative. When he is drunk it does not find useful expression in his thought or speech. When he sobers up or comes out of his self-deception he might plausibly say that he knew all along that it would be disastrous for him to drive. The self-deceptive belief that he will make it home safely can be located in the deceived system, and the knowledge that he probably won't can be located in the deceiving system. One snag remains. If the deceiving system is actively to deceive, then its knowledge of the facts must be operative and available to it. But then the homuncularist must also find a privileged sense in which knowledge is inoperative in self-deception. A strategy suggests itself. Let the deceived system be the analogue of the Freudian ego—the locus of the person's conscious thought, perception, decision, and voluntary control of the body. What is stored in the deceiving system is then hypothesized as not accessible to consciousness and so inoperative and inaccessible from the point of view of the ego or main system. So the homuncularist not only avoids contradiction in his description of the self-deceiver but also appears to be able to explain, in terms of mental compartmentalization, how it is that the self-deceiver could believe propositions that are contradictory.

If another model of self-deception were produced then this account of the duality involved in self-deception might seem forced. One can make perfectly good sense of conscious belief that p and unacknowledged knowledge of the contrary without thinking that there are particular loci within the mind which are the respective subjects of attitudes of these sorts, as if "consciousness," "preconsciousness," and "unconsciousness" were names for layers or compartments of the mind.

One reason for thinking that another model should be produced is that the homuncular explanation replaces a contradictory description of the self-deceiver with a host of psychological puzzles. How could the deceiving subsystem have the capacities required to perpetrate the deception? For example, do such deceiving subsystems have a much higher alcohol tolerance than their hosts? Is that why they seem particularly active when one is drunk? Why should the deceiving subsystem be interested in the deception? Does it like lying for its own sake? Or does it suppose that it knows what it is best for the deceived system to believe?

Again, how does the deceiving system engage in an extended campaign of deception, employing various stratagems to alter the beliefs of the deceived system, without the deceived system's somehow noticing? If the deceived system somehow notices then the deception cannot succeed without the collusion of the deceived system. However, to speak of the collusion of the deceived system in its own deception simply reintroduces the original problem. The deceived system is now both (partial) agent and patient in the deception. Must we now recognize within the deceived system a deceiving subsystem and a deceived subsystem? If so, we face a dilemma: either a completely unexplanatory regress of subsystems of subsystems or the termination of the regress with a deceived subsystem stupid enough not to notice the strategies of deception and so one for which the question of collusion does not arise. The latter may always seem to be the way out until we reflect on the fact that the knowing, *complex*, and deceiving subsystem must have a curious kind of self-effacing motivation both to deceive the stupid and *simple* subsystem *and* to let it speak for and guide the whole person on the issue in question. Often self-deception involves a matter vital to the self as a whole, e.g., whether one will survive the drive home tonight. It is hard then to see why the wiser, deceiving subsystem should stand aside and let its foolish victim's belief control subsequent inference and action.

In fact homuncularism is a premature response to the surface paradox of self-deception. A dubious presupposition does lurk behind the familiar construal of the paradox. To be deceived is sometimes just to be *misled* without being *intentionally* misled or lied to. The self-deceiver is a self-misleader. As a result of his own activity he gets into a state in which he is misled, at least at the level of conscious belief. But the presupposition that generates the paradox is that this activity must be thought of as the intentional act of lying to oneself so that self-deception is just the reflexive case of lying. Evidently, *as the surface paradox shows*, nothing could be *that*. The homuncularist holds to the presupposition that the intentional act of lying is involved but drops the strict reflexive condition. If self-misleading is to be lying then the best one can do is to have parts of the self play the roles of liar and liar's victim. (Some have suggested that temporal parts of the self over time could play this role, but as we shall see this will not provide a general account.)[4]

The suggestion I wish to explore is that the surface paradox and deeper paradoxes of self-deception (i.e., those developed by Bernard Williams, by Sartre in a different passage, and by Donald Davidson)[5] arise because as theorists of self-deception we tend to over-rationalize mental processes that are purposive but not intentional. These are processes that serve some interests of the self-deceiver, processes whose existence within the self-deceiver's psychic economy depends upon this fact, but processes that are not necessarily initiated by the self-deceiver for the sake of those interests or for any other reason. If we call mental processes that are purposive but not initiated for and from a reason *subintentional* processes then we can say that our over-rationalization of self-deception consists in assimilating subintentional processes to intentional acts, where an intentional act is a process initiated and directed by an agent because he recognizes that it serves a specific interest of his.[6] Faced with the subintentional processes of division, denial, repression, removal of appropriate affect, wishful perception, wishful memory, and wishful thought, the theorist whose only model for things done by an agent is that of the intentional act will multiply subagents complete with their own interests and action plans. Self-deception is an important test case for such a theorist since the very characterization of someone as self-deceived suggests both mental division and self-directed agency. If the subagency or homuncularist picture applies anywhere it should apply here. However, as I shall argue, little in the way of plausible interests and action plans can be constructed in order to carry out the program of representing self-deception as an intentional act of a lying subagency. In any case, this would misrepresent what we are censuring when we censure someone for self-deception. For in censuring the self-deceiver we do not blame any subagency for simply lying, nor are we mixing such blame with sympathy for an innocent victim of the lying subagency.

The recognition of subintentional mental processes points the way out of the so-called paradoxes of self-deception and avoids an implausible homuncularism. The subintentional mental process involved in wishful thinking and self-deception is an instance of a nonaccidental mental regularity: anxious desire that *p,* or more generally anxiety concerning *p,* generates the belief that *p.* Deeper morals about the nature of the mind emerge from the recognition of such nonaccidental, purpose-serving, mental regularities—mental tropisms, as I shall call them.

The existence and ubiquity of mental tropisms whose relata do not stand in any rational relation falsifies a certain view of the mental which is gaining currency. This *interpretive view* of mental states and events has it that there is nothing more to being in a mental state or undergoing a mental change than being apt to have that state or change attributed to one within an adequate interpretive theory, i.e., a theory that takes one's behavior (including speech behavior) as evidence and develops under the holistic constraint of construing much of that behavior as intentional action caused by rationalizing beliefs and desires that it is reasonable to suppose the subject has, given his environment and basic drives. On this conception, when we attribute a mental state to another, we are not locating within him an instance of a mental natural kind or property that as such enters into characteristic causal relations in accord with nonaccidental psychological or psychophysical regularities. On the view in question there are no natural mental properties and so no lawlike psychological or psychophysical regularities. Instead, attributions of mental states and changes have a point only within a whole pattern of potential reason-explanations, i.e., explanations that exhibit the subject as a rational agent pursuing what is reasonable from his point of view. Fitting into a pattern of reason-explanation that serve to interpret their subject is thus a constitutive condition of something's being a mental attribution. More, there can be no other content to the idea that something is a *mental* attribution. In this sense, rationality is constitutive and exhaustive of the mental.

Donald Davidson has done the most to promote this conception of mental attributions.[7] Armed with it he is able to show in a relatively a priori fashion that mental vocabulary needs no special ontology of its own, i.e., that the intentional mental descriptions of an adequate interpretive theory pick out physical event tokens.[8] But, as Davidson recognizes, both mere wishful thinking and self-deception provide prima facie counterexamples to the interpretive view of mental states and events.[9] For they seem to be cases in which desire brings about belief in a characteristic way which on the face of it is not subject to rational explanation. The generated belief could not be the outcome of any practical syllogism with the desire as premise. My suggestion is that the appearances are correct and point to a characteristic, nonaccidental, and nonrational connection between desire and belief—a *mental tropism* or purpose-serving mental mechanism. Finally, it will emerge that such mental tropisms are not peripheral pathologies but are the causal bases of rational and irrational connections alike.

WISHFUL THOUGHT

1. The accusation of self-deception is related to the charge of wishful thinking, a charge that points to motivated belief, i.e, belief adopted not in response to the available evidence but in conformity with what one wants to be the case. Whereas the wishful thinker accepts a proposition without possessing sufficient evidence, or at least without relying upon sufficient evidence that is in his possession, the self-deceiver accepts a proposition against what he at some level recognizes to be the implications of the evidence. Hence it is sometimes said that, whereas the mere wishful thinker is only self-indulgent, the self-deceiver is perverse and duplicitous. He resists the natural implications of the evidence, and in order to do this he employs certain stratagems of denial. A self-deceiver is properly charged with wishful thinking. But to leave the charge at that is to be much less informative and disdainfully self-righteous than one could be.

Self-deception is then a *species* of wishful thought: it is motivated belief in the face of contrary evidence. There is, however, a way of thinking about belief which makes nonsense of the very idea of purely motivated belief, i.e., belief generated from desire and not formed in response to evidence. Thus H. H. Price writes, "[We] cannot strictly be said to believe without evidence, what is so described is not belief but something else."[10] Price's remark suggests an easy way out. Concede the term "belief" to those who wish to tie belief essentially to responses to evidence and recognize a range of attitudes that share the action- and inference-guiding role of belief but not necessarily its (conceded) relation to evidence, so that these attitudes can be generated by desire or, more generally, be under the control of the will.

At this stage this quick dismissal of the worry is too facile. If wishful or self-deceptive thought is to serve its characteristic purpose of reducing anxiety that one's desires will not be satisfied, it must result in one's adopting a cognitive attitude, i.e., an attitude that involves one's taking the world to be a certain way, namely, in accord with or soon to be in accord with one's desires. The doubts about the coherence of talk of a belief's having its origin not in response to evidence but in the will, extend to any sort of attitude that is cognitive, i.e., that involves its subject in taking the world to be a certain way. So for example, when Bernard Williams argues that necessarily I cannot bring it about, just like that, that I believe something independently of the evidence, he gives an argument that would apply to any cognitive attitude, i.e., any attitude that purports to represent reality. Williams writes:

> If I could acquire a belief at will, I could acquire it whether it was true or not; moreover I would know that I could acquire it whether it was true or not. If in full consciousness I could will to acquire a 'belief' irrespective of its truth, it is unclear that before the event I could seriously think of it as a belief, *i.e., as something purporting to represent reality*. At the very least, there must be a restriction on what is the case after the event; since I could not then, in full consciousness, regard this as a belief of mine, i.e., something I take to be true, and also know that I acquired it at will. With regard to no belief could I know—or, if all this is to be done in full consciousness, even suspect—that I had acquired it at will. But if I can acquire beliefs at will, I must know that I am able to do this; and could I know that I was capable of this feat, if with regard to every feat of this kind which I had performed I necessarily had to believe that it had not taken place?[11] (My emphasis.)

The crucial claim in this passage is that I cannot take something to be a belief of mine *and* believe that I acquired it at will. The idea seems to be that, in the simplest case, if I recognize that I have just acquired a "belief" at will, have just conjured up a representation and assented to it, I thereby recognize that I possess no evidence in favor of the truth of that representation so that I cannot then take it to be a true representation of the way reality is. This needs amendment. If someone offers me a million dollars if I can get myself to believe that I will be a millionaire, and I succeed and am about to be given the money, then although I know I acquired the belief at will, I have come to possess sufficient evidence in favor of its truth. I had evidence that if I acquired the belief at will then it would be a true belief. By acquiring the belief at will I simultaneously come to have evidence of its truth. This sort of complication can arise in any case in which acquiring a belief makes it more likely that the believed proposition is true. (See the discussion of positive thinking below.)

What might seem odd is any conscious state that involves one's intentionally coming to believe some proposition *p* while recognizing that one neither presently possesses nor will possess evidence for *p*, so that one has no evidential basis for thinking p true. For then we have an intentional act, e.g., assenting to some representation that p, done without its typical and particularly appropriate reason, namely, that there is evidence for p. However, the atypical is possible, and we should allow for the possibility of one's intentionally coming to believe p out of a desire to believe p which is not itself the result of any sensitivity to the evidence for p—for example, a desire springing from an interest in the causal consequences of one's doxastic states, as opposed to an interest in the truth-values of the propositions one's doxastic states are beliefs in. The appeal of Pascal's wager crucially depends upon the cultivation of such an interest. (See also the discussion of the sophisticate below.) But intentionally coming to believe that p neither out of such interests nor from any evidential reason for p is a contradiction in terms—an intentional act done from and for no reason. How does this bear on the possibility of intentional and immediate wishful thought, i.e., intending to adopt the belief that p, just like that and just because one wants p to be the case?

Any intentional act can be described *as if* it were the outcome of a stretch of practical reasoning from reasons that the agent can be said to have and to have acted because of. This is not to say that prior to each intentional act some reasoning must occur. However, even if practical reasoning did not actually take place prior to some intentional act, our claim that it was an intentional act commits us to the claim that it is possible to *construct* a plausible practical syllogism from beliefs and desires of the agent to the intention to carry out the act. This much follows from the assumption that the agent acted for and from a reason. When the purported intentional act is wishfully acquiring the belief that p or, more generally, wishfully taking p to be the case, what could the associated practical syllogism be? What beliefs in conjunction with the wish or desire that p could rationalize or provide the practical premises for the intention to adopt the attitude of taking p to be the case?

It seems that the relevant belief will have to be some conviction that the acquisition of the belief that p will make p more likely to be true. How otherwise could the acquisition of the belief that p be thought to serve the desire that p? There are cases in which such a conviction is reasonably attributed to the agent, cases in which the belief figures in making itself true. Thus the advocates of autosuggestion think that if they can only believe that they will succeed then they will be more likely to succeed. So they set about trying to inculcate such potentially self-fulfilling beliefs in themselves. William James gives the example of a person who must leap across a deep crevasse.[12] His chance of a successful leap in part depends upon his allaying his own anxiety by convincing himself that he will make a successful leap. So he has reason to try to acquire a belief that cool weighing of the evidence would not support. In some quarters this sort of potentially self-fulfilling wishful thinking is called "positive thinking," and a whole industry of self-help books is built around its advocacy. Whatever its drawbacks and lack of appeal to those of us who are less upbeat in temperament, positive thinking, even when intentionally pursued, is not incoherent.

It would, however, be implausible to suppose that all wishful thinking is some kind of positive thinking. This might be more plausible as a claim about members of a community in which beliefs were thought to be generally self-fulfilling, for example, a community in which ritual magic or voodoo permeated everyday life so that quite generally the symbolic representation of the desired outcome is taken to be efficacious. Even here, if all wishful thought was to be positive thought, it would have to be true that *whenever* someone's desire generated a wishful belief, he had a collateral belief that the generated belief would play some role in the satisfaction of his desire. This is not our situation; we are not *that* superstitious, and our particular superstitions are not perfectly tailored to our wishful thoughts. There is then a residual class of cases of wishful thoughts that are not positive thoughts. Concerning them, Williams seems largely vindicated. Cases of positive thinking apart, nothing could be an intentional act of immediately coming to wishfully believe in the recognized absence of supporting evidence. We could call this the *paradox of wishful thinking or believing* if we liked, but the way out is too obvious to linger long with paradox. Wishful thought, the process that leads from anxious desire that *p* to belief that *p*, is not something done as an intentional act.

A complication arising from Freud's work remains. Consider someone apprised of the existence and function of what Freud called primary process thinking, a representational process that manifests itself in daydreaming and more directed fantasy and which provides a surrogate satisfaction for frustrated desire.[13] Such a person might reason as follows: "I have the unsatisfied desire that *p*. Primary process thought provides a surrogate satisfaction for unsatisfied desire, so I will engage in primary process thought that *p*." This is of course absurdly overexplicit. But that cannot be an objection, since we are simply exploring the *possibility* of constructing a practical syllogism from beliefs and desires of the agent to the act of adopting a wishful belief. The real objection is that even if someone could bring himself to be concerned with assuaging his unsatisfied desires with the appropriate doses of fantasy, as if his own desires were for him mitigatable conditions, the outcome of such practical reasoning would not be wishful thinking. The intentional act prompted by these reasons, the act of engaging in the fantasy that *p*, does not involve one in taking *p* to be the case, any more than pretending that *p* does. One can of course get lost in a fantasy or a pretense, that is, cease to realize that it is such and come to believe that what one was fantasizing or pretending to be the case is the case. This further step would be wishful thinking, but it would not itself be rationalized by any practical reasoning, any more than someone's falling asleep while pretending to be asleep would be rationalized by his reasons for pretending to be asleep.

Consider this example. A nonsuperstitious gambler who wants blackjack (an ace and a ten or a face card) on the hand being dealt to him may find himself fantasizing that a ten or a face card will follow the ace that he has been dealt, but he may have no reason to believe this and is likely not to believe it. If the dealing was interrupted and he was asked to bet a further substantial sum at even money on his getting blackjack, he would typically refuse, knowing that the odds are roughly nine to four against. He has no superstitious belief about the effect of his anticipatory fantasies, but he has anticipatory fantasies nonetheless. Yet they do not in themselves involve him in believing that he will be dealt a ten or a face card next.

Still, all too rapidly even the nonsuperstitious gambler can lose himself in such hopeful fantasies, coming thereby to believe that he will get blackjack on the next hand and betting accordingly. Getting lost in a fantasy in this way is just another name for wishful thinking, and so presents the same problem. Certainly the gambler's desire to be dealt blackjack gives him no reason to believe that he will. The gambler wants blackjack; his coming to believe that he will get blackjack is not something that has any independent or supplementary appeal for him. His interest is in the cards and the payoff, not in some doxastic state he might come to be in. We do not understand his getting lost in his fantasy by treating it as an intentional or rationalizable act. But how then should we understand it?

The gambling example is not peripheral. Repetitive gambling is an arena of action in which wishful thinking is rife. The anxious desire that prompts wishful thought easily arises because there is so much eventful giving of hostages to fortune in relatively short periods of time.[14] Casino proprietors know that the selective reinforcement of anticipatory fantasies of winning can solidify them into the belief that one will win. (Slot machines with their fixed payoff percentages are built around this psychophysical law.) In such a setting the phenomenology of holding out against wishful thinking, in particular resisting the dangerous conviction that one will certainly win in the short run, is the phenomenology of resistance to conditioning or the manipulation of one's attitudes by internal and external rewards. But there is a problem with the simple conditioning model of wishful thinking which has the wishful belief that one will win figure as a rewarding response to one's desire to win. The model I have in mind treats the desire to win as a potentiality to be rewarded by winning. Winning is correlated with the belief that one has won, and we may expect that this belief will acquire some of the rewarding significance of winning itself. Insofar as a belief of the appropriate sort can arise spontaneously (has a certain operant level) its arising in the presence of the appropriate desire will be rewarding, and so beliefs of this sort will tend to arise in the presence of the desire to win. In the jargon of conditioning theorists, the event of a wishful belief's arising or coming about is a reinforced because rewarding operant.

Compare David Pears's account of the functional role of the wishful belief in his recent book *Motivated Irrationality*. Pears writes:

> the explanation must start from the fact that achievement of the real thing would not produce any satisfaction if [one] were unaware of it. The belief is the intermediary, the messenger with the good news, and, when actual achievement causes satisfaction, it is the belief in the achievement that is the immediate cause. The causal linkage makes it possible for [one] to take a short cut to satisfaction: [one] simply manufactures the belief without the real thing.[15]

Such an explanation is not in general adequate. For example, the belief that is correlated with or brings the good news of winning is the belief that one *has* won, whereas the wishful belief correlated with the desire to win is typically anticipatory. It is the belief that one *will* win. Nor is the difficulty to be got around by the Freudian suggestion that primary process thought and hence wishful thought is not significantly tensed but represents a kind of "dream time" that is not determinately past, present, or future. For after all, it is the quite determinately tensed and wishful belief that one *will* win which leads one to bet so recklessly on the *next* hand rather than reach out for one's imagined winnings or do something, whatever it might be, that is intermediate between the two.

No, if we are to understand anticipatory belief as a reinforced operant, we must explain why the arising of a future-tensed belief can be rewarding. The explanation tells us something important about the etiology of wishful thinking and hence of self-deception. A future-tensed belief can reduce anxiety about the future. If this is the rewarding role of anticipatory wishful thought—the reduction of anxiety about a desired outcome—then we should expect anticipatory wishful thought in the presence of the desire that *p* coupled with the fear that not-*p*. This speculation finds some confirmation in the wisdom of those who aim to fight wishful thought. Thus it is said that the gambler who does not want to get carried away with his fantasies must not play with "scared" money (money that he cannot afford to lose) and that he must remind himself that he is in a positive expectation game (otherwise he has no business playing) and has only to make the correct plays and bet well within his bankroll in order to win in the long run. These are, *inter alia*, practical defenses against anxiety and the wishful thought that anxiety generates. Moreover, much of the efficacy of what is presented as positive thinking, i.e., exhortations to believe that one will succeed with the accompanying suggestion that this will make success more likely, derives from the fact that such beliefs tend to reduce debilitating anxiety about the desired outcome. So it is in James's case of the crevasse jumper.

The suggestion is then that we should understand wishful thinking, not as the actual or potential outcome of practical reasoning occurring in the unconscious or in some homuncular part of the mind, but as a mental mechanism or tropism by which a desire that p and accompanying anxiety that not-p set the conditions for the rewarding (because anxiety-reducing) response of coming to believe that p. And now, having properly located and sidestepped the deeper worry about the very possibility of a cognitive attitude like belief being generated by the will, we can deal summarily with Price's objection that such purely motivated belief that p does not really deserve the name of "belief" because it is neither grounded in what one takes to be evidence for p nor reliably connected to the state of affairs that p. Granted, its claims to the title of belief that p do not lie there but in its being a disposition to the occurrent thought that p, in its action-guiding potential, and in its potential to allay anxiety that not-p. Call it "quasi-belief" if you must, but recognize its similarity on the output side to the best grounded beliefs.

The treatment of wishful thought and, by implication, self-deception as the nonintentional outcome of a mental tropism is a rebuff to those who would represent such phenomena as intentional. But knowledge of the existence of a mental mechanism allows one to form plans that intentionally duplicate its typical benefits. A sophisticate could reason that since he wants to reduce his anxiety that not-p he should think that p and dispose himself so to think, i.e., try to believe that p and *not* fear the worst. This would be a case of intentionally aiming at the wishful belief that p for the very reason that it reduces one's anxiety that not-p. It is precisely an interest in the causal consequences of his own doxastic states which is characteristic of our sophisticate. But to regard the sophisticate's reasoning as representing what is essential (if implicit) in every case of wishful thinking is to massively over-rationalize a more primitive phenomenon. The unsophisticated need not be relying upon any beliefs about the relation between belief and anxiety in order to accept the soothing balm of wishful thought. Indeed in the more virulent cases of wishful thought, one is incapable of distancing oneself from one's present anxiety and considering it as an unwanted state of oneself to be treated with the right dose of belief.

Furthermore, there seems to be a conceptual condition on the sophisticate's intentional wishful thinking, a condition that is not satisfied in the ordinary case. The sophisticate engages in or is disposed to engage in the following train of thought:

I anxiously fear that not-p.

I do not want to anxiously fear that not-p.

If I were to come to believe that p then I would not anxiously fear that not-p.

So I will believe that p.

Drawing the conclusion of this train of thought involves the sophisticate's thinking of his believing that p as not prompted by evidential considerations but only by the hope for its soothing balm. Assuming the sophisticate does not pursue belief that p in a way that allows him to forget his reasons for pursuing it, he must recognize that his coming to believe p does not in any way reflect the truth of the matter as to p.[16] But then it is entirely mysterious how one could think that adopting an attitude that one recognized as not in any way reflecting the truth of the matter as to p could help to allay the anxiety that not-p. The sophisticate's practical reasoning is comprehensible only if he believes that his believing that p will make p more likely to be true, e.g., by reducing debilitating anxiety that not-p. Once again, as in James's case, the only kind of rationalizable step from desire that p to believe that p involves positive thinking about p, i.e., thinking in which, for one or another reason, the thinker holds that the desired outcome is made more likely if he believes in it. In other cases there is simply no plausible way to rationalize wishful thinking. The subintentionalist account seems forced upon us.

SELF-DECEPTION

2. Our tentative conclusion is that wishful thought that is not positive thought is not rationalizable and so not intentional. But it does serve a purpose in that it reduces anxiety about the desired outcome. It is reasonable to be less anxious that not-p if one comes to believe that p. So although the efficacy of the wishful thought or belief is intelligible only in terms of a rational connection between the attitudes involved, the generation of the wishful thought is not mediated by any rational connection.

In wishful thought there need not be any appearance of a split within the agent. Someone may simply exploit the slack between inductive evidence and conclusion and wishfully think that the evidence that his wife is unfaithful to him is misleading and is to be otherwise explained. That this was wishful thought on his part rather than conservative thought need not be shown by the existence of some unacknowledged recognition in him that the evidence more or less establishes her infidelity. It can be shown by the fact that when presented with corresponding evidence about other married women he makes the judgment of infidelity.

Once one is no longer theoretically committed to understanding wishful thought as something intentionally done, one need not postulate some degree of recognition in the wishful thinker of what he has done, recognition that then has to be taken as somehow dissociated or sequestered from the mainstream of consciousness in order to avoid having the mainstream entertain what seems an impossible combination, i.e., both the wishful belief and the belief that this belief is wishful and so is not supported by anything that would suggest that it is true. Here we have a prima facie theoretical advantage of the subintentionalist treatment of wishful thought, since there is no direct implication of mental division in the accusation of mere wishful thought.

Things seem otherwise with self-deception strictly so-called. To the extent that the self-deceiver is to be distinguished from the mere wishful thinker by his perversely adopting the wishful belief *despite* his recognition at some level that the evidence is to the contrary, we have reason to regard the self-deceiver as divided. For it is hard to see how anxiety could be reduced by a wishful belief if the wishful belief is copresent in consciousness with the recognition that the evidence is strongly against it. Indeed it is hard to see how the wishful belief could persist in consciousness under these conditions. So it seems that some play must be given to the concept of *repression* in discussing self-decep- tion. If anxiety that not-p produced by recognition of telling evidence for not-p is to be reduced, not only must the wishful belief that p arise, but the recognition of the evidence as more or less establishing the contrary must also be repressed, i.e., the subject must cease consciously acknowledging it. The strategies by which one ceases consciously to acknowledge that one recognizes the evidence to be against one's wishful belief are manifold. One may selectively reappraise and explain away the evidence (rationalization). One may simply avoid thinking about the touchy subject (evasion). One may focus one's attention on invented reasons for p and spring to the advocacy of p whenever opportunity presents itself (overcompensation). Where repres- sive strategies abound, it is plausible to postulate a repressive strategist. But the strategist cannot be the main system, in which the wishful belief allays anxiety. For then the main system would have to aim to put down the threatening belief or recognition of the import of the contrary evidence *in order* that it should cease to be aware of the threatening belief. Consciousness of its reason for repression makes the main system's task of forgetting impossible. Ignorance of its reason makes the task uninteresting. So we seem driven to recognize a subagency distinct from the main system, a subagency that, like Freud's censor or superego, is active in repression.

However, as Sartre maintained in his attack on Freud, it can appear that the Freudian account of repression in self-deception, e.g., the account of repression in self-deceptive resistance to the probings of the analyst, repre- sents no advance over having the main system play the role of repressive agency.[17] If the censor who controls the border traffic between unconscious- ness and consciousness is to successfully repress condemned drives and so resist the analyst, it must be aware of the drive to be repressed in order not to be conscious of these repressed drives. So it seems that the censor's putative project or intention is an impossible one—at the same time to be aware and not to be aware of the repressed desire. Now even if there is reason to doubt this objection of Sartre's to Freud's resort to the censor, say because it is unclear why the *censor* should have to be unaware of the repressed material, Sartre has still highlighted a real difficulty about repression. And this difficulty generalizes, so that we may speak of *a paradox of repression*. No project or action plan can satisfy the condition of simultaneously including awareness and ignorance of the repressed material. Given Sartre's ambition to use the paradox of repression to undermine Freudian pessimism about the scope of conscious choice in our mental life, it is ironic that the way out of the paradox seems to be the same as the way out of the paradox of wishful thought and the surface paradox of self-deception. We should not treat repression, even in its complex manifestations, as an intentional act of some subagency guided by its awareness of its desire to forget. On the contrary, we should understand repression as subintentional, i.e., not guided by reasons but operating for the purpose of reducing anxiety. For where we can find neither a coherent intention in acting nor a coherent intention to be acted upon we cannot discern intentional action.

But before we take this way out of the paradox of repression we must deal with an alternative solution and then (in section 3) with an alternative account of the role of the censor or protective system in self-deception, an account developed by David Pears.

First, why should the condition of *simultaneously* including awareness and ignorance of the repressed material be a natural condition to impose on any repressor's action plan? Surely there are cases of deceiving oneself in which the shadow of forgetfulness falls between the intention and the act.

Forgetfulness can sometimes be planned around. Certain powerful sleeping pills cause retroactive amnesia. One's memory of what one did in the hour or so before taking the pill is very indistinct and sometimes apparently erased completely. Knowing this, one could get up to mischief during such a period and avoid the guilt of the morning after by taking the precaution of rearranging things so that in the morning one will be misled about what one did the night before. This is certainly intentional activity, and if it succeeds it results in the deception of one's later self by an earlier self. Similarly, taking to holy water and rosary beads, i.e., acting as if one accepted the tenets of Catholicism, was Pascal's suggested method of bringing about the belief in those tenets. This is certainly intentional activity, and it can result in the production of a desired belief in one's later self, presumably because it gradually inclines one to view the favorable evidence more sympathetically and not attend to the countervailing evidence. Here we have self-deceptive action plans involving repression and forgetting, and yet nothing paradoxical.

Indeed, it has been suggested[18] that in general the way to avoid the surface paradox of knowing deceiver and unknowing victim's being embodied in the one agent is to exploit the fact that self-deception takes time: in the interim the deceiver can forget what he knew and forget that he set out to mislead himself. This time-lag strategy, however, not only leaves the most puzzling cases of self-deception untreated but also leaves unexplained the most puzzling features of many of the cases it seems to render unparadoxical.

Not all self-deception takes a form in which stages of the self-deceiver's history are successively stages of deceiving, forgetting, and being the victim of deceit. One can simultaneously develop as deceiver and deceived. A case of progressive and self-deceptive alcoholism might be of this sort. As the alcoholic's case worsens and more evidence accumulates, his self-deceptive denials develop concurrently.

Moreover, it cannot be the mere fact that self-deception takes time (if it does take time) that allows the self-deceiver to forget what he knew and forget that he set out to mislead himself. Rather, what is crucial to the cases in which the time delay seems to allow a nonparadoxical description is that the self-deceiver explicitly employs a means to achieve his motivated belief, a means whose operation does not require that the self-deceiver attend to it under the description "means of producing in me the desired belief" or something equivalent. Let us call a means that does not require this kind of monitoring, an *autonomous* means. In the case of nocturnal mischief, the autonomous means is a combination of a process in the external world, the persistence of misleading evidence, and the intended outcome of a drug-induced process of forgetting, a process that is not itself an intentional act and so does not require directive monitoring after the taking of the pill. In the case of Pascal's method, the means is the adoption of a practice itself sufficiently engaging so that past a certain point one need not think of one's participation under the description "means of getting me to believe in the tenets of Catholicism in the absence of sufficient evidence" in order to intend to participate. Past a certain point one just gets carried along.

The phrase "past a certain point" itself masks a puzzling feature of the case. Around the point in question there must be a transition from intending one's participation in the practice under the description "means of getting me to believe in the tenets of Catholicism in the absence of sufficient evidence" to doing it habitually and perhaps under more particular descriptions internal to the practice, e.g., "asking for God's forgiveness." This very transition, which might be called "falling in with the practice," may be compared to getting lost in a fantasy or a pretense, not in order to belittle it but in order to point out that the transition in question involves a kind of forgetfulness that cannot itself be represented as an intentional act, something done from and for a reason. For this forgetfulness simply *occurs* at a certain point, and to represent it as something done for a reason is to allow that it could be monitored as something tending to satisfy and ultimately satisfying an intention. The intention would have to be something like "to forget that my only reason for engaging in this practice is as a means of producing in me belief in the tenets of Catholicism." The paradox of repression simply recrystalizes at the point at which I recognize that this intention is satisfied. I would have to recognize some concurrent act of mine as forgetting that my only reason for engaging in the practice is as a means to produce in me belief in the tenets of Catholicism. That is, I would have to be lucidly aware of what I am supposed to be concurrently forgetting.

The time-lag theory does not illuminate the nature of self-deception, and when it provides a way out of the surface paradox of self-deception it does this by admitting that only subintentional forgettings could produce the intended or desired outcome of having forgotten. But it might be thought that the theory at least has served dialectically to force us to formulate the concept of an autonomous means, which now allows us to qualify our main thesis appropriately. That is, we should say that motivated believings and cessations of conscious belief *that do not employ autonomous means* are not intentional acts but are nonintentional outcomes of mental tropisms.

The restriction does not render the main thesis uninteresting, since it points to a large class of cases that cannot be explained in a certain way. More important, the cases omitted are those in which the means of producing the desired belief operates without one's attending to it. Indeed it is important that one does not intend or monitor the process throughout. But then the operation of the means, although intended to occur, is not itself an intentional act, and neither is the outcome produced by the means, although it is an intended outcome of a process one set in motion. One can describe what one does in the case of nocturnal mischief as "deceiving oneself by arranging misleading evidence and taking the amnestic drug." The description corresponds to a statement of intention that captures one's reason for arranging the misleading evidence and taking the amnestic drug. One intended to deceive oneself by arranging misleading evidence and taking the amnestic drug. But what one *did* in arranging the evidence and taking the drug did not itself constitute self-deception. Only the cooperation of future events made what one did deserve the name of *deceiving oneself* by arranging misleading evidence and taking the amnestic drug. So the main thesis can be stated without restriction: nothing that itself constitutes motivated believing or motivated cessation of (conscious) belief is an intentional act. In the cases of self-deception and repression in which autonomous means are employed, the motivated believing and accompanying repression are constituted by the intentional acts of setting the means in motion *plus* the brute operations of those means culminating in the belief and the forgetting. And this captures the peculiar opacity to intention that self-deception and its associated repressions exhibit. Even when there is a self-deceptive or repressive action plan, no intentional act is *intrinsically* a self-deception or a forgetting. So at least things currently seem to stand.

HOMUNCULARISM REVISITED

3. David Pears has recently offered a response to Sartre's paradox of repression by way of providing a new model of the role of the censor or protective system in self-deception.[19] Pears offers a model in which self-deception is constituted by an intentional act of a lying subagency.

Sartre's mistake, according to Pears, is to suppose that the subagency that does the deceiving and repressing and monitors its success in these projects needs itself to be deceived. Instead, Pears proposes that we should take quite literally a model that locates a protective system as the agent in self-deception, a protective system that operates like a paternalistic liar, protecting the main system or ego for what the protective system takes to be the ego's good. The lying protective system need never deceive itself and so need never be engaged in the contradictory project of trying to believe what it knows to be false. The lying protective system need never produce forgetfulness in itself and so need never aim at forgetting something that having this aim forces it to keep in mind.

Donald Davidson has articulated still another paradox that he takes to show that something like this subsystem model must be the right account of what is going on in all cases of self-deception and wishful thinking.[20] Davidson writes:

> In standard reason explanations, as we have seen, not only do the propositional contents of various beliefs and desires bear appropriate logical relations to one another and to the contents of the belief, attitude or intention they help explain; the actual states of belief and desire cause the explained state or event. In the case of irrationality, the causal relation remains, while the logical relation is missing or distorted. In the cases of irrationality we have been discussing, there is a mental cause that is not a reason for what it causes. So in wishful thinking, a desire causes a belief. But the judgment that a state of affairs is, or would be, desirable, is not a reason to believe that it exists. . . .
>
> If events are related as cause and effect, they remain so no matter in what vocabulary we choose to describe them. Mental or psychological events are such only under a manner of description, for these very events surely are at the same time neurophysiological, and ultimately physical, events, though recognizable and identifiable within these realms only when given neurophysiological or physical descriptions. As we have seen, there is no difficulty in general in explaining mental events by appeal to neurophysiological or physical causes: this is central to the analysis of perception or memory, for example. But when the cause is described in non-mental terms, we necessarily lose touch with what is needed to explain the element of irrationality. For *irrationality* appears only when rationality is evidently appropriate: where both cause and effect have contents that have the sort of logical relations that make for reason or its failure. Events conceived solely in terms of their physical or physiological properties

cannot be judged as reasons, or as in conflict, or as concerned with a subject matter. So we face the following dilemma: if we think of the cause in a neutral mode, disregarding its mental status as a belief or other attitude—if we think of it merely as a force that works on the mind without being identified as part of it—then we fail to explain, or even describe, irrationality. Blind forces are in the category of the non-rational, not the irrational. So, we introduce a mental description of the cause, which thus makes it a candidate for being a reason. *But we still remain outside the only clear pattern of explanation that applies to the mental, for that pattern demands that the cause be more than a candidate for being a reason; it must be a reason, which in the present case it cannot be.* For an explanation of a mental effect we need a mental cause that is also a reason for this effect, but, if we have it, the effect cannot be a case of irrationality. Or so it seems.[21] (My emphasis.)

The pivotal claim driving Davidson's *paradox of irrationality* is that the only clear pattern of explanation in which mental events or states so described can figure requires those mental events or states to be rational causes, i.e., to rationalize what they cause. This is a consequence of the interpretive view of mental states and events. The problem is that wishful and self-deceptive thought seems to involve a characteristic and explanatory causal connection between the desire that *p* and the belief that *p*, but an explanatory connection that is not a rational connection. The anxious desire that *p* is not a reason to believe that *p*. Because the interpretive view counts rationality as both constitutive and exhaustive of the mental, it has trouble finding a place for the very possibility of a *mental* state, anxious desire, which characteristically has irrational *mental* consequences. Nor can the idea of *irrational* (as opposed to arational) consequences be captured if anxious desire and wishful belief are considered as mere physical states.

In fact Davidson seems to back away from the pivotal claim, but in doing so he suggests a way in which it might be defended.

There is, however, a way one mental event can cause another mental event without being a reason for it, and where there is no puzzle and not necessarily any irrationality. This can happen when cause and effect occur in different minds. For example, wishing to have you enter my garden, I grow a beautiful flower there. You crave a look at my flower and enter my garden. My desire caused your craving and action, but my desire was not a reason for your craving, nor a reason on which you acted. (Perhaps you did not even know about my wish.) Mental phenomena may cause other mental phenomena *without being reasons for them,* then, *and still keep their character as mental, provided cause and effect are adequately segregated. The obvious and clear cases are those of social interaction. But I suggest that the idea can be applied to a single mind and person.* Indeed, if we are going to explain irrationality at all, it seems we must assume that the mind can be partitioned into quasi-independent structures.[22] (My emphasis.)

There is a difficulty here. The desire caused the craving and action via a system of intermediate causes that involved the bringing about of an enticing state of affairs, a perception of it, and a subsequent comprehensible desire to explore the enticing state of affairs. In such a case we have a rational connection in the sense of a matching of the salient state of affairs before the eyes and the content of perception, and a subsequent rational connection between the perception of an enticing state of affairs, a standing interest in such states of affairs, and a desire to explore the state of affairs. This is why there is no puzzle in this case as to how one person's desire can cause another's. We have not a mysterious sort of telepathy but a chain of rational causes. This leaves two questions. What is the analogue of such a chain of rational causes in the case of self-deception and wishful thinking? And how does the resort to subsystems within the agent help us to find it?

I suggest that if the segregation, within distinct subsystems, of the relevant mental cause and effect is to do anything to resolve the alleged paradox of irrationality associated with wishful thinking and self-deception, then one must follow Pears and understand these processes as the suggestive implantation of belief in the main system by a protective system. Only then will one have an appropriate analogue of the perceptual link, namely, one person saying something to another who hears what he said and believes it. (The analogy has some appeal. Thomas Reid actually took the receiving of testimony to be a sort of perception via conversation.)[23] In this way the theoretical division of a person into a protective, lying system and a main system that is its gullible victim allows us to reestablish a chain of rational causes. The main system is aware of and reasonably accepts the testimony of the protective system. The protective system's reason for offering this testimony is to allay the anxiety of the main system. So also the protective system may go in for distracting the main system from its anxiety-producing beliefs.

Here we have a homuncularism that solves all the paradoxes of self-deception we have encountered and which seems to represent self-deception (and wishful thinking) as constituted by intentional acts of protective systems. The surface paradox is solved by having distinct subsystems play the respective roles of liar and victim of the lie. The paradox of wishful thinking is solved by having the protective system altruistically set out to allay the main system's anxiety that not-p by inculcating the belief that p in the main system. The paradox of repression is solved by having the protective system altruistically set out to allay the main system's anxiety that p by distracting it from its anxiety-producing belief that not-p. The paradox of irrationality is solved by modeling self-deception (and wishful thought) on interpersonal testimony. If the main strategy of this paper is to work, that is, if we are to use the paradoxes of self-deception to support a tropistic and anti-intentionalist account of the processes involved, then we must discredit the account of self-deception in terms of protective and main subsystems.

This account can be discredited so long as we do not allow its advocates the luxury of hovering noncommittally between the horns of a dilemma: either take the subsystem account literally, in which case it implausibly represents the ordinary self-deceiver as a victim of something like multiple personality, or take it as a metaphor, in which case it provides no way to evade the paradoxes while maintaining that intentional acts constitute self-deception and wishful thinking.

The several difficulties for the subagency account literally construed may be stated as objections to Pears's explicitly worked-out model of a protective system influencing a main system. (It should be emphasized that Pears is not committed to the *general* applicability of this model.)

The main system may be thought of as having the desire for some outcome p and the anxiety that p will not occur. Somehow, as a result of these conditions, a protective system is either generated or set into operation, a protective system that has its own internal rationality directed toward the quasi-altruistic manipulation of the main system. Whereas the inferential processes of the main system are typically introspectable by the self-deceiving person and thereby constitute *his* conscious feelings, thoughts, memories, etc., those in the protective system are not, so that the self-deceiver is not aware of the protective system's manipulation of his beliefs.

Although the system's operations are not introspectable by the self-deceiver and so are not in that sense part of his consciousness, they are not mere instinctual drives, like hunger and thirst, unconsciously pushing the self-deceiver toward outcomes that in fact constitute their satisfaction. The protective system has rather complex beliefs and desires about the main system. In the light of these the protective system acts on the main system by means of various stratagems until it produces the protective belief. That is, the protective system has to have the capacity to manipulate its representations of the main system in practical inference that issues in action on the main system, action that the protective system monitors for its effectiveness. This is Pears's motive for referring to the protective system's operations as *preconscious,* i.e., as involving complex manipulations of representations, manipulations that are not introspectable to the main system and so not part of the self-deceiver's conscious life. The question arises how the protective system could do all this without being conscious of (introspecting) its own operations. After all, it has to compare the outcome it is producing with the outcome it aimed for and act or cease to act accordingly. Any consciousness by the protective system of its own operation is "buried alive," i.e., is not accessible to the consciousness of the main system.

Pears suggests that in wishful and self-deceptive thought such a protective system is either generated or set into operation by the main system's desire for some outcome. The protective system "crystallizes around" the main system's desire. This is puzzling. For it is unclear how the main system's desire that p could give the protective system any reason to produce in the main system the belief that p. The belief that p does not satisfy the desire that p. At most it can reduce the concurrent disturbing anxiety that not-p will obtain. So if any desire of the main system gives the quasi-altruistic protective system a reason to aim to produce in the main system the belief that p, it is the main system's understandable desire to be rid of its anxiety that not-p.

This desire of the main system gives the protective system a reason to aim to produce the wishful belief in the main system only if the protective system is altruistically disposed to the main system. But whence this altruism? Surely *not* from a history of sympathetic identification born of recognition of likeness and fellow feeling. Pears calls it quasi-altruism, thereby suggesting that this is the altruism of concern for the larger unit—the self-deceiver—which includes both the protective, deceiving altruist and the deceived subsystem. But then it must be objected that in many cases of self-deception all but the self-deceived person can see that he would be better off without the protective belief. In such cases the putative actions of the protective system cannot be represented as the outcome of lucid concern for the whole system, which includes it and the main system as parts. Indeed in many such cases the main system and the person as a whole suffer considerably as a result of the putative actions of the protective system, so that the protective system must have a curiously narrowed focus of quasi-altruistic concern.

Take for example the sort of case Freud discusses in the essay "Mourning and Melancholia."[24] One very much wants to love one's mother, and yet one feels hostility toward her for the pain she caused. This conflict generates anxiety that is relieved by the repression of one's hostility toward one's mother. Such repression can be seen as self-deceptive blocking of thought. One ceases to acknowledge or actively entertain one's hostile beliefs, and perhaps one comes to believe that one simply loves one's mother. But as Freud points out, the repressed or unacknowledged hostile beliefs can nonetheless operate to produce unacknowledged guilt experienced as objectless depression and a desire for self-punishment which prompts self-destructive behavior. Here we have a familiar case of self-deceptive resolution of conscious ambivalence and associated anxiety by repression of one's hostile attitudes, with subsequent hell to pay. If a protective system is intentionally repressing the hostile, anxiety-generating belief, and if the effects of repression are often considerably worse than the anxiety produced by the original conflict in the main system, then either the protective system must have a curiously sadistic concern for the main system, involving a readiness to get the main system out of the psychic frying pan and into the fire, or the protective system, despite its otherwise excellent monitoring of the main system, must itself have a curious blind spot that prevents it from seeing the destructive effects of its own characteristic way of reducing anxiety in the main system.

Suppose somehow that these difficulties are solved without making the protective system so limited that it collapses into a tropistic anxiety-reducer, too simple to have motives or intentions.[25] So somehow the protective system's motives are plausibly made to mesh with what it is supposed to do. Concentrate instead on what it is supposed to do, i.e., get the main system to adopt the protective belief. Notice that we invite a regress if we say what is nevertheless plausible, namely, that this is all too easy because the main system is all too ready to accept the protective belief. Such collusion by the main system would itself be wishful acceptance of belief, reproducing within the main system the kind of duality that the intentionalist-gone-homuncularist is trying to keep outside. Instead it must be that the protective system somehow slips the protective belief into the main system, even though the main system's acquiring that belief does not satisfy the main system's ordinary standards of belief acquisition. After all, the main system must be inclined to recognize that the belief does not come from the main system's perceptual input or from its memory or from inference from its other beliefs. The protective belief just pops up. Why does the main system so happily tolerate this?

Moreover, it is clear that getting the main system to adopt the protective belief cannot be something the protective system does directly without employing any particular means. One agency cannot will as a *basic* act of its own that another adopt a belief or ignore evidence or not acknowledge its beliefs. Given this, it is hard to see how wishful thought that involves wishfully exploiting the slack between inductive evidence and conclusion could be brought about simply by the protective system. For the crucial move in such a process is the main system's failing to see that the evidence is sufficient to make the anxiety-provoking conclusion believable. How is this act of the main system explained by anything that the protective system could intentionally do? Well, we may allow for purposes of argument that the protective system can distract, suggest, and cajole, but this leaves the worrying question why the main system is so distractable, suggestable, and biddable in this matter. At a certain point, the protective system's suggestions to the effect that, despite the evidence, *p,* are supposed to be accepted by the main system as sufficient to believe *p.* Why? The main system has no reason to regard these suggestions as reliable testimony. So why does it accept them? The tempting answer is: because it wants to believe *p* and so is all too ready to collude in its own deception. But "collude" is an intentionalist idiom that raises the very difficulties the protective system was postulated to deal with. Should we then postulate within what we were taking to be the main system a second protective system and a more primary system? This would be to make any explanation of self-deceptive and wishful thought forever recede as we try to grasp it. For the very same problems would arise for the actions of the second protective system. We can take as many turns as we want on the intentionalist roundabout, but we will still be left with our original problem: how is it that some main or primary system's desire to believe p leads it to accept suggestions that p as grounds for believing p even though that system has no reason to believe that they are reliable indications that p is true? In short, how could the desire that p lead the main or primary system to be favorably disposed toward believing p? And there seems no other answer but the anti-intentionalist and tropistic one: this is the way our minds work; anxious desire that p simply leads one to be disposed to believe that p.

Finally, the anti-intentionalist and tropistic account does better than the homuncularist account in enabling us to explain the kind of censure involved in accusations of self-deception. On the homuncularist account the deceived and noncolluding main system, a system that has good claim to be the analogue of the Freudian ego, the active controller of the person's conscious thought, speech, and bodily action, is an innocent victim of deception. It is simply lied to. Correspondingly, the protective system is a straightforward, albeit paternalistic, liar. But our accusations of self-deception seem to be accusations of a sort of failure not unlike that involved in cowardly flight from the frightening. For example, in that part of Augustine's orgy of self-accusation in which he confesses his past self-deceptions, he explicitly employs the metaphor of mental flight from horrific features of himself.

> Ponticianus told us this story [of a conversion] and as he spoke, you, O Lord, turned me back upon myself. You took me from behind my own back, where I had placed myself because I did not wish to look upon myself. You stood me face to face with myself, so I might see how foul I was, how deformed and defiled, how covered with stains and sores. I looked, and I was filled with horror but there was no place for me to flee from myself. If I tried to turn my gaze from myself, he still went on with the story that he was telling, and once again you placed me in front of myself and thrust me before my own eyes, so that I might find out my iniquity and hate it. I knew what it was, but I pretended not to; I refused to look at it and put it out of my memory.[26]

Here the self-directed accusation of self-deception is an accusation of mental cowardice, of flight from anxiety (or angst), a failure to contain one's anxiety, a lack of courage in matters epistemic. The homuncularist picture of the self-deceiver prevents us from rationally reconstructing a fitting subject for this sort of censure. The protective system is simply lying. The main system is simply the victim of a paternalistic liar. This does not add up to anything like mental cowardice.

The anti-intentionalist and tropistic account does better. Though mental flight, like physical flight, is typically subintentional, one can still be held responsible for lacking the ability to contain one's anxiety and face the anxiety-provoking or the terrible. The accusation of self-deception is a familiar case of being held responsible for an episode that evidences a defect of character, in this case a lack of the negative power that is reason, i.e., the capacity to inhibit changes in beliefs when those changes are not well grounded in reasons.

Tropisms and Reason

4. The presupposition that drives the paradoxes of self-deception or bad faith is succinctly expressed by Sartre at the beginning of his statement of the surface paradox: "one does not undergo one's bad faith, one is not infected with it. . . . But consciousness affects itself with bad faith. There must be an original intention and a project of bad faith."[27] This is to assume that if self-deception is something *done* rather than merely undergone it must be something intentionally done. We know already from the case of bodily activity that this assumption is false. For example, running our eyes predominantly over the tops and not the bottoms of printed words is something many of us do, since many of us read *by* running our eyes predominantly over the tops of printed words. A way to make this vivid to oneself is to cover the bottom half of a line of print and try to read it and then cover the top half of a similar line of print and try to read it. Now it would be absurd to suggest that using our eyes this way must be something we do intentionally, e.g., for and from the reason that this makes it possible to read more quickly. For many of us, performing the little experiment just outlined gives us the first inkling of what we were up to. But of course the explanation of why this method of reading is unwittingly used by many of us has to do with the fact that it helps us to read faster. The method, once hit upon, persists because it serves a purpose; it is not intentionally employed for that purpose.

Similar things need to be said about the mental process of self-deception by which anxiety that one's desire that *p* will not be satisfied is reduced by one's acquisition of the belief that *p* (wishful thinking) and one's ceasing to acknowledge one's recognition of the evidence that not-*p* (repression). This process is not mediated by intention; rather, processes of this kind persist because they serve the end of reducing anxiety. Hence I speak of a mental tropism, a characteristic pattern of causation between types of mental states, a pattern whose existence within the mind is no more surprising, given what it does for us, than a plant's turning toward the sun.

In fact mental tropisms abound. When the victim of Korsakoff's syndrome confabulates or spontaneously and without deceptive intent fills in the considerable gaps in his memory, we see in operation a process that produces a needed coherence in the patient's remembering of his past, but a process that is not carried on for and from this reason.[28] When we encounter an instance of the phenomenon of so-called "sour grapes," in which the subject's desires are tailored to what he can get in an ad hoc way that reduces the chances of frustration, we see the securing of a comprehensible goal but not intentional activity.[29] When at a reception one's attention suddenly and automatically shifts from the weary discussion of comparative mustards in which one has been idly involved to the nearby conversational group that happens to be discussing one's secret passion, one need not be intentionally turning one's attention to the more interesting exchange. More typically, one has been served by an automatic filtering process that is ordinarily inaccessible to introspection and which determines that what is salient in perception will be what answers to one's interests.

Dogmas die hard, so it is natural to suppose that such tropisms either an peripheral to the mind or represent breakdowns in the otherwise smooth working of the reason machine, the movements of which are properly mediated or guided by reason and are *therefore* different in nature from irrational processes. But this too can be made to seem like a quaint fantasy.

What is it for the normal operations of the mind to be mediated by reason? I suggest that it is just for causal relations to hold between mental states one of which in fact is a reason for another. What is it for mental operations to be *guided* by reason? Just for the reasoner to employ a certain inhibitory capacity—the capacity to inhibit conscious changes in attitude when he recognizes that those changes are not well grounded in reason. Here too we have mental tropisms, characteristic causal processes leading from one kind of attitude to another, tropisms that qualify as rational processes not because of some sui generis manner—rational causation—in which the one attitude causes another but because the one attitude is in fact a reason for the other.

Consider a case of intentional and rational belief change. I explicitly reason from my belief that p and my belief that if p then q to a belief that q. Thanks to my good schooling there takes place in me a causal process the terms of which are mental states whose contents, taken together, conform to *modus ponens*. Indeed, I might have explicitly aimed to guide my thought in accord with *modus ponens*. Then, thanks to my good schooling, there takes place in me a causal process leading *from* my desire so to guide my thought, my belief that p, my belief that if p then q, and my belief that *modus ponens* prescribes that I come to believe q, *to* my coming to believe q. This causal process is relevantly different from the mental tropisms we have been discussing only in involving as antecedent causes mental states that are reasons for my coming to believe q. Given this fact about the terms of the causal process, that causal process *constitutes* my explicitly guiding my thoughts in accord with *modus ponens*. No special kind of event intervening between reasons and my response to them, no special kind of intrinsically rational causation, is needed to make a causal process between mental states a case of rational, and intentional, belief change. Wayward causal cases aside,[30] the existence of a causal process connecting mental states that conform to a rational pattern can itself constitute rational and intentional belief change.

For suppose that what is required over and above causation by states that are in fact reasons for the states or changes they cause is as follows. First, the agent must recognize that he has reasons that support the drawing of a certain conclusion or the performance of an intentional act; second, the agent must will the drawing of the conclusion or will the performance of the act; and third, as a result of the willing, draw the conclusion or perform the act. The special something extra distinguishing rational causal processes from the mere mental tropisms that constitute irrational changes in belief is then supposed to be an intervening act of will rationalized by recognition of sufficient reason. This *could* on occasion go on in a person—he recognizes that he has sufficient reason for an act and he wills that he perform the act in question and he does perform it. But it cannot capture a general condition on rational inference or intentional action. For now we have a causal connection between someone's recognizing that he has reasons to perform a certain act and his willing or coming to intend to perform that act. This is a rational connection—the recognition of reasons rationalizes or gives a point to the willing or the forming of an intention to act. But if a condition on its being a rational connection is its including an intermediate forming of an intention to intend or a willing to will, we are launched on a regress we can never stop without at some point abandoning the general demand for an intervening willing to constitute a rational connection. At some point we must recognize an intentional act that is constituted merely by attitudes causing activity that they rationalize. So in particular, the case of intentionally drawing the logical conclusion from one's beliefs must ultimately turn on the operation of tropisms connecting the attitudes in question. Thanks to innate dispositions, training, and employment of the capacity to inhibit competing irrational operations, certain mental operations conform to good inferential rules but are as blind as the operations of the tropisms that do not conform. If we are to be able to draw any conclusions at all we must in the relevant sense draw some conclusions blindly, which is not to say unintentionally but rather to say without there occurring in us anything more than an automatic response to those reasons, a response that is in fact rationalized by them.

Just as a condition of understanding is that one must at some point respond appropriately to representations without interpreting them in terms of further representations,[31] a condition of reasoning is that one must at some point allow one's reasons to work on one in the appropriate fashion. Better, one's allowing them to work on one in accord with reason is one's reasoning from them, just as responding to one's representations in accord with convention constitutes one's understanding of them.

If this is the truth about rational connections among mental states, then the operations of mental tropisms (blind but purpose-serving connections between mental state types) are not peripheral phenomena but are the basic connections that constitute rationality and irrationality alike. Rational connections are not constitutive and exhaustive of the mental. Rationality could hardly be constitutive and exhaustive, given that minds evolved under conditions in which rational mental tropisms conferred only limited advantages. That a creature whose environment is too complicated for it to get by on the strength of its instincts does better in some ways if it can monitor its desires and rationally exploit means to their satisfaction is no surprise. But it should be no more surprising that such a creature, fallen from simple harmony with nature, does better in other ways if its frequent and debilitating anxieties that its desires will not be satisfied are regularly dealt with by doses of hopeful belief. Though we specially prize reason, it is just one adaptive form mental processes can take.

NOTES

1. See Raphael Demos, "Lying to Oneself," *Journal of Philosophy* 57 (1960):588–595; John Canfield and Patrick McNally, "Paradoxes of Self-Deception," *Analysis* 21 (1961):140–144; Herbert Fingarette, *Self-Deception* (New York: Humanities Press, 1969); David Pears, "The Paradoxes of Self-Deception," *Theorema* 1 (1974):000–000. John Turk Saunders, "The Paradox of Self-Deception," *Philosophy and Phenomenological Research* 35 (1975):559–570; Richard Reilly, "Self-Deception: Resolving the Epistemological Paradox," *Personalist* 57 (1976):391–394; Jeffrey Foss, "Rethinking Self-Deception," *American Philosophical Quarterly* 17 (1980):237–243; David Kipp, "On Self-Deception," *Philosophical Quarterly* 30 (1980):305–317; Mary Haight, *A Study of Self-Deception* (London: Harvester Press, 1980).

2. J. P. Sartre, *Being and Nothingness,* trans. Hazel Barnes (New York: Philosophical Library, 1956), chap. 2.

3. The loci classici of the resort to homuncularist models to explain irrational mental processes are S. Freud, "Repression" (1915), *The Ego and the Id* (1923), and "Splitting of the Ego in the Process of Defence" (1938), all in *The Standard Edition of the Complete Psychological Works,* ed. James Strachey, Anna Freud, Alix Strachey, and Alan Tyson (London: Hogarth Press and The Institute of Psychoanalysis, 1954–1974). David Pears develops a homuncularism specifically tailored to deal with self-deception in *Motivated Irrationality* (Oxford: Oxford Univ. Press, 1985). Both Fingarette and Haight consider the homuncularist response to the surface paradox.

4. R. A. Sorenson, "Self-Deception and Scattered Events," *Mind* 94 (1985):64–69.

5. B. Williams, "Deciding to Believe," reprinted in *Problems of the Self* (Cambridge: Cambridge Univ. Press, 1973); J. P. Sartre, *Being and Nothingness,* chap. 2; D. Davidson, "Paradoxes of Irrationality," in *Philosophical Essays on Freud,* ed. R. Wollheim and J. Hopkins (Cambridge: Cambridge Univ. Press, 1982).

6. For a discussion of subintentional bodily processes and their significance for a theory of the will, see Brian O'Shaughnassey, *The Will* (Cambridge: Cambridge Univ. Press, 1981), vol. 2, chap. 10.

7. See "Mental Events," "Psychology as Philosophy," and "The Material Mind," all reprinted in Davidson's collection of papers, *Essays on Actions and Events* (Oxford: Oxford Univ. Press, 1980). And see "Belief and the Basis of Meaning," and

"Radical Interpretation," both reprinted in Davidson's *Truth and Interpretation* (Oxford: Clarendon Press, 1984). Colin McGinn endorses something like the interpretive view in "Philosophical Materialism," *Synthese* (1980): Daniel Dennett, in "Intentional Systems," reprinted in *Brainstorms* (Cambridge: MIT Press [Bradford Books], 1978) argues that there is no more to one's being in a belief or desire state than it's being the case that the state is attributed to one within an adequate interpretive theory.

8. Davidson, "Mental Events" and "Psychology as Philosophy." I explore this argument and its relations to the interpretive view in "Why Having a Mind Matters," in *The Philosophy of Donald Davidson,* ed. E. LePore and B. McLaughlin (New York: Blackwell, 1985).

9. Davidson, "Paradoxes of Irrationality," p. 289. "An aura of rationality is thus inseparable from these [mental] phenomena, at least as long as they are described in psychological terms. How can we explain or even tolerate as possible, irrational thoughts, actions or emotions?" The phenomenon of wishful thinking prompts Davidson to modify the interpretive view. It would be interesting to explore whether his argument for token physicalism can survive the modification. In any case, I shall suggest that no mere modification of the interpretive view is adequate. Rationality is not constitutive and exhaustive of the mental.

10. H. H. Price, *Perception* (London: Methuen, 1973), p. 140.

11. Williams, "Deciding to Believe," p. 148.

12. William James, "The Will to Believe," in *Essays in Pragmatism,* ed. Alburey Cashell (New York: Hafner, 1948).

13. For Freud's discussion of primary process thought see "The Unconscious" (1915), in *The Standard Edition of the Complete Psychological Works.*

14. For a penetrating analysis of eventfulness and its role in the appeal of gambling see Erving Goffman's essay "Where the Action Is," in *Interaction Ritual* (Harmondsworth, Eng.: Penguin, 1967). Goffman's essay betrays considerable inside knowledge of what is going on in gambling.

15. Pears, *Motivated Irrationality,* p. 11.

16. The need for the assumption will become evident in the next section, where the notion of an autonomous means is introduced.

17. Sartre, *Being and Nothingness,* chap. 2.

18. Sorensen, "Self-Deception and Scattered Events," and D. W. Hamlyn, "Self-Deception," *Proceedings of the Aristotelian Society* 45 (1971):45–60.

19. Pears, *Motivated Irrationality,* chap. 6.

20. Davidson, "Paradoxes of Irrationality."

21. Ibid., pp. 298–300.

22. Ibid., p. 300.

23. Thomas Reid, "Of Social Operations of Mind," essay 1, chap. 8 in *Essays on the Powers of the Human Mind.*

24. Freud, "Mourning and Melancholia" (1915), in *The Standard Edition of the Complete Psychological Works.*

25. When is a system too simple to have intentions, in particular the intention to deceive? This is a complicated matter, but I think that if a system is to be correctly ascribed intentions then the system should have some capacity for practical reasoning and have a means of representing its own desires and beliefs, a means of representing

possible outcomes of action and the extent to which they serve its desires, and a capacity to act upon what it has judged to be the best alternative. Call such a system a *primary homunculus*. Now Daniel Dennett, among others, has suggested that we might take the intentional stance even towards things that are not primary homunculi, e.g., plants. That is to say we might explain the plant's turning toward the sun by attributing to it a desire for sunlight on its leaves and a belief that turning will make this more likely (see his "Intentional Systems"). In some quarters this is called 'homuncular explanation'. Evidently, this sort of homuncular explanation is not at issue in this paper. If any explanatory end is served by understanding a plant as if it has beliefs and desires, as much could be done by so understanding a tropistic anxiety-reducer. However, it is obvious that those who invite the paradoxes of self-deception by explaining self-deception on the model of other-deception are driven to postulate *primary* homunculi, i.e., systems that are rich enough to have intentions, in particular the intention to deceive. In "Machines and the Mental," *Proceedings and Addresses of the American Philosophical Association* 59 (1985), Fred Dretske presents what amounts to an argument that the attributions of beliefs and desires to systems that lack internal representation cannot be literally true. So there may well be problems with taking the intentional stance toward plants or tropistic anxiety-reducers.

26. St. Augustine, *Confessions* VIII, 7–16. I thank Bas van Fraassen for drawing my attention to this passage. It is quoted and discussed in his paper "The Peculiar Effects of Love and Desire," chap. 5 in this volume.

27. Sartre, *Being and Nothingness*, chap. 2.

28. See Nelson Butters and Laird S. Cermak, *Korsakoff's Syndrome* (New York: Academic Press, 1980).

29. This is effectively argued in Jon Elster, *Sour Grapes* (Cambridge: Cambridge Univ. Press, 1983).

30. In wayward causal cases, states that rationalize other states or events cause them, but cause them by a tortuous route employing processes not typical of willing (i.e., that do not typically constitute willing). See D. Davidson, "Freedom to Act," in *Essays on Actions and Events*.

31. This is surely part of the lesson of L. Wittgenstein's *Philosophical Investigations*, section 201, though I shy away from saying what else is going on there.

4

SELF-DECEPTION, RATIONALIZATION, AND REASONS FOR ACTING

ROBERT AUDI

Self-deception is a philosophically challenging subject. It interests psychologists as well as philosophers,[1] and it is widely recognized to constitute a good test case in both fields: a philosophy of mind that cannot account for it is seriously deficient, and a psychology that says nothing about it is at best unwarrantedly narrow. Despite this recognition, there is continuing disagreement over whether self-deception is to be explained, or explained away.[2] Which view one takes largely depends on how one resolves the dilemma that arises as soon as one reflects on the topic. If self-deception is construed literally, it seems to entail that self-deceivers both believe and disbelieve the same proposition: believing it as victims of deception, disbelieving it as perpetrators of that deception. If self-deception is not construed literally, one is hard pressed to explain why it is so called. Philosophers have taken both of these routes, and in each case they have diverged along the way.

Literalists have often sought to show that, and how, believing and disbelieving the same proposition is possible; other literalists have contended that this is irreducibly paradoxical and self-deception thus impossible; still others have argued that taking the term literally does not require endorsing a complete analogy with other-person deception, and that we can thus avoid the paradox. Nonliteralists have sometimes provided analyses of self-deception, sometimes characterized it without quite giving necessary and sufficient conditions, and sometimes argued that since no such conditions are to be found we must be content with noting the features of various kinds of cases. For all this diversity of approach, there is considerable agreement about the territory to be charted. We must at least explain what sort of behavior merits the term; how self-deception is related to thought and action; how its presence affects the person's rationality, moral responsibility, and psychological integrity; and what uses the notion may have in the philosophy of mind or in psychology.

This paper assumes that self-deception, understood literally—though not precisely on the model of one person's deceiving another—is both possible and indeed common. It also assumes that the notion is sufficiently determinate to make a philosophical account possible: while borderline cases may confront any account, the clear cases share certain features. To be sure, "self-deception" is sometimes used loosely. It is also liable to distortion because it provides a convenient way of excusing some of one's own errors or of criticizing other people without calling them dishonest, stupid, blind, or something else felt to be more condemnatory. We should not expect, then, to frame an account that clearly matches every use of the term. What we can achieve is an account that answers the sorts of questions just cited, and perhaps others widely taken to be important in relation to the topic of self-deception.

The specific project of this paper is to clarify connections between self-deception and rationalization, and to bring out the bearing of both on reasons for action. Self-deception surely produces a tendency to rationalize; indeed, rationalization is one of the facets of behavior in which self-deception shows its true character. Why does self-deception produce rationalization? And when it does, does it give the subject reasons for acting? Presumably, a rationalization of an action is nothing if not the provision of a reason for that action. But it is far less clear how one's action is related to a reason one gives in rationalizing it. It should also be noted that if rationalization can be caused by self-deception, it can also produce it. The two turn out to be mutually supporting and, I think, mutually illuminating.

Section 1 sketches an account of self-deception developed in earlier papers and shows why self-deception should be expected to generate rationalizations, which I also briefly explicate. The second section pursues some major connections between self-deception and rationalization. Section 3 explores how rationalization and self-deception are related to reasons for action, to rationality, and, ultimately, to understanding the human agent.

Self-Deception and Rationalization

1. Let me introduce my account of self-deception by locating it in relation to some of the central points of theoretical decision that shape approaches to self-deception. The question of whether self-deceivers must believe and disbelieve the same proposition has been mentioned. This is crucial. Second, one's ontology of self-deception is important: Is it wholly behavioral, a matter of one's actions? Is it, by contrast, a state? Or is it a complex phenomenon straddling both categories? Third, if, like most writers on the subject, one thinks there are both acts and states of self-deception, it matters greatly which of these one takes as fundamental. Should we conceive the state in terms of the acts or vice versa? In either case, there is a fourth question: whether to take cognitive concepts, such as belief and knowledge, as fundamental, or to rely primarily on volitional concepts, such as focusing one's attention and selecting one's sources of evidence. A fifth issue is whether unconscious

elements are to play a role, say in explaining how one can believe and disbelieve the same proposition by making one of the beliefs unconscious. There are other important points of decision, but these are among the most telling.

SELF-DECEPTION

Speaking in terms of these theoretical divisions, my account does not construe self-deception as entailing believing and disbelieving the same proposition; takes the state of self-deception as primary and interprets acts of self-deception as deriving their character from their relation to the state; and uses cognitive concepts, including that of unconscious belief, as its principal building blocks, though it connects them with both motivation and action. The core of the account is this:

A person, S, is in a state of self-deception with respect to a proposition, p, if and only if:

(1) S unconsciously knows that not-p (or has reason to believe, and unconsciously and truly believes, that not-p);
(2) S sincerely avows, or is disposed to avow sincerely, that p; and
(3) S has at least one want that explains, in part, both why S's belief that not-p is unconscious and why S is disposed to avow that p, even when presented with what he sees is evidence against p.[3]

Here unconscious belief is understood in a nontechnical and quite unmysterious sense. It is simply belief which S cannot, without special self-scrutiny or outside help, come to know or believe he has; it is not buried in a realm that only extreme measures, such as psychotherapy, can reach.[4] In every other respect, e.g., in directing behavior and serving as a basis for inferences, the belief can be almost entirely like any other; the often thin and delicate veil between it and unaided consciousness affects it little.

Consider an example. Suppose that Jan is an adolescent girl who has had an unhappy childhood, is subject to depressive moods, and craves attention. She might "attempt" suicide by taking an overdose of aspirin, say, six tablets. The result might be that her parents show alarm and begin to pay more attention to her. She might inform friends about the incident, too, and perhaps tell them, when she feels low, that she is again contemplating suicide. Now, so far the case might be either plain insincerity or genuine contemplation of suicide. But suppose we find out that Jan knew that such doses of aspirin are not normally fatal and that she left conspicuous evidence of her taking the pills (such as the open bottle on the sink). And suppose that her talk of suicide increases as her parents and friends ignore her, yet does not lead to another apparent attempt, and decreases when she gets attention. Imagine, too, that she does not find herself thinking about suicide when she is alone; instead, she thinks about her family and friends and her school activities. At this point, we might doubt that her attempt was genuine and wonder whether she is just lying about suicide to get attention. But suppose we know that she is generally very honest and, in addition, does not in her own consciousness even have the thought that she did not really try to kill herself, or the thought that she is not really contemplating suicide when she says she is. In line with this, we may imagine that when she does say she is contemplating it, she does not have the intention to deceive her hearer, at least not any such intention or motivation that she can discern by ordinary reflection.

In such a case, we have, on one side, evidence that Jan in some way realizes that her "attempt" was not serious and that she is not really contemplating killing herself; and, on the other side, evidence that she is not simply lying when, wrought up, she tells friends that she may kill herself this weekend. I submit that the case could be one of self-deception with respect to the proposition that she is seriously contemplating suicide. When she says this, she is deceiving herself because she knows, unconsciously, that she is not seriously inclined to take her life. But she is also *deceived,* because, in saying this, she is both saying something false and yet not lying, at least not to us: she is, as it were, taken in. She does not quite believe what she says, however. She is too aware of her own behavior and feelings for that; and this is why we do not expect the full range of behavior one would expect from genuine belief, including planning which presupposes that she will die (though in a well-developed case, even planning might be self-deceptively done). Yet her sincere avowal of the proposition is like an expression of belief; normally, in fact, sincerely avowing that p implies believing it. We have, then, both knowledge that not-p and the satisfaction of a major criterion for believing p. The criterion is not a logically sufficient condition, but it is strong enough to make its satisfaction in avowing a false proposition seem like being deceived.

The case also exhibits appropriate motivation. It is completely understandable that Jan should want, and need, attention, and should believe that appearing suicidal is a way to get it. These elements need not even be unconscious; in fact, it is in part because Jan consciously knows of their presence that she can scarcely help grasping, though without being conscious of it, that she is not suicidal. On the other hand, as a decent and honest person, Jan would not want to lie and would recoil from the thought of herself as lying to or manipulating others.[5] Thus, to fulfill her desire for attention in the way she believes will be successful, while maintaining her self-image, she must avoid realizing, or being conscious that, she is not suicidal. We could follow some philosophers and suppose that she also believes she is suicidal. But then we have to explain how she can believe both propositions (which seems at best a bare possibility), and in any event it is surely more reasonable to regard her as reacting normally to the same evidence that we see as belying her threats: such things as her never making a second "attempt" (or making only predictably ineffective attempts), her failing to speak with believable conviction in saying she may kill herself, and her saying it more often or more emphatically, depending on how much visible concern it arouses in us.

So far, my main purpose has been to sketch an account of the state of self-deception. It is also important to see, however, that the account enables us to understand other aspects of self-deception and to distinguish it from similar notions.

First consider *acts of self-deception*. These may be conceived (roughly) as those manifesting, or, in a certain purposive way, conducive to, a state of it. An example of the first sort would be Jan's declining a weekend invitation from a friend on the ground that she may not be alive then; an instance of the second would be her putting out of mind what she knows about the effects of aspirin as she initially "plans" to commit suicide by taking six tablets. One might think that since there are acts of deceiving others by a mere utterance, there are also acts of deceiving oneself at a stroke. I suspect that there are few if any such acts. Moreover, we should not expect the analogy to other-person deception to extend to this; for there is only one person, and the dynamics of self-deception (even given the sort of dissociation my account implies by its appeal to unconscious belief) requires, at least normally, a gradual onset. Nor should it be thought that self-deception is ever identical with an act; the term may be used to refer to patterns of behavior, but neither those patterns nor the existence of acts of self-deception entails that self-deception is ever constituted by an act, any more than the existence of acts of compassion entails that compassion itself is sometimes an act.

The account of self-deception also enables us to understand *being deceiving toward oneself*. This is the sort of behavior by which one gets into self-deception: putting evidence out of mind, concentrating on an exaggeratedly favorable view of oneself, and so on. But it does not entail self-deception. For one thing, it may simply produce *delusion*: one may, e.g., really come to believe that one's motives are noble, without the veiled realization that this is false. Granted, one might first have been in a state of self-deception; but it need not be this way: Joe might simply come to be deceived in believing that *p,* as a *result* of being deceiving with himself, yet not enter self-deception, because he is too wholehearted and there is nothing about him in virtue of which he could be conceived as perpetrating the deception. This is not self-deception; it is *self-caused deception*.

What are we to say of the case where S unconsciously believes something *false,* yet succeeds in getting into a state otherwise like self-deception in which he sincerely avows its negation? Suppose Tom has a masculinity complex and is given good evidence (by acquaintances who are teasing him) that it is only because of fear of rejection that he has not exploited Nancy. He cannot bear the thought, and puts it out of mind; but he cannot resist the evidence, and forms the appropriate (though false) belief. He then seeks evidence that he really held himself back out of decency, and in time he sincerely avows this. This evidence is solid, and he speaks truly, though in so speaking he is not expressing what he really believes. This is successful *self-manipulation,* but it is at best self-deception manqué. For the relevant avowals—those which manifest his having been deceiving with himself and having manipulated himself—are true; he is not deceived in saying what he does in uttering them. We could say, if we like, that he is *unconsciously deceived,* since he is deceived in his unconscious belief. Still, since that belief is the one he holds *qua* manipulator and deceiver, it seems no more correct to say that he is in self-deception than to say that Jack deceives Jill when, in trying to get her to believe *p,* which he mistakenly takes to be false, he induces a true belief. He has been *deceptive,* but his attempt misfires. We could profitably introduce a technical term here, such as *verific deception,* and also speak of verific self-deception; but on balance I think it better simply to note the phenomena in question and, partly because of the way 'deception' and 'self-deception' are success terms, not construe these phenomena as standard forms of deception or self-deception at all.

SELF-DECEPTION AS FERTILE GROUND FOR RATIONALIZATION

If self-deception is conceived as I have proposed, it is to be expected that rationalization, or at least a tendency to rationalize, would be among its effects. Implicitly, I have suggested that, far from being simply irrational, a self-deceiver not only knows something but also exhibits a complex ability, often using considerable skill, in concealing it. I have also suggested that a desire to preserve one's self-image may be important in causing self-deception. If this is so, and if, as seems likely, most people do not like to appear unreasonable, we might expect that rationalization often provides self-deceivers with a way to make otherwise unreasonable behavior seem appropriate. Thus, if Jan is asked by a friend who thinks she is faking, why she has not tried to kill herself during the many months since the last incident, Jan may reply that her parents have been depressed themselves and she cannot take her own life when they are too weak to stand the blow.

The same example illustrates another point: rationalization can help to support self-deception by providing, for *S,* a plausible account of behavior that might otherwise make him realize the falsity of what he sincerely avows. Jan herself, being of normal intelligence, needs an explanation of her not even attempting to carry out any of her numerous threats, else she may question her own sincerity, as she would anyone else's under the same circumstances. Her rationalization helps to keep intact the veil between her consciousness and her knowledge that she is not really suicidal. And in rationalizing, she would normally be expressing something she wholeheartedly believes: that her parents were depressed and that this was a reason for not killing herself at the time. She may even believe that this was the reason *why* she actually did not do so. But suppose that she unconsciously knows that it was not why. Still, in suggesting that it was, as she rationalizes her not having made any attempt for months, she is not lying, except possibly to herself (and lying to oneself is a kind of act of self-deception). She lacks the specific intentions (or other motivation) required for ordinary lying, such as the intention to get the hearer to believe something false. For she knows, though unconsciously, that the statement in question is true; and if this is why she lacks the intention to get the hearer to believe something false, then if she is lying to herself, it is roughly in the sense that she is deceiving herself.

RATIONALIZATION

So far, I have said little about what constitutes rationalization, though I have implied—what I think is uncontroversial—that, minimally, a rationalization of something one has done does not explain *why* one actually did it. Rationalization, at least of particular actions, contrasts with explanation of them (in the success sense of 'explain' rather than merely the attempt sense). It turns out, however, to be nearly as hard to explicate rationalization as to explicate self-deception. Perhaps Freud's view can be fairly readily formulated (though I doubt that); but the notion has a quite active life of its own in standard parlance, and it is this range of uses that I try to capture.

With the example of Jan's appeal to her parents' well-being as background, let me suggest the following account of an agent's rationalizing an action (A) of his:

> A rationalization, by S, of his A-ing, is a purported account of his A-ing, given by him, which (a) offers one or more reasons for his A-ing, (b) represents his A-ing as at least prima facie rational given the reason(s), and (c) does not explain why he A-ed.[6]

Our example illustrates this: Jan takes the fact that her parents are too depressed to deal with her suicide to be a good reason for delaying it, and she offers it as explaining (and perhaps also as justifying) her delay and as rendering her delay reasonable (or rationally appropriate, or something of the sort).

Several comments on this account are in order immediately. First, the term 'rationalization' may also be used propositionally, to refer to what is expressed by a rationalization as just described. Second, the notion of a purported account is intended broadly, but the commonest cases are attempted explanations and attempted justifications. Third, *S* may satisfy (c) without *saying* anything to the effect that, given the reason(s), *A* is at least prima facie rational. Typically, the context will indicate that the factor(s) cited are supposed to show this about the action and *S*'s citing what he does will presuppose that it shows this. Fourth, 'rationalization' as conceived here need not be disapprobative, as it usually is in the Freudian sense, for we are including cases in which, e.g., one quite properly rationalizes an intuitive decision by citing good reasons there were for it which one could have sought had one needed them. Finally, the formulation is meant to *suggest* that rationalizations are normally—and often self-defensively—*motivated* (and this could be readily built into it). Yet the conditions can be satisfied by a purported account that *S* does not give in order to represent the action as rational, and even by a purported account that fails to explain his action owing merely to error with no psychological significance, as where *S* has simply forgotten his real reason for doing something and cites another perfectly ordinary one he had for it. Such cases are not common. But surely one can, under a variety of circumstances, produce an *unintentional rationalization*. In any case, nothing significant in what follows will depend on taking this broad view of rationalization.[7]

In describing our example, I am assuming that Jan appeals to *a reason she has* for delaying; for the fact that her parents are too depressed to deal with her suicide is a reason to delay it, and she *has* it as a reason because she believes this and sees (or is at least capable of seeing) that it counts in favor of her delaying. I also assume that this is not *a reason for which* she in fact delays. For if it is, clearly it *explains,* at least in part, why she delays; and we would then have an explanation rather than a rationalization. Suppose, however, that Jan did not believe, at the time she acted (e.g., abstained from proceeding toward suicide), that her killing herself would be unbearable to her parents. This is still *a reason for* her delaying, since it weighs significantly in favor of delaying. Thus, our account of rationalization would allow her appeal to it to count as rationalizing.

There are writers who hold that an appeal to a reason should not be counted as rationalizing unless *S* at least does not disbelieve that it was a reason for which he acted. One ground for saying this is that we would otherwise assimilate self-deception to lying.[8] But I cannot see why such deceitfulness need do any more than affect the *kind* of rationalization we have. I propose that we distinguish *rationalizations by appeal to (merely) alleged reasons* from *rationalizations by appeal to reasons one had*. The latter are more typical, but the former have the intuitively crucial properties. The former are often, in addition, *deceitful rationalizations,* though a rationalization may also be deceitful because one falsely implies, of a reason one had but did not act on, that it was a reason *for* which one acted. Deceitful rationalizations, in turn, are sometimes self-deceptive, sometimes not, as when S is well aware that he did not have the reason he offers as accounting for his (say) not inviting someone to a meeting. Deceit, then, like self-deception, may occur either with respect to whether one had a reason or with respect to whether one acted *for* that reason. If a number of reasons are cited in rationalizing, the result may be a mixture of reasons S had and did not have. We could call these cases *heterogeneous rationalizations*. They may at the same time be partially or wholly deceitful, depending on what beliefs S has concerning whether he had, or acted for, the reasons in question.

One further complication must be addressed before we explore in detail the connections between self-deception and rationalization. It arises from the complexity of both rationalization and acting for reasons. We often do something for many reasons, just as we sometimes rationalize an action by appeal to many. How should we construe cases in which S offers an account of his A-ing by appeal to several reasons, where some are reasons for which he has acted and some are merely reasons he had for acting? Surely he is to some extent rationalizing; he is, after all, committing himself to at least a partial account of his action by his appeal to the reason(s) he merely had. I propose to call such mixed accounts *partial rationalizations,* since they are in part rationalizations and in part (successful) explanations. This is not to imply that they only *partly rationalize* or *partly explain*. They might adduce a reason S merely had which is sufficiently cogent to rationalize the action fully, i.e., roughly, to make it appear fully rational; and they might also cite a reason for which he acted, that is sufficiently powerful in producing his action to provide a full explanation for it. Here we must be careful, however: because of the possibility of overdetermination, what fully explains, or fully rationalizes, may not yield the whole explanation, or the whole rationalization. Other factors may also be sufficient. The full explainers or rationalizers are then not *complete*: while they do not merely partially explain or partially rationalize, they are only *part of what explains or part of what rationalizes*.

SELF-DECEPTIVE RATIONALIZATION

2. All of the differences we have indicated among kinds of rationalization may affect the way in which self-deception is connected with rationalization. Let us explore some important aspects of this connection.

SELF-DECEPTION AS A ROUTE TO RATIONALIZATION

In pursuing some of the ways in which self-deception generates rationalization, it is useful to consider at least three sorts of variables: the kinds of occasions favorable to this process; the self-deceiver's threshold for rationalization; and the degree of success of the process once it begins. These variables will be addressed in that order.

With respect to favorable occasions, let us first consider those common occasions on which circumstances threaten to penetrate the veil between S's consciousness and his unconscious knowledge. If, e.g., one is deceiving oneself about one's competence in one's work, there will likely be frequent pieces of evidence that go against one's sincere avowal that one is good at the job, and threaten to make one conscious of what one already realizes "deep down." Suppose, e.g., that S hires the wrong person for a task, say because he thinks her bright. Later, asked why he hired someone with so little experience, S might say that he was impressed by a strong, detailed letter from Jones. If S does not want to conclude that he decided incompetently, he will be biased in favor of believing that this was his reason for the hiring, even if it was not. Suppose S does falsely believe this; we would then have a nondeceptive rationalization. If S does not believe it and is quite aware he does not, we would have a deceptive rationalization. Both rationalizations are generated by S's self-deception, because of the way they are ultimately attributable to his desire to view himself as competent (or desires to this effect), and they each function both to nurture this desire and to help in keeping out of consciousness S's realization that he is not good at his job. Both are produced by self-deception; but neither is a *self-deceptive rationalization,* since neither appropriately embodies self-deception. Suppose, however, that S's saying he hired her because he was impressed with Jones' letter was a self-deceptive avowal, since S unconsciously knew that this was not why he did it. Then the very giving of the rationalization is an act of self-deception. I shall take this to be sufficient for its being a self-deceptive rationalization.

There is a second kind of occasion favorable to self-deception's producing rationalization. In these cases, while nothing particularly threatens the veil that preserves one's self-deception, one's behavior or thoughts simply do not seem rational or appropriate, so that a desire to preserve one's general self-image motivates one to find reasons for them. If Joe discovers that he often recalls experiences with Jane, whom he self-deceptively tells himself he is happy to be through with, he may simply feel this is strange, and rationalize that he is recalling the experiences because he likes to recall pleasant times. Granted, some people might feel such recollections to be threatening, e.g. as belying their affirmation that they are happy to be through with Jane. But they need only be felt to be, say, awkward or puzzling in order to generate rationalization. Notice that the rationalization here may be *internal.* If the recollections are not voiced to anyone else, there may be no need to offer the rationalization to anyone else; but one's own standards of rationality, or one's need to maintain a certain view of oneself, may be as demanding as the incredulity or suspicion of others. Rationalization, like self-deception, need not be just for the benefit of others.

A third case, closely related to the first, is a kind of occasion on which one is, so to speak, forced to put one's money where one's mouth is. This need not involve external circumstances. For instance, Jan may simply get to a point at which she feels hopelessly depressed, and in such a way that if she fails, without a suitable explanation, to form a plan to kill herself, she may become conscious that she has never intended to do so. This is a likely time to seek reasons for delaying. She may already have some, e.g. her having promised to meet a friend the next week. Or she may find some, say by discovering how hurtful to her parents it would be to do the deed now. It is possible, of course, that she may actually form a plan to commit suicide *later*, though if she really knows unconsciously that she has not seriously tried to kill herself and the balance of her motivation favors self-preservation, that is unlikely. She might, however, form a *self-deceptive plan*, i.e., roughly, one which she sincerely avows while unconsciously knowing that, e.g., she is not resolute about following it. One might argue that this is not a plan but only self-deception with respect to the proposition that one has a plan; but I am supposing that, for most of the elements in the plan, she does have intentions to carry them out, and has considerable motivation, though not firm intention, to take the last step.

Regarding the self-deceiver's threshold for rationalization, we should note a number of factors. Self-deception always creates a tendency to rationalize in the sorts of cases just described, but people differ in the strength of this tendency. One factor is simply the degree of S's desire, or perhaps felt need, to seem rational. Some people also like, more than others, to explain things or to comment on their own behavior. This applies particularly to the audibly pious: not only those who are religiously pious, but many who regularly express their sense of righteousness, or criticize others for missing the mark. Another factor is S's ability to marshal the reasons he has, to fabricate reasons he does not have, and to avoid the kind of scrutiny, of his consciousness or his behavior, which would expose a rationalization as such, and thus perhaps threaten to lift the veil of self-deception. There are other variables, such as the ability to compartmentalize one's behavior; one's capacity to avoid systematically interpreting one's thought and action; and one's ability to avoid or shorten interactions with people who, like critical older siblings, are likely to expose one to oneself. But we need not discuss the determinants of the threshold for rationalization further; enough has been said to suggest that although self-deception tends to lower this threshold, self-deceivers differ considerably in their thresholds for rationalization. These thresholds also vary from case to case in a single person and, over time, even in a single instance of self-deception.

There are several ways in which the process by which self-deception produces rationalization can be successful, where success is a matter both of how readily and frequently self-deception causes rationalization and of how good the resulting rationalization is, in ways to be indicated. Minimal success occurs when, at least once, S rationalizes on the basis of his self-deception. I say "on the basis of" because self-deception's merely causing a rationalization is not enough: Jan's self-deception may make her anxious, and that may make her feel insecure when queried about a routine act unconnected with her self-deception; this insecurity might then cause her to add a rationalization to buttress an explanation of the act. A rationalization based on self-deception will arise in some sense in the service of that deception, e.g. as obliquely aimed by S at keeping out of consciousness a crucial proposition he unconsciously knows, e.g. that he is not good at his work. It is not that he says to himself something like, "If I don't find an account of my mistaken decision which supports my avowal that I am competent, then I may have to face my incompetence." It is more nearly that his wanting to be, and his wanting to believe he is, competent lead him *both* to do the things that prevent his realization of deficiency from becoming conscious (e.g., his selectively exposing himself to evidence for his competence) and to rationalize away actions of his which point toward the deficiency. The self-deception and rationalization are similarly motivated, one might say; and at least typically the relevant motivation reflects some "ego need." Even when we restrict success in producing rationalizations to those based on self-deception, however, there are still many degrees and kinds of success. Let us consider some.

One factor important to evaluating the (quantitative) success of self-deception in producing rationalization is of course the number of instances in which S gives, or is prepared to give, the rationalization. Another is the number of different rationalizations the self-deception produces. Success is also (qualitatively) greater in proportion to the plausibility of the rationalizations. This has an objective side: the more plausible, the less likely to be rejected by others or, ultimately, by S. But the subjective side is even more important in the preservation of the self-deception: how convincing S himself finds the rationalization(s) to be. A foolish attempt may backfire and lead one to become conscious of one's real reason. (Why am I inventing ridiculous reasons to explain my hiring her?) But if a rationalization is really convincing, it may nicely protect one's self-deception (Jones' letter was really cogent and I even had it at the top of my list of reasons to hire when I made the decision). From this point of view, a self-deceptive rationalization may be less supportive of the underlying self-deception than one that appeals to reasons one genuinely believes explain one's (otherwise telltale) action. Here self-caused deception may work better than self-deception.

By contrast, if self-deception creates only partial rationalization, it is less successful, other things being equal—though it may be that an admixture of truth helps to raise the accompanying falsehoods above suspicion. Similarly, the more readily disconfirmable a rationalization is, the less its production by self-deception is a success (other things being equal). For others, or the subject himself, may discover either that he did not act for the indicated reason(s) or, in the case of fabricated reasons, that he did not have the reasons. This may lead S to see that he has been deceiving himself.

There are, then, many kinds of rationalization attributable to self-deception; and, from the point of view of the preservation of the agent's self-deception and, thereby, of his self-image, self-deception may be more or less successful in generating rationalizations. Not all rationalizations, of course, arise from self-deception. Sometimes rationalization produces self-deception. Exploring how it may do so will help us understand both notions.

RATIONALIZATION AS A ROUTE TO SELF-DECEPTION

We should again consider at least the following three kinds of variables: occasions favorable to rationalization's producing self-deception, S's threshold for passing from rationalization to self-deception, and the (qualitative and quantitative) success of the process by which rationalization produces self-deception when it does so. In exploring these matters, I shall not assume that the relevant rationalization cannot be self-deceptive to begin with (though the examples I cite need not include self-deception); the important point is to see how rationalizations can generate self-deception that they do not initially express.

Not just any instance of rationalization is favorable to self-deception. S may be quite consciously and clearheadedly rationalizing to deceive people about his real reasons and may approve of those reasons and feel no need whatever to protect his ego by accounting for anything he has done. It may be, however, that he rationalizes precisely because he wants to represent himself favorably, and this may in turn be because of, say, fears or insecurity. If, broadly speaking, such ego needs underlie his rationalization, the occasion tends to be favorable to self-deception. Imagine, for instance, that he rationalizes his not taking a stand on an important issue by claiming that doing so would be needlessly divisive, but is aware that he really did it to avoid a fight. Suppose, moreover, that it is important to him to feel that he is courageous, so that he is publicly ashamed of his evasion and privately ashamed of his rationalization. As time passes, he may put out of mind his recollection of the reason for which he acted and focus often on the point that taking a stand would have been divisive. He may also expose himself to others who both accept that point and take it to justify avoiding the issue. In time, his knowledge of why he avoided it may become veiled from his consciousness, and he may be sincere in saying that he acted to avoid divisiveness. One kind of occasion favorable to rationalization's leading to self-deception, then, is the sort in which the former is itself produced in the service of an ego need that can be allayed by becoming self-deceived with respect to the rationalizing reasons.

A second kind of favorable occasion arises when, again assuming the presence of a suitable ego need, rationalizing reasons abound in one's environment or one's thinking, in a way that makes it relatively easy to find *mutually supporting* accounts of one's behavior, in the shadow of which one can veil one's disturbing grasp of the truth. Recall our case of avoiding the issue. Suppose that, at the time when S declined to take a position, the hour was late, the majority disposition was clear, someone neutral would be needed to patch things up afterward, and so on. Other things being equal, rationalization here, whether by appeal to one or to all of these reasons for avoiding the issue, is more likely to produce self-deception.

The third kind of occasion we should note may, but need not, occur together with one or both of the above. I refer to cases in which one is thinking about oneself and, dissatisfied with what one finds, rationalizes as a way to put disturbing actions in a more favorable light. Some such rationalizations might themselves be self-deceptive. But suppose that they are not and that indeed they are less successful than some self-deceptive rationalizations in that they do not relieve one's dissatisfaction. Sometimes a realization that one is rationalizing heightens one's disapproval of oneself and, like a line of residual glue on the crack of a repaired vase, calls attention to what was meant to be hidden. Feeling disappointed with oneself, one might now be inclined to do the sorts of things that conduce to self-deception: selectively expose oneself to information on the matter; stress to oneself the welcome evidence and avoid contemplating the unwelcome; and, in doing this, use the reasons figuring in rationalizations that led one to begin moving toward self-deception.

People differ in the frequency with which they encounter occasions that are favorable to rationalizing or to their becoming self-deceived if they do rationalize. We differ markedly in our thresholds for proceeding from these occasions to self-deception. Other things being equal, this threshold is lower in proportion to (a) S's ability to rationalize convincingly—particularly, but not exclusively, by his own standards; (b) his capacity to evade systematic exploration of his own thoughts and behavior; (c) his ability to assemble what he takes to be information confirming either the elements in his rationalization or the sincere avowals crucial for the self-deception, or both; (d) his ability (and willingness) to bias, say by selective attention, the relative weights of evidence for, versus evidence against, those elements and avowals; and (e) the strength of his relevant desires or needs. While in principle any desire or psychological need could play the appropriate role, those important to one's self-image (roughly, to one's ego) are the typical motivating elements here. Consider, e.g., a desire for a sense of being rational and a need to feel that one is masculine—or feminine, compassionate, brilliant, creative, well liked, etc.

Regarding the success of the process by which rationalization produces self-deception, I am not thinking of success only in the sense of self-deception's resulting; an even more important basis for judging success is the desires or needs of S's that motivate the rationalization in the first place. Three variables deserve special mention in this second, qualitative dimension. First, consider the degree of satisfaction of the relevant desire or need. If S rationalizes his avoiding the issue because he desperately wants to see himself as courageous, then one indication of the success of self-deception produced by that rationalization is the extent to which it fulfills that desire, say by contributing to the range, strength, and conscious visibility of those of his beliefs which seem to him to express evidence, that he is courageous. A second, closely related indication of success here is the extent to which the self-deception *supports* a rationalization producing it. The degree of support depends largely on the kind of rationalization. Imagine that in giving it, S falsely believes not only that he had the reason cited but also that he acted for that reason. Self-deception which helped him maintain both beliefs would support the rationalization better than self-deception that helped him maintain only one of them.

A third measure of success has more bearing on interpersonal contexts. It might be called *underpinning*. I refer to the degree to which the self-deception equips S to withstand the sorts of forces, especially social ones, that would expose the rationalization, for instance comments by others to the effect that he is whitewashing his own conduct. Underpinning tends to vary with the first two measures of success I have cited, but it is affected by others as well. If, e.g., the self-deception is embedded in a great deal of supporting information, then even if some of that information does not support the rationalization directly it may be relevant to rebutting or simply stopping attacks on it. Being able to show, for instance, that others were biased in favor of someone not hired does nothing to support the merits of one's own choice, but may silence their criticism of it. Self-deception about one's own conduct, particularly on an important matter, such as a decision not to revive a relative who suffers heart failure, can be embedded in a host of information about oneself and others, some of it sufficiently general to be used in fending off all manner of criticism of one's motives or self-image.

The success of rationalizations in producing self-deception is also related more directly to the character of the self-deception produced, particularly to its strength. There are many important variables here; I indicate only some quite general dimensions. One is that of *accessibility*: the more readily S can become consciously aware that p, e.g. by unflinchingly acknowledging its truth, the more accessible is his self-deception with respect to p and, other things being equal, the more readily it can be eliminated. This is connected with a second variable: *entrenchment*. The more it would take, say in self-study, to uproot or dissipate the self-deception, the more entrenched it is. High accessibility implies shallow entrenchment; but the notions are not equivalent, since shallow entrenchment may combine with low accessibility where, although S's self-deception would be very difficult for him to discover, there are forces that would dissipate the self-deception without exposing it. For instance, S's needs might change radically and he might simply forget his self-deceptive avowals and cease to be even disposed to repeat them. Similarly, cases of self-deception differ in *resilience*: the strength of S's tendency, after he ceases to be self-deceived about something, such as his courage, to become self-deceived again about the same thing. Resilience is a matter of the kind of person, as well as of the dynamics of the relevant case of self-deception. Some self-deceivers might never regress; others may be well-nigh incorrigible.

The three variables just described—accessibility, entrenchment, and resilience—concern roughly the depth and strength of single cases of self-deception. We must also consider its relation to other psychological elements in the agent. Self-deception may, for instance, exhibit more or less *stratification,* depending on the number and kind of second-order elements. One can have second-order self-deception, being self-deceived about whether—as friends say—one *is* self-deceived; and self-deception may or may not be accompanied by beliefs to the effect that one believes that p, or disbelieves not-p, etc. There are also differences in *systematization,* depending on whether one piece of self-deception is connected with one or more others or with rationalization and other psychological elements, such as desires and beliefs. Self-deception about one's courage could be supported both by rationalizations about faint-hearted deeds and by self-deception about whether one's ideals and competences really express courage. Systematization tends to contribute to, but is not necessary for, *integration*: the degree to which the self-deception fits S's personality, especially his long-term motivation and cognition. Even an isolated case could be well integrated, as where one's only self-deception concerns one's motives for not reviving an aging heart attack victim. Presumably, the overall success with which rationalization produces self-deception should be understood in relation to at least the nine variables I have described. Most often, its overall success, especially from the point of view of serving the desires and needs in which it is grounded, will be greater in proportion to how much it contributes to all of these variables except accessibility. The greater that is, the less stable the self-deception is likely to be, and the less likely it is to help sustain the rationalization that has produced it.

GENERALIZATION OF THE RESULTS

We have seen how self-deception tends to produce rationalization and how rationalizations may generate self-deception. In both cases the agent acts in ways that are intelligible in terms of his desires and needs. Desires and needs either motivate the actions straightforwardly, e.g. when one quite consciously seeks a reason one had for an action in order to present the action in a favorable light, or they produce the actions in some oblique way, e.g. when self-deception arises gradually, not as something intended but as a result of diverse actions individually aimed at such things as putting unpleasant thoughts out of mind, getting others to accept one's story about oneself, and constructing good arguments to support that story. Now if desires and needs produce self-deception and rationalization in the ways we have suggested, and if the latter two play the role they seem to in the psychic economy, we should expect both self-deception and rationalization to concern not only actions, which have been our main focus so far, but any aspect of people or their lives concerning which there can be comparable desires and needs. This is just what we do find.

Take self-deception first. As characterized in section 1, its subject matter is unrestricted. We can be self-deceived about our beliefs or our actions, about others or ourselves, about our property or our character, and so on. Some writers on the topic might object that self-deception is not only *of* the self but, ultimately, at least, *about* it. Perhaps there is a tendency to think that if self-deception somehow serves one's self-image it must be about oneself; but if I have been right, while self-deception is always grounded in the subject's desires or needs, it need not be deception with respect to something about him. Jill could be self-deceived about whether Jack loves his country as well as about whether he loves her. Now if self-deception is unrestricted as to subject matter and is a common route to rationalization, there is some reason to think that rationalization need not be only of *actions* but may be of other things for which having reasons can serve one's desires and needs. There are independent reasons to think this,[9] and rather than argue for it I will proceed directly to illustrating it.

If one can rationalize one's action of avoiding taking a stand, it would be strange if one could not also rationalize one's belief (or, if one does not hold it, *the belief*) that doing so was right. Indeed, if we substitute belief for action in the account of rationalization given above, we get a plausible characterization of *belief rationalization*. The central point is that for beliefs as well as for actions we may distinguish between reasons S merely has for believing and reasons for which S believes, and we find a similar contrast between explaining and nonexplaining reasons. The same holds for desires and all the other propositional attitudes, including even emotions so far as they are propositional.

Thus, there can be (and are) rationalizations of beliefs, desires, emotions, and at least many of the other propositional attitudes. Moreover, self-deception can produce such rationalizations, and they in turn can lead to self-deception. If S is self-deceived with respect to his fear of philosophers, this may lead to his rationalizing. He will almost certainly not rationalize his fear, since, being self-deceived about it, he sincerely avows that he does not have it. But he may rationalize actions, such as his avowals to the effect that he merely dislikes philosophers; beliefs, such as his belief that philosophers are intimidating; and emotions, such as his anger with a philosopher who has shown him mistaken. Rationalizations of elements besides actions may, in turn, produce self-deception.

Given what has been said about how self-deception and rationalization interact, including the points about favorable occasions, thresholds, and success, we should be able to achieve a comparable understanding of the interaction where the relevant rationalization is directed toward something other than an action. The individual cases will of course exhibit some distinctive features, but we need not discuss examples in detail. Instead, I want to conclude this section with a general remark that applies both to self-deception and, by implication, to self-deceptive rationalizations.

As conceived here, self-deception tends to be *unstable*. This is in part because S avows, or is disposed to avow, sincerely, something he (unconsciously) knows is not true. There are at least two important points here. First, by and large we have good enough access to what we do and do not believe so that it takes special conditions, and often special efforts—such as selective exposure to relevant information—to make us capable of being simultaneously sincere (at least in the sense that we are lying at most to ourselves) and mistaken in avowing a belief.[10] Second, we are generally rational enough so that our becoming aware of evidence for a proposition makes us tend, to some degree, to believe it (as the self-deceiver unconsciously does believe the truth he finds somehow unpleasant) and even to *acknowledge* it.

Take a case of self-deception in avowing that one is courageous (p). There is a certain tension here which is characteristic of self-deception and partly explains its typical instability. The sense of evidence against p pulls one away from the deception and threatens to lift the veil concealing from consciousness one's knowledge that one is not courageous, but the desires or needs in which the self-deception is grounded pull against one's grasp of the evidence and threaten to block one's perception of the truth. If the first force prevails, one sees the truth plainly and is no longer deceived; if the second prevails, one passes from self-deception into single-minded delusion and does not see the truth at all. Self-deception exists, I think, only where there is a balance between these two forces. Rationalization helps to keep that balance. It can also create such a balance when it occurs where the appropriate elements are waiting to be so arranged.

On this view of self-deception, it is a phenomenon that manifests a measure of rationality. Indeed, since the subject really does know the relevant truth and does not quite believe what he self-deceivingly avows, the evidence has, in an important way, prevailed. Moreover, viewed as I suggest, self-deception powerfully exhibits the extent to which our beliefs are *not* under the direct control of our wills. Otherwise one could simply refuse to countenance the evidence and could bring oneself to believe what one self-deceivingly avows.

Rationalization also exhibits the agent as to some degree rational: at least he is concerned to adduce reasons, and often he will meet at least moderately high standards of relevance and justificatory support (the purported reason[s] must at least be prima facie relevant, or we have only an attempted rationalization). If we were not minimally rational, as well as complex enough for a kind of dissociation, self-deception would not be possible at all; and if we did not both care about, and have a minimal grasp of, reasons, we could not rationalize. To be sure, self-deceivers and rationalizers may not be paradigms of rational persons, but neither self-deception nor rationalization should be considered utterly inimical to rational agency or intrinsically irrational.[11]

SELF-DECEPTION AND REASONS FOR ACTING

3. Rationalizations of action do not deserve the name unless they produce at least one thing that qualifies as a reason for action. This is one difference between them and *excuses*. Now if rationalizations must produce at least one reason, and if they often manifest our rational capacities, can suitable rationalizations of an action show that it is rational? And can this be so even when the rationalization is produced by, or embodies, self-deception? These are important questions for which we shall have to give complex answers. To see our way more clearly, let us first consider how self-deception provides reasons for action, both through rationalization and otherwise.

SELF-DECEPTION AS A SOURCE OF REASONS FOR ACTING

We have already distinguished reasons one merely has for acting from reasons for which one acts. Both may or may not be reasons there *are* for so acting, in an objective sense implying their conferral, on the type of action in question, of prima facie reasonableness. Reasons one merely has, and reasons for which one acts, are the kinds of reasons that will chiefly concern us. Both kinds are supplied by self-deception. If *S* is deceiving himself out of a desire to see himself as courageous, that desire may provide him with a reason for volunteering for a dangerous job. Suppose he does volunteer. Is this acting *out of* self-deception? It is not natural to call it that, in part because too little of what constitutes the self-deception figures in producing the action: only the motivating desire, which, in addition, is of a common and normal kind.

And while the unconscious knowledge embodied in self-deception certainly can provide a reason for acting—e.g., for not taking on a job so dangerous that only the truly courageous can succeed—we certainly do not think of acting on this sort of reason as acting out of self-deception. By contrast, if S does something which either manifests the self-deception as a whole or seems in some sense designed to preserve it, the case is very different. An instance of the first sort might be S's selectively attending to evidence for his courage. Here his desire to see himself as courageous and his need to support his self-deceptive avowals (perhaps among other things he needs to support) are responsible for the action. An example of the second sort would be S's vehemently arguing against plausible evidence that he lacks courage.

If self-deception can provide not only reasons for action but also reasons *on* which one may act (both in acting out of self-deception and in acting otherwise), do self-deceivers have any control over whether, when they act in line with one or more of these reasons, they do so out of self-deception? In answering this I shall not assume that one ever has *direct* control over which of two or more reasons one has for acting will be a reason for which one acts. But one may have indirect control over this, and self-deception may provide motivation to exercise it. Imagine that by virtue of his desire to seem reasonable, together with his self-deceptive avowals that he avoided the issue because taking a stand would be divisive, S has a reason to mediate between two colleagues who are at odds: he is, after all, on record as strongly opposing division among colleagues, and here is a chance to confirm that he really acts out of this concern. But suppose that he also has reason to mediate because he would benefit if the colleague who shares his view were joined by the other. It might help him in maintaining his self-image if he could see himself as acting to oppose division; this is partly because it would help to keep out of his consciousness his knowledge that he avoided the original issue from cowardice. What he might do, then, is emphasize to himself how his mediating might reduce division; and in deciding to mediate he might explicitly say to himself that he is going to try to make peace, and might keep out of mind (as much as possible) his selfish reason for mediating. When he does mediate, could he then be doing it out of concern to oppose division, or would that claim be self-deceptive rationalization? And how can we tell?

To begin with, while the sort of self-manipulative strategy just sketched might succeed, one could not be confident that it would. From S's concentrating, at the time of action, on one reason he has for it, and putting another reason out of mind, it does not follow that he does not act in part, or even wholly, on the banished reason. One way he might know that the latter is influential is by noticing that as the going gets hard and his efforts flag, the thought of that reason, or of something connected with it, such as his getting what he selfishly wants, seems required to keep him going. But even this is not conclusive, and an ingenious self-deceiver might tell himself that he was merely tempted to act for the wrong reason, and managed to resist. What we would need to know to settle this is nothing less than what he would have done, other things being equal, if he had not had the banished reason. Many factors bear on this. It is often very difficult to gather enough of them to be justifiably certain whether it is so, and both self-deception and rationalization can aid one in avoiding the truth of such propositions.

There is, however, a strong presumption we may make. Where S has a reason for A-ing that represents it as fulfilling (or as likely to fulfill) a particular desire of his, then if he A's intentionally while aware of the connection he takes it to have to the desire, then, other things being equal, he A's at least *in part* for that reason, even if he also does so for another reason. The more vivid the awareness, the stronger the likelihood that the reason is operative, and that, if it is, it plays a significant motivational role. It is not clear whether this is a conceptual truth; I suspect that it is, but it is in any case plausible, particularly for rational persons. For rationality surely *is,* in part, a matter of appropriately responding to the reasons one has when one is suitably aware both of them and of some broadly instrumental relation they bear to something one wants. Thus, in the example just drawn, we would expect the action to be performed for both reasons.

Suppose, on the other hand, we imagine S rationalizing his action deceitfully, by citing reasons there were for his having A-ed, which are not reasons he had, at least not in the sense that they provided potential motivation by virtue of the sort of instrumental connection with desire just indicated. Imagine that, when he mediated, he had the thought that his role as family friend carried a responsibility to the colleagues' spouses to mediate, but had no desire to fulfill this particular responsibility or to do anything else to which he believed fulfilling it would (or might) contribute. Then, the presumption formulated above does not apply. For there is no desire such that his awareness of the obligation should be motivating by virtue of its connection with that desire. This is not to imply that motivation can come only from desire, even if 'desire' is taken broadly enough to be equivalent to wanting; the point is that when a reason lacks the relevant connection with desire, then even if S acts with an awareness of that reason, there is not as strong a presumption that he acts *for* it. S *might* act on this admirable (normative) reason he recognizes; but we do not have compelling reason to expect him to, even if he thinks of it as he acts. That might indeed be an excellent self-deceptive strategy—camouflaging one's real reason for acting by focusing, as one does the deed, on a good reason there is to do it.

A person's not acting for a (nonmotivating) reason he recognized, however, implies little about his tendency to appeal to that reason should he rationalize the action. Indeed, factors S believes were, objectively, reasons to perform the action are a convenient source of rationalizing elements: they do a good job of making the action seem, at least from S's point of view, reasonable, and his citing them suggests, to him anyway, admirable motivation. They are also convenient in supporting self-deception; for it is easy to obfuscate, even to oneself, why one actually did something, particularly much later; and having an objectively good reason to focus on as one's presumptively actuating motive helps to keep buried one's realization of the reason for which one actually did the deed.

Self-deception, then, is not only a fairly direct source both of reasons for acting and of reasons for which one acts, but, by producing rationalizations, an indirect source of further reasons that may turn out to be of either sort. The reasons for acting which, in either of these ways, self-deception provides, may or may not be conscious; and in part because they are sometimes not conscious, it is very difficult to determine which of S's reasons for A-ing is one *for* which he A's. His own beliefs on the matter are not to be ignored; yet they can be mistaken, especially long afterward, and this is so even where there is no self-deception to incline him to attribute certain of his actions to reasons other than the "real," explaining one(s).

It is very hard to generalize about the conditions under which S will act on a particular reason that is provided by his self-deception. For one thing, he may not act out of self-deception at all, since it may exist wholly dispositionally, or at least without producing intentional action (or even nonintentional action of a sort that counts as acting out of self-deception). Moreover, if he does act out of his self-deception, he may be acting for several reasons together. There is also the possibility raised by partial rationalization: that there are reasons that only partially explain his action. We might then have the difficult problem of deciding how much influence each one has in generating (or sustaining) the action. Clearly, self-deception can influence action in complicated ways, and rationalization can compound the difficulties of sorting out and weighing the different influences. Our efforts here are largely conceptual. But if we can see the distinctions clearly, we at least know where to look empirically in trying to understand the agent.

SELF-DECEPTION AND STANDARDS OF RATIONALITY

Self-deception, we saw, requires a certain minimum of rationality and sometimes plays a very significant part in the agent's psychic economy. If, in addition, it provides reasons for action, may it thereby produce rational actions should the agent act in accordance with those reasons? Take, for instance, the case in which the unconscious *knowledge* embodied in self-deception provides a reason on which S acts, as when our cowardly subject declines a highly dangerous assignment because deep down he sees that he cannot manage it. To be sure, he may self-deceptively rationalize this, e.g. by pointing to his having a conflicting obligation. But the rationality of his declining surely does not depend on his rationalizing reasons' being good. If they are not good, he fails to *show* that his action was rational, yet the reason for which he did it may still be sufficient to render it rational. This kind of reason, however, is not the usual sort provided by self-deception, the kind such that acting on it is considered acting out of self-deception. The other cases are more difficult to resolve, and I want to consider some of them briefly (drawing in part on an earlier study).[12]

Perhaps the most general point to be made here is that while the rationality of actions arising out of self-deception is typically more difficult to assess than that of ordinary intentional actions, it does not appear that different criteria of rationality need be employed. One might think that if unconscious beliefs or other unconscious explanatory elements are involved, then we need different criteria of rationality. But if I am right in holding that even unconscious beliefs may be appropriate responses to evidence—which is typically how they count (when true) as the unconscious knowledge in virtue of which the self-deceiver deceives—then perhaps other unconscious propositional attitudes are also rational. This, at least, is what I am assuming. I also assume that unconscious elements can render an action rational if they motivate it in the right way, as a rational belief does an action based on it. There may be a sense in which action arising from self-deception is a test case for criteria of rationality—it certainly poses a challenge to them—but it does not require special criteria.

Another important general point is that there is a profound difference between particular actions and action-types, and what renders one rational may be different from what renders the other rational. Let me first develop this point with respect to rationalization and then apply it to action arising from self-deception.[13] When Joe rationalizes his avoiding the issue by citing the need to prevent division, may we conclude that the avoidance was rational, assuming the cited reason is a good one? The question is ambiguous: is the reference to the type, *avoiding the issue,* which might be instantiated by him (or others) on different occasions, or is it to his particular action of avoidance? It makes perfect sense to say that his rationalization shows that the type, *avoiding the issue,* was a reasonable (kind of) thing to do, yet deny that *his doing it* was reasonable. This is precisely what I claim (and have defended elsewhere).[14] On my view, a reason one has for an action renders that action rational only if one performs the action at least in part for that reason. Note that unless we say this we must allow that a rational action can be performed for very bad reasons, e.g. on the basis of irrational beliefs and foolish desires, so long as *S* has a good enough reason for it. I would call this irrationally doing something which, in the circumstances, is a rational kind of thing to do. The view is parallel to Kant's thesis that a deed is moral only if done out of a sense of duty, not merely in accordance with it.

SELF-DECEPTION AND ACTING RATIONALLY

If the two general points I have stressed are correct, then whether an action produced by self-deception is rational will depend not on what reasons for it are provided by the self-deception but on the reasons *for* which it is performed (together with some other factors, such as moral and prudential considerations, that cannot be discussed here). Let us consider what are perhaps the most typical cases of actions produced by self-deception. One is the case in which *S* is in effect putting his money where his mouth is: doing something in order to conform his behavior to his self-deceptive avowal, say one to the effect that he is not frightened by philosophers. Another is self-deceptive rationalization, as when Joe self-deceptively says that he avoided the issue because taking a stand would have been divisive. There is also the artificial focusing of attention on considerations favorable to sustaining the self-deceptive avowals, such as concentrating on why a stand would have been divisive and on how, on other occasions, one acted to avoid division. Similarly, *S* may evade conditions unfavorable to sustaining those avowals, e.g. the company of suspicious friends or the recollection of occasions on which he behaved fearfully. Some of these cases may be regarded as reducing cognitive dissonance, in that *S* acts to achieve greater harmony among his beliefs and attitudes. Perhaps other reductions of cognitive dissonance may also manifest self-deception, and certainly we have not described all the actions that arise from it. But the examples cited are quite sufficient to give us a sense of how to view the rationality of actions arising from self-deception.

Consider first putting one's money where one's mouth is. Is it irrational to act in support of a self-deceptive avowal? It is often not. But it may be: certainly it is in general reasonable to act in order to live up to the image of oneself one has projected, at least if the image is admirable, as it often is with self-deceivers. Granted, it would not normally be reasonable to act specifically *to live up to a self-deceptive avowal*; it is not even clear how this is possible, since it seems to entail (where the act and avowal are roughly concurrent) a kind of awareness of one's being self-deceived that is inconsistent with one's being so. But this is not what *S* does; such is not the content of his intention (at least not of any conscious motivation). The reason for which he acts may be a perfectly good one. That he would not have that reason if he were not self-deceived neither vitiates the reason nor prevents it from conferring rationality on the action it explains. To be sure, there could be sufficient counterreasons to prevent it from conferring rationality; my claim is that an action is rational in virtue of a reason only if performed for it, but not that every action performed for at least one good reason is rational. Thus, while living up to one's avowal of courage might render taking a stand on a controversial issue rational, it would not warrant doing a daredevil trick for which one knows one is unprepared. Even when self-deception provides good reasons, then, it provides at most defeasible reasons.

With this much said, the other cases may be dealt with more briefly. Self-deception may provide one with a reason to rationalize because, say, one's deeds (as opposed to omissions) are incongruent with one's words, as in the case of the adolescent repeatedly threatening, but never seriously attempting, suicide. Again, if one rationalizes in order to explain one's behavior, doing so may be rational. The *way* one does so, e.g. by citing the kinds of reasons one does, may be foolish, but that is another matter. But should rational persons be rationalizing at all, instead of seriously inquiring into their own motivation? And if self-deception is at the heart of an attempt to rationalize, should we call the attempt rational? It is true that the inquiry might be a better thing for S to do and that self-deception may lead him to irrational action. But if I have been right, self-deception manipulates and partially buries, yet does not wholly overthrow, reason. It is self-protective, and in some cases, like that of the husband who would fall apart if he had to face his wife's no longer loving him, it may be the best protection one has against a blow one could not withstand.

From the point of view of self-interest, then, which is at least one fundamental basis for determining rationality, being in self-deception may be on balance desirable, and some of the ultimately self-protective actions arising from it may also be rational when they are good means to a reasonable end, like preserving an admirable self-image. But if rationalizing, even self-deceptively, is sometimes a rational thing to do, it is risky for the self-deceiver; for even without others' help, he may see through his own rationalization, discover that he is largely speaking for his own benefit, and perhaps grasp what his real reasons are. Certainly, the fact that he is to some degree rational in offering a rationalization does not imply either that he will ultimately accept it himself or that his doing so would be rational.

Similar points may be made about selectively focusing one's attention on relevant evidence, about evading things one perceives as threatening, and about other actions arising from self-deception. And counterparts of many of the points made above hold for nonbehavioral elements that may be produced by self-deception—particularly propositional attitudes, for which I would also argue that they are rational in the light of a reason one has for them only if it is a reason for which one holds (or has) them. For them, too, we should distinguish particular instances, such as S's belief that preventing division is a reason for avoiding a stand, from types, such as *the belief* that it is such a reason. And again, the fact that a type is rational in the light of a reason does not entail that an instance of that type is rational, even when S has the reason.

If his real reason for avoiding the issue is that he wants to be spared unpleasant consequences of joining the issue, and this want is itself based on irrational fear and operates through an irrational assessment of what the consequences will be, then his simply having a reason for this type of action does not make his doing something of that type rational. A rationalizable action need not be rational.

If self-deception is not an intrinsically irrational state, nor even always an undesirable state for a normal person to be in, and if many kinds of actions arising from it can be rational, then we should not be surprised that an action's arising from self-deception does not imply that the agent is not morally responsible for it.[15] Indeed, it does not even imply that S has less than normal self-control in performing the action (though this may hold for some self-deceivers). Partly for this reason, an action's genesis in self-deception also need not provide moral extenuation. We do sometimes talk of someone's being a "victim" of self-deception. But being a victim is not always extenuating, and there is such a thing as highly culpable credulity, which can make the ill-fated dupe a subject more fitted for reproach than for extenuation. In the case of self-deception, one has the added burden of being responsible for both deceiver and dupe. Attributions of moral responsibility for actions arising from self-deception, then, *may* be unaffected by the self-deception; in any event, they are similar to attributions of rationality in being governed by multiple criteria.

CONCLUSION

Self-deception is primarily a state in which a kind of psychological dissociation gives rise to a disparity between what the self-deceiver knows, albeit unconsciously, and what he avows or is disposed to avow. It tends to be an unstable condition, and to exist only so long as there is a balance between the pressure of the evidence, to which the self-deceiver's knowledge is typically a rational response, and the strength of his defenses in maintaining the veil that camouflages that knowledge from his consciousness. Self-deception is rarely if ever a static phenomenon. Like a craving for reassurance, it usually gives rise to efforts to satisfy the desires or needs that underlie it. It produces many kinds of behavior. Rationalizations are among the most important of them. In addition to being intrinsically interesting, rationalizations often support the self-deception that produces them, and they often reveal much about the agent: what he values, believes, and wants; even what ego need is responsible for his self-deception.

Rationalizations are not simply products of self-deception, however; they may produce it themselves, even if they are not self-deceptive to begin with. Self-deception is fertile ground for rationalization. This is because rationalization can so well supply reasons for action—or belief, desire, emotion, and other psychological elements which protect the subject These reasons protect in at least two ways. They cloak both the motivation and the needs actually underlying the actions or other elements; and they help to keep buried whatever unconscious knowledge the subject has concerning those reasons or other elements. But rationalizations are also fertile ground for self-deception: they provide, for instance, considerations on which one can focus in putting out of mind, and gradually pushing beyond conscious access, knowledge, beliefs, desires, and emotions that it is painful to acknowledge as one's own.

Plainly self-deception, so conceived, can have a role in maintaining not only the subject's comfort, but even his sanity, or at least his ability to function without drastic interference from guilt-ridden thoughts or distracting preoccupations. Moreover, if self-deception both embodies knowledge and leads one to want to see oneself as, for instance, reasonable, it should not be a surprise that it provides one with reasons for acting and, at times, leads one to act rationally. Some rational acts of this sort are guided by the unconscious knowledge; others are directed toward living up to the self-deceptive but often high-minded avowal; and still others are aimed at finding or interpreting relevant evidence: an activity that can be admirably rational even if the evidence gathered is not impartially assessed. In some cases in which self-deception leads one to seek rationalizations, one undertakes this search rationally; the rationalization one produces may then be plausible or foolish, and it may support one's self-deception or, occasionally, expose it by somehow pointing to what it was meant to hide.

Self-deception and rationalization are, in an important way, manifestations of, though also typically defects in, our rational makeup. But it would be a mistake to think that when they provide reasons for action, and the agent acts in accordance with those reasons, he thereby acts rationally. It is vital to distinguish between reasons one simply has for doing something, and reasons for which one does it. A rationalizing reason, and many of the reasons for acting provided by self-deception, are only of the former kind. One may act in accordance with them while acting for very poor reasons. We then have an irrational action that the agent can rationalize; at best he has irrationally done what is a rational kind of thing to do. Similar points hold for the propositional attitudes, which bear counterpart relations to self-deception and rationalization. Both self-deception and rationalization can provide one with an account of oneself that can be used in meeting criticism; but if the defensive reasons they yield are only reasons one has, then they do not support the rationality of the actions they rationalize, and they cannot absolve one of moral responsibility for them. They can veil, from others and even oneself, what one is really like; but whether one's action is rational and how, in general, one's overall rationality is to be assessed depend on how one's behavior is attributable to one and not on the portrait one can paint of it.[16]

NOTES

1. For a wide range of recent papers on self-deception, by psychologists as well as philosophers, see *Self-Deception and Self-Understanding,* ed. Mike W. Martin (Lawrence, Kans.: University Press of Kansas, 1985).

2. See, e.g., M. R. Haight, *A Study of Self-Deception* (Sussex: Harvester Press, and Atlantic Highlands, N.J.: Humanities Press, 1980); some authors in Martin, op. cit., take a similar view, though most of them, philosophers *and* psychologists, think self-deception possible.

3. I have developed this account in "Self-Deception, Action, and Will," *Erkenntnis* 18 (1982):133–158, and "Self-Deception and Rationality," in Martin, op. cit. Martin takes acts of self-deception, rather than the state, as fundamental, and develops a different view. See, e.g., his "Demystifying Doublethink: Self-Deception, Truth, and Freedom in *1984,*" *Social Theory and Practice* 10 (1984):319–331, in which he characterizes self-deception as a "refusal to acknowledge the truth to ourselves," where such refusals include persuading oneself into false beliefs, holding inconsistent beliefs, being willfully ignorant, having phony attitudes or emotions, or engaging in inauthentic self-pretense. For a detailed account that makes motivated false belief central in self-deception and is intended to contrast with mine on several points, see Alfred Mele, "Self-Deception," *Philosophical Quarterly* 33 (1983):365–377. For Mele, the self-deceiver has a desire that *p* (which is actually false) be true; he thus manipulates apparently relevant data in a way that causes him to believe *p* (p. 370). This surely can lead to self-deception, but more must be said if we are to distinguish self-deception from self-caused deception.

4. I have discussed unconscious belief in some detail in "Self-Deception, Action, and Will," cited in note 3. For an account of believing which makes clear sense of this notion, and indicates how our multiple criteria for it permit both discovering unconscious beliefs and conceiving them as beliefs in essentially the same sense as conscious ones, see my paper "The Concept of Believing," *The Personalist* 57 (1972):43–62.

5. Her reaction to this thought would depend on many factors, including her ability to rationalize it away (as we shall see below), and normally self-deception would prevent its occurring to her. Kent Bach goes so far as to argue that a person self-deceived with respect to *p* avoids "the sustained or recurrent thought that *p*" (e.g., that she will kill herself). See "An Analysis of Self-Deception," *Philosophy and Phenomenological Research* 41 (1981):351–370, esp. pp. 362–365. But while it is important to recognize a *tendency* toward such avoidance, *S* may even focus on the thought in a sustained way provided he has adequate defenses.

6. This formulation is developed and defended in my "Rationalization and Rationality," *Synthese* 65 (1981):159–184.

7. For a narrower conception of rationalization which does make motivation necessary (and may in other ways be closer to Freud's than mine), see Béla Szabados, "The Self, Its Passions and Self-Deception," in Martin's collection cited in note 1. Szabados says, e.g., that a rationalization "is a form of justification prompted by a mixture of desire and fear such that the rationalizer tries to put his action, conviction, or emotion into a better light than it would otherwise appear to himself and to those significant others whose opinions matter to him" (p. 155).

8. See, e.g., Andrew Oldenquist, *Normative Behavior* (Washington, D.C.: University Press of America, 1983), esp. pp. 155–160, in which he contrasts rationalization with insincerity and requires that a rationalizer be "mistaken" (not deceitful) if we are to call the reason he offers a rationalization (p. 156).

9. In "Rationalization and Rationality," cited in note 6, I have argued that the notion of rationalization applies to propositional attitudes other than belief.

10. There is a kind of privileged access here, but the privilege is highly limited, as I have argued in "The Limits of Self-Knowledge," *Canadian Journal of Philosophy* 4 (1974):253–267.

11. For contrasting perspectives on the rationality of both self-deception and rationalization, see Bach, op. cit., who speaks at one point of "the irrationality of the rationalizing self-deceiver" (p. 359), and Jon Elster, *Sour Grapes: Studies in the Subversion of Rationality* (Cambridge: Cambridge Univ. Press, 1983), esp. pp. 148–157. My views on this are defended and elaborated in my papers cited in notes 3 and 6. For related discussion, including defense of the view that self-deception is not necessarily evil or irrational, see John King-Farlow and Richard Bosley, "Self-Formation and the Mean," in Martin, op. cit. Also relevant to the relation of self-deception and rationality is Amélie Oksenberg Rorty's "Self-Deception, Akrasia and Irrationality," *Social Science Information* 19 (1980):905–922.

12. See my "Self-Deception and Rationality," cited in note 3.

13. Here I draw on my "Rationalization and Rationality," cited in note 6.

14. Ibid., esp. pp. 170–178.

15. Self-deception in relation to moral responsibility is discussed at length in my "Self-Deception, Action, and Will," cited in note 3.

16. For helpful comments on an earlier version of this paper I am grateful to Mike W. Martin, Alfred Mele, and Allison Lea Nespor.

Part II

THE EPISTEMIC DIMENSION OF SELF-DECEPTION

5

THE PECULIAR EFFECTS OF LOVE AND DESIRE[1]

BAS C. VAN FRAASSEN

> Who can untie this most twisted and intricate mass of knots?
> —St. Augustine, *Confessions* II–10

To write about self-deception, I must choose a very personal style, since I bring no professional qualification to the subject, nor much learning. How self-deception is even possible is of course the first philosophical question about it. Every approach to this subject leads quickly back to the inconsistency borne in its name. Yet logical puzzles about how one could possibly believe one thing and know its opposite seem to me almost a travesty of the perplexities we feel about the phenomenon, or cluster of phenomena, we refer to as self-deception. The threat they pose, I have come to think, lies not there but in our sense that their possibility undermines any defense against skeptical doubts—not of the global kind we tend to dismiss as philosophical *vieux jeux* but of a much more intimate sort. My idea here is to look closely at some of those phenomena, after only a few pages of general reflection.

FREDERIC MOREAU AND MME. ARNOUX

1. Which phenomena, exactly, should we look at? This question cannot be answered by a definition of self-deception; at the preliminary stage all we can have is a rough demarcation. If I say that you deceived yourself, I imply that you had a false opinion, and that you arrived at it in a way that makes you culpable. For if I deceived someone else, he or she would have a false opinion, and would have arrived at it in a way that made me culpable. In central cases of deception the deceiver knows that the opinion in question is false, or at least, is of the contrary opinion. Hence in the clearest cases of self-deception we must also be able to say, "You really knew all along; or at least, if you had faced the issue honestly and explicitly, you would have

had to acknowledge the truth." But not all cases are like this. Suppose that a certain bridge is dangerous, and I do not know this, that I really have no evidence that makes it less likely than not, for me, that the bridge is safe. But suppose in addition that I think it would be very good for me if you believed the bridge to be safe, and I successfully persuade you to believe this falsehood. Then I have certainly deceived you, although I did not know that the information was false. Similarly I expect that there can be cases of self-deception in which the person cannot correctly be said to have known or even recognized the truth as the most likely. The main requirement for it to be (self-) deception, as opposed to unintentional (self-) misleading, is that he be culpable of persuading himself by epistemically unfair means or practices. This leaves us unsure of the boundary with wishful thinking, but it may be correct to call that a limiting case of self-deception.

An accusation does not, for its effectiveness, depend on the verifiability or falsifiability of the charge. This was proved at the stake and in the House Committee on Un-American Activities. If we harbor radical doubts about whether there is a coherent concept of the self-deceiver, we doubt at least that it is in principle possible to give nontrivial, adequate truth conditions for attributions of self-deception. Although an accusation always *purports* to state a solid sort of fact, such a radical doubt would not remove the possibility of charges and accusations of self-deception. It would, however, undermine such accusations (you cannot harbor the doubt and also take the accusation seriously) while explaining the language-game as a (mere) mechanism of accusation. The learned would explain the vulgar game, but their explanation would prevent them from taking part.

Such a position has the usual drawback that it is exceedingly difficult to forsake the game. I shall turn to examples below; meanwhile it will probably be agreed that we often want to say of others that they do deceive themselves, and of ourselves that we did but do no longer. Those claims may sound patently false to the audience: consider "For years I deceived myself, thinking I did not love my daughter, but really all the neglect and harsh words and the misery I caused her sprang from love and were for her own good . . ." But the automatic reaction ("I think that is false!") is equally incompatible with the radical doubts outlined above. And what do you say when someone just does not come to an inevitable conclusion, and hypotheses of dim wit or dissimulation are ruled out? "To me the evidence is clear, and you have the evidence also; the facts are staring you in the face; I see it must be more comfortable to reject my conclusion, but you are deceiving yourself if you do." What else is there to say?

This second example points to a different way to exploit the idea of accusation. An accusation can consist in a moral or quasi-moral evaluation of commonly admitted facts. To deny the accusation can then take the form of admitting those facts, but rejecting the evaluation. The obvious examples are: to admit killing but deny murder, to admit falsehood but deny deception. And the denial can take the form of either advancing a contrary evaluation of the same sort, or denying the applicability of that *sort* of evaluation at all.

This too has a difficulty: in the case of self-deception, the (quasi-) moral evaluation would have to be of the formation of belief or the weighing of evidence—or so it would seem. There are indeed two traditions in epistemology that differ on this, but the one for which it would make sense (*voluntarism*) has, I think, never been a popular one. For most writers on the subject, weighing evidence and determining what is credible is construed on the model of arithmetic—or at best, Archimedean statics. You may not be very good at sums—but that is stupidity or ignorance. It would be very hard, I think, to explain self-deception this way if we could be relevantly guilty only of deliberately careless or incompetent arithmetic.

I do not wish to continue in this vein of exploring general possibilities for an account of self-deception in the abstract. Let us go to the facts themselves, for a while. Of course, let us approach them a little systematically, or we'll just get lost. We need to choose something, tentatively, to go on.

2. Let me hazard a first guess. There is something theoretical about the ideas of thought, opinion, and belief, and also something nontheoretical. If I want to accuse you (or myself) of self-deception, I can make the charge prima facie irrefutable by skillful trade on the consequent ambiguities.

In the first place, attribution of thought or thinking need not carry any implications of conscious mental activity at all. (I am not suggesting that there exists unconscious mental activity: let us leave such hypotheses to psychologists.) For example, if you ask me, "How are you?" and I reply, "Happy," I do imply that I am happy, and was happy already when you asked me, but not that there were conscious feelings or thoughts of a relevant sort preceding my answer. I was happy already; now I realize it, as I answer you. Even if I look at the sky and say, "I think it will rain," or look at you and say, "You clearly think this will spoil our walk," I attribute no conscious mental activity preceding my words either to me or to you. I merely attribute opinions. Think of how irrelevant it would be if you replied, "Not at all; that is false, for I was thinking about something else entirely, about dragons as a matter of fact." For it is possible that both are true: that you *are* thinking about dragons, and that you *do* think rain will spoil our walk.

For there is also conscious thought, which is, or is like, talking to oneself *sotto voce*. It happens as you walk along the street, deeply engrossed; it happens in little pauses between the sentences I am now writing, as I sculpt the next, though many of these sentences are just written without such a prelude. And since this activity (let me call it thought "*s.v.*" for "*sotto voce*") is so much like speech, it offers itself at once as a base from which to make the usual, standard inference from what a person says to what he thinks (in the sense of: what he opines).

The function of thought *s.v.* is, I think, mainly preparation. I prepare for writing the next sentence or paragraph by trying out phrases in my mind; also for writing a paper, or part thereof, by trying out schemes and outlines *s.v.* Suppose now that as I walk along the street, deeply engrossed, eyes unseeing and shoulders hunched, the subject that so engrosses me is my relations with *Mme. X.* She has told me this morning that I am merely deceiving myself if I think that I still love her, that I only have to look at my own actions and gauge my own inclinations to perceive the truth. In my mind I am speaking to her eloquently and at great length, explaining how I have always felt, how she misperceived my earlier ardor and even more my present preoccupation with work and desire to travel. I hear her voice, I see her laughing at me, with more amusement than bitterness, clearly showing that she had escaped these bonds sometime before. I suspect her of incredible infidelities, of really loving her husband after all; I swear my affections have never faltered. And now, tell me if there is one single test by which these exclamations *s.v.* are not to be counted as the purest, most sincere, and most privileged expressions of belief, if anything could be?

If there is to be any inference at all from what I say sincerely, without qualification or reservation, without constraint or possibility of gain or loss, to what I really think or believe, then such an inference must surely be correct *a fortiori* now. For now I am my own sole audience, and my only aim is to rehearse a problem crucial to my own life and to my action and happiness henceforth. This thought *s.v.* is apparently preparation—that is its normal function—for speech out loud, which, if performed, may have the most far-reaching consequences for my own life. And yet, here I am, sounding like a cheap lawyer, distorting the truth to suit the impressions he is paid to create, on behalf of a client without integrity, before a judge so corrupt that he will let go unchallenged the most improbable of claims. Not only that; I half realize I will not say or write these things, except perhaps for those accusations that, if true, will go some way to justify my own actions, or make them look better.

The normal function of thought *s.v.* is in such a case abrogated. It is then a pretended speech in my own defense, before a pretended tribunal consisting of *Mme. X* (now compliant, now skeptical, as my rhetorical moves require for their setting), myself, and the world. Later, looking back on these sad episodes, I will again think *s.v.,* appear before the tribunal of my mind, and tell stories that explain what really happened. In some I will shine, and in some I shall be as guilty as if I had constructed and run Dachau single-handedly. Depending on how traumatic the episodes were, the number and diversity of mutually contradictory reconstructions in memory, performed at the tribunal in my mind, may be quite extensive.

One crucial point about these pleas and stories that makes it possible for them to live in my mind is that so many of their lines attribute to me and to *Mme. X* thought that is not *s.v.* and attribute intentions, motives, and feelings in the same way, without necessarily implying any conscious mental activity. The point is that I can attribute thought and feeling with total impunity as far as details are concerned. For it is entirely consistent to say that you or I thought or felt this or that yesterday, while admitting we had no conscious awareness of any such thought or feeling and engaged in no action that bore explicit witness to it.

The paradigm inference to what a person thinks is from what he or she says, when there is no contraindication of gain from the effect of the saying itself. As soon as we *doubt* that self-deception is really possible, we must take thought *s.v.* to be very strongly qualified as a base for such an inference. If you say to me that you (too) love *Mme. X,* the effect you want to have on me may have more to do with what you say than your belief concerning its content. But what if you say it out loud, alone, in the middle of a forest? *A fortiori,* what if you think it *s.v.?* But (here comes the catch) if thought *s.v.* is such a very good base for that inference, and if we can evaluate it "from outside" (in memory, in our own case) as deceptive, rhetorical, lying, flouting all ethical standards for debate, then we can conclude that the person is engaged in a deception practiced on no audience but himself. These shoddy arguments, dismissals and distortions of evidence, and comforting opinions with no claim to warrant, we must then conclude to be really *his.* So, to sum up the argument: if you doubt the possibility of literal self-deception, this doubt makes it impossible to explain away the very phenomenon that, if taken seriously, gives us overwhelming reasons to say that self-deception is regrettably pervasive in situations of stress.

We have an alternative, though I don't think it is very palatable. It is to reject as a mistake of the vulgar, that paradigm inference to what a person thinks or believes. This surely results in an almost complete skepticism about inferences from thought *s.v.,* let alone from speech however sincere, etc., etc., to what anyone (even oneself) really thinks or feels. I say "almost complete skepticism," because two paragraphs ago I had to say "as far as details are concerned." Of course, the story in the large is made up of details, but it is less easy to be skeptical about less detailed matters. This is a matter of degree, but there are limits. In André Gide's *Strait Is the Gate,* Alissa writes in her journal about Jerome:

> I strive to act according to reason, but at the moment of action the reasons that made me act escape me, or appear foolish; I no longer believe in them.

The reasons that make me fly from him? I no longer believe in them. . . . And
yet I fly from him, sadly and without understanding why I fly.

We have already, perhaps, concluded that the reasons she gave were not the
real reasons; although she was sincerely persuaded of them, she was deceived.
But did Alissa really love Jerome? Did Jerome love Alissa? Did Juliette love
Jerome? Perhaps in the end we are disinclined to say *yes* to any of these. But
the disinclination is not of equal strength; we are under the impression that
in trying to answer such questions, we are weighing various relevant factors,
and they are not the same. In any case, no opinion based on the text can
imply that Jerome loved Juliette. Conscious avowal, thought *s.v.*, and actions
and behavior almost uniformly speak against it. No, it would be too farfetched;
the novel has strained our credulity too far already.

Well, if it is so farfetched, why have I wasted more than three words on
it? Because it can't be ruled out, except by bludgeoning it with common
sense, and refusals that are just a bit too loud to be mere denials. Reasonable
skepticism about what human beings really thought or felt, even ourselves,
has its limits—but they are not theoretical limits.

3. The story of *Mme. X* that I sketched above does not exist. What I mean is:
there is no such story. One recurrent reason for the misgivings I feel with the
philosophy of mind is that it often uses as data, examples that do not exist.
An example exists if it is made up, you will say; and that is right. An example
could be a real happening or a story. But a cartoonlike sketch of a story
is neither. Both in real life and in real literature, the observer finds himself in a context so rich that—despite the clear limitations on what he can
observe—he has a basis for conclusions about thought and emotion. Cartoonlike sketches, however, do not generally give him such a base, but only *assert*
that he has such a base. Examples so sketched are like Harlequin romances:
they give the reader simply the conclusions he is supposed to reach. Any
philosophical conclusions reached by such means are, I think, sheer moon-
shine, just as are conclusions about love and marriage based on Harlequin
romances. They are only the opinions of the author, thinly disguised in dramatic form. There is no saying what conclusions we would reach if we came
upon a factually similar episode in real life or literature. Possibly there is also
a good way of proceeding by sketched examples: to ask the reader to take
them as pointers to real episodes in his or her own and acquaintances' lives
or in literature. But then the conclusions drawn by the author from his or her
sketches must be carefully checked against the readers' own, genuinely known
instances. Moreover, they must be ones the readers *can* check—that rules out
most science fiction examples, and many others as well.

I want to point to a real episode in literature, to which the *Mme. X* story
(as I continue it below) bears some distant relation. In Gustave Flaubert's

Sentimental Education, Frederic Moreau falls in love with Mme. Arnoux, and although she is unattainable, there is never anyone who can supplant her in his heart. This sentimental education of Frederic covers eleven years, from 1840 to 1851; near the end he can say to Rosanette, "I have never loved anyone but her." Then many years go by:

> He travelled.
> He came to know the melancholy of the steam boat, the cold awakening in the tent, the tedium of landscapes, and ruins, the bitterness of interrupted friendships.
> He returned.
> He went into society, and he had other loves. But the ever-present memory of the first made them insipid; and besides, the violence of desire, the very flower of feeling, had gone. His intellectual ambitions had also dwindled. Years went by; and he endured the idleness of his mind and the inertia of his heart.
> Towards the end of March 1867, at nightfall, he was alone in his study when a woman came in. (p. 389)

It is Mme. Arnoux. The scene that follows puts the lie to everything Frederic has pretended. Or does it? They speak of love as of a lost treasure; he feels a violent desire for her, but does not want her for fear of disgust later. "Besides, what a nuisance it would be! And partly out of prudence and partly to avoid degrading his ideal, he turned on his heel and started rolling a cigarette."

Much can change in sixteen years, must change; this scene does not mean that he did not love her *then*. But what about that contention—which we are surely meant to understand as his—that the ever-present memory of his first love made the others insipid? Did that story begin to play a role in certain defenses, hiding the disinclination for a more exacting emotional life? And looking further back, was that love for Mme. Arnoux, never consummated and never pursued beyond very strict bounds, not present mainly in the "official" role in which it helped define his relations with others, such as Rosanette and Mme. Dambreuse? In reflections such as these we can see the mechanisms of accusation roll ponderously into action—the first and primary function of our attributions of self-deception to someone else. The doubts raised have as *one* obvious resolution the conclusion that Frederic deceives himself.

I am not in a position to resolve these doubts with any certitude and propose that we continue for now, naively, with that most difficult question: could there be self-deception in emotion? Suppose we continue with the story, unfortunately not of such literary merit, of my affair with *Mme. X.* Imagine that the scene I have already described happened long ago. Years later (*She traveled. She came to know the melancholy of steamboats, cold awakening in tents, . . .*) she let me know she wished to see me again. I wrote that I had never forgotten her, that all loves had been insipid beside the memory of hers, that we could meet upon her return, a month hence. One week before the meeting, I fell violently in love with a woman I met on the Metro. I was delirious; she was not out of my thoughts for a moment. A few months later it was hard to recapture this feeling; it had ended peaceably enough. Meanwhile, one may imagine with what mixed feelings I approached the meeting with *Mme. X.* It was strange to meet her again: at the same time as if we had never left each other, as if no time had elapsed, and also as if we were strangers, doubtful that we had any way of gauging each other's feelings. As it happened I did not actually have to reveal to her how inextricably my heart was now involved with someone else. Before the end of the first evening, she said ruefully that the many weeks that had elapsed since she wrote to me had undoubtedly been a mistake; one should always act on one's great impulses, but she had been afraid. Meanwhile, she and Ricardo, a traveler on the same steamboat by which she had come home, had realized how uniquely suited they were for each other, romance blossoming into love . . .

What shall we say of this narrator and his paramour? Did they not really have the emotions they avowed? Let us consider only his infatuation with the woman he met on the Metro. By every test one can imagine, in speech, thought *s.v.,* behavior, decisions made day by day, one has to admit that the evidence is overwhelming that he really had those feelings, that he wanted her, experienced tenderness and compassion, cared for her, had no greater joy than to see her joy—you, reader, may supply whatever criteria I omit. So his immediate feelings were real, if any are. He was perhaps mistaken in thinking (as he surely did?) that they would last, but that is not the point at issue. Nevertheless, this infatuation was as effective a defense against the very *possibility* of reconciliation with *Mme. X* as can be imagined. And so it was with her feelings for Ricardo, which, we should perhaps add, lasted not much longer.

Imagine, in contrast, a slightly different scenario. Suppose that instead of becoming preoccupied with another woman, our narrator had stayed totally preoccupied with the coming meeting, but had contemplated day and night *Mme. X*'s past treacheries, real or imagined, and developed baroque hypotheses about her present plots and motives and sexual involvements. Suppose that he had convinced himself that even as he thought about her so ardently and tortuously, she was having a shipboard affair with someone on the journey home, some fascinating Latin, with a name like Roberto or Ricardo—all without the slightest shred of evidence. We would say that he was deceiving himself, just as much as a hypochondriac who refuses to acknowledge the evidence of his good health and sees pathological symptoms everywhere. And we would know why. Despite his letter (but how shall we explain that?) there was nothing he wanted less than a reconciliation with *Mme. X,* or the exacting future this might bring in train. (But how are we to explain his making all the arrangements to meet her, and speaking already of subsequent meetings?) The two scenarios are not really so different. He was deceiving himself.

4. Now we have two stories, one real by Flaubert and the other only sketched, in which the main character was apparently deceived about his own emotions. In the latter we concluded that he was deceiving himself when he thought and said that he wanted to meet *Mme. X* again, that he still felt very strongly about her, that he was happy at the prospect of meeting her. And also of course when he thought that he was in love with the other woman, that being in her presence was an end in itself, the delight of being entranced with someone for whom he cared deeply. (I preserved certain similarities with *A Sentimental Education* to draw on your memories of something closer to reality.) So this character was deceived on the very subject to which epistemology has traditionally given him privileged access. But is *our* situation (qua philosophical spectators of the collaboration between writer and reader in the preceding section) really so simple?

It will not have escaped you that at certain points the argument was distinctly weak, and the weaknesses glossed over by bits of persuasive rhetoric. By what process did we (you, reader, and I, alternately character, narrator, and critic) reach this conclusion about the character's self-deception? It is essential that we inspect this process closely, because we wish to have it as an example of how, in reality, such conclusions are reached about others and ourselves. So let us look again, for a moment, at the preceding section.

I hope that you did not become impatient with me for tailoring the story of *Mme. X* to my didactic purposes as I went along. To be able to do that is surely the exact and only reason why a philosopher makes up his own examples rather than drawing on real literature and life? At the beginning of the *Phaedo,* Socrates (who has been writing poetry while awaiting execution) explains that poetry and philosophy are totally different because the poet makes up stories and fables. The reader immediately recalls stories of Socrates' and notices in fact that a very few lines before, broaching the nature of pleasure and pain, Socrates has sketched a fable of a double-bodied (two-backed?) beast. I was only following Socrates' practice rather than his preaching therefore when I sketched a story in the service of philosophy. My tailoring of the story was never capricious, but provided the vehicle for an argument that moves by its own internal necessity; isn't that true? And I was quite honest about it; little would have been gained anyway if I had done all the tailoring beforehand and dished up the whole story at once, at the outset. You would have seen through that anyway.

The point I wanted to lead you to was that the emotions the character felt for the woman he met on the Metro were subjectively no less and no more real than were (in the alternate plot) his suspicions and dreadful certainties about *Mme. X*'s betrayals. They had also exactly that same efficacy, which makes the accusation of self deception spring to our lips. In neither case can he (allow himself to) "know what he is doing"—i.e., sabotaging the possibility of reconciliation—but he is doing it nevertheless, and the facts are there before his eyes as clearly as before ours. But *it is the reader who says this,* the accuser who adds an explanation to the events depicted, who imposes an interpretation on what happens, who gives primacy (in his or her reading) to the defensive function that he or she (the reader) attributes to those feelings and thoughts. If that was not clear to you at the time, was it perhaps because I, the writer, switched so naturally from role to role, speaking at certain points even with the voice of a reader of the story I had just held up before us?

That the reader could have reached different conclusions is evident. The sudden infatuation on the Metro could be seen as a fear reaction: the way the relationship with *Mme. X* had ended is still in his mind, the memories of agony, reproach and self-reproach, the sense of loss and defeat, the mourning and grief over lost dreams. There must inevitably be fear—of failure, of renewed rejection, of a return to those tortures.

> O, the mind, mind has mountains; cliffs of fall
> Frightful, sheer, no-man-fathomed. Hold them cheap
> May who ne'er hung there.

And if in fear he grasped for some safety, some harbor or firm ground, that was not a sign that he did not deeply want reconciliation. The accusing reader, in the preceding section, discarded or ignored such and similar alternative explanations, and concluded instead that this man deceived himself about wanting to make a reconciliation possible.

This accusing reader is not omniscient. He or she—more specifically, you—may have motives that do not bear close scrutiny. So let us be objective. Let us examine one another, you the reader and I the writer, with particular attention to what happened as we journeyed together through that story of *Mme. X.*

This accusing reader, who ended section 3 with "He is deceiving himself," is not omniscient. What motives lie hidden from our scrutiny? Have you, accusing reader, been betrayed by another's inconstancy; do you now have a stake in saying angrily that this man in my story was betraying and deceiving himself and everyone around him? Why were you so ready to accuse him of self-deception—implying that no, he was not really in love with this siren of the subways; no (in the alternate plot) he was not really the tortured subject of painful doubts, but only rationalizing his unwillingness to be receptive to *Mme. X*'s approach? Were you perhaps basing your verdict less on evidence than on an identification with *Mme. X,* seen (at least until late in the section) as the person wronged?

And what of me, the writer? Did I help you to this verdict by obligingly presenting, tailor-made, only those bits of evidence that fitted exactly the "real" story you constructed as a gloss on my own? Was I in fact disingenuous in *this* section too, when I outlined the reasons why a philosopher must sometimes make up his own stories rather than rely on literature or reality? (You noticed, of course, how defensively verbose that paragraph was?) A novel would not so compliantly have provided only the evidence tailor-made for one explanatory hypothesis—and reality would not have either.

Indeed, now that the doubts have sprung up, we must notice that the narrator of that story was also its main character (for the story is in the first person) as well as the writer of the section. We must surely see now how convenient it would have been for this protagonist to believe afterward that he had not really wanted a reconciliation with *Mme. X*. This conclusion, after all, allows him to discard such soul-rending possibilities as that he really wanted her terribly, and that a reconciliation would have finally led them to the love fate had reserved for them, could they only have accepted it—that his infatuation on the Metro had sprung from fear, or stupidity, and that he was unworthy of or unable to accept the great gift life had once more held out to him. And we notice sadly that the conclusion of that accusing reader, "He deceived himself" (referring not to the final diagnosis but to the infatuation begun on the Metro) gives the main character precisely that conclusion, so convenient for his later peace of mind.

But when the story purports to be a memory of one's own past, then protagonist, narrator, reader, writer, and critic are all one and the same. Where shall I stand, when the text of my life deconstructs itself at every turn of the page?

5. All these rhetorical questions may have exhausted you a little. But you saw well enough, didn't you, that they were rhetorical? That is to say: I was really presenting you with a new story, the story of how a writer and reader had collaborated in drawing the conclusion of self-deception, in a process that was a far cry from an argument moving by its own internal necessity. Indeed, this fictional writer and reader (for of course, nothing like that really happened when I wrote, and you read, section 3!) were deceiving themselves. The writer purported to be writing a story that could show us, by its verisimilitude, the phenomenon of a person self-deceived with respect to his own emotions. This scenario, once created, could be held up in place of a bit of reality, a neutral object there for inspection by everyone, and everyone would see the same thing. This purport was false; the compliant reader was deceived. Or rather, he deceived himself, because not only the writer's carefully selective presentation of data but also the reader's readiness to fit these data into a scenario of treachery were needed to arrive at that conclusion. (*You see*

what I meant about philosophy of mind done by the method of sketches of examples'!)

This new example was one of self-deception in the interpretation of a story that was (perhaps, or perhaps not) about self-deception also. In thought *s.v.* every part of this could have happened, with writer, narrator, main character, and reader all one and the same person, reflecting on his own past. Recall that person, walking along the street early on in the *Mme. X* story. Totally engrossed in a self-justificatory speech *s.v.*, he plays his own lawyer, judge, jury, general public, and on top of all that, the voice and eyes of a compliantly listening *Mme. X* present at this tribunal. Perhaps he walks along another street, years later, totally engrossed, his thought *s.v.* now duplicating more or less our section 3. Now he plays, in effect, the role of writer, narrator, character, etc., in the story of his past so far. Here he finally concludes that he was deceiving himself when he came to the conclusion that his affair of the Metro was a case of self-deception about his own emotions. He concludes it was motivated by the desire to feel sure, in retrospect, that he had not really wanted the reconciliation with *Mme. X* and that therefore he had not really lost anything when the (apparent?) attempt at reconciliation was a failure.

We see therefore that the phenomena of self-deception are extremely complex, and not really touched by sophisticated little discussions about how to believe both *p* and not-*p*. The past is a kaleidoscope into which I look in memory. The hand that turns the kaleidoscope is perhaps more skillful at influencing the changing patterns than I would like to admit. Under these conditions, there is some reason for despair: not only about our ability to know where we have been and what we have done or even seen but also about the very possibility of finding significant, nontrivial truth conditions for such a statement as "He deceived himself." After all, if he did not know the truth, belief in a falsehood was not deception but error. One may object here that the deception lay in the idea that he had adequate evidence for this falsehood, while really he had better evidence for the truth. My story about stories inside stories was meant in part to preempt this reply. If *he* could not infer from his own felt emotions, actions, desires, speech, and thought *s.v* that he was (or was not) really in love with the woman of the Metro and/or did (or did not) really want a reconciliation with *Mme. X,* then we never have sufficient reason for belief in such propositions. The truth about what evidence I have, or how it should be counted or weighed in the balance—a tortuous enough topic in the epistemically more hygienic case of scientific methodology—seems no easier to know than the conclusions themselves. If he tells me afterward *that the evidence was unambiguously and overwhelmingly in favor of the conclusion* that he really wanted the reconciliation but had been taken by surprise, on his way there, by a love so deep and beautiful that he was helpless in its grasp—then I doubt him just as much as if he had simply said that the conclusion was true. I just don't believe it. "He is culpable; he was deceiving himself and everyone around him," I say, and no attempt to shift the discussion to confirmation theory can budge me. (What *can* budge me, especially if he and I are closely connected or identical, is accusations of self-deception in the way I arrived at *that* conclusion.)

In the first section I did my best to explain the difficulties with a skeptical position about self-deception. The skeptical doubts about self-knowledge we have now come to seem worse than the ones I discussed there. They also have to do with the way in which thought, belief, and emotion are partly theoretical and partly nontheoretical, of course. Beside the problems we have now about the very possibility of defining the conditions under which "He deceives himself" is true, there are also strong doubts about whether (if there are such conditions) we could ever have adequate reason for thinking they obtain. This is a problem that goes beyond the philosophical *problématique*: if I have come to the conclusion that I was deceiving myself in some respect, why should I think I won't come—in a rational fashion—to a contrary opinion after thinking some more? The skeptical doubts of *this* sort are neither based on general considerations nor general in nature. They arise if we take it for granted that self-deception makes sense and is possible, but pay attention to the whole horizon of doubts surrounding any such story. Once the possibility of self-deception is taken seriously it undermines all stories (about oneself, but also one's own stories about others), including those that attribute self-deception. We are in a quandary, personal as well as philosophical.

Dell'Opinione, Regina del Mondo

6. I want to make a new beginning, and draw on another source altogether. Today, of course, the whole of Western literature occupies itself with romantic or at least sexual love, whereas once upon a time it dealt entirely with war. Compare, if you will, Homer with Barbara Pym, *The Song of Roland* with *À la Recherche du Temps Perdu*. To our writers today, it seems, love is the only battlefield. (Perhaps this is not altogether accurate; I am no expert. In philosophy facts never matter too much anyway, only the ideas; isn't that so?) However, in those battles where sword rang against sword, the heroes were all men broad and bold, not much given to introspection. Whatever truth there is in all this supports the impression that self-deception is a new and recent concept, having come to light only when writing turned from the spectacle of glancing blows to those more intimate ones of glance intercepted by glance. But—and here is my point—that impression totally ignores another literature, turned even further inward, focused on battles fought in loneliness. For once upon a time, too, not all literature was secular. To recall this quickly dispels the impression that the idea of self-deception is novel, the phenomenon only recently noticed, or the philosophical question—*how is self-deception even possible?*—new.

My knowledge of this other literature, surely as old as any, is even more limited, and I must proceed somewhat differently from before. Let me begin by citing the totally conscious, explicit description by Pascal of how we deceive ourselves:

> The nature of self-love and of this human self is to love only self and consider only self. But what is it to do? It cannot prevent the object of its love from being full of faults and wretchedness: it wants to be great and sees that it is small; it wants to be happy and sees that it is wretched. . . . The predicament in which it thus finds itself arouses in it the most unjust and criminal passion that could possibly be imagined, for it conceives a deadly hatred for the truth which rebukes it and convinces it of its faults. It would like to do away with this truth, and not being able to destroy it as such, it destroys it, as best it can, in the consciousness of itself and others; that is, it takes every care to hide its faults both from itself and others. . . .
>
> It is no doubt an evil to be full of faults, but it is still greater evil to be full of them and unwilling to recognize them, since this entails the further evil of self-delusion. (*Pensées,* fragment 100, pp. 347–348)

Pascal is as close to us as Descartes, the Port-Royal Logic, and the probability calculus. But reading Pascal we hear the echoes of St. Paul: "For if anyone thinks himself to be something, whereas he is nothing, he deceives himself" (*Letter to the Galatians* 6:3). We also hear echoes of St. Augustine examining his own blindness before conversion, and also afterward:

> I did not know these things at that time, nor did I advert to them. They beat upon my eyes on every side, and yet I did not see them. (*Confessions* III–7)

> Why am I hurt more by abuse cast upon myself than by that cast in my presence with the equal injustice upon another? Am I in ignorance of this also? Does it amount to this, that I deceive myself, and do not do the truth before you in my heart and on my tongue? (*Confessions* X–37, 62)

If we found ourselves inextricably entangled in the treacheries of the mind, so did Augustine: "Who can untie this most twisted and intricate mass of knots?" (*Confessions* II–10).

Let me try to offer an explanation of how religious writers engaged in such self-scrutiny arrived at our questions—what is self-deception and how is it possible at all?—and of what sort of answer they appear to give.

7. We are very safe if there really is no limit to hypotheses of self-deception, and if there is no final arbiter between them. In George Crabbe's poem "The Parting Hour," analyzed by J. Hillis Miller, the returned sailor remembers his capture by pirates, his wife and his children in Spain, and the life he led there once he had gained his freedom by marrying and converting to

Catholicism—the life there that he had fled, to return eventually, aged worn, and crippled, to Protestantism and reunion with his first love.[2] But the dreams and longings of his old age are exactly of this Spanish wife and of the sunshine in which he lived and loved with the vigor of his youth. We feel the shameful waste and loss of a life lived at each point in alienation from the present, oriented to future or to past but always in the desire for somewhere he is not. I mention this story to conjure up the unbearable sense of loss of someone who gave up a country, family, and peace in the arms of someone who loved him, for an uncertain future, and the unbearable regret after the choice has been made and become irreversible. But unbearable? Nothing is unbearable if you can convince yourself that the loss you regret is only the loss of an illusion. If this man could look back to those Spanish eyes and "realize" they would not have waited for him, convince himself that the memories of happiness are really of an illusion, of a blindness to the bitter lines around that Spanish mouth, of a time in which he deceived himself (or about which, in his recent memories, he indulged in self-delusion)—then there was no real loss after all. And once he tries, if he tries, he will soon have ample evidence to sustain this "realization." The hypothesis that you were deceived *can* bring consolation rather than despair; and this haven, it seemed above, is always accessible.

The religious writers to whom I have now directed our attention deny us this sad refuge of skepticism: they assert that there *are* limits, there is an end to deception. They once were lost but now are found; there is a truth to which they once were blind, but now they see. They describe graphically the state of blindness, and blame it on themselves, as a delusion for which the deluded person is responsible. And they also describe graphically the undeceived state, and what they saw once undeceived. Their philosophical problem is the paradigm problem of self-deception: how could they have been blind, or have made themselves blind, to what was there plain and clear for anyone with eyes to see? Their accounts carry an absolute, if implicit, rejection of the idea that all such states, the later as well as the earlier—any state at all of subjective certainty and conviction—are equally vulnerable to the hypothesis of self-deception.

I say the descriptions are graphic; I do not mean that they are philosophically transparent. Nor can I say that their attempts to solve the problem have an immediate or satisfying finality. Augustine writes:

In all that bitterness, which in accordance with your mercy resulted from our worldly deeds, when we sought to know the reason why we should suffer such things, darkness confronted us. Groaning, we turned away, and we said "How long shall these things last?" Often we said this, but even as we spoke, we did not give up our worldly ways. For as yet there shone forth nothing certain, which, such ways forsaken, we might reach out to and grasp. (*Confessions* VI–10, 17)

Ponticianus told us this story [of a conversion], and as he spoke, you, O Lord, turned me back upon myself. You took me from behind my own back, where I had placed myself because I did not wish to look upon myself. You stood me face to face with myself, so I might see how foul I was, how deformed and defiled, how covered with stains and sores. I looked, and I was filled with horror, but there was no place for me to flee to away from myself. If I tried to turn my gaze from myself, he still went on with the story that he was telling, and once again you placed me in front of myself, and thrust me before my own eyes, so that I might find out my iniquity and hate it. I knew what it was, but I pretended not to; I refused to look at it, and put it out of my memory. (*Confessions* VIII–7, 16)

[T]he day had come when I stood stripped naked before myself. (*Confessions* VIII–7, 18)

At crucial points the description of the experience becomes metaphorical, but the point is clear: there was a truth about himself that he did not see before and does see now. When he did not see it he was mistaken about himself, and this mistake was no mere mistake but was due to a refusal "to look" and to willful, wish-fulfilling acceptance of a rosier picture maintained against and in the face of the facts he did not face.

8. It is also characteristic of these writers that what they see in their past is a situation so desperate that the despair would be unbearable if it *were* faced (alone). Accordingly they hypothesize mechanisms of self-deception in analogy to avoidance, flight, and escape characteristic of other, more familiar failures of courage. The mechanisms must, however, be means of mental rather than physical flight, and must be drawn from familiar types of mental activity. Their hypotheses relate accordingly to distortions of imagination, opinion, and desire or value. This is very clear in Pascal, who may be regarded after all as a pioneer of decision theory. Let me quote from him first to establish the view, similar to Augustine's, of the real truth about the human situation, and then to show the ways, less metaphorical than Augustine's, in which he suggests explanations. First, the undeceived view:

When I see the blind and wretched state of man, when I survey the whole universe in its dumbness and man left to himself with no light, as though lost in this corner of the universe . . . I am moved to terror, like a man transported in his sleep to some terrifying desert island, who wakes up quite lost and with no means to escape. Then I marvel that so wretched a state does not drive people to despair. (*Pensées,* fragment 198, p. 88)

One needs no great sublimity of soul to realize that in this life there is no true and solid satisfaction, that all our pleasures are mere vanity, that our afflictions are infinite, and finally that death which threatens us at every moment must in a few years infallibly face us. . . . Nothing could be more real, or more dreadful than that. (*Pensées,* fragment 427, p. 157)

Next we find him wondering how it is *possible* for people to be in this situation, and yet not in despair. He is inevitably led to suspect deception and pretense:

> Thus the fact that there exist men who are indifferent to the loss of their being and the peril of an eternity of wretchedness is against nature. With everything else they are quite different; they fear the most trifling things, foresee and feel them; and the same man who spends so many days in fury and despair at losing some office or at some imaginary affront to his honour is the very one who knows that he is going to lose everything through death but feels neither anxiety nor emotion. It is a monstrous thing to see one and the same heart at once so sensitive to minor things and so strangely insensitive to the greatest. It is an incomprehensible spell, an supernatural torpor. . . . Man's nature must have undergone a strange reversal for him to glory in being in a state in which it seems incredible that any single person should be. Yet experience has shown me so many like this that it would be surprising if we did not know that most of those concerned in this are pretending and are not really what they seem. (*Pensées,* fragment 427, p. 159)

He echoes here St. Augustine's "Whence comes this monstrous state?" (*Confessions* VIII–9, 21). Elsewhere (in the passage from *Pensées,* fragment 198, which I quoted above) he says, "Then these lost and wretched creatures look around and find some attractive objects to which they become addicted and attached." The first hypothesis is therefore of a distortion of desire or value judgments, which results in a disproportionately high valuation of something trifling. This distortion of judgment is not possible without a certain blindness or myopia as well, i.e., without ignoring much of our total situation and focusing on what is near and obvious alone. He gives a simpler, more familiar sort of example, designed perhaps to show how distortion of value judgments and of perception (in some wide sense) cannot be disentangled: "How is it that this man so distressed at the death of his wife and his only son, deeply worried by some great feud, is not gloomy at the moment and is seen to be so free from all these painful and disturbing thoughts? There is no cause for surprise: he has just had a ball served to him and he must return it to his opponent" (*Pensées,* fragment 522, p. 214).

Nor is it possible to disentangle imagination and opinion; they are distorted and distorting, in unison. In a long and searing commentary on the disguises sustained by imagination, Pascal writes scornfully: "Imagination decides everything: it creates beauty, justice and happiness, which is the world's supreme good. I should dearly like to see the Italian book, of which I know only the title, worth many books in itself, *Dell' opinione regina del mondo.* Without knowing the book, I support its views . . . " (*Pensées,* fragment 44,

p. 41). Imagination, he says here, is the dominant faculty, "master of error and falsehood, all the more deceptive for not being invariably so."

9. Let us try to sum up, in a preliminary way, how these writers view the phenomena. *First,* as I said, they identify a certain appreciation of our situation in the world as the correct one, the truth, not vulnerable to further charges of self-deception. This *appreciation* (a term I shall use to mean both perception and evaluation) is one they have come to themselves, and forms the point of view from which they evaluate the others (including that of their earlier selves). *Second,* it is possible for anyone to see the situation this way, and it is really surprising that people don't see things as they really are, for "they beat upon [their] eyes on every side." *Third,* they agree also that it is actually very difficult to see the truth—they do not assume that our minds or personal histories are transparent to us. The surprise must be about the apparent difficulty: how is it possible not to see the truth, and how can it be that it is in fact so rarely faced? The surprise is also with the contrast: how can a person attend so closely to (comparatively) small issues and be oblivious of the large ones? The *normal, usual* state is one of ignorance and deception about oneself.

But this must also mean that normal, rational functioning can go on well enough in a state of self-deception. When Pascal examines the work of the imagination, he does not uncover pathological functions: as he describes it, imagination has a role in the normal, rational processes of formation of opinions and decisions.

I think the first point is a very important one. Not only is it the stopping point that keeps these authors from sinking into the quandary that caught us in the first part of this essay ("Frederic Moreau and Mme. Arnoux"), but perhaps there is a secular, "relativized" version that can help us in our quandary too. This secular version would be: the attribution of self-deception makes sense only from the point of view (one appreciation of the facts) of someone who does not share it. That entails, correctly, that I could never rationally and truly say, "I am now self-deceived about so and so in such and such a particular way." It does allow, also correctly, that I could say that I have been so self-deceived, or even that I think I must now be deceiving myself about something, though I don't know what. (The "preface" paradox notwithstanding, I can say that one of my present beliefs must be false, though I don't know which. It is also possible to say that my present appreciation of the facts must be mistaken, although I can't yet see how, and that from the correct appreciation it will appear that I was now guilty of having persuaded myself in some culpable fashion.)

To insist on this will not remove the doubt whether my present conclusions about myself are ever invulnerable from charges of self-deception. But it does mean that when my appreciation of the situation is consistent (even in the broad sense of being free from glaring inequity in my treatment of different subjects), I shall have a certain measure of safety. For in such a case I can be sure that the charge of self-deception cannot be warranted by appeal to features of my present appreciation, but only by a point of view that I do not (yet) share. We glimpse here the possibility of a position that does not "deconstruct itself."

Let me elaborate a little. The worst fear is that I would always be in a position in which I can be convicted *on my own grounds* that there is serious reason to doubt my conclusions about myself. We have removed this, leaving only two other fears that are simply not theoretically removable (and we must live with them). The first is the fear that if I examine my own appreciation more closely, I will find inconsistencies or glaring inequities. The second is that I will at some later time encounter in someone else, or even in myself, an appreciation according to which I was not simply mistaken but culpably mistaken in my present one. These two fears the religious writers also overcame, but admittedly not by reason alone.

10. I omitted from the list in section 9 the important fourth point in the story told by these religious writers. That is that the truth, the real state of fallen humanity, is unbearable. This is also the beginning of their answer to the puzzle: how is it possible to be so deceived? For if the truth is unbearable, it is not possible to live while facing it. And here they can link up with more mundane cases again, for it is appropriate to look at less extreme ones. Such is Pascal's widower, so distressed at the death of his wife and son, yet at present not gloomy at all. "There is no cause for surprise: he has just had a ball served to him and he must return it to his opponent." This person is not unaware of the facts, but he is not currently facing them. We can quickly marshal other cases: escape into daydream, or recourse to magic and superstition, or a headlong plunge into work, career, infatuation, parties . . . any of the many effective creations of illusion that "make life worthwhile again."

What is needed is an account of normal, rational functioning of opinion, desire, and decision which gives substance to this view. For it is at first sight really startling: it says that self-deception proceeds by exactly the same means as rational changes of mind, mood, and behavior.

In Pascal's *Pensées,* not solely in its famous wager, we find the beginnings of decision theory. Let me sketch this sort of analysis of one's situation, as we might today. A person faced with a decision has first of all an *opinion* about the current state of nature: what the relevant facts are like. Second, he *imagines* a set of alternative actions. Unfortunately, his imagination is limited, so some possible actions open to him may fail to be included. The opinion above may also have such limits: he imagines various ways in which the world may be, and these may not exhaust all possibilities, logically speaking. Thus imagination enters in two ways. Let $S_1, \ldots, S_n$ be the states of nature he imagines as possible; his opinion consists in judgments of the form "S_k is

$Q(k, m)$ as likely to be actual as S_m"; the number $Q(k, m)$ is called his *odds* for S_k against S_m. In addition, let the set of actions he imagines as possible be $A_1, \ldots, A_q$. His imagination steps in to supply possible outcomes of these actions; let these be $C_1, \ldots, C_r$. His opinion then contains further judgments of form "If the actual state of nature is S_n and I do action A_m, then C_n is $Q(k, m, n, p)$ as likely to occur as C_p", thus entering further odds. Now, why should this situation be unbearable to him?

Well, one of the actions imagined as possible is to kill his mother, and one of the outcomes imagined may be to be guilty of not avenging his father and, moreover, to be torn apart by the Furies. Such was Orestes' situation. In addition, the factual judgments constituting his opinion entailed that he could not avoid the latter outcome without performing matricide. Given his values, moral judgments, and desires, his love for mother and father alike, action and outcome are unbearable to contemplate. Besides imagination and belief or opinion, therefore, there is a third ingredient, or sort of ingredient: value, moral sense, desire.

Fallen humanity's situation is unbearable in a different, if related, way. The state of nature includes much about him, namely, his own character and past actions: everything that is settled so far. He is not entirely definite about which is the actual state, though some seem likelier than others. In addition, he evaluates some as despicable or regrettable. In addition also, looking at his possible actions and their outcomes, and hence, at the accessible future states of affairs, he sees again much that is despicable, regrettable, and frightful. But even more, the limits of these three imagined sets, *sub specie* his opinion, are such that he has "nowhere to turn": he sees no escape from the regrettable, despicable, and frightful. Hence his situation is unbearable.

That is, it is unbearable as long as he or she is objective. He seeks frantically for an escape from the inescapable, within his own power, and objectivity is lost. He *does* find a way to escape, a way fully allowed by the above abstract theory. The situation in which he finds himself is unbearable, after all, in virtue of the collaboration of three ingredients. It is unbearable in part because transformations of the situation by means of an action are not envisaged as leading to one more bearable. So "normal" escape is not possible. But the situation could be transformed in a way other than through action: namely, through changing the imagined sets of possibilities, or the opinions concerning them, or the values and desires that define their significance for him. Of course, one cannot do most of this while knowing what one is doing. For in the light of one's present opinions and values, different opinions and values are mistaken. Hence from one's present point of view, the result of the transformation would be a delusion or a perversion.

It will be objected at once that such an escape would be pathological and easily distinguished from escape through action. Certainly, many such "subjective" transformations of the situation must have recourse to the irrational. Yet the objection does not stand. For each such subjective change can be, and under certain circumstances will be, the rational and correct response. If we postulated moreover that no one is ever in a problem situation without a rational solution, it would even *follow* that "normal" escape through action is impossible only if some such subjective transformation is rationally required.

Let us consider examples. Sometimes one is trapped by limited imagination: there *are* ways out, but the agent was not imaginative enough (and perhaps no one so far had ever been!) to see them. Salvation may come through the imaginative construction of a richer world-picture, a richer set of possible states of nature or of actions. But from the preceding point of view, two classifications of this escape are possible: alchemy or science. Think of a secular reaction to an imagination that calls up a paradise in the hereafter or atonement through sacrifice, or anyone's reaction to the purchase of a lottery ticket. The imagination has suddenly hit on something else to be brought into the picture. And the lottery ticket may win a million dollars. The foolish dabblings with wooden wings and smelly little engines may lead to the first powered flight, followed by the era of true aviation. The escape mechanism is the same.

Of course, it is not enough for imagination to provide a richer set of alternatives, if the new ones are allocated no credence. All the neighbors laughed when the poor man bought the lottery ticket, or those dabblers invested their energy and resources in heavier-than-air flying machines. The agents themselves must have found it a little less incredible—though in an unbearable situation, even a little credence may suffice for such a wager. The transformation of opinion by something other than minimal adjustment to the evidence must be per se within the bounds of rationality, if my current argument is to succeed. I think it is, and have argued for it elsewhere.[3] But it is easy to see that self-deception can also result in this way—as well as foolish hopes and superstitions of all sorts.

The most powerful transformation of all is the emotional, which effects a transvaluation of all values. The situation is unbearable because all outcomes of all envisaged actions are just different forms of misery. But why are they misery? Because they satisfy no desire, and harbor threats of more deprivation later. But which desires, what satisfactions? Suppose that as the situation is first defined, only one sort of outcome is acceptable: a reconciliation with *Mme. X,* a return to the love and trust and affection of the past. When it seems no avenue is open that leads to this, suspicion, blame, and anger may spell sudden salvation. For suddenly there is a new *sort* of alternative (or a new cross-classification of the same outcomes as envisaged before), which gives satisfaction: e.g., the alternatives in which the protagonist rightly and strongly rejects her, and bitterly lets her know how she deserves rejection. The very same action that before was ranked with cutting off one's own hands, now (in anger) ranks as the way to satisfaction.

When is this transformation through emotion to be lauded as rational and when to be depreciated as irrational defense or self-deception? We could insist on truth as a criterion: the situation has been correctly changed exactly if, as a matter of fact, *Mme. X* deserves rejection. It is rational to revalue the options by anger exactly if the resulting valuation is objectively correct. Quite apart from the difficulty of bringing factual truth and objective value together, there is also this problem: the criteria of rationality should be such that self-policing is in principle possible. Irrationality cannot be due to ignorance. Self-deception cannot be a matter of factual accident, outside the agent's ken. The religious view has no difficulty here: the real facts, the real values may stare one in the face—and the criterion of evident truth, admitted or denied, can replace that of truth. Thus abstractly stated, this view can also be secular. But there will be many gaps—many cases in which the truth is not evident. And there is the general problem of distinguishing evident truth from great but wrong certainty, certainty that is *especially great while one is in the grip of emotion*. From the point of view held preceding the anger, pity, tenderness, fear, or other emotion, the subsequent valuation is of course wrong, and from the one that accompanies the emotion, right. If criteria of rationality must allow of self-policing, they cannot distinguish in such a case.

We are driven again to the conclusion that the distinction between the case of a "correct" change in the emotive perception of the situation and that of a self-deceiving, rationalizing, or self-justifying change, must come from outside. Such an admonition as, "But don't you see how she is suffering? Don't harden your heart!" or its contrary, "But don't you see how she has been leading you up the garden path again? Take hold of yourself!" reflects a definite emotive and evaluative perception of the situation. However, only giving in to the emotion of tenderness or pity on the one hand, or of anger on the other hand, can effect the admonished change. For the protagonist has to come to see *Mme. X* as deserving sympathy, or rejection, respectively—and this change in emotive perception *is* emotion. It is not a result of emotion that could equally be achieved by deliberation alone; it *is* emotion.

On Faith in Things Unseen

11. *We have now an answer, albeit a little sketchy, to the first philosophical question: how is self-deception possible?* I am not unhappy with the answer; indeed I am quite convinced that the normal functions involved in rational opinion and decision clearly allow for this possibility. This answer presupposes a nonparadoxical identification of the phenomenon, something like: to

be of a false opinion, and to maintain and support this opinion in a fashion that makes one culpable of wrong-doing (such as biased selection, presentation, or weighing of evidence) of the sort characteristically involved in deception. And such an identification in turn presupposes an exterior viewpoint: the evaluation of someone as self-deceived in some way must be from within an appreciation of the situation that differs from his or her own (though it could be one's own somewhat later).

As we discussed the phenomenon of self-deception, however, the "secondary" problem of skeptical doubt became more and more pressing. Are there no limits to self-deception? Does the very possibility of self-deception not automatically rule out the possibility of self-knowledge? Well, perhaps knowledge is too theoretical or idealized a concept to worry us. But the problem still remains. For if self-deception is always possible, consider the plight of the poor subject who has begun to wonder if he has not perhaps come to some opinion by deceiving himself. He begins to investigate more closely, to weigh the evidence, to imagine new hypotheses of sorts not hitherto entertained. Unfortunately, it is exactly in these processes that self-deception always finds its means. For one selects, but not explicitly or consciously, what aspects to attend to more closely; the weights to give to different bits of evidence are not "written into" that evidence but must be supplied by oneself; and the imagination—ah, the imagination! So active in directions pleasing to oneself, or alternatively frightening, servant of wishes and fears, itself the flawed mother of the flawed queen of the world! Under these conditions, how shall we ever find a spot of safety, secure from distrust of one's own opinion?

The religious writers, as I pointed out in the second part, assume or recognize such a secure vision of the world, the single truth against which all other views are measured. But it is admittedly not reached by reason; the certainty found is one of illumination. I accommodated this momentarily by noting the important role, played in attributions of self-deception, of an exterior viewpoint, different from that of the accused. This does not solve the skeptical problem; at best it underlines it. Yet we can't very well offer faith as a solution—faith, the sum of our hopes and evidence of things unseen, is not a *philosophical* solution to skepticism. And apart from that, the religious writer surely has his own skeptical problem. Should an angel appear and speak to us, what credentials establish him as an angel? And if words spoken with the voice of an angel strike certainty in the heart, so to speak, who is to say whether his own certainty is so come by? For, despite Descartes' proofs, we have no a priori certainty of the sources of our certainties.

12. Faith, I said, is not a *philosophical* solution to the skeptical problem. But what is a philosophical solution to a philosophical problem? What we can hope for is a wider perspective, in which the initial double bind appears

to be due to demands or presuppositions that we need not share. And that sort of solution, I do think, is to be found in Augustine. I am now referring not to his *Confessions* but to the first work he wrote after conversion, the work called *Against the Academics*.

13. To describe Augustine's response to the Academic philosophy—the Pyrrhonist skepticism of the Third Academy, handed on through Sextus Empiricus and Cicero, and popular in the late Roman empire—I should first describe the skeptical problem as he found it. I shall begin with the story of the Stoic "criterion" and the critique it received in the Academy, then state the problem faced by those critics.[4] At first sight, Augustine's reaction seems naive and inadequate; but I think that in the final analysis, it proposes a form of voluntarist epistemology that deserves to be taken seriously.

How shall we distinguish the true from the false? This problem arises acutely already for simple judgments of perception: "That is Helen standing on the shore," "There is a snake in that corner." To say that sense perception is the final arbiter in questions of what is true does not solve the problem—it only pushes it back, for we are often mistaken in just such simple judgments. Chrysippus provided the definitive version of the Stoic solution. He draws a distinction between sensation and judgment. The former is a change in the soul, produced in a way that is not subject to the will. A judgment is something we form, in general—through by no means always—deliberately. This is where error may arise, and the function of the will in Chrysippus' account is to explain perceptual error. Some judgments, however, are forced by sensation—these are called *irresistible perceptions,* and that irresistibility is the mark of truth. The criterion of truth lies exactly in those judgments that are not formed deliberately, in which the will plays no part, but which are forced irresistibly upon us.

There is good prima facie reason to accept the account. Is there any way that I could, at this moment, believe, deliberately form the judgment, that there is an elephant sitting on the table before me? No. Certain simple perceptual judgments are forced upon me by my present sensory experience, and I *cannot* believe something with which they conflict. This does not imply that belief is not subject to the will. Larceny presumably is; and if I am sitting in a warm bath in my own bathtub, in my own home, I cannot steal. The preconditions are not met. Our present experience may be relevant to belief in just that way. However, Chrysippus intends something more: certain judgments are irresistible, made so by sensation. *Seeing is believing.* And finally, most important, irresistibility is the mark of truth.

The New Academy, under Arcesilas and later Carneades, attacked the Stoic doctrine in a number of ways. Because the conclusion for which they argued was that belief is never rationally compelled, and is really better not to have, they do not seem to have considered the question whether, during given experiences, some beliefs may be impossible simply because some preconditions of belief are not met. Certainly they comment indirectly, because they insist that, given any belief, they can find reasons to show that a belief in the opposite is at least as rational. Doing so produces "equilibrium" in which agnosticism recommends itself. So apparently their contrary view is here that *the feeling of irresistibility comes not so much from sensation by itself, as from sensation in the context of a limited range of contemplated possibilities.* The irresistibility disappears when you think deeply enough about all the possible ways in which the judgment could be false.

Let us put this in some perspective. The Stoics, noting the irresistibility of certain judgments at certain times, attribute this to sensations. But it is clear that if I were in a different state, or had had different previous experience, the same sensations could force different judgments. After talking and thinking about snakes all evening, I "see" one on the veranda the moment I open the door. Of course, at the moment of judgment, it is not within my power to change the preceding evening. But which alternatives I presently contemplate it is within my power to determine. By considering various new possibilities and inventing new hypotheses, judgments that were at first accompanied by that feeling of irresistibility may lose it. And when they do, the preconditions for forming opposed judgments may be met. Having seen this, however, the idea that such irresistibility is the mark of truth loses its charm. False judgments are at times accompanied by such feelings every bit as strong as those that marked the true. The rationale behind the skeptics' attack is that which judgments we arrive at in experience depends in part on the contemplated hypotheses and possibilities. Any sort of optical illusion will bear this out, but ropes seen as snakes will do as well.[5]

Nevertheless, Arcesilas is left with a serious problem. It seems that, in immediate experience, seeing *is* believing. If you see a horse rushing toward you at full gallop, you jump aside. What better evidence that the sensation *produced* belief? If we lived in epistemic equilibrium, we would not form those impetuous judgments of perception, but we would die. So not only do we apparently rely on our ability to arrive at true beliefs, but we ought to rely on it—suspension of judgment would automatically lead to suspension of action. Thus Arcesilas ends up with the problem of giving an account of practical action. It is clear how he would react to the argument—by inference from other skeptical reactions to other points. For the skeptics readily admit that they have the same feelings of conviction as other men do, and that they naturally act on them. They deny only that in doing so, they implicitly disown skeptical doubt. For even if the feelings are momentarily irresistible, this need not lead one to *endorse* the judgment. There is no reason to say that seeing *is* believing, when the only evidence we have is that we act just as we would if we did believe, immediately, what we saw. The alternative hypothesis, which produces skeptical equilibrium here, is that we rely not on our ability to arrive quickly at true perceptual beliefs, but instead on an ability to correct our impetuous mistakes as quickly.

So endorsement, not action, is the criterion of belief for Arcesilas. The problem remains acute, however, for if we do not act on our beliefs, what do we act on? If belief is not the guide to life, what is? Carneades, the head of the Third Academy, developed the constructive alternative answer to these questions. He explicitly developed an account of *probability* as *the criterion for the conduct of life*. (See Sextus Empiricus, *Against the Logicians* I, pp. 166–173: "These were the arguments that Carneades set out in detail . . . to prove the non-existence of the criterion (of truth); yet as he, too, himself requires a criterion for the conduct of life and for the attainment of happiness, he is practically compelled on his own account to frame a theory about it." The basic idea is that what appears to us in experience gives greater or less probability to various possible judgments that occur to us (the irresistible appearance is replaced by the probable appearance at the bottom of the epistemic ladder), and we act on these probabilities—endorsement never being involved in the step from seeing to acting.

This one-sentence summary does not do justice to his account, for he did not merely degrade the epistemic status of irresistible perceptions from indubitable truth to probability. In addition he took away their criterial role; for the immediate judgments have, for him, the lowest level of probability, and are relied on least. It is tempting to compare his view with such a view as Richard Jeffrey's that the epistemic subject does not give probability 1 to any contingent proposition, and acts merely to maximize expected utility. (Jeffrey himself has done so.) What Carneades did have was a rough division into levels of probability, or perhaps of evidential support, and the recognition that within each of these levels, distinctions of more-and-less are possible. In any case, as a consistent skeptic, Carneades must have proposed this merely as a contrary hypothesis, to be used in the method of equilibrium, against the Stoic position.

In that alternative account, Carneades envisages us as giving least credence to the judgments made spontaneously in response to experience. We immediately subject them to the test of corroboration. Someone smiles across a crowded room; I rise a little hesitantly and say, "Isn't that Peter?" When he comes near, I just extend my hand and say, "Why, hello, Peter!" But later even well-corroborated judgments can be submitted to further inquiry "as in a court of law"—for "no presentation is ever simple in form but, like links in a chain, one hangs from another" (op. cit., pp. 176, 182). One ends by giving assent (*syncatathesis*) to judgments that survive an active inquiry, similar to the practice "at assembly-meetings when the People makes inquiry about each of those who desire to be magistrates" (loc. cit.). But it is clear that this assent—so described by Sextus—is not the endorsement that Ar-

cesilas says we should withhold; it is merely a practical assent, an acknowledgment of willingness to act.

14. To understand Augustine, I think, we should be subversive and ask
whether belief is possible for the skeptic. It is clear enough that Arcesilas
and Carneades thought that people do reach full belief—but are foolish to do
so. Are these negative evaluations of belief compelled by their account of
endorsement and practical assent, or merely concomitant?

When St. Augustine was converted to Christianity, he immediately wrote
Against the Academics, attacking the skeptical philosophy of the New
Academy. What is most noteworthy, but little noted, is how much of the
skeptical philosophy Augustine accepts as correct. To be sure, he argues
against it that we can have certainty, but of eternal truths (he gives the
arithmetic example that $2x = x + x$ for all x) and egocentric ones (I am
alive, I exist, I think). For perception and the natural world, he agrees to all
the skeptical arguments. There, no belief is rationally compelling, nor any
evidence. But he adds that we do have beliefs about the empirical world,
takes it for granted that this is rational, and concludes that rational belief
is shot through and through with leaps of faith. Is this really a consistent
position?

To examine this question, we must look into the Academics' reasons for
counting full belief irrational. A moderate skepticism can be summarized in
four tenets:

(1) seeing is not believing: experience does not force belief (in the sense
    of endorsement);
(2) nothing gives any empirical proposition the automatic right to accep-
    tance, or would compel all rational beings to believe it;
(3) nothing gives any accepted proposition the automatic right to con-
    tinued acceptance, or immunity from revision;
(4) rational action and decision can be based on the probable, while
    judgment as to truth is suspended.

There is nothing in these four tenets that implies that having beliefs is
irrational. It is implied that if you are concerned only to have your behavior
and deliberation qualify as rational, you need never have a full belief. But
neither need you ever reach an aesthetic judgment or have a capacity for
aesthetic appreciation—to give only one other sort of example—so this does
not suffice to make belief irrational.

The fifth, hidden tenet that characterized the skeptics and led them to that
conclusion was a certain view of life, happiness, and wisdom. For note that
(1) through (4) also establish that no empirical proposition is absolutely

beyond doubt. Hence if you form a full belief, then you court the danger of being wrong, of being contradicted by further appearances. This is a perturbing experience, all too common in ordinary lives, and the basis of all unhappiness—what is it to be unhappy but to be deceived in one's expectations? Wisdom consists, not only for the skeptics but for their rivals in antiquity, in guarding against the very danger of unhappiness, in the ability to lead a happy life, that is, a life free from perturbation, whether by actual *contretemps* or the apprehension thereof. Needless to say, Augustine did not share this view of life—it may not be unfair to say that this disagreement is the exact mark of the passing of the Pagan world, the coming of the Christian era. Yet this was the reasoning that led to the further tacit principle:

(5) if something is not beyond reasonable doubt, then it is irrational to believe it.

So we may conclude at least that it is consistent for Augustine to accept the main skeptical arguments against empirical beliefs while holding that one can rationally have such beliefs. We will require from him, however, two things: reasons for having (empirical) beliefs *at all,* and an account of the epistemic process that makes the role of belief explicit. As to the first, I have found no direct answer in his writings, and I do not feel that I can rigorously extrapolate one. But Augustine does give quite an explicit answer to the second, and provides indeed an account of belief that is as definite as Carneades' account of practical assent. I may sum it up in four points.

(1) The will plays a crucial role in perception (*Trinity* XI, 2, and *De Musica* VI, 5, as well as sundry passages in *Against the Academics* and *On the Freedom of the Will*). In his analysis, perception has three distinguishable aspects: the content (object seen), the experience or act (the seeing), and the attention, which is the part played by the will. In other words, sensation is, as the Greeks said, a change in the soul—but there is no perception of the object sensed unless attention is focused on it, so as to make the information available information. Hence Augustine says that the action of the will "binds together" the act and the content. All this is quite metaphorical or analogical (which is typical of the way we describe mental phenomena), but I think that the point is a good one: deliberate selection, to a large extent under our control even if *usually* automatic, is an essential part of perceptual experience.

(2) The criterion of belief is endorsement or explicit assent, and this is subject to the will: "for what else is it to believe but to assent to the truth of what is propounded? Consent being a matter of the will" (*On the Spirit and the Letter,* 54). Not unexpectedly he is quite clear that to say this does not mean that consent is necessarily easy, or that one believes the moment one wants to believe—these being points that theologians typically discuss at length.

(3) Reason(ing) is subject to criteria of evaluation closely linked with, or analogous to, those of moral judgment. This point is one that emerges already in the skeptics' discussions, and especially in the description of the Carneadean threefold process of putting into question, resolving doubts, and giving assent. In this process of inquiry and decision one can be timid, prudent, courageous, impulsive, impetuous, steadfast, stubborn, or swayed by every breeze. Augustine goes further, for he argues that the very process presupposes some measure of traditional moral virtues:

> Reason is the gaze of the soul, but . . . the gaze itself cannot turn [the soul] toward the light unless these three things endure, namely: *Faith,* by which it believes that the thing on which the gaze is to be fixed is of such a nature that when it is seen it will beget happiness; *Hope,* by which it trusts that it will see, if only it gazes intently; *Love,* by which it yearns to see and enjoy. (*Soliloquies* I, 13)

We have here an implicit criticism of Carneades' account; for why should one engage in scrutiny and inquiry? Why worry about strengthening the evidential support for propositions before acting on them, unless one believes that this will be beneficial? We may put it paradoxically, but pointedly, as follows: *if the only connection between probability and rationality is that it is a principle of rationality to act on probabilities, then there is no significant connection.* A principle without a point has no status.

(4) All belief is shot through and through with leaps of faith. This view, amply illustrated in his *On Belief in Things Unseen,* is clearly a necessary consequence of Augustine's acceptance of the main skeptical arguments. But since he simply takes for granted that much of what ordinarily passes for rational belief is rational, he can also conclude that these leaps do not make the belief irrational.

Yet the leap of faith is the paradigm of going beyond where rationality leaves off. To reconcile these two points, we must clearly distinguish *rational* from *justified,* and *justified* from *compelled.* Consider an argument in which these are not distinguished: "justification of belief is through evidence; but of course you cannot be justified by evidence in believing more than what that evidence justifies; therefore, it is irrational to go beyond the evidence." I think everyone will recognize this argument as a fallacy, and locate the crucial ambiguity. The evidence may certainly give us good reason to believe a hypothesis even though it does not rule out all contrary hypotheses. Just as in practical decisions, the most prudent decision is not necessarily the moral one to make, so also in epistemic decisions, the most prudent policy of belief formation may not be the wisest. Rationality is at most bridled irrationality, and the process of rational inquiry does involve venture, commitment, enterprise, willingness to take a chance. If our belief, and belief change, is by and large rational, then rationality *is* shot through and through with leaps of faith.

15. So we are finally left with the conclusion that disagreement with the skeptics is in the view of life. To disarm the skeptics' final move, one must say that, on one's own view of life, genuine epistemic *engagement* has its own value, and is to be preferred to a life of utilitarian calculation and prudence—what Bradley called a shopkeeper's life of always a little bit more, a little bit less. There is no escape from skepticism in theory; skepticism has no theoretical limits. This is a conclusion I also asserted in section 2. Reasonable skepticism about what anyone really thought or felt has its limits—but they are not theoretical limits. At some point, reactions to skepticism, whether refusing or giving in to its seductive offers of momentary peace and safety, equally become matters of decision, attitudes, and will. Self-deception for example, is possible, and so certainty about what one felt or really thought, or about how one arrived at one's opinions, may in any given case be an illusion. But this is finally only one instance, if the most extreme, the closest to home, of that danger which lurks everywhere. There is no need to counsel us to live dangerously; we do. The question is how to live with that danger—seeking to remain in the safest position possible, the skeptic's solution, is no more *theoretically* justifiable than any other. Of course, the converse of skepticism is faith—to give in to skepticism is to refuse faith, to refuse skepticism is a leap of faith. This is as true in personal matters (Is it love? Does he trust me? Do I really feel that, or am I pretending even to myself?) as in ideology or religion.[6]

Courage and the End of Philosophy

16. Thinking about self-deception we felt ourselves powerless, not against global skepticism—which allows life to go on as normal, except for philosophers—but very specific, disabling, local skeptical doubts. Telling and recognizing the truth about oneself, about one's own opinions, emotions, and attitudes, appeared insuperably difficult. And that takes the thrill out of every joy—for joy lives on unreflective certainty—and increases the sting in every guilt and anguish. Unfortunately for the philosopher, local, even little skeptical doubts soon threaten to swallow the whole world. But perhaps that is not so unfortunate, if in refutations of skepticism we can find defense against the local sorts as well.

There are two sorts of refutation of skepticism—I think we should call them the idealist and the voluntarist. The former supply a defense against global skepticism only, for they purport to demonstrate that the doubt is incoherent, and the demonstration hinges on the global nature of the doubt. Such are, in our day, the refutations offered by Donald Davidson and Hilary Putnam. The voluntarist, of which I have followed Augustine's version in some detail now, characterizes capitulation to skepticism as a failure of will,

of courage, of faith. G. E. Moore's, which looks at first sight so different—
"look, here is one hand, and here is another"—is also of this type. How can
we resist the slide into doubt, except by reaffirming faith? And faith lives in
every moment of everyone's epistemic life. I can *see* my hand, but I can only
believe in it as the means for lifting the cup, breaking the bread, touching a
hand. The belief is verifiable; indeed, the very next moment may put it to
the test, so to affirm this faith is not the empty posturing of the metaphysical
world-maker. But the point is easily taken too far, as by Jean-Paul Sartre's
communist Brunet in the prison camp in *Iron in the Soul*:

> "Schneider" he said without raising his voice. "It is *conceivable* that . . . the
> roof of this hut might fall on your head, but that does not mean you spend your
> time keeping a wary eye on the ceiling. . . . When you stretch out your hand
> to grasp your mess-tin, the mere fact of that gesture postulates a universal
> determinism. (p. 338)

No, it does not. Our opinions need only be very modest to sustain practical
life. But, if the voluntarist story is correct, Brunet is pointing to a clear and
inextricable feature—though of course the word "postulate" comes more
naturally to him than "faith." Either way, Brunet's remark points to the role
of the will, and thus leads to the diagnosis of disabling doubts as a failure of
will.

17. Whatever happened to Frederic Moreau? He grew old, settled down to
a life of tired idleness and reminiscences with his old friend Deslauriers. As
they exhumed their youth, they asked each other after every sentence, "Do
you remember?" In their memories, real happiness was reserved for scenes
in boyhood, when they were just becoming young men, their derring-do when
every act was still more symbolic than real, surrounded by a halo of limitless
possibilities. Frederic's life had after all been only a sort of life, the lost
dream of a love lived with Mme. Arnoux always putting the meager realities
to shame. So now those realities are discounted: no, life had never lived up
to those glories of the imagination, for which courage and fate had proved
insufficient.

And what happened to our narrator, whose courage had failed crucially at
every step with *Mme. X*? Here we enter the garden of forking paths; many
things happened.

His love of Flaubert led him to take up the mannerisms of the Second
Empire: a cane, a hat, a daybook to record anecdotes, memories, and fantasies. Late one afternoon we see him writing in his daybook: I remember
still that day I walked along the street, my mind a court in which I fought
furiously to answer *Mme. X*'s charge that I no longer loved her. Again I hear
her voice, gently telling me that I merely deceived myself if I thought that I

still loved her. I hear myself answering with many passionate fallacies, before a tribunal scandalously biased in my favor. Then, years later, when she wrote that she wished to see me again, I continued this self-deception when I replied—surely believing what I wrote—that I had never forgotten her, that all loves had been insipid beside the memory of hers. But then . . . what a disaster. How could I have kept myself so much in the dark about what I really felt and wanted? To think that I escaped blindly into an infatuation with someone else—just to avoid admitting that I really had been living a lie all along.

Or was *that* story, about how I deceived myself about being all that time still in love with *Mme. X,* the real self-deception? Was it simply unbearable for me, after all, to think afterward that I had lost her love just when fate finally offered it again, by not being courageous enough? Why did I not, when she came back, affirm my faith, commit myself utterly, however dangerous it seemed to place my life again in *Mme. X*'s none too reliable hands? Ah, well, who is to say? In the end, age having taken its toll, I prefer to think back to days long before those. I remember the time when I was still a boy but almost a man, when every action seemed charged with significance, when every step in the rustling autumn leaves carried me forward into life and its limitless possibilities. And then those days a little later, my first days in Paris, lamplight reflected in the wet November leaves, my first glimpse of *Mme. X,* . . . In this old age, calm after the storms, I have anyway the final courage not to regret my lost life.

So he writes in his daybook, having propped his cane against the desk, smiling at this fantasy that he has just written, about how he will grow old and become even more like Frederic Moreau. Then he closes the daybook and leaves the study—it is New Year's Eve. A warm excitement lights up his eyes as the valet brings his coat. Walking down the steps, he smiles at the disappearance of those illusions, doubts, and dreams once fed by cowardice but now dispelled. And he wonders what a hypothetical reader would surmise in reading his real story: that he is stepping out to meet *Mme. X,* or the refound love of the Metro, or someone else, met much later? Or something else altogether, since he had not even known what to hope for? But it does not matter; every New Year's Eve he has had to admit that the year before he could not have foretold the year to come. Once he had found the courage to believe, everything else was added onto him, even effortless certainty of what to believe.

18. The importance of the voluntarist refutation of skepticism is that its reflections are immediately relevant to local skeptical doubts as well. Yes, it is true that the possibility of self-deception undermines certainty about oneself; but no, it does not follow that the only rational course is to renounce all confidence in one's own appreciation of the facts. Yes, the facts are ambigu-

ous, and confidence may ebb; alternative interpretations may leap like leopards from every tree, every step of the way. But no, there is no failure of rationality in the very phenomena of trust, confidence, and affirmation.

Philosophical solutions never give practical guidance. Once we look into just how the mere possibility of self-deception undermines certainty, it brings to light the indispensable role of will—courage, faith—to sustain any appreciation of what there is. But courage to believe what? Courage to hold to an opinion increasingly difficult to act on, or courage to sacrifice it? The solution is *not* that this question has a "right" answer, *but* that this is the right question. The guidance philosophy cannot give would, if such an a prioristic discipline could give it, remove the role of courage altogether.

NOTES

Bibliographical note: The texts cited come in many translations, of which the following are representative: André Gide, *Strait Is the Gate,* trans. D. Bussy (New York: Knopf, 1965); Gustave Flaubert, *A Sentimental Education,* trans. A. Goldsmith (New York: Dutton, 1961); Blaise Pascal, *Pensées,* trans. A. J. Krailsheimer (Hammondsworth: Penguin, 1966); St. Augustine, *Confessions,* trans. R. S. Pine-Coffin (Baltimore: Penguin, 1961); *Soliloquies* and *On the Spirit and the Letter,* in *Basic Writings of St. Augustine,* ed. W. J. Oates (New York: Random House, 1948); *Sextus Empiricus,* trans. R. G. Bury (Cambridge: Harvard Univ. Press, 1967); Jean-Paul Sartre, *Iron in the Soul* (pub. in the U.S. as *Troubled Sleep*), trans. G. Hopkins (Hammondsworth: Penguin, 1958). The quoted lines of poetry are from "No worst, there is none," in *The Poems of Gerard Manley Hopkins,* ed. W. H. Gardner and N. H. Mackenzie (Oxford: Oxford Univ. Press, 1967), p. 100. The verse from *Galatians* is essentially the same in the three or four Bible translations I have consulted.

1. I want to thank Mark Johnston for many helpful comments and criticisms of an earlier draft.

2. George Crabbe, "The Parting Hour," in G. Crabbe, *Tales, 1812, and Other Selected Poems,* ed. H. Mills (Cambridge: Cambridge Univ. Press, 1967), pp. 136–147; J. Hillis Miller, "The Ethics of Reading: Vast Gaps and Parting Hours," in *American Criticism in the Poststructuralist Age,* ed. Ira Konigsberg (Ann Arbor: University of Michigan Slavic Pub., 1981), pp. 19–35.

3. Bas van Fraassen, "Belief and the Will," *Journal of Philosophy* 81 (1984):235–256.

4. The main sources are Sextus Empiricus, *Against the Logicians* I, and *Outlines of Pyrrhonism*; and Cicero, *Academic Questions* II.

5. See Sextus Empiricus, *Against the Logicians* I, 162–163, 170–171, 180–181, and 187–189.

6. The view of our epistemic situation which I have pursued and elaborated here is not meant to exist in isolation from more theoretical concerns. Epistemological problems, encountered in one area of reflection, soon reveal tendrils and shoots in many others. To end, then, by linking this discussion to the article cited in note 3, let me repeat from it a quotation from William James' "The Will to Believe" in which he contests W. K. Clifford's contention that it is wrong always, everywhere, and for everyone to believe anything on insufficient evidence. Clifford holds up the scientist as (professionally) living by this creed, but James insists that the scientist's two aims, to believe truth and avoid error, must be pursued each at the cost of the other. James concludes:

he who says 'Better go without belief forever than believe a lie!' merely shows his own preponderant private horror of becoming a dupe. He may be critical of many of his desires and fears, but this fear he slavishly obeys . . . a certain lightness of heart seems healthier than this excessive nervousness. . . . At any rate, it seems the fittest thing for the empiricist philosopher. (*Essays in Pragmatism* [New York: Hafner, 1948], p. 100)

6

SELF-DECEPTION AS RATIONALIZATION

DAVID H. SANFORD

When the editors invited me to contribute to this volume, I had recently completed an essay on infinite regress arguments, which maintains that we often misperceive our own desire structures. As I started to develop an account of self-deception from this, a look at philosophical literature on the topic neither convinced me that I was on the wrong track nor taught me that just the same track had been traveled before.[1] Discussions similar to mine tend to treat as secondary what I view as primary. The following passage by Terence Penelhum captures what I regard as essential to self-deception:

> The appraisal of the object furnishes justification, if there is any, for being pleased at the object (sometimes even for enjoying it). This generates a higher-level type of self-deception, viz., the invention of reasons which render the pleasures we already take more acceptable to ourselves or to others. A man may tell himself his new car is a bargain in order to justify his pleasure in it, and in order to lend some degree of weight to his arguments with his wife over the expense. In such cases the indulgence in a self-consciously irrational pleasure is a more honest state of mind—the thirst for rationality is a major source of lies.[2]

Penelhum provides no more details about this car-buyer, and I think the case can be filled out in several ways that involve different kinds of self-deception. However the case is filled out, it includes the following mistake: the car-buyer thinks he takes pleasure in his new car because it is a bargain, but the real reason for his pleasure is something else. I shall say that the car-buyer's belief that his new car is a bargain is an *ostensible* reason for his taking pleasure in a new car. While use of the term "ostensible" implies that appearance in the respect in question does not correspond to reality, in some contexts it is not self-contradictory to say, "In this case, the ostensible reason turned out to be the real reason." Also, when we normally call someone's professed reason "ostensible," we do not imply that he is self-deceived about his reason. He may only be attempting to deceive others while knowing perfectly well what he is up to. For the purposes of this essay, I should like *ostensible* to be understood in a narrower sense: one's ostensible reason always functions differently from the way one takes it to function. Professed reasons that are also genuine, and those that are professed with a conscious intention to deceive, will not be called ostensible. Ostensible reasons figure prominently in the kind of self-deception called *rationalization*.

Penelhum's example is intended to illustrate "the invention of reasons." There is room here for inventions of several kinds, but in any case the car-buyer invents a false theory to explain and justify the pleasure he takes in his new car. A better theory would mention something else, perhaps the fantasies that preoccupied him at age twelve. We need not agree, however, that the pleasure is irrational to agree that the source of self-deception is the thirst for rationality. A pleasure need not be irrational just because it is misunderstood. The car-buyer does not accept the real reason for his pleasure, either because he is totally ignorant of it or because he more or less consciously rejects it. If he rejects it, or would reject it if he were aware of it, there is room for still more distinctions. Would almost any sensible person agree that he ought to reject it, or that he ought not to reject it? Or, as seems most likely in this case, would there be disagreement on the issue? The car-buyer, in any event, needs a reason he can accept, and the car's being a bargain is such a reason.

Even if the misunderstood pleasure is not itself irrational, it would be irrational to work great financial hardship on the family in order to buy an unneeded new car. But the irrationality of financial recklessness is something else. It can be dangerous in the pursuit of even the most high-minded, refined, and completely understood pleasures. The pleasure a musician takes in her newly acquired violin may involve no self-deception although it was only through self-deception that she convinced herself that she could somehow afford an instrument costing over a hundred thousand dollars.

If the car-buyer does not know why he finds buying and having a new car so exciting and realizes, moreover, that he does not know, then he may honestly experience pleasure that he knows he does not fully understand. He would then have, in one respect, self-knowledge of the kind Socrates claimed to distinguish himself from most others: he would know that he does not know.

When Penelhum talks about "the invention of reasons," I suspect he has in mind an invention in addition to the one I have discussed. The car-buyer invents the belief that his new car is a bargain. The lie, which here has the thirst for rationality as a source, is the second-order belief that one believes the car to be a bargain. The car-buyer somehow really knows that the car is not a bargain, but he deceives himself into thinking that it is. This is the kind of self-deception philosophers often take as a paradigm, and its paradoxical appearance they typically attempt to explain away. I shall return to self-deception of this sort, but here I want to insist that it is inessential to the kind of self-deception I described first. The car-buyer's belief that he believes the car to be a bargain can be perfectly correct, even though his belief that the car is a bargain is only the ostensible reason for his taking pleasure in the car. We need not suppose that his belief that the car is a bargain flies in the face of his evidence or in the face of evidence that should sway him if only he took the trouble to obtain it. We may suppose, on the contrary, that his belief is both well supported and true. He has consulted last April's *Consumer Reports* and the latest *Edmund's New Car Prices*. He correctly believes that he could not reasonably expect to buy this car for much less. In so far as a new car of this kind can be a bargain, his is a bargain. Still, that isn't the real reason he is getting such a kick out of his new car. The real reason is something else.

Without abandoning the supposition that the car-buyer really believes that his car is a bargain, let us now consider a different story about how he acquires this belief. The belief is not true; the car could have been bought for considerably less. Neither is the belief well supported. Usually wary of high-pressure salesmen, the car-buyer was quick to believe the dealer's fervent assurances that the car was a bargain. Anticipation of how the belief might serve as a reason played an essential role in the production of the belief. I shall say in this case that the car-buyer's belief is an *anticipating* reason for his pleasure.

I shall not apply the term *anticipating* just whenever the desire to have a reason for something figures somehow in the production of a belief. We often search for reasons to back up our prior hunches, opinions, and convictions. It is when the interpretation of the evidence, or putative evidence, is biased by the anticipation of supporting something that the resulting biased belief is anticipating. When one has an anticipating belief one supposes to be based on evidence, then if one had no motive for wanting evidence that points in a certain direction, one would generally regard the evidence as insufficient grounds for the belief.

Beliefs are often based, or at least thought to be based, on evidence. But I want to apply the terms *anticipating* and *ostensible* to many mental states in addition to beliefs, states to which questions of evidence and evidential support are often irrelevant. I shall use *attitude* as a very general term to refer to any mental state under the following conditions. If having a mental state can be regarded as the reason, or part of the reason, for having another, then both count as attitudes. Attitudes include beliefs, pleasures, desires, intentions, judgments, suspicions, evaluations, attractions, enjoyments, fascinations, displeasures, resentments, repulsions, indifferences, hopes, fears, and so forth.

Mistakes about one's own desire structure are common. A desire taken to be for something only for the sake of a second thing can really be for the sake of a third thing, either instead of or in addition to the second. More specific varieties of this general kind of mistake include the following: a desire taken to be for something only for its own sake is really for the sake of something else; a desire taken to be for something only for the sake of something else is really for something for its own sake. These mistakes all involve desires that are both anticipating and ostensible. Another variation of the car-buyer example will illustrate the phenomenon. Instead of our asking him, or his asking himself, why he takes pleasure in his new car, we ask the related question why he wanted a new car. "Because I wanted a bargain" is as unacceptable an answer to him as it is to us. He realizes that a general desire for useful bargains can be more easily and deeply satisfied by buying items other than new cars. The car-buyer answers rather, and answers sincerely, that he wants dependable transportation. He believes that his new car is dependable; and we may add, if we like, that this belief is both well supported and true. It is not true, however, that he wants a new car because he wants dependable transportation. He understands the real reason for his wanting a new car as little as he understands the real reasons for his taking pleasure in it. The desire for dependable transportation is only the ostensible reason for his wanting a new car; and it is also an anticipating reason, since his desire for dependable transportation arose out of his need for an acceptable way to fit his desire for a new car into his desire structure. If he had not wanted a new car, he would not have focused on the desirability of dependable transportation. This example could naturally involve a second attitude that is both anticipating and ostensible, namely, the belief that his present car was undependable. (As we know too well, desires, especially desires poorly understood, can be satisfied without producing the expected satisfaction. The car-buyer in all the versions of our example is fortunate, from the viewpoint of hedonism; for he really does take pleasure in his new car despite his poor understanding of his desire to have a new car.)

So far as I have described the examples, the ostensible reasons do not really function at all to support what the car-buyer takes them to support. I also want reasons that play a real but derivative role, while the subject takes them to play a primary role, to count as ostensible. Suppose the car-buyer could not take pleasure in his car without thinking he had some sort of acceptable reason. Since he does not accept the primary reason for his pleasure, success at rationalization is a necessary condition of his feeling pleasure. His belief that the new car is a bargain satisfies this necessary condition. Another reason might have worked as well in other circumstances, but some such reason has to be available for him to be pleased. His belief that the car is a bargain thus plays a genuine role in explaining his pleasure, but it is a role he misunderstands. The belief only enables him to experience pleasure that has another source he does not acknowledge. He takes the reason to be a sufficient condition for his having an attitude when the reason actually only satisfies a necessary condition of his having the attitude. I shall also call such reasons *ostensible*. Generally, one's attitude A is an ostensible reason for one's attitude B when one overestimates how much one's having attitude A contributes to the reason for one's having attitude B.

Anticipating reasons may be described at the same level of generality. One's attitude A is an anticipating reason for one's attitude B when an essential factor in the final adoption of attitude *A* is that having attitude *A* helps provide what one takes to be an acceptable reason for having attitude *B*.

An attitude can be ostensible without being anticipating or anticipating without being ostensible. The car-buyer would naturally like to believe that his new car gets good mileage. When he calculates its mileage for the first time, he miscalculates—makes a mistake in subtraction—and comes up with a result that is too high, though not so high as to be incredible. We who balance our own checkbooks and prepare our own tax returns are familiar with such mistakes. They are due to a desire to reach a conclusion of a certain kind, so one's acceptance of a miscalculation in such a case counts as the acceptance of an anticipating reason. But the reason is rarely ostensible. The car-buyer has no merely ostensible reason for believing that his new car gets twenty-eight miles to the gallon. His belief about his car's mileage really is based on the results of his calculation. This is at best a questionable case of self-deception.

Frederick Siegler describes a similar case involving a perceptual mistake.

> If A simply mistakes my dog for his, even if this could be due to a desire that the dog be his dog and when he fears and suspects that it might be mine, it is difficult to think of such a case as one of self-deception, and this is because when one's desires and fears distort perception we are inclined to think of there being a psychological distortion which results in mistake of which the person himself normally is not aware.[3]

This character has no merely ostensible reason for thinking that the dog is his. He thinks it is his only because he thinks (mistakenly) that he can see that it is his. I am more inclined than Siegler to count this as a case of self-deception, but I admit that it is not a clear case.

When an anticipating belief concerns the weight or strength of evidence, then one "jumps to a conclusion" or accepts some conclusion on a *pretext*. Such anticipating attitudes need not be ostensible with respect to the conclusion accepted. The conclusion sometimes really is accepted on the basis of the putative evidence. Still, if the subject thinks he has reasons for taking the evidence to support a certain conclusion, these reasons can be both anticipating and ostensible. They are anticipating because his desire to have adequate support for the conclusion plays an essential and biasing role in his finally coming to think that he has it. They are ostensible if this desire, or something else yet unmentioned, provides the real reason for his accepting the conclusion. The car-buyer thinks that his long experience with automobiles grounds his belief that the noise his old car has been making recently is a good indication that it will soon require expensive repairs. In fact his long experience with automobiles has nothing to do with it. He believes this noise is an ominous sign only because he needs a reason for replacing his old car.

In the clearest cases of self-deception of the kind called *rationalization*, an attitude is both ostensible and anticipating. Although some rationalizations are so implausible that a second, higher-level rationalization is required to protect the subject from the awareness that he is deceiving himself, successful rationalizations are generally plausible. In each of the following bits of sincerely accepted monologue, while everything could be as it appears, a paradigm of rationalization could also be involved:

"I like thumbing through the magazines in the supermarket checkout line because of my sociological interest in the current preoccupations of popular culture."

"I choose not to submit a paper to the Program Committee because I believe it is appropriate only for younger, less experienced writers to submit papers."

"I will recommend so-and-so for promotion because I find her papers to be well written, original, and important."

"I will recommend that so-and-so not be reappointed because I find his papers to be carelessly written, unoriginal, and uninteresting."

"I like to go jogging at least four times a week only because I think it is good for my heart and lungs."

Rationalization involves false beliefs about relations between one's attitudes. These attitudes include beliefs, which are either true or false, but are by no means restricted to beliefs. When a case of self-deception involves an anticipating, ostensible reason concerning the relation between attitudes that are not beliefs, there is still a false belief involved, a second-order attitude. Examples in which the only relevant false beliefs are second-order attitudes are useful in making some negative points about self-deception. There need be no readily available strong evidence against second-order false beliefs, and there need be no reason to suppose that the self-deceived person "really knows" things to be other than he believes them to be. Self-deception does not in general require belief in the face of evidence or a conflict between what one in some sense knows and what one believes. This point is also supported by examples in which the ostensible reason concerns a belief. I think my daughters would really enjoy going to tonight's baseball game. This is my reason, I think, for wanting to take them to the game. But the real order of dependence is the reverse of this. While I am not so self-ignorant that I fail to realize that I would like to go myself, I do not quite realize that I am unlikely to indulge this desire without some additional reason for doing so. My belief that they would enjoy going serves to justify my acting on my desire to take them. They do not manifestly hate going to baseball games, so my belief is not absurd. It may even be true. The point is that I have it because it rationalizes a desire of mine, while I mistakenly think that I have the desire because I have the belief. There may well be lots about my desire of which I am ignorant, but there need be nothing that I really know but am trying to cover up. I do not really know, in particular, that I think they would enjoy going to the game because I would like to have an acceptable reason for taking them.

The fact that one can be self-deceived without hiding from some truth that one really knows does not show that there is an asymmetry between self-deception and other-deception. Others can be as ignorant of my genuine attitude structure as I am myself, and my publicly professed reasons can be as convincing to others as they are to myself.

"Deception," like many "-tion" words, easily admits of a process-product shift. It can refer either to the state of being deceived or to the process that results in a state of being deceived. When "deception" is applied to a process, the process is usually thought of as deliberate. There is indeed an asymmetry between self-deception and other-deception. While there is no appearance of paradox in the deliberate attempt of one person to deceive another, there appears to many, myself included, to be a paradox in deliberate self-deception. I do not want to deny that there is such a thing as deliberate self-deception, and in this essay I forgo a discussion of attempts to explain away its apparently paradoxical nature. I do deny that the deliberate attempt to deceive oneself is essential to being self-deceived. One can be in the state of being self-deceived without in any way, consciously or unconsciously, attempting to get oneself into this state. More generally, one can be deceived in a certain respect without there being anyone, oneself or another, who attempts to bring about the deception. We are deceived when we are misled by appearances. It is primitive anthropomorphism to think of every deceptive appearance as set up with the intention to deceive. The state of being deceived does not in general require that there be a deliberate process with the state as its intended outcome, and the state of being self-deceived in particular requires no such process.

If it is granted that in rationalization there need be no tension between knowledge of an unpleasant or somehow unacceptable truth and a contrary belief masking this knowledge, one may still suspect that such tension is central to kinds of self-deception that do not involve rationalization. I shall attempt to cast doubt on the existence of self-deception that is free of rationalization.

It is only appropriate that I should have qualms about this attempt since my own activity is an excellent candidate for being an instance of the phenomenon I am discussing. Those who defend theories often provide striking examples of rationalization. Although the defender of the theory thinks he regards the theory as adequate because he thinks there are no genuine counterexamples, his treatment of putative counterexamples is actually heavily biased by his fondness for the theory. A theory that proposes to tell us the essence of *being self-deceived* should be especially suspect. There is no prior reason for thinking it has an essence. Perhaps *being self-deceived* is a "family resemblance" concept, one which applies for related but distinguishable reasons in different cases but does not apply for just the same reason in every case. The only effective way to refute this suggestion is to produce an adequate account of the kind it implies is unavailable. Given the realization that one's opinions are often anticipating and their uses in supporting conclusions are often merely ostensible, what can one do but continue to give reasons as best one can? My reasons for regarding rationalization as essential to self-deception consist in examinations of representative examples in which rationalization is absent.

Consider first someone who sincerely professes friendly feeling about someone but whose verbal behavior around this person often exhibits a pattern of domination and cruelty. Need this be a case of self-deception? A combination of affection and hostility toward the same object is common enough. The professed friendly feeling may be genuine, although it is certainly in conflict with the cruel, belittling jokes and domineering behavior often exhibited. Given that the subject does not recognize the existence or extent of his cruelty, it does not follow that he has mistaken beliefs about his cruelty. So far as the case has been described, it need not involve the subject's having an opinion on the topic one way or the other. Mere lack of self-awareness is not self-deception. An adult who is oblivious to his cruel behavior, having no opinion about it one way or the other, is in this respect abnormally childish. But a normal kindergartner can be quite capable of fairly subtle verbal cruelty unaccompanied by any reflection or opinion about what he or she is up to. Perceptive teachers, parents, and older children who try to foster more self-awareness in the younger child are not thereby trying to diminish self-deception in the child. The thirst for rationality must be cultivated before it can become a major source of lies.

An adult who makes cruel jokes without recognizing them as cruel will normally have a biased, distorted opinion about what he is up to. It is the misperception, rather than the lack of awareness of the nature of one's own behavior, which constitutes self-deception in this case. The subject's belief that he is "only kidding," just making small talk, merely engaging in the sort of banter that is a normal and benign form of verbal interaction, is both anticipating and ostensible. It is ostensible because the real reason for his behavior is something else, unrecognized. It is anticipating because a need for an acceptable explanation of his own behavior influences his perception of it.

Must someone who is self-deceived in this way "really know" that his jokes are cruel? I think we are not forced to find a place for such suppressed self-knowledge. There may or may not be conscious qualms and suspicions. If there are not, we need not postulate unconscious qualms. Although it ought to be obvious to the subject that he habitually disparages his companion, it may not be at all obvious. One who is self-deceived may systematically underestimate the psychological effect of his jokes, and there is room for different degrees of variation between the mistaken estimation and the truth. Someone who quite realizes he is engaged in verbal aggression can still misperceive the depth and hurtfulness of his thrusts.

Such misperception can occur even when the jokes are reflexive. The habitual maker of self-deprecating jokes can have some awareness of what he is doing without realizing the full extent of his self-aggression. In his sermon "Upon Self-Deceit," Butler emphasizes that by its means people "palliate their vices and follies to themselves."[4] We know it is also by its means that people overestimate their own follies and vices. Self-hatred can cloud one's perception of reality as much as self-love. What makes a reason ostensible is its difference from the real reason. An ostensible reason may be more worthy than the real reason, or less worthy, or neither. So long as self-deception is regarded as a kind of lying to oneself, it appears, as a kind of lying, to be immoral. When it is regarded, as I suggest, as a kind of misapprehension of one's attitude structures, it ceases to appear to be an intrinsically immoral failing. It is the moral status of the particular attitudes involved and the actions they motivate which determines the moral status of particular instances of self-deception. As some of my examples are intended to illustrate, self-deception can occur in morally insignificant contexts.

Now I turn to an example of someone who believes something in the teeth of evidence that points in the opposite direction. John Canfield and Don Gustafson sketch the following example: "Suppose that Jones is presented with overwhelming evidence proving that his son is guilty of a crime, but that in the face of this evidence Jones refuses to admit that his son is guilty. Here we would say, truly, that Jones is deceiving himself."[5] Canfield and Gustafson take this example to illustrate their claim that to deceive oneself about *p* is to believe *p* under belief-adverse circumstances. Penelhum discusses this suggestion as follows:

> But the self-deceiver must also *know* the evidence; or else we have not self-deception but ignorance. Further, if he knows the evidence yet does not accept what it points to, this might be because he does not *see* what it points to, and then we have stupidity or naivete; so the self-deceiver must not only know the strong evidence, but see what it points to. But if he has, knows, and sees the import of, strong evidence, what is left for him to do to believe what it points to? The notion of acceptance seems to add nothing in such a context; for the criteria for saying that he really does see where the evidence points and the criteria for saying he accepts the conclusion to which it points are the same. (p. 258)

I think this last claim is mistaken. With the purpose of pointing out the importance of rationalization in self-deceit, I shall elaborate the Jones example to show that the notion of acceptance does add something in the context Penelhum describes.

The gambling debts of Jones's son, Sonny, had become very worrisome to everyone in the family, including Sonny. One day both Sonny and his car were gone. So was Jones's valuable stamp collection. There has been no word about the stamp collection, the car, or Sonny. Jones says that he does not believe Sonny took the stamp collection; and this is one of the common cases in which a syntactically external negation is understood to function internally as well, so "I don't believe p" is understood to imply "I disbelieve p." Jones believes that Sonny did not take the stamp collection.

As the example is described so far, it contains no unexpected details. Now I shall provide some more information about Jones's psychological state. On one hand, he quite realizes not only that his strong feelings about Sonny influence his reluctance to admit that Sonny is a thief but also that his strong feelings about the relation between Sonny and himself make him especially reluctant to admit that Sonny has stolen *from him*. On the other hand, the father does not claim to have any special insight into his son's character which outweighs the evidence that he stole the stamp collection. Although the father thinks there is some other explanation for the disappearance of the stamp collection, he has no specific alternative hypothesis in mind which he regards as more likely than the obvious hypothesis that Sonny stole the stamps.

The father knows what the evidence is. He sees where it points. He admits that the evidence supports the conclusion that Sonny stole the stamp collection. He admits that those who accept this conclusion on the evidence have a reasonable belief. He says he does not accept the conclusion himself, and I want to take him at his word. He does not have the inconsistent beliefs that Sonny stole the stamps and that Sonny did not steal the stamps. He believes only the second, that Sonny did not steal the stamps. Although he is willing to admit that this is an unreasonable belief, it is not in the present circumstances within his power to give it up. The father accepts that the conclusion that Sonny stole the stamps is well-supported, but he does not accept the conclusion. That is an additional step he does not take.

No doubt this example is psychologically unlikely and extreme. I think it is nevertheless coherent. From my point of view, the most interesting feature of the example is that the father has no relevant anticipating or ostensible reasons. Given that Sonny did indeed steal his father's stamp collection, the father does have a false belief about that. But the father has no relevant false beliefs about himself, about the reasons for his having one belief and not having the opposite belief.

I suggest that this example, as elaborated, is not at all a clear case of self-deception. When we fill in the original sketch of Canfield and Gustafson to produce a clear case of self-deception, we add an element of rationalization. The father is unwilling to admit that his belief is unreasonable. He denies that the evidence offers very strong support for the conclusion that Sonny stole the stamp collection. His estimation of the evidence is both anticipating, because he wants to avoid admitting the true strength of the evidence, and ostensible, since the real reasons for his refusing to accept the conclusion are not his evaluations of the evidence. His typical misperception reverses the true direction of dependence. He thinks it is because he judges the evidence to be inadequate that he does not accept the conclusion that Sonny is a thief, but actually it is because he wants to avoid the conclusion that he judges the evidence to be inadequate. He may in addition hold that a particular alternative hypothesis to explain the stamp collection's disappearance is more likely. The objectively preposterous hypothesis appears plausible to him mainly because it is an alternative to the hypothesis he wants to avoid.

Now let us suppose that the father in the original case gets some additional evidence. He is informed by the police that Sonny has been arrested in a nearby city while attempting to sell the stamp collection to a dealer. I think the story could be coherently continued in the same way: the father admits that this new evidence is even stronger, but he still believes that Sonny is innocent. But I will not force the father into this extreme position. I continue the story, rather, by allowing the father not to hold out against the new evidence. He comes to believe what others believed all along. While he is willing to admit that they really *knew* all along, he does not say that he himself knew all along. He does say, just to make the case difficult for the view of self-deception I am attempting to defend, that he deceived himself about Sonny's innocence. This self-ascription of self-deception sounds natural, in the circumstances, and if it is correct it undermines my suggestion that an element of rationalization is necessary for genuine self-deception. But I think we should not be too eager to assume that it is correct. Self-ascriptions of self-deception are not especially privileged. Like many other kinds of self-ascription, they can be sincere but mistaken. A sincere self-ascription of self-deception, that is, can itself be a case of self-deception. I shall illustrate this with a new example.

Fairs and carnivals often have games in which success consists in the performance of a task that does not appear to be so difficult. One wins by shooting away with a rapid-fire BB gun all of a small star on a paper target or by completely covering a painted circle with five smaller circles. The operator of the circle-covering game frequently demonstrates that the large circle can be completely covered, and I suppose it is physically possible to shoot away the entire star. But both feats are extremely difficult for a nonexpert. The motivation for playing these games often illustrates, incidentally, a common pattern of self-deception. The prize for a single success is typically a huge but sleezy stuffed animal. Although some players think they want to win the prize because they want to have it, the actual direction of dependence between their desires runs in the opposite direction: they want to have the prize because they want to *win* it. (Compare: "Although she doesn't really want to serve as president of the organization, she wants very much to be *elected* president of the organization.") Whether or not I rationalized my desire to win a prize is unimportant to the point of this example. I did want to win it. But even though I attached a very high subjective value to winning, I realized that each attempt was a very bad bet, a long shot in which the possible gain, if assigned an appropriate financial value, did not justify the financial risk. I have known about midway games for a long time, and I was not naive about their true difficulty. I did not think that I had suddenly acquired some special skill or knack. I did not temporarily forget or somehow bracket my reason for thinking that it was virtually impossible for me to win. I nevertheless spent a few dollars in the attempt.

Recounting my midway misadventure a bit later, I say, "As usual, I deceived myself into thinking I could shoot away the star." Although this bit of mild self-deprecation is intended to entertain, it is not deliberately insincere. It is nevertheless mistaken. Given my earlier experience with such games and others' testimonial evidence, if I had overestimated my chances of winning, I would have deceived myself. But I never overestimated my chances. Despite a correct estimation of my chances, I spent good money attempting, against very long odds, to win. While the matter is not serious, and my self-ascription of self-deception does not mask a very deep discomfort, it does mask something. It is more difficult to accommodate my actual behavior to my self-image than to regard myself as temporarily blind to my real chances. Since I believe that self-deceit with respect to the import of evidence is a nearly universal condition, I don't mind so much attributing to myself a misestimation of evidence in this instance, for I am not particularly ashamed of my motivating desire to win the silly game. I do not, however, have a satisfactory explanation of my violating the precept that estimated probability should be a guide to action.

Jones may have a similar difficulty in explaining to himself his belief in Sonny's innocence. There are two alternative hypotheses: he was blind to the import of the strong circumstantial evidence; he appreciated the strength of the evidence, but nevertheless believed that Sonny was innocent. By hypothesis, the second is correct. But the first may be easier for Jones to deal with. He would rather think of himself as unreasonably misestimating the strength of the evidence than as unreasonably maintaining a belief at odds with strong evidence whose strength he estimates correctly. When he finally comes to the sad realization that Sonny did steal the stamp collection, his admission that he deceived himself may serve to protect him from recognizing his true cognitive structure.

But let us suppose, contrary to my most recent suggestion, that Jones does not have a distorted view of his former attitude toward the evidence. He says that he deceived himself simply because he held a belief in the teeth of evidence whose strength he estimated correctly. Then, although as I said earlier, my reluctance may be an instance of the phenomenon I am discussing, I am still reluctant to admit that his self-ascription is correct. Jones was wrong about Sonny, but he was not wrong in any relevant way about himself. He was not self-deceived. Or, if he was, then the final version of his story serves as a counterexample to my central contention.

That contention, in summary, is that being self-deceived consists in one's misapprehending the structure of one's attitudes, in one's taking the having of one attitude to explain the having of another when the true explanation is something else. Such misapprehension does not require inconsistent beliefs or a belief in conflict with what one really knows.

NOTES

1. I consider no accounts of self-deception published after the summer of 1983, when I completed this essay. (The promptness of my response to the editors' invitation revealed to me how eager I was to escape from another project.) The view that we often misperceive our own desire structures occurs in an examination of Aristotle's infinite regress argument that there cannot be a desire without there being something desired for its own sake. See my "Infinite Regress Arguments," in *Principles of Philosophical Reasoning,* ed. James H. Fetzer (Totowa, N.J.: Roman and Allanheld, 1984), pp. 93–117.

2. T. Penelhum, "Pleasure and Falsity," in *Philosophy of Mind,* ed. Stuart Hampshire (New York: Harper and Row, 1966), p. 261. Penelhum's paper first appeared in *American Philosophical Quarterly* 1 (1964):81–91.

3. F. Siegler, "An Analysis of Self-Deception," *Nous* 2 (1968):161.

4. Sermon X of *Fifteen Sermons,* in *The Works of Joseph Butler,* ed. W. E. Gladstone (Oxford: Clarendon Press, 1896), 2:175.

5. J. Canfield and D. Gustafson, "Self-Deception," *Analysis* 23 (1962):35.

7

PARTISANSHIP

Adam Morton

Gambles with Rationality

1. It is a platitude, I hope, that if you want to learn anything interesting about the world you have to take a risk of being wrong. The risk isn't trivial: the danger run by the most carefully formed belief, obtained by the most reasonable and reliable method, is still real. There is always what Isaac Levi has called a gamble with truth.[1] The more you want, the more you pay: the lure is the possibility of knowledge and the price is the likelihood of being wrong. What I will argue for is an extension of this. The price is higher than the platitude describes it: if you want to learn something *interesting* about the world then the price of the most effective way of achieving this end may be counted not only in truth but in rationality. There is a gamble with rationality too: the best strategy for acquiring knowledge may commit its participants to courses of action that can result in their acting and reasoning irrationally. This is a dramatic way of describing a consequence of some not terribly controversial facts about the structure of scientific inquiry, but it is also a fairly clear feature of personal and political commitments. Irrationality there tends to take the form of self deception. These commitments may therefore seem not fully rational. My hope is that the comparison with the same phenomenon in the scientific context will show that this need not be the case, that in love and politics one can rationally run a deliberate risk of irrationality.

My strategy will be to begin with the examples from science—concentrating on the rationality of commitment to a theoretical tradition or a research program—and then to apply some of my conclusions to the (even) more tangled cases of commitment to a person or an ideology. One unifying theme will be the relations between desires and beliefs. It is essential to my argument that there are rational connections between what one wants and what one thinks— connections that explain one's belief and explain it as rational, though typically they cannot serve as justifications of it—and that the influence of desire over belief does not just consist in what David Pears dismisses as "the usual short circuit described so well by Freud."[2]

Scientific Partisanship

2. Scientists have commitments as well as beliefs. This is an inevitable result of the fact that science is a social enterprise, and has as its inevitable result that the most reasonable way of doing science (and thus the most reasonable way of learning about most of the world) bears an unavoidable risk of irrationality. Or so I shall argue. Let me begin with the sociality of science.

No individual can act out the whole scientific enterprise. But if some superhumanly intelligent and protean agent could play all the epistemic roles required in the formation and confirmation of scientific theories, then she would be doing just that: playing a number of distinct roles, dividing herself into a scientific community. Something like this conclusion emerges from almost all contemporary discussions of scientific method. For whatever route of escape one takes from ancient inductivism (Karl Popper's, W. V. Quine's, Thomas Kuhn's, Imre Lakatos's) one ends up with this conclusion at least: there is a variety of epistemic functions, a variety of stages along a route that a proposition (theory, hypothesis, idea) takes toward final acceptance, and what happens in them is essentially different. For example, on my schematization of the process (essentially Lakatos filtered through Quine)[3] one begins with initial conjecturing, in response to preexisting tensions and anomalies but subject to very little rational constraint, followed by careful reformulation, then by experimental and theoretical tests, and eventually—if all goes well— by inclusion into orthodoxy. There are rational constraints, different ones, on each of these stages.

I don't want to present more details of the picture. If I did, the aura of cozy uncontroversiality would immediately dissolve. I want, though, to draw some consequences that follow, I think, from just about any way of filling in the details.

(a) These functions, these stages toward acceptance, can be carried out by different people. In fact, they are usually best carried out by different people. So we have, crudely speaking, experimentalists and theoreticians (of both the kind who invent theory and the kind who work with theory) and sage codifiers of orthodoxy. Each group does its job with what it is given and hands something on to the next. (Cyclically: the codifiers hand on anomolies to the conjecturers.)

(b) As a result of (a), scientific investigations usually proceed in terms of a division of labor among people doing essentially different tasks. Scientists work in teams organized in varying degrees of tightness. A position in a team is a node in a network: it involves taking in and sending on information, adding and processing in between, and it requires a grasp of the overall purposes and structure of the network. You have to have some idea of who else is doing what and why. Otherwise you wouldn't know what to do. This grasp is necessarily imperfect. Otherwise a team would not be necessary.

(c) At many nodes of the network, that is, in performing many of these epistemic functions, factors besides simple weight of evidence play an essential role. Someone makes a conjecture and others then reformulate it. They do so in accordance with a guiding conception of what a good, intelligible, testable, respectable hypothesis should look like. Then others subject it to tests. They first see if it is a hypothesis of a sort that is worth taking seriously enough to test. You don't bother testing variations of the phlogiston idea or new chemical tests for transubstantiation. There are also rules of thumb about which kinds of hypothesis are best tested in which ways, and which kinds of test, of which stringency, will be of use to the theoreticians. Theoreticians, of the kind who work out the theoretical consequences and acceptability of theories, employ a similar range of guiding ideas and rules of thumb. And the final absorption of an idea into orthodoxy requires the use of standards and traditions of codification, reflecting ideas about the kinds of information that will be of use to the general project.

Cooperating scientists, then, need what I have called 'guiding conceptions', 'rules of thumb', 'standards and traditions', and so on. These are all glimpses of the intentions of the whole project, each from the perspective of a particular node in the system. Or, more realistically, if you could gather them all together and add them all up you would get something, a rather messy something, which you could glorify with the title of The Overall Intention.

There is, obviously, almost never a unique, or a best, way of formulating these background ideas, guiding conceptions, and so on. If one's aim is simply, say, to understand the etiology of various human cancers then the very general outline of biological science will not answer basic practical questions like: should you look first of all at viruses, should you look for a common origin for cancers of very different tissues, should you start with pathological tissues or first investigate the processes by which normal cells differentiate into specialized sublines and maintain an ordered and subordinated cooperation, . . . The questions multiply. There is obviously no a priori way of answering them. Following up any one of the possible lines of investigation will take all the time and intelligence of a number of people. So a further division of labor is inevitable, not just within teams but *between* teams. Different groups of researchers will work with different presuppositions, different aims.

It follows from this that different research groups will very often think of each other as *wrong,* misguided about what constitutes a sensible approach to the problem. A newly minted research worker, about to join one team or another, will not think of their characteristic feature as rightness or wrongness. The thought will be just: this is the way they do it here. But as long as this is the way the thought presents itself, the researcher will be hampered in carrying out the function to which he is assigned. The thought will be at once too diffuse for the specifics of the job—no graspable 'this way' can capture the overall mentality of a working research program—and too cerebral—it will not motivate in the way that is required to produce ideas and overcome obstacles. Instead, once recruits are socialized to a particular role in the team, they have internalized a large number of norms: these are the characteristics of a reasonable hypothesis, this is how one goes about testing one, and so on, and closely related to these, a set of *desires*: these are the general characteristics of the hypothesis we want to establish (why? because we want to discover the truth and we're committed to seeing the truth along these lines), these are views we want to refute, and so on.

Some such desires are ways in which individuals represent the general scientific strategy of the whole program. Others, though, are less epistemic. For example, one reason for taking seriously the possible involvement of viruses in human cancers is the connection between viruses, the immune system, and vaccines. Where there is a virus there is the hope of a vaccine. This makes it reasonable to put devotion and ingenuity into formulating viral hypotheses, searching for confirmation of them, and defending and reformulating them against recalcitrant evidence. Desire does not lead to belief here alone or directly: other beliefs, both of a theoretical and an observational kind, are needed, and the eventual belief need not represent anything like the original wished-for situation. But, still, the fact that someone starts off with a certain desire is an essential part of the reason why he ends up with a certain belief. And one obvious case of this is obviously consistent with the agent's rationality: that in which a desire leads one to take seriously a certain possibility which, properly formulated and tested, turns out to have evidence on its side.

It ought to be possible for members of rival research teams to see each other as reasonable, but wrong, misguided. For, after all, a member of a differing team is reaching different conclusions as a result of different assumptions, originally fairly arbitrary ones, about the most profitable strategy for unraveling the phenomena in question, and these are in the end different presumptions about the form that the truth behind the phenomena is likely to take. After all, it then looks like any other dispute between reasonable, understanding, self-conscious people. But to describe it like this is to miss the essential difficulty of the situation. If you are a member of one team then members of another will: take seriously hypotheses that seem to you not worth consideration, consider them supported by what you consider misconstruals of the evidence, and integrate them into the common theoretical background in a way that seems to you to show a misunderstanding of the structure and direction of the theories involved. These are things that can easily be signs of incompetence, stupidity, or unreasonableness. To see whether they are or not in any particular case, you have to get a grip on the theoretical context of the other: his rules of thumb and guiding conceptions. This is hard not only because of the distasteful qualities of the beliefs involved, but also because no one knows them all! They are spread throughout the other team or tradition, scattered where they are needed to tell people what to do. And partly because of this diffusion, they are not formulated, carefully expressed, or written down; some of them are the private property of the less articulate subspecies of the other team. So for all your gentlemanly resolve to see the other side as merely differing and deeply wrong, rather than irrational, confused, or stupid, you know that they may *be* that, and you may never be able to tell.

Moreover there *are* dangers to one's rationality inherent in cooperative science, and their effects are hard to distinguish—even from within a research program—from those of intelligent adherence. They are the obvious consequences of partisanship: overestimation of the objective support for one's favored views, blindness to the evidence for rival views, failures to see either the explanatory appeal of an unappetizing rival theory or the explanatory bankruptcy of one's own. The important point is not that these blindnesses and misjudgments exist, nor even that they are inevitable for people working in teams and with programs, but rather that they are of a piece with the essential functioning of programs implemented in groups.

Of course, the difficulty of judging the rationality of those engaged in a rival project is closely linked to that of judging the rationality of one's own project. For it is reasonable for a project to continue when it is still among the live options for unraveling the questions at hand, and unreasonable when it is not. That is what the bankruptcy of a research program consists in: the smallness of the likelihood that it will provide explanations of the phenomena it aims to explain, compared to the likelihood of rival programs. The estimation of this likelihood is rarely uncontroversial, which is just another way of saying that the evaluations of a program from the outside and the inside are likely to be different. And, most importantly, it is a comparative matter: to know how reasonable one's program is one needs to have some idea of the standing of the alternatives. Very often, in spite of all the problems I have mentioned, there is a rough consensus in a subject about the relative vitality of the various alternatives, and sometimes it is perfectly clear that one of the alternatives is now hopeless. Perfectly clear, that is, to all except those working in the hopeless program. They, trapped within its rules of thumb and guiding assumptions, may not be able to see its hopelessness. For them the gamble with rationality has been lost. They enrolled in an enterprise that promised them a justified understanding of some phenomenon, and then not only failed to deliver but supplied an invisibly defective substitute. But that does not mean they were not justified in the original enrollment, not even if they understood the chance of this outcome.

There are three general consequences of this situation. (1) the appearance of the border area between the clearly rational and the clearly irrational changes as one approaches it. From a distance, there seem to be clear cases on either side, then a steep descent to a short, boggy lowland in between the two slopes. But at ground level and in the midst of the terrain, as any rambler could tell you, things are not that simple. The slopes on either side are not so uniform and the definite heights on either side are obscured by the smaller features, so that it is often far from obvious where between the two extremes one is.

The commitment to a research program—scientific partisanship—puts one on the ground where one cannot survey the terrain: to make the commitment one must accept the danger that one will wander onto the other slope without knowing it, and without having committed any obvious navigational error.

(2) Desire *should* influence belief. One's beliefs are shaped by more than the evidence available and the theoretical background. For it is perfectly reasonable, indeed it is unavoidable if one is to do science of any sophistication, to be moved by: a desire that a particular kind of theory eventually provide the best explanation of a phenomenon; a desire that a particular kind of theory *not* prove to be the best explanation; a desire that the explanation of a phenomenon prove applicable to some practical concern; and so on. Of course, there are rational and irrational ways in which desires can influence beliefs. And of course there are desires that cannot easily and rationally affect beliefs, for example the desire that the efforts of some particular person or group provide or not provide a successful theory. (I don't want to say that such desires can have no rational effect on belief. The next section suggests that there are such effects.) The delicacy of the distinction between the legitimate and the illegitimate effects of desire on belief is the main reason why it is so hard to know where you are between the obvious extremes.

Another way to put (2) is to say that agents' desires not only can explain why they believe what they do; desires can also be part of explanations why they are rational to believe as they do. And if you are asked, "Why do you believe that?" you can quite fairly include in your answer an account of how you came to have a commitment to a particular program or tradition of theorizing, and how that commitment led you, via conjecture, evidence, and reformulation, to your belief. That is not to say that such an explanation will very often serve as a justification of your belief. But that is another matter.

(3) The original aim of a research program is rather indefinite. It is not that a particular theory should prove true, let alone that a particular group of researchers should succeed. It is rather that some as yet undevised theory of some usually pretty broad kind, e.g., a viral theory of cancer or a deterministic underpinning for quantum mechanics, should adequately account for present and future data. The diffuseness of this aim is the reason why it fits quite naturally into a reasonable strategy for gaining knowledge: one is not committing oneself in advance to any particular conclusions. But it is also the main

source of the dangers of the situation, for it is hard to work with something so vague, and inevitable that one will assimilate it to some degree to some more definite and less epistemically legitimate aim.

PERSONAL COMMITMENTS

3. Now consider more ordinary kinds of irrationality, those that result from loyalties and commitments. It is the most familiar fact of social life that people defend their own good names and those of people they are attached to. And it is equally familiar that this often results in beliefs that are blatantly contradicted by obvious evidence, although the mechanisms and strategies of this irrationality are notoriously unobvious. I think it is not too hard to see that analogues of (1), (2), and (3) above, apply in this case too, and for very similar reasons.

The most important of the three here is (2), the relevance of desire. For although (1) may be readily granted, if it is taken just as asserting that personal commitments make it hard to know how near to irrationality one is, (2) asserts that the desires that are part of such commitments can rationally influence the beliefs that one forms. And this is more controversial. The most interesting way to defend it is to stretch an analogy between the scientific and the personal case, as follows. When one enters into a commitment to a person, such as that of love or parenthood or even some kinds of colleagueship, one acquires a desire to think well of them. The attributes one may want a person to have are very varied. There is always some evaluative element: one wants the person to be capable, worthy, or at least minimally decent. One special case is that in which the person one is committed to is oneself. Then it is just a matter of self-respect that one wants oneself to be mildly capable and minimally decent, and of course one would like a lot more. Now these desires are essentially vague. They are like the diffuse objects of point (3): one does not want the person to have this or that very specific virtue but just wants them to turn out to be in some way or other a suitable object of affection or respect. One is thus entering into something like a research program. The aim is to show that the eventually best explanation of the person's actions is provided by an account of them that represents them as in some way good or admirable. The exact virtues involved will depend on the ways in which one interprets the evidence as it arrives.

If this is one's program, then one's reactions to information about the person involved will follow some obvious lines. Their successes will of course be explained in terms of their virtues, but, much more significantly, each different success should lead to a refinement, elaboration, or reconsideration of the exact form of the virtue. And too simple and obvious deductions from failures and misdeeds will be resisted.

There are reliable reports that your loved one voted Tory, or stole from a famine collection box. The reports are reliable enough that were you uncommitted you would be justified simply in believing that he or she is a rotten person. But given your commitment you will not be pushed so quickly to that conclusion. Your commitment commits you to resist it. There may be alternative explanations of the action consistent with the loved one's being the kind of person you wanted them to be. Perhaps it was tactical voting, designed to elect someone so terrible he would utterly discredit his party. Perhaps the collection box was fraudulently labeled, and after the theft the money was donated to real famine relief. Another strategy would be to accept the facts at face value and to revise your conception of the kind of virtue the loved one possesses. Perhaps the loved one is politically naive because all their good sense goes into work and into care for friends. Perhaps the loved one's devotion to friends is so touchingly, if foolishly, great that they will steal from the starving—no doubt intending to repay it—in order to buy a present.

Either of these strategies might succeed. But to adopt them is to assume a responsibility. You cannot just entertain these perhapses; to suggest any of them obliges you to search for evidence of its truth, and to see how much plausibility it has, given what else you know of the person, indeed what else you know of humanity. If you live up to this responsibility you may be disappointed; the conjecture may be unsupportable. You may also succeed; in that case an interesting truth about the person, one that allows the person better to come to terms with themself and allows you better to define your affection, is discovered. And that is why this response to a commitment is rational: not only does it follow essentially the same pattern as a research program in natural science, but, as in science, it is the only way available to us in which some interesting and important truths can become known.

The response can also be irrational, and in two ways. One can fail to do the necessary thinking and checking. And one can fail to see that it is not working, that the aim of finding an explanation of the person's actions which preserves their honor is hopeless, that this research program is bankrupt. In that case the influence of desire on belief has been illegitimate. But it is important to see that the illegitimacy is related to—in fact is produced by a sometimes very slight deviation from—the necessary and legitimate influence of desire on belief, which certainly takes more forms than "the usual short circuit." Our situation is more interesting, and more difficult, than that.

The general outline of the situation is much as it is in scientific partisanship. The source of the commitment is different, though, and one way in which this shows is in the relation between explanation and justification. An explanation of the reasonable belief of a scientific partisan will refer to the desires that are part of their commitment, but if you turn this explanation into a justification of the belief, the result will not usually be very convincing to someone who doesn't share the commitment. (Mind you, I doubt that much justification can actually succeed across a very great difference of theoretical commitment, even given very similar beliefs, but I cannot follow this up here.) But with commitments to people the situation is somewhat different. Suppose that I am defending my conviction that someone is decent, appearances to the contrary, by means of a strategy of alternative explanations of their apparent misdeeds, and the strategy is working, in that the alternative hypotheses are dealing with the evidence adequately. Then I can also justify the beliefs that result; I can give you reason to share them by showing that the evidence can be explained by the hypotheses I have formed and that their greater complexity is counterbalanced by the advantage of being able to think of the person in question as decent.

It is the a priori reasonableness of thinking of someone as decent—the irrationality of avoidable hatred—that makes this possible. We cannot so easily convert explanations into justification if the direction of the strategy, though perfectly rational, is toward defending someone's marvelousness rather than their decency or adequacy. Thinking of it this way suggests that in a way there *is* something analogous in scientific rationality, though it is so basic it is rarely visible. This is the a priori reasonableness of a commitment to seeing the world as intelligible. An even faintly scientific explanation of a phenomenon is often more complicated and less obviously consistent with the evidence than an explanation in terms of good and bad luck, fate, or mystical powers. If one is trying to justify one's belief in a particular scientific explanation rather than a mystical one, it is perfectly reasonable to cite one's commitment to interpreting the world as intelligible, even before there is good evidence that the domain in question is in fact intelligible.

One cannot get terribly far with these 'transcendental' considerations, whether they are directed at the intelligibility of the world or the decency of human beings. But their existence does at any rate support two general points. First, some of what passes as deep metaphysical belief may instead be taken simply as a kind of desire: the desire, for example, to see the world as not mysterious and people as not evil. And second, even though an explanation of a belief as rational depends essentially on the agent's desires, it can sometimes be presented as a context-independent justification of that belief.

POLITICAL PARTISANSHIP

4. It is fairly obvious how the analysis of scientific and personal partisanship extends to the case of political partisanship—the possession by political agents of intentions to defend political positions of various general kinds before these positions are exactly formulated, let alone supported by evidence. And the conditions under which it is rational will also be roughly parallel.

The differences between the three cases are as important as their similarities, though. One way of describing the differences is in terms of the human resources that are made use of and the kinds of irrationality that are risked. Scientific partisanship exploits intellectual differences between people, differences both of belief and of skill. And its dangers arise most fundamentally out of the subtlety of the different attitudes to a proposition—as conjecture, hypothesis, theory, or established doctrine—attached to these different skills—meticulousness, originality, erudition, rigor, and so on. Personal partisanship exploits the strength of human attachments and the resources of human social intuition. These underlie our resourcefulness in devising explanations of our own and other's actions, and thus underlie the typical pitfalls of personal partisanship, which arise from the disparity between the wealth of hypotheses we can make to explain an action and our limited power to confirm or eliminate them. In political partisanship what is exploited is the sense of injustice and the emotions of loyalty and solidarity. The corresponding pitfalls are those of inexplicitness, of failing to transform a commitment into a testable belief. Let me explain (but more briefly this time).

Again the natural device is to think of a political commitment as a research program. The aim is to show that a theory of a certain general sort, or from some broadly defined tradition, will prove to be a guiding description of a satisfactory social arrangement. What do 'guiding' and 'satisfactory' mean? Well, their content is not really fixed by the nature of the commitment. One is just committed to the view that one's initial conviction that that particular ideology or movement (socialism, say, or an adherence to individual rights) will lead to a systematic description of what outrages one about the present state of the world, and a usable prescription of action to be taken to improve things. The commitment is to *finding* useful diagnoses. So one cannot stop with the general picture of how one would like to be able to think and judge; one has to find ways of turning one's commitment into beliefs that can at the same time serve the intended function and be given objective confirmation.

I think that in our society the most natural form for these beliefs is as beliefs about actual and possible economies. Marx was right to that extent: the responsibility to turn one's political convictions into something for which reasons can be given is most naturally fulfilled first by finding economic theories that help reveal what doesn't work in the present and what is promising for the future, and then by trying to find good evidence for them—and evidence against those of others. (It is here that the familiar advantages and problems of scientific partisanship enter.) I take it that classical Marxian economics does not have much going for it, that monetarist theories are damaged by the crude evidence of economies such as those of Britain and Chile, and that there is a general dissatisfaction these days with most of the alternatives, directed largely at unrealistic assumptions about competition and about the ways in which individuals and firms make decisions. The result is not that there are not useful, powerful, and even predictive economic theories available but that there is a lack of the kind of theories that give substance to political convictions. And that is one of the sources of the ungroundedness of present-day political life, the tendency for political ideology either to be simply dogmatic or to collapse into vague moralizing and good will.

The obligation imposed by political partisanship can thus be hard to carry out. One has to search for beliefs that satisfy one's commitment yet are supported by evidence, and they may be hard to find. But the obligation must be assumed, for it is the way in which we can reconcile our need to have reasons for our beliefs with the inevitable influence of political temperament. Different people have different political beliefs and commitments in part because they *are* different people, with different dispositions toward complacency, sympathy, outrage, optimism, and caution. This alone does not make their commitments or their beliefs irrational. What is required for their beliefs not to *become* irrational, though, is for temperament to inspire inquiry, so that in the light of experience the enlightening force or the bankruptcy of a developed theory can become evident.

FACTS AND VALUES

5. There have been two closely related themes in this paper. One is the idea of a gamble with rationality, that in order to have a chance of acquiring some valuable kinds of knowledge one will often have to risk not just being wrong but being irrational. The other is the idea of the legitimacy of various connections between desire and belief, that there are perfectly rational ways in which what one wants can influence what one believes. This latter phenomenon is the main reason for the gamble described in the first theme. But now it might seem that the breadth of the range of cases to which the latter idea is applicable, including personal and political commitments as well as scientific inquiry, rather undercuts the initial description of the gamble. For the payoff of the gamble was to be knowledge. That was what lured one into, and made it reasonable to accept, the risk of irrationality. But in the personal and political cases, and others like them, that might seem clearly wrong. It is not the desire for knowledge that moves one there.

No, of course it is not. And I could reformulate the first theme so that it had a more general appearance, describing the rationality of accepting a risk of irrationality in most enterprises directed at most kinds of good. But there is something to be gained by not doing this. For there is something very significant about the fact that the processes I have described begin with desire and end with belief. In each of the three kinds of partisanship I have described, a belief is produced in the working out of a desire. If all goes well, enough conditions will be met that the belief will be made a reasonable one for the person to hold, given their commitments. And if all goes extraordinarily well, the belief will be supported in a way that will convince, or at any rate worry, those who do not share the commitment. This was clearest with political partisanship: one begins with a commitment to a tradition and a set of social emotions, and one aims at a social and economic theory that will make good that tradition and justify those emotions.

The project may fail. No such justifiable beliefs may be found, either because ingenuity and insight are not equal to the task of finding them (as I suggested is the present situation of political economy) or because what beliefs do result may not actually be supported by the evidence one bases them on. These are the two dangers of falsehood and irrationality. I have been presenting them as dangers for the person involved. But they are also dangers for the desires, commitments, or traditions themselves. For a desire that proves itself incapable of generating justified beliefs is in a pretty clear way discredited. It doesn't lead anywhere; people subscribing to it will not have something they can convince others of.

Racism is an example of this. Even a hundred years ago it was not entirely obvious that the various allegiances and prejudices that go with an attachment to one's own race might not work themselves out through anthropology and psychology, so that there would be valuable scientific theories that were racist in underlying motivation, if not in explicit content. But the very fact that that program has failed—the facts were not there and the theories didn't work—discredits the whole motivation. Sometimes the opposite happens, and a surprising or subversive desire is vindicated when it gives rise to testable and enlightening theories. An example of this, rather different from others I have used, is the partial rehabilitation of lust as a motive in human affairs, deriving from the successes of a program, originally pretty eccentric, of showing how central it is in our motivation and how futile it is to ignore it.[4]

Thus although what we want is usually more general than knowledge, what we stand to gain—or lose—is not just the satisfaction but also the vindication of our desires. And this cannot happen unless we connect our desires with methods and procedures whose natural end is the acquisition of knowledge.[5]

NOTES

1. Isaac Levi, *Gambling with Truth* (New York: Routledge, 1967). I am appropriating Levi's terminology while ignoring some of his doctrine, since for him the utilities involved are purely 'epistemic'. This is relevant to the question of the relation between the explanation and the justification of belief, dealt with very sketchily in section 3 below. See also part 1 of Levi's *Decisions and Revisions* (Cambridge: Cambridge Univ. Press, 1984).

2. David Pears, *Motivated Irrationality* (Oxford: Oxford Univ. Press, 1984), p. 54.

3. Imre Lakatos, *The Methodology of Scientific Research Programmes,* ed. J. Worrall and G. Currie (Cambridge: Cambridge Univ. Press, 1978), especially chap. 1. W. V. Quine, *Word and Object* (Cambridge: MIT Press, 1960), especially chap. 1.

4. Much of this section is my development of something Ronald de Sousa said to me. I don't know what he would think of what I have done with it.

5. Discussions with Peter Railton and Rex Hollowell made me throw away parts of an early draft of section 2, and comments of Keith Graham and David Milligan showed me how to improve sections 3 and 4. Contact with Paula Boddington's greater knowledge of the literature on self-deception has shown me that I would be foolish to try to discuss it.

8

EPISTEMIC DIMENSIONS OF
SELF-DECEPTION

Frederick F. Schmitt

Self-deception has long been recognized to be psychologically perplexing and morally troubling.[1] Discussions of self-deception commonly try to resolve some psychological perplexity or prosecute or dismiss a moral objection. The psychological and moral dimensions of self-deception do not, however, exhaust its philosophical interest. Self-deception also has epistemic dimensions, which, though often recognized, have received far less attention.[2] In this paper I propose to chart some of these dimensions.

In sections 1 and 2, I will argue that deception and (by instantiation) self-deception are themselves epistemic conditions, and I will draw out some epistemic perplexities of self-deception to which the proposed epistemic conditions give rise. In sections 3 and 4, I will explain the respects in which deception and self-deception can be counted epistemically objectionable. These respects arise from the epistemic conditions elaborated in the earlier sections.

In each case, I will begin with a discussion of deception, and I will take it as a working hypothesis that self-deception is deception in which one deceives oneself. The psychological perplexities of self-deception have driven more than one writer to conclude that self-deception cannot be an instance of deception.[3] If such perplexities can be resolved in no other way, I have no quarrel with this move. But these psychological perplexities are not my topic here, and I think we ought to deviate from the working hypothesis only if we are forced to do so.[4] At any rate, I believe it is worth exploring the character of self-deception as an instance of deception, checking whether perplexities that arise on this hypothesis can be resolved on their own ground. But I hope that what I have to say about self-deception as an instance of deception will carry over to plausible deviations from the model of deception in light of the psychological perplexities.

Deception and Justification

1. I wish to argue in this section that deception is an epistemic condition. I do not claim that there is a unique ordinary use of "deception." I believe there

are several uses. I wish to show rather that our intuitions about one use of "deception" are best explained by adverting to epistemic conditions. I do not claim that there is a unique set of epistemic conditions which defines this use: our intuitions about this use are pliable enough to fit a number of epistemic conditions that differ from one another along several dimensions. Instead I will select one set of conditions which deserves close attention. What is crucial is that these conditions supply our intuitions with a rationale in virtue of the theoretical role the conditions play in the epistemic evaluation of deception.

Let me begin by asking what epistemic state Holmes must be in to deceive Watson into believing a false proposition p concerning the outcome of a fair lottery. Would it be enough for Holmes merely to guess that the proposition is false? Suppose that in this lottery a ticket is drawn from one hundred tickets, each of which is either red or green. Holmes knows that there are fifty red tickets and fifty green tickets. Holmes must guess the outcome, and for no good reason he guesses red. He then undertakes to make Watson believe that the winning ticket will be green by producing (misleading) evidence that one hundred tickets are green.[5] As it happens, Holmes is right. Does Holmes succeed in deceiving Watson into believing that the winning ticket is green? Certainly there is a sense in which Watson is deceived in his belief, but this is clear only in the sense in which "deceived in his belief" means "has a false belief." Nearly everyone to whom I have presented this case has had a similar reaction, one of resistance to saying that Holmes deceives Watson; he may try to deceive Watson, but it doesn't seem that he succeeds. There is a use of "deception" on which the deceiver's guess is not enough for deception.

Now let us increase the ratio of red to green tickets known to Holmes. Suppose there are sixty red tickets and forty green tickets. Does Holmes succeed in deceiving Watson into believing that the winner is green? Here I find that resistance to saying so fades into hesitation: "Well, Holmes is no longer merely guessing, but it's not right to say firmly that he deceives Watson," say my sources. Suppose there are ninety red tickets and ten green tickets. Hesitation gives way to enthusiasm: "I'm strongly inclined to say he does deceive Watson." What if there are only red tickets? Enthusiasm shades into resolution.

What would explain the variation in our intuitions about these cases? Evidently our enthusiasm for assigning deception varies with Holmes's degree of justification for the belief that the winning ticket is red. We need a hypothesis that explains this variation.[6] One hypothesis that does so is that deception requires that the deceiver be justified in believing not-p.[7] This explains the variation if our enthusiasm for attributing justification to the deceiver also varies with the degree of justification for not-p. And I believe our enthusiasm for attributing justification does so vary.

There is one possible hitch in the present explanation of the variation. On one view of justification, there is a fixed high degree of justification, less than an absolute maximum, that is sufficient for justification. On such a view, enthusiasm for attributing justification to Holmes should reach resolution at that high degree, somewhat before there are only red tickets. And on a variety of views of justification, justification is in many cases reached at a degree less than the absolute maximum, though that degree varies from case to case. If any of these views is assumed, then, according to our hypothesis, our enthusiasm for attributing deception in these cases should reach resolution *before* there are only red tickets. Whether our hypothesis is correct, then, depends on whether our enthusiasm in these cases reaches resolution before there are only red tickets. I don't find my own intuitions on this matter firm enough to be able to say whether this consequence holds. But since it is extremely difficult to identify cases in which justification is reached at a degree less than the absolute maximum, it does not seem that having firm intuitions in particular cases would help much in testing our hypothesis. I am not inclined, then, to take this possible hitch as a serious objection at present. I would like to propose that an individual S deceives an individual x into believing p only if S is justified in believing not-p.

I would like to turn now from the deceiver to the relation between deceiver and deceived and propose, with greater caution, that this relation must also meet an epistemic condition. In paradigmatic cases of deception, the deceiver must transmit justification for believing p to the deceived. More generally, the deceiver must arrange things so that justification for believing p is available to the deceived.

Suppose Holmes knows that there are only red tickets in the lottery, and he undertakes to make Watson believe that the winning ticket is green. However, he does so by stimulating Watson's cerebral cortex with an electrode. In this case, assuming it is possible, I don't think we would say that Holmes *deceives* Watson into believing p. Evidently, to count as deception, Holmes's effort must appeal to some extent to Watson's reason and get Watson to arrive at his belief by reasoning.

In paradigmatic cases of deception, the deceiver transmits evidence in favor of believing p to the deceived or supplies the deceived with justification by lending authority to the belief p, and I would claim that in such cases our enthusiasm for attributing deception varies with the quality of the evidence transmitted.[8] Let us consider a paradigmatic case of deception, in which Holmes knows that there are only red tickets, believes that Watson requires good evidence to be made to believe that the winning ticket is green, and accordingly supplies such evidence by claiming that there are only green tickets. Watson, having no reason to doubt Holmes, takes there to be such evidence and accordingly comes to believe that the winning ticket is green on the basis of this evidence. We can imagine a sequence of cases that fall short of this case in the quality of the evidence, and our enthusiasm for attributing deception declines with the decline in quality. Consider what we would say if Holmes offered Watson evidence that there are ten red and ninety green tickets, or forty red and sixty green, or forty-nine red and fifty-one green. With this much description to go on, most people to whom I have presented this sequence are increasingly hesitant to attribute deception as the sequence progresses.

The most obvious hypothesis that would explain why our enthusiasm for attributing deception varies with the quality of the evidence is that it varies with the degree of justification offered to the deceived. Of course, the preceding cases are unusually simple in that Watson does not already possess evidence for or against p. The present hypothesis would entail that, when Watson possesses such evidence, Holmes must supply enough evidence for p to make the evidence Watson already possesses sufficient to outweigh the evidence Watson possesses against p. I believe that our intuitions confirm this consequence when the above cases are modified to allow for evidence possessed by Watson.

I think the present hypothesis provides the correct explanation of our intuitions about these cases, but it is not easy to make it stick. For the last cases in the sequence seem possible only if we make some additional assumptions, and our hesitancy to attribute deception might be traced to these assumptions. For one thing, we can scarcely imagine that Watson will believe p on the basis of such slim evidence unless we assume that he has misheard the evidence transmitted by Holmes, or that he has heard only Holmes's endorsement of the conclusion and has reasoned by appeal to authority, or that he believes it is sufficient evidence but is simply incompetent to judge which evidence is good. In any of these cases, I think we would hesitate to attribute deception to Holmes. The problem is that it might be claimed that the reason we hesitate to attribute deception in these instances is not, as suggested earlier, that Holmes fails to supply sufficient evidence, but that communication breaks down, or that Watson in effect deceives himself through incompetence. Either way Holmes fails to be the prime cause of Watson's belief p and therefore does not deceive Watson.[9]

But I would respond to this claim by saying that if our hesitation to attribute deception in these instances is to be explained by these factors, and not by Holmes's failure to supply sufficient evidence, then we ought to hesitate to attribute deception when Holmes supplies sufficient evidence (only green tickets) and these further conditions prevail. But I do not think we do hesitate equally in this case. I think we have a greater tendency to attribute deception when Holmes supplies sufficient evidence even if Watson mishears the evidence, or reasons by appeal to authority, or is incompetent to judge. Holmes can deceive Watson by supplying sufficient evidence even if Watson does not take full account of that evidence. And notice that pinning our hesitation to attribute deception on the latter factor would commit us to a most implausible view—that a person who is epistemically incompetent cannot be deceived, no matter what evidence is offered. Thus, on my reading of our intuitions, we hesitate to attribute deception in the earlier case because Holmes fails to transmit sufficient evidence.

I believe similar remarks can be made about other kinds of deception, kinds not involving the transmission of evidence. Holmes may deceive Watson into believing that a green ticket will win by planting misleading clues or by concealing clues that favor p. Holmes may arrange it so that Watson overhears a conversation in which lottery officials say that the lottery is rigged in favor of a green ticket. In these cases, Holmes ensures that Watson has enough evidence for p available to him to counter the evidence against p that he possesses. Deception of this sort requires that Holmes make available to Watson evidence sufficient to justify p in the presence of the evidence Watson possesses for and against p.

If what I have said is right, certain common intuitions about deception are most plausibly explained by supposing that deception, at least in one form, is itself an epistemic condition requiring that the deceiver be justified in believing not-p and make justification for p available to the deceived. I repeat my earlier proviso that it is no part of my conclusion that such epistemic deception is the only kind of deception, or that the epistemic use of "deception" is the only use. I do not wish to deny, for example, that if Holmes intentionally offers Watson insufficient evidence, knowing Watson's incompetence in such matters, and Watson believes p as a result, then it would be within bounds to call this deception. Certainly it would be correct to say in this case that Holmes *dupes* Watson into believing p. I would myself prefer to consider duplicity to be exclusive of deception, but I cannot see that anything important turns on how we assign the terms to the conditions. What matters is that there are theoretical reasons for marking off the conditions, reasons that provide a rationale for assigning deception in the way we do and thus for having the intuitions we have. I would now like to consider what these theoretical reasons might be.

We must ask what function the epistemic notion of deception plays in evaluation. A deceiver's intention in deception is to make the deceived believe a false proposition. Certainly we want to be able to refer to conditions that entail that this intention is fulfilled. But there are types of conditions which cut across the divide between fulfilled and unfulfilled intentions, and which we would expect to be a special focus of evaluation. These are types in which false belief normally results.[10]

I wish to propose that epistemic deception as earlier defined is one such type. It is plausible to suppose that if a person is justified in believing not-p and makes justification for believing p available to another, then false belief normally results. At least, this is plausible if we assume that justified beliefs are normally true. This assumption is strongly suggested by the view that a belief is justified only if it is highly probable, assuming that probability is tendency to be true; for it would be surprising if beliefs that tend to be true were not normally true. If justified beliefs are normally true, then a deceiver who is justified in believing not-p will normally make the deceived believe a proposition that is in fact false. The interest of the requirement that the deceiver make justification for p available is that such a condition normally results in a false belief that p.

There is good reason to expect that epistemic deception, as we have defined it, is evaluatively significant. Perhaps an ideal system of epistemic evaluation would succeed in discouraging individuals from attempting to produce false beliefs just when these beliefs are in fact false. Such a system would employ a notion of deception that entails the falsity of p.[11] And no doubt we do in fact have a use for such a falsity-entailing notion of deception: though our own errors in assigning truth-values to beliefs will guarantee that we fall short of the ideal, we will be correct often enough that we will generally discourage individuals from attempting to produce false beliefs in those instances in which the beliefs are indeed false. But this falsity-entailing mode of evaluation has two important limitations. One is that it can effectively curb attempts to produce a false belief that p only if evaluators believe not-p and are normally correct. It seems, however, that false beliefs are likely to succeed in inverse proportion to the dissemination of the evidence for and against p: targets of deception are more likely to be deceived when they do not have access to evidence from sources independent of the would-be deceiver. The more likely the success of attempted deception, the more valuable it is for evaluators to be able to criticize would-be deceivers effectively, but the less likely it is that evaluators will succeed in criticism or even criticize at all if they are limited to the falsity-entailing mode of evaluation. For they are less likely to believe not-p the less the extent of the dissemination of the evidence for and against p. And, since success in falsity-entailing criticism requires that the evidence available to the evaluators be sufficient for arriving at a correct belief as to whether p, the evaluators are less likely to succeed the less the dissemination of the evidence for and against p. If, on the other hand, evaluators employ the epistemic notion of deception outlined above, they need not believe p, and need not obtain evidence for and against p, but may proceed by comparing the justification belonging to the would-be deceiver with that transmitted to the deceived.

The other limitation of the falsity-entailing mode of evaluation is that it cannot be used to curb conditions that normally produce false beliefs in instances in which these conditions do not in fact result in false beliefs because the would-be deceiver falsely believes p. This is a limitation because we are concerned not just to prevent would-be deceivers from producing false belief but to discourage conditions that normally have this result. In short, it would seem that we need an evaluative notion that does not entail falsity but does entail conditions that normally produce false beliefs—such a notion as the epistemic notion of deception outlined above. I conclude that there is a use, and a significant one, for the epistemic notion of deception.

SELF-DECEPTION AND JUSTIFICATION:
SOME EPISTEMIC PERPLEXITIES

2. If there is genuine self-deception, properly so called, it must consist of deceiving oneself into believing some proposition. To apply the account just proposed, I deceive myself into believing p only if I am justified in believing not-p and I make available to myself justification for believing p. Of course, I also believe not-p, and I believe p. In this section I wish to treat a perplexity associated with this condition.

The perplexity arises in normal cases of self-deception, if these are like normal cases of deception. In normal cases of deception, the deceiver is justified in believing not-p and succeeds in making the deceived believe p by supplying evidence for p which comes to be possessed by the deceived and to justify p. Then we would expect that in a normal case of self-deception, I would not only make evidence for p available to myself but I would possess that evidence and thus be justified in believing that p.[12] Suppose I deceive myself into believing that I am not a glutton. I would normally be justified in believing that I am a glutton and also justified in believing the contrary. But how can I be justified in believing p and also be justified in believing not-p? If I am justified in believing that I am a glutton, the total evidence in my possession supports gluttony. But if I am justified in believing the contrary, then the total evidence in my possession supports the contrary. And the total evidence cannot both support gluttony and support the contrary. It would seem that normal self-deception is impossible.

The solution I wish to propose is to distinguish the possessed evidence relevant to the justification of the belief not-p from the possessed evidence relevant to the justification of the belief p. If the latter evidence need not contain all of the former evidence, then it is possible for the former to favor not-p while the latter favors p, and S can be justified in believing not-p while also being justified in believing p.

On what ground might we distinguish the possessed evidence relevant to the justification of the belief p from the possessed evidence relevant to the justification of the belief not-p? There are two sorts of possessed evidence relevant to the justification of a belief: reasons evidence—evidence concerning p which serves as reasons for believing p (on one view: evidence that is input for the process that forms the belief p); and background evidence against p whose possession diminishes the justification for p. Obviously the first sort of evidence will differ for the belief p and the belief not-p in a case of self-deception: the subject's reasons for believing p will not be the same as his reasons for believing not-p, since the former favor p and the latter not-p. The question is whether the remaining evidence relevant to the justification of the belief p, evidence against p, must include all the evidence that serves as reasons for believing not-p (e.g., because such evidence is possessed).

The answer is that background evidence against p does not count as relevant to the justification of p merely in virtue of possession by S. If S possesses evidence counter to p, but despite persistent care in considering the evidence for and against p, is psychologically unable to access some part of that counterevidence, then S's justification for believing p is not undermined by that possessed evidence. More broadly, whether possessed counterevidence is relevant to the justification of a belief depends on the epistemic cost of accessing the evidence in memory and considering its bearing on the belief.[13]

If it were an easy matter to access all the background evidence one has in one's possession and bring it to bear on the belief, then there would be no reason to restrict the relevant background evidence to a subset of what one possesses. But accessing evidence is no easy matter, and one often has to struggle even to come up with the very evidence that formed one's opinion. There is a point to limiting the subject's liability in justification to those pieces of possessed evidence it is epistemically cost-effective to take into account (or more cautiously: to pieces of a kind that it is normally cost-effective to take into account). We simply do not want to discourage forming a belief in the absence of costly consideration of possessed evidence. An account of justification that makes all possessed counterevidence relevant would do that.

If relevant possession is a function of the epistemic cost of accessing and bringing evidence to bear, then it varies with this cost and thus with the belief to be justified. In particular, if beliefs have different evidential histories, they will be causally related to the evidence in different ways, and this can make it more or less difficult to access and bring the evidence to bear on the beliefs. Imagine that the total evidence I possess favors the conclusion that I am a glutton, and I believe this as a consequence of possessing this evidence. In the meantime, I associate with other gluttons and come to find them repulsive, and eventually react to gluttony with disgust. Since my self-image does not tolerate disgusting vices, I have increasing incentive to shield myself from the possessed evidence that I am a glutton. My weighting of the evidence begins to shift toward the conclusion that I am not a glutton, and in the end I convince myself that I am not.[14]

The mere fact that I weight the evidence in a certain way can make it epistemically costly for me to access and bring the possessed evidence for gluttony to bear.[15] Psychological difficulties can exact epistemic costs and make certain actions epistemically unreasonable, even when these difficulties are artificial. We may say that there is no possessed evidence *relative to* the belief that I am not a glutton which undermines my justification for this belief, so I am justified. For all my possessed evidence is accessible at the time I form the belief; and later developments do not increase the accessible possessed evidence against p that can be brought to bear on the belief p. The evidence for gluttony in my possession, on the other hand, is no longer possessed relative to the belief that I am not a glutton. For that evidence does not enter into the causation of the belief—is indeed excluded from it; and the process of exclusion is one which makes it costly to bring the evidence to bear on the belief.

I foresee resistance to this defense of self-deception. It might be objected that psychological costs do not necessarily amount to epistemic costs. It might even be claimed that psychologically inaccessible evidence against p can nevertheless undermine justification for p in just the way that physically inaccessible evidence against p sometimes preempts knowledge that p. I want to agree that there is some force to this objection. There is something to the intuition that if I destroy a packet that I believe might contain (and, let us assume, does contain) evidence against my belief that I am not a glutton, then I fail to know that I am not a glutton, despite the fact that this evidence is "too costly" to retrieve—can no longer be retrieved. And similarly, there is some force to the intuition that if I suppress the possessed evidence that I am a glutton, my belief that I am not is not justified. The intuition seems especially strong if the suppression is intentional. Then the way that my belief that I am not a glutton comes to be justified involves some epistemically irresponsible actions, and any belief that results from epistemically irresponsible actions cannot be justified.

But I believe we can accommodate this intuition and still save self-deception. To do so, we need to examine a peculiarity of the notion of justification. It is easiest to see this peculiarity if we assume a particular view of justification—that a belief is justified only if it has an estimable history (e.g., is formed as a result of a sequence of inferences that preserve or tend to preserve truth). On this view, a belief can fail to be justified because some segment of its history falls short of the required standard (some inference in the sequence does not tend to preserve truth). On such a view, as several writers have noted, there may be reason to speak of a belief that fails before some point, as estimable from that point onward (if all inferences from a certain inference onward tend to preserve truth).[16] And there seems to be a sense in which a belief counts as justified if it is estimable from a certain point onward, even though, taking its whole history into account, we would not describe it as justified. If, from a certain point onward, the history of a belief is estimable, we may say that it is now justified as from that point. (This way of relativizing justification can be generalized to nonhistorical accounts of justification by relativizing not to times but to circumstances—e.g., on coherentism, one could be justified as from one subsystem of beliefs, but not from another.)

If we understand the factors that can make the history of a belief fail to be estimable as including whatever access the subject had to evidence for and against p, we may apply the idea of relativizing justification to the case of self-deception. We may say that my belief that I am not a glutton is currently justified as from a time t' after which I have had no access to the evidence for gluttony, but this belief is currently unjustified as from any earlier time t since at all these times I had access to the evidence for gluttony.[17]

The suggestion is then that common cases of self-deception require only that my belief p be justified as from some time. This suggestion would reconcile my being justified in believing that I am a glutton with my being justified in believing that I am not a glutton, even if my evidence for p relative to the first belief is not enough for current justification as from every time in the past. On the present proposal, possessing evidence for p relative to a belief p is sufficient to justify p as from any time at and after which the total possessed evidence against p is suppressed. The above objection, then, shows at most that self-deception is impossible if it requires that I be justified in believing p as from all times in the past. It does not show that self-deception is impossible if it requires only that I be justified as from some time in the past.[18]

There is some question whether in relativizing justification to times we have not lost a great deal. I imagine the persistent critic will object that justification as from a time is no genuine justification at all: if evidence against p can no longer be brought to bear because it has been irresponsibly suppressed, this cannot save the belief p from epistemic criticism. No doubt such a belief remains susceptible to epistemic criticism. But I think the right response is that there are different kinds of epistemic criticism, and there is a use for criticism as from a time. Insusceptibility to criticism as from some time may be quite enough for the evaluative purposes the epistemic notion of self-deception is designed to serve. If justification for p functions to generate the belief p, then it is quite enough to ensure that there is a time after which evidence against p cannot be brought to bear on the consideration of the belief p. The inaccessibility of such evidence will enhance the chance that the deceived will form the belief p. Of course, to say that the deceived is justified in believing p as from a time is not to say the subject is absolved from blame for believing p when the total evidence he possesses concerning p favors its contrary.[19] Still less is it to say that there is not something objectionable about the epistemic conditions the subject satisfies. The requirement of justification as from a time is admittedly a modest one, but not without its function in deception.

What Is Wrong with Deception?

3. In epistemic deception, and by instantiation self-deception, intending to produce a false belief normally results in a false belief. This is obviously one

thing wrong with epistemic deception and self-deception. There is, however, quite a bit more to the evaluative story. In identifying conditions in which intending to produce a false belief normally results in false belief, we locate conditions whose satisfaction is a good deal worse than their normal consequences. The reason lies in the fact that these conditions are epistemic conditions.

Very roughly, epistemic conditions not only produce true beliefs; they *function* to produce true beliefs. That is, minimally, their maintenance and promotion as conditions, and as desirable conditions, is a consequence of their success in producing true beliefs. (To assert this is, I grant, to embrace a version of sociological functionalism, but I believe such a view can be defended from recent criticisms.)[20] For example, the function of making justification available to oneself or others, as in the transmission or arrangement of evidence, is to produce true beliefs. But in deception, the intended result of making justification available is to produce false beliefs. In deception, then, making justification available to oneself or others tends to undermine its own function.

More exactly, Holmes is able to deceive Watson, and I am able to deceive myself, because there are epistemic norms to which people generally conform, which make it possible to make justification available to oneself or others. The function of these norms is to facilitate the formation of true beliefs. What is objectionable about deception and self-deception is that the conditions of deception rely on these norms to result normally in false beliefs, thus undermining their function.

I think it would be most helpful to begin by illustrating these points with the case of interpersonal deception involving the transmission of justification. I will then generalize to the arrangement of evidence.

The norms to which I refer govern activities within the social epistemic enterprise. Individuals are to a large degree isolated from the information in their environments and have access to that information only through the exercise of belief-forming processes involving the use of organs of perception, perceptual processing, and reasoning. Individuals do not generally have the ability to develop the use of these processes, or even to exercise the processes, on their own. Such processes require significant amounts of information for their development and exercise, and individuals depend on the collaboration of others to obtain this information. Furthermore, the exercise of these processes uses considerable cognitive resources. Since individuals have only limited resources, they are limited in the information they can acquire through most processes.[21]

The social epistemic enterprise surmounts these limitations by a system of information sharing.[22] With information sharing, individuals need no longer use considerable resources to acquire the information they need. They may access the same information using relatively minimal perceptual processing and reasoning by receiving information from other individuals. If an individual is to make significant progress in her individual epistemic enterprise, it seems she must take part in such information sharing.

We may see deception as undermining the norms that regulate the social epistemic enterprise.[23] Most prominent among these are two epistemic norms of transmission.

(1) The norm of *justificatory correspondence* consists of a pair of requirements: (a) individuals are to transmit justification for *p* only if they are justified in believing *p*, and (b) individuals are to transmit a denial of having justification for *p* (or a justification that entails a failure of justification for *p*) only if they are *not* justified in believing *p*. Deception violates both (a) and (b). Violations of (a) and (b) are not by themselves much to get concerned about. Though it is an offense to transmit justification for *p* if one is not justified in believing *p*, an individual can commit the offense merely by transmitting while failing to be justified in believing *p* (and similarly an individual can transmit the denial of having justification for *p* when he is justified in believing *p*, merely by transmitting while being justified in believing *p*). This is an offense because it will normally fail to result in a true belief, and so does tend to undermine (a) and (b). However, the offense of deception is more significant. It involves violating (a) and (b) at one and the same time: the deceiver transmits justification for *p* though not justified in believing *p*, and at the same time transmits the denial of having justification for not-*p* though justified in believing not-*p*. This is a worse transgression of justificatory correspondence than the preceding offenses because simultaneous violation of (a) and (b) will normally result in a false belief, rather than merely failing to result normally in a true belief. Deception has a greater tendency to undermine the function of (a) and (b).

(2) According to the norm of *justificatory trust,* individuals are to believe *p* if they receive justification for *p*. Deception tends to undermine conformity to justificatory trust in the sense that, when the deception is uncovered, the deceived (and perhaps others as well) gains some reason to be wary of conforming to the norm.[24]

Let us now modify this account of what is wrong with deception in transmission to cover other cases of deception. There is also the sort of case in which Holmes deceives Watson into believing *p* by arranging things so that Watson happens upon sufficient evidence for *p*—e.g., Holmes arranges for Watson to overhear a conversation in which the lottery officials falsely claim that there are only green tickets. Here there is no transmission of justification or authority, so we cannot explain what is wrong with such a deception by appeal to the above norms. Even so, what is wrong evidently parallels what is wrong with deception by transmission. By arranging things so that Watson happens upon sufficient evidence for *p*, Holmes interferes with the course Watson's inquiry would normally take and prevents him from acquiring sufficient evidence for not-p. Further, Holmes causes Watson to acquire justification for p when he (Holmes) is not justified in believing p. These actions violate a norm analogous to justificatory correspondence, and thus tend to undermine the social epistemic enterprise. More than this, they tend to undermine a norm analogous to justificatory trust, on which the subject is to assume no foul play in the arrangement of evidence. It is not always— perhaps not even very often—required that a person in possession of sufficient evidence for a proposition transmit justification or authority for that proposition to others, even in circumstances in which others can make very good use of that justification or authority. But the success of the social epistemic enterprise requires that subjects in possession of justification normally not arrange things so that others acquire evidence to the contrary. When Holmes arranges things so that Watson acquires misleading evidence, this action is in effect a substitute for the epistemically helpful action of transmitting justification he is in a position to perform. It is a substitute in the sense that the two actions cannot both have their intended effect. What the social epistemic enterprise requires is a norm to the effect that subjects in possession of justification for not-p not perform any action which in this sense substitutes for the transmission of justification or authority for not-p.

WHAT IS WRONG WITH SELF-DECEPTION?

4. Self-deception is much like the case in which Holmes arranges for Watson to overhear the lottery officials claiming there are only green tickets. To deceive myself into thinking I'm not a glutton, I might begin with an appreciation of the evidence of my gluttony, and propelled by a growing distaste for gluttony, I might arrange my thoughts and observations of my environment in such a way that I come to weight the evidence and to gather further evidence so as to favor my not being a glutton. I might systematically relax my attention when I recount the episodes in which I overconsume food, and I might make a special effort to recall those instances in which I have shown restraint in the consumption of food or abstained from eating when I very much wanted to eat. As a result of the habits I develop in thinking this way, I come to weight the evidence I possess in favor of my not being a glutton. In self-deception, one forms a certain set of mind consisting of habits of attention, rehearsal, recall, reconsideration, and consequently of weighting the evidence, and this set results in weighting the evidence in favor of the proposition p, even though the evidence one possesses is already weighted in favor of not-p.

I wish to propose, accordingly, that what is wrong with self-deception parallels what is wrong with interpersonal deception in which the deceiver arranges things so that the deceived happens upon evidence for p. On this proposal, we trace what is wrong with self-deception to the way that a set of mind violates and undermines norms that make the personal epistemic enterprise possible.[25]

As I emphasized earlier, arranging things so that a person acquires evidence for *p,* whether by transmission or other manipulation of the environment, functions in the social epistemic enterprise to supply information that the person would otherwise not acquire and to which in many cases she would otherwise not have access. People are naturally informationally isolated, and norms of arrangement and transmission are needed to bridge this isolation. Let us ask whether there is a similar informational isolation within individuals and whether it must be remedied by similar norms.

In describing the mind, information-processing psychology has recently attributed a central role to informational isolation, and some of these recent developments will help us here. These developments seem to show that there are systems of belief that are informationally isolated from one another, that the arrangement of evidence and consequently the set of mind that produces it is instrumental in managing this isolation, and that such management requires norms governing set of mind.

Let us note first, however, that the most far-reaching development concerning informational isolation will not help here. I refer to the emerging modular picture of the mind, on which the mind consists of a number of distinct faculties, each of which processes information belonging only to certain subject matters (domain-specificity) and remains to an extent informationally isolated from other faculties (i.e., incapable of accessing the contents or outputs of these faculties, at least in any manner controlled by the subject).[26] Unfortunately, the faculties for which the evidence for modularity is best—sensory input systems, linguistic systems, and emotional systems—are not suitable for our purposes. Such faculties do not generally form beliefs or take beliefs as inputs, as they would have to do to be governed by norms that restrict set of mind, since in deception at least, set of mind takes beliefs as inputs and yields beliefs as outputs. Rather, they take as inputs what Stich has called subdoxastic states, propositional attitudes that are inferentially isolated from other propositional attitudes and are not susceptible to modification in light of collateral information available from long-term memory; and they yield as outputs percepts, images, verbal expressions, subvocalizations, or emotions.[27] Moreover, modular systems count as genuine faculties; they are fixtures of the mind. Among other things, this entails that the chief problems of resource conservation to which they give rise are solved by cognitive strategies that are not sufficiently optional to fall under norms. Their limited ability to process information is handled by their restriction to inputs that are subdoxastic states, thus inferentially isolated, and to processing that is domain-specific, allowing domain-specific problem-solving strategies to be built into the system. Modular systems do not, then, conserve resources by conforming to norms that govern set of mind.

I do believe, however, that beliefs are informationally isolated, and that such isolation is managed by norms of set. Set functions in such a way as to reduce the amount of information an individual must process to reach a conclusion on a given topic. Individuals must constantly form beliefs on a great diversity of topics. One function of central processing is to form beliefs, given information from sensory, linguistic, and emotional systems, and from long-term memory. But central processing is limited in its informational load, both by its rate of processing and by the capacity of short-term and buffer memory. It can supply all the desired conclusions only if it is quite selective in the information it chooses to process. This inevitably involves ignoring much information that would be taken into account on any plausible epistemic conditions of processing with larger capacity. And it entails forgoing much processing that enhances reliability—e.g., persistent efforts at retrieval and recall, extended deliberation, and reconsideration. The beliefs that result from central processing belong to a belief system that is informationally isolated in the sense that, in the formation of these beliefs, only a small portion of the information it would be epistemically ideal to process can be processed.

Set, then, is an efficiency measure that enables the individual to arrive at more beliefs than would be possible without artificially imposed limitations on the information load of central processing. These limitations entail limitations on accuracy. To achieve accuracy that meets modest absolute standards the subject must take care to choose the information to be processed in a way that makes good use of the limited facilities. The strategies of set are determined by the desired balance of efficiency and accuracy. Efficiency and the load of information may differ markedly from one topic to the next, so different solutions to the problem of efficiency may be required for different topics, and set may be restricted to particular topics. But the development and maintenance of set itself uses cognitive resources. So efficiency is bound to involve repetition of the elements of set across topics.

The most intensely studied elements of set are heuristics in reasoning and problem solving, such as Amos Tversky and Daniel Kahneman's representativeness, availability, and anchoring heuristics.[28] Other frequently studied elements in set include primacy, recency, and halo effects, and the truncation of statistical reasoning (ignoring the base rate, violating the law of large numbers, etc.).[29] All these elements contribute to efficiency in reasoning at the expense of some accuracy. They are all pervasive features of reasoning, and they function to conserve resources without inflicting gross damage. This is not to say that the elements in set always embody an optimal balance between efficiency and accuracy.[30] But these elements could hardly be as pervasive as they are if they did not afford a level of achievement that is satisfactory overall for the conduct of human life. And it seems even safer to say that set itself is generally a desirable feature of cognition.

These observations lead to the conclusion that set performs a function in the personal epistemic enterprise somewhat (though obviously not closely)

analogous to that of the arrangement and transmission of evidence in the social epistemic enterprise. Just as individuals are informationally isolated by
the limited capacity of perceptual processing, systems of belief are informationally isolated by the limited capacity of central processing.[31] Just as the
arrangement and transmission of evidence functions to facilitate more conclusions within these limits, set functions to the same end. And set works in a
manner roughly similar to that of the arrangement and transmission of evidence: by relieving information load for each conclusion. It is appropriate to
speculate, then, that set will be governed by norms that ensure that it serves
its function, just as the norms of arrangement and transmission ensure that
these perform their analogous services.

Now, set falls short of the optimal performance of its function to the extent
that its operation entails a duplication of processing that consumes resources,
and it tends to undermine its function to the extent that this duplication leads
to false beliefs. Of course there is often a point to rehearsing, recalling, or
reconsidering evidence for and against p even after the subject has acquired
justification for not-p and come to believe not-p as a result. But such rehearsal,
recall, and reconsideration duplicate processing unless collateral information
warrants a second look at the evidence. And even if there is such collateral
information, if these activities result in the formation of a belief, other beliefs
must be revised accordingly. If the subject uses set to engage in these
activities without warrant, this diminishes the efficiency of central processing;
and if, having formed the belief, the subject fails to revise accordingly, he
tends to undermine the function of set.

The intrapersonal norm analogous to justificatory correspondence in interpersonal arrangement would constrain set in virtue of what the subject is
justified in believing. In particular, when S is already justified in a belief as
to whether p, the norm would rule out using set to reach conclusions as to
whether p merely by selective rehearsal, recall, and reconsideration of the
evidence, in the absence of collateral information warranting these activities.
This does not forbid set that ignores relevant information or deflects possessed
evidence favoring what one is justified in believing. Nor does it forbid using
set in a manner that leads to the denial of what one is justified in believing.
It seems to me doubtful that it is ever appropriate to use set to revise particular
beliefs under descriptions of their representational contents alone. (Of course
it *is* appropriate to use set to revise justified beliefs, but as described by their
evidential properties, not by their representational content alone.) But we
need not take a stand on this issue.

To turn now to the norm analogous to justificatory trust, we would require
forming beliefs in accordance with set. It is worth noting that this norm,
unlike justificatory trust, might not be one that can be satisfied in a piecemeal
fashion. Though certain kinds of set are themselves optional, it might not be
optional to form particular beliefs in accordance with a certain set once it is

formed. Though set is a habit, it might not have the optional character of most noncognitive habits. The proposed norm ensures efficiency by requiring us to form beliefs in accordance with set as a matter of course.

Self-deception, we can see, undermines these intrapersonal norms in much the way that deception undermines their interpersonal counterparts. It violates the analogue of justificatory correspondence: it involves using set to deny what one is justified in believing, by mere selective rehearsal, recall, and reconsideration, without warranting collateral information. And it tends to undermine the analogue of justificatory trust: when it is uncovered, an individual tends to become cautious about relying on set in forming beliefs. Of course, ceasing to rely on that particular set might be quite appropriate, just as ceasing to rely on a deceiver might be appropriate. But the discovery of self-deception in one instance of set might carry over to other instances and tend to erode reliance on set.

It goes without saying that I am not denying the personal epistemic enterprise can and does tolerate widespread self-deception. Self-deception is tolerable if its undermining effect on norms is attenuated or isolated. Particular instances of self-deception tend to undermine the norms to the extent that they tend to be discovered and to the extent that discovery tends to bring caution in relying on set in other cases. But self-deception on certain topics tends not to be discovered. For example, social propriety rules out extensive negative feedback from others concerning one's character traits and idiosyncrasies of personal behavior, so that one tends not to discover one's own self-deception on these matters, though of course one discovers that of others. (Compare this with job performance, which is normally submitted to routine formal evaluations: here gross self-deception does not often last long.) And the effect of discovering self-deception on certain topics tends to be isolated: beliefs about one's personal idiosyncrasies are inferentially isolated from most of what one believes; we tend to think of such beliefs as involving specialized set, and mistrust of this set tends not to carry over to other topics.

Our normative account of self-deception is a natural extension of the normative account of interpersonal deception. Despite the interpersonal character of the harm done by interpersonal deception, what is wrong with self-deception is in the end roughly like what is wrong with interpersonal deception.[32]

NOTES

1. I would like to thank Robert Audi, Hugh Chandler, Brian McLaughlin, and Alfred Mele for helpful comments.

2. Among those who have recognized the epistemic dimension of self-deception are Terence Panelhum, "Pleasure and Falsity," *American Philosophical Quarterly* 1 (1964):81–91; Frederick Siegler, "An Analysis of Self-Deception," *Nous* 2 (1968):

147–164; Robert Audi, "Epistemic Disavowals and Self-Deception," *Personalist* 57 (1976):378–385; Jeffrey Foss, "Rethinking Self-Deception," *American Philosophical Quarterly* 17 (1980):237–243; Kent Bach, "An Analysis of Self-Deception," *Philosophy and Phenomenological Research* 41 (1981):351–370; and Robert Audi, "Self-Deception, Action, and Will," *Erkenntnis* 18 (1982):133–158.

3. See for example Mary R. Haight, *A Study of Self-Deception* (Atlantic Highlands, N.J.: Humanities Press, 1980).

4. Equally, I ignore the issue whether self-deception requires intentionally deceiving oneself into believing *p*. For some troubling objections to an affirmative answer, see Alfred Mele, "Self-Deception," *Philosophical Quarterly* 33 (1983):365–377.

5. For reasons of expository convenience, I will slip without notice between various uses of "evidence": evidence as a piece of hardware whose existence provides reason to believe *p*, a fact that supplies reason to believe *p*, a proposition corresponding to such a reason, and a belief on the basis of which the subject may believe *p*. So far as I can see, the context easily identifies the use. I don't assume that propositional evidence must be true. The reader who thinks so may read occurrences of "evidence" as "would-be evidence." I don't wish to assume that a person can be justified only by possessing evidence. There may be perceptual reasons that cannot be given a propositional reading.

6. Note that the hypothesis that deception requires an absolute maximum (or perfect) degree of justification—only red tickets—offers no explanation of our willingness to attribute deception in the cases in which the degree of justification is less than an absolute maximum.

7. There is an alternative hypothesis that explains the variation in our enthusiasm for attributing deception in these cases: deception requires that the deceiver *know* that not-*p*. Such a hypothesis predicts that our enthusiasm for attributing deception will increase with the degree of justification for not-*p*. This is true even if justification requires only a high degree of justification, less than an absolute maximum. For knowledge requires more than justification, as the many recent discussions of Gettier cases, cases of failed knowledge, show. One possible explanation for our hesitation would assume that knowledge requires us to rule out relevant possibilities contrary to not-*p* (in this case, the possibility that a green ticket will be drawn), and whether a contrary possibility is relevant varies with its probability: then the lower the ratio of reds to greens, the more we tend to count the possibility that a green ticket will be drawn as relevant, and the less we are inclined to attribute knowledge. Note that the explanation here does not depend on the requirement that knowledge entails truth. We would do as well in our explanation if we said that deception requires knowledge*, a state that differs from knowledge only in not requiring truth.

8. Deception typically involves not only supplying sufficient evidence for *p* but arranging things so that the counterevidence that is available to *S* is unavailable to *x*.

9. It might be urged that there is another sort of problem with this reading of our intuitions, having to do not with how Watson receives the evidence but with how Holmes transmits it. We must imagine, in the last cases in the sequence, that though Holmes believes Watson is convinced only by sufficient evidence, Holmes nevertheless transmits insufficient evidence. But we can scarcely imagine this unless we assume that Holmes produced such evidence only through inadvertence or incompetence in judging which evidence is sufficient. And it might be claimed, again, that

the source of our hesitation to attribute deception is this breakdown before transmission, rather than the failure to transmit sufficient evidence itself. Whatever the merits of this claim, it is clear that we cannot argue for it on the same ground as the earlier argument, for explaining the failure of deception by appeal to a breakdown in reception would entail that Holmes is not the prime cause of Watson's belief that p. I do not think the analogous premise is true here: even if Holmes is inadvertent or incompetent in producing evidence, he is still the prime cause of Watson's belief. I am inclined to doubt that there is any reason to assign our hesitation to the breakdown before transmission rather than the failure to transmit sufficient evidence. In any case, such a breakdown implies a failure to transmit sufficient evidence (or at least the likelihood of such a failure), so even if it is the correct explanation, we may still conclude that transmitting sufficient evidence (or at least the likelihood of doing so) is necessary for Holmes to deceive Watson in the particular way he tries.

10. We might want instead to speak of the types in which false belief is objectively *likely* to result.

11. It is worth noting that there are two reasons to resist requiring that deception entails the falsity of p. One is that we seem to be able to assign deception in cases in which the truth or falsity of p will never be known. If Holmes mistakenly believes that Goldbach's conjecture has been proved, and he causes Watson to believe the negation of Goldbach's conjecture, then there is some temptation to say that he deceives Watson even if it turns out that Goldbach's conjecture is false, so long as the conjecture will never be proved. A second reason for resisting the requirement is that it has a curious consequence: it implies that S cannot deceive x into believing that x is deceived into believing something. For doing so would require that it is false that x is deceived into believing something; but then S could not deceive x into believing something, contrary to what is required. To my ears this consequence sounds harsh.

12. Many of the cases that pass for self-deception do not involve the subject's actual possession of the evidence for not-p: there is evidence for not-p in the subject's environment but the subject chooses not to seek or acquire such evidence. In such cases the subject is not justified in believing not-p. I do not propose to include these cases under the heading "self-deception," but even if they are not counted as cases of self-deception, they are so similar that they deserve to be called *self-paradeception*. If self-paradeception requires the belief that not-p, then it suffers from the same psychological perplexities as self-deception. In any case, it is epistemically perplexing in ways akin to those I discuss below.

13. See Keith Lehrer, *Knowledge* (Oxford: Oxford Univ. Press, 1974), for a discussion of epistemic cost.

14. It may be asked how it is possible for me to change my weighting of the evidence and still be justified in believing not-p. The answer is that my weighting does not change *simpliciter*, but only relative to the belief that p; I revert to my old weighting when considering the belief that not-p. I will pass on numerous questions here: whether self-deception requires that I value certain evidence more highly and not merely that I count it more highly in determining what to believe; whether self-deception involves weighting certain evidence less or merely ignoring it; and whether self-deception necessarily involves having inconsistent beliefs about proper weights.

15. Note that the fact that in self-deception the belief not-p is itself deeply suppressed is not a problem here. It is true that it is costly to bring possessed evidence for and against p to bear on a suppressed belief: this may even require extraordinary techniques like psychotherapy and hypnosis. But the belief that not-p may remain justified when suppressed in virtue of the evidence that provides the subject's reasons for believing not-p: reasons justify even when they cannot be brought to bear. (Does evidence counter to not-p count against the justification of the suppressed belief? One way to make it do so is to introduce counterfactual cost: counterevidence counts against the belief if, were the belief to be considered, the counterevidence would not be costly to access and bring to bear.)

16. See Alvin Goldman, "What Is Justified Belief?" in *Justification and Knowledge,* ed. George Pappas (Dordrecht: Reidel, 1979), pp. 1–23; and Hilary Kornblith, "Justification and Responsible Belief," *Philosophical Review* 92 (1983):33–48. The "as from" terminology is Kornblith's.

17. My belief that I am a glutton is of course justified as from every time because the reasons for it remain reasons and the counterevidence does not increase.

18. It might be objected that my defense of the possibility of self-deception rests on the assumption that self-deception involves a temporal succession of justification: first I am justified in believing not-p, then I am justified in believing p. But of course there need be no succession. If I ensure that from the very outset I do not possess evidence against p relative to the belief p, then I am justified in believing p from the start. In this case, I am (at each time) justified in believing p as from every time in the past. For then there is no time as from which I am not justified in believing p. I think, though, that this merely calls for a slightly different defense, relativizing justification to a set of circumstances rather than a time. In the present case, I am currently justified as from all times in the past, but I am not justified as from the set of circumstances which includes the causes of my not being able to consider the evidence against p.

19. But I do not assume that all instances of self-deception involve epistemically blameworthy or irresponsible behavior. In some instances the subject may not be able to help intending to produce a false belief, or may be able to help it but only at considerable epistemic cost.

20. For an extended critique of sociological functionalism, see Jon Elster, *Ulysses and the Sirens* (Cambridge: Cambridge Univ. Press, 1979). I believe the tools for a proper defense are to be found in Robert Cummins, *The Nature of Psychological Explanation* (Cambridge, Mass.: MIT Press [Bradford Books], 1983).

21. For interesting discussion of these matters see C. A. J. Coady, "Testimony and Observation," *American Philosophical Quarterly* 10 (1973):149–155.

22. For a discussion of the conditions in which such information sharing is possible, see Michael Welbourne, "The Community of Knowledge," *Philosophical Quarterly* 31 (1981):302–314. See also Keith Lehrer and Carl Wagner, *Rational Consensus in Science and Society* (Dordrecht: Reidel, 1981). I discuss related matters in "Justification, Sociality, and Autonomy," *Synthese* 73 (1987):43–85.

23. See David Lewis, "Language and Languages," Minnesota Studies in the Philosophy of Science, Vol. VII, *Language, Mind and Knowledge,* ed. Keith Gunderson (Minneapolis: Univ. of Minnesota Press, 1975), for an argument that similar norms must be current in a population if it is to count as speaking a language.

24. Different kinds of deception undermine the norms of transmission to different degrees, depending on how frequently they are discovered. E.g., normally, the more justification the deceiver has for believing not-p, the more evidence against p is available to the deceived, and the more likely the deceived is to acquire this evidence and have his justification for believing p overturned. In such circumstances, discovery of the deception is correspondingly more likely. (Similar remarks may be made about deception in which the deceiver knows not-p, or in which p is false.) Let it also be noted that varying the degrees of transmitted justification for p has an ambiguous effect on the extent to which deception undermines the norms of transmission. Increasing the transmitted justification of p will decrease the likelihood that available counterevidence will overturn the justification for p; but by the same token, in those instances in which justification is overturned, the reversal will involve greater cognitive dissonance, and we can expect the deceived to be less trusting in future cases. Decreasing the transmitted justification for p will increase the likelihood that available counterevidence will overturn the justification for p, but decrease cognitive dissonance in reversal, so that the effect on trust is less powerful, though more common.

25. It is worth noting that what is wrong with self-deception in a wide range of cases is closely analogous to what is wrong with interpersonal deception involving the transmission of justification or authority. There are norms that govern the intrapersonal transmission of authority. In certain respects memory involves the transmission of authority from a time t at which we possess evidence for the belief not-p to a later time t' by which we have lost the evidence we earlier possessed. We are justified at the later time by something that might be called authority through memory. We evaluate ourselves as justified in such instances because we have fairly reliable ways of identifying current beliefs for which we once possessed evidence, or at any rate fairly reliable confidence in such beliefs, even though we no longer possess evidence. And if we are fairly reliable in this, such beliefs will normally be true. And there is good reason not to insist that justification requires the retention of evidence: we don't have the capacity to remember evidence for all of the beliefs for which we have good use. Thus, there are norms designed to protect the transmission of authority through memory, and these norms parallel the norms of interpersonal transmission. Self-deception involving the transmission of authority through memory violates these norms.

26. For a vigorous defense of modularity, see Jerry Fodor, *The Modularity of Mind* (Cambridge, Mass.: MIT Press, 1983).

27. Stephen Stich, "Beliefs and Subdoxastic States," *Philosophy of Science* 45 (1978):499–518.

28. See the articles by Tversky and Kahneman in *Judgement Under Uncertainty: Heuristics and Biases,* ed. Daniel Kahneman, Paul Slovic, and Amos Tversky (Cambridge: Cambridge Univ. Press, 1982).

29. For empirical evidence for these heuristics, see Richard Nisbett and Lee Ross, *Human Inference: Strategies and Shortcomings of Social Judgment* (Englewood Cliffs, N.J.: Prentice-Hall, 1980).

30. Psychologists often speak of a trade-off between speed and accuracy in belief formation. (For an excellent discussion, see Robert G. Pachella, "The Interpretation of Reaction Time in Information-Processing Research," in *Human Information Processing: Tutorials in Performance and Cognition,* ed. Barry H. Kantowitz [Hillsdale, N.J.: Lawrence Erlbaum, 1974], pp. 41–82.) But speed is relevant here only to the

extent that it bears on informational load. And there are informational limitations on central processing that are independent of speed: no matter how long one takes, one still cannot take all relevant information into account because there are too many factors to juggle. These limitations seem to be absolute, despite the phenomenon of chunking in short-term memory, which enables subjects to store increasing quantities of information (measured in bits) in the face of syntactical limitations.

31. The assumption of an informationally limited central processor is a key assumption of information-processing psychology. The case for such a processor is overwhelming. See Fodor for a sketch of the argument. For some resistance to the view, see Howard Gardner, *Frames of Mind* (New York: Basic Books, 1984).

32. I should respond to some apparent difficulties. It might be asked whether the norms to which I appeal here do not undermine their own point in the case of self-deception. If these norms function to make accurate belief-formation less costly, then similar norms can function to make it less costly to revise beliefs. But then beliefs that are self-deceived will not be costly to revise, and the damage done will not be great, contrary to our normative account. This incorrectly assumes, however, that the cost referred to in the account of justification is the same as that referred to in the normative account. The former cost is the cost of accessing the counterevidence; the latter is that of forming beliefs without set. The latter cost could be high even though the former is low.

It might also be asked whether the present explanation of what is wrong with self-deception is consistent with our earlier argument that self-deception is possible. Our normative account assumes that conformity to the norms governing set is voluntary—that is, access to counterevidence is voluntary. Yet self-deception is possible on our account only if justification is relative to a time in virtue of the fact that we do not have the option of accessing just any counterevidence. Our account of justification seems to require that counterevidence be rendered impossible to access, but our normative account seems to require that it be possible to access. But there is no genuine inconsistency here. First, our normative account assumes only that set is voluntary; it does not follow that accessing counterevidence concealed by set is voluntary once set is formed. Second, justification requires only that counterevidence be too costly to access, but the normative account agrees that counterevidence is rendered too costly when it is defeated by set.

Part III

THE PSYCHOLOGY OF
SELF-DECEPTION

9

SELF-DECEPTION AND BAD FAITH

Allen W. Wood

The Problem of Self-Deception

1. Self-deception is so undeniable a fact of human life that if anyone tried to deny its existence, the proper response would be to accuse this person of it. But Jean-Paul Sartre begins his famous discussion of bad faith in *Being and Nothingness* by raising a problem about how self-deception is possible.[1] In general, to lie or deceive someone is not simply to tell that person something false or to create a false belief in that person. In order to lie or deceive someone, I must myself disbelieve what I am telling that person, or disbelieve what I am causing the other to believe—typically, I must *know* that it is false. Accordingly, Sartre says, when I deceive or lie to myself,

> I must as deceiver know the truth that is masked for me as the one deceived. Better yet, I must know that truth very precisely, in order to hide it from myself the more carefully—and this not at two different moments of temporality, which would permit us to reestablish a semblance of duality, but in the unitary structure of one and the same project. (BN 87–88/89)

This means, however, that I must believe something as victim of the lie which as liar I disbelieve. It now looks as if self-deception cannot occur; a self-deceiver must simultaneously believe and disbelieve the same proposition, and this looks like a contradiction.

One straightforward way out of the contradiction immediately presents itself. For in general it is not a contradiction to say that a thing simultaneously has two contradictory properties, if one says that it has them in two different respects. I may be both hot and cold at the same time, that is, hot in my forehead and cold in my feet; a piece of prose may be good and bad at the same time, that is, good in the ideas it expresses, but bad in its grammar, spelling, and punctuation. Accordingly, one way out of the problem about self-deception is to say that when I believe and disbelieve the same proposition, I do so in two different respects. But not just any distinction of this kind will do, because any system of beliefs involving the simultaneous belief and disbelief in the same proposition will be inherently unstable in a way that the state of self-deception is not inherently unstable. A stable condition of self-deception seems to require that there be in a single person two distinct subsystems of belief, one of which involves the belief in a proposition and the other disbelief in it. Self-deception thus seems to require us to hypothesize what we may call a "divided mind."

The commonest way to do this is to distinguish a subsystem of *conscious* beliefs from a subsystem of *unconscious* beliefs. When I deceive myself into believing that *p,* then what happens is that I consciously believe that *p,* but unconsciously I disbelieve *p* (or know *p* to be false). In self-deception my unconscious mind is aware of the falsity of what my conscious mind believes, and it hides this falsity from my conscious mind. Freud, for example, holds that certain mental processes are kept out of our conscious mind by unconscious mechanisms of "repression." Sartre, however, rejects this solution to the problem he raises, along with the whole concept of unconscious mental processes. Because of this, he is committed to accounting for self-deception as an entirely *conscious* process. And the special Sartrian concept of "bad faith" (*mauvaise foi*) refers to this wholly conscious type of self-deception.

Sartre's discussion of bad faith in *Being and Nothingness* is designed to serve the larger ends of the book, and so the concept of bad faith is developed in paradoxical terms, as part of his ontology of consciousness or the "for itself," whose being is "to be what it is not and not to be what it is." This makes it less than wholly clear what bad faith is, or how Sartre thinks he has solved his problem about self-deception.

In § 2 of this essay we will critically examine Sartre's reasons for rejecting the Freudian appeal to the unconscious in solving the problem of bad faith. In § 3 we will look briefly at Sartre's famous description of several examples of self-deception or bad faith, and see how much his solution to his problem is illuminated by his attempt to relate it to his theory of human freedom. In §§ 4–5 we will try to develop Sartre's concept of bad faith and see how it is supposed to solve the problem of self-deception. And in § 6 we will decide how successful the solution is.

UNCONSCIOUS DECEPTION

2. The Freudian theory of repression is a great deal more than a solution to Sartre's problem about self-deception, and it is not clear that Sartre has correctly interpreted Freud's account of the mechanisms by which repression works. But beyond a brief consideration of Freud's reasons for believing in unconscious mental processes, it will suffice for our purposes simply to take up the Freudian solution to Sartre's problem in the (perhaps caricatured) form in which Sartre presents it. For even in this form we will see that it easily withstands Sartre's objections.

As Sartre depicts it, the Freudian solution is this: My mind includes not only an ego or consciousness, but also an id, a set of instincts and drives. These drives are originally unconscious, but they display themselves to my consciousness in the form of "conscious symbols," such as desires and impulses, which take the form of "real psychic facts" (BN 88–89/90–91). At the "border" between the conscious mind and the unconscious mind there is a part of me which acts as a "censor," (conceived, at least half-seriously, as a sort of psychic customs office or passport control). The censor decides which desires are to be permitted entry into consciousness, and it also determines the form in which my instincts appear as facts of consciousness (BN 88–90/91–93). The censor has cognitive access to the instincts, it knows the real truth about them; it also has access to the psychic facts as they exist for consciousness, and is capable of selecting these on the basis of the conscious states (e.g., beliefs, emotions) that will result from them. On this model, when we deceive ourselves, what happens is that our consciousness forms a belief that the censor has brought about in it, and that the censor knows to be false. In self-deception, I as deceiver am the censor, while as victim of the deception I am ego or consciousness. The ego and the censor represent belief systems divided from each other, and this is what makes self-deception possible.

There are many things in this picture which Sartre cannot accept. He scorns the "mythology" of physiologically determined instincts and drives (BN 91/93; cf. BN 707/784). He also rejects the whole conception of "psychic givens" (BN 17/11), and in particular rejects the idea that any conative or motivational states, however "basic," can be given to us as brute psychic facts independent of our choices (BN 516–519/567–569). Sartre's attack on the Freudian solution to his problem, however, is directed at difficulties that it allegedly incurs in its account of the censor's activities.

"The censor, in order to apply its activity with discernment, must know what it is repressing. If we renounce in fact all those metaphors that represent repression as an interaction of blind forces, we are forced to admit that the censor must *choose*, and in order to choose, it must *represent itself*" (BN 91/93). If it is to carry out its activities, Sartre alleges, the censor must have a second-order knowledge both of the activities themselves and of the information it uses in acting. Not only must it know the truth about the drives it is repressing but it must also represent itself as knowing, it must know that it knows; not only must it select which drives are to become conscious and choose the form in which these drives are to appear in consciousness but it must also represent itself as choosing, it must know that it is making these choices.

Why does Sartre think the Freudian must grant the censor this second-order knowledge?[2] Sartre himself seems to think that all knowing and choosing involve second-order knowledge of themselves (BN 18/12),[3] but a Freudian need not agree. Sartre seems on the right track in suggesting that the censor needs such knowledge "in order to apply its activity with discernment," but to clinch his case this suggestion would have to be spelled out in more detail.

Sartre's next step is to claim that the second-order knowledge that the censor must have must be *conscious* knowledge, on the ground that "all knowing is consciousness of knowing" (BN 91/93). From this he argues that the censor's knowledge must belong to the same consciousness as the false beliefs the censor is creating. Hence the censor's consciousness can only be "consciousness (of) the tendency to repress, but precisely *in order not to be conscious of it*." (BN 91–92/94). But that is only to say that the *censor*, entirely on the conscious level, is deceiving itself. The problem about self-deception has returned in its original form.

This argument, however, assumes both that the censor must have second-order knowledge of its activities and that this second-order knowledge must be *conscious*. But the Freudian has been given no reason for accepting these assumptions, and especially the second. One reason that might be given is to be found in an explication of the distinction between the conscious and the unconscious given by Colin McGinn.[4] For McGinn, not to be conscious that you believe *p* is simply not to have the second-order knowledge that you believe *p*. From this it would follow that if the censor has the second-order knowledge of its knowledge or its activities, then it is *eo ipso* conscious of them. But surely all this shows is that McGinn's way of drawing the distinction between the conscious and the unconscious is defective. For why could there not be unconscious mental processes involving second-order knowledge of themselves which is also unconscious? If we suppose that I have second-order knowledge of a mental state, that should not by itself decide one way or the other whether either the state or the knowledge of it is conscious.

Another argument Sartre might use is this: If the explanation for the repression or disguising of my knowledge that *p* requires the act of a censor, then if my knowledge of that act is also supposed to be repressed or disguised (rendered unconscious), this must in turn require the act of a second censor. And if the act of this second censor is to be rendered unconscious this will require yet another act of censorship, and so on. Either we face a vicious regress or else we are forced at some point to imagine an act of censorship performed consciously. But this argument overlooks the obvious possibility that the censor's act might be *self*-repressing. (If it were not, it is hard to see how it could accomplish its aim.) We postulate a "censor" (that is, a subsystem of beliefs and mental activities independent of my consciousness) in order to explain how I can believe something consciously which I at the same time disbelieve, and whose falsity I hide from myself. But there is no need to postulate a third subsystem to explain the censor's keeping its knowledge and activity out of consciousness, because there is no incoherence in the censor's system of mental activity. Hence there is no need for the regress to begin.

Of course the Freudian can grant the obvious fact that in actual cases of self-deception there is nearly always some awareness of the processes through which the deception is maintained. For instance, in the conversation between Ivan Karamazov and Smerdyakov before Ivan's departure for Moscow, the two men make a compact: if Ivan announces the intention to go to Tchermashnya, then Smerdyakov will murder their father, Fyodor Pavlovich, while Ivan is away. Throughout the conversation, and even while he is agreeing to the compact, Ivan prevents himself from becoming consciously aware of its terms, or even of its existence. He does this largely through a single device: when there is a danger that Ivan will become consciously aware of what Smerdyakov is proposing, Ivan loses his temper and demands that Smerdyakov stop insinuating and state clearly and explicitly what he means.[5] Ivan is clearly conscious of his own anger, impatience, and his conscious desire that everything between Smerdyakov and himself should be kept wholly explicit and aboveboard. Since these are in fact the devices by which Ivan prevents the compact from entering his consciousness, Ivan is in a sense conscious of what the "censor" in him is doing.

But this is not the kind of consciousness of the censor's acts which Sartre's argument requires Ivan to have. For Ivan is not conscious of these desires and emotions *as* devices for keeping his knowledge of the murder compact out of his consciousness—indeed, they seem to Ivan to be no more than expressions of his fervent desire that there should be nothing at all unstated or merely implied in his relations with Smerdyakov, and hence Ivan's awareness of the devices by which he deceives himself only contributes further to the deception. What Sartre thinks the Freudian must concede is that the self-deceiver is consciously aware of the censor's acts of repression precisely *as acts of repression,* as the keeping out of consciousness of what is to be repressed. But why should Sartre think that the Freudian must concede this?

The answer to this question, I am afraid, is disappointingly simple and, from the standpoint of Sartre's argument, flatly question begging. Sartre thinks that the censor's mental activity must be conscious because he holds as a dogma that *all* mental activity must be conscious. Sartre's frequent references to the "transparency of consciousness" are really assertions that the mental is reducible to the conscious. For Sartre, there can be no unconscious knowledge at all (BN 91/93), no unconscious believing (BN 117–118/121–122), no unconscious intending (BN 20/14). The dogma that the mental is reducible to the conscious belongs to the phenomenologist's peculiar interpretation of the project of founding everything on what is self-evident, and then taking for granted (what is far from self-evident) that mental processes, both their occurrence and their nature, are something self-evident, or at least something that can be made self-evident by the right epistemic techniques.

As one sympathetic interpreter describes it, Sartre's rejection of the Freudian unconscious is due to Sartre's "mistrust of the hypothetical," and especially of scientific hypotheses.[6] In effect, Sartre simply accepts Descartes' definition of "thought" (his inclusive term for mental) as "everything which we are aware of as happening within us in so far as we have awareness of it."[7]

Strictly speaking, this definition does not even allow for latent or dispositional mental states, for dispositional knowledge, belief, desire, and so on. If Descartes can account for such dispositional mental states at all, it must be by saying that they are not mental but *bodily* states (perhaps states of my brain which dispose my mind to have certain occurrent thoughts at certain times). It is not clear that even this account of dispositional mental states would be open to Sartre, since he entertains a radical skepticism about dispositions generally, derived partly from Hume and partly from Hegel (BN 33–34/29, 139–142/147–150). Descartes himself does not adhere consistently to his definition of the mental, since he believes in innate ideas, which are plainly supposed to be dispositional states, and states of the mind rather than the body.[8]

A more moderate version of the Cartesian view of mind would hold that all mental states are either states of consciousness or else dispositions to have states of consciousness. Freud is well aware of this view as a source of "philosophical" objections to his concept of unconscious mental activity, to which he responds frequently and thoughtfully, not without condescension. Freud points out that we do not hesitate to ascribe mental states (and occurrent states, not merely dispositional ones) to other people on the basis of their behavior, despite the fact that we ourselves are not conscious of these states. The same principle, however, he says, might be applied to ourselves: on the basis of our own behavior, and in the same way we infer mental states from the behavior of others, we might ascribe to ourselves mental states of which we are not conscious.[9] Such unconscious mental states, Freud argues, turn out to be reasonable hypotheses, even necessary ones, which are required in certain cases to fill in the gaps between conscious states.[10] The states whose existence we may infer in this way, he says, are not merely dispositions to conscious states (these dispositions Freud calls "preconscious" states) but themselves occurrent or "active" states, some of which remain unconscious however strongly active they may be in their influence on our behavior.[11]

Freud is convinced that the web of unconscious mental states which is required to explain people's behavior is sufficiently large and complex that it makes sense to regard unconsciousness as "a regular and inevitable phase in the processes constituting our mental activity; every mental act begins as an unconscious one, and it may remain so or go on developing into consciousness, according as it meets with resistance or not"; far from its being true that consciousness is the hallmark of the mental, Freud maintains that "what is mental is in itself unconscious."[12]

Freud's concept of the mental harmonizes well with contemporary functionalist accounts of mind, which treat categories of mental events and activities as states of an organism, distinguished by the functional role they play in the physical mechanisms through which the organism processes its informational input and generates its behavioral output. Mental states need not be conscious in order to perform their functions; indeed, sometimes they can perform them better if they remain unconscious. When this is so, a theory of the organism's mental functioning ought to be able to explain why. And this is what Freudian psychology tries to do.

Freud acknowledges that this ambitious role for unconscious states in people's mental lives must be established by a complex set of inferences, each of which must be tested for its soundness;[13] and many people are rightly skeptical of some of Freud's claims about our unconscious memories, wishes, and decisions. But surely there is no good reason in principle why the workings of our minds might not be explained better by a theory attributing unconscious mental states to us than by one limiting itself to conscious mental states. For example, the hypothesis of an unconscious subsystem of mental activities acting on our conscious beliefs provides one plausible way of solving Sartre's problem about self-deception and explaining how self-deception is possible. Whether self-deception works in some such way in real life is an empirical question. There is nothing either original or persuasive in Sartre's attempt to reject the Freudian unconscious a priori on philosophical grounds.

FACTICITY AND TRANSCENDENCE

3. Once he has dismissed the Freudian solution to his problem, Sartre makes a new start by describing several cases in which he thinks we will recognize self-deceptive conduct at work. The examples are well known, even famous. A woman ignores the sexual overtones of her escort's conduct because she does not want to "break the troubled and unstable harmony that makes for the charm of the hour" (BN 95/97). She seems not to notice when he takes her hand, because at that moment she happens to be pure intellect, divorced from her body. Then there is the waiter in the café who plays at being a waiter in a café in order to persuade himself that he is nothing more than that. There is the homosexual who refuses to acknowledge that he is a pederast, insisting that his case is "different"; and, finally, there is his friend, the champion of sincerity, who tries to get him to admit that he is a pederast and no more than that (BN 94–108/96–112). Sartre describes these examples so skillfully and vividly that it is easy to overlook the fact that they do not tell us much about self-deception. They neither provide a clear solution to Sartre's problem about self-deception nor support his claim that self-deception must be a wholly conscious phenomenon. In fact, they are little more than a series of illustrations of Sartre's own radical and idiosyncratic views about human freedom. What they say about self-deception is almost incidental.

In each case, Sartre claims, the self-deceptive behavior turns on a distinction between "facticity" and "transcendence": between the brute givens of my situation (my body, my occupation, my past) and the total freedom in which I confront these givens as someone who must *be* the person given through them and yet must be that person freely, unconstrained in any way by them. The self-deceivers in these examples are all depicted as exploiting this inevitable ambiguity in the nature of free selfhood. The woman "transcends" her body and the homosexual his past behavior. Both have a truth on their side when they dissociate themselves from their "facticity," but each misinterprets this truth so that it turns into a falsehood. The woman uses her freedom in relation to her body as an excuse for disavowing responsibility for the decision she must make about what she will do with her body; the homosexual uses his freedom in the face of his past to disavow the only plausible interpretation of that past. On the other side, the waiter and the champion of sincerity recognize that one cannot flee from one's facticity, that one must *be* that facticity. Yet they interpret this truth in such a way as to deny our total freedom in the face of facticity. The waiter wants to become nothing more than the social role in which he has cast himself (and has been cast by others); the champion of sincerity wants his friend not only to admit the pattern represented by his past behavior but also to identify himself wholly with this past, disavowing his freedom in the face of the past.

There seem to be significant philosophical issues between Sartre and the waiter or the champion of sincerity, and it is not self-evident that Sartre is right about these issues. The waiter behaves as he does because he wants to *realize* his condition (BN 99/102), that is, to actualize himself, to live a life in a way which is consonant with his nature. Of course Sartre thinks that human freedom precludes having a "nature" in this sense; and it is easy to make fun of the aspiration to actualize one's nature when that nature is identified with being a waiter in a café. But it is not quite so easy to discredit a theory of self-actualization as it is put forward by Aristotle or Aquinas, or even by F. H. Bradley or T. H. Green. Likewise, it is far from self-evident that to be a homosexual never means anything more than to have a certain past, in the face of which we are always totally free to reconstitute our desires through a radically new choice of ourselves. But even if Sartre were right on the philosophical issues, that would not necessarily show that those who disagree with him are victims of self-deception.[14]

What is worse than this, however, is that Sartre's philosophically loaded discussion of his examples contributes nothing at all to the solution of his original problem about self-deception. The common pattern in the examples is that the self-deceiver misinterprets a truth drawn from the Sartrian ontology of consciousness.[15] What he or she believes is true taken in one sense, but not in the sense in which he or she takes it. ("I am not my past" is true, but not in the way in which the homosexual interprets it; "I am my past" is true, but not in the way in which the champion of sincerity interprets it; and likewise for the other examples.)

Mistakes of this kind, however, do not necessarily involve self-deception at all—in philosophy we run across them all the time. Self-deception occurs in such a case only if I assent to a statement that I *know* I am interpreting in a false sense while nevertheless *believing* the statement on that interpretation. But if this is what has happened, then we simply have one more kind of case—and not a distinctive, or a fundamental, or even an especially illuminating kind—in which an individual believes a proposition while disbelieving it (knowing it to be false). It contributes nothing to resolving Sartre's problem about self-deception that the subject matter of the simultaneous belief and disbelief is the dubious Sartrian ontology of free selfhood.

Sartre identifies "the unity we find in the different aspects of bad faith" as "a certain art of forming contradictory concepts, which is to say, concepts that unite in themselves an idea and the negation of that idea. The basic concept thus engendered utilizes the double property of human being, that of being a *facticity* and a *transcendence*" (BN 95/98). Does Sartre really expect us to believe that every case of self-deception involves attributing a contradictory concept to something? And does he think that all contradictory concepts derive from the facticity-transcendence relation? Neither claim has much plausibility, and neither receives any real defense from Sartre. But leaving that aside, my attribution of a contradictory concept to something counts as a case of self-deception only if I believe the attribution while at the same time knowing that the concept is contradictory and that a proposition ascribing a contradictory concept to something must be false—that is, only if I believe the self-contradictory proposition and simultaneously disbelieve it (because I realize it is self-contradictory). Once again, even if it is correct that all self-deception concerns the facticity-transcendence relation, we are still no closer to a solution of Sartre's problem about self-deception.

THE PROJECT OF BELIEVING

4. Sartre's problem about self-deception arises because it seems that in order to deceive myself I must simultaneously believe and disbelieve the same proposition at the same time, and this looks like a contradiction. But it looks like a contradiction because it looks as if believing *p* entails not disbelieving *p* and vice versa. I will suggest that Sartre's own solution, presented briefly in the section entitled "The 'Faith' of Bad Faith," operates by questioning this assumption.

How might we argue that there is no contradiction in saying that I simultaneously (and consciously) believe and disbelieve the same proposition? We might say that it is not a contradiction for me to believe and disbelieve *p*, just as it is not a contradiction for me simultaneously to want X and to want not-X. When Don Giovanni asks Zerlina to give him her hand, Zerlina reports her mental state as "*Vorrei e non vorrei.*" This would be a self-contradictory report if it is taken to mean: "I want to give you my hand and it is false that I want to give you my hand." But it is not self-contradictory if what it says is: "I want to give you my hand and I want not to give you my hand." What Zerlina is reporting is a conflict between two wants. The two things she wants cannot both occur at the same time (she cannot at the same time both give Don Giovanni her hand and not give Don Giovanni her hand), but there is no contradiction in her consciously wanting both things at the same time.

The obvious problem with this suggestion is that while it seems perfectly possible to be wholly conscious of conflicting wants coexisting in oneself, the same does not seem to be possible with contradictory beliefs. If I am shown a contradiction between two of my beliefs, then my reaction—like Zerlina's—is confusion, but not the same kind of confusion. Zerlina's recognition of her conflicting wants does not necessarily weaken either of the wants or cause her to doubt that they conflict. But when someone claims that two of my beliefs conflict, then that either tends to weaken at least one of the beliefs or else causes me to doubt that there really is a conflict between them. Of course I can be *inclined* to believe p and also to disbelieve p, but this is not a state of both believing and disbelieving p: rather, it is a state of being *uncertain*. The remark "I believe it and I don't," seems to make sense only if it is taken as an expression either of such uncertainty or else as a report of my vacillation over time between incompatible beliefs ("I believe it and I don't: one day I will find myself believing it, but then the next day I will tell myself that it can't be true").

We can, of course, describe Zerlina's state too as one of being uncertain what she wants. But this is misleading if it suggests that she is unsure whether or not she wants the thing in question (i.e., to give Don Giovanni her hand). For that suggestion is simply false: Zerlina does quite strongly want to give him her hand, and at the same time she quite strongly wants not to give it to him, and she is painfully conscious of the strength of both wants. Zerlina is uncertain about what to *do*, because although she can both want and not want the same thing, she can't both do and not do the same thing. She must make up her mind not about what she wants (that's clear enough), but rather about what she will do in the face of her conflicting wants.

Believing, however, appears to be in this regard like doing, and unlike wanting. Just as you can't do and not do the same thing at the same time (unless you do them in different respects or with different parts of yourself—e.g., saying 'No' with your lips and 'Yes' with your eyes), so you can't believe and disbelieve the same thing at the same time unless you believe two different things in two different respects (e.g., consciously and unconsciously).

It is well for Sartre, therefore, that he does not try to solve his problem about self-deception by arguing that believing is in this respect like wanting. But his solution does resemble this abortive one. Both work by arguing that the two apparently contradictory doxastic states involved in self-deception are really compatible, and arguing this through an appeal to something allegedly special about the nature of believing and disbelieving. "The true problem of bad faith comes evidently from the fact that bad faith is *faith*," that is, belief. "But if we take belief as the adherence of being to its object when the object is not given or is given indistinctly, then bad faith is belief, and the essential problem of bad faith is a problem of belief" (BN 108/112). The problem of self-deception, as we have seen, is that it looks like a contradiction for me to believe p and yet at the same time and in the same respect to disbelieve p. Sartre maintains, however, that the *typical* case of belief is one in which belief is combined with disbelief. "To believe is not to believe," he declares. "No belief is enough belief, one never believes what one believes. . . . No belief, strictly speaking, is ever able to believe enough" (BN 110/114).

As in the case of Zerlina, these assertions would be self-contradictory if we took Sartre to be saying: "One believes p and (at the same time and in the same respect) it is false that one believes p." But there is not necessarily a contradiction if what Sartre means is: "One believes p and (at the same time and in the same respect) one disbelieves p." This is not necessarily self-contradictory if sense can be made of the idea that I can simultaneously and in the same respect believe and disbelieve p, so that my disbelieving p does not entail that it is false that I believe p.

Sense can be made of this if we recognize that Sartre is alluding to what might be called the *imperfection* of beliefs, taking that term in its etymological meaning. That is, he is describing belief as a project that all too often fails, which falls short and is consciously left incomplete, owing to the unfortunate circumstances of our lives. When this happens, what we are left with as beliefs are things that are made to do the job of beliefs but which we recognize as insufficient to do this job. Insofar as what must serve as the belief that p is forced to serve in this capacity it may be said that I believe p. But insofar as I recognize this same item as insufficient to do the job of a belief, I consciously disbelieve p. As a result, it can be simultaneously true that I believe p and that I disbelieve p, since my disbelieving p does not entail that it is false that I believe p.

We must note to begin with that Sartre uses the term "belief" in an unusually narrow sense. "Belief," he has told us, is to be understood "as the adherence of being to its object when the object is not given or is given indistinctly." Because this sense of "belief" is artificially narrow and because it will be necessary below to use "belief" and its cognates in their ordinary senses as well as in Sartre's special sense, I propose to refer to "belief" and its cognates, when used in Sartre's sense, as "belief*."

We do not believe* what is self-evident or undeniable on the basis of the evidence presented to us. Belief* is only what we believe on the basis of inadequate, mixed, or ambiguous evidence. A belief* is not something for which we can claim "an intuition accompanied by evidence" (BN 109/114). You do not believe* anything for which the evidence you have is so overwhelming that you have no choice but to believe it. Exactly which of our beliefs we count as beliefs* depends on how charitable an epistemology we subscribe to, how high its standards are, and what we think meets those standards.[16] But for my own part, I would claim to believe, though not to believe*, such things as that $2 + 2 = 4$, that Napoléon died before I was born, that there are at least five automobiles now in Paris, and that right now my eyes are focused on a piece of paper with words written on it.

Belief* is something that we to some degree sustain in ourselves, something we hold at least to some degree by choice. Hence Sartre associates belief* with "faith" in a religious sense. "*I believe it* means I give way to [*je me laisser aller à*] my impulses to rest confidence in it; I decide to believe it and to maintain myself in that decision, I conduct myself as if I were certain of it, all in the synthetic unity of the same attitude" (BN 109/114).

Sartre's claim that "to believe is not to believe" is thus really the claim that all belief* is *imperfect,* that it falls short of what it has to be to perform the function of belief. But what is this function? We may look at all believing (including believing*) as a way of dealing with the world, and more especially with facts about this world as they present themselves to us in the form of direct sense information, reports heard or read, pieces of reasoning presented to or engaged in by our minds—in short, what we call, in relation to our beliefs, the "evidence" for them. Every belief is an attempt to "integrate" that evidence into a coherent whole. A belief of course tries to be consistent with all the evidence, but it also tries to explain this evidence, and it tries to do so in a tidy and nonarbitrary way. Finally, it tries to win out in a competition, using the above criteria as its standards, with other possibilities for belief which we see as alternatives to it.

We do not bother to form beliefs about everything, perhaps not even about everything concerning which we have evidence available to us. On the whole, we form beliefs about things that matter to us, things concerning which we need to integrate the evidence because we need to establish a settled way of reacting to the world—where "reacting" includes verbal behavior, and even tacit speech or thought directed only to ourselves. The function of believing is to give ourselves a stable way of reacting to the world in the face of the evidence. A belief best performs this function when it fully integrates all the evidence that the believer faces.

A belief*, however, is by definition a response to the world not totally fixed by the evidence, perhaps even one integrating some pieces of evidence while clashing with others. A belief* is something I hold in the clear consciousness that other, alternative beliefs* are also open to me, while no belief that is not a belief* is open to me. Whatever I believe*, the evidence I face will be less than fully integrated, my world will be less than fully intelligible, and there will be a distinct danger of instability, ambiguity, and tension in my reactions to it. From the standpoint of the project of believing, this result is unsatisfactory. To believe* is always to fall short of success in the project one has in every believing.

Now we can see why Sartre might hold that "to believe is not to believe," that "no belief is enough belief," that "we never believe what we believe." All belief* is imperfect, a project we are unable to complete. To believe* is not to succeed in doing what every believing—and that includes every believing*—tries to do. No belief* does enough of what beliefs* aim at doing. What we believe* never does the job a belief* is supposed to do, and so in that sense we never quite believe* what we believe*.

Sartre thinks our consciousness of the imperfection of our beliefs* becomes especially acute when we reflect on them, when we become aware of them *as* beliefs*. "To know that one believes is no longer to believe. Hence to believe is no longer to believe because it is only to believe" (BN 110/114). In becoming aware that my belief* is only belief*, I become aware that it is I who maintain myself in my belief*, and I see clearly too that nothing in the state of the evidence prevents me equally from adopting this or that alternative belief*. But to see that is already to see myself as not quite believing what I have defined myself as believing. It is in this act of reflection that we are most clearly aware of the complete compatibility, in all cases of belief*, of believing and disbelieving the same proposition, and even the reciprocal dependence of belief and disbelief in these cases.

If we could regularly achieve a perfect integration of the evidence we face, so that beliefs* were a rarity, merely a marginal phenomenon in human life, then the phenomenon of faith (good faith or bad faith), would not be central to our dealings with the world. But I think Sartre is convinced that the human condition is sufficiently shot through with complexities, ambiguities, uncertainties, and tensions that we cannot live without believing*, that a wide range of our responses to the world must consist of beliefs* that are conscious of their own inadequacy. Moreover, these complexities, ambiguities, and uncertainties often hit us right where we live, in our beliefs about ourselves, about our character traits and the meaning of our actions, in our beliefs about our relations to others, in our beliefs about what is worth living for, beliefs about morality and philosophy, politics and religion. If Sartre is right about this— if in the things that matter we almost never find ourselves in the enviable position of the perfect knower, with our reactions to the world fixed scientifically by a complete integration of the evidence—then the typical case of believing is after all a case of believing*.

GOOD FAITH AND BAD FAITH

5. The imperfection of belief*, the fact that no belief* ever succeeds in being what it needs to be, is what makes bad faith possible. Every belief* is faith, but not every belief* is bad faith. Sartre insists that there is also the possibility of good faith, and that good faith is belief* every bit as much as bad faith is. Both good faith and bad faith come to terms with the fact that we must believe* and with the fact that no belief* is ever enough, that we never quite believe* what we believe*. But good faith and bad faith come to terms with the imperfection of belief* in different ways.

Both good faith and bad faith want to flee the imperfection of belief*. The difference is that "good faith wants to flee the 'not believing what one believes' into being; bad faith flees being into the 'not believing what one believes'" (BN 111/115). What this seems to mean is that good faith is forever discontent with its own imperfection and strives to complete the project of believing, it believes* but only in order to convert its belief* into an integral response to the world. Good faith therefore involves "critical thought," its beliefs* are always open to revision in the light of new evidence; good faith even strives to alter its beliefs* whenever the alteration brings it closer to completing the project of believing.

Bad faith, by contrast, is less quixotic and self-alienated, more realistic, more modest in its demands; it may be less "rational," but it is more reasonable. Bad faith realizes that the condition of "not believing what one believes" is inescapable, that all belief* is inevitably a decision in a situation of ambiguity. It is resigned to the fact that whatever it says it believes will be something that fails fully to integrate its world. So it is "resigned in advance to not being fulfilled by the evidence," and all evidence for it becomes "unpersuasive evidence," since belief* can never rest solely or squarely on the evidence anyway (BN 109/113).

Bad faith defines itself as believing* something that at the same time it quite consciously disbelieves, insofar as its belief* fails to integrate certain elements of its world, leaving them outside its belief* and clashing with it.

> No belief is enough belief, one never believes what one believes. And consequently the primitive project of bad faith is only the employment of this self-destruction of the fact of consciousness. If all belief in good faith is an impossible belief, then there is a place for every impossible belief. My inability to believe I am courageous will not deter me, since no belief, strictly speaking, is ever able to believe enough. As *my* belief I shall define this impossible belief. Certainly I cannot hide from myself that I believe in order not to believe, and that I do not believe *in order to* believe. But this subtle and total annihilation of bad faith by itself cannot surprise me: it exists as the foundation of all faith. (BN 110/114–115)

Both bad faith and good faith are counterexamples to the central assumption behind Sartre's problem of self-deception: the assumption that there is a contradiction in consciously believing and disbelieving the same proposition at the same time. For both good faith and bad faith involve belief*, a state of mind in which believing some proposition *p* (adopting it as one's integrating response to the world) can without contradiction coexist consciously with disbelieving *p* (recognizing its inadequacy as an integrating response to the world). The difference between good faith and bad faith, and the reason why we may call the one and not the other a form of "self-deception," is that in good faith the project of belief is still being carried on in earnest, belief* is still striving to perform its function as integrating evidence for a stable response to the world, even if its striving is unsuccessful. In bad faith, however, this is no longer the case. In bad faith, belief* has become content with itself as belief*.

But why then do people fall into bad faith? Why should I consciously be content with a belief* that fails to complete the project of believing*? The answer is obvious enough. For our beliefs are often called upon to do far more than integrate the evidence. Beliefs also interact with our desires, wishes, feelings, and emotions, which make demands on them which diverge from the demands placed on belief by the evidence. Bad faith is a state in which we consciously satisfy these extraneous demands. It is open to us to satisfy them because we can never do more than believe*, and that liberates us to some degree from the cruel constraints of the evidence. For bad faith, as for the honest Kant, it is well that we cannot know, but must believe*.

But if believing can serve to satisfy our desires and cater to our feelings, why not treat these as functions coequal with that of integrating the evidence? The answer to this question is clear enough in cases of belief which are not cases of belief*. Where beliefs successfully integrate our response to the world, there is no room for selecting them on the basis of their service to other needs, and people do not worry about whether they are doing any good or harm by holding the beliefs they hold. It is only where belief has admittedly failed, where it has taken the consciously imperfect form of belief*, that the question can arise, and only there that bad faith's answer is an option at all. The question whether anything except the evidence should determine what we believe is a question that can be raised only in bad faith.

Yet in a sense the question remains a real one, because it is part of what Sartre calls "the *Weltanschauung* of bad faith" to behave as if the function of believing is as much to cater to our desires and feelings as it is to conform to the evidence and produce an integral response to the world (BN 108/113). Because bad faith has its own *Weltanschauung*, it is not surprising that it should have its defenders too. We see this *Weltanschauung* exhibited often enough, perhaps most conspicuously by a certain style of tender-minded religious apologetics, but in other places too—in that aestheticism that calls it philistine not to prefer the beauty of poetic fancies to the petty facts and displeasing truths of science, or in that comfortable Humean skepticism that counsels us to ignore shrill reason in matters of belief and follow the mellower promptings of nature. It would be the topic for another paper to say precisely what (if anything) is wrong with bad faith or its *Weltanschauung,* as exemplified by the apologists, aesthetes, and careless skeptics. For now it will be enough if we merely recognize them for what they are.[17]

BAD FAITH AS A FORM OF SELF-DECEPTION

6. How successfully does Sartre's conception of bad faith solve his problem about self-deception? We have seen that in belief*, in good faith as well as bad faith, Sartre has given us a counterexample to the central assumption behind his problem: he has shown how believing something can coexist consciously with disbelieving the same thing. In bad faith, Sartre has also displayed for us a case of belief* in which the pressure of wishes, emotions, and so on, might consciously influence belief, bringing about a state we are probably inclined to describe as "self-deception." Yet there is no need to appeal to either a divided mind or unconscious mental processes in explaining how bad faith works.

Despite Sartre's success on this point, I doubt that his concept of bad faith can account for all the phenomena of self-deception, even for all the phenomena Sartre himself appears to recognize. It cannot, for example, account for a case in which "I as deceiver know the truth that is masked for me as the one deceived, and know that truth precisely, in order to hide it from myself the more carefully" (BN 87–88/89). In bad faith, I disbelieve what I believe* to the extent that I recognize my belief* as an imperfect attempt to produce an integral response to the world. But bad faith is not a case in which I disbelieve what I believe* in the stronger sense of *knowing* that what I believe is false while nevertheless believing it. If there are cases of self-deception which involve this stronger sort of disbelief of what one believes, then we can give no account of them in terms of bad faith alone.

The devices available to Sartrian bad faith seem, on the whole, to be restricted to what Harry Stack Sullivan calls "selective inattention."[18] In bad faith, I maintain my belief by consciously attending to those aspects of the world that the belief integrates, and directing my attention away from those aspects that clash with my belief. (I permit myself do this *consciously* because I am aware in advance that I cannot do more than believe*, and that whatever belief* I hold I will have to be selective in this way.) Sartre's own description of the woman in bad faith exhibits a clear preference for selective inattention as the device by which her state is maintained.[19] But it is doubtful that selective inattention by itself can satisfactorily explain her success in deceiving herself, because it cannot account for its own selectiveness. As Sartre himself depicts her, the woman *knows* her companion's intentions, and uses this knowledge to select what to attend to in his behavior, so as to avoid becoming conscious of what she knows. Some sort of "divided mind" explanation, most likely involving unconscious knowledge and unconscious choices, seems required to account for this conduct.

Bad faith and self-deception involving unconscious mental processes seem to be two quite distinct and equally tenable ways of responding to Sartre's problem about self-deception. But in the actual conduct of self-deception, is bad faith wholly distinct from self-deception involving unconscious processes?

Consider the case of Mr. Nicholas Bulstrode, the pious, prosperous, and respected banker in George Eliot's *Middlemarch*. Bulstrode was not always so rich, however, or so respectable. And his past comes back to haunt him in the form of the sickly, bibulous, and garrulous Raffles, who knows too much about how Bulstrode made his money, and forces himself on Bulstrode as an unwelcome houseguest by threatening to tell what he knows. Dr. Lydgate has told Bulstrode that Raffles' illness is not at present life-threatening, but Lydgate has warned Bulstrode repeatedly not to allow Raffles to indulge his taste for brandy, since in his present diseased state this might be very dangerous. Bulstrode admits to himself his desire for Raffles' death, but as a God-fearing man he vows not to let this desire influence his conduct: he will obey the doctor's orders.

> Should Providence in this case award death, there was no sin in contemplating death as the desirable issue—if we kept his hands from hastening it—if he scrupulously did what was prescribed. Even here there might be a mistake; human prescriptions were fallible things; Lydgate had said that treatment had hastened death—why not his own method of treatment? But of course intention was everything in the question of right and wrong. (M, p. 644)[20]

Wearied by the thought of what Raffles' loose tongue might do to his reputation in the town, Bulstrode decides not to watch the night with his patient, but to go early to bed, putting the sick man in the care of his servant, Mrs. Abel, who knows nothing of Dr. Lydgate's orders but what the master has told her. But then when Mrs. Abel urges that Raffles be given the brandy he craves, Bulstrode strangely fails to mention Dr. Lydgate's orders (has he forgotten them?) and gives her the key to the wine cooler where the brandy is to be found. Before Dr. Lydgate sees him again, Raffles has sunk into a sleep from which he will never wake. When the end comes, however, Bulstrode's conscience is at rest, "soothed by the enfolding wing of secrecy, which seemed then like an angel sent down for his relief" (M, p. 650). Bulstrode accordingly offers his sincerest prayers of gratitude to Providence, which has chosen to release him from the cause of his anxiety. As to his own behavior in the matter, "Who could say that the death of Raffles has been hastened? Who knew what would have saved him?" (M, p. 651).

Bulstrode surely *knows* (at some level) that by letting Raffles have the brandy, he has killed him; but consciously he does not let himself believe it, for he is a Christian and a man of conscience, who could not bear the thought of committing a cold-blooded murder. He conceals from himself the link between his conduct and the consummation of his desire, although the link is plain enough to him.

> A man vows, and yet will not cast away the means of breaking his vow. Is it that he distinctly means to break it? Not at all; but the desires which tend to break it are at work in him dimly, and make their way into his imagination, and relax his muscles in the very moments when he is telling himself over again the reasons for his vow (M, p. 647).

Even in his inmost prayers, we are told, Bulstrode cannot "unravel the confused promptings of the last four-and-twenty hours"; but then private prayer, after all, "is inaudible speech, and speech is representative; who can represent himself just as he is, even in his own reflections?" (M, p. 650).

Bulstrode's state is not merely one of bad faith; his self-deception requires for its explanation some appeal to a "divided mind," some sort of partition between what Bulstrode unconsciously knows and what he consciously makes himself believe. But bad faith is plainly there too, in his conscious thoughts. On the one hand, there is the attitude of cautious doubt, used in the manner of bad faith to show that he does not *have* to believe what it would prove inconvenient or painful to believe: "Human prescriptions were fallible things," "Who could say that the death of Raffles had been hastened? Who knew what would have saved him?" Bulstrode makes full use of "the common trick of desire—which avails itself of any irrelevant skepticism, finding larger room for itself in all uncertainty about effects, in every obscurity that looks like the absence of law" (M, p. 645).

On the other hand, there is also bad faith's selective appeal to argument and evidence, its use of plausible arguments that one nevertheless knows in advance can never be wholly convincing. In Bulstrode's case, these arguments take a special form because he is a man who values not only righteousness but also the appearance of righteousness, and who values both so highly that he has gotten out of the habit of distinguishing sharply between them: "For who, after all, can know how much of this most inward life is made up of the thoughts he believes other men to have about him?" (M, p. 629). Hence Bulstrode has a certain weakness for arguments that might perhaps convince others, even if not himself—yet they are offered precisely to himself, and not to others. Thus, just as Bulstrode tells Dr. Lydgate the next day, "I was over-worn, and left [Raffles] under Mrs. Abel's care," (M, p. 651) so he had told himself the night before, "It was excusable in him, that he should forget part of an order, in his present wearied condition" (M, p. 649).

In Mr. Bulstrode, some form of self-deception involving a divided mind seems not only to coexist with bad faith, but even to use bad faith for its ends. Bad faith serves as the solicitor, as it were, for thoughts and deeds Mr. Bulstrode refuses to acknowledge, representing the interests of these thoughts and deeds before the forum of Mr. Bulstrode's consciousness. We may suspect that it is not uncommon for bad faith to be employed in this way as the conscious agent of some deeper form of self-deception.

NOTES

1. References to *Being and Nothingness* will employ the abbreviation "BN" and will cite both the French text, Jean-Paul Sartre, *L'Être et le Néant* (Paris: Editions Gallimard, 1949), and the standard English translation, *Being and Nothingness*, trans. Hazel Barnes (New York: Pocket Books, 1966). The pagination in the French will be cited first and then the pagination in the English, separated by a slash (/). All translations from *Being and Nothingness* in this paper are my own.

2. David Pears, "Motivated Irrationality, Freudian Theory and Cognitive Dissonance," in *Philosophical Essays on Freud,* ed. Richard Wollheim and James Hopkins (Cambridge Univ. Press, 1982), pp. 273–274, supplies in Sartre's behalf the argument that if the censor were ignorant of its own knowledge and activity then this ignorance would have to be explained by a process of repression, thus leading to an infinite regress. But I find this neither persuasive nor in Sartre's text. For all that has been shown, the censor might just happen to be ignorant of its own cognitive states and activities, without any process of repression or self-deception entering in.

3. Actually, Sartre *rejects* the formula (which he attributes to Alain): "To know is to know that one knows." But he rejects it because he interprets the word "knows" very narrowly, as expressing a relation between a subject and an object *different* from it. Hence Sartre thinks that Alain's formula entails that all knowing of knowing must be "reflective," or "positional"—involving an objectification of the self and an act of distinguishing it from the consciousness for which it is—whereas Sartre wants to insist that every mental state is "prereflectively," "nonpositionally," and hence "noncognitively" conscious of itself—conscious of itself while completely coinciding with itself (BN 16–23/9–17). This, however, is not a denial of the thesis that "to know is to know that one knows" as it is usually understood, but is instead an unusually strong form of its affirmation, since it affirms not only that there is second-order knowledge but also that this second-order knowledge must be *conscious*.

4. Colin McGinn, "Action and Its Explanation," in *Philosophical Problems in Psychology,* ed. Neil Bolton (London: Methuen, 1979), pp. 20–42.

5. Fyodor Dostoyevski, *The Brothers Karamazov,* trans. Constance Garnett (New York: Random House, 1950), pp. 314–325.

6. Peter Caws, *Sartre* (London: Routledge and Kegan Paul, 1979), p. 81.

7. J. Cottingham, R. Stoothoff, and D. Murdoch, trans. and eds. *Philosophical Writings of Descartes* (Cambridge: Cambridge Univ. Press, 1986), 1:195.

8. *Philosophical Writings of Descartes,* 1:303–304.

9. Sigmund Freud, *An Autobiographical Study,* trans. James Strachey (New York: W. W. Norton, 1963), pp. 58–59.

10. Sigmund Freud, *An Outline of Psychoanalysis,* trans. James Strachey (New York: W. W. Norton, 1949), pp. 105–106.

11. John Rickman, ed., *A General Selection from the Works of Sigmund Freud* (Garden City, N.Y.: Doubleday, 1957), pp. 46–53.

12. *A General Selection from the Works of Sigmund Freud,* p. 51; Freud, *An Outline of Psychoanalysis,* p. 35.

13. Freud, *An Outline of Psychoanalysis,* pp. 106–107.

14. This is an objection brought against Sartre by Arthur Danto, *Jean-Paul Sartre* (New York: Viking Press, 1975), pp. 76–79.

15. The initial description of the case of the woman in fact illustrates not the ambiguity of facticity and transcendence but only the original problem. The woman "knows very well the intentions that the man to whom she is speaking nourishes regarding her. She knows also that she will have to make a decision sooner or later" (BN 94/96). But she does not want to make the decision and would find it unpleasant to be aware of the man's intentions, so she "refuses to take his desire for what it is," and "postpones the moment of decision as long as possible" (BN 94–95/97). These are clear examples of someone who believes two propositions (namely, that the man's intentions are merely respectful and that there is no need to make any decision about whether she will go to bed with him) while also disbelieving them—*knowing* that they are false. As far as I can see, Sartre never gives an account of these central examples of the woman's self-deception in terms of her exploitation of the facticity-transcendence relation.

16. Belief* seems to be very close to what Locke calls "Faith, or Opinion," as opposed to "Knowledge." John Locke, *An Essay Concerning Human Understanding,* edited by Peter H. Nidditch (Oxford: Clarendon Press, 1975), pp. 536–537. Locke thinks we have "knowledge" of our own existence, of God's existence, of certain truths of mathematics and metaphysics, and (in his charitable rather than his stricter moods) of the existence of corporeal bodies while we are actually sensing them. But he denies that we ever have anything more than "faith" or "opinion" concerning the existence of other minds or these same bodies at any time when we are not actually sensing them. I suspect that most of us are less certain than Locke is about God (even if we believe in him), and more certain about other people's minds and about bodies we have very recently sensed.

17. "Bad faith does not preserve the norms and the criteria of truth as they are accepted by the critical thought of good faith. The thing it decides first, in effect, is the nature of truth" (BN 108–109/113). These remarks may mislead. They are accurate if they are taken as describing the unreflective conduct characteristic of bad faith, but they are false if they are taken to indicate a catalog of beliefs that someone in bad faith must hold. It would even undermine Sartre's project of solving his problem about self-deception on the conscious level if he thought that when you are in bad faith you must have *deceived yourself* about the essential function of belief and its proper standards—believing one thing about these matters while knowing that your belief is false. For this would make bad faith rest on a kind of self-deception for which, as

we shall see in § 6, Sartre has no account. Fortunately, however, there is no need for him to make the claims that would get him into this trouble.

18. Harry Stack Sullivan, *Clinical Studies in Psychiatry* (New York: W. W. Norton, 1956), chap. 3.

19. "She interests herself only in what is discrete and respectful in her companion's attitude," "She does not take his conduct as part of the 'first approach'," "She refuses to take his desire for what it is," "She does not *notice* that she is leaving [her hand in his]" (BN 94/96–97).

20. George Eliot, *Middlemarch* (New York: Bantam Books, 1985), abbreviated throughout as "M" and cited by page number.

PSYCHOANALYSIS AND SELF-DECEPTION

Psychoanalysis is often thought to be relevant to problems of self-deception. Is it? It certainly appears to be if we are talking about the elimination of self-deception or the explanation of its occurrence. Psychoanalytic therapy, if successful, can diminish one's tendency toward self-deception; and psychoanalytic theory, if true, explains the psychological mechanisms of at least some forms of self-deception. Is psychoanalysis, however, relevant to *philosophical* problems of self-deception? It would appear not, at least not to the problem most discussed in recent philosophical literature: that of providing a paradox-free analysis of the concept. Whether construed as a psychological theory, a therapeutic technique, or a method of discovery, psychoanalysis seems not to be in competition with philosophical analyses. I think, however, that appearances here are misleading. One thing I hope to show is this: *if* psychoanalytic theory is true, it creates a problem for, and perhaps refutes, almost all of the recent philosophical analyses of "self-deception." The theory also provides at least a partial resolution of some of the self-deception paradoxes.

Although I will say something about the evidence, I do not intend to argue in support of the theory. The main issue I will be discussing is a hypothetical one: if the theory (or, rather, a certain part of it) is true, what bearing does this have on certain philosophical analyses of "self-deception"? I assume that this can be of interest even to those, such as myself, who are skeptical about psychoanalysis. One does not have to be a behaviorist or a Christian to have at least a detached interest in the question whether operant conditioning theory is incompatible with free choice or whether Christian theology has certain implications for morality.

PSYCHOANALYTIC CASE STUDIES

1. Consider some cases of self-deception discussed in the psychoanalytic literature.

CASE 1: THE MAN WHO WOULD NOT
GIVE HIS NAME

Herbert Strean (1984) discusses a patient who refused to give his name to his analyst for over a year and a half. The patient, Mr. A., had sought analytic treatment for many reasons. He had just been fired from his job, he was depressed, and he suffered from many phobias and physical problems. At the end of his first interview, he pointed out that he would not be able to pursue treatment if the analyst insisted on knowing his name. When asked the reason for his concern, he replied, apparently sincerely, "The government frequently makes check-ups on people, and if they found out that I was in psychoanalytic treatment, I'd never get a job" (Strean 1984, 411). From the first session to the 217th, he continued to express his fear that the analyst would insist on knowing his name. In the course of the analysis, however, it was revealed that the patient was not aware of his true motive. According to the analyst, his concern about revealing his identity masked his strong unconscious wish to be raped. When he was able to face up to his wish to be raped, to be a woman who would give up her virginity, he was able to tell the analyst his name.

CASE 2: WHY NIXON TAPED HIMSELF

Alan Rothenberg (1976) asks why Richard Nixon ordered electronic devices to record his private, often self-incriminating conversations, which would threaten his presidency if they were made public. By analyzing Nixon's behavior and speeches, Rothenberg pieces together a psychoanalytic explanation in terms of unconscious, infantile wishes. The tapes, Rothenberg speculates, may have been Nixon's "detrimental substitute" for his masochistic self-voyeurism. As Freud pointed out, if one is deprived of forbidden sexual objects, the voyeuristic instinct may eventually gain some expression, but only at the cost of suffering and only if fixed upon a substitute object that is painful. For Nixon, the substitute object was the tapes.

Rothenberg notes that the tapes may have also served a second function: to provide a defense against Nixon's masochistic self-voyeurism. The tapes would present an enormous threat (or promise) of negative exhibitionism if they should ever be released. That Nixon had premonitions of the versatile, self-destructive potential of the tapes, Rothenberg points out, may well have unconsciously figured in his original decision to tape himself.

Rothenberg does not claim to know what Nixon thinks his motive for taping was. Nixon may have convinced himself that he was trying to provide a useful record for posterity or that he acted for some other reason. Whatever his perceived motive (or motives), however, Nixon has deceived himself about why he taped himself, assuming that the psychoanalytic explanation is correct. Given that his real motives (i.e., the ones that actually moved him) were unconscious, he could not at the time of the taping have known what they were.

CASE 3. THE MISGUIDED VEGETARIAN

Professor S. has refrained from eating meat for many years and believes that he has done so because he has remained convinced by solid moral arguments. The arguments pertain to the interests and rights of animals and the suffering they endure while being raised for slaughter. Professor S. believes that even if he has other reasons for being a vegetarian, the cogency of the moral arguments is crucial; if he were to repudiate these arguments, he thinks, he might once again eat meat.

The term "Professor S." is not intended to refer to anyone in particular; let it refer to any vegetarian professor who has the aforementioned beliefs about his or her motives. If Stanley Friedman (1975) is right, any such vegetarian is likely to be a victim of self-deception. On Friedman's account, vegetarianism is at least partly, if not primarily, a defense against unconscious cannibalistic wishes. These wishes may not be causally sufficient, Friedman notes; other conflicts may also play a causal role in the etiology of vegetarianism. Having cannibalistic wishes, however, according to Friedman, is clearly a *necessary* condition. Consequently, if he is right, *all* vegetarians refrain from eating meat at least partly because of the need to defend against cannibalistic urges. Philosophers who believe that they are being swayed only by the moral arguments are rationalizing and are deceiving themselves.

CASE 4. THE CASE OF A SEVERE PHYSICIAN-PHOBIA

Paul Meehl (1983) describes a woman he treated for a full-blown physician-phobia. The phobia prevented her from seeing a doctor for several years despite her admitted need for a physical examination. The patient believed that her fear of doctors was due to the psychic trauma she suffered after having a hysterectomy several years earlier. In fact, if Meehl is right, the phobia was caused by a repressed memory of a much earlier event.

After seventy-five or eighty sessions of psychoanalysis, Meehl inferred that when the patient was a child, an examining physician had discovered that she had masturbated and had confronted her with that fact. In a later session, the woman recalled the earlier examination, the doctor's question about masturbation, and her answer. The morning after the release of the repressed memory, she made an appointment with a doctor and apparently kept it. Meehl considers the woman's vivid recall of the early examination, plus her making an appointment with her doctor, to be grounds for preferring his explanation of her aversion to doctors to her explanation (i.e., that regarding the traumatic hysterectomy).

CASE 5. WHY "CHOCK FULL O'NUTS" DOES NOT PERMIT TIPPING

Leon Bloom (1962) holds that there is a relation between tipping and impotence. On his theory, tipping is a confession of guilt about oedipal desires toward the mother-waiter who serves the child. As an example of the tipping-impotence connection, Bloom describes his visit to a fast-food restaurant in New York. Two signs in the restaurant reflect the management's policies: "Hands never touch the food you eat at Chock Full O'Nuts" and "Tipping is not permitted." According to Bloom, in the unconscious of the person responsible for both policies, a connection has been made between touching and tipping; so, the familiar injunction against the former has been extended to the latter. The connection is brought about by unconsciously equating one of the meanings of "tipping" with "touching." "Tipping," in one sense, means *to touch lightly*. In premature ejaculation, Bloom points out, the slightest touch can bring on an orgasm. What apparently happened, assuming that Bloom is correct, is that the person responsible for the restaurant's policies had an unconscious fear of premature ejaculation; because he feared touching, and unconsciously associated it with tipping, he decided to prohibit tipping.

In discussing the above cases, I have assumed that the subjects had a belief about why they behaved as they did. In cases 1, 3, and 4, the subjects explicitly stated an explanation of their behavior; in the remaining cases, it seems plausible to assume that the subjects thought that they had certain motives. Richard Nixon, for example, has had a good deal of time to reflect on why he taped himself; it would be very surprising if he has not reached any conclusion about his motive (or motives). It would be even more surprising if *no* philosopher-vegetarian had formed a belief about why he or she does not eat meat. The case of the restaurant executive who prohibited tipping is more speculative; perhaps a committee made the decision or perhaps the policy had no rationale. If either is true, then the case is not relevant to the point I want to make; but it is plausible to assume that if one man made the decision, then he believes it was made for a certain reason. I am also assuming that in each case, the subject's belief about what motivated him is incorrect, and that the psychoanalytic explanation is correct. I have offered no proof for this assumption, but that does not matter: I merely wish to argue at this point that *if* the psychoanalytic explanations are correct, then recent analyses of "self-deception" are problematic. The question of providing evidence for the psychoanalytic hypotheses will be discussed later.

Finally, we need to ask if the above cases really do involve self-deception (assuming that the psychoanalytic hypotheses are correct). It seems to me that at least some of them do, although all are different from the cases typically discussed in the philosophic literature. The more usual cases concern such examples as: a mother who believes that her son is honest despite strong evidence to the contrary; a man who distorts and refuses to accept evidence that he is terminally ill; and a woman who refuses to accept evidence that her lover has been unfaithful. In the psychoanalytic cases, the subjects have false beliefs not about others but about themselves. However, why should that matter? Even if psychoanalytic theory is totally wrong, many (perhaps most) cases of self-deception involve false beliefs about oneself. The man who persists in believing that he is quite handsome even though he is not and the alcoholic who believes that he has no drinking problem may deceive themselves just as much as those whose self-deception concerns other people.

Another feature of the psychoanalytic cases is that they involve unconscious motives. Many ordinary cases of self-deception, however, involve motives that the subjects are unaware of. Why should it matter that in one case the motive is "deeply" unconscious (it is the result of repression and cannot easily be brought to consciousness) and in another case is "unconscious" in a non-Freudian sense (the subject is simply unaware of his or her motive)? For example, suppose that a man periodically gives money to charity and believes that he does so for purely altruistic reasons. He desires to help the needy, and, he believes, this is all that motivates him in making donations. Suppose, however, that he shows in other ways that he has little concern for poor people; that he donates *only* when his bosses are aware of his donation; that he refuses to donate to similar causes when asked to do so anonymously; and that he does other things that he does not normally do in order to convince his bosses that he is a decent fellow. If we were aware of this pattern of behavior we would suspect that this person does not give to charity to help the poor, or at least that this is not his main motive. Let us assume, furthermore, that our suspicion would be correct. This is a familiar kind of case of self-deception. People like to think well of themselves; they sometimes credit themselves with fine motives that they do not have, or that play minor roles in explaining their behavior. Yet, the fact that they are unaware of their true motives does not mean they are not deceiving themselves. Why is it not self-deception, then, when the real motive lies deeply buried in the person's unconscious? Suppose, for example, that our charity-giver's motive was not to impress his bosses but to make amends for unconscious oedipal urges to have sex with his mother. He would still, it seems to me, be deceiving himself about his motivation; it is just that the psychological explanation of the self-deception would be different. More generally, I see no reason to admit that people can deceive themselves about their motives when their true motives lie in their preconscious (they are simply unaware of it) and yet deny that self-deception can occur when the real motive lies in the unconscious.

It might also be complained that someone who is moved by unconscious motives acts very differently from someone who deliberately lies to another person. The first person, unlike the liar, does not deliberately try to deceive anyone, not even himself. The man who tries to impress his bosses with his donations to charity, however, is not (or at least need not be) trying to deceive himself, and yet he is guilty of self-deception. There is no evidence, moreover, that in most cases, the self-deceiver deliberately tries to deceive himself. I want to believe, for example, that the woman I love also loves me. So, I put the best interpretation I can on what is really very weak evidence, and I end up deceiving myself. That was not my goal, however: what I wanted was to shore up my belief that my affection would be returned.

There might be at least one important difference between the psychoanalytic and nonpsychoanalytic cases. If someone's motive is in his unconscious, then it seems plausible to say that he is not morally responsible for his self-deception. Some philosophers contend that in the nonpsychoanalytic cases, the self-deceiver *is* morally responsible for his self-deception and for the behavior that flows from it. Not everyone agrees about this point, but if it is correct, this does not show that the psychoanalytic cases are not cases of self-deception. It is a general feature of psychoanalytic theory that if it correctly explains human action, then there appears to be no moral responsibility in many cases where we (perhaps mistakenly) hold people accountable. If I often deceive other people because of an unconscious motive, it is arguable that I am not morally responsible for my deception, but that does not mean that I am not deceiving people. Of course, it might be argued that I am morally responsible for my deception of others even when my motive is unconscious, but that can be argued for self-deception as well. I conclude, then, that there *may* be an important moral difference between psychoanalytic and nonpsychoanalytic cases of self-deception, but this does not show that the former are not genuine cases of self-deception.

I turn next to some standard analyses of "self-deception."

ANALYSES OF "SELF-DECEPTION"

THE NEGATIVE CONTRIBUTION

2.1 There is more than one way to classify philosophical analyses of "self-deception," but for my purpose it is useful to distinguish between *inconsistent belief* and *evidential* analyses. Philosophers who give the first sort of analysis tend to draw an important analogy between cases of other-deception and self-deception: in both cases, p and not-p are believed. When I deceive another about p, I believe p and bring about his or her belief that not-p; when I deceive myself about p, I believe p but convince myself that not-p. To say that the self-deceiver believes that p and not-p implies no contradiction, but it does call for some explanation. Raphael Demos (1960), in one of the classic papers on self-deception, explains this odd result as follows. Self-deception entails that B believes both p and not-p at the same time, but this is possible because there are two kinds of awareness: simple awareness and awareness with attending or noticing. The self-deceiver may be *simply aware* of his belief that p without, at the same time, noticing or focusing his attention on his belief. This failure to notice his belief that p permits him to believe that not-p. Several philosophers have criticized Demos' account, but have kept his requirement that the self-deceiver believe both p and not-p. Jeffrey Foss (1980) goes further, requiring in addition that he who deceives himself about p also *knows* (as well as believes) that not-p. On his account,

(A) Jones deceives himself about p just in case:

    (1) Jones brings it about that he believes that p ($_jB_p$), and

    (2) Jones knows that not-p ($_jK_{-p}$).

Robert Audi (1982) also requires belief that p and belief that not-p, but he stipulates that one of the beliefs must be unconscious. In speaking of unconscious beliefs, however, he is not presupposing psychoanalytic theory: the belief may be unconscious in a nonpsychoanalytic sense. His analysis is:

(B) S deceives himself about p if and only if:

    (1) S unconsciously knows that not-p (or has reason to believe, and unconsciously and truly believes, not-p);

    (2) S sincerely avows, or is disposed to avow sincerely, that p; and

    (3) S has at least one want that explains in part why the belief that not-p is unconscious, why S is disposed to disavow a belief that not-p, and why S is disposed to avow p even when presented with what he sees as evidence against it.

Whatever the merits of the above analyses, they all encounter problems in the psychoanalytic cases: those in which someone deceives himself into thinking that he acted because of a certain conscious motive when, unknown to him, an unconscious motive was the cause or primary cause of his behavior. For example, in case 1 (The Man Who Would Not Give His Name), the client convinced himself that p: "I am refusing to give my name in order to prevent the government from finding out that I am undergoing psychoanalysis." If the psychoanalyst is right, p is false; an unconscious wish to be raped, perhaps along with other unconscious wishes having nothing to do with the government, was the real motivating factor. There is no reason to believe, however, that the client believed not-p.

In case 2, we are not told how Richard Nixon explains his taping, but that does not matter as long as his explanation is incorrect. Assume, for example, that Nixon believes p: "I taped myself in order to provide an objective record for posterity." Again, if the psychoanalytic account is right, then p (or whatever account Nixon consciously believes) is false. As far as we know, however, there is no reason to think that Nixon also believes that not-p (or the negation of whatever explanatory statement he does consciously accept). The same point can be made about the other cases. The subjects believe p (a statement about what motivates their behavior) but do not believe not-p. That could not happen if any of the above analyses of "self-deception" were correct, given that they all require that the self-deceiver believe both p and not-p.

One could reply that in each of the psychoanalytic cases, the subject *does* believe not-p, but believes it unconsciously. This reply would fit nicely with Audi's analysis (analysis B), which requires that the belief that not-p be unconscious, but it would also be consistent with Foss' analysis (analysis A).

There are problems, however, in holding that the subjects in the psychoanalytic cases all unconsciously believe that not-p. In the first place, it seems gratuitous to insist that they do; there seems no reason to postulate this belief except to save one or more of the above analyses from counterexample. In this respect, the psychoanalytic cases are different from the standard cases that motivate the "inconsistent belief" analyses. Consider, for example, Jones, who deceives himself into thinking that his beloved really loves him, despite much contrary evidence: she tells him she does not, she has returned all his love letters unanswered, and she has married someone else. Unless we have some other plausible account of self-deception, there is some reason to say that at some level, or in some way, Jones does believe, or at least once believed, that his beloved does *not* love him. How else can we explain the appropriateness of saying that Jones is deceiving himself rather than making a simple error or engaging in wishful thinking? I do not want to insist on this point, but I concede that in this sort of case, there is some plausibility in attributing to Jones inconsistent beliefs. In the psychoanalytic cases, however, there is no need to postulate inconsistency. The subject has a theory about his own behavior; he explains it in terms of some motive that appears to him to have been the main (and perhaps only) motivating factor. The explanation of how he deceives himself is this: he has no conscious access to the real motive behind his behavior unless he undergoes psychoanalysis, for he has repressed that motive. He has an unconscious wish, if the Freudian account is correct, but he need not have the unconscious belief that this wish played a causal role, for example, in his refusing to give his name or in his taping himself. It is possible that he has such a belief, but its postulation plays no role in explaining how he deceives himself.

In the second place, the postulation is very implausible. It is not implausible to say that a man has a motive he is unaware of; the case of the charity-giver discussed earlier is a plausible example. If there is evidence for Freudian theory, it is also not implausible to say that people are often moved by motives and wishes that are repressed and inaccessible to consciousness. It is quite different, however, and very implausible in the absence of any evidence, to attribute to people the *sorts* of unconscious belief that we are discussing; we would require people *characteristically* to hold, in cases of psychoanalytic self-deception, conscious theories about their behavior and unconscious theories that negate the conscious ones. Nixon, we would need to say, believes consciously "I taped myself in order to provide an objective record for posterity" and also believes unconsciously "It is false that I taped myself in order to provide an objective record for posterity." The unconscious, on this view, would be the repository not only of instinctive urges and repressed wishes but also of true causal hypotheses about human behavior. Every time I deceive myself into thinking that some conscious motive rather than an unconscious one explains my behavior, I unconsciously accept the true hypothesis that that conscious motive did not cause my behavior. To postulate such unconscious beliefs in *all* cases of Freudian self-deception is gratuitous and implausible.

If we are not willing to postulate inconsistent beliefs in the psychoanalytic cases, we can turn to a second kind of analysis, one that explains self-deception in evidential terms. An early account of this kind (Canfield and Gustafson 1962) holds that:

> (C) Jones deceives himself about *p* if and only if: Jones believes that *p* under belief-adverse circumstances such that the evidence Jones has does not warrant belief in *p*.

Terence Penelhum (1964) argues that this account is insufficient because it does not distinguish self-deception from, for example, making a simple mistake about the evidence. He includes the following conditions: belief in the face of strong evidence, the subject's knowledge of the evidence, the subject's recognition of the import of the evidence, and the falsity of the subject's belief. Subject to certain qualification (e.g., that the self-deception be about matters other than one's own inner states), the account can be reconstructed as follows:

> (D) Jones deceives himself about *p* if and only if he:
>
> (1) believes *p* in the face of strong counterevidence;
> (2) knows of the counterevidence;
> (3) recognizes the import of the evidence; and
> (4) *p* is false.

Béla Szabados (1974) and Foss (1980) reject analysis (D) as being insufficient because it fails to distinguish self-deception from mere lying or vacillating. A more complicated evidential analysis is offered by Alfred Mele (1983):

(E) S deceives himself about p only if:

    (1) the belief that p which S acquires is false;

    (2) S's desiring that p leads S to manipulate (i.e., to treat inappropriately) a datum or data relevant, or at least seemingly relevant, to the truth-value of p; and

    (3) this manipulation is a cause of S's acquiring the belief that p.

To obtain sufficient conditions, Mele adds one more requirement, a complicated condition about "accidental intermediaries." This condition need not be discussed here: it is the necessary conditions that interest me.

There are other ways to analyze "self-deception" in terms of avoiding or manipulating counterevidence, but they all encounter the same problem. In many cases of self-deception, there is no counterevidence, or at least none that the person is aware of or could easily become aware of. If the philosopher who is a vegetarian deceives himself about why he does not eat meat, and if the psychoanalytic account is correct but unknown to him, then he need not have any counterevidence to his own explanation of his behavior. If Richard Nixon deceives himself in thinking "I taped myself in order to provide an objective record for posterity," he need not have any counterevidence to his belief. In general, if someone believes that he or she acted because of some conscious motive, there need not be, and often will not be, any counterevidence to that belief; however, if psychoanalytic theory is correct, in many such cases people deceive themselves about what in fact motivated them. In many such cases, it was an unconscious desire that caused the person to act. Evidence that the conscious desire was not the most important causal factor is not likely to be known to the person unless he or she undergoes psychoanalysis.

It might be said in defense of Penelhum's (1964) account that it was not intended to cover self-deception about one's own mental states. Consequently, the psychoanalytic cases are not genuine counterexamples. It is also true that all of the above analyses can be made immune to the psychoanalytic counterexamples by simply adding an exception clause: the account applies except when the subject is deceived about his motives. However, all such analyses, including Penelhum's, would then be seriously incomplete. They would fail to cover one of the most prevalent kinds of cases of self-deception, assuming that psychoanalytic theory is correct. The psychoanalytic cases, then, show either that the evidential analyses are incorrect or that they are seriously incomplete in that they fail to provide necessary conditions for all, or even most, cases of self-deception.

There are other analyses that do not fit in either the "inconsistent belief" or "evidential" category. For example, James Peterman (1983) suggests the following:

(F) A deceives himself about p if and only if:

(1) A believes that p;
(2) it is false that p;
(3) A might have recognized that p is false had he thought about p more carefully;
(4) a part of the explanation for A's belief that p is that A desires that p;
(5) A mistakenly believes that he believes that p because it is reasonable to do so; and
(6) a part of the explanation of A's belief 5 is his desire that p.

An important ingredient in Peterman's analysis—perhaps the key ingredient—is condition 3. However, that condition is not met in the typical psychoanalytic case. The man who would not give his name to his analyst could not discover merely by thinking about it that he was wrong about his reason for his refusal. In any case where repression is the mechanism that accounts for the self-deception, mere reflection will be insufficient for discovering one's error. If psychoanalytic theory is correct, psychoanalytic therapy will usually be necessary, but may not be sufficient (if the ego is not adequately strengthened, the person may never come to believe that he was mistaken). Reflection alone will not suffice to eliminate the self-deception.

One last account to be considered is due to Kent Bach (1981):

(G) Over t_1–t_2, S deceives himself about not-p if and only if, over t_1–t_2:

(1) S desires that not-p;
(2) S believes that p (or that he has strong evidence for p);
(3) conditions 1 and 2 combine to motivate him to avoid, and he does avoid, the sustained or recurrent thought that p; and
(4) if condition 3 is satisfied by S's avoiding the sustained or recurrent thought of p, then even if the sustained or recurrent thought of p were to occur to him during t_1–t_2, conditions 1 and 2 would still motivate S to avoid the sustained or recurrent thought that p.

One thing that is unusual about Bach's account is that it permits someone to be self-deceived about not-p without the person believing that not-p. Consider an example Bach uses. A man believes p, "My wife will never return to me." The man desires that not-p, "It is false that my wife will never return to me," but he need not believe it. Provided that he meets condition

4, it is enough that his desire that not-p combine with his belief that p to motivate him to avoid the sustained thought that p, and that he be successful in avoiding this thought. Because Bach's analysis does not require the deceiver to have a false belief that not-p, or even to believe that not-p, other philosophers are likely to argue that his account does not provide sufficient conditions. Whether or not that is correct, the conditions are not necessary if the psychoanalytic cases of self-deception are genuine. Consider, for example, the first case study I discussed and the proposition expressed by p, "I am refusing to give my name in order to prevent the government from finding out that I am undergoing psychoanalysis." The patient did believe p, but he did not avoid the sustained or recurrent thought that p. On the contrary, when the analyst asked him why he would not give his name, he readily expressed the thought that p. In addition, there is no reason to think that he desired that not-p. Unlike the man who desired that his wife would return, this man, as far as we know, did not desire that his own explanation of his behavior be incorrect. More generally, in most psychoanalytic cases, Bach's conditions 1 and 3 will not be met. Where p expresses a proposition about the conscious motive behind one's behavior, one will generally not desire that the proposition be false or avoid the sustained or recurrent thought that p is true.

I have tried to show that the psychoanalytic cases of self-deception pose a problem for many of the recent analyses of the concept. All of the analyses that I have considered state one or more putative necessary conditions that are typically not met in the psychoanalytic cases. One response might be to modify or eliminate the offending necessary condition: to drop the requirement, for example, that the self-deceiver believe p and not-p, or the requirement that he in some way manipulate evidence contrary to his belief. If we respond in this way, however, we run the risk of rendering the analysis insufficient and, in some instances, of destroying whatever was valuable in it. However, it is possible that one or more of these analyses can be modified so as to accommodate the psychoanalytic cases. *If* that is possible for a particular analysis, then for that analysis, such cases of self-deception pose only a superficial problem and do not provide a deep refutation. Nevertheless, until it can be shown that the psychoanalytic cases are not genuine cases of self-deception or that they can be accommodated by modifying a particular analysis, such cases, if they occur, pose a problem for all of the analyses I have discussed.

THE POSITIVE CONTRIBUTION

2.2 Besides presenting a challenge to recent analyses, psychoanalysis is relevant to self-deception in a more positive way. What motivates most analyses is the following dilemma, or something very much like it. If self-deception is very different from deception of others, then it is not clear that it involves genuine *deception*, but if it is not very different, then it gives rise to apparent paradoxes. For example, in deceiving another, the deceiver believes p and deliberately tries to convince another that not-p; but where the deceiver and deceived are one, it seems paradoxical to say that the deceiver believes p and yet deliberately tries to get the soon-to-be-deceived person to believe that not-p.

Psychoanalytic theory suggests the following resolution of the above dilemma. For a wide range cases, self-deception is unlike other-deception: there are not, or at least need not be, inconsistent beliefs. The self-deceiver does not believe that p while deliberately trying to get the deceived (himself) to believe that not-p. Hence, at least one apparent paradox is eliminated. However, self-deception *is* like other-deception in one important respect: there is a deliberate attempt to hide the truth; it is this element that makes the use of the term *deception* appropriate. During the oedipal phase, for example, a child has desires that the ego finds unacceptable. The ego hides these desires by repressing them into the child's unconscious. The repressed wishes persist, but so long as the person's defense mechanisms work smoothly, the resulting behavior may be non-neurotic and nonpsychotic. The person who reflects on the causes of this behavior, however, is likely to deceive himself. In the initial act of repression, and in the continued repression of the unacceptable wishes, the person will have to hide the truth from his conscious self. He will have done something that prevents his coming to know that these repressed wishes, in combination with certain defense mechanisms, cause certain sorts of behavior. He is likely to believe, instead, that the behavior is caused by certain conscious motives.

Does speaking of "hiding the truth" imply that the person both knows the truth and does not know it? If it does, then an apparent paradox reemerges. *Hiding the truth,* however, does not have this implication. What the self-deceiver hides from his conscious self is his unconscious wish. He does not hide the truth that behavior B is caused by unconscious motive M. He need not be aware of this truth, nor need he believe that it is the truth. All he need believe is that behavior B is caused by a certain conscious motive; he need not also believe the negation of this proposition.

So, one positive contribution psychoanalytic theory can make to the topic of self-deception is to show how self-deception can occur without paradox. However, the theory does not offer a conceptual analysis of "self-deception"; nor does it eliminate the need for such an analysis. Although the theory purports to explain many cases of self-deception, it does not, even if true, explain all. There will be many other cases of self-deception that do not involve the operation of unconscious desires. Jones may, for example, distort the evidence that his girlfriend has been unfaithful or that he has a terminal disease; he may distort the evidence because he consciously desires that these states of affairs not exist. There may, then, still be a need to analyze "self-deception" in order to eliminate apparent paradoxes that arise in cases outside of the range of psychoanalytic theory. Consequently, although psychoanalysis may, if correct, make a positive contribution to philosophical problems associated with self-deception—it shows how self-deception can occur in a nonparadoxical way—the contribution is a limited one. It does not resolve all of the philosophical problems, nor does it render a conceptual analysis unnecessary.

Of course, even if psychoanalysis had nothing to say about the paradoxes, it would still be important to the study of self-deception in several other ways. First, if the theory is true, there is a great deal more self-deception then we normally think. Besides the psychoanalytic cases of self-deception about one's motives, there will be many other cases where people deceive themselves about their emotions, goals, character traits, fantasies, dreams, neurotic problems, and slips of the tongue and pen. I think I know how I feel about my parents, for example; but if psychoanalytic theory is true, I may well be mistaken. Smith believes that most people are extremely selfish; in fact, *he* has this trait and projects it to other people. Jones thinks he knows what his life's goals are; psychoanalytic theory tells us that he deceives himself.

A second important contribution is that psychoanalytic theory provides a psychological explanation, for a wide range of cases, of how self-deception occurs. It does so not only via the theory of repression but also by providing a detailed account of other Freudian defense mechanisms and by explaining the etiology of neurosis, the meaning of dreams, and the origins of slips.

Third, psychoanalytic therapy, if it is effective, helps us to eliminate self-deception. It can help us gain important insights into our unconscious desires; if our personality economy is radically restructured, therapy can also permanently diminish our disposition to deceive ourselves in the future.

In sum, if the theory is true and the therapy effective, psychoanalysis, as has long been recognized, offers important contributions to the psychology and treatment of self-deception. If what I have argued is right, the theory also is relevant to philosophic discussions of the subject: it has a limited positive role to play in showing how self-deception can occur without even seeming paradoxical, and it is of greater negative use in criticizing certain analyses of the concept of self-deception.

So far, I have argued for hypothetical conclusions: psychoanalysis is relevant to self-deception in certain ways *if* the theory is true and the therapy is effective. What are the grounds, however, for thinking the theory true or the therapy effective?

THE EVIDENTIAL QUESTION

3. In the psychoanalytic case studies I discussed, were the authors correct in explaining the subjects' behavior in terms of unconscious motivation? That

question need not be answered if we understand the philosophic analyses as stating putative logically necessary and sufficient conditions. If interpreted in this way—which, I believe, is how some of the authors intended to be understood—the analyses must hold in all possible worlds, or they are incorrect. A case of self-deception that occurs in some possible world, then, refutes any analysis that is inconsistent with its occurrence. So long as the psychoanalytic cases are possible cases of self-deception, that is sufficient to make them relevant to the philosophical analyses. We need not argue that any such case occurs in the actual world. It should be added, however, that psychoanalytic theory or psychoanalytic case studies have no unique role to play in refuting such philosophical analyses. Counterexamples of a nonpsychoanalytic kind, even if they be taken from fairy tales, could serve just as well. Perhaps there is a heuristic advantage in appealing to a well-known theory that is so readily applicable to self-deception, but from a logical point of view, a newly concocted theory or example would be just as relevant.

Not everyone writing today would equate philosophical analysis of a concept with a statement of logically necessary and sufficient conditions. Some would be content to state truth conditions for the application of a concept in the actual world; putative counterexamples that are possible but never actual are irrelevant. So, let us understand analyses of "self-deception" in this way. If the psychoanalytic cases are to constitute counterexamples, they must actually occur. The question of the evidence for the psychoanalytic interpretations, then, does arise.

In one of the cases I discussed, that of the woman with a fear of doctors, Meehl (1983) argues for his interpretation in terms of the dramatic clinical effect that immediately followed the presentation of his interpretation. Once the woman gained insight into the cause of her problem and the repression was lifted, she was able to make an appointment with a doctor. Meehl's argument is interesting, but, as I have tried to show elsewhere (Erwin 1985), it does not support his interpretation alone. There are other plausible ones that fit the same facts. In the other cases, the authors offer no argument whatsoever to support their interpretations. I suppose that in each case, if the author were asked, he would defend his hypothesis as a plausible conjecture, *given* the evidence for Freudian theory. We would then need to ask about *that* evidence. In fact, so long as psychoanalytic theory can be supported, it is not necessary to vindicate any of the hypotheses from the five cases I have discussed; other cases could be found in the psychoanalytic literature.

It is also not necessary to defend *all* of Freudian theory. As Paul Kline (1981) points out, Freudian theory is a collection of mini-theories; one can consistently accept some hypotheses and reject others (or be agnostic about them). Kline (1981) and Seymour Fisher and Roger Greenberg (1977) argue for a core component of Freudian theory but do not try to defend every single Freudian hypothesis. To solidify the points I made about psychoanalytic theory and self-deception, it is not even necessary to argue for all of the Freudian hypotheses that they defend. Roughly put, it is enough to argue for the following: that a Freudian (i.e., a dynamic) unconscious exists; that unconscious events play an important causal role in explaining both neurotic and non-neurotic behavior; that repression occurs frequently; and that some of the other Freudian defense mechanisms operate widely in human affairs. This very minimal version of Freudian theory is accepted by almost all who accept any version of psychoanalytic theory; so, for our purposes, it is not necessary to talk about different kinds of psychoanalytic theory.

How strong is the evidence for this minimal version of psychoanalytic theory? Opinion is obviously still divided, but many writers who are familiar with the evidence are convinced that it supports central parts of Freudian theory (including the parts relevant to self-deception). In the preface to his new book on psychoanalysis and cognitive psychology, Matthew Erdelyi (1985) writes (p. xi): "The clinical psychology of today is closer to psychoanalysis than it was a decade ago and—as I have no doubt the future will bear out—rapidly converging upon it. Psychology, as a whole, seems poised on the brink of rediscovering psychoanalysis—or of reinventing major portions of it." As already noted, Kline (1981) and Fisher and Greenberg (1977) also claim that the evidence has now confirmed central parts of Freudian theory. Although many other examples could be cited, I think the foregoing is sufficient to show, what perhaps needs no demonstration, that some serious investigators believe that some important parts of Freudian theory have now been confirmed. Psychoanalysis, then, is unlike, say, phrenology, which is not widely defended today. It may be of no interest to argue that if the claims of phrenologists are true, then certain philosophic analyses are incorrect, but the demonstration of an analogous hypothetical claim for psychoanalysis is of some interest, given the continued appeal of the latter.

For my purposes, then, I need not argue that the evidence really does support psychoanalysis; to show that the hypothetical claim I have been arguing for is of some interest, it is enough to show that competent, knowledgeable investigators believe that it does. Some philosophers, however, have tried to go beyond a demonstration of a hypothetical conclusion and argue that because psychoanalytic theory is true, a certain philosophical result holds. A well-known case is John Hosper's (1974) appeal to Freudian theory to show that there is little or no free choice. Others who write on psychoanalysis and self-deception have generally taken for granted that Freudian theory is correct. If, however, we want to take the final step and argue that because the theory is true something of interest holds about self-deception, then we do have to take seriously the evidential question. How strong is the evidence for Freudian theory? In my view, it is not strong at all. There has long been disagreement about the quality of the main body of evidence, the clinical evidence, but Adolf Grünbaum (1984) has now shown in great detail that it is "remarkably weak" (p. 278). One could appeal to the experimental evidence, but I have tried to show that that evidence is also extremely weak (Erwin 1986, 1988; see also Hans Eysenck and Glenn Wilson 1973; Eysenck 1985). As to the claim that psychoanalytic therapy is useful for eliminating self-deception or producing other therapeutic benefits, firm evidence that this is so does not exist (Erwin 1980; Rachman and Wilson 1980; Kline 1981).

REFERENCES

Audi, R. 1982. "Self-Deception, Action, and Will," *Erkenntnis* 18:133–158.
Bach, K. 1981. "An Analysis of Self-Deception," *Philosophy and Phenomenological Research* 41:351–370.
Bloom, L. 1962. "Further Thoughts on Tipping," *Psychoanalysis and the Psychoanalytic Review* 149:135–137.
Canfield, J., and D. Gustafson. 1962. "Self-Deception," *Analysis* 23:32–36.
Demos, R. 1960. "Lying to Oneself," *Journal of Philosophy* 57:588–595.
Erdelyi, M. 1985. *Psychoanalysis: Freud's Cognitive Psychology.* New York: W. H. Freeman.
Erwin, E. 1980. "Psychoanalytic Therapy: The Eysenck Argument," *American Psychologist* 35:435–443.
———. 1985. "Holistic Psychotherapies. What Works?" In *Examining Holistic Medicine,* edited by D. Stalker and C. Glymour. Buffalo, N.Y.: Prometheus Books.
———. 1986. "Psychotherapy and Freudian Psychology." In *Hans Eysenck: A Psychologist Searching for a Scientific Basis for Human Behavior,* edited by S. Modgil and C. Modgil. Philadelphia: Falmer Press.
———. 1988. Psychoanalysis: Clinical vs. Experimental Evidence." In *Psychoanalysis and the Philosophy of Mind,* edited by P. Clark and C. Wright. Oxford: Blackwell.
Eysenck, H. J. 1985. *The Decline and Fall of the Freudian Empire.* New York: Viking Press.
Eysenck, H. J., and G. Wilson. 1973. *The Experimental Study of Freudian Theories.* New York: Methuen.
Fisher, S., and R. Greenberg. 1977. *The Scientific Credibility of Freud's Theories and Therapy.* New York: Basic Books.
Foss, J. 1980. "Rethinking Self-Deception," *American Philosophical Quarterly* 17:237–243.
Friedman, S. 1975. "On Vegetarianism," *Journal of the American Psychoanalytic Association* 23:396–406.
Grünbaum, A. 1984. *The Foundations of Psychoanalysis: A Philosophical Critique.* Berkeley, Los Angeles, London: University of California Press.
Hospers, J. 1974. "Psychoanalysis and Moral Responsibility." In *The Problems of Philosophy, 2nd Edition,* edited by W. Alston and R. Brandt. Newton, Mass.: Allyn and Bacon.
Kline, P. 1981. *Fact and Fantasy in Freudian Theory.* New York: Methuen.

Meehl, P. 1983. "Subjectivity in Psychoanalytic Inference: The Nagging Persistence of Wilhelm Fliess's Achensee Question." In *Testing Scientific Theories*. Minnesota Studies in the Philosophy of Science, vol. 10, edited by J. Earman. Minneapolis: University of Minnesota Press.

Mele, A. 1983. "Self-Deception," *Philosophical Quarterly* 33:365–377.

Penelhum, T. 1964. "Pleasure and Falsity," *American Philosophical Quarterly* 1:81–91.

Peterman, J. 1983. "Self-Deception and the Problem of Avoidance," *Southern Journal of Philosophy* 21:565–574.

Rachman, S., and G. T. Wilson. 1980. *The Effects of Psychological Therapy*. New York: Pergamon Press.

Rothenberg, A. 1976. "Why Nixon Taped Himself: Infantile Fantasies Behind Watergate," *Psychoanalytic Review* 62:201–223.

Strean, H. 1984. "The Patient Who Would Not Tell His Name," *Psychoanalytic Quarterly* 53:410–420.

Szabados, B. 1974. "Self-Deception," *Canadian Journal of Philosophy* 4:51–68.

11

FREUD ON UNCONSCIOUS AFFECTS, MOURNING, AND THE EROTIC MIND

LEILA TOV-RUACH

"It is surely of the essence of an emotion that we should feel it, that is, that it should enter consciousness. . . . For . . . feelings, and affects to be unconscious would be out of the question."[1] As coming from Freud, the view that there are no unconscious affects is astonishing. After all, according to popular understanding, it is Freud who—if anyone—has insisted that a person can love or hate without recognizing his condition. "It may happen that an affect or emotion is perceived but misconstrued. By repression of its proper presentation (i.e., its ideational content), it is forced to become connected with another idea. . . . Its ideational presentation undergoes repression."[2] Certainly Freud's case studies present the best evidence for the persistent and canny substitution of one presentation for another, cases where someone is ignorant, and perhaps even systematically, willfully ignorant, of the true objects of his affects. In some cases one object is substituted for another: the clerk's (forbidden) hatred of his father is expressed by his hating his boss. There also appear to be cases where one affect is substituted for another: sons who hate the father whom they believe they love, fathers whose fear for their daughters' safety are a transposition of their own sexual attachments, colleagues who harbor murderous hatred for one another under the surface of elaborate respect or jovial banter. Even in his analysis of nonpathological cases, in the account of the etiology and specificity of adult love—its origins in the family drama that characteristically fix the objects of love—Freud appears to allow that we can be persistently and systematically ignorant of our affects. What, then, could he mean by denying that there are unconscious affects? Is it a defensible claim within his system? Is it a defensible claim independently of that system?

Although Freud would consider most psychological states that are normally classified as emotions to be affects, his notion of *Affekt* is both broader and narrower than the folk-psychological notion of emotion. It is broader in that it includes conditions which, like irritation, surliness, and excitation, are feelings and sensations that need not have characteristic proper objects. It is narrower in that some basic psychological conditions standardly considered emotions in folk psychology—love, for instance—are, on Freud's classification, sometimes direct manifestations of instinctual drives and sometimes by-products of the frustration of those drives. When love is the direct expression of libidinal energy, it need not be experienced as an affect; if it is felt, or is accompanied by feelings, those felt libidinal energies would be physiologically and phenomenologically distinguishable from the longing feeling associated with the affect of love.[3] Freud sometimes treats an affect as an independent, self-contained psychological event with a specific sort of etiology and function in releasing or expressing blocked libidinal energy. But sometimes he treats it as essentially and identificationally conjoined with an idea: an affect is then the felt qualia of the idea, the "charge" of the idea as a dynamic force with a functional role that can be phenomenologically experienced.

Sometimes several problems are better than one: by rubbing them together, one can generate a bit of light. Freud's surprising doctrine on unconscious affects becomes somewhat less puzzling if we put it together with three other surprising views. I want first to try to make sense of the claim that there are no unconscious affects, relating this view to Freud's discussion of the phenomena of identificational mourning. With a fuller account of the Freudian canon of explanation in hand, we can understand Freud's concerns about whether affect-laden memories of childhood seduction are fantasized or real. Finally, we should be in a better position to reconsider whether the presumed submergence of affect during the "latency" period is self-deceptive.

I

Freud's chronicles of the unacknowledged rage of a son against his father, a daughter's denial of her jealousy of her mother, chronicles of (what appear to be) self-deceptive—or at the very least systematically misunderstood—affects, do not, on his understanding of the matter, constitute examples of unconscious affects. Although these psychological conditions are often misdiagnosed, although someone can often be mistaken about the true target or object of her feelings, and can even substitute one feeling for another, she experiences her condition affectively. To understand Freud's distinction between an affect, its object, its aim, and its function, we need, alas, to sketch one of the mainsprings of classical Freudian theory: the theory of drives. It is an almost ludicrously simple theory, resting on an almost breathtakingly simple image that provides the model—a sometimes Procrustean model—of endogenous action.

Behavior has its origin in—sometimes Freud speaks of it as a manifestation of—a set of drives. The most basic, most general drive is that of organic survival: it is expressed in a host of more specific drives, for food, for bodily maintenance, and for protection. Each of these generates and sometimes is expressed in yet more specific, intentionally individuated and identified motivating forces. Although drives have proper satisfactions and proper objects, they are the most general and plastic energetic origins of action. Their energies can be directed and redirected, and the objects that satisfy them are substitutable and fungible. The drive for nourishment has food as its natural object, eating as its natural expression, and digesting as its natural satisfaction. But even in this basic, simple process, satisfying the original drive allows latitude for substitution: synthesized chemicals can serve as food; intravenous feeding can bypass the usual forms of eating and digesting. Indeed drives are sufficiently general and plastic to allow even contrary realizations and expressions (*The Antithetical Sense of Primal Terms,* SE 11:153). Hunger can manifest itself not only by imagining elaborate feasts but also by elaborate rituals of refusing food. In themselves, drives are blind. They do not carry their own interpretations: a person need not be consciously aware of their aim or objects. All behavior—even such a mechanical, physically caused behavior as hiccuping—can be given intentional significance by an agent. A person can treat such behavior *as if* it were voluntary, and thus elicit defensive reactions against forbidden behavior and thoughts.[4] Although actions are identified by their intentional descriptions, and the same piece of behavior can, under different intentional descriptions, designate distinctive actions, at least some actions have standard or fundamental normative intentional descriptions.

The prolonged, physically and psychologically vulnerable dependence of infancy produces acute psychological problems whose resolutions require, and are expressed in, a vast range of symbolic activities and attitudes. An infant's dependence on those who feed and nurture it generates problems—and images—that center around ingestion and incorporation. The problems of nourishment are followed by those of muscular control, expressed in the struggles for physical and psychological power and mastery.[5] Each of these sets of problems is double-faced: the organism is itself affected not only by the objects with which it interacts but also by its own activity in interaction. Not only the food digested but the processes of digesting affect the organism. This double-faced character of the expression of drives makes activity and passivity coordinate: every event experienced as a passive response can also be experienced as an outcome and expression of the organism's own activity. This Spinozistic inheritance has obvious consequences for Freud's theory of affects: when the natural expression of a drive is blocked, the body undergoes a set of physiological modifications that are experienced as affects, that is, as a set of distinctive sensations. For Freud, as for Spinoza, an affective reaction can be transformed into an active expression of an endogenous drive when the person's intentional description of her behavior connects it to her libidinal energy. In any case, the consequences of organic interaction with the environment do not remain localized at the point of interaction: every modification is the "active cause" of changes that are individuated by their etiology.

These elaborations are consequences of Freud's attempts to combine a mechanistic model with an organic one: his psychodynamic theory borrows heavily from, and attempts to unify, Aristotle's psychology with Hobbes' mechanism. He wants to combine the advantages of Hobbes' functionalist identification of psychological states with an Aristotelian intentionalist identification of actions. He adopts and develops Aristotle's view that genetically and socially determined psychophysical development—the acquisition of habits of action and of mind—affects the intentionality of actions and interactions. He adopts and develops Hobbes' mechanistic account of motivational energy as a quantum of force with direction and momentum. Following the mechanistic picture, Freud characterizes an organism as a homeostatic system functionally organized to preserve its quantum and balance of energy. The system is constructed in such a way that it discharges the excess energy produced by invading stimuli. Because psychic energy is neither created nor destroyed, substitute channels are found when direct reactions to stimuli are blocked.

On this model, the energetic force of psychological states is distinguishable from their ideational contents. Identifying actions that have been determined by vectorial resolutions of forces does not require reference to their intentionally described energetic origins. Part of our problem in interpreting Freud's claim that there are no unconscious affects is the problem of reconciling an Aristotelian intentionalist with a Hobbesian extensionalist identification of psychological activities—the problem of giving an account of the relation between the intentional object of a psychological state and its functional role.

Identifying psychological states requires four parameters or variables:

(a) the impetus—the amount of energy;
(b) the aim—the character of the satisfaction involved;
(c) the object intentionally described;
(d) the source

(*Instincts and Their Vicissitudes,* SE 14:126).

Because these identifying factors are independent of one another, transformations can occur in one without affecting the others. So, for instance, the object of a psychological state can be replaced by a symbolic substitute without affecting the impetus; and the impetus can be reconstructed—reapportioned within the psychological field—without affecting the aim. Much of the Freudian canon of explanation consists in the set of rules governing the transformation and substitution of libidinal energy: the strategies of drive satisfaction. For our purposes, the significant rules can be characterized as rules for the transformation of energy and rules for the translation of ideational content. The rules for the transformation of energy are formally elegant, involving simple spatial redirections. The direction of the energy can be internalized or externalized; its charge can be changed from positive to negative; the relation can be active or passive. (*Instincts and Their Vicissitudes,* SE 14:126) The rules for the translation of ideational or intentional content are much more complex: they permit idiosyncratic symbolization from sources lying in an individual's psychological history, as well as in standard cultural allusions.

The energetic force of a drive remains constant until it is expressed or discharged. It is directly discharged when it is expressed in the sort of behavior that characteristically brings the satisfaction that is its instinctual aim. When the direct expression of a drive is blocked, its redirections will have an affective charge, no matter what form they take. Dreams, fantasies, symbolic ritual acts, or sublimated activities—indirect expressions of a blocked drive—carry an affective charge that releases the original energy. And it is *that*—the affective charge—which can't be unconscious. Affects just are the by-products, the effects of blocked or frustrated drives. They are a kind of psychophysical explosion, a feeling that expresses and releases the energies of the pent-up drive.

> An affect . . . represents that part of the instinct which has become detached from the idea. . . . [It] corresponds with processes of discharge the final expression of which is perceived as feeling. . . . Affectivity manifests itself essentially in motor (i.e. secretory and circulatory) discharge resulting in an (internal) alteration of the subject's own body without reference to the outer world. (*Repression,* SE 14:91, 111)

It is precisely their being felt and experienced that releases the force of the drive, and that identifies the psychological condition as an affect.

We are now in a better position to see why Freud thinks that his examples of unacknowledged hatreds, displaced loves, and transformed angers are compatible with his insistence that there are no unconscious affects. The *affect*—the feeling—is (virtually by definition) consciously experienced as such. But all the surrounding material—the original drive, the object, the direction, even the tonal quality as positive or negative, active or passive, projected or introjected—can be transformed, displaced, or substituted to fit the rest of the person's psychological condition: to avoid what is forbidden, to follow habitual, encoded symbolization, and so on. It is about all of this surrounding material, rather than about the presence or absence of the affect, that a person can be self-deceived. "The ideational material has undergone displacements and substitutions, whereas the affects have remained unaltered" (*Interpretation of Dreams,* SE 14:461).

Sometimes Freud speaks of affects as distinctive, nonintentional psychological states, those which succeed in discharging the energy of blocked drives in a specific way: by felt somatic modifications that have no reference to the outer world. But sometimes he says that all indirect expressions of frustrated drives—even those which, like dreams, fantasies, and ritual actions, are essentially attached to an ideational content—carry an affective discharge. But what distinguishes a direct from an indirect release of a drive, particularly if drives are plastic and fungibly satisfiable? What differentiates the redirected or sublimated satisfaction of a drive from an indirect expression of its frustration? Why introduce affects as special events at all? How do they differ from other forms of release? Why wouldn't fantasies, dreams, and redirected activity be sufficient to release the energy of a drive? And why can't someone be mistaken about whether she is in an affective condition?

As long as someone can deny the translation or symbolization of an ideational content or deny that an energetic drive has been transformed, then affects—individuated by their ideational content—can be as unconscious as anything else. The affect is then not identifiable independently of the ideational content to which it attaches, any more than the ideational content is fully identifiable independently of its etiology. This is the solution that follows the Aristotelian intentionalist strand in Freud's thought. But following the mechanistic, functionalist Hobbesian line—a line that Freud considers necessary for the possibility of the redirection and transformation of psychic energy—requires him to separate the energy of a psychological state from its ideational content. And it is this, the mechanistic rather than the organicist version of his theory of drives, that leads him to insist on the impossibility of unconscious affects.

There is a set of related problems: if the affect just is the experience of discharged energy that had been blocked, then there can be no question of its appropriateness to its object or even to its cause. It is not even clear how qualitative distinctions among affects are identified. To the extent that affects just are "motor discharges," they can be distinguished from one another only by the nonintentional sensations associated with their various physiological conditions. "The release of affects as a centrifugal process directed towards the interior of the body and analogous to the processes of motor and secretory innervation" only allows a nonintentional criterion for the differentiation of affects (*Interpretation of Dreams*, 467–468). But if affects are only identifiable and distinguishable by physically based, nonintentional sensations, then an affect cannot be used to recover a repressed idea. When Freud speaks of the inappropriateness of an affect, or of the singular absence of an appropriate affect, however, he clearly envisages a closer connection between its energy and its content. ("If the affect and the idea are incompatible in their character and intensity, one's waking judgment is at a loss" [*Interpretation of Dreams*, 459–461]. Indeed only if there *is* a proper connection between an affect and its idea is there a reason to repress or displace the idea, to replace the real with a manifest content. And only if there is a proper connection can an affect be used to "give us a pointer as to how we can find the missing (i.e., the censored or repressed) thoughts. . . . The affect [helps us] seek out the idea which belongs to it but which has been repressed and replaced by a substitute" [Ibid.].) At least in *Interpretation of Dreams,* Freud means to make the close connection between an affect and its ideational content a pivotal diagnostic and therapeutic tool. Because the affect remains the same when the idea is changed, it can be used to recover the original idea; when the idea is again connected to its original affect, some affective disorder can be corrected. Nowhere is Freud's struggle between the mechanistic-associationistic and the cognitive-intentional views sharper than in the tension arising out of his attempts to explain how an affect that has become detached from an idea can be used to recover the repressed idea.[6]

II

Before the situation improves, it must get worse. It might seem that either every psychological state is affective (because it involves the transformation and redirection of blocked drives) or there are no purely affective states (because drives are always somehow expressed). If every case of successfully redirected energy that requires patterned ignorance and misdescription involves the suppression of material that is also implicitly recognized, then self-deception lurks virtually everywhere. Or self-deception is nowhere, because the mechanisms that explain denial, or repression, or the censorship of unconscious material do not represent the activities of *the self.* There is no such single entity. If on one hand "the self" is a complex whole, composed of more or less integrated subsystems, it does not, *as that whole,* deceive itself: one subsystem systematically misleads others. If on the other hand "the self" is the well-developed ego, then there is no self-deception, because the ego is the subsystem that attempts to integrate all others. If affects are just the nonintentional sensations consciously experienced as the result of blocked drives, then self-deception could only consist in an attempt at verbal denial—a denial manifestly invalidated by the rest of the person's behavior. But if affects are also identified by their ideational content, then self-deception can only involve systematic misdescription or misidentification of the object of the affect.

Freud's discussion of mourning—and his puzzling failure to connect two sorts of identificational imitation—provides an illuminating example of his indecision about how to resolve the problems that emerge from his views on unconscious affects. In discussing the connection between mourning and identification, Freud observes that the mourner often takes on the *persona—* the habits and gestures, intonation patterns, and sometimes attitudes—of the person she has lost. He speculates that this identification attempts to recreate the lost object.[7]

Though it is basic to the explanatory canon, the term *identity* is rarely characterized with any precision: it is vaguely used to cover a wide range of senses. Freud's use of the term can be reconstructed, in such a way as to give us some understanding of what it is for a set of traits, ideals, and habits to be central to a person's identity. What Freud treats as structure can be interpreted in dynamic and defensive terms. A trait, object relation, attitude or belief, concern, or ideal is central to a person's *identity* when it is essential to her survival as the sort of person she is. The preservation and expression of that trait (attitude, concern, object relation, ideal) is motivationally central: a threat to it directly mobilizes the strategies of defensive maneuvers exercised in self-preservation, without requiring any other pleasure-bound, pain-avoiding motivation. Exercising, enhancing, defending, promoting, and expressing those traits (etc.) is constitutively and directly motivating independently of any other satisfactions or ends. As it stands, this rough characterization allows that someone might be mistaken about what is essential or central to her identity, either falsely believing that a trait (etc.) is central when it is not, or falsely believing that a trait (etc.) is not central when it is. At least some traits essential to a person's identity can be extensionally identified; sometimes that identification can significantly differ from the person's own conception of what is essential to her identity, even when the behavioral expression of the two are the same. Yet understanding the systematic pattern of a person's actions and thoughts requires not only understanding what is effectively identificational (in the sense sketched above) but also her conception of what is essential to her, including active ideals that she tries, but fails, to realize.[8]

Freud does not draw the obvious consequence of his theory: the hidden proper object of mourning is the self that has been diminished or transformed by the loss. The reason he does not draw this consequence is that when mourning is expressed as an affect, it does not have a proper object. The energy released at the frustration or blockage of a drive bears no representational relation to the objects or aims of the original drive; nor does it represent the causes of its repression. Freud does not face the problem of why those forms of mourning that recreate, internalize, and act out the life of the lost object are not experienced or felt as affects. On the one hand, such mourning is surely fused with felt grief. On the other hand, it might seem as if identificational mourning does not conform to the conditions of affectivity: it is externally and representationally rather than internally directed. In that case the fact that the mourner can be systematically unaware of reproducing the lost object, and can even deny the loss, does not disconfirm Freud's claim that there are no unconscious affects. When mourning is expressed by assuming and acting out a lost identity, it is not expressed as an affect. Perhaps

Freud can have it both ways: the two forms of mourning—the affective and the behavioral—might be psychologically fused while being analytically distinguishable.

Still there is a problem. Identifying with the lost object, the mourner defends herself by recreating and imitating what has been lost. What was necessary or essential to her identity is magically preserved. This defense must be disguised to be successful, particularly in that, all along, the real but obscure object of mourning is the dear self, whose identity has been threatened by the loss. Following this line of thought would lead Freud to preserve the strong connection between an affect and its object: for it is precisely by imitating and preserving the lost object that damage to the self is avoided. *For this process to work successfully, the person must be systematically unaware of what she is doing.* For if she were fully conscious of the fiction, she would not succeed in defending herself against the threat to her identity. Presumably Freud would have to argue that insofar as mourning is behavioral, it can be unconscious or self-deceptive; but insofar as it is affective, it cannot be.

The labyrinthine intricacy of Freud's view appears even more dramatically when, after the first account of the phenomena of mourning, he remarks that the mourner's attempt to incorporate the lost object is very similar to the sort of identification and imitation that newly married women make: they often acquire and imitate their husbands' traits, opinions, and gestures (*Mourning and Melancholia,* SE 14). He notes, without developing the matter, that there appears to be an asymmetry in the acquisition of traits when couples live together. The woman tends to identify with and imitate the man; rarely does the man take on the traits of the woman. Surprisingly, Freud simply mentions this as yet another form of identification, without exploring the possibility that far from being an independent phenomenon, this type of imitative identification is an instance of self-deceptive mourning.[9] Why does Freud conjoin the two phenomena without connecting them and without elaborating or explaining his observation? Why did he introduce this phenomenon of wifely imitation in the middle of a discussion of the identificational processes that take place in mourning?

In the course of describing and analyzing this process of identificational mourning, Freud remarks that the choice of a sexual object appears not only to influence the development of the ego of women, but also to affect their character, that is, their identity. There seems, he says, to be an intrusive relation between identification and object-choice. Women tend to imitate and identify with the objects of their attachments even when the cathexis is anaclictic and not particularly loving.

Of course there may be many other explanations for this imitative identification. Characteristically, the woman is socially and economically dependent on her husband. Especially when there is a marked difference in age, the wife is often formed by her husband (cf. Freud's educative letters to his fiancée) and formed for him (cf. Rousseau's highly influential *Émile*). Without being aware of doing so, the women may well be placating or complying with or wooing (those whom they experience as) their superiors. But because there is good reason to think that there is overdetermination in this area, I want to explore the possibility that such imitative identification is mourning, with the affect submerged or denied. Our question will then be: is the woman self-deceived when she is unaware of, and would deny, her mourning?

Freud believes that we acquire our conceptions and expectations of love from our early experiences: the particular tonal character of parental nurturing serves as the paradigmatic model for all that we later consider to be affectional bonding. Characteristically, the kind of love that newly coupled men receive from their women tends to include the sort of attentive nurturing they received from their mothers.[10] Standardly, men are fed and preened by wives who follow maternal patterns down to the details of attending to clothing. But unless they are narcissistic types, women rarely receive this sort of attention, even when they are well loved. Standardly and conventionally, a man's ardor is greater before sexual partnership is established, while a woman's affections are more strongly bonded afterward. On Freud's account, this difference is a function of the differences between male and female genital development: male genital drives are physically developed in adolescence, while female sexuality only matures with experience. Once the couple are established sexual partners, the man not only receives sexual satisfaction: he also reliably receives the kind of nurturing care on which he comes to depend, and which he associates with love. As long as he receives both kinds of attention, he need not experience any affect of love or longing.

But the woman's story is somewhat different. Although in the best cases, her awakened genital drives are satisfied, her need for nurturance is not. Even though the man provides for her financially, he does not actually tend or attend to her as he did during their courtship. But since the woman also formed her conceptions and expectations of loving bonding from parental nurturing, she experiences her husband's bonding as incomplete. She has lost the man who courted her. This is why many women are puzzled by what seems to them as their husbands' withdrawal, while men are puzzled by what seems to them to be their wives' excessively clinging emotionality. The men cannot understand why their women fail to recognize that love is thoroughly expressed in action and in sexuality, in satisfaction rather than in longing. Freud provides the materials for explaining the phenomena. To the extent that some of her needs for nurturance—needs she associated with physical bonding—are frustrated, the newly married woman experiences longing love as a mode of mourning. To the extent that her sense of herself has been bound up with her husband, her identity is threatened by what she experiences as a loss. She often tries to woo her husband back by what is usually counterproductive clinging—the sort of clinging a child evinces when it experiences the withdrawal of a parent—or, like other mourners, she attempts to identify with, and to recreate, the suitor she has lost. The more helpless she is to express that love effectively, the more powerfully felt it becomes.

If the newly wed wife is mourning, she is usually either systematically unaware of, or self-deceived about, the true nature of her affective condition. She may well have reason to deny that her diffuse longing and its accompanying identificational imitation are varieties of mourning, deflections of her sense of diminished identity. If she finds that her continued expressions of melancholic love distance her husband, she may repress the feeling as well as the expression. Yet her imitative identificational behavior may express mourning, as well as the acknowledgment of power. If there are such cases of repression, Freud's denial of unconscious affects must, at the very least, be hedged.

III

Freud's difficult vacillation over the theory of childhood seduction—the problem whether adult reports of childhood seductions are bona fide memories of whether they are fantasies—also provides an argument that Freud should accept rather than reject the existence of unconscious affects.

Setting aside those cases of actual physical seduction, does it follow that all other cases of reported childhood seduction are fantasies based on wish, subjected to the usual set of projective transformations? No; I believe it does not follow. The very large area that combines reality, interpretation, and fantasy provides ample documentation of self-deceptive or unconscious affects.

This, I believe, is a naturalistic story about parent-child seductive interaction. In the course of giving their children physical and nurturing care—bathing them, combing their hair, dressing them and so on—parents often come to form an erotic attachment to their children. Finding them delectable, seductive, they may often have erotic fantasies and wishes of which they are only marginally aware. They might simply wish to extend and prolong their caresses and in an obscure way want to arouse the child to return caresses. Though such wishes and fantasies would normally be suppressed and not overtly enacted, still the parent's arousal may be sufficient to change her or his expression and gestures in a subtle but observable way. An intent that is not expressed in overt action can nevertheless be observably manifest to a sensitive child. A child might not only notice but respond to such subtle changes in the features of an erotically aroused adult. The child would of course not understand the latent intent, because it would have no way of assimilating this to other experiences. The event would present something unknown and frightening, both because it is unknown and because it carries an unassimilable, responding, excited charge. Particularly because the subtle traces of erotic arousal sometimes can superficially resemble the subtle traces of repressed anger, the child might find the undigested, uninterpreted, unacknowledged experiences difficult and unresolvable. Frequently repeated, sometimes highly charged, such experiences might be strong enough to produce anxiety requiring working out in dreams and fantasies whose own internal psychological momentum might magnify it.

Once the child acquires the categories and concepts of sexual life, new explanations can retrospectively be applied to the unabsorbed eroticised experience. The stories of childhood seduction can sometimes fall in that important area between fantasy and reality: the child has correctly recognized the latent and submerged content of an interaction, and has done so at a time when it cannot mark the all-important distinction between an intention that is overtly expressed in behavior and one that is psychologically real but behaviorally sublimated or repressed. Since the distinctions between mood, intention, and action are learned only gradually, and are indeed always being reinterpreted, it is not surprising that the child confuses a real tonality with a realized action. In the absence of any correcting experience, the adult continues the child's confusion, reporting something that falls between memory and fantasy.

What has this to do with unconscious affects? It suggests, though of course it does not prove, that an adult who has reworked such erotically charged experience is recounting and reporting affectively charged memories that can, but need not be, experienced affectively. Sometimes, indeed, it can be just the very deadpan *absence* of affect in situations that, presumptively, are strongly affect-laden that reveals the person's psychological struggles. If it is genuinely possible to report and behaviorally manifest *the absence of affect* in situations that appear in every respect to conform to the model of blocked—affectively redirected—energies, it would seem that a person could be self-deceived about *whether* she is affected, as well as about *what* affects her.

IV

Yet again, things must get worse before they get better. Before trying to resolve Freud's problems about unconscious affects, let us see what the mystery of latency can contribute to the story.

The apparent blankness of the latency period presents a puzzling lacuna in Freud's account of the psychodynamics of development. Why should there be such a long dormant period at a time of important physical and intellectual change? Following the general dictum that all psychophysical and intellectual changes are psychosexually significant, it seems implausible that this period should be developmentally blank, centered primarily on consolidation. As Anna Freud was later to suggest in her account of intellectual development, thought processes can become affectively charged to express and release psychodynamic conflicts. A child's success in developing a powerful, affective and richly subtle intellectual and imaginative life depends on her being systematically unaware of the psychosexual functions of those processes, of the ways her thought expresses and releases psychodynamic conflicts. But systematic ignorance—patterned repressive discrimination of attention— requires scanning for forbidden material, which involves implicit admission of its import. The success of sublimated activity appears to depend on denials and repressions of affect that are suspiciously like self-deception. And if the intellectualization of libidinal processes and conflicts is not affectively experienced, then not only ideas but also affects themselves can be unconscious.

The latency stage occurs between the end of anal stage and the beginning of the genital stage, after habits of psychophysical self-control and mastery have been developed and consolidated. The activities of the oral stage—introjection and projection, absorption and rejection—have been integrated and expanded onto a larger somatic and psychological field. Before puberty focuses on the issues of genitality, a person's central psychological work consists in developing characteristic intellectual patterns of thought, imagination, and fantasy: it is the period for the formation of psycho-intellectual strategies for elaborating, transforming, and gratifying instinctual processes. The metaphors central to the earlier stages remain: seeing is a way of absorbing and introjecting the world, imagining is a way of mastering and controlling it, speaking and writing are expressions, expulsions, explosions. The eye and the mind become eroticized during the latency stage. What we cannot have, we can imagine. What we cannot destroy, we can deconstruct. It is the stage for the development of thought at the service of defense. But it is also the stage in which thought, imagination, and fantasy come to be sources of—and not merely avenues for—independent autoerotic satisfaction. The child develops habits of categorization and association, characteristic narratives of symbolic thought and action, patterns of substitute gratification. Rituals of play and games form expectations of roles and attitudes: life is seen as combat, adventure, or exploration; one's role is that of leader, follower, or observer; the world affords opportunities or frustrations; events unfold with fateful necessity or largely by accident and chance; other players are comrades or kinfolk, mysterious strangers, allies, enemies, superiors or inferiors, primarily men or primarily women, or indifferently men or women. Communication is largely verbal or nonverbal, direct or symbolic; the tone is playful, devious, ironic, or serious. The primary strategies of defense are intellectual or physical, political or aesthetic. (Of course these alternatives are meant to be suggestive rather than exclusive or exhaustive.)

Why didn't Freud recognize the eroticization of the eye and the mind, of language and modes of communication? Of course in one sense it was he who introduced this idea: thought is a means toward, and eventually itself becomes, a form of gratification: the redirection and satisfaction of instinctual drives. Fantasy and the imagination originally provide substitute gratification; but when they have become eroticized, they provide direct as well as substitute satisfaction. When Freud discusses the eroticization of thought, he dampens the distinction between the energy of a psychological state and its content (*Instincts and Their Vicissitudes,* SE 14). But even though his analyses of scoptophobic and linguistic disorders amply document the eroticization of the eye, language, and the imagination, his commitment to one version of the Hobbesian mechanistic model prevents his accepting the consequences of his insight. While Freud gives an account of general somatic eroticization, the erogenous zones include the mouth, the anus, and the genitals, but not—except in pathological cases—the eyes and ears. Freud's continued commitment to the mechanization of the biological model—the buildup and release of energetic charges—explains his surprising failure to connect his theory of the development of erotically charged intellectual processes with his theory of the role of erogenous zones in psychodynamic development.

With considerable strain and some Procrustean cutting, Freud can interpret his theory of the activities of mouth, anus, and genitals within his mechanistic model: the mouth devours and spits, the anus constricts or defecates, and genital tension mounts and is orgastically released. Here the problems of theory become dramatic: what are the criteria for *release*? Do eating and defecating really conform to the excitation-and-release model? Each seems to involve a different model of release. In any case, however wide the latitude of the mechanistic model of excitation, accumulation, tension, and release, the eroticised eyes, ears, and mind do not follow it.

One might attempt to combine the two strands of Freud's theory by distinguishing the phenomenological from the ontological enterprise.[11] The separation of an affect from its ideational content, required by the Hobbesian approach, is introspective and phenomenological; the connection between the two, required on the Aristotelian view, is ontological and conceptual. This would be a pretty solution if it were true. But does an introspective-phenomenological account really reveal the separability of an affect and its content? The phenomenological feel of affects seems content-bound and variable with the details of the individuation of their objects: someone's affective feelings toward (just this) newborn child are radically different from his affective feelings toward that child when she is six, or ten, or twenty. And these are different from his affective feelings toward his brother's children at six, ten, and twenty. And these again are different from the affective feelings one has toward the children of one's friends. Introspectively, affective feelings are protean indeed: but protean because they are bound up with, rather than disconnected from, their ideational content, which itself varies with the psychodynamic role played by that ideational content.

We can distinguish affect types (rage, love, or fear, for example) from individuated ideas-and-affects identified by their etiology and functional roles (for instance, a child's particular fear of a particular church spire on a particular occasion). The former permit the substitution of objects and allow for functionally equivalent replacements (hate for love, gratitude for envy); the latter do not. Even though an affect type is characterised by associated typical intentional objects (sibling jealousy, for instance), it can be detached from its particular objects (brothers, sisters). The minuet graces of transformations (the change of charge from positive to negative, from active to passive, from projective to introjective) and the rich thesaurus of translations of objects (the substitutions of sons for brothers, kings for fathers, gloves for mothers, church spires for kings) all take place on the level of affect types. Only on that level is it possible to reidentify "the same" affect under its transformations and "the same" content under its translations. But individuated affects are radically transformed by every transformation: someone's horror of a particular church spire just is different from his horror of his maternal uncle's beard at a particular time, under particular circumstances. This is not important news: it is a trivial consequence of the discernibility of distinct individuals.

Freud can retain the advantages of the physiologically oriented mechanistic model—the advantages of accounting for the redirection of energy from one content to another—with the advantages of the cognitive model according to which individual psychological states (and the behavior and actions that express them) are intentionally identified. The mechanistic model applies at a general level, the level of typical description: at that level, ideational contents of psychological states are substitutable; indeed it is sometimes just their substitutability that allows them to play their appropriate functional roles. Sometimes psychological states themselves—and not merely their ideational contents—are functionally substitutable. So, for some (but not for all) purposes hate can play the same functional role as love, love the same role as envy. The stringency of conditions for the reidentification of a psychological state varies with the level of detail at which its functional role is described. So, for some purposes, an affect can be identified by its generalized functional role: for this purpose, hate need not be distinguished from love. But for other purposes—purposes that require a more detailed and individuated description of functional roles—the two affects are distinguished. *When the functional role that a psychological state plays essentially requires its having a specific intentional content, then the affective charge of the state cannot be separated from its ideational content. When the functional role of a psychological state can be played without any particular intentional content (and perhaps even without any particular type of intentional content) then it can be identified*

independently of that intentional content. Because the criteria for reidentification need not reduce to the criteria for individuation, a psychological state
can be identified at different levels of generality for different explanatory
purposes. So, for some explanatory purposes, it can be separated from the
particular intentional contents that individuate it, and for others not.

When affects are identified independently of their intentional contents—
when they are identified by their functional roles most generally characterized—they cannot be unconscious. They cannot be unconscious because at
that level of generality, there is nothing to them but their affective feel: no
affective feel, no affect. At *that* level of generality, affects are not individuated, not even as affect types: characterised so generally, the functional
role of hate is not distinguished from that of love. But when affects are
identified by their intentional contents, a person can be as self-deceived about
her affect as she can be about its intentional content. If the content is translated
or substituted, so can the affect be; if the content is repressed, so can the
affect be. One of the attractions of this solution is that it gives us a way of
saying that at one level of description—as playing a generalized functional
role—an affect cannot be unconscious, but at another level of description, it
can be. Is it the same affect which, at one level of generality, is unconscious,
and at another level, is not? The answer depends upon the generality of the
question. At a general level of reidentification—one which allows the substitution of intentions *salve functione*—"the same affect" can, under one description, be unconscious, and on another, not. But affects individuated by their
intentions cannot be both conscious and unconscious.

NOTES

1. *The Unconscious* (1915), vol. 14 of the *Standard Edition of the Complete
Works of Sigmund Freud*, ed. James Strachey, 23 vols., (London: Hogarth Press,
1966–74). Henceforth, all references to this edition will be given in the text as "SE."
Freud's use of the term *Affekt* derives from Spinoza's *affectus,* a reactive modification
contrasted to the active expression of *conatus.*

2. Ibid., p. 110. Without systematically distinguishing them, Freud sometimes
speaks of the *idea (Idee)*, sometimes the *concept (Begriff)* or *content (Inhalt)*, sometimes the *presentation* or *representation (Vorstellung)*, sometimes the *object (Objekt)*
of psychological states. In all cases, he is referring to intentional objects.

3. Since Freud sometimes suggests that drives are themselves *felt,* and that their
being felt is part of their operation, he owes us an account of the difference between
the felt experience of the expression of a drive and the felt experience of its frustration.

4. The Talmudic strand that Freud shares with Spinoza is central here: a mechanistic account of behavior is compatible with an open-ended and revisionist intentional,
ideational, or cognitive description of that behavior.

5. Freud is greatly indebted to Rousseau's account of the effects of dependence:

it produces a kind of anxiety that in turn generates a cycle of vulnerability to, and defiance of the powers and opinions of others.

6. Brian McLaughlin has suggested this formulation for the difference between the two strands in Freud's theory: "A given state is an affect in virtue of having a functional role F [that of releasing the energy of a blocked drive]; that state is a state of *love* in virtue of having a functional role, F'; it is a state of *loving one's mother* by virtue of having a functional role F''. Being in an affective state is essentially open to consciousness. Any F'' state is also F'; and any F' state is also F. But an F state need not be F'; nor need an F' state be F''. So while being in an affective state F is essentially open to consciousness, a person might be in F' or F'', without being aware of being in a certain type of affective state and without being aware of the particular content of that state." (Though essentially aware of being in some sort of affective state, a person can mistake his anger for love, and his anger for his father as an anger for his boss.)

Ronald de Sousa has suggested that there might be interesting parallels between this aspect of Freud's theory—the view that affects are sensed experiences of physiological changes—and the James-Lange account of emotions as the sensations of bodily states.

7. Mourning at death is, of course not the only kind of mourning. There are losses in separation, alienation, the death of affection, even in the perception of dramatic or radical change in the objects central to a person's identity. There are even losses of fantasy objects and losses of fantasy relations. Whatever is perceived or experienced as the kind of loss that affects a person's conception of what is essential to her sense of herself presents an occasion for mourning.

8. Clearly it is not necessary that a person loves what she mourns or that she loves what she takes to be centrally identificational. Someone can, for instance, mourn the transformation of a family home or neighborhood which, in childhood, brought pain and misery; or she can mourn the loss of a hated enemy. Her sense of herself, her identity, had been bound up with him, or with her hatred of him, even though she not only hated the villain but hated hating him.

9. This interpretation of the gender-linked asymmetry of mourning is borne out by the differences between the mourning of widowers and that of widows: widowers who have lost their primary nurturers, as well as their friends and partners, often suffer affective debility and disorientation, while widows who must learn how to manage their financial affairs appear to suffer in more straightforwardly practical, less affect-ridden ways. Of course when such practical difficulties are symbolically highly charged—as often they are—they become affectively laden.

10. Freud took marriage to be the central model of the kind of bonding he described. But of course the phenomena are more general: even men and women who form relatively bracketed and short-lived alliances exemplify the patterns Freud characterizes as marital. It is not always the *woman* who follows the pattern Freud describes: it can be Marcel in relation to Albertine, one male homosexual to another, or a nurturing man to a narcissistic woman. But even such variations on the standard type exemplify the plot Freud sketches, when the suitable substitutions are made.

11. Cf. Anne Thompson, "Affects and Ideas in Freud's Early Writings" (unpublished paper).

12. Ronald de Sousa, Lawrence Friedman, Brian McLaughlin and Ruth Nevo contributed useful comments on this paper. An earlier and shortened version of the paper appeared in *Hebrew University Studies in Literature and the Arts,* vol. 14, no. 1, ed. Nevo and Besserman, under the title "Mixing Memory and Desire: Freud on Unconscious Mourning."

12

TOWARD A COMPUTATIONAL ACCOUNT OF *AKRASIA* AND SELF-DECEPTION

GEORGES REY

In memory of Eunice Belgum.

Common mentalistic explanation seems to depend upon the plausibility of some version of a law of practical reason: e.g., people (try to) do what they believe will best secure what they most prefer. A great many objections have been raised against the existence of any such law. Some of them might be regarded as external to mental theory generally, in that they charge the whole of it with being vacuous, unprincipled, indeterminate, or "a failed research program" (Churchland 1981). Some of the objections are, however, more internal: close attention to the full details of our mental lives shows laws of practical reason to be implausible. These objections frequently focus upon the disturbing phenomena of "*akrasia*" or "weakness of the will" (I shall use the former term so as not to prejudice an account), and the related phenomena of self-deception. In cases of *akrasia,* people seem straightforwardly to fail to act on their highest preference: thinking work to be more important than a movie, I nevertheless go to the movie. In self-deception people seem straightforwardly to fail to act in accordance with the attitudes they sincerely avow: sincerely claiming her lover to be intelligent, someone nevertheless seldom takes his views seriously, condescends to him in discussion, hesitates in recommending him for a job; she "conceals from herself" her real opinion. If a law of practical reason is to explain both what people say and what they do, such cases can appear to render the whole project of assigning beliefs and preferences incoherent: the *akratēs* seems both to think that a certain act is best and not think it is best; the self-deceiver, both to believe and not believe that a particular claim is true.

A full reply to the external objections probably depends upon fuller, more detailed experimentation with mentalistic psychology than is presently available, experimentation whose success or failure it would be rash to prejudge. But there are promises of replies, particularly in recent computational theories of mind. Although we lack as yet a satisfactory formulation of a law that captures the rationalizing relation as it is realized in human beings, I think it is reasonable to expect some such law(s) to be formulated in detailed computational models of mental processes. I shall provide a sketch of such a computational account in section 1 below. Elsewhere, I should like to show how this account provides replies to many of the external objections. In this paper what I want to explore is how it affords a reply to the internal ones.

Contrary to claims that I will discuss in section 2, *akrasia* and self-deception are genuine phenomena that present a peculiar challenge for mentalistic explanation: we seem to understand these phenomena mentalistically despite their apparent conflict with plausible mentalistic laws. A natural response to the problems is to divide the mind into different subsystems. However, most attempts to do so, I argue in section 3, either lack independent motivation or fail to mark a distinction relevant to the phenomena.[1] In section 4, I propose a division of the mind that I believe to be free of these defects. Borrowing on recent experimental evidence, I argue that the problems posed by *akrasia* and self-deception lie not with practical reason but rather with too uncritical a presumption about the reliability of self-attributions of attitudes. This presumption has a number of sources. One traditional one is the Cartesian insistence on the self-transparency of the mind. But another, more prominent in recent literature, is a conflation of two independent bases for the attribution of propositional attitudes, the verbal and the explanatory, and a related failure to appreciate two kinds of attitudes, the avowed and the central, to which those bases give rise. There are important reasons to maintain these latter distinctions, and I try to show in section 5 how a computational model of the mind offers a clear way of doing so. I conclude in section 6 that an account of *akrasia* and self-deception, far from being incompatible with practical reason, can be shown to accord naturally with it.

A COMPUTATIONAL ACCOUNT OF PRACTICAL REASON

1. The computational model of mentation that I think shows great promise is the representational model that has been proposed by Gilbert Harman (1970) and, independently, by J. A. Fodor (1975). The main advantage of this model is its intelligibility: it is relatively clear how we might program a machine to perform the requisite computations on formally specified representations. It is largely an empirical question whether people's minds may be regarded as a computer of this sort. Fodor (1975, 27–53) argues that present cognitive psychologists are committed to such a model if they are to make sense of their accounts of such processes as practical reasoning, confirmation, and perception.

Fodor (1975, 28–29) presents the following computational account of practical reason: the agent believes she's in situation S; that (basic) actions $B_1 \ldots B_i$ are open to her in S; and that $C_1 \ldots C_i$ are the likely consequences of $B_1 \ldots B_i$, ordered according to her preferences. On the basis of these beliefs, she computes hypotheticals of the form 'if B_i then prob $(C_i) = j$', and then selects one of B_i as a (e.g., decision-theoretic) function of those probabilities and her preference ordering. If she can in fact perform B_i in S, then this process brings about that performance.

Fodor proposes taking this model quite literally:[2] the agent's brain is to be understood as a computer storing and performing operations upon actual sentences (or other forms of representation) that express these hypotheticals, behavioral options, probabilities, and preferred consequences. Different propositional attitudes are distinguished by (inter alia) the different operations that may be performed on such sentences in the above and other (e.g., deductive, inductive/abductive) computations, as well as by the different propositions those sentences express. The belief that p and the preference that q, for example, might be defined in terms of operations B and P, that an agent, x, might perform upon sentences, σ and τ, that express propositions p and q. I.e.:

x believes that p iff ($\exists \sigma$) ($xB\sigma$ & σ means that p), and
x prefers that q iff ($\exists \tau$) ($xP\tau$ & τ means that q).

We can (although we needn't) imagine that B and P involve actually storing σ and τ at specific addresses[3] that are accessed at appropriate times in the execution of the above process of practical reasoning. Later in this paper I shall consider other operations in addition to B and P that might be introduced in a similar fashion. I shall not be concerned with the 'means that' relation that is elsewhere the locus of much important discussion.[4]

Fodor's formulation of an account of practical reason is obviously a first approximation, wanting, at least in the human case, considerable emendation. For example, there is no reason to think that we know yet the particular terms in which such laws ought to be couched. Fodor follows philosophical practice in using, e.g., 'believes' and 'prefers'. But these terms are obviously too dispositional: a person may believe that p in the sense that, were she relaxing in her living room, she might then say that p; but that's no assurance that she'll bear it in mind (i.e., compute upon it) in the fray. In view particularly of the causal significance of B and P, actual instances of practical reason will need terms more like 'notice' than 'think' or 'believe'; and it will need to allow for, e.g., degrees of belief and for changes of attitude over time. 'Prefers', too, covers a multitude of temptations: 'wishes', 'wants', 'craves', 'loathes', 'values highly', 'believes good', 'thinks best'. This very generality of the terms, though, will permit sufficiently general accounts of *akrasia* and self-deception below.

But there mustn't be too much latitude. Critics of mentalistic explanation often complain that laws of practical reason are so loose as to be circular:

people may do what they most prefer, but that is only because what they most prefer is determined only by what they in fact do. Such a conception, however, ignores the substantial intricacy of mental attributions. Practical reason, particularly on Fodor's account, consists of a law that relates innumerable instances of beliefs, preferences, and acts, each instance providing independent evidence for the others. A belief may combine with other preferences to rationalize and explain one array of acts, and a preference may combine with other beliefs to rationalize and explain another array. Wanting water explains why, if I think there's some to the left, I turn left, and why, if I think there's some to the right, I turn right. Believing there's some to the right explains why, if I want some, I turn right, and, if I want to avoid some, I turn elsewhere. Furthermore, this network involves not only practical but also other forms of reasoning (deductive, inductive/abductive) whose execution in varying degrees, particularly on a real-time computational model, is open to still further independent test. And the entire network is further constrained by the actual habits, needs, and physiology of the organism, not only under actual but under all manner of ideal conditions that a viable *ceteris paribus* clause permits.[5] If one seriously bears in mind all these constraints, it is hard to formulate a law of practical reason that, far from being circular, has a chance of being *true*.

THE INTERNAL PROBLEMS

2. I think people do worry about circularities in attitude ascriptions because of problems that arise in much of the ordinary practice of such ascriptions. For ordinarily we rely heavily on what an agent says. But this reliance is what raises what I have called the internal problems for practical reason, the problems of *akrasia* and self-deception: these are cases in which people do not appear to act in accordance with their expressed beliefs and highest preferences. The internal problems take on a special significance when we try to make sense of these phenomena while insisting upon the possibility of independent evidence of mental states.

A traditional reaction to *akrasia* brings out this significance. Socrates, Aristotle, and, more recently, R. M. Hare have been associated[6] with various forms of "prescriptivism," which denies the very possibility of people intentionally performing acts other than the ones they think best. At the moment of action, prescriptivists claim, the relevant considerations recommending the better act are somehow not fully in the agent's mind: she has temporarily forgotten them (Socrates), or they have become merely "potential" (Aristotle), or she is engaged in one or another form of "backsliding"—hypocrisy, permitting a special dispensation for oneself, using 'ought' in some off-color way (Hare). A serious problem with these accounts is that they seem circular and ad hoc. No *independent evidence* is provided for the momentary lapses, backslidings, or other problems to which they appeal· the only reason we have to suppose the belief has lapsed, gone potential, or slid back, is simply that the agent acts akratically. Worse, as evidence *against* any such lapse, there are the *akratēs'* frequent reports that at the time of the act they are not forgetting or neglecting anything (tell people you're writing a paper on weakness of the will and they invariably offer themselves as first-hand authorities). And then there are all the effects of the supposedly lapsed belief: an akratic act is often performed with greater or lesser fervor, and accompanied by feelings and signs of shame, disgust, glee (not all of us, after all, succumb to temptation with the "calm and finesse" of which J. L. Austin [1964, 58] boasted). But if the belief that some other course of action is to be preferred has ceased being actual, then what could possibly account for these further features? It is difficult to resist the feeling that prescriptivists are in the grip of the very kind of circular theorizing that critics of mentalistic explanation fear.

In loosening the grip of that circle, as Donald Davidson has admirably done over the last twenty years, we shouldn't, however, abandon all hope of applying practical reason to these problematic areas. But, in an influential article on *akrasia* and in a recent discussion of self-deception, Davidson (1980, 1985) seems to do just this. He views each of them as involving violations of general maxims of rationality. Weakness of will consists of someone judging that an action is best all things considered, but not judging it best and so acting *sans phrases*. It violates what he calls a "principle of continence": "perform the act judged best on the basis of all relevant reasons" (1980, 40–41). Self-deception he analyzes as a species of what he calls "weakness of the warrant," involving a violation of the "requirement of total evidence": "give your credence to the hypothesis supported by all available relevant evidence" (1980, 41; 1985, 140). He concludes that at least in the case of weakness of the will, "the attempt to read reason into behavior is necessarily subject to a degree of frustration. What is special in incontinence is that the actor cannot understand himself: he recognizes in his behavior something essentially surd" (p. 42).

But if *akrasia* is really so surd, why are people not more baffled by it? Davidson's account of *akrasia* assimilates it to actions for which there might exist no intelligible mentalistic explanation at all. Consider, for example, someone who, wanting to live and knowing a certain medicine will kill her while curing her disease, takes it anyway: she does this for a reason—her belief in the cure—but simply neglects to take into account the further, overriding reason ("taking it is better than not," she judges, even though "all things considered it would be better not"). This sort of behavior *would* be surd: one might well despair of any rationalizing explanation of it. But such a case, as it stands, is not a case of *akrasia*.[7] What *akrasia* presents us with are cases that, despite a surface irrationality, do seem to be in some way rationally comprehensible. This is in part because of further facts Davidson omits from his analysis. We seem to understand all too well the effects of habits, self-interest, strong desires, and how these things can cause and "rationalize" an agent's judgments and actions somehow despite her better judgment.[8] The philosophical puzzle consists in part in understanding that understanding, and in explaining why we aren't ordinarily puzzled.

This rational comprehensibility of *akrasia* is related to the issue of precisely what sort of irrationality we ought to ascribe to the *akratēs* and the self-deceiver. Davidson himself rightly observes that "we don't want to explain incontinence as a simple logical blunder" (1980, 40); nor presumably does self-deception arise from a failure to appreciate the law of noncontradiction. The *akratēs* and the self-deceiver can often *think* at some level perfectly clearly: the *akratēs* genuinely thinks that, all things considered, she ought to perform a certain act;[9] the self-deceiver, that a certain claim is wholly justified (the self-deceived, like the paranoid, can often provide dazzling justifications of his claims, and can innocently deny the inconsistencies we impute to him).[10] But violating obvious rational maxims of the sort Davidson cites would seem to involve just as serious errors in thought as violating laws of logic. Certainly they are errors that the agent could explicitly avoid in conscious thought and argument. The problem would seem to lie not with the patterns of thoughts themselves but rather with their lack of integration into the rest of the agent's psychology: in the case of the *akratēs,* with her acts; in the case of the self-deceiver, with other things that we have independent reason to think he knows.

Dividing the Soul

3. It is partly in order to distinguish *akrasia* and self-deception from outright irrationality that people have often been led to divide the soul. Davidson himself has recently been so led: "the idea is that if parts of the mind are to some degree independent, we can understand how they are able to harbour inconsistencies" (1982, 300). He offers no specific suggestions, but tradition is rich with them: the *akratēs* fails to resist his "lower," "animal" inclinations; "the spirit is willing, but the flesh is weak"; "'Tis one thing to know virtue, and another to conform the will to it" (Hume, *Treatise,* bk. 3, pt. 1, sec. 1); the self-deceiver "unconsciously" believes what she consciously denies. Though crude, these distinctions seem to me to be on to something right. But they do seem to suffer from the same circularity that plagues prescriptivism. What, after all, is "spirit" or "will" other than that which is supposed to bring about conformity to virtuous knowledge? What are "unconscious" attitudes other than just those that protect the self-deceiver from outright self-contradiction?

A division of the mind that does enjoy some independent motivation, and has figured in a number of recent philosophical discussions, is that between first-order and second-order attitudes. Richard Jeffrey (1983) uses it to explain *akrasia,* which he claims results when an act issues from a first-order preference for *p* despite a second-order preference not to prefer *p*. Analogously, one might suppose, self-deception consists in an agent's believing *p,* but believing that she believes not-*p*.[11]

This approach, I think, nicely draws attention to the very aspect of cases of *akrasia* and self-deception that it neglects: this is what might be called the *endorsement* involved in the attitude articulated by the agent. The *akratēs* endorses a certain course of action with which she fails to comply; the self-deceiver endorses a certain belief that he in some sense doesn't really have. The second-order approach can be regarded as a proposal to assimilate an agent's endorsement of an *n*-ary attitude to an $(n + 1)$-th belief or preference about that attitude. Some sense of what endorsement might be emerges from considering ways in which this proposal fails.

Suppose someone is tempted by some appetite to act against his better judgment. Appetites seldom exist entirely by themselves; they are often accompanied by meta-appetites that the appetite itself be sustained to the moment of satisfaction. Despite my diet, not only do I crave chocolates but I also crave to continue to so crave right up to the very moment that I eat one. Given how difficult regulating one's meta-cravings can be, I may go on to crave to crave to crave . . . to arbitrary depths of nesting and depravity. But, for all these nested cravings, I still might not judge that I *ought* to eat chocolates. This is brought out by the fact that I'm not to be counted akratic when I forsake all these nested cravings and stick to my diet instead. Unendorsed preferences can nest themselves indefinitely without ever securing endorsement, and so do not capture that endorsement.

Acting against second-order desires is not, then, sufficient for *akrasia*. Nor is it necessary: I may have first-order desires that I endorse, but about which I may have no second-order desires one way or the other. I might, for example, wish to be by the sea, and this wish may in fact play an important role in my life: I may feel it profoundly and sacrifice many things to satisfy it. But it doesn't follow that I *want* to have this wish. I might never have considered *that* as an option. Or I might wish that I would cease to love the sea and come to prefer more conveniently located mountains instead. However, for all my lack of love for my love of the sea, I still count as akratic when one fine day I languish lazily in bed instead of going sailing as I think I ought.

Nor are nested beliefs necessary or sufficient for self-deception. A self-deceiver could simply be the victim of first-order wishful thinking with no second order attitudes at all (I wish that she loved me, though I know she doesn't; so I come to believe she loves me nonetheless). Or the self-deceiver might suffer from a *mistaken* second-order belief without the corresponding first-order endorsement: a devout theist might believe that, sinner that she is, she hasn't really attained the faith. She believes that she doesn't really believe in God, but, when asked, does sincerely assert what she in fact genuinely believes, namely, that God exists. People, that is, may be *deceived about themselves* without, however, being *self-deceptive,* i.e., without actually making sincere claims that they don't believe.[12]

These cases seem to me strongly to suggest that an endorsement should not be understood as a second-order attitude. Rather, it is a kind of first-order attitude itself: my lack of endorsement of the chocolates is a failure of an attitude not toward myself but toward *the chocolates*; my endorsement of the sea is an attitude I have toward the *sea*; the devout believer, whatever her attitudes toward her own attitudes, does have the appropriate attitude toward *God.* So it seems doubtful that any account in terms of nested attitudes will do the work we need.

Kent Bach (1981), in his account of self-deception, invokes a different distinction that initially might appear to avoid this problem. He distinguishes "thinking" from "believing" in roughly the way that other philosophers have distinguished "occurrent" from merely "dispositional" belief (p. 354).[13] He identifies self-deception as a particular discrepancy between one's thoughts and one's beliefs. *Akrasia,* we might extrapolate, consists in a discrepancy between what one occurrently and what one dispositionally desires.

There are a number of problems with this distinction as Bach draws it. In the first place, by assimilating it to the distinction drawn, e.g., by William Alston (1967, 402) and Alvin Goldman (1970, 86) between occurrent and dispositional belief, Bach risks depriving genuine beliefs of causal powers in the absence of the corresponding thoughts. Goldman (1970, 88), for example, claims that "standing [dispositional] wants and beliefs do not by themselves cause acts. . . . [They] can cause action only by becoming activated, that is, by being manifested in occurrent wants and beliefs." This view accords with the examples Bach provides of purely dispositional beliefs that one has never entertained, e.g., that kangaroos are bigger than cockatoos (p. 354): surely that belief was never causally active until one "thought" of it (one "believed" it only in the sense that one would quickly have inferred it from other beliefs had the occasion arisen).

But it is clear from other remarks—e.g., "[a person's] thoughts do not invariably correspond to his beliefs" (p. 355)—that Bach intends beliefs to be able to have a life of their own. If they do, however, he must supply an independent characterization of "thoughts." He does supply this to some extent, but, in order to mark a sufficient contrast with "belief," he focuses on examples of momentary impulses and vacillations, such as being "momentarily deceived by a loud bang into thinking a gun had been fired or tempted by a piece of flattery into thinking one's lost youth had returned" (p. 357).

These kinds of cases contrast sharply with the cases of self-deception in which he rightly appeals to "the sustained or recurrent thought that p" (pp. 363–365).[14] Unfortunately, these latter are precisely cases in which it is harder to sustain the difference between thinking and believing: sincerely and sustainedly thinking that p—one might say, *endorsing p*—unlike impulse and vacillation, is usually taken as evidence for the belief that p. So precisely in those cases in which his distinction is most needed, it collapses.

Nevertheless, I think Bach is on the right track. What we want, I think, is some combination of Bach's "thoughts" and the "endorsement" that some but not all genuine beliefs involve.

CENTRAL AND AVOWED ATTITUDES

4. Cases of *akrasia* and self-deception present us with some sort of gap between thought and act, or, in any event, between what an agent *claims* to think and how she behaves. Now this latter gap *has* been independently observed. Besides the standard clinical literature regarding people's unconscious beliefs and motives, there is now a sizable number of "self-attribution" experiments detailing different ways in which people "tell more than they can know." Subjects in these experiments have been shown to be sensitive to, but entirely unaware of, such factors as cognitive dissonance (Festinger 1957), expectation (Darley and Berschied 1967), numbers of bystanders (Latané and Darley 1970), pupillary dilation (Hess 1975), positional and "halo" effects (Nisbett and Wilson 1977), and subliminal cues in problem solving and semantic disambiguation (Maier 1931; Zajonc 1968; Lackner and Garrett 1972). Instead of noticing these factors, the subjects frequently "introspect" material that can be independently shown to be irrelevant, and, even when asked about the relevant material, explicitly deny that it played any role. The positional effect is as good an example as any: fifty-two subjects asked to choose among four *identical* pairs of nylon stockings presented in a left-right array tended overwhelmingly (four to one) to choose the right-most pair, without one of them mentioning position as affecting them. Instead:

> when asked directly about a possible effect of the position of the article, virtually all subjects denied it, usually with a worried glance at the interviewer suggesting that they felt either that they had misunderstood the question or were dealing with a madman. (Nisbett and Wilson 1977, 244)

Other experiments deal with systematic errors in reasoning and the demonstrably mistaken accounts subjects provide of them (Wason and Johnson-Laird 1972; Wason and Evans 1975); cases of "blindsight" and extremely rapid visual perception in which subjects are able to make visual discriminations and recognitions apparently without conscious sensory experience (Weiskrantz, Warrington, and Saunders 1974); and, perhaps most dramatically, cases of hypnotic suggestion in which subjects respond to whispered commands and even to "painful sensations," of all of which they claim to be unaware (Hilgard 1977).

Stephen Stich (1983) argues that cases in which there is a demonstrable discrepancy between what is said and what is done lead to a breakdown of ordinary mentalistic ways of talk, of so-called "folk psychology." He claims that "it is a fundamental tenet of folk psychology that *the very same* state which underlies the sincere assertion of 'p' also may lead to a variety of non-verbal behaviors" (p. 231). He goes on to cite some of the above results as evidence that "*our* cognitive system keeps two sets of books," from which he concludes that "this is a finding for which folk psychology is radically unprepared . . . and under those circumstances I am strongly inclined to say that *there are no such things as beliefs*" (p. 231).

Stich supplies surprisingly little argument for this claim. Presumably he takes it to be a consequence of the close connection he claims exists between thought and (natural)[15] language: "A belief that *p* is a belief-like state similar to the one which we would *normally express by uttering 'p'*" (p. 231; see also pp. 79–81). Others feel this connection: Davidson (1980, 86) writes, "If someone who knows English says honestly 'Snow is white', then he believes snow is white," and, elsewhere (1984, 170), he rejects ascribing propositional attitudes to nonlinguistic animals.

But is thought really so closely tied not merely to language but to actual language *use*? It is hard to believe that animals don't have attitudes or that the above experimenters' own accounts of their results, namely, as showing there are *nonconscious* attitudes, are incoherent. What makes it so hard is that in both sorts of cases the attribution of attitudes has such *explanatory power*. Attributing beliefs and preferences to Norman Malcolm's (1972) dog that, chasing a squirrel, barks up the wrong tree is not merely picturesque; it is explanatory precisely in the way we considered earlier. We could, for example, systematically alter the direction of the dog's bark by altering (with decoy squirrels) his beliefs, or (with some well-placed bones) his preferences. Similarly, attributing nonconscious beliefs and preferences to the subjects in the self-attribution experiments often permits us to apply practical reason in a way that explains the results and predicts how they would differ were those beliefs and preferences to differ. Many of these attributions may be mistaken; but certainly they *make sense*. What attribution of nonconscious or nonverbalizable beliefs and preferences to people or animals does is to bring out the *explanatory* basis implicit in many of our ordinary ascriptions of attitudes: we are justified in attributing attitudes to an agent as part of an inference to the best explanation of her behavior and whatever else we know about her. Ordinarily, this explanatory basis may coincide, nearly enough, with the verbal basis so emphasized by Davidson and Stich. What the self-attribution experiments do is to show how the two bases may diverge.[16]

Having said all this, let me now take some of it back. The above account can invite the assumption that the verbal basis, being merely one piece of the total evidential story, is entirely subordinate to the full explanatory basis. We are justified in taking a person's saying that p as evidence of her believing that p if and only if the best explanation of her so saying is her so believing. It is hard to take exception to this line if one thinks justification in general involves inference to the best explanation. But strict adherence to it in the case of attitude ascription raises certain difficulties, difficulties that I think provide reason to preserve something like the independent verbal basis claimed by Davidson and Stich.

Consider how the explanation of someone's sincerely saying 'p' is supposed to go. Along the lines (and subject to all the qualifications) of practical reason that I have sketched, a natural suggestion is: she says 'p' because she believes p and most prefers to say whatever she believes. But this won't do; it doesn't have quite the right form for practical reason. Compare: she says 'p' because she has 'p' inscribed on her blouse and most prefers to say whatever is inscribed on her blouse. This latter is no explanation by practical reason unless we assume that she *believes* 'p' is inscribed on her blouse; indeed, that belief, even without the inscription, would do. Just so: the former explanation requires not that she actually believes p but rather that she *believes that she believes* it. But what reason do we have to believe that?

There are those (e.g., Sartre 1953, 93; Hintikka 1962) who think the "logic" of belief insures it: believing that p simply entails that you believe that you believe it. And so there is a reliable path from the belief that p to the production of an assertion that p. But too much psychological evidence tells against this further principle: someone may believe that p but never have bothered to have noticed that fact; or, as in the above attribution experiments, people may simply be mistaken about the beliefs that are influencing them. More generally, Daniel Dennett (1978, 273–276) discusses how animals might be first-order without being second-order intentional systems. Certainly a system might realize Fodor's program of practical reason—and other programs for deduction and induction—without intentional idioms specifically appearing in the descriptions of acts and consequences.

Furthermore, someone's saying 'p' will not be evidence that she believes p unless we also have reason to think that she does in fact believe what she believes she believes. However much the "logic" of belief may take us from a belief to a belief in that belief, certainly it doesn't take us back again. *Insofar as belief is regarded as purely an explanatory attitude,* it's not at all clear that an agent should be in any better position for knowing about it in her own case than she might be with respect to the states that explain her own digestion or metabolism. Why should we think a person has any sort of privileged access to the actual causal springs of her action? But, if she doesn't, if her believing that p and her believing that she believes it are so distinct, we are left with the problem of justifying our inference from someone's saying 'p' to her believing it.

The explanatory basis for attitude ascription seems to invite, that is, a peculiar dissociation of a person from her own beliefs. Arthur Collins (1979) argues that this dissociation tells against the entire computational/representational account of mind that I have been presuming:

> [Were believing that p identical to having 'p' inscribed in one's brain], the question, "Is p inscribed in my brain?" must have the force of "Do I believe that p?" From this it follows that, within the framework of the materialist account of belief, a subject can raise the question, "Do I believe that p?" and resolve this question definitively without taking any stand at all on the question, "Is it the case that p?" (p. 240)

One might complain that Collins' argument confuses epistemic and metaphysical modalities: the identity theorist he opposes could reply that if the proposed identity were in fact true when the situation imagined by Collins, while epistemically possible, is not metaphysically so. Indeed, if the identity were true then someone discovering that p was inscribed in her head would simply be someone for whom the question of p itself *would* be settled, should she only notice.[17] Collins begs the question against the identity theorist by supposing otherwise.

Despite this fallacious argument, I think there is something right in Collins' recognition of a special force in many (although he is wrong to think in all) standard first-person uses of at least some attitude ascriptions. Without there being any semantic ambiguity, speakers can utter sentences of the form 'I believe that p' with systematically different intentions. The literal meaning of the words, of course, involves merely the attribution of a mental state[18] to a particular individual, namely oneself; and they could be uttered with merely this intention. But the sentence is, as Collins suggests, more usually uttered as an alternative way of simply saying p: it "commits" the agent not so much to *believing that he believes p* as actually to *believing p* itself. Conversely, saying 'p' is often a way of saying 'I believe that p' ("Do you believe it's going to snow?" "No, it's going to rain"). Indeed, it is only this frequent pragmatic equivalence between the two forms that gives rise to "Moore's paradox" of someone saying "p is true, but I don't believe it"—otherwise, what's the problem? A similar commitment to a desire or preference is involved with standard uses of 'I want' or 'I prefer' and perhaps even with 'I think such and such is good': by so saying, the agent is not merely observing but to some extent "committing" herself to so wanting or preferring (which is not to say, with the prescriptivists, that she need abide by this commitment). We might call these latter uses of first-person reflexive attitude sentences *expressions* of those attitudes, as opposed to mere *reports* of them.

This distinction between reports and expressions is closely related to the distinction between the verbal and explanatory bases for attitude ascription that we have been considering. Both distinctions might clearly emerge together after one of the self-attribution experiments. A participant in the stocking experiment could be moved by the explanatory force of Nisbett and Wilson's (1977, 244) speculation that people nonconsciously prefer objects viewed later in an array. She might conclude on that basis that she, too, must have this nonconscious belief and so assert, "(I guess) I believe objects viewed later are better than earlier ones," or "(I guess) I prefer the later objects," much as an "educated" neurotic might acquiesce to the nonconscious motives ascribed to him by his therapist. But (as the optional use of 'I guess' helps make explicit) her *reports* of her beliefs or preferences in this way would have to be distinguished from *expressions* of them that she might produce using the very same words. These expressions would not be based upon her conscious acceptance of the explanatory speculations but would simply be a way of her saying that earlier objects are better than later ones. In the case of the educated neurotic, one wants to distinguish his acquiesencing to the therapist's ascriptions from his genuinely *admitting* (with, say, the appropriate feelings and "commitment") the ascribed attitudes. In *reporting* a belief, a person makes a first-person attitude ascription from an unusual third-person point of view; *expressing* the belief, whether by saying 'p' or 'I believe that p', is usually done "directly," from the first-person.[19]

When Stich thinks of a belief as a state that we would normally express by uttering 'p', he would seem to be collapsing the third-person to this first-person point of view, and with it the difference between reports and expressions. This may be why he finds so little room in his account for the purely explanatory basis suggested by the self-attribution experiments. There is this to be said, though, for that collapse: as a result of sincerely expressing, and so "committing" herself to certain beliefs and preferences, it would seem that someone must *have* those beliefs and preferences, at least "at some level." Otherwise she couldn't be *mistaken* in saying, as evidently the subjects in the experiment did, "Of course I don't think objects viewed later are better"; at worst she simply would be behaving misleadingly. Avowing 'p' or 'I believe that p' or 'I prefer that p' would seem to be *constitutive* of *some* kind of attitude toward p itself.

Such an attitude is not idle. It plays a significant role in our moral and social lives. Arguments, votes, examinations, affidavits, testimony in courts of law, parliamentary proceedings, marriage ceremonies: these are the most obvious cases in which people's avowals are taken very seriously, sometimes more seriously than whatever attitudes the best psychological theory might ascribe to them. When I "swear to tell the truth," I don't swear to make inferences to the best explanation of my behavior, but only to be sincere, that I may be taken at my word. Similarly, a person can't be held to wholly nonconscious promises or contracts even were it possible to form them: a serious promise just is a particular avowal.[20] The seriousness with which we take people at their word would seem to be related to the importance we attach to their moral and social "autonomy." At any rate, given the moral and social arrangements to which not only Kantians are committed, there would seem to be something more than merely legally wrong with allowing psychological research to change people's votes, reject their answers on examinations, void their contracts, rescind their vows of marriage, or convict them of perjury merely on the grounds that they really don't believe what they sincerely avow. Perhaps in view of some of the things I have said about the explanatory nature of belief, we oughtn't to take avowals quite as seriously as Davidson and Stich insist; but it is hard to see not according them some special status.[21] We should, that is, distinguish what I shall call "central" attitudes from "avowed" ones: central attitudes are the ones attributed on the basis of the best (mentalistic) explanation of the agent's behavior, that form the basis in turn for "reports" of attitudes; "avowed" attitudes are attributed on the verbal basis, and form in turn the basis for "expressions."

Avowed attitudes begin, I think, to capture the "endorsement" attitudes I earlier claimed we need for understanding *akrasia* and self-deception. To endorse *p* would seem to involve at least some sort of "inner" avowal of it. But we will not have gotten much closer to an understanding of this attitude until we can imagine what sort of difference in psychological structure this difference between avowed and central attitudes might reflect. The phenomenal differences are too elusive to help us out here; and behavioral differences won't do, since what we actually *say* may be a report, an expression, or neither.

SOME OTHER OPERATIONS

5. Defining the distinction between central and avowed attitudes is no different from defining other states and processes whose natures are embedded in explanatory roles, such as diseases, metabolism, or, in a more psychological vein, the distinction between perception and thought (cf. Putnam 1975). Just as we infer from a variety of behavioral and phenomenological symptoms *some* distinction between sensory experience and belief, so might we infer from similar evidence—particularly from the work cited by Nisbett and Wilson—the distinction between central and avowed attitudes. In both cases, the ultimate characterizations of the distinctions will probably not be in the behavioral or phenomenological terms by which they are introduced, but in terms of the best account(s) of the mind and brain. If, as I suggested in section

1, the best such account is in fact a computational one, then we can expect
that the distinction between the central and the avowed—as, for that matter,
between perception and thought—will ultimately be drawn in terms of the
computational architecture of the brain.[22]

Indeed, I think the computational model provides precisely the machinery
that we need. In particular, in addition to the computational operations B and
P that I introduced in section 1, we can suppose there are other operations,
AB and AP, such that:

x avowedly believes that p iff ($\exists \sigma$) (xABσ & σ means that p) and
x avowedly prefers that p iff ($\exists \tau$) (xAPτ & τ means that p)

As in the case of B and P, one way to think of AB and AP would be in terms
of internal addresses to which they might have access. Taking seriously the
"two sets of books" Stich fears we keep, we could regard a person as a
computer having two sets of addresses:[23] the "central" set, a set of addresses
that contains the contents of attitudes that enter through B and P into instances
of practical reasoning that largely determine one's acts in the fashion that
Fodor described; and the "avowal" set, a set of special addresses that specifically provides the contents, accessed by AB and AP, that serve as the basis
for sincere assertions and other functions in which one is to be taken at one's
word (oaths, promises, examinations).[24] I shall say that a person *centrally*
believes or prefers the contents that are represented by the sentences accessed
by the B and P operations; and that she *avowedly* believes or prefers, or
simply "avows" (explicitly or merely "inwardly"), the contents represented
by the sentences accessed by the AB and AP operations.[25] To a first approximation, one could say that, *ceteris paribus,* a person avowedly believes that
p if she would sincerely and decidedly assert p if asked; she avowedly prefers
p to q if she would similarly assert that she does. This can't be regarded as
a satisfactory *definition* of avowed belief: the *ceteris paribus* clause is too
generous, ruling out, for example, defects in an agent's grasp of her natural
language whereby she may fail to *say* what she genuinely avows.[26] That is
why, here as elsewhere, we need to go beyond behavioral criteria for the
requisite definitions, in particular to the terms of computational architecture,
i.e., to AB and AP, in addition to B and P.

Once we have these computational distinctions, it is clear that what is
avowed need not be identical to what is believed: i.e., that someone's accessing a sentence by operation B need not entail her being able to access it by
AB. In the case of much verbal behavior, of course, both relations may be
involved, but in different ways. When someone verbally *expresses* an n-th
order attitude she may do so because she has a central $(n + 1)$-th order
preference to produce a natural language expression of (some of) her avowals.
When she *reports* an n-th order attitude (e.g., "I guess I believe later objects

are preferable to earlier ones."), she *expresses* an $(n + 1)$-th order avowal regarding an n-th order self-attribution. She could perform either or both of these acts without both AB and B accessing the very same sentence (token, type, or translation), without, for example, the contents of an avowal address corresponding to the contents of any central ones.

Avowals, however, need not be produced only through instances of central practical reasoning of these sorts. They may interact with other psychological processes in myriad ways. Some avowals may be a standard cause (and in some instances partially constitutive)[27] of certain feelings of guilt and shame. Some reasoning processes may involve only A-like operations, as when one passes through a piece of reasoning "merely intellectually," and so comes to avow things that one doesn't centrally believe. Such reasonings may even be practical: one avowedly thinks about the best thing to do and straightaway does it. In these and in more "automatic" ways, avowal operations may be able to function to varying degrees independently of the central ones—e.g., leading someone sometimes merely to "blurt out" his avowals, in the absence of central preferences to do so, perhaps even despite central preferences to do otherwise.

Of course, except in cases of pathological dissociation, the two systems are presumably not completely independent: most people seem to enjoy a fair degree of computational and cognitive integration. But, notoriously, pieces of our psychology can become isolated from one another; not only may avowed attitudes become computationally independent of central ones generally, but, within both central and avowed attitudes, different subsets of them may become in varying degrees computationally independent of one another (as when one doesn't notice, and may even be unable to resolve, contradictions in what one avows or between different ways one acts on different occasions).[28] The distinction between central and avowed attitudes is perforce a crude one, intended here not to rule out further divisions and complexities but only to resist the simplicity suggested by tradition, ordinary talk, and an excessive concern with the unity of the self. (I shall, though, return to the issues of identity and personal identification below.)

The contents of avowals are presumably determined in a variety of ways. Both AB and B operations appear to have reliable access to the output of sensory modules as well as to various stages of explicit problem solving, imagining, and decision making. But many stages seem to be inaccessible at least to AB: notoriously, we are hard put to describe the rules we seem to use for such processes as recognizing patterns, making inferences, coordinating our motions. What the self-attribution experiments can be taken to show is that avowal contents can often be the result of AB's having access not to actual stages of internal processing but rather to *speculations* about those stages: people seem often to avow attitudes they merely (centrally) *believe* people like themselves (ought to) hold.[29] Sometimes this speculation seems to be affected by motive: what we avow can presumably also be affected by (central) desires, e.g., to please, comply, impress, intimidate, see ourselves as we wish others to see us. Supporting our ordinary suspicions of such effects, Ruben Gur and Harold Sackheim (1979) found that discrepancies between subjects' conscious misidentifications and nonconscious correct identifications (as indicated by Galvanic Skin Responses) of voices as their own or others were a function of their independently manipulated self-esteem (they misidentified their own voices as others' when they thought ill of themselves, and others' voices as their own when they thought well of themselves). Such phenomena are, of course, the very stuff of self-deception, to which we shall shortly return. The point here is only to emphasize the complexity of the psychology that may generally determine what we avow.

In view of all this complexity, it might seem that we are even worse off than we supposed in explaining how saying that p could be the nearly definitive evidence we ordinarily take it to be of the belief that p. But the point of the distinction I'm drawing is precisely to protect what we avow from that complexity: the reason we can so nearly take people at their word is that sincerely asserting that p is, *ceteris paribus, constitutive* of a *kind* of belief that p, namely, an avowed belief. What would be a mistake would be to suppose, as Davidson and Stich could be said to do, that it is constitutive, or even a very reliable indication, of a corresponding central belief. This supposition would be warranted only in those cases in which we might have additional reason to think that a person's avowed attitudes, at least about certain domains, as a matter of fact coincide with her central ones.

Does this model even tempt us to suppose with Stich that "there is no such thing as belief"? We don't seem to be similarly tempted when we discover that pretheoretic uses of 'jade' divide into two (Putnam 1975): there are simply two kinds of jade. Similarly, then, there are simply two kinds of belief (and other attitudes).[30] The burden of proof would seem to be with Stich to show what in folk psychology is genuinely resistant to such a view. Behaviorists are fond of pointing out how excessively friendly folk psychology is to homunculi, a friendliness borne out by our earlier, familiar quote from Hume. Why should these modest computational subsystems pose any threat? Perhaps the fear is that, without avowals, ascriptions of attitudes will become viciously circular. But, as I argued in section 1, this fear ignores the intricate cross-checking on which any particular ascription depends. Indeed, as should be clear from the evidence cited from the psychological literature, the proposed distinction is one with abundant independent justification. Given the evident divergence between what people avow and what they do, the distinction in effect simply shifts the burden of proof to those who claim that the two coincide. Perhaps all that my account amounts to is a denial of an uncritical Cartesianism that persists in our thinking about the mind.[31]

6. This computational model of the distinction between central and avowed attitudes provides. I think, a clear and independently motivated basis for an account of *akrasia* and self-deception. As with other accounts, these phenomena become species of discrepancies between the two kinds of attitudes. But not just any discrepancy will do. Mere self-*ignorance,* as when someone believes her grammar is other than it is, need not involve any *weakness* or *deception.* Self-deception arises when the discrepancy is motivated. For this to be possible, a number of other psychological states need to be present, and, as in any case of deception, some of them need to be second-order and reflexive. The following should serve as a first approximation of self-deception: an agent centrally holds some attitude that p and knows that she does; but, preferring not to avow it, she prevents herself from doing so, sometimes bringing herself to avow not-p instead.[32] Thus, someone may condescend to her lover because she centrally believes him a fool; but, being centrally ashamed, she prevents herself from avowing it, avowing instead a belief in his intelligence.[33] On this account, self-deception looks a little like insincerity, but is to be distinguished from it: whereas in self-deception what's believed is not avowed, in insincerity what is (in my sense) avowed is verbally denied (repeated insincerity, of course, may lead to self-deception, as we come avowedly to believe what we hear ourselves say).[34]

Within this model we can distinguish a variety of kinds and levels of self-deception. As we saw in an earlier example, someone may be entirely self-aware upon intimate introspection in his living room, but, motives aroused, he may be self-deceived in the fray; or someone may be able to avow attitudes in the presence of some people but not others. What is accessible by AB and AP, and thus one's self-deceptions, may in these and other ways involve a relation to a context. And there is the sophisticated self-deception open particularly to our educated neurotic: he centrally believes p, avows 'I believe that p' as a *report,* but fails to *express,* i.e., avow p itself ("I should tell you I care only about myself," he says truly, but with self-deceived avowed concern for his audience).

Akrasia involves more avowed knowledge than self-deception. As A. Rorty (1980*a*) has emphasized in her discussion of the "reflexive condition," "not only does the akratic agent have preferences, but he must be capable of recognizing—i.e., avowing—them *as his* preferences" (p. 345). For *akrasia,* familiarly enough, involves a consciously recognized losing battle between avowals. When Willie Sutton leaves his monogrammed handkerchief at the bank-teller's window, centrally but not avowedly wishing to be caught, he is simply ignorant. He needn't be self-deceptive: although he has the first-order desire to be caught, the second-order reflexive idea that he wants to be caught may not have centrally occurred to him, and so his ignorance can hardly be explained by a central desire not to avow that want. And since he does not avow it, he is not akratic: he cannot struggle with and "succumb to a temptation" of which he is entirely unaware. Of course, after a few visits to his therapist, who suggests to him the presence of this desire to be caught, he may come to have a further central desire not to avow that desire, and so come to deceive himself. If this doesn't happen, the content of the desire may eventually be avowed, creating for him an avowed conflict between it and the desire to stay out of jail. Avowing the latter to be the more important, he may then try to act accordingly, but nevertheless fail and act akratically. *Akrasia* occurs when someone avows all the relevant preferences, avows one to be higher than the other, but still centrally values the other over the one.

Many people (e.g., Sartre 1953, 90ff.; Thalberg 1982, 257ff.) worry about just who on such accounts is deceiving whom, or, in cases of *akrasia,* about who has the different desires (e.g., Matthews 1984).[35] On the proposed account it is perfectly intelligible that one is deceiving oneself: what is centrally believed is being intentionally withheld from being avowed; in *akrasia,* what is centrally most preferred is not avowedly so. It is as though one has adopted a policy about what can be "publicly" (even if inwardly) expressed, much as in a single government the executive might regulate the information available to the press officer (cf. Dennett 1978, 151–152). The fact that it is a single person with simply different kinds of attitudes permits us to distinguish self-deception and *akrasia* from self-contradiction and irrationality.

A person may, of course, choose not to *identify with* the central but only with the avowed attitudes. This identification is perhaps not surprising, since if I am *asked* about my attitudes, or consciously think about them, what I will express are the contents of avowals; and these are likely also to be the contents I would ascribe to myself in self-reports (but they might not be: I could, like the subject in the stocking experiment or the educated neurotic, merely *report* on what I take to be my central, unavowed attitudes). This identification with avowals may also be encouraged by our sense of our autonomy. It at least feels as if we can exert more control over avowals than over central attitudes: we seem to be able to "think" and "concede" many things "at will" that it may be none too easy to believe centrally, a fact that is no doubt related to the greater autonomy and responsibility that is attached to avowals in our social and moral relations.[36] This may in part be what leads us to place such great stock in our avowals, and so to be strongly motivated, as we are in self-deception, to shape our avowals to desired conceptions of ourselves.

The connection here with free will can make it seem as though at least morally one *ought* to identify with one's avowed self, and regard the central self as so much (in Kant's phrase) "pathology" or mere luck. But this identification overlooks the complex relations that may exist between avowed and central attitudes. On the one hand, one doesn't want to be overly burdened with the biases, superstitions, and stupidities that one may centrally believe despite one's better (avowed) judgment; but, on the other hand, one oughtn't to be swayed by now this, now that bit of explicit reasoning. *Akrasia* in this way can save our lives: having read a little philosophy, someone may avow complete skepticism about the external world, other minds, and the causal nexus, but fortunately find herself unable to act accordingly.[37] Much that people find important but "ineffable"—things that they "know in their hearts" but cannot say—may be due to subtle and complex central attitudes that are not easily avowable, but that they might find important to identify with in this second-order way. However, there is no reason to decide this issue of identification here. Just as avowals themselves are caught up in social relations, so are the identifications we make with them. Different identifications may be required for different legal, moral, or personal relations.[38] There is no obvious need for a person to *identify* with the person with whom she may nonetheless be identical.

In view of the complexity of the relations between central and avowed attitudes, I think we ought not presume with Davidson (1985, 139–40, 148) and David Pears (1982, 264) that the *akratēs* and the self-deceiver are *ispo facto* irrational. The heart may have its reasons that avowed reason may not know. Whether the agent or her acts are irrational depends upon the rationality of the central policies she has adopted about what she ought and ought not avow, which might in turn depend upon the role of her avowals in the whole of her psychic economy. As Davidson (1985, 143) himself notes, self-deception may be "benign," but one might even say "intelligent," when it involves one's attitudes toward family and friends, or attitudes necessary for living with oneself: having evidence that I have six months to live, I may centrally realize the useless torment the avowal will cause me, and so mercifully prevent the fact from being avowed (see Rorty 1988). One might (but needn't) criticize the *akratēs* or the self-deceiver morally or characterologically for such policies: but there needn't (although there might) be some error in *reason*. Indeed, where central attitudes are, as they sometimes may well be, *more* rational than those that are avowed, *akrasia* and self-deception may themselves be rational: A. O. Rorty (1980*b,* 201) provides the nice example of the religious youth who (to use my terms), despite his central absorption with the years of Enlightenment rationality, avows religious texts as a guide to action beyond all reason and mere mortal morality. When he self-deceptively avows that some religious act ought to be performed, and then akratically fails to perform it, he may be acting nonetheless rationally.[39]

It is not surprising that *akrasia* and self-deception, despite their similarities on my account, should ordinarily be distinguished. The means of coping with them are different. In cases of *akrasia* there is our peculiar ability to "try harder." Although it is by no means clear how we are to understand this ability, it is evidently something we can and do make use of in attempting to act on our highest avowed preference. "Will" on this view involves developing a central preference so to act: paraphrasing Hume, we might say that it is one thing to avow the good, another to conform one's central attitudes to it.[40] Its exercise, however, like its lack, *akrasia*, requires that we be able to avow the competing preference. But this, of course, is precisely what is unavailable to us in self-deception. The techniques of avoiding this latter difficulty are much less clear. While in the cases of contextual self-deceptions we may come to remember the admissions of franker moments, the uncovering of a thoroughgoing self-deception may require the insights of friends, therapists, novelists.

Self-deception and *akrasia* may cooperate with each other, and people may flicker back and forth between them. I may centrally prefer most of all to go to the movies, despite my avowal of the greater importance of work. One way to avoid the impending *akrasia*, of course, would be to reevaluate that importance. Centrally realizing *that*, I may then centrally arrange to avow all manner of sophistry rationalizing away the importance of, say, work on this particular evening: *akrasia* would then give way to self-deception. Perhaps only for a while; long enough to buy a ticket. A little later—conveniently too much later—the ruse may begin to fail, and I may be swallowed up by the familiar feelings of guilt, remorse, and anxiety about my editor's impending deadline. It is perhaps this particular phenomenology that best fits the prescriptivistic accounts, which so emphasize forgetting and backsliding. Whether most episodes described as akratic are like these flickerings between genuine *akrasia* and mere self-deception is a further empirical issue that need not concern us here.[41] An advantage of the proposed model is that it leaves many such possibilities open.

Unlike the prescriptivistic accounts, however, my account also allows for plain open-eyed wrongdoing, as when one lies in bed clearly avowing to oneself the importance of getting up, but fails to do so. And it allows that this may happen even while the avowed thought of the better act remains causally efficacious. Sentences expressing the contents of avowals may fail to be accessed by B and P in the execution of practical reasoning; but they may affect the course of that reasoning and other psychological processes in other ways. The central content that getting up is the avowedly better act may combine with central preferences regarding avowals—recalcitrance, contempt, "Evil be my good"—and so determine by other instances of practical reason further acts in defiance of the avowal. Centrally noticing that I'm still lying in bed avowing the importance of getting up, I am discomfited, exasperated, glad, and so pull the covers around me more tightly. It is precisely these details that can provide independent evidence for the retention of the avowed material, and so save this view from the circularities that plague many of the alternatives.

Someone might complain, however, that my account merely replaces one problem with another. For instead of the problems of *akrasia* and self-deception, we could be said to be left now with the problems of continence and self-awareness: how do we manage to get our avowed and central attitudes to coincide? The advantage of this problem over the previous one is that it is no longer particularly philosophical: there is no paradox here, nor any counterexample to a law of practical reason. There is simply the practical problem of learning how to do so.[42]

NOTES

1. The reader interested only in my positive view, and not in the motivation it receives from my criticisms of alternatives, could pass over sections 2 and 3.

2. Just *how* literally we need to take Fodor's hypothesis is a complicated issue into which I hope there is little need to enter here. The properties of a sentential model that seem to me to recommend it are its capabilities of (a) expressing structured propositions; (b) capturing rational (e.g., deductive, inductive/abductive, practical) relations into which attitudes enter; (c) individuating attitudes sufficiently finely to distinguish, e.g., synonymous descriptions, coreferential names, and indexicals; (d) explaining how attitudes can be causally efficacious; and, most importantly for present purposes, (e) permitting different roles and access relations for different attitudes. Perhaps there are other theories that exhibit these properties. Perhaps Fodor's hypothesis describes only a "virtual machine" that is realized, say, by a "connectionist" network in such a fashion that the sentences he posits correspond to no actual physical object in the brain. (For discussion, see e.g., Loar 1981; Peacocke 1983, Pylyshyn 1984; Cummins 1986.) I suspect there would be a straightforward translation of anything I say in this paper to any such alternative account.

3. S. Schiffer (1980), for example, considers the sentences as being stored in what he calls a "Yes-Box." For purposes here, an address may be regarded as simply a place where some coded material is stored in a computer for purposes of access in the execution of some computation. It could be a single localizable physical place, but need not be. What is important about addresses in a computational system is that they are *functional*, and are individuated by the computations and accessibility relations into which they enter: the computer is programmed to access the material that is "in" them, regardless of whether all of what's in them happens to be in one continuous physical place.

4. At the useful suggestion of Brian McLaughlin, my formulations in this paragraph are modeled on H. Field (1978), who, there and elsewhere (Field 1977), devotes his attention to the 'means that' relation. For a representative sampling of much recent discussions of this latter topic, see French, Uehling, and Wettstein (1979), as well the work cited in note 5 below.

5. I have in mind here particularly the role that may well be played by ideal epistemic conditions in fixing the semantic content of a person's assertions, or the inscriptions in her brain. Such a condition plays a role in the currently fashionable "detection" theories of semantics of such writers as D. Stampe (1977), R. Stalnaker

(1984), Fodor (1987), and G. Rey (1986). I believe idealization also plays an important role in answering skeptical challenges like those Saul Kripke (1982, *pace* 28 ff.) attributes to Wittgenstein. In all such roles, of course, the *ceteris paribus* clause is a commitment to explaining apparent exceptions to the idealization by appeal to independently establishable interference.

6. Prescriptivism is one fairly natural interpretation of the Socratic view presented at *Protagoras* 352c–e, and of Aristotle's view in bk. 7 of the *Nicomachean Ethics,* an interpretation developed and defended in Eunice Belgum (1976). But it is not the only interpretation: see, e.g., G. Santas (1969) and James Bogen and J. M. E. Moravcsik (1982). Hare's view is set out in Hare (1964, chap. 5) and in Hare (1963, 83).

7. Davidson (1980, 30), reasonably enough, wants not to restrict *akrasia* too narrowly—e.g., to "reason being overwhelmed by appetite," or "virtue by passion." And he does usefully draw attention to cases, like that of the late-night tooth brusher (p. 30), that philosophers have often neglected. But he draws the class much too broadly if he really means to include even cases like that of my genuinely surd medicine taker, or just anyone who acts only on some arbitrary subset of the totality of her reasons. Incidentally, it bears mentioning that these latter sorts of cases are not to be confused with the quite common case of people's failing to act on the totality of reasons *available* to them. It is of course not at all uncommon for someone to fail to bear in mind at a particular time all the considerations that she actually (dispositionally) knows bear upon a particular decision to act at that time; as I emphasized in section 1, what is important for practical reason on the computational model are the considerations that are *actively considered. Akrasia* is presumably problematic because the agent fails to act in accordance with *them.* In claiming that the relevant knowledge has become simply "potential," prescriptivists like Aristotle, I think, risk missing this point.

8. Davidson (1980) does allow for, but oddly dismisses, the relevance of these sorts of explanations. Immediately preceding the passage quoted above, he writes: "If [the question of akrasia] is a request for a psychological explanation, then the answers will no doubt refer to the interesting phenomena familiar from most discussions of incontinence: self-deception, overpowering desires, lack of imagination, and the rest" (p. 42). But the problem is how to make sense of these answers in a way that preserves the comprehensibility of the mentalistic explanation and the rationality of the agent. (Perhaps he is less concerned with these problems than others of us, given his general view of the "anomalousness of the mental" [Davidson 1980, 208ff.].) Notice that Davidson (1985) could claim that, despite their formal similarity, self-deception is not as surd as *akrasia,* since the practical reasons the agent has for deceiving herself do fully rationalize the self-deception. So in the case of self-deception Davidson could account for why we are not baffled by it. But, to anticipate my next objection, he still would owe us an account of how the self-deceiver does not seem to be thereby making an error in thought, failing to be cognitively rational. Practical reason, after all, is usually a way for an agent to select an action, not a belief.

9. Davidson (1982, 304) writes, "The standard case of akrasia is one in which the agent knows what he is doing, and why, and knows that it is not for the best, and why. He acknowledges his own irrationality." (See also Davidson 1985, 139–140,

148.) But *what* irrationality? If he does in fact know all those things, it is difficult to see what *error* the *akratēs* is making (notice in *this* description, the judgment that the chosen act is not for the best is *sans phrases*). As Davidson describes him *here,* it is as though, mind made up to do one thing, he then observes (with horror?) his body doing something quite different, acting on some, but not all the reasons he has been considering, helplessly dancing a tango when he decided to dance a jig. This is not *akrasia* but perhaps a purely neurological disorder.

10. There are other ways in which the *akratēs* and the self-deceiver may also be rational that seem to be not adequately captured on Davidson's account: both self-deception and *akrasia* may also be rational strategies in view of the whole of an agent's psychic economy (see, e.g., A. Rorty 1988), a point I will discuss in section 6 of this paper. None of my remarks here, however, should be taken to foreclose the possibility that people can be genuinely irrational, perhaps even believe contradictions.

11. Rob Cummins, Eva Kittay, Steve Leeds, and Eddy Zemach (in conversations) helpfully pressed a conflict between first- and second-order attitudes as an account of *akrasia* and/or self-deception. Nested attitudes have also been invoked on behalf of free will in H. Frankfurt (1971), and as the locus of ideal self-identification in P. Railton (1986), roles for which, for the reasons I raise here, I fear they may be similarly unsuited.

12. Such a situation of course invites "Moore's paradox": someone saying something of the form "*p* is true, but I don't believe it." I discuss this in the next section.

13. Bach (1981, 354) denies, however, that "thoughts," or so-called "occurrent beliefs," are kinds of belief. In this way he hopes to save the self-deceiver from self-contradiction.

14. The contrast is even sharper in Bach's "final illustration": "Consider someone who, whenever the prospect of traveling by air arises, develops acute anxiety about flying even though he believes that commercial flying is as safe as many other things he does without fear. Even while realizing the irrationality of it, he cannot help thinking that flying is dangerous" (1981, 357). Even if these thoughts are "sustained and recurrent," insofar as the agent doesn't seriously *endorse* their contents, I find it hard to regard him as self-deceptive. He seems simply the victim of disturbing thought episodes, like a person haunted by hallucinations to which he doesn't succumb.

15. The debate about the connection between thought and language is often muddied by an equivocation between natural and internal languages. That thought might require the latter, as Fodor and Harman argue, does not *entail* that it requires the former, even if someone—like Harman—might further claim that the two coincide. In the passages quoted here from Stich and from Davidson, the context strongly suggests they have natural language in mind. For the classic statement associating thought and natural language, see Wilfrid Sellars (1956).

16. T. Horgan and J. Woodward (1985), in an excellent defense against Stich's attack on folk psychology, also wonder (pp. 207–208) why Stich doesn't consider unconscious attitudes. It is worth noting that, unlike Davidson, Stich (1983, 104–106), does allow that dumb animals may have beliefs. I suspect that Stich believes that our only hold on the concept of belief is through expressions in natural language, and that when we claim an animal believes *p,* we are committed to the counterfactual claim that, *were the animal capable of speech,* it could express that belief by saying *p* in

its natural language: after all, it is in a "belief-like state similar to the one which we would *normally express by uttering 'p'*", so if it were like us in being able to express such states at all, it would presumably do as we do. Thus, admitting animal beliefs does not entail admitting unconscious ones, since even a linguistic agent may be unable to express the latter in words. Unconscious beliefs are a paradigm of beliefs ascribed on the basis not of language but of explanation.

Davidson (1982, 305) does admit the attribution of unconscious mental states on precisely the explanatory basis I advocate here, which he acknowledges to be so well exploited by Freud. But, as seems to me to be the case with Freud, this admission is reluctant, as though the *standard* case were provided only by the verbal basis. What I want to do is to reverse this presumption.

17. Collins might seize here on 'notice' instead of 'believe': noticing that *p* can't be the same as having '*p*' inscribed somewhere in your head, since you could notice that '*p*' is inscribed in your head without noticing that (you notice that) *p*. But here the opacity fallacy that Collins is also committing is quite plain: noticing that *p* doesn't entail noticing that *q*, even where *p* and *q* are *logically* equivalent (see, e.g., Bealer 1982, 69–74). Thus, noticing something's a circle doesn't entail noticing it's a locus of coplanar points equidistant from a given point. Similarly, noticing that '*p*' is inscribed in my head doesn't entail noticing that I'm noticing that *p*, even if the event of my noticing that *p* is identical to the event of '*p*' being inscribed in my head.

18. I ignore Collins' further conclusion (1979, 243) that belief cannot be a state of mind, since it is based upon the same fallacies as those discussed above.

19. This distinction between reports and expressions of attitudes is not the same as the related distinction emphasized by a number of recent philosophers (e.g., Lewis 1979; Perry 1979; Chisholm 1981) between ordinary and "indirect," or "emphatic reflexive," or *de se* self-attributions (as in "I believe that I myself [and not merely the son of Noël Rey] am over thirty"). The relation between the two distinctions deserves more comment than is possible here. Suffice it to say that self-*expressions* employing attitude terms are presumably always *de se*. Self-*reports* probably usually are, but needn't be: I could report on my own attitudes in a fashion that did not essentially involve the use of "I." This issue may be connected with the agent's sense of identification, discussed a little more in section 6 below.

20. This is not to say that there mightn't be *implicit* promises and contracts, which need not involve any specific nonconscious attitudes, and which presumably arise only in the context of some avowed conventions of promise keeping; hence my use of 'wholly'.

21. In a more epistemic vein, Raymond Smullyan (1983) has also drawn attention to the importance of expressing as opposed to merely reporting on one's beliefs. Along the lines already drawn by Collins, he imagines (pp. 62–75) a scientist relying entirely on a brain-reading machine to tell himself what he thinks about a particular issue, and wonders on what reasonable basis such a scientist could come to accept the testimony of such a machine. Somewhere along the line it would seem that he would need (at least "internally") to express and not merely report on such a belief, if only to check whether the machine is reliable. Notice that his "acceptance" of a claim as reasonable need not involve a belief of the sort that might determine much of his behavior: in his heart a biologist might really be a creationist—this might in part explain his

religious observances—while nonetheless sincerely avowing evolutionary theory in responsible professional matters. The role in epistemology of what I am calling avowals deserves, however, much more discussion than can be provided here.

22. The particular proposal that psychological states might be defined in terms of computational (or, more generally, functional) architecture is developed in Pylyshyn (1984), and, as a way of distinguishing perception from thought, in Fodor (1983). Philosophers wanting a more a priori account might, of course, complain that by so wedding our psychological terms to actual human architecture we deprive ourselves of the opportunity of applying them to beings without that architecture. But it is by no means clear that we ought to be worried by this deprivation: beings with a very different architecture from ours might well not have many of our psychological states, e.g., of *perception*, or of emotion (see Rey 1980, 192–193), or of *akrasia* and self-deception.

23. The sets need not be disjoint. They are determined merely by the operations to which they are accessible, and it could certainly turn out in many cases (e.g., accurate introspections and perceptual reports) that one and the same address is accessed by both central and avowal operations. In those kinds of cases, we would have then a clear basis for claiming that the agent has "privileged access" to those states that are in fact causing her behavior.

24. Dennett (1969, 118–119) comes close to the computational account I have in mind when, in his account of consciousness, he distinguishes the content that is effective in directing behavior ("awareness-2") from the content of a speech center ("awareness-1"), and (in Dennett 1978, 150–157) between "computational access" and "public access" to information in a computational system. Consciousness, however, is not the function of AB. At best, that an attitude is *available* to consciousness may be a necessary condition of its being avowed, but it isn't sufficient: there are many conscious events—disturbing images, impulsive thoughts, vacillating suppositions—that do not involve the "commitment" to any sort of belief or avowal. Moreover, though all avowals may be available to consciousness, not all conscious beliefs and preferences may directly reflect the content of avowal addresses. Our "educated" neurotic would seem to be consciously aware of believing and preferring all sorts of things that he still might not avow. Dennett's account does not restrict itself sufficiently for the purposes at hand.

Elsewhere, Dennett (1978, chap. 16), following Ronald de Sousa (1971, 54–56) suggests a different distinction, between "belief" and "opinion." Whereas beliefs may admit of degree and wax and wane with changing evidence in a way largely independent of one's will, opinion involves "making up one's mind" and "committing oneself" to a certain attitude. I see no reason, however, to identify this distinction with the one I am drawing between AB and B: both, either, or neither may admit of degree, and both may involve "making up one's mind." It certainly won't account for *akrasia* and self-deception as he proposes (p. 307): the *akratēs* may just as much "make up his mind" to smoke as to judge that smoking is a bad idea; and the self-deceiver can "make up her mind" both in believing *p* and in believing not-*p*.

Perhaps the distinction I want to draw could be regarded as a combination of Dennett's distinctions: avowed beliefs are the ones someone has "made up her mind" to (be prepared to) *assert*. Not just any verbal dispositions will suffice (that is what is wrong with the first two distinctions), nor will just any decision do (that is what is lacking in the third). What is needed are dispositions involving what we've "made up our mind" to (be prepared to) assert as expressive of our attitudes.

25. Herbert Fingarette (1969) distinguishes one's "engagements" from one's "avowals," the former being attributed on the basis of "the totality of the conduct" (p. 88), the latter on the basis of how one "define[s] one's personal identity for oneself" (p. 70). (Throughout those pages, Fingarette discusses in rich detail avowals and their social roles along lines similar to those I sketched earlier.) Watson (1977, 320–321), developing some remarks of Santas' (1971), also distinguishes "evaluation" from "motivational" senses of 'wants', or those wants that one "ranks" in a particular way, from those that actually determine one's acts. There has always seemed to me something right about these distinctions, although it was not clear to me how, particularly in the face of skepticism about *akrasia* and about the identities of the relevant agencies (e.g., Sartre 1953, 90ff.; Thalberg 1982, esp. pp. 257ff.), they were coherently to be made out. The computational model I am proposing seems to me to afford an unusually clear way of doing so.

26. In terms of the model sketched here, certain internal sentences might be available at the addresses that are accessed by AB and AP, but there may be defects in the procedures whereby those sentences are translated into expressions in natural language. (For a sketch of the kind of account I have in mind of natural language processing, see Fodor 1975, 58–79.) Such examples need by no means be limited to "verbal slips." Philosophically, an interesting source of discrepancy between what gets said and what might be genuinely avowed can occur because of various sorts of confusions, due for example to people's failures to appreciate the conventions and distinctions of their language, or the consequences of what they say. As Rogers Albritton often makes vivid, some of the power of Wittgenstein's later work consists in drawing philosophers' attention to ways in which they not only tell much more than they can know, but often say much more than they avowedly believe, e.g., in contra-causal free will, in a personal soul, in unlimited epistemic possibility, in unrestricted application of the law of excluded middle. Jonathan Adler has reminded me, though, that while what philosophers *say* may not properly express what they genuinely avow, it may coincide with what they centrally believe.

27. I discuss ways in which cognitive states may be partially constitutive of emotional states in Rey (1980, 175–176, 188–189).

28. Fodor (1983) discusses what in the present context are extreme examples of the kind of computational independence I have in mind when he discusses the "cognitive impenetrability" of what he regards as the sensory and language "modules" in the functional architecture of the mind. A good example is the resistance of, say, the Müller-Lyer illusion to our beliefs about the actual equality of the length of the two lines. Conceivably, the central and the avowal systems could in some cases be modularized in this way.

29. This is the hypothesis Nisbett and Wilson (1977) themselves advance. We needn't endorse here what seems to be their extreme suggestion that there is no difference between the epistemological position of the first person and a third person. For useful discussion and further experimental examination of the conditions under which people are reliable, see Ericsson and Simon (1984) and Wilson and Stone (unpublished).

30. In discussion, some people have balked at regarding avowals as a kind of belief. There is this to be said for my usage: it accords with what Davidson, Stich, and many others have thought was constitutive of belief; it accords with the important social practices and functions of belief that I discussed earlier; and it allows us to understand in what way self-deception is a kind of *deception*. But if someone (e.g., Audi 1988) wanted not to regard avowals as kinds of beliefs, I see no deep objection. The issue may be entirely verbal, as in the case of 'jade'.

31. See R. Rorty's (1979) discussion of "the glassy essence," and related claims about the self-transparency of the mind, the best recent examples of which are perhaps Sartre's (1953, 89, 93–94) claims about the "total translucency of consciousness." Sartre recognizes that these claims lead to difficulties in understanding self-deception.

32. I emphasize that this is a first approximation, intended to capture a large class of cases. Some people may want to include under self-deception various forms of "wishful thinking," which could be regarded as a kind of "deep" self-deception, consisting not in a discrepancy between a central and an avowed attitudes but simply in central, motivated irrationalities. Much of the subtle discussion in Pears (1982) could perhaps be regarded as addressed to this form. See Davidson (1985, 144) for reasons for distinguishing wishful thinking from self-deception.

33. Bach (1981, 357–362) provides a useful discussion of three ways this may occur: what he calls "rationalization," "evasion," and "jamming." He thinks, however, that these processes can't rationalize the self-deception: "Surely [the self-deceiver] does not reason, 'Although I believe that *p,* since I desire that not-*p,* I will avoid the thought that *p* whenever *p* comes to mind.' If that were what self-deception involved, it would be intolerably paradoxical" (p. 364). Similarly, because of the difficulties in attributing blatantly inconsistent beliefs to an agent whose belief that *p* we might infer from her sustained thought that *p,* Bach (pp. 354, 364) also peculiarly restricts self-deception to merely a passive form, i.e., to an agent's *failing* to "think" a conclusion for which she has sufficient warrant. These areas are perhaps where the distinction between *avowals* (as opposed to mere "thoughts") and central beliefs is most conspicuous. For if an avowal involves differently accessible content, as opposed to content that is merely activated, then there is no paradox in observing that people often do not want to avow, and so are led by practical reasoning not to avow, what they centrally believe, avowing the negation of what they believe instead.

34. Another consideration I would mention in behalf of my account is that it affords a clear way of making sense of insincerity. For the sorts of reasons I discussed earlier, we can't say that people are insincere merely when they say "not-*p*" while they believe *p*, or even believe that they believe *p,* or even when they *consciously* believe (that they believe) *p*: for if the conscious belief is merely a *report* of (e.g., what some psychologist has convinced the agent to be) a belief, the agent can't be held to be insincere. People can only be convicted of insincerity or perjury when the belief is one they deny when they are nevertheless quite prepared to *express* it.

35. These worries are very often raised with regard to Freudian accounts of these phenomena. It is a topic for quite another paper to show how much of what Freud wanted to say both about these phenomena and generally about, e.g., ego, id, superego, and primary and secondary processing, might be saved from these and other worries by computational (in place of his inappropriately "hydraulic") models of the mind.

36. In this regard, it is worth comparing Jean-Paul Sartre's distinction between "*en soi*" and "*pour soi*" to the distinction between reports and expressions, and so to the distinction between central and avowed attitudes; see esp. Sartre (1953, 90ff.). It can certainly *seem* as though avowals can be *creative* of a self that didn't exist prior to them: cf. E. M. Forster's remark, "How am I to know what I think until I hear what I say?"

37. It may be rational in such cases for her to develop a meta-view of her own psychology whereby she trusts her central "intuitions," despite her inability to provide any avowable first-order justification for them. Of course, were she to avow such a principle, she would not be akratic were she to act on her intuitions despite the other "best" arguments.

38. See Sigmund Freud (1953) and G. Matthews (1981) for interesting discussions of the related problem of taking responsibility for one's dreamt thoughts and "acts."

39. Other interesting examples are easily accommodated on my model. The akratic act need not be done in behalf of Appetite as against Reason: there is A. O. Rorty's (1980*b*, 198) tragic case of the *bon vivant* who, as I would put it, akratically forgoes central and avowed pleasures as a result of the central persistence of puritanical qualms. Similarly, when Davidson (1980, 30) gets up out of bed to brush his teeth despite his avowed judgment that he ought to remain contentedly in bed, he presumably is acting against pleasure on a central preference sustained by habit and/or an obsessive concern with his health. What are ruled out on my account are genuinely surd actions, like those of the medicine taker I discussed in section II, that are merely rationalized by some *arbitrary* subset of the totality of an agent's reasons. There are probably such acts. I simply see no reason to regard them as akratic.

40. If we are particularly Kantian, we might even insist with H. Frankfurt (1971) that, for the act to be freely willed, we must manage to perform it as a (causal) result of a second-order avowed desire to act in accordance with one's highest first-order desire.

41. I leave open as well the complicated issue of *akrasia* of belief, which may also involve complex combinations of self-deception and *akrasia*; see A. O. Rorty (1980*a*).

42. Much in this paper emerged from fruitful and enjoyable discussions with the late Eunice Belgum about her defense of Aristotle's account of *akrasia* (Belgum 1976), an account she would probably still prefer to any I have presented here. I have also gained more than merely many of the experiments and examples I've cited from talks with Eleanor Saunders and with Amélie Rorty: an earlier version of this paper served as a commentary on her American Philosophical Association presentation of Rorty 1980*a*. Still another version was read at a symposium on self-deception at the June 1986 meeting of the Society for Philosophy and Psychology. Brian McLaughlin commented very helpfully there and at several other times. The present version has benefited from comments of Jonathan Adler, Rob Cummins, Dale Jamieson, and Terry Winant, and from the thoughtful editing of Elizabeth Robertson.

REFERENCES

Alston, W. 1967. "Motives and Motivation." In *The Encyclopedia of Philosophy*, edited by P. Edwards, pp. 399–409. New York: Macmillan.

Audi, R. 1988. "Self-Deception, Rationalization, and Reasons for Acting." Chapter 4 in this anthology.

Austin, J. L. 1964. "A Plea for Excuses." In *Ordinary Language,* edited by V. C. Chappell, pp. 41–63. Englewood Cliffs, N.J.: Prentice-Hall.

Bach, K. 1981. "An Analysis of Self-Deception," *Philosophy and Phenomenological Research* 41 (March):351–370.

Bealer, G. 1982. *Quality and Concept.* Oxford: Clarendon Press.

———. 1984. "Mind and Anti-Mind." In *Midwest Studies in Philosophy, IX,* edited by P. French, T. Uehling, and H. Wettstein, pp. 283–328. Minneapolis: University of Minnesota Press.

Belgum, E. 1976. "Knowing Better: An Account of Akrasia." Ph.D. dissertation, Harvard University.

Bogen, J., and J. Moravcsik. 1982. "Aristotle's Forbidden Sweets," *Journal of the History of Philosophy* (April):111–129.

Chisholm, R. 1981. *The First Person.* Minneapolis: University of Minnesota Press.

Churchland, P. 1981. "Eliminative Materialism and Propositional Attitudes," *Journal of Philosophy* 78, no. 2:67–89.

Collins, A. 1979. "Why Beliefs Can't Be Sentences in the Head," *Journal of Philosophy* 76, no. 5:225–242.

Cummins, R. 1986. "Inexplicit Information." In *Problems in the Representation of Knowledge and Belief,* edited by M. Brand and M. Harnish. Tucson: University of Arizona Press.

Darley, J. M., and E. Berscheid. 1967. "Increased Liking as a Result of the Anticipation of Personal Contact," *Human Relations* 20:29–40.

Davidson, D. 1980. *Essays on Actions and Events.* Oxford: Oxford University Press.

———. 1982. "Paradoxes of Irrationality." In *Philosophical Essays on Freud,* edited by R. Wollheim and James Hopkins, pp. 289–305. Cambridge: Cambridge University Press.

———. 1984. *Inquiries into Truth and Interpretation.* Oxford: Clarendon Press.

———. 1985. "Deception and Division." In *Actions and Events, Perspectives on the Philosophy of Donald Davidson,* edited by E. LePore and B. P. McLaughlin. Oxford: Blackwell.

Dennett, D. 1969. *Content and Consciousness,* London: Routledge and Kegan Paul.

———. 1978. *Brainstorms.* Cambridge: MIT Press (Bradford Books).

de Sousa, R. 1971. "How to Give a Piece of Your Mind; or, a Logic of Belief and Assent," *Review of Metaphysics* 25:52–79.

Ericsson, K., and H. Simon. 1984. *Protocol Analysis: Verbal Reports as Data.* Cambridge: MIT Press (Bradford Books).

Festinger, L. 1957. *Cognitive Dissonance.* Stanford, Calif.: Stanford University Press.

Field, H. 1977. "Logic, Meaning, and Conceptual Role," *Journal of Philosophy* 74 (July):379–408.

———. 1978. "Mental Representation." In *Readings in Philosophy of Psychology,* vol. 2, edited by N. Block, pp. 78–114. Cambridge: Harvard University Press.

Fingarette, H. 1969. *Self-Deception.* London: Routledge and Kegan Paul.

Fodor, J. A. 1975. *The Language of Thought.* New York: Crowell.

———. 1983. *The Modularity of Mind.* Cambridge: MIT Press (Bradford Books).

———. 1987. *Psychosemantics,* Cambridge: MIT Press (Bradford Books).

Frankfurt, H. 1971. "Freedom of the Will and the Concept of a Person," *Journal of Philosophy* 68:5–20.

French, P., T. Uehling, and H. Wettstein. 1979. *Contemporary Perspectives in the Philosophy of Language*. Minneapolis: University of Minnesota Press.

Freud, S. 1953. "Moral Responsibility for the Content of Dreams," one of "Some Additional Notes upon Dream Interpretation as a Whole." In *Collected Papers,* vol. 5, edited by J. Strachey, pp. 154–157. London: Hogarth Press.

Goldman, A. 1970. *A Theory of Human Action*. Englewood Cliffs, N.J.: Prentice-Hall.

Gur, R., and H. Sackheim. 1979. "Self-Deception: A Concept in Search of a Phenomenon," *Journal of Personality and Social Psychology* 37, no. 2:147–169.

Hare, R. M. 1963. *Freedom and Reason*. New York: Oxford University Press.

———. 1964. *The Language of Morals*. New York: Oxford Univ. Press.

Harman, G. 1970. *Thought*. Princeton, N.J.: Princeton University Press.

Hess, R. 1975. "The Role of Pupil Size in Communication," *Scientific American* 233, no. 5:110–118.

Hilgard, E. 1977. *Divided Consciousness: Multiple Controls in Human Thought and Action*. New York: Wiley and Sons.

Hintikka, J. 1962. *Knowledge and Belief: An Introduction to the Logic of the Two Notions*. Ithaca, N.Y.: Cornell University Press.

Horgan, T., and J. Woodward. 1985. "Folk Psychology Is Here to Stay," *Philosophical Review* 94, no. 2:197–225.

Jeffrey, R. 1983. "Preference Among Preferences." In *The Logic of Decision,* 2d ed., pp. 214–227. Chicago: University of Chicago Press.

Kripke, S. 1982. *Wittgenstein on Rules and Private Language*. Cambridge: Harvard University Press.

Lackner, J. R., and M. Garrett. 1972. "Resolving Ambiguity: Effects of Biasing Context in the Unattended Ear," *Cognition* 1:359–372.

Latané, B., and J. M. Darley. 1970. *The Unresponsive Bystander: Why Doesn't He Help?* New York: Appleton-Century-Crofts.

Lewis, D. 1979. "Attitudes *de dicto* and *de se,*" *Philosophical Review* 88:513–543.

Loar, B. 1981. *Mind and Meaning*. Cambridge: Cambridge University Press.

Maier, N. 1931. "Reasoning in Humans: II. The Solution of a Problem and Its Appearance in Consciousness," *Journal of Comparative Psychology* 12:181–194.

Malcolm, N. 1972. "Thoughtless Brutes," *Proceedings and Addresses of the American Philosophical Association,* pp. 5–20.

Matthews, G. 1981. "On Being Immoral in a Dream," *Philosophy* 56:47–54.

———. 1984. "It Is No Longer I that Do It . . . ," *Faith and Philosophy,* Jan. 1984:44–49.

Nisbett, R., and T. Wilson. 1977. "On Saying More than We Can Know," *Psychological Review,* 84, no. 3:231–259.

Peacocke, C. 1983. *Sense and Content: Experience, Thought, and their Relations*. Oxford: Clarendon Press.

Perry, J. 1979. "The Problem of the Essential Indexical," *Nous* 13:3–21.

Pears, D. 1982. "Motivated Irrationality, Freudian Theory, and Cognitive Dissonance." In *Philosophical Essays on Freud,* edited by R. Wollheim and J. Hopkins, pp. 264–288. Cambridge: Cambridge University Press.

Putnam, H. 1975. *Mind, Language, and Reality.* Vol. 2 of *Philosophical Papers.* Cambridge: Cambridge University Press.

Pylyshyn, Z. 1984. *Computation and Cognition,* Cambridge: MIT Press (Bradford Books).

Railton, P. 1986. "Facts and Values." Paper delivered at the Morris Colloquium, at the Dept. of Philosophy, University of Colorado, Boulder, Colorado, March 1986.

Rey, G. 1980. "Functionalism and the Emotions." In *Explaining Emotions* edited by A. Rorty, pp. 163–195. Berkeley, Los Angeles, London: University of California Press.

———. 1986. "What's Really Going on in Searle's 'Chinese Room'," *Philosophical Studies* 50:169–185.

Rorty, A. O. 1980*a.* "Where Does the Akratic Break Take Place?" *Australasian Journal of Philosophy* 58, no. 4:333–346.

———. 1980*b.* "Akrasia and Conflict," *Inquiry* 23:193–212.

———. 1988. "The Deceptive Self: Liars, Layers, and Lairs." Chapter 1 in this anthology.

Rorty, R. 1979. *Philosophy and the Mirror of Nature.* Princeton, N.J.: Princeton University Press.

Santas, G. 1969. "Aristotle on Practical Inference, the Explanation of Action, and Akrasia," *Phronesis* 14:50–61.

Santas, G. 1971. "Plato's *Protagoras* and Explanations of Weakness." In *The Philosophy of Socrates,* edited by G. Vlastos, pp. 264–298. Garden City, N.Y.: Doubleday Anchor.

Sartre, J. P. 1953. *Being and Nothingness.* Translated by Hazel Barnes. New York: Washington Square.

Schiffer, S. 1980. "Truth and the Theory of Content. In *Meaning and Understanding,* edited by H. Parret and J. Bourveresse. Berlin: deGruyter.

Sellars, W. 1956. "Empiricism and the Philosophy of Mind." In Minnesota Studies in the Philosophy of Science, vol. 1, *The Foundations of Science and the Concepts of Psychology and Psychoanalysis,* edited by H. Feigl and M. Scriven, pp. 253–329. Minneapolis: University of Minnesota Press.

Smullyan, R. 1983. "An Epistemological Nightmare." In *5000 B.C. and Other Philosophical Fantasies,* pp. 62–75. New York: St. Martin's Press.

Stalnaker, R. 1984. *Inquiry.* Cambridge: MIT Press (Bradford Books).

Stampe, D. 1977. "Towards a Causal Theory of Linguistic Representation." In *Contemporary Perspectives in the Philosophy of Language,* edited by P. French, T. Uehling, and H. Wettstein, pp. 42–63. Minneapolis: University of Minnesota Press.

Stich, S. 1983. *From Folk Psychology to Cognitive Science: The Case Against Belief.* Cambridge: MIT Press (Bradford Books).

Thalberg, I. 1982. "Freud's Antinomies of the Self." In *Philosophical Essays on Freud,* edited by Richard Wollheim and James Hopkins, pp. 241–263. Cambridge: Cambridge University Press.

Wason, P., and J. Evans. 1975. "Dual Processes in Reasoning," *Cognition* 3, no. 2:141–154.

Wason, P., and P. Johnson-Laird. 1972. *Psychology of Reasoning: Structure and*

Content. London: B. T. Batsford.

Watson, G. 1977. "Scepticism About Weakness of Will," *Philosophical Review* 86:316–339.

Weiskrantz, L., E. K. Warrington, and M. D. Saunders. 1974. "Visual Capacity in the Hemianopic Field Following a Restricted Occipital Ablation." *Brain* 97:709–728.

Wilson, T., and J. Stone. Unpublished. "Limitations of Self-Knowledge: More on Telling More Than We Can Know."

Zajonc, R. 1968. "The Attitudinal Effects of Mere Exposure," *Journal of Personality and Social Psychology* 8, no. 2, pt. 2:1–27.

13

PSEUDORATIONALITY[1]

ADRIAN M. S. PIPER

I want to argue that self-deception is a species of a more general phenomenon, which I shall call *pseudorationality,* which in turn is necessitated by what I shall describe as our *highest-order disposition to literal self-preservation.* By "literal self-preservation," I mean preservation of the rational intelligibility of the self, in the face of recalcitrant facts that invariably threaten it. (The preservation of bodily integrity against physical assault—the familiar, meta-phorical sense of "self-preservation"—is a necessary but not sufficient condition of literal self-preservation in this sense.) By a "highest-order disposition," I mean a disposition that constrains any other disposition or motive we may have. Although I have touched upon some of these issues elsewhere,[2] all of this will need to be spelled out and defended at some length. But the basic idea, briefly, is this. Perhaps under Hume's influence,[3] we tend to conceive of theoretical reasoning as a kind of contingent mental operation, conscious or unconscious, which we perform on sentential propositions.[4] Whether or not we perform it is often thought to depend on such contingent factors as training (e.g., whether or not we have had a course in first-order logic), personality (e.g., whether or not we persevere in reasoning when the going gets rough), or the presence or absence of some object of desire we must calculate how to achieve. This Humean conception situates theoretical reason at a considerable remove from the kinds of factors—emotions, dispositions, desires, and so forth—we ordinarily recognize as capable of causal efficacy. It thus practically forecloses the possibility that theoretical reason might be motivationally effective in behavior. At least it is difficult to imagine how anything so seemingly remote from causation could be.

Some Kantians seem to accept the Humean picture. They assert that moral principles are motivationally effective only for an agent who is fully rational, where "full rationality" just means being moved by the thought of certain propositions.[5] The implication is clear that this stipulation does not purport to approximate the empirical facts of human psychology. Actual human agents who adopt such principles but fail to act on them are then portrayed as suffering from some (perhaps extended) form of *akrasia.*

I think the Humean conception is incomplete: theoretical reason is, as Kant saw, intimately tied to certain necessary conditions of selfhood and agency. However, what I shall claim to be the necessary connection between agency and theoretical reason confronts every such agent with the dilemma of her own imperfection: we cannot possibly make rationally intelligible everything that happens to us or everything we feel and do, without threatening the coherence of that which we *do* think we understand rationally. So we cannot possibly integrate all such events without undermining our agency. Rather than do this, we systematically distort and truncate our understanding, with the help of our rational capacities themselves, so as to achieve the illusion of rationality. This is, as a rough first approximation, what I mean by *pseudorationality*.

We do not strictly *have* to engage in pseudorationality. It is psychologically open to most of us simply to endure the anxiety, confusion, and power-lessness that often accompany reminders of our subjective fallibility. It is in our interests to do this. But reminders of our subjective fallibility are much harder to endure, if being right is more important to us than being genuinely rational; i.e., if we have a favored theory of our experience to vindicate. And they are even harder to endure if what reminds us of our subjective fallibility is our own enigmatic or personally unacceptable behavior, rather than some enigmatic or unexpected event in the world. For our own anomalous behavior poses a more immediate threat to our agency than enigmatic external events, and so calls forth an even more intensified mobilization of the resources of pseudorationality to withstand it.

This is part of what makes self-deception a difficult and central problem for moral theory: no matter how fully developed or compelling our favored moral theory may be, it is useless to us if we are psychologically incapable of admitting to having violated it. "A conscience," Alice Hamilton observed, "may be a terrible thing in a man who has no humility, who can never say, 'I might be mistaken.'" It may be even worse in one who has sufficiently mastered the philosophical reflex to be able to say this without, nevertheless, entertaining it as a serious possibility. Reflective self-knowledge may there-fore seem to be the antidote. But if self-knowledge, i.e., being right about oneself, is morally even more important to one than being right about other things, then the lure of self-deception will be all the more pernicious and compelling.

Kant saw this quite clearly. He saw that the really pressing motivational problem for actual moral agents is not *akrasia*, but rather self-deception. *Akrasia* presupposes that we know our motives, our obligations, and hence our moral derelictions with respect to them. But the more importance we accord to such self-knowledge, the more susceptible we are to self-deception about what our moral obligations are, and whether we have fulfilled them.[6] And of course self-knowledge *is* morally very important to most of us: we console ourselves with the thought that we may not be morally perfect, but at least we know what we are doing wrong.

Rather than examining the morality of self-deception, I want to consider the relation of self-deception to our favored theories in general, and reach some conclusions that will apply *inter alia* to moral theory.[7] I shall suggest that the greater the consolation we derive from the certainty of self-knowledge, the more susceptible we are to self-deception, because our inability fully to satisfy the demands of theoretical rationality requires it. But here, too, we do not *have* to deceive ourselves, any more than we have to engage in pseudorationality more generally. It is psychologically open to us to abdicate the aspiration to inviolable agency or to infallibility or to unalloyed moral rectitude by opting for a policy of *epistemic audacity*. If we are really serious about avoiding self-deception, this is in fact the only choice we have.

SOME UNARGUED ASSUMPTIONS[8]

1. First, I shall say that an event, object, or state of affairs (henceforth a "thing") is *rationally intelligible* to us if we can recognize it as an instance of some concept. To *recognize* something is to perceive it as familiar, i.e., as the same as or similar to something you've perceived before. If something is in no respect like anything you've perceived before, then you cannot identify it at all.

Second, the requirement of rational intelligibility implies what I shall call a *holistic regress*. This consists in two epistemic facts about us. First, nothing can be rationally intelligible to us in isolation from things to which we recognize it as similar and other things from which we recognize it as differentiated (thus its holism). And second, in order for us to have a concept of the kind of thing some thing or property is, we must have or be able to acquire a host of further concepts of the higher-order kinds of things that kind of thing itself is (thus its regressiveness). For example, if we recognize a thing as red, we must be able to recognize it as a certain color.

Third, the holism of the holistic regress implies that we cannot conceive a thing or property simultaneously as what it is and what it is not, i.e., that all the concepts by which we make sense of the world at a particular moment must simultaneously satisfy the law of noncontradiction.[9] This means that I must conceive all the things and properties that are simultaneously rationally intelligible to me as logically consistent with one another.[10] Call this the requirement of *horizontal consistency*.

Fourth, the regressiveness of the holistic regress implies that I must conceive the higher-order properties by which I recognize something, as logically entailed by the relevant lower-order ones as a matter of conceptual necessity.

Call this the requirement of *vertical consistency*.[11] I shall say more about vertical consistency in section 2 below.

Finally, I shall refer to the property of being an experience I have as the *self-consciousness property* of things I in fact experience, including both things in the external world and my own intentional states. If I could not recognize each of these things as having the self-consciousness property, I could not conceive any of them as my experiences.[12] To conceive an experience as mine is to conceive it as having the character it has partially *in virtue of my nature*. An agent who lacks the concept of the self-consciousness property lacks the recognition of herself as partially responsible for the character of those experiences. She views things as happening *to* her, but not in any part *from* her. Without an implicit recognition of her collaboration in the character of her experiences, she lacks a necessary condition of being motivated intentionally to alter them, i.e., to act. She therefore lacks a necessary condition for motivationally effective agency—but not just in the ordinary sense of being incapable of intentional physical behavior. She lacks it as well in the more pervasive sense in which we ordinarily conceive ourselves actively to *do* things like think, feel, infer, and search our memories.[13] So if I am an agent, each thing that is rationally intelligible to me at a given moment must, as a matter of conceptual necessity, instantiate the highest-order concept of an experience I have. Hence this highest-order concept must also satisfy the requirements of horizontal and vertical consistency.

These five premises jointly imply that if we are successfully to make coherent sense of things, including our own actions, we must, in conceiving those things, satisfy the law of noncontradiction in the ways the requirements of horizontal and vertical consistency specify. This is part of the sense in which the requirements of theoretical reason apply not just to sentential propositions but also, and more fundamentally, to those concepts of their constituents that form an agent's perspective at a particular moment: theoretical rationality is to this extent a necessary condition of agency. But then whether an agent is rational or not cannot depend solely upon contingent factors such as training or personality that some normal human agents have and others lack. An agent who is not theoretically rational in the minimal sense to which satisfaction of the requirements of horizontal and vertical consistency commit us cannot make sense of the world at all.

This may seem to be a very strong thesis. For it implies that, at any given moment, we must conceive the things and properties we experience in such a way as to satisfy the requirements of theoretical reason, whether they do so in fact or not. And this, in turn, suggests that we are unable to detect logical inconsistencies in our experience, or at least are extremely averse to doing so. In particular, this thesis suggests that we cannot conceive *ourselves* at a particular moment as simultaneously desiring contradictory objects, or as simultaneously believing contradictory propositions, even if in fact we do.

If this is true, it means that self-deception is just as inevitable as self-consciousness. For in situations in which we may simultaneously hold such contradictory beliefs, it implies that it is psychologically impossible for us to see this. These are the claims I want to defend in the following sections.

LITERAL SELF-PRESERVATION

2. Suppose, then, that you are in New York, making your way down West Broadway, where anything may happen, and you suddenly encounter—what? It is large, mottled gray, prickly, shapeless, undulating, and it moos at you. You have at the disposal of your current perspective certain concepts of higher-order properties that might enable you to recognize this entity—street sculpture, advertising gimmick, genetic mutation, three-martini lunch hallucination, tropical plant, Mayor Koch, etc.; but it is not immediately evident which one would suffice in these circumstances, or if any of them would. It is tempting to think that this is just the sort of case that belies the necessity of the requirement of vertical consistency to rational intelligibility. For in this case, it may seem, you must know at least that you have encountered a gray blob, even though you don't know what higher-order kind of gray blob it is.

But reconsider. If it is unclear which of those higher-order properties now at your disposal would enable you to recognize this entity, any of them might. If it is unclear whether any of them would, none of them might. If none of them did, concepts that would enable you to recognize this entity would not form part of your current perspective. In this case, you could not be said to experience this entity at all. If it is unclear whether any of the concepts constitutive of your current perspective would enable you to recognize this entity or not, then you can in fact neither identify this entity as a kind with which you are already familiar nor differentiate any such kind from it. The recalcitrance of this entity to identification in terms of the properties currently at your cognitive disposal calls into question *all* the concepts that form your current perspective: if they do not clearly fail to identify this entity, neither can they clearly succeed in identifying any other. So if you cannot now ascertain whether this entity is a three-martini lunch hallucination, a tropical plant, or Mayor Koch, you cannot ascertain whether it is a gray blob or not, either; or whether, if it is not, anything else could be.

This conclusion may seem to be too strong. Surely, it might be objected, it does not follow from the fact that you do not know what something is that you therefore do not know what anything is. Indeed it does not. But the preceding narrative does not address the question what or how you *know,* or even what propositional *beliefs* you have, but rather a presupposition of both of those questions. It addresses the question whether, if you cannot successfully *recognize* something you experience in terms of the concepts at your disposal, you can successfully recognize anything else you encounter at the same time; and concludes that the answer is no. If you cannot recognize something in terms of the concepts at your disposal, you cannot identify it as having the properties of which you have those concepts. In this case, propositional beliefs about, and *a fortiori* propositional knowledge of, that thing are impossible.

Again it might be objected that it does not follow from the possibility that your identification of one thing is incorrect that your identification of everything else is called into question. Indeed it does not; yet again the objection misses the point. The preceding narrative does not address the question whether your identification of something is *correct* or not, or, therefore, the question of the fallibility of your other identifications, but rather a presupposition of both of those questions. It addresses the question whether, if you fail to make something you experience *rationally intelligible* relative to everything else you experience at the same time, you can succeed in making anything else rationally intelligible at that time, despite this one failure. The preceding narrative concludes that the answer is no. If you cannot recognize something as the same as or different from something else, then you cannot identify that second thing relative to it. Hence the question whether you have identified either one of them correctly or not does not arise.

But this may seem unsatisfactory. For it *must* be in some sense possible for us to recognize an unfamiliar thing in terms of its lower-order properties, independently of our ability to identify it in terms of higher-order ones; otherwise how could we ever come to recognize and eventually categorize unfamiliar things at all? The implication would seem to be that if we were truly to adhere to the requirement of vertical consistency, we could never learn anything new. I want to defer addressing this valid objection until later in the discussion, after I have developed a more fine-grained taxonomy of agent's perspectives than that which we now have. At that point I shall suggest that it is, indeed, much more difficult for some agents than for others to learn anything new, about themselves or anything else, even if, like the gray blob on West Broadway, it is staring them in the face.

That you do not experience what is rationally unintelligible to you at all is why it would be a mistake to take the conclusion of the preceding narrative to be that your encounter with a gray blob on West Broadway will necessarily plunge you into madness. The preceding narrative has been intended, rather, to suggest that we have a very deeply ingrained, motivationally effective aversion to rational unintelligibility, because it threatens the rational coherence of the self as having that experience. We have already seen that an agent must, as a matter of conceptual necessity, finally be able to conceive of everything that happens to her consciously as her experience, in order to conceive of herself as capable of altering what happens to her, and so in order to exercise her agency. The preceding narrative shows us that, conversely, an agent who cannot conceive of her experiences in a rationally intelligible form cannot conceive of them as her experience at all, and so similarly lacks the agency necessary to change them. An agent who experiences events that she cannot make rationally intelligible in terms of the concepts that constitute her perspective at a given moment *loses her perspective on those events*: she confuses them with others, and all of them with herself. That is, she confuses all of those events with the rationally intelligible cognitive and conative events that constitute her perspective at a given moment. But a self that confuses unintelligible external or internal events with itself loses the ability to distinguish those events from itself, and with it the ability to defend its rational integrity against them, and so, finally, the ability to act intentionally in response to them. That is why your most likely initial reaction to encountering a gray blob on West Broadway will be neither madness nor annoyance, but instead temporary cognitive and conative paralysis.

It is this cognitive and conative paralysis, and the loss of unified selfhood and agency it threatens, that motivate us either to render a perceived conceptual anomaly rationally intelligible at any cost—even at the cost of plausibility, accuracy, and truth—or else to suppress the perception altogether. I shall refer to these strategies for preserving selfhood and agency against the threat of disintegration as *pseudorational* strategies. Below I shall try to say in greater detail in what these consist, and why they should be viewed as integral to theoretical rationality.

First consider the objective of these strategies, i.e., the preservation of rationally integrated agency—or, as I shall call it, *literal self-preservation*. As we have seen, literal self-preservation just is the preservation of the rational intelligibility of our experience in the form necessary for agency, i.e., as self-conscious experience. We have also seen that this, in turn, requires that the ways we conceptualize our experiences satisfy the requirements of horizontal and vertical consistency, however else they may differ. These requirements, I have suggested, are the familiar requirements of theoretical reason applied to the substantive and predicative constituents of declarative propositions we occurrently believe. This means that literal self-preservation is, in effect, preservation of theoretical rationality as motivationally overriding in the structure of the self. Theoretical rationality is *motivationally overriding* in that it constrains and is a necessary condition of any other motive an agent may have. For without it, there would be no agent to be motivated to perform any particular action whatsoever. So literal self-preservation must be a biologically fundamental disposition that any such action—and any more particular motivation for it—must presuppose.[14] Since it enables us to preserve the consistency of the highest-order concept of our selves as having our experiences, and so constrains all other motives we as agents can have, I shall describe it as a *highest-order disposition to literal self-preservation*.

That literal self-preservation, i.e., the preservation of the theoretical rationality of the self, is in this sense motivationally overriding in the structure of the self, may help to explain why, when confronted by a conceptual anomaly, we are more inclined either to suppress it from consciousness altogether or to distort or truncate the concepts constitutive of our perspective in order to accommodate it. For the alternative would be passively to acquiesce in the threat of unintelligibility, disorientation, and ego-disintegration that such an anomaly represents. By definition, such an inclination towards biological self-defeat could have no survival value whatsoever.

That literal self-preservation has biological survival value implies, of course, that it has *value,* i.e., that it is, for us, a normative good. But we have just seen that literal self-preservation just is the preservation of the rational intelligibility of one's experience, i.e., satisfaction of the requirements of horizontal and vertical consistency. This means that what we often refer to as descriptive or explanatory coherence is itself a normative good— one we must achieve to some degree before we can even strive to achieve any other. Now in some ways this may seem to be an impossible task. We are continually assaulted, if not by the presence of gray blobs, by other internal and external experiences that test the psychological strength of the self to withstand them, or its cognitive flexibility to accommodate them within the constraints of rational intelligibility. And we must take it as a given that we can neither withstand all such events—on pain of the fate that frequently befalls ostriches who bury their heads in the sand—nor accommodate all of them—on pain of the fate that befalls overladen computers, whose simulated cognitive psychoses bear a touching resemblance to our own. On the other hand, theoretical reason is all we have for coping with such cognitive assaults. So the requirements of theoretical reason must be systematically attenuated and bent somewhat in order to do so. Its consistency requirements must remain in force, but be made easier to satisfy; the stringency of those requirements must be upheld, yet tempered by rational loopholes. The result is not rational intelligibility in the sense described above, but rather pseudorationality. Let us now examine how the strategies of pseudorationality function.

Pseudorationality

3. The pseudorational strategies I want to target are three in number: denial, dissociation, and rationalization respectively. There are probably others, but I believe these three are primary, for reasons that will become clear in what follows. But briefly, *denial* is our imperfect attempt to satisfy the comprehensive requirement of rational intelligibility, whereas *dissociation* is our imperfect attempt to satisfy the requirement of horizontal consistency, and *rationalization* our imperfect attempt to satisfy the requirement of vertical consistency.

We have already seen how what I shall refer to as *denial* might operate in cases in which the arsenal of concepts constitutive of an agent's perspective is completely inadequate to identify a conceptual anomaly: if one has no concepts even remotely appropriate for coping cognitively with the thing in question, one will simply fail to register that thing as an experience one has. Here the preservation of rational intelligibility, i.e., literal self-preservation, requires that one remain oblivious to the thing's presence.

But now contrast this case with one in which denial is required, not in order to preserve the rational intelligibility of one's experience as such, but rather the rational intelligibility of *a certain interpretation or theory of* one's experience. The distinction can be limned as follows. I may be able to make sense of everything I experience *as my experience,* without trying or being able to make sense of it as confirming the *theory* that, say, it's a jungle out there or that everything happens for a reason or that I am a serious person, or some more sophisticated theory of human nature or the physical world or myself. In the first case, the rational intelligibility of my experience is a function of its horizontal and vertical consistency relation to the highest-order concept of the self-consciousness property *simpliciter*: all the experiences I have are mutually consistent with one another relative to the concept of their being my experiences. This is the only highest-order concept that unifies all of them. I shall describe someone who conceives her experience in this way as a *naïf.*

The naïf lacks what I shall describe as a *personal investment* in any particular theory of her experience. I shall say that an agent A is personally invested in something t if (1) t's existence is a source of personal pleasure, satisfaction, or security to A; (2) t's nonexistence elicits feelings of dejection, deprivation, or anxiety from A; and (3) these feelings are to be explained by A's identification with t. *A identifies with t* if A is disposed to identify t *as* personally meaningful or valuable to A.[15] Since the naïf lacks a personal investment in any particular theory of her experience, she is less prone to encounter genuine conceptual anomalies. For the only requirement something must meet in order to be rationally intelligible as one of her experiences is that it must be the kind of thing she *can,* in fact, experience. Included among the lower-order concepts that constitute the naïf's perspective are the commonsense observational ones of size, shape, color, etc., we all share. But absent from that perspective are higher-order concepts that qualify and restrict the scope of those observational concepts to any particular *theory* of the kind of thing one can in fact experience. Since the naïf lacks higher-order pet theories that restrict what qualifies as, say, contemporary art, the possible mutant effects of radioactive fallout, Mayor Koch's attention-getting devices, etc., that a mottled gray, mooing blob on West Broadway might violate, she has less cause to suppress recognition of such a blob than you or I. But we already know, from folklore and history as well as from personal experience, that naïfs, and children, often see many things, not just the emperor's sartorial desolation, that the rest of us systematically overlook.

Contrast the second case, in which I do have a personal investment in some favored theory of my experience.[16] This case is different. For here the rational intelligibility of my experience is a function of its horizontal and vertical consistency relative to *two* higher-order concepts, the mutual relation of which may vary. First, there is the concept of things as experiences I have, and second, there is the concept of things as confirming my favored theory of my experience. What is the relation between these two? There are at least three possibilities.

We have already seen (section 2) that the second concept could not dominate the first without violating a necessary condition of agency. Of course this does not mean it cannot dominate the first, period. By an *ideologue*, I shall mean someone who regards her experience as an instantiation of her theory, rather than the other way around. She thus has a sense of mystical inevitability about herself, as an impersonal force in the world that, like other such forces, behaves in the ways her theory predicts. The ideologue may seem to have the concept of the self-consciousness property, in that she recognizes things that happen to her as experiences she has. But in fact this recognition is hollow, because she does not, in so doing, recognize things as happening to her precisely in that form *in virtue of her nature*. Instead, she thinks her experience has the character it does in virtue of the forces, specified in the theory, that determine her nature. And she interprets her own active responses to that experience in similarly impersonal terms, not in terms of personal motivations to alter it. Because the ideologue accepts no responsibility for the particular character of her experience, in fact she does *not* fully grasp the concept of the self-consciousness property. Hence she abdicates a necessary condition of motivationally effective agency: her thoughts, feelings, and impulses are to her a series of *aha-Erlebnisse,* forced upon her by her situation; and she is, to varying degrees, propelled into action by impersonal internal forces that are beyond her intentional control.

For the ideologue, a conceptual anomaly is intolerable. By threatening the rational intelligibility of her favored theory of her experience, it threatens, so far as she is concerned, not only the rational intelligibility of that experience itself, but thereby the rational intelligibility of the universe and her predestined place in it. Because she regards her own experience as an instance of her theory, rather than the other way around, it is not open to her to rethink her perspective on the world as independent of that world itself. Her perspective is such that she views it as fully determined by that world, in the ways specified by the theory that purportedly describes it. To undermine the theory, then, is to undermine everything at once. For the ideologue, conceptual anomalies do not exist. I shall say more shortly about some more subtle pseudorational mechanisms by which they are made to disappear.

Like the ideologue, the character I shall describe as the *solipsist* also attempts to make all her experiences rationally intelligible, relative both to her favored theory and to the concept of the self-consciousness property. But by contrast with the ideologue, the solipsist reverses the relation between them, for she recognizes her favored theory, and its confirmation by her experiences, as itself an experience she has. So even if her theory that, say, it's a jungle out there or that she is a serious person does, in fact, make all of her experience rationally intelligible, she conceives it as doing so *in virtue of her nature,* i.e., as itself an experience she has: her favored theory is subordinate to the highest-order concept of the self-consciousness property. Because of this order of priorities, the solipsist's investment in any such theory can never be more than tentative, and her attitude toward it never more than pragmatic. If the theory makes sense of what is *already* rationally intelligible as her experience, well and good. If it is undermined by a conceptual anomaly, then it is to be modified or replaced. But this is merely to restate what we already know about solipsists, namely that they are, on the one hand, inclined to skepticism about higher-order explanatory theories, and on the other, fondly attached to the observational data those theories are recruited to explain.

Like the naïf, the solipsist has less trouble with conceptual anomalies than the ideologue. For since she recognizes even her favored theory to have the character it does in virtue of her nature, her personal investment in it cannot be so absolute as to blind her to the possibility of its—and her—limitations. And since she lacks such an overriding personal investment in her favored theory, its modification or eventual replacement by a theory better able to accommodate the existence of gray blobs is more a matter of regret than anxiety or panic. Finally, since her conceptualization of her experience as hers takes priority over her conceptualization of it in terms of any such tentatively held theory, she is, like the naïf, freer to recognize a gray blob simply for what it is.

The figure for whom the relation between the concepts of the self-consciousness property and of her favored theory as confirmed by her experience presents a genuine dilemma is one I shall call the *dogmatist.* Luckily, this dilemma is one the dogmatist is unusually well-equipped to solve. For the dogmatist, the relation between these two concepts is one of uneasy parity: both are of the highest order in the dogmatist's perspective; neither is subordinate to the other. The dogmatist both conceptualizes all of her experience as hers and conceptualizes it as instantiating her favored theory. The dogmatist would not deny that her experiences have the particular character they have in virtue of her nature. Nor would she deny that they have that character in virtue of the truth of her favored theory. Rather, the dogmatist would congratulate herself on the good fortune of being so constituted that the way she experiences the world is, in fact, the way it is. Thus for the dogmatist, these two concepts are materially equivalent.

The notion of being personally invested in one's favored theory about the world has special poignancy in the case of the dogmatist. For the dogmatist is someone who does derive very great pleasure, satisfaction, and security from her favored theory of her experience (indeed, the dogmatist may feel instinctively that it is the only genuine source of security to be had); and these feelings are, of course, to be explained by her identification with her favored theory. But notice that the higher-order priority she gives to her favored theory implies her identification with it in an even stronger sense than that required by the definition of personal investment. Her favored theory of her experience is not just personally meaningful or valuable to her; it *is* her at the deepest level of self-identification. For as we have just seen, she assumes that the way she experiences the world is, in fact, the way her theory depicts it; and that this, in turn, is the way it is.

Conceptual anomalies that threaten or undermine the rational intelligibility of the dogmatist's favored theory are correspondingly anxiety producing. For in so doing, they undermine the dogmatist's conception of her own experience, and the rational intelligibility of that experience itself. Thus the dogmatist is like the naïf and the ideologue (and unlike the solipsist), in that all three are made more susceptible to rational self-disintegration by their unqualified attachment to the concepts that constitute their perspectives. But the dogmatist is like the ideologue (but unlike the naïf and the solipsist), in that the personal investment of both in favored theories of their experience constricts the scope of their experience, and so brings the threat of rational self-disintegration that much closer. Because the favored theory with which the dogmatist strongly identifies restricts the range of concepts by which to make sense of those realities, her perspective on them is correspondingly less open-ended, more rigid, and therefore more fragile. The constriction and fragility of the dogmatist's perspective creates more occasions on which she may encounter conceptual anomalies, to the extent that her favored theory excludes more from its scope of rational intelligibility: modern art, ESP, the inscrutable cultural Other, avant-garde styles of self-presentation, play, astrology, jokes, interpersonal theater, agitprop cultural subversion, and her own delinquent impulses must be either explained (or explained away) by her theory or else consigned to conceptual oblivion. It is for the dogmatist, as for the ideologue, then, that the gray blob on West Broadway may present a real problem.

We can now distinguish three circumstances in which denial may be an expected response to the presence of a conceptual anomaly; only the last is, strictly speaking, a *pseudorational* response. First, it may function, as it does for the naïf, to eradicate from consciousness something that is anomalous relative even to the most comprehensive and flexible concept one has, namely the concept of something as an experience one has. Something that is not recognizable in these terms is by definition conceptually inaccessible, and so is not a candidate for rational intelligibility in the first place.

Second, denial may function as it does for the solipsist, who is in a loose sense a member of the scientific community, in that her favored theory of her experience has been tested, confirmed, and consensually validated to some extent by that community (macroscopic determinism might exemplify such a theory). Something that is a conceptual anomaly relative to such a theory still may be an experience one has, but the weight of consensus and scientific method militate against acknowledging it as such. Under these circumstances, the anomaly may be a candidate for rational intelligibility, but the solipsist's skepticism, plus the weight of theoretical reason itself, is against it. Here again, denial is consistent with the requirements of theoretical reason.

Third, denial may function as it does for the dogmatist or the ideologue, whose theories may or may not receive consensual validation, but whose theoretical biases in either case would not survive disinterested critical scrutiny. To determine this here we may, but need not, appeal to rational method. We have a commonsense, lay criterion for distinguishing that which is so obscure or genuinely enigmatic as to be rationally inaccessible, from that which is intersubjectively obvious, namely, *third-person disinterested recognition*. If a third party, similarly equipped both culturally and cognitively, but lacking the dogmatist's personal investment in her favored theory, can make the thing rationally intelligible relative to her own perspective, whereas the dogmatist cannot relative to hers, then the dogmatist's difficulty is not that the thing in question is conceptually anomalous, but that her favored theory is just too restrictive or parochial to accommodate it. In this case, her denial of the thing in order to preserve the rational intelligibility of her theory is a pseudorational strategy.

Because she identifies her experience with her theory, rather than conceiving her experience as subordinate to it, the dogmatist has, in addition to pseudorational denial, cognitive resources for meeting such challenges that the ideologue lacks. We have already seen that because the latter lacks a necessary condition of agency, she lacks the conception of herself as actively *doing* things like thinking, inferring, and searching her memory. This is not to say that she does not do these things at all; just that she does not conceive herself as doing them. Hence by contrast with the solipsist, the ideologue does not conceive herself as capable of revising or rethinking her favored theory—or, by contrast with the dogmatist, as capable of rearranging it to fit the facts.

The dogmatist has the same cognitive resources for conceptually rearranging things as she had for arranging them in the first place, in order to satisfy the two consistency requirements of rational intelligibility. And she is more highly motivated to do so by the fragility and constriction of her theory and her self-protectiveness toward it. That is, the dogmatist does not just have a biologically fundamental *disposition* to render her experiences horizontally and vertically consistent, as the rational intelligibility of those experiences requires. In addition, she has a contingent but central *desire* to render her experiences horizontally and vertically consistent, relative to the requirements and constraints of her favored theory of those experiences. And the more parochial her theory, the stronger this desire must be. Thus the requirements of horizontal and vertical consistency afford the dogmatist the option of two more subtle pseudorational strategies, in addition to blanket denial, for dealing with conceptual anomalies. And her natural disposition to satisfy these requirements, together with her personal investment in her favored theory, motivates her to exercise those strategies.

From now on, in discussing these two further pseudorational strategies, I shall speak not just about the dogmatist but also about *us*. This is not because I think anyone who is likely to read this essay is purely and simply a dogmatist in the sense in which I have described one. Obviously, the naïf, the ideologue, the solipsist and the dogmatist are all equally caricatures, abstracted from more complex agents whose dispositions and perspectives may change from moment to moment, and who are capable of exhibiting the characteristics of each. But I do think that anyone likely to read this essay probably does have a favored theory of her or his experience, however nascent or inchoate, a theory in which she or he is, to varying degrees, personally invested. So I hope to be analyzing cognitive phenomena that all of us will recognize.

Our disposition to satisfy the requirement of horizontal consistency supplies us with the pseudorational strategy I shall dub *dissociation*. Recall that horizontal consistency requires us to conceive all our experience at a given moment as mutually logically consistent, i.e., as satisfying the law of noncontradiction. Relative to a favored theory of that experience, this is to require, first, that the theory be horizontally consistent, and second, that all our experience be recognizable in the theory's terms. A conceptual anomaly is then by definition anything that defies recognition in these terms. In dissociation, the anomaly is then identified in terms of the negation of some or all of the concepts that constitute the theory; thus the horizontal consistency of our experience is preserved.

This is one juncture that separates the dogmatist from the solipsist. The solipsist's tentative investment in her theory allows her greater detachment from it, which enables her more easily to rethink or revise it in order to accommodate what appears to be a conceptual anomaly. By contrast, the dogmatist's personal investment and self-identification with her theory makes her reluctant to abdicate or modify it, and inclines her to construe her theory, and therefore the events and phenomena it explains, honorifically, as normative goods. Relative to these, the negation of her theory that a conceptual anomaly represents is to be dismissed not only as intrinsically alien and inscrutable but therefore as *insignificant,* without value, and so unworthy of further attention.

Reconsider, for example, the gray blob on West Broadway. There are, obviously, a variety of ways of making sense of this entity, and we have considered some of them. But it is equally easy to construct a rather arid theory of one's experience in which there is simply no room for such things: a theory, say, in which there are two sexes, three races, a circumscribed set of acceptable roles and relations among them, an equally circumscribed set of acceptable norms of behavior, dress, and creative expression, and a further division of the human race into those who observe these standards and those who do not. Not only gray blobs but much else that is of interest, not just in our contemporary subcultures but in other ones as well, will then fall outside the pale of this theory. Again, someone with a personal investment in such a theory similarly will tend to dissociate such phenomena from the realm of the meaningful and important, and consign them instead to the status of intrinsic and uninteresting conceptual enigma (assuming that these perceived enigmas do not allow their existence to be denied altogether).

Yet a third way of dealing pseudorationally with conceptual anomalies is what I shall describe as *rationalization,* a degenerate form of vertical consistency. Recall that vertical consistency requires us to preserve transitivity from the lower-order concepts by which we identify something to the higher-order ones they imply. Relative to a favored theory of our experience, this is to require, first, that the lower- and higher-order concepts of the theory be vertically consistent, and second, that any experience recognizable in terms of its lower-order concepts instantiate the relevant higher-order ones as well. Now any theory even ostensibly worth its salt must include, among its lower-order concepts, the observational concepts by which we commonsensically interpret our experience—of shape, color, size, and so forth—however otherwise parochial that theory may be. But this means that even a parochial theory of one's experience can exclude through its lower-order concepts only genuine conceptual anomalies, of the kind that might trouble the naïf or the solipsist. It cannot exclude gray blobs simply by fiat.

This may explain the valid objection, noted earlier but not addressed, to the case of the gray blob on West Broadway as originally narrated. Surely, we felt, if we have the lower-order concepts of grayness, shapelessness, mooing things, and so forth, we can recognize the thing in question as a gray blob, even if we cannot say what higher-order kind of gray blob it is. Indeed, parochial theories were characterized as precisely those that made into conceptual anomalies things that were well within the range of rational intelligibility from a theoretically disinterested perspective. The need for rationalization arises because the commonsense rational intelligibility of these things at lower conceptual orders puts pressure on the theory's higher-order concepts to accommodate them, on pain of violating the requirement of vertical consistency and so of revealing the conceptual inadequacy of the theory. The dilemma for one who is personally and dogmatically invested in such a theory is that she must accommodate the anomaly without seeming to revise the higher-order concepts of her favored theory; this dilemma is what separates the dogmatist from the solipsist. It is for the dogmatist that rationalization is of greatest use: it is the process by which one stretches, distorts, or truncates the customary scope of instantiation of the higher-order concepts of one's theory, in order to accommodate the recalcitrant phenomenon within the theory's scope of rational intelligibility. More generally, *rationalization* consists in applying a higher-order concept too broadly or too narrowly to something, ignoring or minimizing properties of the thing that do not instantiate this concept, and magnifying properties of it that do.

For example, consider once more the gray blob on West Broadway. Again it is easy to imagine a theory of a particularly self-righteous and sour-minded sort, according to which this blob is, like much else on West Broadway, nothing but one more capitalist plot to poison the minds of the unsuspecting masses and fill the coffers of media devils. The beauty of any favored theory of one's experience is a boon for the personal investor in particularly parochial ones, namely the versatility of its constituent concepts. Pseudorationality, if not genuine rationality, is an available resource for literal self-preservation for even the most dogmatic and narrow-minded among us. For as Humpty Dumpty knew, we are free to use concepts in any way we like.

SELF-DECEPTION

4. Now, finally, I shall try to cash out my claim that self-deception is a particular kind of pseudorationality. In particular, I shall argue that self-deception is pseudorationality about a particular kind of theory in which we have a personal investment, namely our personal self-conception.

First I want to show that not all dogmatic pseudorationalizers are self-deceivers. Consider a cult member. A cult member self-identifies with a dogmatic and parochial theory of her experience, a theory in which her degree of personal investment necessitates denial, dissociation, or rationalization of dissonant data in order to preserve the rational intelligibility of her experience. Nevertheless, such an individual might be completely *selfless* in the sense that her pseudorationality is motivated solely by her dogmatic allegiance to the theory, and not by considerations of personal vanity or self-esteem. She might, indeed, simultaneously exhibit all the beneficent virtues to a particularly high degree: devotion to others, compassion, generosity, humility, modesty, and so forth; virtues that lead us to deplore all the more their being squandered in the service of the dogmatic theory that deludes her. To call her selfless is not to say she lacks a self, for it is precisely the virtuous characteristics of the self she expresses whose waste we deplore. Rather, it is to say that her self-identification with her favored theory is not itself motivated by self-aggrandizing considerations. While she defends herself by pseudorationally defending her theory, the defense of her theory is not intended to redound to her own greater glory. Conversely, although an assault on her theory is an assault on the rational coherence of her self, she does not perceive such an assault as an *insult* or as denigrating her own value. Her responses to such an assault include anxiety and panic, not rancor or resentment. That the cult member's personal investment in her theory is to be explained by her selfless self-identification with it, *but not* her self-aggrandizement by it, underwrites the intuition that this case is, indeed, most naturally described as a case of *delusion,* not self-deception. To identify it as a case of self-deception would be conceptually peculiar.

The implications are two. First, although all self-deceivers are dogmatic pseudorationalizers, not all dogmatic pseudorationalizers are self-deceivers. The cult member has everything it takes to be a pseudorationalizer, but lacks a certain feature conceptually necessary to being identified as a self-deceiver. Second, therefore, self-deceivers are dogmatic pseudorationalizers of a certain kind: they are pseudorationalizers with a personal investment in a certain *kind* of dogmatic theory, namely one with two mutually dependent parts. The first, explicit part is a dogmatic and parochial theory of their experience, of the sort already discussed. The second part, however, is often left implicit: it is a theory of who they are, how they behave, and how they relate socially to others. For the self-deceiver, this second part of the theory is the source of the vanity and self-aggrandizement the cult member was shown to lack.

This second part of the theory is not to be confused with the self-consciousness property. The latter is merely the concept of one's self as having one's experiences; the former is a substantive conception of the *kind* of self one is, for example, that one is a serious person. I shall refer to this as the agent's *self-conception.* The agent's self-conception includes the properties she thinks accurately describe her psychologically, socially, and morally, and the more complex principles she thinks govern her behavior and relations with others at a given moment. Any agent may have a self-conception, and not all self-conceptions function as does the self-deceiver's.

A self-conception, the unstated second part of the self-deceiver's theory, is mutually dependent with the first, in that the validity of the first is a necessary and sufficient condition, in the self-deceiver's eyes, of the validity of the second. This is because, typically, the first part, the dogmatic theory of her experience, includes in it honorific status for persons of the kind she conceives herself to be. According to this analysis, then, a self-deceiver is a pseudorationalizer who conceives of herself as a good and valuable person if and only if the dogmatic theory of her experience she espouses is the correct one. Nazis, racists, sexists, anti-Semites, and other elitists of various kinds are all obvious examples of individuals we would identify as (at the very least) self-deceived according to these criteria. But there are many other dogmatic theories of one's experience that may function similarly to align one on the side of the angels, as it were, depending on one's social values. It may be that, held by the right agent, any such theory may, in that agent's eyes, confer on her the exalted status of being holier than thou.[17]

Now one implication of the foregoing characterization of self-deception as a species of pseudorationality is that a certain familiar analysis of self-deception, as believing that not-p because one wants to, even though one knows in some sense that p, is inadequate to the psychological facts. For if the familiar analysis is right, either we must continually vacillate between believing that p and believing that not-p, adjusting our current perspective, favored theory of our experience, and self-conception accordingly in order to preserve horizontal and vertical consistency, which is psychologically implausible, or else our personal investment in believing that not-p must lead us pseudorationally to deny, dissociate, or rationalize p in order to maintain the belief that not-p. In this case, I would argue, it is not true that we also "in some sense" believe or know that p. For to have any such belief would presuppose the rational intelligibility of p that our pseudorational mechanisms are designed to obliterate.

The second implication of the foregoing characterization is that, even if we *could* be said "in some sense" to believe or know that p while believing not-p because we want to, as the familiar analysis would have it, this analysis could not in any case provide a sufficient condition of self-deception. For according to the familiar analysis, we would have to identify the cult member as self-deceived, which, as I have suggested, seems conceptually peculiar. In addition, one's desire to believe the falsehood not-p must be, specifically, a desire for self-aggrandizement, to which belief in the falsehood is a means. This is to argue that in addition to deception of the self by the self, self-deception intrinsically involves deception *about* the self that deceives.[18]

Is there any pseudorationality recognizable as self-deception that does *not* involve self-aggrandizement as a motive? I doubt it, but remain open to persuasive counterexamples. Consider two kinds of case, nonpersonal and personal. First the nonpersonal case: suppose I have a personal investment in the theory that it's a jungle out there. Also suppose, for the sake of argument, that this theory is false. My investment in it then may be explained either by the generally oppressive experiences I and most everyone else seem to be having or by the fact that this theory excuses my own failures and moral turpitude. Only in the second case does it make sense to describe me as self-deceived. Now take the personal case. Suppose I have a personal investment in the theory that my spouse is a good person. Again suppose this theory to be false. Again my investment in it may be explained in at least one of two ways: either by my spouse's resourcefulness in maintaining an appearance of virtue and guilelessness, which elicits my love and respect, or by the fact that my recognition of his moral turpitude would reflect negatively on my conception of my own tastes, preferences, and susceptibility to moral corruption. If my spouse is recognizably a bad person, then either I have vicious tastes—say, a fascination with evil—or else I am morally unconcerned by the close proximity of evil. Again it seems to me that only in the latter case does it make sense to describe me as self-deceived.[19] Hence self-deception does not depend on the nature of the theory in which one has a personal investment but rather on the motive that causes the investment. My claim is that it always involves a desire to buttress another theory, namely an honorific self-conception.

Now I want to consider a case that is identifiable as one of self-deception according to these criteria, and test the capacity of the foregoing analysis to explain it. Take the hero of André Pieyre de Mandiargues's *The Margin*. Sigismond, while on a business trip in Barcelona, has received an ominous letter from the servant of Sergine, his wife. As he begins to open the letter, his eyes alight on these sentences: "She ran to the wind tower. She climbed the spiral staircase. She threw herself from the top. She died right away." He decides not to read the letter just yet, and puts it in a prominent place on his hotel dresser. For the next three days, he drifts through the streets of Barcelona, reveling in its museums, architecture, and unsavory nightlife. Some of his experiences recall to him with disgust his dead father's depravities. Often he finds himself imagining Sergine's sturdily impassive reactions to the situations he encounters, responding as he imagines she would, and reminiscing fondly about episodes in their life together. Every morning he returns to his hotel room, naps, notices the letter, and goes out again. Sometimes he thinks about the letter there in his hotel room while engaged in very different pursuits. His revelry is gradually brought to a halt as his companion of the night deserts him, his pleasures grow stale, and the image of the unopened letter becomes more persistent. Finally he returns to the hotel, and opens and reads the letter, to learn that his only child, Elie, has drowned in an accident, and that Sergine, immediately upon discovering this, has committed suicide. He quits his hotel, drives away from Barcelona, and pulls over to the side of the highway, where he, too, commits suicide by shooting himself in the heart.

Now on the familiar analysis of self-deception, we would be forced to describe Sigismond's state during his three days of revelry and dissipation as one in which he in some sense knew that Sergine had committed suicide, but convinced himself that she had not, because he loved her and did not want her to abandon him, and so both believed (perhaps unconsciously) that she had and believed that she had not. But this just seems completely inadequate to handle the complexity of the case. He may not have wanted her to commit suicide, but surely this desire would ordinarily motivate him to ascertain whether she had or not, and, if so, why. And if he believed she had, why did he spend three days partying in Barcelona before committing suicide himself?

I would suggest a different analysis. First, the functioning of the pseudorational mechanisms themselves: the sanguinity of Sigismond's perspective is violated by the intimation of tragic news about his wife, in the form of the letter. He pseudorationally *denies* this intimation, with the help of the distractions and novelties his stay in Barcelona provides. Relative to the fragile and studied innocence of his perspective, he regards the physical presence of the letter on his hotel dresser as a potential threat, which he pseudorationally *dissociates* as an inscrutable, enigmatic object that regularly intrudes on his guilelessness, only to be repeatedly dismissed. The exhaustion of his resources for denial forces him to confront the contents of the letter, in the hope of integrating it into the sanguine perspective he has, with the aid of these pseudorational mechanisms, so tenuously maintained. This proves to be impossible. Sigismond's avoidance of the contents of the letter is not predicated on his unconscious knowledge of its contents, but rather on his cognitive inability to make its contents rationally intelligible relative to the constraints of his perspective. These contents are threatening to him not because he already knows what they are but because he cannot find the conceptual resources for figuring out what they are without violating the dogmatic assumptions in which he is personally invested.

Second, the personal investment that motivates Sigismond's pseudorationality: it is very hard to understand the point of Sigismond's pseudorational behavior without knowing the self-conception its presence threatened. After all, he cares deeply about Sergine; why wouldn't he hasten to find out whether the phrases in the letter actually referred to her, and, if so, what had motivated her suicide? The implication is that it could not have been news of Sergine's suicide alone that he was avoiding. Without reference to his self-conception, it is similarly difficult to understand why the contents of the letter lead him to commit suicide himself. After all, his affection for his son, Elie, was rather distant to begin with; and although Sergine's suicide must be a terrible blow, he obviously is not without resources for containing his loneliness. The implication is that it was not just the combination of his wife's and his son's deaths itself that led him to this end. Without reference to the self-conception in which Sigismond is personally invested, we cannot quite understand why he has been so energetically motivated to deceive himself in the first place.

The description of the case provides evidence for what this self-conception is. We know, for example, that he feels both attracted and repelled by the thought of his own father, and that he does not give a thought to his own son's safety after receiving the letter. We also know that he is, on the one hand, deeply attached to his wife, and on the other, untroubled by occasional, casual betrayals of her. Although his recollections of her include no demonstrative expressions of her love or affection for him, we know that he assumes that she is attached to him as well, and ignorant or tolerant of these dalliances. We can say, then, that he has a deep personal investment in the conception of himself as Sergine's beloved and of their bond as intimate, loving, and durable, and that he views his extramarital activities as unproblematic and is untroubled by Sergine's likely reactions to them. We also know that he feels some distaste for, or at least detachment from, the role of father, and is emotionally indifferent toward his son.

That this self-conception is pseudorational is suggested, first, by the distance and impassivity of Sergine's responses as Sigismond has recalled them. They do not provide evidence of her emotional attachment to him at all. His assumption that she does love him is sustained by *rationalization,* by misconceiving her imperviousness as itself the way she expresses her love for him. This rationalization enables him falsely to assume that she loves him, because she does not correct it by telling him explicitly that she does not.

Second, the pseudorationality of Sigismond's self-conception is evinced by Sergine's having committed suicide immediately upon Elie's death. For the implication is clear that without her son, Sergine's life is no longer worth living; and her husband, despite his attentions to her, does not make it so. Sergine's suicide nullifies by a single act the importance of his commitment to her as he conceived it, and thereby his value and importance in his own eyes. It is not simply the combination of her suicide and his son's death that drives Sigismond to suicide, but the now-inescapable realization that he meant so little to her that his love provided her with no consolation or further reason to live. In demonstrating through her suicide that he provided *her* with no reason to live, Sergine has taken away *his* reason to live. Sigismond is goaded to suicide by the realization that his self-conception as the valued and beloved object of her devotion was false. This is the truth that he went to such lengths to avoid, that Sergine's suicide makes inescapable, and that makes his own suicide inescapable as well.

What makes Sigismond a self-deceiver, then, is not just that he manages to avoid unpleasant truths because he prefers not to know them, as the familiar analysis would have it. What makes him a self-deceiver is his self-aggrandizing self-conception, sustained by denial, dissociation, and rationalization: by a studied obliviousness to the conclusive, tragic evidence of his wife's indifference; by dissociation of the letter that contains it; and by rationalization of the earlier unresponsiveness to him that otherwise would have indicated it. His personal investment in his pseudorational self-conception is self-deceptive because it enables him to avoid recognition of who he really is.

But why is it in general so important for the self-deceiver to avoid self-knowledge? I would suggest that this is to be explained, quite simply, by the self-deceiver's personal investment in her self-conception, in conjunction with the disparity between that self-conception and what the pseudorationalized evidence in fact suggests to be a less exalted truth. Earlier I suggested that our highest-order disposition of literal self-preservation made the horizontal and vertical consistency of our favored theory of our experience tantamount to a normative good, and disposed us to ascribe to it, and to the things it explains, an almost honorific status. I also argued that a particularly fragile or parochial theory elicits an even more intensely self-protective desire to preserve it, proportional to one's personal investment in it. For these reasons, the self-deceiver is particularly recalcitrant and impervious to any attempts of her own to survey and critically revise her own pseudorational self-conception. Her investment in it is too great, and increases not only with its fragility, but with the bogus value it confers on her. I think that this is why the project of convincing a self-deceiver that she is self-deceived often seems such an exasperating and futile one: the self-deceiver has not only the rational intelligibility of her experience, but her self-conception as a valuable person, to protect.

But the same vigilance and self-protectiveness that leads the self-deceiver so strenuously to avoid self-knowledge leads her to value it all the more. For of course her pseudorational self-conception would become a source of intense humiliation to her if it were revealed to be false. The revelation that one is not as nice, smart, or popular as one thought is a shaming experience in which one's deficiencies are exposed to the ridicule of the cruelest and most unsympathetic spectator of all. To avoid this revelation, one must be very humble on principle, like Uriah Heep, very vigilant, like St. Augustine, or, like the self-deceiver, very resourceful in one's commitment to truth. As Sigismond's case suggests, self-deception, and pseudorationality more generally, requires energy, perseverance, an inquiring mind, a good grasp of the data, and a deep desire for epistemic rectitude. In order to avoid the humiliation of self-discovery, the self-deceiver needs not only to excise the damaging evidence that portends it but also to believe that the pseudorational mechanisms by which she does so themselves rather bespeak her honesty, sincerity, and perspicacity. Thus may self-reflection and a commitment to truth supply a disguise for pseudorationality for the self-deceiver. Her pseudorational self-conception, then, provides not only a source of bogus value for the self-deceiver, but the illusion of a limited but impregnable scope of personal infallibility that enhances it. This is what I meant when I suggested, at the beginning of this discussion, that the self-deceiver would rather be right than rational.

Now against such self-deception, as well as other forms of pseudorationality, philosophers of a Humean persuasion, such as Henry Sidgwick, John Rawls, Richard Brandt, Stephen Darwall, and of course, David Hume himself[20] have urged a palliative, i.e., vivid reflection on the relevant data in a calm and composed setting. But if the mechanisms of pseudorationality function as I have suggested, the Humean palliative may in many cases amount to little more than ineffectual bootstrap-pulling. For the whole point of exercising our pseudorational resources is to *restrict* what counts as relevant data to the psychologically and theoretically palatable. If the self-deceiver, and the pseudorational agent more generally, had appropriate conceptual access to these data in the first place, vivid reflection on them would be unnecessary. For the self-deceiver, vivid reflection on the relevant data is an occasion for pseudorationality, not an antidote to it.

What hope is there, then, for the self-deceiver—and, indeed for us all—to avoid or ameliorate self-deception, if reflective self-scrutiny is ineffective? I shall close this discussion by advocating a thoroughgoing policy of what I shall call *epistemic audacity*. By this I mean, simply, having the courage of one's convictions; being willing to test one's favored theory of one's experience more generally, as well as of oneself, against circumstances or aspects of one's own behavior that one perceives as challenging or threatening it. For we do, at least, have conceptual access to these observational data. We are all familiar with the sinking of the stomach, increased heartrate, or tightening of the throat that motivates us to ignore such behavior, or turn away from such circumstances, or dismiss them summarily as unimportant or without value, or explain them uneasily in familiar terms that nevertheless do not seem entirely to fit. Perhaps *these* are the data that genuinely deserve our reflection, more than any peculiar to the circumstances in question: the anxiety and discomfort that accompany intimations of our confusion, fallibility, or inadequacy. The suggestion is that most of us can stand much greater doses of these feelings than we may think, and might be better off in the end for doing so. The real threat, of course, is the cognitive and conative paralysis, or self-disintegration, or madness broached earlier. But a little madness is not necessarily a dangerous thing, if it forces us to rethink and restructure the dogmatic theory that crippled our vision in the first place.

NOTES

1. The term is Kant's. See *The Critique of Pure Reason,* trans. Norman Kemp Smith (New York: St. Martin's Press, 1970), A 311/B 368, A 339/B 397, passim. Work on this paper was partially supported by an Andrew Mellon Post-Doctoral Fellowship at Stanford University, 1982–84. It is exerpted from chaps. 11 and 12 of a longer manuscript in progress, *Rationality and the Structure of the Self* (henceforth *RSS*). I have benefited from discussion and criticisms of the relevant parts of these chapters by Akeel Bilgrami, Paul Boghossian, Don Loeb, Barry Loewer, David Reid-Maxfield, and Sigrun Svavarsdottir. Jeffrey Evans supplied important criticisms, insights, and psychologically relevant data for an earlier version of this paper. I would also like to thank Amélie Rorty for suggestions and criticisms that have both improved this version and made me aware of how very much more there is to say about the topics discussed, and Brian McLaughlin for his care and patience in reading a number of such versions.

2. See my "Two Conceptions of the Self," *Philosophical Studies* 48, no. 2. (September 1985):173–197; reprinted in *The Philosopher's Annual VIII* (1985), secs. 3–5.

3. I discuss Hume's conception of theoretical reason in "Hume on Rational Final Ends" (forthcoming).

4. I am grateful to Akeel Bilgrami and William Frankena for pressing this view in conversation. I speak of sentential propositions rather than sentences in order to avoid the implication that one must have or use a language in order to be theoretically rational. The significance of this will become clearer in what follows.

5. Alan Donagan relies on this assumption throughout his *Theory of Morality* (Chicago: Univ. of Chicago Press, 1977); see especially chaps. 2.3, 7.1, 7.3–4, and 7.6. For a resourceful elaboration and defense of this view, see Christine Korsgaard, "Skepticism About Practical Reason," *Journal of Philosophy* 83, no. 1 (January 1986):5–25.

6. See the footnote to A 551 in Kant's *Critique of Pure Reason* (op. cit.), and the further elaborated claim in Kant's *Groundwork of the Metaphysic of Morals,* trans. H. J. Paton (New York: Harper Torchbooks, 1964), at *Ak.* 407–408. Also see Kant's description of a brand of self-deception at *Ak.* 424–425, and compare it with his characterization of man's natural propensity to evil in *Religion Within the Limits of Reason Alone,* trans. T. M. Greene and H. H. Hudson (New York: Harper Torchbooks, 1960), pp. 27–29. For further remarks on the inevitability of self-deception and the inscrutability of our own motives, see the latter work, pp. 17, 33–34, 46, 56–57, 70, 78, 85, and 90–91. I am indebted to Henry Allison for pointing out to me the importance of Kant's preoccupation with self-deception.

7. The implication is that a moral theory is a theory like any other, the terms of which do not differ from other theories in their semantic status. In "The Meaning of 'Ought' and the Loss of Innocence" (unpublished paper, 1986), I argue that moral theories are false descriptive theories whose normative force is to be explained by our deeply rooted psychological attachments to them.

8. For a defense of these, see my *RSS,* chap. 11, and another short paper exerpted from it, "Rationality and the Structure of the Self," presented, with Akeel Bilgrami commenting, to the Association for the Philosophy of the Unconscious, at the Eastern Division Meeting of the American Philosophical Association, Boston, Mass., 1986; the University of Minnesota Philosophy Department, November 1987; the Columbia University Philosophy Department, March 1988; and the Character and Morality Conference, with Nancy Sherman commenting, hosted by Radcliffe and Wellesley Colleges, April 1988; and forthcoming in a volume to be edited by Amélie Rorty and Owen Flanagan.

This discussion in turn attempts to flesh out more systematically some ideas sketched very roughly in sect. 3 of my "Two Conceptions of the Self" (op. cit.) and *RSS,* chap. 12. The notion of the holistic regress and the theoretically rational requirements of horizontal and vertical consistency introduced in the following pages draw heavily on Kant's conception of theoretical reason as developed in the Dialectic of *The Critique of Pure Reason.* See especially A 299/B 355–A 308/B 364, A 322, A 330–332, A 337, B 378–379, B 383, B 387–388, B 437, A 643/B 671–A 669/B 697, "The Regulative Employment of the Ideas of Pure Reason"; compare B 93–94, B105–106 on judgments as functions for unifying our representations. I discuss the interpretation of these passages, and Kant's view of reason more generally, in "Kant's Idea of Reason" (unpublished paper, 1986). In what follows, I do not claim to interpret Kant, but merely to develop some ideas that can be found in Kant's writings. Nevertheless,

I shall try to navigate between the Scylla of technical issues in the philosophy of language and the Charybdis of Kant exegesis. My frequent references to Kant are thus intended to provide historical and motivational context for these ideas, not to represent them as what Kant actually meant (nor even, necessarily, what he should have meant).

9. Note that what satisfies the law of noncontradiction is not the relation as we conceive it between things *and* their higher-order properties. So this requirement cannot be expressed by the relation between a predicate letter and the objects that fix its extension, thus:

$$(1) \quad (x) -(Fx \ \& - Fx).$$

What is required to satisfy the law of noncontradiction here is rather our concepts of the objects assigned to individual variables, i.e., our concepts of things and properties themselves. Not just sentential propositions, but any rationally intelligible thing t assigned to an individual variable a must satisfy the requirement that

$$(2) \quad -(a \ \& -a);$$

i.e., we must conceive it as self-identical. The holistic regress implies that we can recognize things and properties as self-identical only if we can identify them in terms of higher-order properties that are themselves self-identical.

10. Of course this does not mean that they *are in fact* logically consistent with one another, just that I *must conceive* them as being so.

11. In standard notation, the requirement of vertical consistency would run roughly as follows. Given an individual variable a to which t is assigned, and terms F and G with the extensions P and P^1 respectively,

$$(3) \quad Fa \rightarrow [(x) \ (Fx \rightarrow Gx) \rightarrow Ga]$$

It is important not to confuse the requirement of vertical consistency with a claim about the transitivity of relations among predicates generally: not every predicate is of a higher or lower order than every other predicate. Rather, the requirement of vertical consistency is a transitivity claim about the relation between our concepts of the lower- and higher-order properties of a thing, i.e., those that satisfy (3). I am indebted to Wayne Davis for alerting me to notational errors in an earlier formulation of the requirements of horizontal and vertical consistency.

12. Of course this does not mean that they would not *be* my experiences, just that I could not thus conceive them.

13. For these reasons, I do not see how Bernard Williams can claim that "When I think about the world and try to decide the truth about it, . . . I make statements, or ask questions, . . . [which] . . . have first-personal shadows, . . . [b]ut these are derivative, merely reflexive counterparts to the thoughts that do not mention me. I occur in them, so to speak, only in the role of one who has this thought" (*Ethics and the Limits of Philosophy* [Cambridge, Mass.: Harvard Univ. Press, 1985], p. 67). If I did not occur in such statements in the role of one who had this thought, I would be unable to act on any thought I had. So I think Williams is too quick to differentiate the "I" of theoretical deliberation as necessarily impersonal from the "I" of practical

deliberation as necessarily personal. I have tried to show elsewhere ("Moral Theory and Moral Alienation," *Journal of Philosophy* 84, no. 2 [February 1987]:102–118) that impersonality in deliberation is usually a function of psychological factors, not moral or philosophical ones.

14. For this reason, it would be a mistake to confuse this disposition with a *desire* for literal self-preservation; the very idea is incoherent. For however we understand the notion of a desire—whether as an occurrent, internal event, or as a "pro-attitude" as do, for example, Donald Davidson ("Actions, Reasons, and Causes," in *Readings in the Theory of Action,* eds. Norman S. Care and Charles Landesman [Bloomington: Indiana Univ. Press, 1968]) and Alvin Goldman (*A Theory of Human Action* [Englewood Cliffs, N.J.: Prentice-Hall, 1970]), or as itself a disposition to experience certain occurrent, internal events under certain circumstances (as do Richard Brandt and Jaegwon Kim in "Wants as Explanations of Actions," in Care and Landesman, *Readings in the Theory of Action*), eds., or as a merely theoretical construct (as does David Lewis in "Radical Interpretation," *Philosophical Papers, Volume 1* (New York: Oxford Univ. Press, 1983)—a desire must be in any case something that some agent has. So it cannot be the same as that disposition that is required by the continuing existence of that agent to begin with. The disposition to literal self-preservation must be presupposed by any desire an agent has, because it must be presupposed by motivationally effective agency. If it is a necessary presupposition of desire, it cannot be the same as desire.

For the same reason, it would be a mistake to suppose that the preservation of the theoretically rational intelligibility of the self might be a mere means to the satisfaction of some further desire. There can be no doubt that the disposition to literal self-preservation has *at least* instrumental value, since it is a necessary precondition of any of the ends an agent adopts, and so *a fortiori* of those she actively tries to achieve at a given moment. But it also *precludes* the adoption of any ends or beliefs that are themselves inconsistent with the rest of her experiences. For example, consider the hero of Henry James' "The Last of the Valerii," a young Roman count of ancient lineage who unearths a pagan statue on his family's estate. The statue evokes in him the desire to engage in ancient and, to him, completely inexplicable Dionysian rituals. He finds himself compelled to perform these rites nightly from dusk until dawn. Tormented by impulses that, although harmless, are to him completely unintelligible and inconsistent with the other desires and habits that characterize him as a modern European, he has the statue reburied almost immediately, rather than utilize his wealth and freedom to indulge these anomalous impulses. The biologically fundamental disposition to literal self-preservation requires the suppression not only of external but of internal events that violate the requirements of horizontal and vertical consistency, on pain of cognitive and conative paralysis—or, at worst, madness. I have profited from discussing these objections with Louis Loeb and Paul Guyer.

15. I discuss the definition of personal investment at greater length in "Moral Theory and Moral Alienation" (op. cit.).

16. Does it matter whether my favored theory of my experience is normative or explanatory? The preceding remarks suggest not. Any powerful explanatory theory also prescribes a way things are supposed to, i.e., *should* work under ideal conditions, and so contain a normative component. And any full-blooded normative theory also explains a way things *would* work if conditions were, in fact, ideal, and so contains

an explanatory component (this point is developed at greater length in my paper "The Meaning of 'Ought' and the Loss of Innocence," and with reference specifically to Kant's Categorical Imperative in my "Kant's Idea of Reason"). Part of what we do by attempting to make things rationally intelligible in the terms given by our favored theory of our experience is to assess the extent to which the real measures up to the ideal—or, to put it in Hegel's infamous terms, the extent to which the actual is rational.

17. I doubt the difficulty of imagining alternatives to this way of thinking about oneself. For example, one might derive a great deal of self-esteem from being an academic, because one enjoys teaching and research, and believes one can make a valuable social contribution by engaging in them, without thereby supposing that academics, and so oneself, are any *more* important or valuable in the total scheme of things than janitors or secretaries or postal clerks.

18. Also see Amélie O. Rorty, "Belief and Self-Deception," *Inquiry* 15 (1972): 387–410. Rorty has since repudiated this view.

19. Of course there are further, large questions about whether or not, in the absence of vicious tastes, one can be said to love a person one recognizes as unregenerately bad, and in general about what our commitment to recognizably and incorrigibly morally flawed others consists in. I am indebted to Brian McLaughlin for this example.

20. See David Hume, *A Treatise of Human Nature,* ed. L. A. Selby-Bigge (Oxford: Clarendon Press, 1968), bk. 3, sec. 3, p. 603 (and my "Hume on Rational Final Ends" for a systematic discussion); Henry Sidgwick, *The Methods of Ethics* (New York: Dover, 1966), Bk. I, chap. 1, pp. 13–14, and chap. 8, p. 101, passim; John Rawls, *A Theory of Justice* (Cambridge, Mass.: Harvard Univ. Press, 1971), chap. 7, sec. 64, p. 417; Richard Brandt, *A Theory of the Good and the Right* (New York: Oxford Univ. Press, 1979), chap. 1.1, pp. 11–13, chap. 4, pp. 111–113; and Stephen Darwall, *Impartial Reason* (Ithaca: Cornell Univ. Press, 1983), chap. 8, pp. 85–86, 91–93.

14

EMOTION AND SELF-DECEPTION

RONALD B. DE SOUSA

> -But lest you are my enemy
>   I must inquire!
> -No matter, so there is but fire
>   In you, in me.
> —W. B. Yeats, "The Mask"

> -I can call spirits from the vasty deep.
> -Why, so can I, or so can any man.
> But will they come when you do call for them?
> —Shakespeare, *Henry IV*, Part I

Earnest pretense is the royal road to sincere faith. Or so we are enjoined to think by that vast literature of *exhortation,* which recommends the cultivation of certain sorts of behaviors as a means of inducing desirable states of mind. Thus Pascal's advice to the religious skeptic: practice *as if* you believed, and you will find yourself believing. A particularly intriguing special case of this strategy is this: once an emotion has been induced by such methods, it sometimes succeeds in actually making true the very fact that justifies it. I shall refer to this as *bootstrapping*. An innocent example of bootstrapping in this sense is the edge given by self-confidence in competitive situations. But not all instances are so unproblematic.

In this paper I want to explore the grey area where bootstrapping shades into self-deception. For practical purposes, we may characterize self-deception in a preliminary way as the purposive act of entertaining a belief that one has good ground for holding most likely false, in the service of some more comfortable state of mind. To clarify what is involved in more general terms, I begin with two cases of problematic rationality. One, I shall argue, is indeed irrational, involving a clear violation of a certain kind of consistency. The other is a legitimate if somewhat bizarre use of the boot strap principle.

Here then are two stories. The first is about Niels Bohr. I have borrowed it from Jon Elster:

> Niels Bohr at one time is said to have had a horseshoe over his door. Upon being asked whether he really believed that horseshoes bring luck, he answered, "No, but I am told that they bring luck even to those who do not believe in them."[1]

The second story is about me. It illustrates the *placebo paradox*:

> I take vitamin C to ward off colds. What I have read about it has convinced me
> that, *pace* Linus Pauling, vitamin C is a *placebo*. But I believe in placebos. That
> belief is a rational one, because I have read in *Scientific American* that placebos
> are surprisingly effective.

The stories have a superficial similarity. Both exemplify bootstrapping.
Are their protagonists rational? As Elster points out, Niels Bohr can be shown
to be irrational according to Jaako Hintikka's principles of *doxastic rationality*: "If your beliefs are to be consistent, it must also be possible for all your
beliefs to turn out to be true without forcing you to give up any of them."[2]
The principle of doxastic consistency appealed to also serves to explain the
irrationality of Moore's paradox ("*p*, but I don't believe that *p*"). Doxastically
consistent belief requires not only that what one believes be consistent but
that it be consistent with one's believing it. Niels Bohr is doxastically inconsistent. He is explicitly committed to the following:

(1) NB believes that horseshoes will not bring luck, and

(2) Horseshoes bring luck (even) to those who believe that horseshoes will
not bring luck.

Both (1) and (2) could be true. But doxastic consistency requires in addition
that it be possible for all of Niels Bohr's beliefs to be true *while also believed
by him*. In that sense Niels Bohr is also (doxastically) committed to:

(3) Niels Bohr believes (1) and (2).

And the conjunction of (1) through (3) describes a straightforwardly inconsistent set of beliefs: that is to say, if (3) is true then *something that NB
believes is bound to be false*.

But consider now my own case. I am explicitly committed to the following:

(1′) RdS believes that vitamin C is chemically inert, and

(2′) Chemically inert substances sometimes cure colds for those who believe they will do so, and

(2′a) I believe that vitamin C will cure my cold.

Proposition (2′) was learned from *Scientific American*. So phrased, (1′), (2′),
and (2′a) do not give rise to inconsistency if we suppose me to believe all of
them. Now if we add (3′):

(3′) RdS believes (1′), (2′), and (2′a)

we do not get a straightforwardly inconsistent belief set. Propositions (1′)
through (3′) are not doxastically inconsistent.

Still, aren't they *weird*? Am I not irrational in some other way? The feeling
that this is so rests on the fact that (2′a), the belief that vitamin C will be
effective (even though it is chemically inert) is *itself irrational*. To which I
answer: yes, it's irrational if by that you mean that it is *groundless*. I have
no good reason to believe (2′a). Certainly (2′) by itself does not support it,
not is it even enough to cause the belief (2′a). So much is evidenced by the

fact that I don't believe that just *any* chemically inert substance will cure my colds. My confidence must be powered by some independent prejudice in favor of vitamin C. And that prejudice, given the truth of (1'), is quite irrational.

Note, however, three points in defense of my sanity: (a) groundless beliefs are sometimes true, (b) not all my beliefs can be grounded, and there may well be some that are intrinsically rational, though they are not arrived at by argument, and (c) in this case I actually have scientific evidence that it may well be true, even though it's groundless. Isn't that ground enough?

We have then, if my defense is sound, a case of successful bootstrapping, where a belief (or "feeling" in the broad sense) is rationally founded on a nonrational base.[3] Many cases of self-deception involve something like bootstrapping. Consider this case. You have been at the seaside a few weeks, long enough, in fact, to have become rather tired of lying in the sun and swimming. Nevertheless you are aware that you will not get another chance for a whole year or more. And so, wearily, you drag yourself to the beach like a dutiful drudge, and spend another day sunning and bathing. You do it because you know that *next week,* when you are back in the sultry city, you will be sorry if you didn't. But now what does happen next week? You are longing to go to the beach, but you can't. Because you did go that day last week, it seems to you that you can count your last week's swim as satisfying this week's desire. Isn't this a bit like my hopes for vitamin C? Is it rational? Intuitions may differ here, but there are considerations on both sides.

In favor of rating the dutiful bather and the deliberate placebo-taker as rational is this consideration: as human beings and manipulators of symbols we are inevitably and very properly the *creators of our own values.* And so it is quite right that for any given desire we should be allowed essentially to define the conditions of its satisfaction. On the other side, we must allow some reality to the possibility of self-deception. And merely to decree that a desire *ostensibly* having a certain object (to go swimming today, for example) can be magically satisfied by something quite different (to *have gone* swimming a week ago), is surely a case of self-deception.

One possible diagnosis of the ambivalence one feels in such cases is that our contrasting intuitions relate to different conceptions of rationality. I want to distinguish three kinds or levels of rationality: the strategic, the cognitive, and the axiological. In brief the distinction is this: when we assess a representational state or course of action in the light of the probable value of its *consequences,* we are evaluating its *strategic* rationality. (The classical theory of strategic rationality is Bayesian decision theory, in which we estimate the desirability of a possible course of action by summing all its possible consequences, weighted by their probability.) An assessment is purely *cognitive,* by contrast, if it is concerned only with the adequacy of the state to some objective state of the world of which it purports to be *true.* In order to leave open here the question of the nature of the criteria of rationality to which emotions are subject, I propose to call *axiological rationality* whatever branch or level of rationality is concerned with the appropriateness of an emotion to its object. In my sense axiology is concerned with more than merely two-dimensional assessments of value. Different emotions, that is, might be assessed in terms of different kinds or dimensions of value of which the emotions in question are quasi-cognitions.

In terms of that threefold distinction, then, it may be that our conflicting intuitions are due to the fact that the bather's case and the placebo paradox involve strategic rationality built on the foundation of *cognitive* irrationality: we begin with an inadequate representation of the world, but then make the best of it in our practical decisions. But this does not automatically tell us how things stand in the case of *axiological* rationality.[4] For this reason, matters are liable to become more complicated when we come to ask whether emotions *themselves* can be subject to self-deception. This amounts to asking whether, in addition to the assessment of cognitive rationality to which we might subject the beliefs involved in an emotion, and the assessment of strategic rationality to which we might subject the attendant desires, there is an irreducible sense in which we can be emotionally self-deceived. If there is, I shall say that the irrationality involved in those cases is *axiological*.

The contrast I have in mind is this. In standard cases of self-deception the role of the emotions is a commonplace. Emotions obviously play a crucial role in *akrasia,* or weakness of will. Moreover vanity, envy, ambition, grief, resentment, apprehension, despair, lust, jealousy, and anger all induce us to connive in the clouding of our vision. But this confines emotions to a causal or motivational role in episodes or self-deception focusing on *belief*.[5] Insofar as emotions involve cognitions, they might be said to be *derivatively* subject to self-deception. This comes a little closer. But I am interested in making sense of an emotion's being *directly* self-deceptive. Shading into these cases are ones where we are self-deceived *about* our own emotions. In those cases the very nature of the emotion may be affected, by something like the bootstrapping principle. But the "intrinsic" cases I am looking for would be different from both of those.

We should not assume, in any case, that every instance of self-deception will fall squarely into one category or the other. Emotions provide a framework for our beliefs, bringing some into the spotlight and relegating others to the shade. (When I am irritated at your neatness I may continue to believe that you are generous and kind. But that will seem a very minor part of your total personality, dominated as it is by your more important faults of being fussy and demanding. At other times, though, I shall weigh these things differently.) In such cases the choice of description between self-deceived beliefs and self-deceived emotion may be rather arbitrary. Here is an example. Consider the character of the spy and defector Guy Burgess. One is led to surmise that he extended his mastery of deception to himself. But should we say he held a self-deceptive *belief* that the Soviets had a better system? Or should we describe him as indulging a self-deceptive belief *about* his emotions—mistaking for a love of socialism, perhaps, his hatred of Eton? Or, third, should we say that the latter emotion had actually become self-deceptively *converted* into the former, yielding a case of a full, intrinsically self-deceived emotion?[6]

What follows is a preliminary catalogue of the types of cases that might be described as affecting emotions themselves, as opposed to (a) beliefs that emotions might distort, (b) false beliefs about one's own emotions, or (c) false beliefs on which they might be founded. Each is based on one or more of the following characteristics of emotions.

(i) As William James first pointed out, the *experience* of emotion is closely tied to its *expression*.

(ii) The process by which emotions are learned involves what I call *paradigm scenarios*. These work roughly as follows. We are first made familiar with the vocabulary of emotions by the association of our own instinctive responses with complex situations of our childhood, reinforced with stories and fairy tales, and later supplemented and refined by art and literature. Paradigm scenarios involve two aspects: first, a situation type providing the characteristic *objects* of the specific emotion type; and second, a repertoire of characteristic or "normal" *responses* to the situation. It is in large part in virtue of the response component of the scenarios that emotions are commonly held to *motivate*; but this is, in fact, back-to-front. For the emotion often takes its name from the response disposition ("The baby is in a jealous rage") and is only afterwards assumed to cause it. There is little doubt that a child is genetically programmed to respond in specific ways to the certain situational components of paradigm scenarios. An essential part of education consists in identifying these responses, providing the child with a name for them in that context, and thus teaching it that it is experiencing a particular emotion.

(iii) We tend to mold our self-ascriptions of emotions to our implicit theories about rational emotion. In some ways, then, we are led into self-deception by our theories.

(iv) Both the existence of paradigm scenarios and our need to have *theories* about emotion lend an important *social dimension* to our emotions. This gives rise to what I shall call *ideologies of emotions*.

SELF-FEIGNING

Erving Goffman has pointed out that a rough distinction may be made among forms of deception. One kind consists in the deliberate distortion of information that one (explicitly and intentionally) "*gives*": this is lying or "deceit."

The other deals with information that one "gives off." This class comprises a "wide range of action that others can treat as symptomatic of the actor, the expectation being that the action was performed for reasons other than the information conveyed in this way."[7] Deliberate misinformation by means of this type of communication is pretending or "feigning." Expressions of emotion are typically treated as "given off." So it may be fruitful to look for a kind of self-deception that bears the same relation to *feigning,* as self-deceived belief bears to *deceit*: a kind in which self-deceivers are taken in not by their own lies but by their own *pretenses*. This will be one approach I shall take. It would lead to nothing very novel, however, if pretending to oneself resulted merely in having false beliefs. Its significance in the present context derives from my argument for the independence of axiology. If that is sustained, then emotions can admit of error without reducing to mistaken beliefs. That, as we shall see, is precisely the description that cases of self-feigning call for.

An essential outcome of emotional learning is the potential for nonverbal communication.[8] Our expressive repertoire, like any other device of communication, can be used deceptively.[9] There is but a short step from here to the possibility of self-deception as being fooled by one's own pretense, or "self-feigning." Recalling some features of the James-Lange theory of emotions will enable us to take that step.

According to James, an emotion is essentially the awareness of one's own bodily changes. One of the chief arguments against James is that identical physico—chemical stimuli produce divergent emotions depending on the situational and epistemic context.[10] But if we reinterpret the bodily changes involved to include those that amount to, or normally determine, the *expressive* motor events associated with the emotion, we can say that *what we feel* in an emotional state *is the expressive set of our body*. This is not to say that what we feel is all there is to an emotion, for that would leave out the semantic aspect: an emotion *means* a formal object, that is, a property characteristic of a paradigm scenario, and *ascribes* it to a target. It does imply, with common sense and against prevalent philosophical doctrine, that we can commonly *identify* our emotions *by* what we feel. Against this version of the James-Lange view the standard objections have no force. Now in cases in which the expressive set is deceptive, and where the deception is not consciously acted out, it is not hard to see how one could take one's own expressive state for the corresponding emotion.[11] (This is what is being imputed when someone is accused of histrionics.) On this account, we can see how self-feigning is not merely a matter of acquiring false beliefs about one's own emotions. Rather it *induces* an emotion, which is itself erroneous in its ascription of a characteristic property to an object. We have then a possible mechanism for emotional self-deception of the type advertised above.

What, however, are the typical occasions of its manifestation? A partial answer to this question will lead to a second form of fallibility.

TRANSFERENCE AND DETACHABILITY

Sometimes a situation or target evokes an expressive response that is not appropriate to it as a whole, but merely triggered by some partial aspect. The response has been associated with a paradigm scenario, defining an emotion that is then *read into* the present situation. This is what psychoanalysts call *transference*. The classic case of transference, of course, takes place in the analytic situation, in which the patient characteristically "falls in love" with the doctor regardless of the latter's lovableness. According to Freud, "the patient does not remember anything of what he has forgotten and repressed, but acts it out . . . and in the end we understand that this is his way of remembering."[12] In other words, transference is not merely mechanical repetition triggered by a stimulus, but has a semantic structure of its own, akin to that of memory. Its defining feature is that it lacks *detachability*—in a sense now to be explained—from the paradigm scenario.

DETACHABILITY

The use of a predicate can be said to be detachable from its learning context in this sense. Suppose I learn a color word from a chart. I may at first associate the word 'red' with that particular patch on the chart. But that is not yet to have learned the meaning of 'red'. Once learned, the word is cut loose from its associations with the color chart. It now simply refers to the color. The learning situation does not remain encrusted in the meaning of 'red', though for some time it may be more or less vividly remembered and affect the *connotation*—as opposed to the (Fregean) *sense*—of the word.[13] This contrasts with the semantic structure characteristic of *symbols,* typified by religious rites and the objects used in them. The worship evoked in the faithful *by* the bread and wine is directed *at* the body and blood of Christ. The sense of the ritual depends on an essential reference to the original ceremony. For the more thorough sects, indeed, the bond of symbolization is strengthened into identity by the power of transubstantiation: the bread *is* the body. So for the patient: (unconsciously) the doctor *is* the parent. The difference is that the average neurotic cannot *endorse* the identification once its role is brought to full consciousness, and seeks to be cured of rather than sustained in that identification. Detachability seems to emerge as a *norm* for the semantics of emotion, an ideal often thwarted by our tendency to symbolic interpretation.

This account treats symbol-semantics as an undesirable affection of emotions. But perhaps this is only therapeutic prejudice, which should not be taken for granted. The neurotic and the religious do not have a monopoly on transference. As Freud put it, transference "consists of new editions of old traits and . . . repeats infantile reactions. But this is the essential character of

every state of being in love. There is no such state which does not reproduce
infantile prototypes" (TL, p. 168). The origin of emotions in paradigm scenarios implies the possibility of extending that observation to emotions other
than love. Two questions can then be raised: first, whether transference emotions are *authentic*—whether they are the emotions they advertise themselves
to be—and second, whether their real targets (and motivating aspects) are
their ostensible ones.

It is tempting, for the sake of simplicity, to take a hard line on both questions: emotions are always what they seem, and their objects are always the
ostensible ones. And if this means that some emotions are inappropriate, then
things are just as we know them.

The origin of emotions in paradigm scenarios allows us another theoretical
option here. That is to say that the actual paradigm situation is always the
real object of subsequent emotions. This latter option is unrealistic, however;
it is comparable to saying that our color words *really* refer to the patch on
the color chart. Better then to go with the former option, so long as we remember that in some cases the *content* of the emotion must be interpreted in
terms of a reference to an object or target other than the ostensible one. This
allows for judgments of degree in respect of the relative role of the present
and the past in shaping present content. There are degrees of pathology or
self-feigning, in which trouble with the semantical relation to the *target*—the
thing or person to whom the emotion is directed—is reassigned to the *content*
or character of the emotion.[14]

In respect of content, taking phenomenology at face value is less plausible.
Freud sometimes appears to think otherwise: "We have no right to dispute,"
he says, that transference love "has the character of a 'genuine' love." But
his reason is perplexing: "lacking to a high degree in a regard for reality [it]
is less sensible, less concerned about consequences and more blind in its
valuations . . . precisely what is essential about being in love" (TL, pp.
168–169). But "less" than what? Freud seems to change thought in mid-
sentence: he starts out to say that one would expect normal love to be more
sensible than neurotic love, but switches to thinking all love equally crazy.
If this is so, then the "genuineness" even of normal emotions is bought at the
price of their wholesale and systematic inappropriateness—an unwelcome
implausibility. Besides, Freud also thinks that emotions, like actions, can be
reinterpreted as something other than they seem: transference love is itself
sometimes a disguise for resistance (since it can function to distract the patient
from the analytic task) (DT, pp. 101ff.).[15] And common sense also avails
itself of this possibility of reinterpretation.

What criteria should guide reinterpretation? The origin of emotions in paradigm scenarios implies that each person's emotional "dialect" will be subtly
different. For the content of emotions for which two people have the same
name will depend on their individual temperaments and the specific details of

their learning experiences. When we interpret one another's emotions, therefore, we have a Whorfian problem of translation: our "dialects" determine different experiences. So when can we place credence in interpretation?

Freud's answer is confusing, as we have seen. But we can construct an answer on his behalf by looking at his strategy in a related domain. He thought of the "plasticity of instinct" as an essential and pervasive characteristic of the human psyche, manifested in normal development. The plasticity of instinct is involved in *sublimation,* and also in *perversions.* What is the difference between them? Ultimately they are sorted out on evaluative grounds: sublimations have redeeming social value, perversions are antisocial or by consensus found aesthetically repellent.[16]

Much the same is true of commonsense judgments of authenticity and appropriateness. We are often content to infer what emotions people *must* be having from our knowledge of the situations in which they find themselves. Far from granting any privileged access to the subject in this area, if there is a discrepancy between the conclusion of such an inference and the subject's declaration, this last is more commonly taken to be self-deceived. Allowances are made for variabilities of individual temperament, reactivity, style, upbringing, and so forth; but ultimately the barrier between the neurotic, intrinsically erroneous emotion and the normal one is drawn along *conventional* lines. And this is—up to a point—as it should be: for intuitively the difference between mere transference and authentic emotion is in whether the ostensible object is actually, in its present relation to the subject, fitting for the emotion that it occasions. Otherwise it is merely acting as a trigger for something to which it is only accidentally connected. Nevertheless, the conventional source of assessments of emotion is also the source of an important category of self-deception in emotions. It will be my main concern in the rest of this paper.

THE IDEOLOGY OF EMOTIONS

The thesis that emotions are somehow socially determined can be understood in several ways (so much so that one might be forgiven for suspecting that it derives its plausibility from one interpretation, and its interest from another, quite disjoint interpretation). In the simplest sense it might simply mean that we wouldn't *notice* emotional phenomena unless they had a public name. In this sense we sometimes say that something "isn't real unless it is recognized." How we classify it when we do recognize it may then differ from culture to culture. There is something here of the bootstrap effect. Recall La Rochefoucauld's epigram to the effect that few people would ever fall in love if they hadn't read about it. This kind of social dependency of emotions has something to do with people's tendency to imitate and follow fashions, to "be conventional" in the sense in which being conventional contrasts with being eccentric. Some people have claimed that emotions are in this sense *culturally relative,* so that their expression, their significance, and presumably even their subjective feel differ from one culture to another. One advocate of cultural relativity puts it this way: "the fact of the matter is that most standard emotional reactions are socially constructed or institutionalized patterns of response."[17] But do these conventions in fact *define* these emotions, or do they *interpret* them in some way that might allow for correctness or incorrectness? The latter is the less radical view. But it carries with it new possibilities for self-deception. Sometimes our own beliefs as to the proper structure of an emotion may cause us to *rationalize* it when it does not meet those criteria. Here is an example. Bernie admires Jan. What he admires her *for* is that when she was six years old she played solo violin with the Toronto Symphony Orchestra. However, Bernie is mistaken. The story on which his belief rests is a stubborn legend, which persists in circulating in spite of Jan's denials. Now when Bernie discovers that the ground for his admiration was a false belief, he may still *feel* a kind of residual admiration; but since he knows that admiration needs a motivating aspect he may just *invent* one. He may just think of her vaguely as someone extraordinarily accomplished in the Arts, without recalling the source of that belief.[18]

The implicit second-order theory about how emotions *ought* to be justified will turn this from a case of emotion lacking a focus into a case of an emotion with *illusory* focus. Bernie resembles the recipient of a posthypnotic suggestion, who on following the suggestion confabulates a pretext, so as to be able to interpret his own action as rational according to normal criteria.

We are not inclined to think that because the mistake is socially generated it is not a mistake at all. Misinformation is just another risk entailed by the opportunities of information afforded by social intercourse. This is just a special case of the general rule that the more we are (categorially) rational, the greater is our potential for (evaluative) irrationality. Being *categorially* rational is a matter of being the sort of thing that is capable of rationality, and therefore also of irrationality. It contrasts with being nonrational, in the sense that a stone is nonrational, whereas the contrast to *evaluative* rationality is *irrationality.* You have to be categorially rational in order to be irrational; and the more sophisticated is your understanding of how emotions can be assessed for rationality, the greater the risk of irrationality.[19]

On the most radical interpretation of the social determinants of emotions, which seems to be espoused by Naomi Scheman,[20] emotions are like moves in a game; they have literally no existence at all outside of the conventions that *define* the game. A move in chess is not some previously unnoticed slice of the world. If the convention is lost, the move doesn't merely fail to be named and noticed: it fails to *exist.* The conventions involved here are *constitutive* ones, not rules of etiquette.

This extreme contextualist view has little appeal as a *theory* of emotions.

But it is useful in reminding us of the relative autonomy of different levels of analysis. What phenomenologically is an individual phenomenon may be rooted in social determinants without ceasing to be an individual phenomenon; social phenomena, in turn, may be impossible to relate in detail to the equally indispensable factors that underlie them on the biological level. A comparison with language may once again be instructive here. Our capacity to learn a language is biological and innate, but our particular language is entirely learned. But there is also an important disanalogy: I don't know what it would mean to claim that some particular human language somehow *distorted reality*.[21] Of emotions, by contrast, it makes perfectly good sense. If that is true, then emotions can only claim a level of social relativity lower than that of language. Nevertheless, as the following examples show, that level of social dependency does make possible some distinctive forms of emotional self-deception.

Two Examples from the Natural History of Sexism

Different paradigm scenarios can generate subtly different emotional repertoires. In some cases this is systematized by the process of socialization to differentiate whole social groups. Gender socialization, the deepest level of sexism, provides an example whose importance transcends philosophical illustration. A vivid case can be made about such general sentiments as *love*.[22] But love, whose characterization involves whole complexes of particular feelings, expectations, long-term patterns of intercourse, and social sanctions, while offering all the wider scope for the promotion of sexual inequality, is arguably too complex to be called "an emotion." Here I focus on two more specific emotions: *anger* and *jealousy*.

The paradigm scenarios for anger differ between men and women in respect of both its expression and its criteria of appropriateness. An angry man is a manly man, but an angry woman is a "fury" or a "bitch." This is necessarily reflected *in the quality of the emotion itself*: a man will experience an episode of anger characteristically as indignation. A woman will feel it as something less moralistic, guilt-laden frustration, perhaps, or sadness. Insofar as the conception of gender stereotypes that underlies these differences is purely conventional mystification, the emotions that embody them are paradigms of self-deceptive ones. And they illustrate the fact that in what I have been calling self-deceived emotions the self mostly connives rather than originates. We are responsible only to the extent that we are generally motivated to conform to the social and gender roles assigned to us, and that we allow ourselves to be taken in by the self-feigning that this necessarily requires.

The case of jealousy is more complicated,[23] but exemplifies the same points. A man's jealousy is traditionally an assertion of his property rights, and something of that survives in the emotional tone of jealousy as felt by many contemporary men. A woman's, on the other hand, "is regarded as nearly equivalent to shrewishness, fishwifery" (Farber, p. 182). It is not taken as seriously (there is no feminine of "cuckold"). Underlying the surface ideology, according to Dinnerstein's persuasive speculations, is the fact that "the symbolic shock value of the other's physical infidelity is far less absolute for her than for him" (Dinnerstein, p. 42). In the original scenarios in which mother-raised men and mother-raised women have learned both their sense of self and the emotions provoked when it is threatened, girls are able to identify with their mothers more than boys. Consequently a woman is likely to feel "that she carries within herself a source of the magic early parental richness" (ibid.). By contrast, the man's attitude stems "from the mother-raised boy's sense that the original, most primitive source of life will always lie outside himself, that to be sure of reliable access to it he must have exclusive access to a woman" (Dinnerstein, p. 43).

Not only is the very experience of jealousy for men and women tinged with the different consequences of this mystification, but the attempt to eliminate jealousy is also fraught with divergent meanings. For a man, to overcome jealousy is to overcome possessiveness. But for a woman, the effort described in the very same terms may simply play into the possessiveness of the male and thus reinforce the sexist mystification. This discrepancy adds yet another level of self-deception. This results from the assumption, fostered by the homonymy of "jealousy" in its feminine and masculine senses, that the task of achieving greater rationality of emotions is the same task for both. Hence the complex emotions that may be tied to an expectation of reciprocity in the elimination of jealousy may once again be self-deceived.

THE DIALECTIC OF FUNGIBILITY

The acquisition of a conceptual scheme requires a capacity for general representation, at varying levels of specificity. (Hence Plato's emphasis on "collection and division" as the key to conceptual progress in the *Sophist*.) But general representation allows only quasi-intentionality. Full intentionality implies a capacity for singular reference.[24] The psychological correlate of these semantical facts is that we are prepared, by infantile attachment to certain classes of pleasures and comforts—certain *qualities*—for the acquisition of nonfungible attachment.[25]

It is obviously a crucially important fact about early psychosexual development, in need of explanation, that general desires for fungible satisfactions become focused on a particular person or persons. There is then a further developmental question about how it is possible to transfer (or replace) this affection, whose target is a parent, onto a new and equally nonfungible target. That the new target—ideally the spouse—be nonfungible is part of the ideology of love in most cultures.[26] The ideology of love is therefore directly contrary to the general desirability of emotional fungibility. For the properties on which human attachment is based are not qualitative, but *historical*. They are always transference emotions in a sense different from the one Freud intended: their ideology requires that we generalize not from a fungible scenario, but from an individual *target* as the essential component of a succession of constitutive scenarios. All this generates two sorts of self-deceptive possibilities. One is that a desire for fungible sexual satisfaction, because it advertises itself as "love," should be *experienced* as nonfungible ("I *feel* that I love you forever"). The other is its converse: an ideology constructed out of the desire to avoid the dangers of the former ideology, which denies the need for nonfungible attachment, or even its possibility. But if psychoanalysts are right about the connections between the capacity for attachment and other aspects of human fulfillment, then the zipless fuck[27] may also be delusive as an alternative ideology of love—and delusive in the very same ideologically conditioned way.

I must now face two problems. The first is terminological. Admitting that the phenomena I have described exist, why call them *self*-deception? Are they not rather a form of mystification in which the individual is merely the victim of a socialized ideology? No. For the ideology that infects the content of an emotion can do so only if it has been internalized. It comes from outside myself, to be sure—but so does most of what I call "myself." To attack it requires "consciousness raising," in the sense in which that term is restricted to the bringing into consciousness of facts *about myself* which then come up for endorsement as avowed parts of my identity.

THE PHONY PARADOX

But this answer suggests a graver problem. I have spoken as if consciousness-raising provided an avenue of escape from emotional self-deception. Yet in my account both appropriate emotions and self-deceptive ones have their origin in paradigm scenarios. Some forms of self-deception seem to lodge in the very semantic structure of emotion, or in an ideology that has the same source whether it is constructive or distorting. How then can I leave conceptual room for the distinction between normal, authentic emotions, and hypocritical, self-feigning, or ideologically self-deceived emotions? A theory of emotions that finds them to be learned as social *roles* must still find a place for those that we denigrate as *mere role playing*. When, in short, is an emotion *phony*?

Once again, the axiological level of reality required to make sense of emotional self-deception cannot be pried apart from the question of *human nature*. And at the core of that notion there is the ambivalence generated by the fact of bootstrapping: we make some things valuable by caring about them, but at least some of these things we should not care about if we thought there was nothing "out there" objectively *worth* caring about. What is authentic and what is phony has much to do with individual autonomy; but the cult of individual autonomy can itself be phony, if it takes no account of the constraints and possibilities of human nature. A good instance of this is André Gide's story about a man in pursuit of the *acte gratuit*. Gide's character, not wanting to be a slave to any determinism of passion or reason, decides to commit a completely unmotivated crime. The story demonstrates, of course, the self-defeating nature of the project, but in its attempt to escape from human nature itself the aspiration would be pointless even if it were coherent.[28]

I conclude with three remarks about escaping various forms of emotional self-deception—including that which might derive from the assumption that our emotional life can never change, because it is rooted in our paradigm scenarios.

The access we have to our emotions, in the crucial aspects that have concerned us here, is more difficult than access to either will or belief. Of course, as has often been noted, a change of belief can radically alter an emotion. But this touches only the cognitive aspect, not the distinctively axiological element, which I have claimed constitutes the idiosyncratic core of emotions as quasi-cognitions. We have no more direct access to the content of our emotions than we have voluntary control over the past situations in which we learned them. So one form of the phony is just this: the pretense of complete control, which can be made at various levels of awareness. We do have some indirect control, however: we can regestalt even those early paradigms. Sometimes we do it willy-nilly, forced by fresh vision to change our emotional attitudes to our past, now seeing what seemed domineering as protective, what seemed weak as gentle, what seemed principled as priggish.

In coaxing or badgering ourselves into such regestalting, we should remind ourselves of the crucial role and example of the *aesthetic* emotions. Aesthetic emotions seem to be an exception to the general rule that paradigm scenarios go back to infancy. I am inclined to think that they constitute emergent emotional structures, which bear witness to our capacity for fresh emotional experience, built on, but not out of, preexisting emotional repertoires. Emotions more or less mechanically constructed in the latter way, out of ready-made atoms, are also phony. Fresh emotions are not necessarily unreflective: on the contrary, the emotions of the unreflective are threatened with cliché.

Verbal argument is not useless in this process of examination. Consciousness-raising—that paradigm of philosophy—largely consists in propositional description and redescription. But we must carefully note its limitations. Verbal argument is not a powerful tool at the level of the immediate content of emotions. It doesn't help much to repeat, like an incantation, "This isn't really frightening," "There is really no reason to be angry/jealous/depressed/envious/sad." It helps a bit more to draw out the similarities with other paradigm scenarios, redescribing not the emotion but the situation: "He's being intimidating only because he's shy." But the level at which the effort of rational description is most useful is where I have argued much of the harm is done: at the meta-level of *ideology*. It is at least in part in searching out assumptions *about* emotions—about their peremptoriness, about their naturalness, about their transparency to the subject, about their identity or "biologically determined" differences between males and females—that we are most likely to transform and reform their experienced content and emerge from self-deception. In this sort of life examination, philosophical analysis merges with psychoanalysis, and each can strengthen the other's promise of therapeutic virtue. In the realm of the emotions, nothing is more phony than the simple life.[29]

NOTES

1. Jon Elster, *Sour Grapes* (Cambridge: Cambridge Univ. Press, 1983), p. 5. Elster cites as the source of the story E. Segre, *From X-rays to Quarks* (San Francisco: Freeman, 1980).

2. See Jaako Hintikka, *Knowledge and Belief* (Ithaca: Cornell Univ. Press, 1962), p. 24.

3. Jon Elster's case of sour grapes is a social kin to the placebo paradox:

> For the utilitarian, there would be no welfare loss if the fox were excluded from consumption of the grapes, since he thought them sour anyway. But of course the cause of his holding them to be sour was his conviction that he would be excluded from consuming them, and then it is difficult to justify the allocation by invoking his preferences. (Elster, *Sour Grapes,* p. 109)

4. Note that to grant that something is a case of self-deception may not *ipso facto* condemn it as altogether irrational. Self-deception is sometimes strategically rational even where it is not cognitively rational. But I am here adopting the working assumption that the axiological level is sui generis. Axiological rationality could go either way.

5. The best treatment of self-deception I know to date remains that of Herbert Fingarette in *Self-Deception* (London: Routledge and Kegan Paul, 1969). It takes a more inclusive view than most. I have discussed it in a review in *Inquiry* 13 (1970):308–321.

6. Katherine Ashenburg drew my attention to the ambiguities of this case.

7. Erving Goffman, *The Presentation of Self in Everyday Life* (Garden City: Doubleday Anchor, 1970), pp. 308–321.

8. Indeed, we are free to speculate that this may be one important biological

function of emotion. We unreflectively assume that our capacity to feel emotions precedes both our need and our capacity to express them. But the naturalness of some expressive behavior suggests that, on the contrary, emotions might have evolved for their communication value. On the cross-cultural constancy of some emotion expressions, see Carroll E. Izard, *Human Emotions* (New York and London: Plenum Press, 1977), p. 7.

9. This might be little more than the "injury feigning" of those birds that "pretend" to be wounded, dragging a wing along the ground to distract an enemy from their brood. See E. O. Wilson, *Sociobiology* (Cambridge, Mass.: Harvard Univ. Press, 1975), p. 122.

10. See William James, "What Is an Emotion?" *Mind* 19:188–204; S. Schachter and J. E. Singer, "Cognitive, Social, and Physiological Determinants of Emotional States," *Psychological Review* 69 (1962):379–399.

11. A related view is defended by Kendall L. Walton in "Fearing Fictions," *Journal of Philosophy* 75, no. 1 (January 1978):5–27. Walton discusses cases in which suspension of disbelief is no real belief, but involves real emotion. But it is not exactly the same emotion as would be generated in the presence of belief. See below on the "ideology of emotions."

12. Sigmund Freud, "Remembering, Repeating, and Working Through," in the *Standard Edition of the Psychological Works* (London: Hogarth Press, 1958), 12:250. See also in the same volume "Transference Love" (henceforth "TL") and "The Dynamics of Transference" ("DT").

13. See G. Frege, "Sense and Reference," in *Translations from the Philosophical Writings of Gottlob Frege,* ed. P. Geach and M. Black (Oxford: Basil Blackwell, 1952), pp. 56–78.

14. In some therapeutic contexts, however, it may be important to insist on the emotion's *reference* to another object: an emotion might be repetitive and neurotic precisely because it has been *spuriously* detached from its target or object, and the first step might be to bring this into focus.

15. Note that there is no implication here that we have reached a rock bottom of interpretation. Resistance can itself be a form of transference.

16. This is greatly oversimplified. For an account of some of the complexities of Freud's actual account, see my "Norms and the Normal," in *Philosophical Essays on Freud,* ed. Richard Wollheim and James Hopkins (Cambridge: Cambridge Univ. Press, 1982), pp. 139–162. The strategy of supplementing a structural account with normative criteria is found in Aristotle's treatment of *akrasia.* He points out (*Nicomachean Ethics,* bk. 7, chap. 5) that if an act is noble, we don't call it *akrasia,* even though it might strictly involve the same psychological mechanism. For by definition "*akrasia . . .* deserves blame."

17. James R. Averill, "Emotion and Anxiety: Sociocultural, Biological, and Psychological Determinants," in *Explaining Emotions,* ed. A. O. Rorty (Berkeley, Los Angeles, London: Univ. of California Press, 1980), p. 47.

18. Here is a curious psychological finding. Tell people that *p,* and let them infer that *q*; then inform them that *p* was actually false. Still, they are likely to continue to believe that *q,* forgetting that the ground for it was worthless. The case envisaged in the text is similar, except for featuring inertia of emotion rather than of inferred belief. For many other examples of rationalization, see R. Nisbett and T. Wilson, "Telling

More than We Can Know: Verbal Reports on Mental Processes," *Psychological Review* 84 (1977):321–359.

19. This is not to say that children cannot be surprisingly sophisticated about the normal structure of emotions and their function in mediating between the social and the autonomous self. Witness Hannah, at 4 years, whose mother had asked, "Do you ever get mad at yourself?" "No, why should I? I have you to do it for me."

20. Scheman states:

Some examples of individualistic states are being five feet tall, having pneumonia, missing three teeth, and having some immediate subjective experience. . . . Being the most popular girl in the class or a major-general or divorced are not individualistic states: nor, I want to argue, are being in love or angry or generous. (Naomi Scheman, "Individualism and the Objects of Psychology," in *Discovering Reality,* ed. S. Harding and M. B. Hintikka [Dordrecht: Reidel, 1983], p. 226)

21. This claim has been made, of course, in particular by B. L. Whorf, *Language, Thought, and Reality.* But in his claim that "Standard Average European" languages were bound to distort the reality of quantum mechanics, which North American Indian languages naturally captured, he provided the perfect *reductio* of his own view.

22. For a brilliant attack on "falling in love" as an inherently self-delusive emotion based on sexist ideology, see Simone de Beauvoir, "The Woman in Love," in *The Second Sex* (New York: Random House, Vintage, 1974), pp. 712–743.

23. For a good discussion of jealousy, see Leila Tov-Ruach, "Jealousy, Attention, and Loss," and Jerry Neu, "Jealous Thoughts," both in A. O. Rorty, ed., *Explaining Emotions* (cited in note 17 above). Illuminating treatments of jealousy are also to be found in Leslie Farber, "On Jealousy," in *Lying, Despair, Jealousy, Envy, Sex, Suicide, Drugs, and the Good Life* (New York: Harper and Row, 1976), and especially in Dorothy Dinnerstein, *The Mermaid and the Minotaur* (New York: Harper and Row, 1976). My sketch draws on the latter two works, with references in the text.

24. For more on various grades of intentionality, culminating in the capacity to make singular reference, see my "Teleology and the Great Shift," *Journal of Philosophy* 87 (1984):647–653, or chap. 4 in my *The Rationality of Emotion* (Cambridge: MIT Press [A Bradford Book], 1987).

25. An object is said to be *fungible* if it belongs to an equivalence class any member of which can substitute for any other in the fulfillment of a contract. Money is the paradigm fungible: individual dollar bills are not material to a debt. On the other hand if you lend me a vase and I return another, I have not strictly returned what I borrowed, though I may have offered an adequate substitute.

26. But not in all:

Dr. Aubrey Richards, an anthropologist who lived among the Bemba of Northern Rhodesia in the 1930's, once related to a group of them an English folk tale about a young prince who climbed glass mountains, crossed chasms, and fought dragons, all to obtain the hand of a maiden he loved. The Bemba were plainly bewildered, but remained silent. Finally an old chief spoke up, voicing the feelings of all present in the simplest of questions: "Why not take another girl?" he asked. (Morton Hunt, *The Natural History of Love* [New York: Alfred A. Knopf, 1959], p. 10)

27. The term is taken from Erica Jong, *Fear of Flying* (New York: Holt, Rinehart and Winston, 1973). But the concept has long been aloft.

28. See André Gide, *Les Caves du Vatican*.

29. The present paper is adapted from a chapter draft of the author's *The Rationality of Emotion* (cited in note 24 above). An early version was first published as "Self-Deceptive Emotions," *Journal of Philosophy* 75 (1978):684–697, and reprinted in A. O. Rorty, ed., *Explaining Emotions* (cited in note 17 above). Thanks are due to Amélie Rorty for discussion, ideas, and inspiration lavished over many years, and to Brian McLaughlin for helpful comments on a previous draft.

Part IV

THE SOCIAL DIMENSION
OF SELF-DECEPTION

15

IDEOLOGY, FALSE CONSCIOUSNESS, AND SOCIAL ILLUSION

ALLEN W. WOOD

The Marxian concept of ideology is not an especially clear one, and there is relatively little space in the texts of Marx and Engels devoted to explaining it. Since Marx's time, moreover, we have become accustomed to using the term "ideology" to denote important Marxian concepts for which Marx himself did not employ it, but which have retained their currency and usefulness in social theory and popular social thought, even among some of those who regard Marxian historical materialism and Marx's critique of capitalism as outmoded, unscientific, or otherwise discredited. As Freud was later to do, Marx changed our way of thinking about ourselves by making us aware of ways in which our conception of ourselves is systematically distorted by illusions, forms of deception, or motivated irrationality, whose removal is exceedingly difficult and requires practical conquest, enlightenment, and self-development as well as theoretical self-understanding.

The Marxian concept of ideology has spawned a great variety of different conceptions not found in Marx, such as Gyorgy Lukacs' concept of "reification," Louis Althusser's concept of ideology as an "imaginary lived relation between men and their world," and Jürgen Habermas' concept of ideology as distorted communication (to mention only three).[1] In this paper I will attempt no survey of such conceptions, but will restrict myself to concepts of ideology found in Marx's own theories. It would be too restrictive to consider only those concepts that Marx normally designated by the term "ideology," because this term has in the meantime come to denote important Marxian concepts for which Marx seldom employed it. But it will be well to begin by considering the concept of ideology as Marx found and adopted it.

IDEOLOGY: THE SCIENCE OF IDEAS, MENTAL LABOR, AND THE DOMINION OF THOUGHT

1. The word "ideology" (*idéologie*) was first used in 1796 by Antoine-Louis-Claude Destutt de Tracy (1754–1836). For Destutt, "ideology" was a science,

the science that studies the origin of ideas. Destutt's project was to trace all ideas to their origins in sensation, thus refuting scientifically all claims in behalf of "innate" ideas made by metaphysicians and showing these claims to be the result of mere prejudices. Despite Marx's contempt for him, Destutt anticipated the Marxian conception of ideology when he attributed many of people's prejudices to social class interests.[2] Owing to Destutt's revolutionary sympathies, he and his followers were subject to the wrath and scorn of Napoléon, who used the terms *idéologie* and *idéologue* as terms of abuse, stigmatizing *idéologues* as tedious intellectuals engaged in pointless and fruitless disputations. Marx was thinking of Napoléon's sense of the term, as some explicit references in his earliest uses of it indicate (see CW 1:244, 4:23).[3] Marx continues to use the term "ideologue" to refer to people who play a certain role in the social division of labor, namely, the performance of mental as opposed to manual labor (CW 5:59–60). This seems to be the sense in which Marx and Engels speak of priests as "the first form of ideologues" (CW 5:45), and also the sense the term carries in *The Communist Manifesto,* when Marx and Engels speak (apparently referring to themselves among others) of those "bourgeois ideologues" who have risen to a theoretical comprehension of the historical process, and have been thereby led to transfer their allegiance to the proletariat (CW 6:494).

The German Ideology, however, seems at times to be using "ideology" in a sense more closely related to its original one as referring to a proposed "science of ideas and their development." They are thinking not of Destutt's empiricist project of tracing all ideas back to their origin in sensation but rather of the German idealist project of showing how ideas evolve transcendentally out of one another a priori. Even more, they are thinking of the view of Hegel and his followers that the course of the world, and especially of human history, is determined by the development of ideas. Ideologues, they say, "agree in their belief in the dominion of thoughts [*Gedankenherrschaft*]," agree in "regarding the world as ruled by ideas, ideas and concepts as the determining principles" (MEW 3:14, CW 5:24). This usage may also hint at "ideologue" in the sense of "mental laborer," however, if the suggestion is that ideologues believe in the dominion of thoughts because they happen to be in the business of producing thoughts. (Marx often attributes to people the narrow-minded propensity to exaggerate the importance of their own social roles, or to see things only from their own distorted social perspective: see CW 5:60, 6:501–504.)

In *The German Ideology* Marx and Engels are interested in the belief in dominion of thoughts chiefly because they are concerned to reject it as a theory of society and history. "It is not consciousness that determines life, but life that determines consciousness" (MEW 3:27, CW 5:37). "Ideology," then, becomes the name for a philosophical view (the belief in the dominion of thoughts) to which they are opposing their own newly developed materialist conception of history. In the writings of Marx, "ideology" usually refers either to this philosophical view or to the products of mental laborers who (Marx thinks) generally share the view either tacitly or explicitly. But once the materialist conception of history is established, the term "ideology" will also occasionally be used to stand for an important theoretical concept related to the theory's account of the nature of social consciousness.

HISTORICAL MATERIALISM

2. According to the conception of history first developed in *The German Ideology,* the basis of human history is not the development of ideas, nor even that of political institutions, but rather the development of what Hegel called "civil society," the economic sphere, the sphere of human productive capacities and, corresponding to them, of the social relationships within which people produce and appropriate, which Marx and Engels call the "form of intercourse" (*Verkehrsform*) or the "relations of production" (MEW 3:44–45, CW 5:50). The materialist theory views history as divided into epochs, each characterized by a distinct form of intercourse or set of production relations. These relations define a set of economic roles, whose most crucial feature is that the relations assign ownership (effective control) over the means, process, and fruits of production to the occupants of certain roles, while excluding the occupants of other roles.

These differences are the basis of class differences in society. Classes are social groups whose members are assigned by the production relations to a common situation, giving them certain common interests (CW 6:211). Marx distinguishes, however, between merely potential classes (classes *an sich*), groups assigned a common economic situation by the production relations, and actual classes (classes *für sich*), groups that have become in some manner conscious of their common plight and organized to promote their common interests, so that they are represented as a class by an identifiable political movement (CW 5:77, 6:211, 11:187). For Marx, class interests properly speaking are not simply the interests shared by members of the social groups defined by production relations but instead the political goals of the movements representing these groups (CW 11:173). In this way, class interests become "general interests" over and above the individual interests of the class's particular members, which can sometimes demand the sacrifice of individual interests (CW 5:245).

On the materialist theory, social change comes about because the social relations of production are not static, but are compelled from time to time to undergo alterations, sometimes quite sudden and drastic ones. The explanation for these alterations lies in the social powers of production, the arsenal of productive techniques and capacities, including human knowledge and methods of cooperation and embodied in tools and other material means of production. These powers on the whole tend to grow. At any stage of their development, the employment and further growth of the productive powers of society is facilitated more by some historically viable social relations of production than by others. Eventually, any given set of social relations will become obsolete, dysfunctional in relation either to the existing productive powers or to their further expansion. A social revolution consists in the transformation of the social relations of production which is required by the growth of productive powers, either by their past growth or by their tendency to further development (CW 5:52; cf. SW 182–183).

Productive powers, however, do not make revolutions. The mechanism by which the adjustment of social relations to productive powers is effected is the class struggle. The struggle of classes, as we have seen, is really for Marx the struggle of the political movements representing them. The long-term goals of these movements, however, are not determined by the momentary consciousness of their members, neither by that of the leaders of the movement nor by that of the masses they represent. Instead, it is determined by the nature of the social changes that a movement can effect given its historical situation (CW 4:37). Marx identifies the long-term interests of a class with the establishment and defense of a certain set of production relations in society. That class tends to win out in the struggle whose long-term interests are identified with the set of production relations that, under the historical circumstances, best correspond to the state of development of the social powers of production. "The class struggle is the proximate driving force of history" (MEW 34:407). It is only the "proximate" driving force of history because its outcome is in turn determined by the tension between production relations and productive powers.

The Marxian claim that "life determines consciousness" means, in the context of this theory, that the ideas characteristic of a historical epoch reflect the interests of the epoch's most prominent classes. More specifically, these ideas are symptomatic of the state of the class struggle, and constitute the form in which people become conscious of this struggle.

> It is not men's consciousness that determines their being, but their being that determines their consciousness. . . . [Thus] in considering [an epoch of social revolution], we should always distinguish the material transformation of the economic conditions of production . . . from the legal, political, religious, aesthetic, or philosophical, in short, the ideological forms in which men become conscious of the conflict and fight it out. (MEW 13:9, SW 183)

It would not be plausible to take the term "ideological" here as a reference either to the supposed science of ideas or to those who believe in the dominion of thoughts, since there is no reason to think that this science or such believers have a monopoly on the forms of consciousness in which social revolutions are fought out. It might indicate only that the forms of consciousness indicated are produced by mental laborers: jurists, politicians, priests, artists, and philosophers. But likelier still, the term "ideological" is being used to express something more, something which is more intimately linked to the materialist conception of history.

Because Marx and Engels hold that "social consciousness" is "determined" by "life" or "social being," they take it to be one of the tasks of a materialist science of history to explain "ideological forms" in terms of productive powers, production relations, and the class struggle.

> This conception of history depends on presenting the actual process of production, starting from the material production of life itself, conceiving the form of intercourse connected with and created by this mode of production, i.e., by civil society in its different stages, as the foundation of all history, describing it in its action as the state, and also explaining how all the different theoretical products and forms of consciousness, religion, philosophy, morality, etc., etc., arise out of it, and following their formation process from this foundation . . . ; it does not explain practice from the idea but explains the formation of ideas from material practice. (MEW 3:37–38, CW 5:53–54)

By providing such explanations, historical materialism will refute "ideology" in the sense of a belief in the dominion of thoughts. But the term "ideology" may also be used to characterize those ideas that are the objects of the proposed materialist explanations. This is very likely the import of the term "ideological forms" used in the passage quoted in the previous paragraph. We may call ideology in this sense "functional ideology."[4]

FUNCTIONAL IDEOLOGY AND ITS MATERIALIST EXPLANATION

3. If we examine their usage closely, it is striking that Marx and Engels do not more often use the term "ideology" to express the conception of functional ideology. Nearly always, their use of the term involves reference either to some form of the belief in the dominion of thoughts or else to the fact that the thoughts in question are products of a distinctive category of mental laborer. It will be apparent on brief reflection that there is no need for functional ideology to have either of these characteristics. Marx has no reason to limit his materialist explanations to ideas produced by specialized mental laborers or to expressions of a theory of history he rejects. In one prominent passage, Marx even points out that the "superstructure of different and characteristic feelings, illusions, ways of thinking, and views of life" that pertain to a given class are "created and shaped by the *whole class* from its material foundations and from the corresponding social relations" (MEW 8:139, CW 11:128, emphasis added). We will follow subsequent tradition, however,

in using the term "ideology" to designate functional ideology (what Marx here calls the "superstructure"), irrespective of who creates it or of its affiliation with idealist theories of history.[5]

How does historical materialism propose to explain ideology in this sense? Marx's repeated statements that people's social consciousness is determined by their social being, together with his utter rejection of the "ideological" notion that ideas make history, has led many to read him as holding that human consciousness is purely epiphenomenal in relation to the economic sphere, that ideas never exercise any real influence at all on what goes on in the economic sphere. On such an interpretation, of course, it is impossible to understand how Marx himself could have regarded his theoretical work as a practical help to the working-class movement. The interpretation also conflicts with many casual statements by both Marx and Engels to the effect that of course the economic, political, and ideal spheres all exert an influence on one another, which it is the task of historical materialism to trace (CW 5:53, SC 460, G 88). Such an interpretation is best suited to the purposes of those who want to show after a cursory reading that Marx's theory of history is not worth serious study.

Marx's theory becomes intelligible, however, if we recognize that the "determination" of social consciousness by the class struggle, like the "determination" of relations of production by productive powers, involves a species of teleological or functional explanation, rather than a causal determination.[6] The theory holds that production relations change in such a way as to *facilitate* the employment and growth of productive powers, and it proposes to explain ideological forms through the way they *further* the interests of classes. These explanatory goals are not only compatible with the assumption that production relations exert causal influence on productive powers and that ideology exerts an influence on the class struggle; they positively *require* that there should be such an influence.

The explanations are based on the existence of *tendencies*: a tendency for productive powers to be employed efficiently and to expand, and a tendency for class interests to get themselves satisfied through the thoughts and behavior of social agents. Marx thinks that such tendencies are real, empirically verifiable features of the social world. The existence of such tendencies presumably also requires the existence of causal mechanisms through which people's ideas are adjusted to the needs of class movements, just as the existence of the tendency for a warm-blooded animal to maintain a constant body temperature requires mechanisms for generating and losing body heat and for the adjustment of heat production to heat loss. But just as it is easier to perceive the tendency to maintain constant body temperature than to trace the mechanisms through which it operates, so it is easier to perceive the tendency for ideas to serve class interests than to comprehend the complex mechanisms by which that tendency operates. Historical materialism is a theoretical program cast in terms of the more readily observable tendencies and in terms of functional or teleological explanations which may be based on them.

The program does, however, explicitly include on its agenda a study of the mechanisms by which these tendencies are fulfilled, and the detailed history of the process by which ideologies are actually generated. As we saw above, Marx and Engels propose to "explain how different theoretical products and forms of consciousness arise out of the material mode of production and to follow their formation process from this foundation" (MEW 3:37–38, CW 5:53–54). But this is an exceedingly ambitious aim, and it cannot be said that Marx or Engels ever did more than provide programmatic suggestions as to how it might be fulfilled. In effect, to fulfill it completely would be to provide a detailed and empirically verified theory telling us why certain ideas become current, fashionable, or trendy. It is not surprising that Marx did not succeed in doing this. No one else has ever been able to do it either.[7]

FALSE CONSCIOUSNESS AND SOCIAL ILLUSION

4. If "ideology" refers to functional ideology, then there is no reason why the beliefs included in "ideology" must be false, unscientific, or in any other way epistemically defective. There is no reason in principle why class interests may not be served by the dissemination of scientific knowledge. Marx in fact appears to believe that the dissemination of scientific knowledge about the origins, laws of motion, and future tendencies of capitalism will serve the needs of the proletarian class, and he seems ready to apply his materialist theory of history in this way to a social explanation of its own genesis: historical materialism was discovered and became current when and where it was because its discovery and currency promote the interests of the revolutionary proletariat. If Marx seems reluctant to call his own theory "ideology" and uses the term "ideology" in such a way that it suggests views that are false or unscientific, then that is probably a sign that "ideology" for him refers not to functional ideology but to belief in the dominion of thoughts. For later Marxists, however, who tend to use "ideology" in the sense of functional ideology, the explanation will have to be different.

It is a commonplace in Marxist thinking that ideology involves "false consciousness." But the term "false consciousness" is seldom if ever used by Marx, and plays no role in his own account of ideology.[8] The one text in which this term does play such a role occurs in a well-known letter of Engels' to Franz Mehring, written some ten years after Marx's death: "Ideology is a process carried out by the so-called thinker with consciousness, but with a false consciousness. The real driving forces that move him remain unknown to him; otherwise, it would not be an ideological process. Thus he imagines to himself false or apparent driving forces" (MEW 39:97, SC 459). In this passage, Engels makes it a necessary condition for something to be ideology that it involve "false consciousness." "False consciousness," however, here refers to the falsity or illusory character of the supposed "driving forces" to which the ideological thinker attributes his own ideas. "False consciousness" here is thus the ignorance of, or the possession of false beliefs about, what explains the form of social consciousness one has.

It seems very likely that Engels is thinking here of "ideology" in the sense of the belief in the dominion of thoughts. That would explain why an "ideologist" is necessarily ignorant of the material "driving forces" of his own thinking. For to believe in the dominion of thoughts is to believe that thoughts and conceptions rule the world and have their own proper course of development, which is independent of the development of productive forces, production relations, and the struggles of social classes; hence it is to deny on principle the existence of the "driving forces" to which historical materialism attributes one's own thinking. This is a much narrower meaning of "false consciousness" than the one that is current in more recent Marxist discourse. No doubt Marxists regard the belief in the dominion of thoughts and other false theories about the explanation of one's social consciousness as a form of false consciousness, but they do not restrict false consciousness to this, as Engels does. Instead, they apply the term to a wide variety of false, mystified, or distorted beliefs people have about themselves, the world, and social relationships whose social prominence is to be explained by the economic or class function these beliefs serve.

Although Marx and Engels do not use "false consciousness" in this sense, they plainly do hold that the forms of social consciousness whose prominence is to be explained by their class function do typically distort or falsify reality in systematic ways. The dominant ideology in any epoch of class society is a dominant "illusion" (*Illusion, Schein*) (MEW 3:46–47, 48, 49; CW 5:55, 59–60, 62). Historical materialism even takes upon itself the task of explaining the fact of this illusion: "If in all ideology human beings and their relations appear to be standing on their head as in a *camera obscura,* this phenomenon is produced by their historical life-process, just as the inversion of an object on the retina is produced by their immediate physical life-process" (MEW 3:26, CW 5:36). Marx sees his materialist science of history as the theoretical weapon of the proletariat, whose historical mission is the liberation of humanity from class society. Part of this liberation, however, is the liberation of people from socially created illusions about themselves and their condition, so that as social beings they may also be autonomous beings acting with rational understanding of the true meaning of what they do.

These illusions exist, in Marx's view, because societies and classes need them. People are subject to them because social relations of production require for their survival and smooth functioning that the people who are subject to them be unable to see them for what they are. For Marx this is especially true of class societies, whose relations of production involve the oppression of one class by another. Oppression is one reason why societies need illusions, because oppression works best when it is hidden—not only from the oppressed but also from the oppressors, who would not be as effective in maintaining the relations from which they benefit if they saw them as oppressive.

Not all social illusions are conservative for Marx. Some serve the interests of revolutionary classes by serving as justifications for their revolutionary activity and representing their social aspirations in a favorable light. For example, bourgeois ideologies that represented the interest of the bourgeois class as the universal interest of all society helped the rising bourgeoisie destroy feudal aristocratic and guild privileges (CW 5:60–61). In a similar way, the interests of particular classes, in Marx's view, tend in class ideology to represent themselves as the universal interests of all society (CW 11:130–131). As long as class society persists, however, phrases such as "the general interest," "the common interest," and "the universal interest of all society" have no referent. All interests in class society are particular interests. Phrases like "the general interest" in class society always serve an exclusively ideological purpose, namely that of representing the particular interest of one class as general for the purpose of persuading people to accept the rule of a particular class (CW 5:61).

Unlike previous classes, in Marx's view, the proletariat is capable of advancing its interests without the need for the illusion that its interests are universal ones; not, however, because it is the truly "universal class," but because it is the class whose historic mission it is to abolish class society. Only when class society has been abolished altogether will the interests of the (erstwhile) proletariat cease to be particular class interests asserted against the interest of a ruling class (CW 5:77).[9] It is notable that Marx also credits the bourgeoisie with playing a role in ridding humanity of the need for illusions by reducing all exploitation to its fundamental—that is, purely economic—form, thus enabling people finally "to regard their life situation and mutual relations with sober eyes" (CW 6:487).

A second (if overlapping) reason why class society, and especially bourgeois society, needs illusions is *alienation*—the fact that social relations of production impose on people a mode of life that is crippled, stunted, unfree, a life that prevents the development and exercise of their essential human capacities. If the social relations are to be maintained, people must be prevented from coming to recognize this fact, or if they do recognize it, they must be given a suitably mystifying interpretation of their experience of it. This latter function is accomplished not only by illusions about the workings of society but also by illusions about human nature itself and the human condition—for instance, by certain religious illusions.

People whose lives are alienated—impoverished and empty—often tend to sense this fact, to experience themselves as worthless and their lives as devoid of dignity. Certain religious illusions serve the psychological function of interpreting this alienation so as to make it bearable and of offering supposed remedies for it—very much as magic and religion in societies with primitive science and technology both interpret people's powerlessness over against the natural world and provide them with imaginary remedies for it, such as entreaties and sacrifices to the gods and the ritual deeds of witch doctors. Both in "primitive" and in "civilized" religion, the illusion of having some sort of access to the mysterious powers that govern our fate and of having achieved "salvation" from our alienated condition can often be quite effective on the psychological level, even though it leaves the real state of powerlessness or alienation entirely untouched.

Religious illusions in alienated bourgeois society simultaneously serve a socially integrative function by reconciling people to the social relations that are responsible for their alienation. For example, religion explains people's sense of spiritual frustration and unfulfillment as due to their "self-will" and their "sinful" desires (such as those for autonomy, material well-being, and earthly happiness, which are frustrated in existing society); it represents a blind adherence to archaic religious laws (interpreted, of course, so as to buttress the prevailing social relations) as the path to liberation and superstitious faith in the supernatural as the means to achieve spiritual fulfillment.

Illusions of this kind are a particularly effective way to protect alienating social relations from the instability threatened by alienation, since they put people's efforts at ending alienation in the service of precisely those social relations that cause it. Such illusions, of course, not only distort people's perceptions of the alienation to which they are subject but also themselves constitute a significant part of that alienation, since to be subject to them is by itself to be spiritually degraded, crippled both in one's understanding of one's condition and in one's practical orientation to it, and thus deprived of important aspects of the fulfillment of one's human nature. Individual members of an alienated society may reject religious beliefs as illusions, but in Marx's view such illusions will continue to be socially prominent because as long as society is alienated in real life the illusions fulfill a psychological need on the part of alienated individuals and a structurally defensive need on the part of the society.

IDEOLOGY AND OBJECTIVE SOCIAL ILLUSION

5. Some social illusions for Marx take the form of direct factual misinformation, false theories, mystifying philosophical interpretations, and aesthetic imaginings. When these are conservative, they have the effect of diverting attention from the facts of oppression and alienation, and of either defusing

social discontent or directing people's energies to the defense of the prevailing social forms. When they are revolutionary, they correspondingly focus on the defects and irrationalities of the status quo, portray the aspirations of the revolutionary class in a uniformly favorable light, and divert attention from the inevitable costs of revolutionary change. The term "illusion" must also be understood broadly here, and not interpreted in too narrowly cognitive a sense. Since the function of ideology is to affect people's practice, it may be doubted whether all these ideological distortions can be reduced to or adequately portrayed simply in terms of false beliefs. Marx refers to the ideological "superstructure" as consisting not only of beliefs but also of "feelings" and "ways of thinking" (CW 11:128). Ideology operates not only by supplying people with false beliefs but also by affording them a systematically biased selection of correct information, by distorting ways of processing the information they have, and by encouraging associations between perceived reality and certain sentiments or affectively colored images.

These forms of illusion, however, all consist simply in people's having certain mental contents or processes, and they are all produced by human thought, often by a specialized class of ideologues (mental laborers). There is another species of social illusion discussed in Marx's writings, however, which is not in this same sense merely subjective in nature or simply a product of human thinking. In Marx's view, social reality can sometimes present *itself* in a false or illusory form, so that the illusion exists prior to all theorizing, and even persists for someone who is in possession of a correct theory.[10]

The best known example of such an illusion is the "fetishism of commodities." Religious fetishes, Marx says, are "products of the human brain" that

> appear as independently living beings, entering into relations both with one another and with human beings. In the world of commodities it is the same with the products of the human hand. This I call the 'fetishism' which adheres to the products of labor as soon as they are produced as commodities and which is therefore inseparable from commodity production. (MEW 23:86–87, C 1:72)

Commodities are useful objects (use-values) produced by human labor for exchange. In a society based on commodity production (a market economy), the social relations between cooperative human producers are made a function of the exchange relation (the exchange-value) of their products. It is no illusion that in a commodity-producing society, the social relations between producers are governed by the exchange relations between their products: "the relations connecting the labor of one individual with that of the rest appear not as direct social relations between laboring individuals, but as *what they are,* thinglike relations between persons and social relations between things" (MEW 23:87, C 1:73). The illusion is that this capacity of people's products to regulate their social relations belongs to the products simply as use-values, as objects capable of satisfying human wants. Thus in a commodity-producing society, my social relation to others—my capacity to command their labor and my susceptibility to having my labor commanded by them—appears by nature to be a function of the utility of the objects I have to offer for sale.

This is an illusion because commodities have the power to regulate social relations between persons not in virtue of their natural or useful properties but only in virtue of their social character as commodities, as objects produced for exchange. In a feudal society, as Marx points out, products of labor do not have that power, despite their use-value; social relations here appear directly as relations of personal dependence and subjection, not as a consequence of relations between things. The products of labor will once again lack the power to determine social relations when society becomes a "community of free individuals, carrying on their work with the means of production in common, in which the labor power of all the different individuals is consciously applied as the combined social labor power" (MEW 23:91–93, C 1:77–78, T 3:484). As long as people's production is dominated by the exchange relation, the social relations between them will inevitably appear to arise out of the natural properties of the commodities they have to sell. "What is mysterious about a commodity is simply that in it the social character of men's labor is reflected back to them as an objective character of its product, as a social-natural property" (MEW 23:86, C 1:72).

The distinctively "objective" features of this illusion are, first, that the illusion is not due to people's adoption of false economic or social theories, but simply to the commodity form that products take, and second, that even intellectual comprehension of the illusion through a correct theory does not do away with the false appearance.

> The recent scientific discovery that products of labor, insofar as they are values, are merely expressions in real material form of the human labor expended in their production, is epoch-making in the history of humanity's development. But it by no means chases away the objective illusion [*gegenständlichen Schein*] concerning the social character of labor. (MEW 23:88, C 1:74)

A normal perceiver is still subject to the illusion even when in possession of the truth of the matter and of a correct theoretical explanation of it. For Marx, the social world, like the physical world, is capable of generating false appearances (similar to optical illusions). Marx compares the illusion involved in commodity fetishism to the appearance that air is composed of a single gas and that the sun revolves around the earth (C 1:74, 316). The difference is that objective physical illusions depend only on the constitution of the physical world and of our senses; objective social illusions, however, depend on historically transitory features of society. In Marx's view it is both possible and desirable for people to create a society in which their relations are transparent, immediately perceived for what they are and not encumbered with objective social illusions.

The fetishism of commodities is the best-known example of objective social illusion, but it is far from being the only example presented in Marx's writings. Others include the illusion that laborers are paid for the whole time that they labor (C 1:539–540), that machinery and raw materials are capital (C 3:815), that labor-intensive industries produce no more surplus value than others (C 3:168), and that land has value and enters as capital into the costs of production (C 3:623, 810). All these illusions follow a single pattern: they all represent social forms as identical with the material economic contents they organize. Capitalism is especially prolific in generating such illusions because in capitalism social relations of production appear in a directly economic form, as opposed to the personal or political form they assume in slave society or feudalism. This means that people's social roles appear to coincide directly with people's roles in the productive process, and thus to be inseparably bound to the material constituents and activities that form that process.

Marx never applies the term "ideology" to objective social illusion. But this is completely understandable when we recall the restrictive sense in which Marx uses the term. Objective social illusions are clearly ideology in the sense of socially prevalent illusion or false consciousness, and they certainly do seem to be, or to involve, functional ideologies, that is, forms of social consciousness that may be explained by the way they contribute to the stability of the mode of production and promote (ruling) class interests. Marx does not call them "ideology," however, simply because they neither are products of a class of mental laborers nor involve any belief in the dominion of thoughts.

IDEOLOGY AND SELF-DECEPTION

6. In this paper I have tried to expound Marx's theory of ideology in the broad sense of social consciousness and social illusion, but it is well beyond the scope of the paper to assess (let alone to defend) the many controversial claims involved in the theory. The materialist conception of history is a challenging programmatic hypothesis, but still not a widely accepted view, and Marx's class analysis of modern society, at least in the form he presented it, seems in certain respects quite outdated in the late twentieth century. In any case, a theory that holds that many socially prevalent ideas, beliefs, and perceptions are pernicious illusions could hardly expect to escape controversy, and Marx himself often calls attention to the fact that his theoretical consequences are paradoxical and offensive to common sense and prevailing beliefs.

One central, striking, even paradoxical idea in Marx's theory, however, has proven impossible to dislodge: the idea that our social life and practice is not transparent or immediately intelligible but opaque and systematically distorted by social forces, that social life subjects people to systematic illusions serviceable to the interests of certain social groups. This idea, as I said earlier, like the idea of the Freudian unconscious, forces itself on us as a troubling inevitability with which any modern self-understanding must reckon. Both ideas, moreover, are associated in people's minds with the notion of self-deception. The final question, therefore, which I want to address is: What is the relation between ideology and self-deception?

This question unfortunately requires us to come to some understanding of what we mean by "self-deception." I will understand "self-deception" as a certain species of motivated irrationality, thus as belonging to the same genus as *akrasia,* or weakness of will. Self-deception may be distinguished from *akrasia,* however, by the fact that in self-deception we are forced to account for the irrationality by supposing that the subject's mind is in some way "divided," so that the motives and the mechanism producing the irrationality are excluded from the subject's conscious awareness.[11] This exclusion is motivated, as when I have good grounds for believing p but believe not-p instead because I wish not-p to be true or find it comforting or consoling to believe not-p. Sometimes, however, people (religious believers, for example) hold on to a belief in the teeth of the evidence because they find the belief consoling, and yet seem to remain all the while quite conscious of what they are doing. This may be a case of motivated irrationality, but it is not a case of self-deception except insofar as the maintenance of the belief requires that the believers distort their reading of the evidence or exclude some of it from consciousness in ways they do not admit to themselves. The fact that the distortion or exclusion is something that occurs under the pressure of need indicates that it is an *accomplishment* of the mind in a way that acts done out of *akrasia* are not, and that it requires some significant effort and the expenditure of psychic energy.

Ideology, as we have developed the conception above, is any form of consciousness that distorts or falsifies people's perception of reality, and whose social prominence is explained by its functionality for the prevailing mode of production or for the promotion of the interests of a social class. To the extent that ideology distorts reality, and especially to the extent that it tends to hide its own distorting influence, ideology may be regarded as a form of *deception.* Some cases of ideology, however, look like cases in which self-deception is very much in place. Ruling-class ideologies typically represent members of the ruling class in a favorable light, making them feel good about the privileges they enjoy and representing the sufferings of the "less fortunate" either as inevitable or as something deserved. It is easy to see how such beliefs could answer to the wishes of ruling-class members, and how such people could hold them in the way we have described as self-deception.

Marx often calls attention to ideologies that are taught to an oppressed class by the paid representatives of a ruling class (priests, journalists, academics, pedagogues), and serve the ruling class by deceiving the oppressed about their condition. In such cases the oppressed do not appear to be victims of *self*-deception, since the distortion is imposed on them from without, and there seems to be no motive (such as wish fulfillment) which would induce the oppressed to adopt beliefs that it is directly against their interest for them to have. This kind of ideology looks more like straightforward lying than like self-deception. This ignores, however, the fact that those who are oppressed may derive a kind of comfort from believing that their sufferings are unavoidable or deserved, and that it may prove very distressing to them to realize that their condition is both unjustifiable and alterable, especially if altering it is seen as difficult, costly, and risky. Ideology, even ideologies that deceive the oppressed, often prove functional because they provide comfort and consolation, and are the sorts of things people wish were true. They are illusions to which people are subject, Marx says, because they are subject to a condition that needs illusions (CW 3:176). Illusions people need often operate through self-deception.

Despite these considerations, I doubt that self-deception plays a role in most ideology. For although self-deception provides a mechanism that might be serviceable to ideology, it is doubtful whether ideology often stands in need of this mechanism. Cases of self-deception are cases in which the psychically upsetting awareness is dangerously close at hand, and fairly drastic steps must be taken by the individual's psyche if the danger is to be averted. A social order whose functional ideology depended on mechanisms of self-deception in its individual members would be far less secure than one which found other ways of inducing the necessary illusions in them. When the observance of a society's norms of conduct is made to depend largely on mechanisms of individual self-deception or repression, the norms will be observed only very imperfectly. (Restrictive norms of sexual behavior provide a good illustration of this.) A mode of production that is forced to entrust its chief functional ideologies to such mechanisms must be either one without serious inner conflicts or else one tottering on the brink of destruction.

That societies do not need to depend on self-deception is easy enough to see when we reflect on the following considerations. Social orders and their prospects for change, and the needs, interests, aspirations, and capacities of human individuals are all complex matters. The truth about them is not easy to discover, and not easy to confirm once it is discovered. Social orders that are changing, moreover, represent a moving target in this respect; the truth about them, even if once discovered and verified, is not likely to last for long. Where this is the case, it is easy to see that there would very likely be differences of opinion about how people are to understand themselves and their societies, even among inquirers whose views were not distorted by such things as personal vanity, interest, or partisanship. Various sets of ideas favorable to social stability or to the interests of a given class are bound to be available, and they will tend to be socially prominent if the social mechanisms regulating the production and dissemination of ideas tend to favor them.

Every society requires some mechanisms to select which ideas are to form part of the pedagogical and scientific orthodoxy of the society, and which subjects, theories, and hypotheses are to receive the most resources for research.[12] Such mechanisms typically (almost inevitably) involve choices between rival theories, made by people who do not themselves possess as much expertise as do those who produce the rival theories between which they choose (such people as politicians, bureaucrats, editors, those who fund research and publication, or just plain consumers). It is natural for such people's choices to be influenced by convictions, held honestly and without self-deception, which harmonize with their class interests or prejudices. The theories that they tend to prefer will be those harmonizing with these convictions. Their preference for these scientific theories gives respectability to the theories, while the fact that these theories are generally preferred lends support to the convictions that harmonize with class interests. Self-deception, of course, may often be involved in the production of theories, or in the selection made by those to whom the social order leaves such choices to be made, or in both at once. But it is not difficult to understand how prevalent ideas would tend to harmonize with class interests and the needs of the mode of production even if self-deception were not a factor at all.

The notion that ideology operates through self-deception leads naturally to the presumption that where people are "honest," where they do not experience the psychic tension and do not need to invest the psychic energy characteristic of self-deception, ideology cannot be operating. This presumption, however, is one of the errors that give ideology the cloak of invisibility which it needs in order to do its work. The notion that ideology operates through self-deception is itself a piece of ideology.

NOTES

In citing works of Marx and Engels, I will use the following abbreviations, normally citing both the German text and a standard English translation in the case of a direct translation, and otherwise the English version only. All translations of quotations, however, are my own.

MEW   *Marx Engels Werke* (Berlin, 1961–1966), cited by volume and page number.

CW   *Marx Engels Collected Works* (New York, 1975-), cited by volume and page number.

C   *Capital* (New York, 1967), cited by volume and page number.

G   *Grundrisse* (Moscow, 1939); English translation by Martin Nicolaus (Harmondsworth, 1973), cited by page number in the English translation.

SC   *Selected Correspondence 1846–1895* (New York, 1965), cited by page number.

SW   *Selected Works* (in one volume) (New York, 1968), cited by page number.

T   *Theories of Surplus Value* (Moscow, 1971), cited by volume and page number.

1. Gyorgy Lukacs, *History and Class Consciousness,* trans. Rodney Livingstone (Cambridge, Mass., 1972), pp. 83–222; Louis Althusser, *For Marx,* trans. Ben Brewster (New York, 1970), pp. 231–236; Juergen Habermas, "Vorbereitende Bemerkungen zu einer Theorie der kommunikativen Kompetenz," in *Theorie der Gesellschaft oder Sozialtechnologie?* ed. J. Habermas and Niklas Luhmann (Frankfurt, 1971), pp. 101–141.

2. "Destutt de Tracy, the fishblooded bourgeois doctrinaire. . . . " (MEW 23:677, C 1:648). For Destutt's anticipation of the Marxian conception of ideology, see Emmet Kennedy, *A Philosophe in the Age of Revolution: Destutt de Tracy and the Origins of "Ideology"* (Philadelphia, 1978), p. 206.

3. These passages are discussed by Louis Dupre, *Marx's Social Critique of Culture* (New Haven, 1983), pp. 219–220.

4. Compare my *Karl Marx* (London, 1981), pp. 117–122. In that very brief discussion of ideology, I distinguished (1) "functional ideology" from two other senses of the term: (2) "historical idealism"—belief in the dominion of thoughts—and (3) "ideological illusion"—the incomprehension by a form of social consciousness of its own material (economic and class) foundations. I did not mention there the two other senses of "ideology" and its cognates that we have noted in this paper: ideology as (4) the science (or pseudoscience) of ideas, and (5) the products of a class of mental laborers. My treatment of ideological illusion was also rather simplified, and oriented especially to the prominent text of Engels (to be discussed below) in which the term "false consciousness" is used.

5. Marx's use of "superstructure" in this passage is apparently at odds with his use of it in the famous 1859 "Preface," where it designates the system of legal and political institutions, explicitly distinguished from the corresponding "forms of social consciousness" (SW 182).

6. See my *Karl Marx,* chap. 7, and G. A. Cohen, *Karl Marx's Theory of History* (Princeton, 1978), chaps. 9 and 10.

7. There thus need be no disagreement between Marx and Jon Elster on two points that Elster uses to criticize Marx: (1) that the kinds of historical materialist explanations that appeal to tendencies are a "temporary necessity," used only because more detailed explanations of the mechanisms behind these tendencies are not available, and (2) that wherever such explanations are employed, it is presupposed as a condition of their validity that there are such mechanisms at work, even if we are unable to identify them. See Jon Elster, *Making Sense of Marx* (Cambridge, 1985), pp. 6–7. Elster, however, appears not to be entirely consistent. He sometimes grants that a functional explanation is permissible "if one insists on the necessary existence of some underlying mechanism" (p. 7), and he admits that one can provide reasons for thinking that there is a mechanism without being able to specify one (p. 28). Yet at other points he insists that "to explain is to provide a *mechanism*" (p. 5), which entails that functional explanations in terms of tendencies do not explain at all, even if we insist that they operate through some underlying mechanism. This, of course, is not consistent with Marx, and it seems unduly restrictive besides.

8. John Plamenatz, in his book *Ideology* (London, 1970), states repeatedly (pp. 23, 79, 89, 124) that Marx called ideology "false consciousness," but cites not one text in support of this claim.

9. There is, of course, one text (CW 3:186) in which Marx does refer to the proletariat as the "universal class"; it is often cited as providing unique insight into Marx's conception of the proletariat. The text *is* unique in Marx's writings, because it was produced in 1843 and thus predates Marx's historical materialist account of class ideology, which brings with it the repudiation of this whole universalistic and moralistic conception of the proletariat. See my article "Justice and Class Interests," *Philosophica* 33 (1984):9–22.

10. My account of the concept of objective social illusion and its exemplification in the fetishism of commodities follows closely that of G. A. Cohen in *Karl Marx's Theory of History,* chap. 5 and appendix 1, although my discussion of these matters contains some minor points of divergence from his (for example, I believe his accounts of religious fetishism and of the illusion involved in commodity fetishism are not quite accurate to the text of *Capital*). I will also have no occasion here to discuss the central thesis Cohen attributes to Marx, that science requires that there be a discrepancy between reality and appearance.

11. See David Pears, "Motivated Irrationality, Freudian Theory and Cognitive Dissonance," in *Philosophical Essays on Freud,* ed. Richard Wollheim and James Hopkins (Cambridge, England, 1982), pp. 264–270.

12. Some such mechanisms will be more restrictive than others on what opinions people are permitted to express. But some sort of relative selection between opinions is a necessity, even in the most liberal and open-minded society, if the work of scientists and educators is to go on at all. Further, societies without formal press censorship can often be just as effective at suppressing information about the misdeeds of their governments as societies in which there is repressive state management of information. In the U.S., news media and academic scholarship are often self-censoring. The conceptions of "fairness" and "objectivity" prevailing in the media have nothing to do with standards of epistemic appraisal, but consist rather in accu-

rately reflecting the balance of power between the institutions and groups powerful enough to demand an effective hearing for their ideological distortions of the truth. The ideologies of these institutions and groups count as "respectable" however little intellectual merit they have, and views falling outside them are normally available only in publications with a very tiny circulation. These claims are well-documented regarding U.S. involvement in third-world fascism, terrorism, and genocide. See Noam Chomsky and Edward S. Herman, *The Washington Connection and Third World Fascism* (Boston, 1979), especially pp. 71–79. There are many good reasons for favoring a society in which there is freedom of expression, but the idea that in such a society the truth must prevail is not one of them.

16

THE SOCIAL CONTEXT OF SELF-DECEPTION

Rom Harré

In this paper I am going to attempt a social constructionist theory of self-deception. To begin with I propose to treat the concept of self-deception within the framework of a commonsense understanding. When we say that someone is deceiving himself we mean, I believe, that his expressed opinions are contrary either to some more fundamental beliefs that we suppose him to have or, subtly, to his own best interests. The former of these contrasts is, at least at first sight, an individualistic notion, while the second is social. However, to pursue a social constructionist account of either of these contrasts further, it will be necessary to set out in some detail the theory of self that is characteristic of that point of view.

A Social Constructionist Conception of Self

1. The distinction upon which the whole of the social constructionist view rests is that between the public fact of identity of a human being as a person and an individual's sense of that identity. The fact of personal identity is, I believe, a public and social matter and is ontologically grounded in the concept of the person. I take a person to be a publicly identifiable being with a characteristic combination of linguistic capacities and moral qualities, most of the latter having to do with responsibility. These aspects of the concept of a person that reflect the moral order within which the level and range of personal responsibility is defined will turn out to be highly culturally dependent. One simple and more obvious way in which the concept of a person is culturally dependent turns on the degree to which responsibility for an individual's actions is taken as a personal or a community matter.

A society that recognizes individuals as the source of action may still treat, for example, families, as the locus of moral responsibility. One might quote the apocryphal Eskimo phrase, "I did it; we are responsible."

It is conceivable, that is, logically possible within the general metaphysics of persons, that there is a tribe who have no self-awareness and whose mental life is exhausted by their public conversation. For such a tribe, the public, collectively identified person coincides with the self. But most human tribes consist of people with a sense of their own identity, individual by individual. Having been warned by J. Sabini and M. Silver (1982) of the complex incoherence of any attempt to pick out the proper realm of the psychological through the use of the distinction between subjectivity and objectivity, I propose to contrast the sense of self with the fact of identity just in terms of the distinction between that which is private and that which is public. I take our sense of identity to be personal in the sense of private-individual aspect of mind. The basic social constructionist thesis is that that sense is made available to the members of a culture through an ontological myth, namely, a belief in the existence of a self.

So the first theme of social constructionism is the contrast between that kind of identity that human beings have as members of a community engaged in a conversation within a moral order of rights, duties, obligations, and conceptions of human worth, some of whose acts may be conveyed through material practices, and the organization of perception, thought, feeling, recollection, and so on, with respect to a sense of identity which can be neatly capsulated in the phrase "a sense of self." It is that which Doris Lessing described as "continuing to burn" behind a multiplicity of different roles.

I have already hinted in the foregoing that persons and selves are comprehended within our rhetorics as belonging to the same ontological category, namely, individuatable beings. But according to social constructionism the former are real while the latter are (indispensable) fictions. The *various* culturally distinct versions of self which can be identified in the cognitive and material practices of mankind are theoretical concepts whose referents are fictions. To go further into this idea we must draw on the general theory of theoretical concepts from nonlogicist philosophy of science.

It has now become widely accepted, outside the hard core of conservative logicists, that the theoretical concepts of a science are not arbitrary interpretations of a logical calculus but are independently meaningful. Their semantics is to be understood in terms of analogical relationships with prior sets of concepts. The prior sets are frequently referred to as source analogues or source models. To illustrate the idea with a simple example, Darwin's concept of natural selection is a theoretical conception built by analogy with the empirically grounded concept of domestic selection. Darwin takes some trouble at the beginning of *Origin of Species* to build up the sense of the concept of domestic selection by illustrating its use with a great many examples drawn from farm and field, pigeon loft and garden. The theoretical developments in his book open with the careful analogical construction of the concept of natural selection on the basis of the intensional semantics of the concept of domestic selection which he has so carefully analyzed. This account frees theoretical concepts from any immediate referential attachment to real-world entities. Or to put the matter another way: our understanding of theoretical concepts arises by a process internal to theorizing by building on an already existing concept. Only thus can we allow for the question whether such concepts have referents to be considered independently of how they get their meaning.

A powerful theoretical concept, modeled on a well-established empirical concept, may have all sorts of organising power in the conceptual field of a science, and yet the question of the existence of putative real-world referents corresponding to it may remain open.

Social constructionism says that the self, which appears in talk about our private sense of identity, is a theoretical concept of just that kind. Each culture creates such a concept(s) on the basis of the existing person-concepts characteristic of its public life. In this way concepts of self have a well-established meaning. This meaning does not arise through the denotation of the concept of self but via its relation with the public concept of person. Social constructionists can see no reason for differing from Hume, Kant, and Ryle in their well-grounded opinion that the sense of self is not referential and indeed could not be. For Hume, there is no impression corresponding to the idea. For Ryle, the self is systematically elusive. In social constructionist terms the concept of self is a theoretical concept, and the entity corresponding to it in a realist reading of subjective, self-reflective talk is a hypothetical entity that has not, and indeed could not, be revealed in the course of any empirical investigation. This is the groundwork on which those phenomena that are currently called 'self-deceptions' will be investigated.

The organization of experience, feeling, cognition, and so on, into unified manifolds is best understood, I believe, by some revamped version of the Kantian conception of the syntheses. Indeed, the developmental psychology of L. S. Vygotsky (1978) could, with reason, be looked upon as a version of the Kantian idea that each individual mind is a result of a synthesis of a mere flux of fragments of experience. For social constructionists, the Kantian syntheses are psychologically real. That is, the unities of thought and feeling, action, etc., which are the empirical grounds of the individual sense of self, are not given, nor are they the result of a natural maturation. According to social constructionism, the syntheses of the fluxes of various kinds of human experience into manifolds are the result of a social process and mirror something of the public world.

It will be no surprise to learn that it is the public-collective concept of person that is thought to be mirrored in the unities of the synthetic manifolds. Kant's way of locating the transcendental ego can be interpreted, perhaps with a measure of charity, as a version of the idea that it is a theoretical concept. After all, he says it is an idea and not an intuition. But Kant seems to have thought that the origin of the syntheses lay in the activity of the noumenal self. The process that he broke down into concept, category, and schematism, as the means through which the activity of the noumenal self is realized in the syntheses of inner and outer experience, was, so to say, internally derived. Social constructionism, as opposed to Kant, holds that the syntheses are the product of interpersonal actions and that the source of their schematisms lies in features of the social milieu and personal conversations meaningful within it.

In this way there is a distinction of great moment between the larger Kantian theory and its social constructionist alternative, even though the latter is, from the point of view of the syntheses of the manifolds in the various kinds of unity which Kant recognized, wholly sympathetic to Kant's great idea (Harre' 1983).

Now, in order to understand what in the social milieu is the source of the structure that interpersonal activity causes to be imposed upon the undifferentiated flux of infant experience, we must return to the basic idea of the role of the concept of a person. Once this step has been made it is possible to ask in a wholly empirical spirit what, in the social world, in interpersonal action, could be the bearers or vehicles of the concept. It is possible to ask, further, which of those vehicles would be that by which other collective organization of discourse around persons can become a private and individual organization of thoughts and feelings around selves.

The most obvious candidate for such a vehicle is the language through which social interaction, and in particular those activities that are manifestations of the local moral order, is realized. So my first detailed suggestions will have to do with the analysis of referential practices in conversational speech acts, that is, the theory of pronominal functions. I propose to show that there are very characteristic features of the way human conversation develops that lead almost inevitably to the opening up of a gap between public reference and personal acts of self-predication. This gap opens up via the social practice of commenting upon the epistemic and moral qualities of what other people believe and do. In short, I hope to show that the practices of interpersonal commentary are the source of a structure of intrapersonal commentary. The self is a fiction carried by the concept of a transcendental ego through which self-predication is made intelligible to the very being who acquires this practice.

One final preliminary point is in order before I turn to the detailed examination of the grammar of pronominal functions. There is a third social constructionist idea useful for this analysis, namely, psychological symbiosis. I can introduce the idea by drawing a contrast between two ways of describing a mother's relationship to the infant with whom she is interacting. In what might be called the 'separate identity' view, a mother's interference in the efforts made by her infant to converse, to carry out simple tasks, and so on, is described as 'helping'. In this way of putting the matter, the mother and the infant are conceived as separate social beings, and the interaction between them is described in such moralistic terms. Conceived as psychological symbiosis, the mother's efforts are no longer thought of as giving aid to an independent, active being but as complementing and supplementing the activities of one component of a dyad. Only the mother-infant dyad is a complete social being, with whom the mother, as another being, *in propria persona,* so to say, is interacting. So when the mother interprets an infant's efforts to speak or gives a 'helping hand' to one who is trying to carry out some physical task, this is not to be construed as one human being helping another, but as one-half of a dyadically structured individual contributing its part to the total activities of that dyad considered as a social individual.

Once this conception is adopted, the whole framework within which developmental psychology is to be pursued changes quite radically. The process of maturation occurs, for the most part, in conditions in which the infant as a component of a dyad is being treated as a wholly responsible being. Development assists in the transfer of skills, knowledge, etc., from one part of a complete social individual to another. A case can be made out for the claim that there are none of the amazingly complicated processes described by Piaget as assimilation/accommodation, but merely the imitative accumulation of the component parts of cognitive structures which simply 'click' into a coherent whole when an infant has acquired the necessary totality. So no more complex and esoteric interpersonal psychological process than imitation need be invoked. The well-known phenomenon of discontinuous development, that is, the sudden occurrence of big steps in sophistication, is explained by the equally unproblematic phenomenon of the forming up into structures of the various independent components, once they have all been acquired.

The idea of psychological symbiosis is perhaps not crucial to the theory of self-deception, but it has been worth adding at this point since many of the ideas of the social constructionist view ultimately depend upon a non-Piagetian theory of development.

The Referential Logic of Interpersonal Discourse

2. The kind of interpersonal discourse that I have in mind in the discussions to follow is the commonplace exchange of performative utterances that goes on in ordinary conversations—pleas, requests, refusals, invitations, acceptances, insults, apologies, and so on—the components of a discourse. It is so obvious as to be hardly worth remarking that the social force of any given utterance is determined not only by the conventions governing its ordinary use but also by the place that it occupies in the conversational matrix. It may require several conversational turns before one is certain whether a remark should be taken as an insult or a joke. This feature of conversation means

that the analysis of a discourse in terms of illocutionary force requires attention to quite extended sequences of social acts. It cannot be done utterance by utterance (Clarke 1984). For practical purposes, of course, I shall discuss utterances produced in the course of imaginary conversations and allow the intuition of the reader to fill out the rest of the exchange in such a way that my arbitrary assignment of illocutionary force makes sense.

A further proviso must be entered. It is necessary to take account of the fact that overt grammatical forms may be poor indicators of the kind of social functions that sentences are being used to perform. For example, it is a commonplace of sociolinguistics that the question form is by no means almost always used for queries. A sentence in question form can be used as an order, as an invitation, and so on. The examples I will draw on will be in English, a language that separates the bearers of the pronominal function into lexically distinctive pronouns, although verbs remain by and large uninflected. But it is the pronominal function that I am interested in, not the specific rules governing the grammatical pronouns of English. In Latin languages, for instance Spanish, the pronominal function is largely carried out through the inflections of the verb. Pronouns are used for what grammarians call 'focusing': "*Ti quiero*" is "I love you," but "*Yo ti quiero*" is "*I* love you," "*Yo*" simply being a 'focusing device'. This is an obvious and commonplace point, but I have noticed that in discussing these issues in predominantly English-speaking circles, there is a tendency to identify the logic of the pronominal function with the grammar of what we take to be unproblematic pronouns. To avoid any further possibility of confusion I shall speak of 'referential' rather than 'pronominal' functions and simply take for granted that the reader is sufficiently apprised of the way referential functions are managed in languages spoken south of the Pyrenees and of the fact that the pronouns as used in those languages, by and large, are not their main bearers.

Let us begin with a group of performative utterances that I shall call the 'uptake markers.' For example, in the course of a conversation I might respond to what you have just said by saying, "Yes, I follow you," or "I understand, go on," etc. Now a statement like "I get it" has two main uses in ordinary conversation so far as I can see—a performative use as a speech act and a descriptive use as a self-attribution. The facility of a performative use does not depend on the truth of the descriptive use. When in a conversation I say, "Yes, I understand, go on," there are two kinds of response that the speaker could make as the next step in the conversation, taking account of the perlocutionary effect of previous illocutionary utterances. In saying, "I understand you," I might have been doing the equivalent of nodding, I might have been sympathizing, I might have been showing that I was following you, and so on. On that reading the speaker is encouraged to continue his or her exposition. Alternatively, the remark could be taken in a descriptive sense. This would be revealed if the speaker (say, a teacher) suddenly turned on the interlocuter (a pupil) and demanded, "Prove it; prove you understand me." Of course, in that case, what is required is some demonstration by the listener that the speaker's utterances have indeed been understood—that is, a demonstration of the interlocuter's proper state of mind. In the second case we can think of the remark "Yes, I understand you" as describing a psychological phenomenon which has occurred in the mind of the interlocuter.

Common though such utterances are, even more common is a complex form involving two uses of the first person, for example, "I think I understand you." Such a statement, I believe, is itself a performative, and indeed it is obvious enough that it is a weaker form of the embedded "I understand you," were it to stand alone. So, we can divide it into two parts, the overall statement "I think I understand you" and the embedded utterance "I understand you." My claim is that the weaker performative is created from the stronger performative by epistemically qualifying the descriptive twin of that original. Or to put this another way: when the utterance "I understand you" is embedded in the sentence frame "I think . . . ," its performative force is suspended, and it can be read only as a putative descriptive statement about the speaker's state of mind. This thesis can be confirmed by looking more closely at the grounds for the weak performative and at the evidence for the truth or falsity of "I understand you" treated as a descriptive statement. Logicians are familiar with the idea of referential opacity, which occurs in contexts like "I believe that the Atlantians colonized England before the Romans." Such a statement can be true even if it is as a matter of fact false that the Atlantians colonized England. The truth-value of the embedding statement is not a function of a truth-value that is embedded within it. Reference of the embedded statement is, so to say, suspended. My examples are intended to highlight a phenomenon that I shall call 'illocutionary opacity', an analogy with the referential opacity of belief contexts.

To illustrate the way in which evidence operates on such statements I need to emphasize that the embedding frame, for example, "I think . . . ," is a way of epistemically qualifying that which is embedded. To take another case, suppose someone says, "I think I am going to be sick." We can call this whole statement 'b' and compare it with the utterance "I am going to be sick," which I shall call 'a'. Clearly "I am going to be sick" can be taken, and often is taken, as a warning, but it might also be taken, descriptively, as a prediction. The more complex statement, 'b', is also a warning, but a weaker one, and it may also be, though rarely I think, taken as a weaker prediction. Suppose the statement 'b' is challenged by an onlooker who says, "Are you sure?"; then the sufferer might be inclined to offer some evidence for 'a', possibly in terms of a report of a nauseated feeling or some other matter that is relevant to the truth or falsity of the statement 'a', now considered as a prediction. This offering, which is *evidence* for 'a', is coupled with a sincerity condition, part of the felicity conditions for the issuing of the weaker warning, 'b'. Embedded in "I think I am going to be sick," 'a' is not a performative; it is a descriptive or predictive statement. The weaker warning, 'b', is created by the epistemic qualification of 'a'.

I would like to illustrate this with a third example. Compare "I am not sure that I understand you" with "I understand you." The larger statement, 'b', is a performative and its illocutionary force clearly arises by the epistemic qualification of 'a'. In considering 'a' as epistemically qualified we have to take into account evidence for 'a', which in many cases may be a mental state.

Now this form of expression, which is very characteristic of English, brings to the fore two different referential functions performed by the use of the pronoun "I." When "I" stands at the beginning of a simple performative, the illocutionary force or social act is indexed as properly the responsibility of the speaker. The indexical "I" is such that the sense of the sentence has to be completed, or indeed can only be completed, by someone who has knowledge of the particular occasion of that utterance. Similarly, in the complex performative of type 'b' above, the use of "I," which introduces the whole statement, is, I would claim, indexical in just the same way as the "I" that introduces the simpler performative. However, in a descriptive or predictive reading of the sentence 'a' (which, standing alone, was used to express the simpler performative) as embedded in the complex sentence, "I" refers to a subject of predication. In particular, when the simpler utterance is embedded in the more complex and the illocutionary force is suspended, we have no option but to treat the embedded "I" referentially. Now the question, of course, is whether there is a real referent to which that referential *use* refers.

According to the social constructionist thesis, the personal practice of self-examination is a special case of, and parasitic upon, the social practice of the critical examination of the conversational contributions of others. So, if we are to understand fully the logical grammar of sentences such as "I am not sure I understand you," "I think I am going to be sick," or "I believe I am falling in love with you," we must compare them with statements like "I think he is falling in love with you," "I am afraid he is going to be sick," and "I am not sure he understands you." In these cases the descriptive or predictive force of the embedded statement is entirely transparent since the third person is not capable of functioning indexically to introduce a performative. If I say, "He promised to marry you," I am usually reporting upon his act, not vicariously performing one for him. It is possible to imagine an episode in which my statement does indeed commit him to a certain course of action, but I choose to ignore such out-of-the-way occasions.

The theory that I promised in section 2 can now be invoked to give an account of the referential function of the embedded pronoun. In most cases, the kind of evidence that a speaker would use for acts of self-examination would be some form of self-reflection of the kinds of feelings, the kinds of grounds, etc., upon which the simpler performative, had it been uttered, would have been based. Of what are those feelings, those judgments and so on, to be predicated? One simple and popular doctrine is that they are to be predicated of the very same entity, namely, the person, as are the public acts and performatives of a speaker. But I think I have already given sufficient grounds in discussing the distinction we maintain in our culture between the fact of personal identity and the sense of self to suggest that that answer will not do.

I believe that the self theory that we learn in the course of acquiring our language and within the material practices and moral exhortations in which we are embedded in our daily life, tends to the inculcation of a belief that the unities of thought, feeling, and action, which constitute our sense of self, are not only structural but ontological. It takes philosophers to remind us that we have no empirical grounds for these ontological beliefs.

To sum up this section of the argument, I will consider the dialogue between two persons, Alpha and Beta.

ALPHA: I am not sure that I trust you.
BETA: Why, what have I done?
ALPHA: Well, you let me down before.

Now Alpha's second statement brings forward the evidence on which the embedded '*a*', "I trust you" is judged a false description of Alpha's current state. The content of Alpha's second statement, "Well, you let me down before," expresses part of the felicity conditions of the complex, weak performative '*b*', "I(1) am not sure that I(2) trust you," which is the whole statement that Alpha first made. The weaker performative, '*b*', is created by the epistemic qualification of '*a*', the stronger performative. Occurrence(1) of the first person "I" is indexical, labeling the speech act as that of 'the speaker', but occurrence(2) is referential, referring to a subject of predication of mental states, and this is because the *qualification is epistemic*. The indexical referent of "I(1)" is a publicly identifiable and collectively defined person around whom cluster social acts and actions. The denotational referent of "I(2)" is the supposed center of a cluster of mental states. The first center is the person, the second is the self. But the self is not an object. It is a concept providing for the synthetic unities of thought, feeling, and action.

THE GENERAL THEORY OF MONODRAMA

3. As long ago as 1923, T. Evreinof proposed a psychological theory based upon the idea that there was a thoroughgoing reciprocity between the forms of staged drama and the structure of individual minds. Evreinof's book, *The Theatre as Life,* now strikes us as somewhat naive. Nevertheless, he did at-

tempt a practical application of his theories and wrote plays for the Parisian theater in which the dramatis personae were essentially *Id, Ego,* and *Super-ego.* And, of course, he has not been the last to indulge in this conceit. A more recent statement of the monodramatic principle we owe to J. S. Bruner (1979). He says:

> There is within each person a cast of characters—an aesthetic, a frightened child, a little man, even an onlooker, sometimes a Renaissance man. The great works of the theatre are decompositions of such a cast, the rendering into external drama. The life too can be described as a script, constantly rewritten, guiding and unfolding internal drama. (p. 137)

The point of view of this paper is monodramatic but takes exactly the opposite tack. It seems to me that both Evreinof and Bruner supposed that the structure of the mind was given and the dramas of the stage and everyday life were projections onto the social world of that structure. On the contrary, I believe that the cast of characters that can fancifully be supposed as the components of the human mind, is borrowed from episodes of real life. Our attempt to understand the ways in which we carry out such activities as self-criticism and self-exhortation, and the kind of language in which the "I" addresses, exhorts, and criticizes the "me," must be understood by reference to a linguistic practice borrowed from that developed for social purposes of exhortation, criticism, and the like, in which the commentator or critic and the actor are different persons. The decomposition of the self, I believe, can only be a reflection of a multiplicity of persons and social episodes. According to the monodramatic view, though, the concept of self-deception can be made sense of only with a model drawn from typical social episodes frame within the moral order of the community in which the self-deceiver lives and the language that he or she speaks.

According to this point of view we may not take for granted that there is any such thing as a universal phenomenon of self-deception. There may be, but the theory requires that every such psychological phenomenon be considered within the framework of a particular society.

The first step, then, will be to consider the various ways in which we can deceive one another. Broadly speaking there are two, though they may have immensely complex variations depending upon whether speech or action predominates as the vehicle of deception. One can lie or, more potently, one can simply fail to disclose. This distinction is now enshrined in English law. Not only is it an offense actively to deceive a client about the state of something that is being sold—for example a house—but it is also an offense to fail to reveal conditions that are known only to the vendor. Both are conceived of as forms of deception. It is only too obvious that the notion of deception here is epistemic—that is, the victim is prevented in some way or another from knowing what he or she has a right to know. So, as in many phenomena that have a place in the economy of our psychology, the simple epistemic definition must be supplemented by some reference to the moral order of the local community. Recently, in a psychology lecture, Jos Jaspers pointed out that the commitment of a speaker to the truth of his or her utterance is a highly culturally variable matter. By and large, in Anglo-Saxon and Scandinavian milieus, speakers intend the hearer to take their remarks literally and they make a commitment in line with that intention. But this is far from true south of the Alps, and the further east one goes the less does that commitment form part of the Gricean conditions of conversation. Along with those changes in conditions must of course go the difference in the cultural conventions concerning deception. It has become a philosophical commonplace that a culture that did not recognize the difference between truth and falsity would not survive since all practical conversational practices would be stultified.

So it is clear that the notorious Indian or Greek who, in response to an inquiry, tells the inquirer what he or she thinks the inquirer would *like* to know, or simply expresses himself or herself firmly and authoritatively as part of an exercise of self-presentation, must at the same time be operating within a cultural matrix that preserves truth and falsity, at least at some level and for the purpose of some language games.

It will follow from this that if self-deception is somehow or other to be conceived in terms of the unfolding of episodes in which one person deceives another, then it is likely that no cultural universal will be revealed by whatever studies in self-deception we may undertake. But the crucial question is this: is it right to assimilate self-deception to such activities as self-criticism and self-exhortation?

ADMISSION OF SELF-DISCOVERY

4. The contexts in which performatives of admission occur will repay close study. For example, consider the statement "It took me ages to admit to myself that I couldn't do it . . . that I had betrayed my best friend, etc." These are the kinds of statements that seem to me to be unproblematically self-referential in the way that encourages the use of the concept of self-deception. So one explanation of the conditions under which such a statement would be made would be that they indicate moments of revelation prior to which the speaker was deceiving himself or herself. I will suggest in the spirit of the theory expounded so far that the philosophical grammar of this class of statements does not warrant an ontological gloss on the double use of the pronoun. Let us turn to a public statement with much the same content, such as "I think you have been fooling yourself," and the kinds of reasons that might be given for so assessing somebody's past condition. For example, it

might be that the speaker wants to get the listener to admit that he or she has not got the necessary resources or talent, or whatever is required to do what he or she has been proposing. So a useful response might be, "Well, I now realize that I can't do this thing," or "I have to admit (to you) that I can't do it, having once thought I could." These mark in various ways the transition in the state of knowledge of the speaker. What, then, are we to make of the iterated pronouns in "I think I am fooling myself," or "I think I have been fooling myself"?

If we consider these kinds of statements just with respect to the kind of illocutionary point that they would have in a conversation or a monologue, or even a confession to a third party, it seems to me clear that this should be understood in terms not of psychology but of rhetoric. That is, they are in various ways a rhetorical framing in terms of an *acceptable* public-collective model, in which there are mild accusations and reproaches, reminders and observations, to draw attention to the fact that someone has, or had, false beliefs about his or her past, talents, and resources. This is a commonplace kind of conversational gambit, and we might discuss it further, were we so minded, in terms of such concepts as candor and tact.

But there is no doubt from the literature—for instance, as summed up in Herbert Fingarette's study (1969)—that this monodramatic grammar is, at least implicitly, read as an indication, or perhaps even a description, of an interaction between two self-like components of a single human being, or in Fingarette's more muted version of the theory, two psychological centers around which knowledge and belief cluster. According to the argument of this paper, that is a reading controlled by the theory, a theory that is quite widespread among the speakers of languages that iterate pronouns or functionally identical first-person inflections. However, if we take the rhetorical analysis seriously then we may have doubts about the ontologizing of a useful grammatical model which is used to express lightly to one's friends that they have not devoted enough care to examining their resources, critically assessing their memories of past events, or summing up their talents and capacities.

All of this runs counter to the idea that psychodynamics has demonstrated that there are genuine cases of knowing but not acknowledging. This demonstration suggests that (1) the being who knows should be ontologically distinguished from the being who does not acknowledge, (2) that of which the person is not conscious should be distinguished from that of which they are. There are various possible senses in which I could know what I won't acknowledge. For example, I might simply ignore some things that I know, or I may, while being perfectly well aware that I know them, simply fail to acknowledge them, i.e., I may not do anything publicly which commits me to them. There will be various obvious reasons why my public declarations may fall short of candor. As I have argued above, candor and its sibling, tact, are concepts defined for the interpersonal public activities that I sketched at the beginning of this section. In its usual conversation matrix candor is a relationship that stands between one person and another. Taking the mono-dramatic model seriously, we may well ask ourselves who are the entities between which the relation of candor stands if we read "I think I have been fooling myself" as a statement ontologically similar to "I think you have been fooling yourself."

However, I believe that there is a very obvious way of blocking this naive suggestion of ontological similarity, namely, by reference to the phenomenon of hypocrisy. The hypocrite's activities have the same formal structure, I believe, as those of the deceiver. That is, the hypocrite knows or believes one thing and says or does something that is in one way or another incompat-ible with it. The hypocrite is perfectly capable of formulating, indeed probably does formulate to himself or herself, those private beliefs that would have been contradicted by public disclosures had they been allowed to filter into the public arena. And no one has suggested that hypocrisy should be explained in terms of an "I" and a "me" as ontologically distinct beings, the one who believes and the one who says or does, publicly. The commonplace cases of self-deception that are resolved by the candor of a friend (or even of an enemy) I claim are no different in any essential way from hypocrisy. The condition that distinguishes self-deception from deceit, prevarication, and other forms of concealing what one knows behind a contrary public perfor-mance is simply the extent to which the speaker has paid attention to or has taken the trouble to delve into his or her beliefs, resources, talents, and capacities. While hypocrisy is, at least in Anglo-American circles, taken to be a vice, we Anglo-Americans are a little more forgiving of the self-deceiver, though in the moral gloss that I have just given to this psychological phenome-non there is no doubt that self-deception too is, to some extent, reprehensible. My intuition is that we are inclined to think that the self-deceiver ought to have acknowledged those matters that are germane to what the actor in question is proposing or planning to do or is giving expression to.

Erving Goffman (1963) has drawn our attention to an interesting inter-mediate case that lies between hypocrisy and the mildly reprehensible kind of self-deceit that candor resolves. He has remarked on the extent to which people need to present themselves in public in such a way that they conceal certain events in their past, events that would discredit their current public presentation. Goffman calls these events 'stigmata'. In his subtle and enter-taining book he explores the strategies by which discrediting acts are routinely withheld from public display. It may even be that there is a kind of collusion among people to protect one another's public faces by refraining from that kind of public interrogation which, mutually indulged, would reveal the stig-mata that each has so carefully kept from public view. It seems to me that we should not call this hypocrisy, nor should we call it self-deception. It is not hypocrisy because its moral quality differs from that condemned in the behavior of the hypocrite. Nor is it self-deception, because, as Goffman makes clear, the cases he has in mind are those in which the racial origins, educational institutions, ethnic allegiances, and so on, of the people in question, are perfectly well known to those who conceal them and indeed in the most interesting cases to those who collude in the mutual deception, as well as the circumambient society from which they would all be expelled should their stigmata be disclosed.

The main casualty of this kind of rhetorical reading of the illocutionary force of statements modeled upon the public phenomena of candid criticism, comment, and reminder is the idea of an ontologically dual centering of experience. According to the theory I have been advocating there is no such duality; there is only a rhetorical device. Monodrama is a dramatic reflection of public events, not a structural projection of private psychological structures.

The classical accounts of self-deception can be seen as attempts to resolve the problems presented by the apparent psychological acceptability of all of the following four exemplary statements:

(1) A does not know, believe, or remember X.
(2) A himself or herself contrives not to know, believe, or remember X.
(3) A's knowing, believing, or remembering X is a motive for the mental activity described in (2).
(4) A knows, believes, or remembers X.

Thus, A does not know, etc., X only if A does know, etc., X. Freud's solution is to impose the conscious/unconscious distinction on this array of presumed psychological facts. The propositional attitude 'consciously' qualifies the psychological verbs in (1), and so the propositional attitude 'unconsciously' must qualify (4). Once this move is made (1) follows from (4). Statement (2) remains problematic but can be qualified with 'unconsciously' like (4). State-. ment (3) is unaffected by these qualifications since it is a psychologist's hypothesis and, if qualified, would include 'conscious or unconscious.'

To accept this solution we have to accept the psychological reality of an unconscious realm *of the same psychological 'natural kinds' as the conscious realm*. Since the same kinds of psychological processes, e.g., 'motivated contriving', are to be found in the two realms they must, in general, have similar structures. But the phenomenon of self-deception is the most important empirical support for the Freudian theory of the unconscious mind. If there were any more plausible alternative explanations, then that support would fade away. Even if none can be found, a strong whiff of circularity emerges from the above discussion. To express the phenomena of self-deception in such a way as (1) through (4) above seems to be plausible because the

Freudian dichotomy is waiting in the wings to resolve it. So to use that for-mulation to support the scientific claims of the Freudian distinction between conscious and unconscious is, to say the least, dubious.

Fingarette and others have proposed solutions in the mode of monodrama. Perhaps the first step to a monodramatic account in terms of an internal di-chotomy between clusters of beliefs around quasi-persons has already been taken when the phenomena in question are called 'self-*deception*.' 'Deception' is usually used to refer to a lack of candor between persons. The idea of lacking candor toward oneself suggests an inner duality.

The monodramatic reading of the four exemplary statements discussed above resolves the threat of self-contradiction by qualifying the 'A' of (1) as a different quasi-person (A_1) from the 'A_2' of (2), (3), and (4). A_1 is the dupe of the machinations of A_2.

This approach depends upon the reification of the synthetic unities, includ-ing that of apperception, as beings. In the bulk of this paper I have tried to show that apperception is best understood as the grammatical structure of reflexive discourse, rather than a relation between beings. But the practices of self-commentary typical of Judeo-Christian culture are made possible by an organization of thought, feeling, recollection, etc., dependent on each and every one of us coming to believe a theory about ourselves, in which an entity concept of self plays a central role. There is no referent for this concept. The monodramatic analysis of self-deception, since it requires a dual-entity ac-count of self-reflexive discourse, is at best naive, at worst incoherent.

Beyond the grammatical-structure and ontological accounts, a third possi-bility, implicit in all I have argued for, is T. Warner's (1986) 'self-betrayal' account. To return to the four exemplary statements, the self-betrayal account challenges the standard formulation of the problem as it appears in such statements. Statements (1) and (4) are both misdescriptions. There is only one psychological state, that in which A formulates the belief expressed in (4) in such a way that its moral turpitude is concealed. It is not 'hidden behind a veil', but instead A expresses it in a self-justifying (even self-glorifying) *rhetoric* rather than in self-accusing or self-denigrating rhetoric. There are not two 'beings'. There are *two kinds of rhetorics* available to A, and this fact is known both to A and to those who listen to A's remarks. So the difference between honesty and self-deception is not that of psychological levels, one visible and one invisible; nor is it that of trickster and dupe. Rather, it is a difference in moral tone of ways of relating an anecdote concerning the same series of events. The telling in a rhetoric from one cluster excludes the telling in a rhetoric from the other.

And statement (2) above is also a misdescription. A does not 'contrive' not to know X, but rather formulates his or her account of X within a self-glorifying rhetoric. In short, (2) is a meta-misdescription of the psycho-logical basis of self-deception. Now (3) becomes straightforwardly an indication of the kind of reason A might have for adopting a self-justifying rhetoric. It may describe a reason that A would acknowledge.

REFERENCES

Bruner, J. S. 1979. *On Knowing: Essays for the Left Hand, Expanded Edition.* Cambridge, Mass.: Belknap Press of Harvard University Press.

Clarke, D. D. 1984. *Language and Action.* Oxford: Pergamon Press.

Evreinof, T. 1927. *The Theatre as Life.* London: Harrap.

Fingarette, H. 1969. *Self-Deception.* London: Routledge and Kegan Paul; New York: Humanities Press.

Goffman, E. 1963. *Stigma.* Englewood Cliffs, N.J.: Prentice-Hall.

Harre', R. 1983. *Personal Being.* Oxford: Blackwell.

Sabini, J., and M. Silver. 1982. *Moralities of Everyday Life.* New York: Oxford University Press.

Vygotsky, L. S. 1978. *Mind in Society.* Cambridge, Mass., and London: MIT Press.

Warner, T. 1986. "Anger and Other Delusions." In *The Social Construction of Emotions,* edited by R. Harre'. Oxford: Blackwell.

17

SOCIAL SELF-DECEPTIONS

WILLIAM RUDDICK

> He who fools himself fools nobody.
> —from a Chinese fortune cookie

How are we to understand the term 'self' in 'self-deception'? There are at least two ways. On the first, 'self' refers to someone who is both agent and victim—the limiting case of deception. In formal terms, the usual dyadic relation, Dxy ('x deceives y'), becomes the reflexive, Dxx ('x deceives x'). Accordingly, the philosophical task is to explain how a single self can both know and be ignorant of the same proposition; the related psychological problem is to find intrapsychic motives and mechanisms for such double-think. We, or our putative semiselves, must manage somehow to accommodate two contradictory beliefs, or to substitute sham for less respectable, real motives.[1]

The motives and methods for standard cases are rather discreditable: the foolish lover or cuckold, the incredulous mother, the reassuring alcoholic distort or ignore evidence in order to guard cherished false beliefs and imprudent desires. All are charged with "motivated irrationality"[2] or with "wishful thinking grown stubborn and perverse."[3] So diagnosed, the self-deceiver is an anti-Descartes, protecting rather than purging ungrounded beliefs.

Despite the many cases this dyadic account fits, it has a serious individualistic bias. Specifically, this reflexive analysis makes self-deception too intrapsychic, too much a matter of doing something to oneself rather than to the world. It makes self-deception too private: self-deceivers often employ, and even require, social assistance.

I wish to canvass some cases and methods of self-deception that illustrate these social features. And with their help I wish to develop an alternative, "monadic" analysis in which the dyadic Dxx ('x is deceived by x') is replaced by the nonreflexive Sx ('x is self-deceived'). On this monadic reading, the meaning of 'self-deception' is not just a compound of the usual meanings of 'self' and 'deception'. Rather than a doubly referential noun, the 'self' of 'self-deception' is read as an adjectival prefix that modifies the meaning of 'deception'.

With these logical and semantic changes, we will be less tempted to assume that self-deception is a solo performance. We will be better able to see the role that other people play in our self-deceptions. Rather than a paradoxical habit of closeted minds, self-deception appears more social. Rather than moral, epistemic, or metaphysical self-abuse, it can be seen to be a common, even beneficial feature of many joint ventures.

WITTING AND UNWITTING ASSISTANTS

Petrarch's paradigmatic self-deceiver is an innkeeper who lures customers with a sign promising better wine than he serves. But in time he comes to believe his own false advertising.[4] Liars often lose their sense of the truth and come to believe their own lies. How might this happen in this case? Let us suppose that his customers praise his wine, either because they are polite or because their taste is altered by the expectations his sign generated. The innkeeper might overlook or dismiss these possible explanations for their praise and reassess his own initial judgment. With their unwitting help, he comes to think that his wine is as good as his sign suggests.

But is this self-deception? If his sign has corrupted their judgment, then he has deceived them, and they in turn have unknowingly misled him. If they are not deceived but are merely polite, then they have unintentionally misled him. In either case, he has initiated a causal chain that has his own false belief as its last link. But so, too, do gullible people. Can we find special reasons here to eliminate the intermediate links and so to count this as a case in which his attempts to deceive them boomerang?

We would be so justified in this descriptive shortening of the chain of deceptions if deceiving were a transitive relation (that is, by deceiving B, who deceives C, A thereby deceives C). Accordingly, the innkeeper, by corrupting the judgment of his customers, who in turn corrupt his own, would have corrupted himself. The transitivity of deceiving, however, is unclear. As a form of harm, deceiving might be so construed in the law. Someone who harms a second party who, so suffering, harms a third party, would probably be held responsible for both harms. More generally, causal responsibility in the law is transitive. And yet, being causally or legally responsible for such "posterior" harm is not, *eo ipso,* describable as having harmed the victim. There may be further translation rules (backed by certain theories of causality) for condensing talk of "A is the cause of F in B" into "A F'd B." But this is not the occasion to consider them.[5]

These issues do not, of course, arise for the case of polite compliments. If the customers are not deceived but only polite, then there is no chain of deceptions to shorten descriptively on grounds of transitivity. With polite customers, there must be a different basis for the diagnosis of self-deception. The most obvious candidate is the innkeeper's misconstrual of politeness as judicious appraisal. By so mistaking their praise, he makes their remarks misleading, despite their intentions. He turns his customers into unwitting deceivers.

There are, of course, various ways to invite *witting* deception. The gullible person does so by displays of naiveté, of uncritical standards of evidence. The self-deceived are more discriminating: they make it clear that in certain matters they do not want evidence counter to their cherished beliefs and questionable projects. We are all skilled in discouraging criticism, especially people in authority. Consider the biblical King David, Bishop Butler's favorite self-deceiver.

David impregnated a soldier's wife, Bathsheba, and then, in order to conceal his paternity, brought her husband, Uriah, home from the front to sleep with her. But when, out of military zeal, Uriah refused, David arranged his death in an otherwise pointless battle. Sent from God, a fearless prophet, Nathan, confronted David with the tale of a rich sheep owner who commandeered a poor man's only beloved lamb for a feast. David angrily demanded the name of the rich man in order to fine and execute him. When the prophet revealed that the tale was a parable of David's own greedy lust, David saw his sin and accepted God's punishment.[6]

Butler took David's case to be one of monstrous self-deception by an otherwise righteous man.[7] David, he says, allowed sexual passion and self-partiality to blind him, thereby allowing himself to commit "horrid crimes" for which he would have readily condemned anyone else. Such self-partiality is, Butler thinks, the root of all self-deception. Accordingly, he offers us two ways to overcome self-partiality, to "open our moral eyes" and allow our "inner moral light" to illuminate our character and action, namely, the Golden Rule and a hypothetical slander test. The Golden Rule requires us to perform in imagination a double substitution: we are to imagine other agents performing the action we wish to undertake, and ourselves in the situation of those people who would be affected by that action.

His second test requires a different act of imagination: "Suppose then an enemy were to set about defaming you, what part of your character would he single out? What particular scandal, think you, would he be most likely to fix upon you? And what would the world be most ready to believe?"[8] He thinks that if a person does "in plainness and honesty fix upon that part of his character for a particular survey and reflection, he will come to be acquainted, whether he be guilty or innocent in that respect, and how far he is one or the other."

Would these two tests have enabled King David, without a prophet's parable, to detect his own moral monstrosity? Butler admits that some self-deceivers will be too self-partial and too little regarding of others to be able to perform the double substitution required by the Golden Rule. Indeed, could a lustful king with many wives imagine what the loss of an only wife would mean to a common soldier?

Butler thinks that the slander test is better, an "easy and almost sure way to avoid being misled" by self-partiality. He assumes, apparently, that we are better able to imagine what our enemies would say and what the world will believe than we are to imagine the situation and psychology of those we might harm. But suppose our enemies, even our harshest enemies, share our faults. In matters of lust, other kings and courtiers—David's most likely detractors— are likely to make allowances of the very sort David makes for himself. And he might rightly suppose similar indulgence by his most critical subjects, were he to try to imagine their harshest criticisms. (People tend to grant their rulers special sexual license.)

It is no accident that David persists unchecked until a prophet quite alien to his court intervenes. We surround ourselves with or choose the company of those whose views coincide with our own. Hence, our projects come to be questionable only from a perspective we are unlikely or even unable to take. Home remedies are unlikely to work. Even if we can "open our moral eyes," it is unlikely that we will be able to see very much: our associates, out of sympathy or cowardice, tend to keep the lights turned down low.

Joint Self-Deceptions

So far we have examined cases of single self-deceivers assisted by witting or unwitting associates. Self-deception can also be mutual, and the methods communal. Tolstoy writes of impatient relatives: "They all had only one wish that he [Nikolai] would die quickly, and they all did their best to conceal it and went on giving him medicines out of bottles, tried to discover new remedies and doctors, and deceived him and themselves and one another."[9] Self-deception is simpler when others are similarly engaged. If we have any scruples about our projects, joint action will suppress them, or at least discourage their expression. No one acting in concert has an interest in speaking, or producing evidence, against the false belief or questionable desire that each person wants to maintain.

In addition to acting together, we have various ways of *speaking* together to keep scruples and contrary evidence at bay. The jargon that coworkers share in their institutional or professional projects is a most effective means of glossing over disquieting details. For example, nuclear strategists use domestic, sexual, and other metaphors for their apocalyptic scenarios. (Submarine nuclear arsenals are "Christmas tree farms"; the joint firing of many missiles is a "spasm attack" with an "organismic whump.")[10] Likewise, oncologists use euphemism ("serious health problem") and technical preciseness ("stage-IV neoplasm") in talking about fatal cancers. Clinical researchers commonly discount likely side effects of therapy as mere "risks," thereby stressing their uncertainty, while listing improbable improvements as "benefits," thereby seeming to guarantee them.

Hospital review boards (IRB's) often reject research protocols that use such tendentious language on patient consent forms. But patients, even those sensitive to such linguistic practices, seldom object to these expressions of occupational optimism. Both doctor and patient want to believe in the possibility of curing, or at least of arresting, the disease. Each believes that the other, so believing, will try harder. Accordingly, each may mislead the other down a path they both wish to travel, and so diverge further and further from the truth. But to do so, they must also mislead themselves.

For example, a patient might misdescribe his symptoms. Misled, his physician might fallaciously arrive at a hopeful diagnosis. In order to give the patient (and herself) even more hope, she might in turn give him an even rosier prognosis than the misdescribed symptoms support. For this minuet to succeed, they must each make mistaken (and unjustified) assumptions about the other person. (Patient: "She is too shrewd and thorough to be taken in by my misreporting." Physician: "He is too straightforward either to falsify his symptoms or to suspect me of falsifying the prognosis.") So misleading themselves about the other, they manage to engage in misleading each other, thus preserving their joint therapeutic project.

But how can this be a correct description of their engagement? How can one *mislead* oneself? Misleading would seem to require two distinct parties, a leader and a follower. Once again, we stumble upon the reflexive problem. Let us look at a possible solution.

PSEUDOREFLEXIVES

Consider an activity that contrasts with self-deception, namely, self-instruction. Do autodidacts instruct themselves? Clearly not. Instructors impart their knowledge to their students, but, by definition, self-instructors are ignorant of what they are trying to learn. How then does self-instruction proceed? Not in a social vacuum: self-instructors need help—from librarians, "teach yourself" books, programmed texts, and so forth. Such resources, of course, may be instructive, although rarely are they adequate teacher-substitutes. (Witness the autodidact's characteristic failings: mispronunciation, uncritical and spotty knowledge of the subject, opinionated and eccentric judgment.)

Although autodidacts cannot teach themselves, they do perform for themselves (with help) some services that teachers routinely provide their students. They can select texts, set (but not enforce) schedules, even test and grade (if texts provide answers). In short, self-instruction has a few features of instruction; it is, we might say, *near*-instruction—a way of learning akin to instruction. But without instructors it is not instruction, precisely or even metaphorically speaking.

So understood, the term 'self-instruction' is a pseudoreflexive whose proper form is the monadic Sx ('x self-instructs'), not the true reflexive dyadic relation Ixx ('x instructs x'). Correspondingly, the 'self' of 'self-instructs' is not a referential term but rather an adjectival prefix that modifies the sense of 'instructs' and thereby marks self-instruction's distance from paradigmatic cases of instruction. Likewise, there is no need for split personalities, no semiselves dividing the roles of teacher and learner. Nor need we ascribe to the self-instructor prenatal knowledge *á la* Plato. The only psychological prerequisites of self-instruction are the relatively unproblematic desire to learn and the ability to do so without a teacher's rewards and threats. (Further monadic activities, such as self-congratulation and self-reproach, may help but are not necessary.)[11]

Although self-instruction is not (*pace* Butler) a remedy for self-deception, they are contrastive activities: self-instruction is an attempt to overcome one's ignorance; self-deception, to maintain it. Such contrasting pairs of notions invite similar analyses. Is self-deception a form of deception, or is it only a near relative with marked differences as well as some similarities?

DECEPTIVE AND SELF-DECEPTIVE SKILLS

As we have seen, self-deceivers often use deception, and deceivers are often self-deceived (about the costs, risks, and benefits of deception). Although intertwined, deception and self-deception have different goals; hence, they require different skills. Deceivers seek to generate false beliefs in others; self-deceivers, to maintain their own questionable beliefs and pursuits. Accordingly, deceivers need a keen sense of plausibility and of audience. They must know what others are prepared to believe or resist; they must be able to respond quickly and cogently to the doubts of others. Self-deceivers, by contrast, need a capacity for the implausible, for ignoring or misconstruing the remarks of others.

Somewhat paradoxically, deceivers need more self-control than do self-deceivers: they must be able to prevent their voices and faces from subverting the stories they are spinning. They must be able to tell "bold-faced lies," concealing both the truth and their anxious awareness of the truth. They have to improvise calmly and confidently, despite the threat of a widening gap between truth and their fictions. Self-deceivers, by contrast, need no such self-control. Even if they seek to strengthen their own favored beliefs by convincing others, they need neither bravado nor persuasive skills. Rather than persuasion, self-deceivers must practice evasion—evasion of facts or people who might threaten their privileged pursuits.

There are evasive, as well as persuasive, linguistic skills. As noted for defense intellectuals and physicians, the linguistic habits of certain communities help to make self-deceptive misdescription almost effortless and undetectable. But the principal evasive skills of self-deception are epistemic, not linguistic. Self-deceivers must be able to twist the facts, as well as misdescribe them. They must be able to dismiss evidence, not just linguistically launder it. And dismissing evidence often involves adopting odd standards of evidence or forming odd (and unsupported) hypotheses about sources of evidence, including people and their motives. Again, deceivers must be able to get other people right; self-deceivers must be able to get them wrong.

It may be objected that these differences of skill do not show self-deception to differ from deception. The same mental state may be produced by various means. Perhaps so, but it no longer seems clear that self-deception is to be analyzed as a distinctive cognitive state. Its public and social dimensions are not easily absorbed or translated into private, intrapsychic events. If we resist the pull of the Cartesian picture of self-deception and keep its social aspects in view, then skills become as important as whatever "product" those skills produce. Knowing how to avoid threatening facts, for example, becomes as much a part of self-deception as does the false belief we thereby protect. Indeed, even the need for a false belief becomes questionable. If we surrender the dualistic contrast between belief and action, then there can be self-deception without an identifiable false belief. King David's self-deception may be nothing more than a morally insensitive pursuit of Bathsheba. Rather than the divided mind required by the dyadic analysis of self-deception, we may have only single-mindedness. And rather than a false belief, we may have only an irrational or morally flawed project.

Deception, I think, does require the notion of false belief. But even if deception can be equally de-Cartesianed, the difference between deceptive and self-deceptive skills will allow difference enough between deception and "deception" of oneself.

FAULTS OF SELF-DECEPTION

One further difference counts against self-deception as full fledged deception: our prima facie judgments of self-deception are less harsh. Generally, the self-abuser does not use others against their wills or selfishly thwart their projects. Self-deceivers may, as we noted, deceive or in other ways abuse others, but their standard offense is against rationality, not morality. Self-deceivers are thought to be fools, not knaves. Deceivers, by contrast, are taken to be clever and selfish, victimizing others. (Note parallel contrasts between murder and suicide.)[12]

But how irrational is self-deception? At the worst (on the usual dyadic account), self-deceivers persuade themselves that p is true, while continuing to believe that not-p is true. They are thereby charged with the gross irrationality of believing a contradiction; or, if the two beliefs are kept apart in separate mental compartments, the charge is reduced to incoherence. Following Sartre, Herbert Fingarette reduces the charge still further by making self-deception a way of dissociating ourselves from, while persisting in, projects we wish to continue.[13] Rather than as incoherence of beliefs, self-deception is diagnosed as a gap between an agent's self-conception and action.

But how objectionable are such gaps? "Alienating" a project might be a first step toward enlisting the aid of others in reform.[14] More generally, is it always rational to have knowledge of one's motives and circumstances? Accurate knowledge of one's mixed motives or of the probability of failure might well discourage many worthy projects at the outset. Optimists typically eschew such knowledge: for them, it is enough to know that success is possible. The probability of failure is not a concern.

Whether self-deception is irrational or not, it is clearly less so than deception. The psychic costs of deception are higher, and the benefits less. We tend to underestimate not only the likelihood of exposure but also the amount of anxiety, effort, and regret that go into maintaining a lie. Truth *will* out. Self-deception has fewer costs and risks. As noted, it is often effortless and free of anxiety (even on a dyadic account of a subdivided ego). Moreover, self-deception cannot be revealed by slips of the tongue or face. Nor is it easily discovered by others: the stratagems are subtle and indirect, and the "objects" of self-deception are elusive and complex: habitual motivations, character, hopes, probable outcomes are always subject to interpretation and dispute. Mistaking the import of a customer's compliments, or greedy failure to see when enough is enough, is not egregious error. (This complexity also accounts in part for the difficulty of discovering one's own self-deceptions.)

We may conclude that self-deception is less offensive to both morality and rationality. But do these differing critiques show self-deception to be less than full deception, strictly speaking? Perhaps not. But combined with the differing skills required, these different assessments would seem to allow for a monadic reading that gives to the 'deception' of 'self-deception' an altered meaning. And since, on a monadic reading, the 'self' ceases its paradoxical reference to both agent and "victim," we should welcome this alternative.

Why do we have such troublesome pseudoreflexives? Perhaps because they serve to emphasize individual agency and responsibility. By calling learners without teachers "self-taught," we ascribe to them an extra measure of initiative, selection, and control. Likewise, self-deceivers bear more responsibility for their actions than do people who are merely thought of as single-minded, insensitive, or optimistic. Pseudoreflexives are the grammatical preserve of our moral and cultural individualism.

In this tradition, our epigraph would be taken to mean, "He who fools himself fools nobody—but himself." But in a tradition more mindful of the social matrix of all individual actions, it would be read as saying, "He who fools himself fools nobody—at all." I hope to have given some reasons why philosophers in our individualistic tradition should prefer this second ("Chinese") reading.

NOTES

My thanks to the editors, L. A. Kosman, and Derek Parfit for helpful comments on earlier versions.

1. See David Sanford, "Self-Deception as Rationalization" (chap. 6 of this anthology).

2. See David Pears, *Motivated Irrationality* (Oxford: Clarendon Press, 1984), chaps. 1–3.

3. M. R. Haight, *A Study of Self-Deception* (Atlantic Highlands, N.J.: Humanities Press, 1980), p. 2.

4. Petrarch, *Meum Secretum; or, The Soul's Conflict with the Passions,* third dialogue (ca. 1350).

5. See H. L. A. Hart and A. M. Honoré, *Causation in the Law* (Oxford: Clarendon Press, 1959).

6. *The Second Book of Samuel,* chap. 11.

7. Joseph Butler, "Upon Self-Deceit," Sermon X in *The Works of Joseph Butler,* ed. W. E. Gladstone (Oxford: Clarendon Press, 1896), 2:182.

8. Ibid., p. 182.

9. Leo Tolstoy, *Anna Karenina,* trans. David Magarshack (New York: Signet, 1961), bk. 5, 20, p. 505. Tolstoy allows that self-deception may have altruistic motives, or at least benefits for other people: Karenin claims that he tried to deceive himself about Anna's character out of pity for her (bk. 3, 13, p. 287); Anna deceives herself about a divorce from Karenin by devoting herself to the welfare of a destitute English family (bk. 5, 20, p. 505). These are "social" dimensions of self-deception different from those discussed in this paper.

10. See Carol Cohn, "Sex and Death in the Rational World of Defense Intellectuals," *Signs* 12 (Summer 1987):4. For the jargon and other self-deceptive measures among people who select the Pentagon's missile targets, see Henry T. Nash, "The Bureaucratization of Homicide," in *Protest and Survive,* ed. E. P. Thompson and Dan Smith (London: Penguin Books, 1980), pp. 62–75. My current favorite: a government memo speaks of assassination as "complete and total immobilization" (*New York Times,* June 16, 1986, A1).

11. A scholarly account of reflexives would include the middle voice in Greek, the use of '*se*' and '*soi-*' in French, and the use of '*sich*' in Yiddish (by contrast with the German use).

12. In German law, suicide is called self-murder (*Selbst-mordst*). But I suspect that the term strains the language and moral intuitions as much as it would in English. Except in certain religious or feudal societies, suicide is greeted more with sadness than with moral indignation, as an event for psychological rather than criminal investigation.

13. Herbert Fingarette, "Alcoholism and Self-Deception," in *Self-Deception and Self-Understanding,*" ed. Mike W. Martin (Lawrence: University Press of Kansas, 1985), pp. 52–67.

14. Fingarette thinks, to the contrary, that such dissociation allows alcoholics, for instance, to persist without responsibility in their drinking.

18

MIMETIC ENGULFMENT AND SELF-DECEPTION

BRUCE WILSHIRE

I

By *mimetic engulfment* I mean a situation in which humans imitate each other undeliberately. It is reported that infants only two weeks old learn rapidly to imitate adults' facial expressions.[1] It is either highly doubtful or inconceivable that this could be done deliberately. But this mimetic engulfment is not limited to infants' behavior. It has been noted by students of "kinesics" and "body language" that adults often imitate one another without being aware of it, hence, they must be doing it nondeliberately.

We must be very careful, however, in saying that humans imitate one another without being aware of it, because there are various degrees of lack of awareness even in engulfment. It may be that one or more members of a group can, at a certain point, acknowledge what is happening—for example, as they sit, each with arms folded across the chest, someone says, or could say, "Look how we've fallen into the same stance." Let us call this delayed verbal recognition (as realized or as capacity) the least lack of awareness, and the least degree of engulfment. At a greater degree of engulfment the persons involved are not able to acknowledge verbally at any point, not even to themselves, that they are imitating one another—at least not while the episode is occurring. But they could acknowledge it nonverbally, in the sense of mutely recognizing that they are doing it. We call this a second degree of engulfment. At a third degree of engulfment, we suppose that there is no capacity during the episode for even nonverbal acknowledgment to oneself that one has imitated the other; we need only suppose that there has been recognition of the other's stance *as* the other's. At the fourth, and deepest, level of engulfment, we suppose that this recognition of the other's stance involves no recognition of the other's stance as the other's stance—hence no recognition of oneself because no recognition of being other than the other. It is just engulfment-in-such-a-stance. This would be complete engulfment.

It is essential that these distinctions be made, because the type of self-deception I wish to study involves various degrees of mimetic engulfment with others, and because self-deception of any type must involve behavior that is voluntary in *some* sense. Otherwise we have simple mistakes we make about ourselves and our situations—self-mistakes—not self-deception. There must be bad faith, deceit, an intention in some way voluntary to gull and con oneself; and in the type of self-deception I wish to study, the intention to accomplish this will work through one's intention to lose oneself through engulfment in the other, to obscure oneself from oneself through these means.

Aristotle's conception of the voluntary is very broad, and it will help us some. He defined it negatively as any action not done from compulsion or from ignorance.[2] By compulsion he meant some force external to ourselves which renders us helpless to defeat its effect upon us (like a hurricane moving our small ship). By ignorance he meant ignorance of the situation in which we act which is nonculpable, that is, ignorance of things that destructively deflect our actions from their intended ends and of which it cannot reasonably be claimed that we ought to have apprised ourselves of their presence. Voluntary actions constitute an immense set, of which "chosen" acts—voluntary actions preceded by deliberation—are but a small subset. Voluntary actions are all actions that proceed from ourselves rather than from another person or agency, and which are not significantly mediated by factors in our situation of which we ought to have been aware.

This analysis is helpful, but it is not sufficiently fine grained for our purposes. Aristotle's conception of what is internal to one as opposed to external—of self and other, of self and situation—is too rough for us. This renders his notion of nonculpable ignorance too rough. It does not fit some of the facts. An action can arise from oneself and be destructively deflected by *another* of one's intentions of which it *can* be reasonably said that one ought to have been aware of it. *I* want to regard this as a voluntary action. I think we must make room for such actions if we would explain self-*deception*. In definite senses of the terms, we voluntarily and intentionally keep ourselves from fully recognizing our own intentions, and we do this by voluntarily and intentionally keeping ourselves from fully recognizing how we become mimetically engulfed in others.

Now perhaps we can begin to see why the distinctions among degrees of lack of awareness and among degrees of engulfment were made. The fact is we can be *somewhat* aware of intentions to conceal ourselves from ourselves, and *somewhat* aware of losing ourselves in mimetic engulfment with others in order to bring this about. We must very carefully describe phenomenologically these chiaroscuro modes of awareness. In some instances of self-deception it is just because we can verbally acknowledge that our intention with respect to the other is A that we can prevent ourselves from acknowledging what we dimly recognize nonverbally: that our intention with respect to the other is non-A. In instances of self-deception which involve greater degrees of engulfment and of lack of awareness it may be difficult to tell how we voluntarily conceal ourselves from ourselves. Take the third level: here there is no capacity for even nonverbal acknowledgment to self of the intention to conceal one's intentions from oneself in one's mimetic situation with the other. Perhaps we must direct our attention a step backwards to that shadowy area of consciousness in which we voluntarily undermine our capacity for any awareness on any more voluntary and more focally conscious level. At the deepest level of engulfment the greatest philosophical perplexities arise. Here we suppose that there is no recognition of the other as the other, hence no recognition of one's individual self because no recognition of oneself as other than the other. But at a *preceding* moment there may have been enough awareness of self to voluntarily set in motion that mode of interaction which prevents even the capacity for self-awareness to be present in the next.

At this deepest level the most difficult questions arise with regard not only to self-deception but also to identity of self. *Is* there a self at those moments when there is no capacity for self-awareness? Is what we call identity of individual self really, at best, an occasional matter, and is the identity of the corporate individual, the culture, with all its mimetic patterns of attunement— inherited or emergent—the more fundamental identity? The confines of this paper do not allow extended explorations of this sort.[3] I would like to limit myself to a study of self-deception as it occurs in the first, second, and third degrees of mimetic engulfment.

II

How is self-deception possible? How is it possible to *voluntarily* keep one's *own* conscious project, one's own intention, concealed in some degree from oneself? There must be an intention to conceal the intention, and this meta-intention must be concealed. We must hide, and hide the hiding; the very project of self-deception must itself be in self-deception, as Jean-Paul Sartre has said.[4] The logical mind may be inclined to dismiss this out of hand as impossible, inconceivable. But our visceral intuition is that something very like this happens frequently and often with momentous effect. If it is actual it must be possible—now how? First we appropriate a fundamental distinction from William James' phenomenology of consciousness in *The Principles of Psychology*: that between the focus and margin of consciousness.[5] We must finally do justice to the vague, James says. In the field of consciousness the focus is the tiny portion that we clearly perceive or apprehend. Thousands of elements and relations hover in the nebulous fringe; they may become focal the next instant, or they may not. Here is a clue: out of the corner of the eye we can apprehend an intention in the margin as "not to be faced squarely." In our analysis as philosophers doing this paper we are forced to use these words to describe what is being apprehended as having this character, but really it is being apprehended *nonverbally in the margin*. And the intention to *keep* the intention in the nonverbalized margin *is itself* marginal, nonverbalized, unfaced. We hide, and hide the hiding.

In the type of self-deception I wish to discuss, a powerful added factor abets the self-deception of the project of self-deception. It insulates it from the focus—from that which is clearly perceivable by and acknowledgeable to the self, typically verbalizable to the self, and perhaps even to others. It is the other person as apprehended by the self, and with whom the self stands in mimetic attunement or engulfment. It is plausible to suppose that some of the facial expressions imitated nondeliberately by the infant have become permanent imitative tendencies—permanent susceptibilities in certain social situations. Fusion is almost inevitably regressive and archaic. To suppose that the conditions that individuate human bodies (for purposes of pointing them out or for physiological analysis) are also conditions sufficient to establish the *identity* of selves we *call* "individual" is an impossibly crude and question-begging mode of thought.[6]

Even if we maintain that the self is a body (though not one exhaustively analyzable physiologically), it is a body already formed mimetically through others, and which can so allow itself to slip under the influence of others that the person can believe he is only what he believes the other believes him to be. That is, he becomes mimetically engulfed in the other's apparent belief about him. And if the other's supposed belief is counter to what the subject wants to face and believe about himself, this reinforces his own denial. And indeed, if he can construe his mimetic partnership with the other as owing to motivations different from self-concealment—as he so easily can—then he can both hide the to-be-hidden and hide the hiding; the feat is accomplished. All that he can acknowledge is that feature of himself which is the object of the other's supposed construal; he cannot acknowledge his manipulation of self and other which has produced his construal of the other's construal.

Let us start with relatively simple cases. Take what we like to call "frank" discussions. It is possible to accomplish the feat of apprehending one's projects nonthematically and vaguely as the to-be-hidden, and to hide from oneself the hiding of them, if one can allow oneself so to slip under the influence of the other (as one understands the other) that one can believe one is just what the other believes one to be, and the other believes one is not hiding anything. Both persons are being "frank" and "open," so how could one's motivation for undertaking the discussion *possibly* be to hide oneself from oneself and to hide the hiding? Thus the strange aura that hovers about most "frank" discussions, as if it were a cloud of vaporized acid secretly corroding everything. It smells almost sweet. We squirm and love every minute.

We must give concrete and detailed examples. We want to discover the *logos* of the phenomenon itself. Without concrete examples we risk getting carried away in airy abstractions and in exercises in mere distinction-making—even when we think we are being phenomenological—exercises in which we deceive ourselves with the thought that we have exhausted all possible formulations of the problem, and all solutions, and need only watch our *words* carefully to arrive at the correct answer. It is the illusion of verbal omni-competence, verbal totality.

Let us appropriate an example from Sartre and turn it to our own purposes.[7] A young woman is invited out by a man who, she knows, will try skillfully to seduce her. This troubles her. Nevertheless she accepts his invitation, for she finds him attractive, and, while engaged in an intellectual conversation, allows him to take her hand, a move that she knows—in a nonthematic and vague way—sets the seduction in motion. She falls into self-deception. But perhaps the woman is hypocritical, not self-deceived, it might be objected, for she can see that that hand opened to his is *hers* and that *she* has accepted his advances. No, not so she can acknowledge it at the time, and later she may tell us sincerely, "It happened in a dream."

For the young woman's nonthematic sexual project and desires to become nonthematizable for her, she allows herself so to slip under the influence of the other that she believes she is just what he believes her to be, and that he believes her to be incapable of sexual desires and projects. Let us say their conversation is about Platonic love. Since the explicit topic of the conversation is the reverse of what she means to accomplish in the project of self-deception—the conversation is about the value of nonsexual relationships when what she means to accomplish through this is the hiding of sexual desires, the hiding of the hiding, and the establishment of a sexual relationship—then the assertion of the conversation as her goal will subvert her awareness of it as her means (to the opposite), and indeed she will acknowledge it as her goal precisely in order not to be able to acknowledge it as the means that it is. She is pathetically sincere.

The woman does what she deeply wants to do: she imitates his belief about her—or rather what he appears to her to believe about her. And he appears to her to believe this because she tacitly wants him to appear this way. She wants him to appear in such a way that she is relieved of responsibility for herself; indeed, relieved from an awareness of this desire to be relieved. Self-deception is self-reflection that defeats self-reflection; it is Cartesian nightmare.

III

What we have said is correct, I believe, but it is overly simplified because overly intellectualized. It is not simply that the young woman is voluntarily engulfed in the seducer's apparent belief about her. She is mimetically engulfed in his body, as this appears to her.[8] In all likelihood she is acting out archaic responses to those early authority figures who molded her mimetic life. She allows him to stand in for her, and for key figures in her life who stood in for her earlier, and who interpreted her to herself. Here is one of her archaic "roles" into which she can slip nonthematically: "nice little girl for the big, nice man." At this moment she is an individual self in only a compromised sense. The man is a skilled seducer because he understands that she is to become aware of her flesh, but only through the obscuring mediation of his flesh. She and the man conspire to make her aware of her flesh, but not *as* hers, and certainly not *as* her conspiring adult self. She colludes with him to relieve herself of responsibility, and she does this by becoming engulfed in his body.

Recall that I said that I wanted to avoid discussing the deepest level of engulfment in which there is no sense of the other as other, therefore no sense of being other than the other, hence no sense of individual self. It is not going to be easy to achieve this. We have just brushed perilously close to this deepest sense in the preceding paragraph, where we spoke of being an individual self in only a compromised sense. Let us back up a step and affirm solid ground: experience is ineluctably temporal; i.e., for self-deception to *begin* there must be some sense of individual *self*, otherwise we get some sort of radical self-mistaking—a self-obliterating that is not a self-deceiving. But it is possible perhaps to assign some responsibility, which was shirked at an *earlier* moment. We voluntarily set in motion behaviors that we sense will result in self-obliteration, or near self-obliteration, at a later moment.

Indeed, we will find that our painstaking distinction-making among levels of engulfment, while necessary as an initial, heuristic device, is somewhat artificial. In the thick of the phenomena it is very difficult in most cases to decide what level is operant. Was there any moment during the episode in which the woman could acknowledge her self-deceptive project? What is to count as the duration of the episode? Perhaps as she was making up in her bedroom, alone with her mirror, before he arrived, she might have acknowledged what she was doing in going out with him. We would have to know the exact details of her life and situation before we would have any hope at all of knowing. And if we cannot tell if she ever could acknowledge her project, we, of course, cannot tell whether this could be an acknowledgment to both self and another, or whether it could be a verbal acknowledgment, if only to herself. And, of course, there is the vexing question of exactly what we mean whenever we talk of disposition or capacity. If we say that a glass is brittle we mean to attribute to it a disposition, but by this we just mean that it does usually break when dropped. But matters are much more difficult when we are talking about the dispositions or capacities of human beings. Could we suddenly send in a Socrates to ask the young woman about what she was doing? Would she then be able to acknowledge her self-deception?

Well, maybe. But that radically changes the situation. The glass is just that glass, whether being dropped or not, but is the woman with Socrates just the same woman as the one alone with the seducer? At least the question can be asked. We bump into ultimate questions of self-identity again.[9] Could the woman rouse herself from her "dream" while alone with the man? I do not know what would count as decisive evidence either way.[10]

But our structure of distinctions of levels serves some purpose anyway. Not only does it prompt questions, but we can speak roughly of greater and lesser degrees of engulfment and of depth of self-deception. Some cases are like a game: our awareness of our hiding and our hiding of our hiding is almost focal, and we prevent it becoming so just for the fun of it. Perhaps we do so because we are aware that the other is playing the same game and we sense that no destructive consequences could issue from our sport. At the other end of the spectrum is profound, deeply archaic self-deception, which is difficult or impossible to acknowledge even under the most favorable circumstances and with the best will. Let us delve in this latter direction.

In all our examples of self-deception the same general pattern is evident: a voluntary engulfment in the other that presents his view of one as being such that one's motivations in voluntarily engulfing oneself in him are concealed from oneself. We will be exhibiting variations in mimetic engulfment, variations in how we voluntarily confuse and blur together our own desires and feelings and the other's desires and feelings. (Psychiatrists call this "the defense mechanism of projection.") In each case we corrupt our ability to reflectively grasp ourselves by corrupting our ability to utilize what a truly candid and perceptive other might have told us about ourselves.

In the next case the voluntary engulfment is a discounting and discrediting of the other as witness rather than a flattering masquerading of him. (Of course, even in the first case the woman subtly discounts and degrades the man, in counterpoint to his obvious degrading of her, in the sense that she discounts whatever capacities he might have for engaging in a nonseductive relationship.) There is a way in which I condemn another for being picky and squeamish (imagine that we are at dinner together) that discounts him as a witness to my behavior—he is "simply disgusting," an "insensate lump." The more picky I find him, the more my pickiness concerning his pickiness is obscured. The to-be-hidden is my pickiness. The hiding is an absorbing engulfment in the other's pickiness, a repetition of archaic, communal, and habitual modes of rejection. The hiding is itself hidden because in seeing him to be a disgusting, insensate lump I cannot see him seeing me to be anything at all; therefore, I cannot see that I see him this way in order not to see the pickiness in me. I am connivingly merged in the other's apparent blindness. My own pickiness and squeamishness dissolves, blurs, and undermines self-recognition; the experienced world is reduced to a mass of slime. And so on;

e.g., aggression against the other's aggressiveness undermines the capacity for reflective recognition of my aggressiveness.

Let us vary the example slightly. Again, I look down upon the other for what I would condemn myself for if I had not undermined my ability to reflect accurately—let us say this time the voraciousness and sloppiness of my own eating. Self-rejection slips into other-rejection—a magical but in its way very real consumption of the other.[11] The bodies merge experientially because they are colludingly isomorphic, as if two mirror images had collapsed into each other. I condemn another with the very words that, if I could reflect, I would know apply to myself. Indeed, I already know, in the sense that an incompletely individualized self has a prereflective consciousness. The self that refuses to let itself be penetrated by its own knowledge of itself is the self willingly absorbed in a diffused, rejecting, mimetic community shared with the other.[12] My expressivity is knowable for my own reflection only because initially it is known prereflectively through the expressive and responsive bodies of others. Reflection can be undermined if—on the prereflective and sneakingly voluntary level—the other can be either flatteringly masqueraded or discredited as a witness of my bodily being. For since my sense of individual self involves being other than the other and yet also *for* the other, and since he is distorted or discounted as a witness of my behavior, I blur my sense of individual self. Self-rejection that has remained at the prereflective level is dissipated through the atmosphere of one's mood and attitude. One's world is guilty.[13]

It seems plausible to say that a person is capable at one time of bringing a self-deceiving intention to reflective and focal acknowledgment, an intention that at a later moment so blurs or obliterates the self that at that moment the capacity no longer remains. It also seems plausible to say that the capacity is always relative to others in the environment, and the degree of their willingness "to go along with" one's self-deceiving projects. Others who do not bend in the self-deceiving circuit may startle one into recognition of the intention in the margin of consciousness which one has hitherto refused to face.

The question whether one *is* an individual self at all while in the depths of engulfment, I prefer to leave hanging for the time being (and whether there are pressing ethical and legal factors within the culture for assuming a particular self, and whether they contribute to constituting such a self, I likewise leave moot). At least we can say that we ought not to be satisfied with the criterion of individuation of self adequate for everyday purposes, like summoning the right person to court: one body equals one individual self. Just assigning different numbers is sufficient to individuate persons on this basis, and it makes no sense to talk about degrees of individuation; it is all or nothing. We need, I believe, a criterion of identity of individual self which does allow for degrees of individuation, a criterion that accounts for the sense that is made by expressions like "he was not himself" or "she is suffering an identity crisis." What is this criterion? It is an extraordinarily difficult question.

Despite these difficulties we can be fairly certain that there is a continuum of degrees of self-deception and engulfment, and that we can know in which direction it runs. The last example I will give develops Freud's assertion that in the unconscious one's own death is inconceivable, and hence the belief that one does die must be self-deceiving. I think that this is the deepest level of self-deception we have discussed so far.

Let us say that one is providing for his family by planning for his funeral and that he envisions it. The image of himself laid out as a corpse presents itself to him. He must think of this sight as being experienceable if it is to make any sense to him, and he cannot neatly distinguish its being experienceable by him from its being experienceable by anyone. Thus he can prereflectively and self-deceivingly lose himself in that ongoing body of persons that he envisions looking on at his corpse. In this picturing of his funeral his eye looks on at his corpse, but it is an eye that is merged with others' eyes, and it is disowned by him. At an unthematized level of his experience, he thinks himself to be living on with the others; he thinks himself to be immortal; he flees from his death in self-deception. He cannot see that he is doing this just because in thematically seeing himself as dead he cannot see that he is seeing, thinking, or doing anything. In massive mimetic engulfment—in an indefinitely large group—he hides his belief in immortality and hides his hiding.[14]

This is extraordinarily deep self-deception. One reason for its depth is clearly that it derives from basic, universal characteristics: having a particular, mortal body, yet experiencing it unavoidably through the intersubjective structures of the ongoing community of persons as possible experiencers. A corollary of the difficulty is that since the self-deception is presumably universal, there may not be those others who do not "go along with one," and who could, therefore, startle one into self-recognition. Although persons self-deceived about their own deaths may not be self-deceived about others' deaths, and may, therefore, startle them into self-recognition.

IV

This helps us to formulate in a rough way the question: What is that criterion of identity which allows for what is evidently needed—degrees of individuation of self at different times? I do not pretend to have the whole answer. But I do know that it must involve the question of the criterion of identity of the corporate body, the culture.[15] We achieve what we call identity as an individual self only because we incorporate mimetically and nondeliberately others' attitudes and perceptions (including others' attitudes and perceptions of ourselves). Inevitably, then, "what I am" (or its nonverbal equivalent) must include "what we are" (or its nonverbal equivalent). At some moments what distinguishes a self from others is in relative ascendancy, at other moments what is shared. When the latter occurs self-deception can be rampant. It is fostered when the identity of the corporate body involves mimetically induced social role playing, which can be used to mask one's asocial or antisocial or supersocial intentions from oneself—"frank discussions," "strictly intellectual conversations," "just dining together," "prudentially planning one's last rites," etc.

The identity of the particular mimetic community typically conspires to blur one's sense of individuality and to facilitate one's self-deception. Successful role playing is essential to the cohesion and survival of the group. Only the exceptional other who, for some reason, cares for one and is willing to risk ostracism or alienation, will dare to run counter to one's self-deceptive project (perhaps because he or she loves one). In these matters, *compassion* seems to be an essential ingredient in *perceptual capacity*.

It is naively atomistic and nominalistic simply to assert that one *is* a particular self and that to expose self-deception one need only "take hold of oneself." I do not wish to deny that one is a thinking, feeling, imagining body ("the cubic mass of which one feels all the while," as James put it), but I do not see how the kinesthetic sense can be disentangled from the intersubjective structures that condition even one's body image.[16] Body images fuse together, at certain moments dramatically, as Paul Schilder has pointed out.[17] Long ago Aristotle observed that there can be no science of the particular as particular, since science requires universal terms. Particulars must be perceptually intuited. But just what constitutes perceptual intuition of one's own bodily self and situation is a massively difficult question, and I believe it involves the identity of the group. It may be that there is no *pure* particularity or individuality of the self, and the idea that authenticity of self must consist in this is a mistake. It may be that the actual alternatives are these: either a life in which malign engulfment is maximized, i.e., the usual condition in which "the individual" and "the group" conspire to produce self-deception is maximized, or a life in which benign engulfment is maximized, i.e., a life in which the compassionate and perceptive other refuses to be bent out of shape in unavoidable and essential episodes of engulfment.

In the end the analysis of self-deception and identity involves us in basic ethical and, I think, religious questions. For even when we are out of the physical presence of others, it does not follow that we are out of their presence. Others haunt us even then and condition our identity. The religious solution is to believe that authenticity (or salvation) of self consists in holding close to the perfectly compassionate and perceptive other—the Other. Note the prayer of a Tibetan Buddhist master:

> HRI: This illusory aggregate grasped at as self,
> Through meditation becomes the Deity of Great Compassion, Kyanrazig.
> Rising upwards from the heart is wisdom's central path.
> On the crown of my head, in the open space of the Land of Great Bliss,
> Is the Buddha Amitabha, best of guides,
> Surrounded by Buddhas and Bodhisattvas, compassionate and loving.
> In the center of the open eight-petalled lotus of the heart,
> My consciousness, like the egg of the masal bird
> Rests on a shimmering radiance. It emanates upward
> And becomes non-dual with the heart-mind of Amitabha.[18]

That is, the gaze of the other is so deeply constitutive of the self that it is a mistake to try to strip it away. Authenticity consists in merging in the gazing of the all-compassionate and all-perceiving One: being lifted out of the delusory center of ego and being placed in full consciousness where one in fact already is, in the great circle of the community of all sentient beings.[19]

Finally, our basic question about identity involves questions about war and survival. Can we break out of that malign engulfment in corporate egoism that "projects" its guilt onto other corporate bodies and invites mutual aggression and destruction? In order to become who we are each of us has had to be defined by membership in groups that are local. The groups in turn have defined themselves as other than—and, typically, better than—other groups. As "individuals" "project" or "dump" onto other "individuals," so groups do. We are drawn into the massive drama of competition and aggression. How can we identify effectively with humans worldwide with whom we are in fact interdependent?[20] It is bitterly ironical that with all our claims to secular and scientific enlightenment we seem to be as deeply mired in self-deception as any primitive society of persons was ever mired in its practices of scapegoating and sympathetic magic. At least these so-called primitives recognized these practices to be magical, and so were probably less self-deceived than most of us.

NOTES

1. A. Meltzoff and M. K. Moore, "Imitation of Facial and Manual Gestures by Human Neonates," *Science* 198 (Oct. 1977):4312.

2. Aristotle, *Nicomachean Ethics*, bk. 3, chaps. 1 and 2.

3. I explore the question more fully, but not exhaustively, in my *Role Playing*

and Identity: The Limits of Theatre as Metaphor (Bloomington, Ind.: Indiana Univ. Press, 1982).

4. Jean-Paul Sartre, *Being and Nothingness,* trans. Hazel Barnes (New York: Philosophical Library, 1953), pt. 1, chap. 2.

5. William James, "The Stream of Consciousness," chap. 9 in *The Principles of Psychology* (New York: Holt, 1890). See also my *William James and Phenomenology: A Study of 'The Principles of Psychology,'* (Bloomington, Ind.: Indiana Univ. Press, 1968).

6. The concept of self as body-self is developed by M. Merleau-Ponty in *The Phenomenology of Perception,* trans. C. Smith (London: Routledge and Kegan Paul, 1962), and, e.g., by myself in *Role Playing and Identity,* pt. 2.

7. See note 4.

8. What many had perceived intuitively is now established empirically: that readily verbalizable intellectual life does not cohere neatly with perceptual life. This incoherence greatly facilitates self-deception, the concealing of one portion of one's experience from another. Perceptual experience of one's own body is particularly relevant. Depending upon the requirements of any given self-deceiving project, what one's bodily life is doing—what one is doing—either can be discounted as "merely going through the motions" (which seems to be what is going on with the young woman when she allows the man to take her hand) *or,* when one *is* "merely going through the motions," can be represented to oneself as the reality of one's life. (As Ludwig Wittgenstein suggests, in distinguishing attitudes from mere opinions, "You think that after all you must be weaving a piece of cloth: because you are sitting at a loom—even if it is empty—and going through the motions of weaving" (*Philosophical Investigations,* trans. E. Anscombe [New York, 1953], p. 414). Concerning the cleavage between perceptual and verbalizable intellectual life, an experiment has been performed in which a person's writing hand is concealed from his view and another person's hand inserted above it in line with the subject's normal vision of his own hand. The subject is told to draw a straight vertical line. The obviously foreign arm, pencil in hand, veers from the vertical; the subject's concealed hand draws a line veering in the opposite direction, apparently in order to correct it (Erwin Straus, "Embodiment and Excarnation," *Psychological Issues,* monograph 22, vol. 6, no. 2, p. 239). Evidently the subject has a nonverbalized sensory-motor belief attending the sight of the foreign hand, 'That is my hand'—recognizable by him as false *if* the matter is brought to expression by him or others—which has a grip on his behavior that his true and vigorously verbalizable contradictory belief 'That is not my hand' does not dislodge. This suggests that sensory-motor behavior that is intelligent and mental, in a sense, but which resists verbalization can occur; it suggests that the margin of consciousness or even the perceptual focus can flatly oppose the verbalizable focus. I do not here discuss at any length supportive evidence from brain physiology (see Herbert Fingarette, "Selected Bibliography on Cerebral Commissurotomy," in *Self-Deception* (London, 1969). The gist of this evidence is that in situations in which only the nonverbal, nondominant hemisphere of the brain is stimulated, the subject will not be able to say what he perceptually knows. Nevertheless he usually makes an inevitably misleading and abortive attempt to spell out in words these perceptions. The idea is that self-deception may arise when the person knows very well—but only perceptually—what he represses through verbal misdescription and evasion. Most

experimental subjects have had nerves connecting the hemispheres severed. But such dissonance may arise through so-called functional or psychosomatic factors (or so it is conjectured).

9. In episodes of mimetic engulfment I believe we act like sleepwalkers (e.g., in mob behavior—and there are larger and smaller mobs). Imagine: you see somebody sleepwalking and he moves a vase off a table and it breaks. Would it be appropriate for us to say to him after he awakens, "But *you* broke it—I saw you!"? We would be reluctant to say this, I believe, because we would sense that the absence of consciousness of self and world makes it questionable whether any self and any action was involved at all. Now just how similar is mimetic engulfment to sleepwalking? It is an important question that is hard to answer. I acknowledge at least one crucial difference: we probably do not sneakingly intend to fall asleep and then to move a vase off the table. And in the legal sense the woman is awake. But of what philosophical value is this sense? I leave the matter open, yet I do believe that we should press Sartre's comparisons of self-deception and falling asleep as far as we can.

10. Although this may seem to be merely an epistemological point, I do not wish to limit its significance to this. It is basically a conceptual point. That is, following Husserl, we speak of the meaning of an intention (or thought) in terms of the phenomena that would "fill it," or fulfill it (so intention in this broad sense is linked to expectation in a broad sense). Because we are hard pressed to specify which phenomena would count as, e.g., the woman's capacity at any moment to acknowledge her intention (now in the sense of intending to act), we are not clear about the *meaning* of the concepts we are using in describing her.

11. It should not surprise us if this turns out to be a vestigial remain of cannibalistic impulses—a symbolic expression that, nevertheless, given the reality of the eating at the table and the blurring of selves, is quite close to factual reality. Very often self-deception involves the emergence of taboo behavior: cannibalism in this case, and incest in the case of the woman being seduced.

12. The idea of the self that does not let itself be penetrated by its own knowledge of itself is Gabriel Marcel's. See his *The Mystery of Being* (Chicago: Gateway Books, 1960), 1:79 and 119ff.

13. Concerning the inability to localize guilt clearly, see Max Scheler, "On the Tragic," *Cross Currents* 4 (1954):185–187. On the connection between self-deception and what I call tragic choice, see my *Role Playing* (cited in note 3), pp. 173–186 and 209–210.

14. With regard to the Vietnam war Helen Caldicott writes, "Nuclear war and weapons were forgotten, much to everyone's subconscious relief, for to contemplate nuclear war is to entertain the concept of the end of immortality, not just the idea of death" (*Missile Envy* [New York: W. Morrow, 1984], p. 14). This is a shocking passage. Is it sufficiently shocking to knock one out of one's self-deceptive projects with respect to death? Perhaps at some moments. But at other moments the thought of nuclear war is not in our minds, or not forcefully there. Perhaps we can say that the distinct possibility of nuclear war gives us the probably unprecedented opportunity to dislodge this deeply seated project of self-deception with respect to death. Whether we are responsible enough to take it, I do not know.

I should add a qualifier to my words "In massive mimetic engulfment—in an indefinitely large group": if this group consists of all possible human experiencers, then this logically entails, of course, that it is the human race. But psychologically it needn't involve this. Psychologically we tend to equate humanity with our own nation or culture (see my *Role Playing,* p. 296).

15. See preceding note.

16. In a letter to me dated February 2, 1970, John Wild criticized my emerging position and asserted the primacy of direct intuition of one's body, that without which we cannot know the other to be other. In the intervening years I have developed the view that at crucial moments one does not apprehend the other as other, so need have no distinct sense of the particularity of one's own body.

17. Paul Schilder, *The Image and Appearance of the Human Body* (New York: International Universities Press, 1960), p. 123, and pp. 11, 117–178, 249, 254. See also my *Role Playing and Identity,* especially pt. 2.

18. *P'Howa,* according to Rigdzin Longsal Nyingpo, translated in compliance with instructions of Chagdud Tulku Rimpoche (Cottage Grove, Oreg.: Padma Publishing, 1983), p. 1.

19. Notice that I talk of being merged in a gazing, not a gaze. The latter seems to suggest that one might be a gazed-at, an object. I am trying to suggest that authenticity is a benign engulfment, a level of community more fundamental than that which involves the subject/object, self/other split. If it is this, then "projection" from self to other, the sneaking transference of guilt, would be impossible. Perhaps guilt itself would be impossible. The gazing participates lovingly in the life of the gazed-at.

20. I believe with the Buddhists that we are interdependent with nonhuman forms of life also. But I do not pursue this point in this paper.

Addendum

IN WHAT SENSE IS "MIMETIC ENGULFMENT AND
SELF-DECEPTION" PHENOMENOLOGICAL?

Most important, the paper is phenomenological because it develops conceptual points in essential connection with the display of examples of sensuous involvement with phenomena. It eschews the position that examples merely illustrate what can be discovered independently of them through conceptual analysis. But where is the vast scaffolding of Husserlian phenomenology—the transcendental machinery of the "reductions" and the *epoche*? Its spirit has been retained but the structure of its letter abandoned. Its thrust is to break free from the cemented prejudices of commonsense and traditional empirical science, which assume that the meaning of factual reality is embedded in it along with the atoms and molecules. It would restore consciousness to its own freedom, to its own role in the formation of meaning. Indeed, I take Husserl's own notion of "fictive" or "free variation" to be the living kernel of his method. It is a discipline of freely varying phenomenal presentations in "the mind's eye" until the phenomena no longer present themselves as themselves. Their various parameters are traced out to their limits, and their limits marked and connected; hence, through variation we discover the relatively invariable shape of the concept in question. With formal concepts (or "essences") like "triangle" we can precisely discover the "shape" or scope of application, and also that of the various subsorts of the "essence" ("isosceles," "scalene," and so on). With "material essences," like "notch" for example, we cannot precisely determine this; they have "floating spheres" of application. In this article I have employed free variations to expose something of the "shape" of the concept of self-deception. It is very nebulous on its edges, but nevertheless through variations we exposed something of a scaled sequence of shallower and deeper subspecies of it. The absence of any explicit methodological machinery reveals the overlap with hermeneutical phenomenology.

Part V

THE MORAL DIMENSION OF SELF-DECEPTION

19

SELF-DECEPTION, AUTONOMY, AND MORAL CONSTITUTION

Stephen L. Darwall

> And, if people will be wicked, they had better of the two be so from the common vicious passions without such refinements, than from this deep and calm source of delusion; which undermines the whole principle of good; . . . and corrupts conscience, which is the guide of life.[1]

Why is it that self-deception has seemed a matter of fundamental concern to some moral philosophers while others have given it only scant attention? Bishop Butler, from whom the above passage is taken, devoted an entire sermon to "self-deceit." And Kant held that the demand to "know (search, fathom)" oneself is the "foremost command of all duties to oneself."[2] Sincerity with self, he wrote in his notes, "is the formal condition of all virtues."[3] On the other hand, Jeremy Bentham, J. S. Mill, Henry Sidgwick, and G. E. Moore hardly mention self-deception. What explains this remarkable difference?

Since the latter group is composed entirely of consequentialists, and since both Butler and Kant rejected consequentialism, it is tempting to suppose that the explanation must relate to this. Perhaps something about the way deontologists and consequentialists respectively approach philosophizing about ethics explains a profoundly different interest in self-deception. This is on the way to the truth, but it is only a beginning. After all, why would disagreement over the relative priority of the right and the good lead to such contrasting views of the importance of self-deception?

In fact, there is nothing in that bare difference that does explain it. The textbook example of a contemporary deontologist, W. D. Ross, gave no more attention to self-deception than did the great consequentialists. And, while one must be careful in reading historical figures through contemporary categories, Adam Smith would most plausibly be considered a consequentialist even though a chapter of his *Theory of Moral Sentiments* is titled "Of the Nature of Self-Deceit . . ."[4]

We take a step further when we notice that Smith's chapter directly follows one titled "Of the Influence and Authority of Conscience." Butler's ethics are well known for his doctrine that conscience is authoritative. And Kant's discussions of self-deception and of what he called the "foremost command" to know oneself straddle his treatment of conscience in *The Metaphysical Principles of Virtue*.[5] So perhaps moral philosophers who take conscience seriously are also likely to take self-deception seriously, and those unlikely to discuss the former are unlikely to discuss the latter.

But what does it mean to take conscience seriously in this context? Mill, after all, took it seriously in one sense. He chided Bentham for dismissing 'conscience' as "that ill-fated word which scarce even appears but it brings confusion in its train" and for not including it in his account of human motives.[6] Moreover, Mill devoted a whole chapter of *Utilitarianism* to discussing the role of conscience as an internal sanction.[7] But Mill did not concern himself with self-deception.

Perhaps the role he assigned conscience in his moral philosophy explains this. Indeed, I think this is correct. But if it is, we must ask what it is about the role of conscience in Butler, Kant, and Adam Smith, as opposed to Mill, that lead the former group to worry about self-deception in the way they did and Mill did not. Moreover, not every moral philosopher who has taken self-deception seriously is happily thought of as giving conscience a fundamental role. Jean-Paul Sartre is one example; his discussion of self-deception is notable though he would hardly have referred to conscience in expressing his views.[8]

We are left with our question: What explains the differential interest in self-deception? In what follows I shall argue that no less than a difference in fundamental approach explains the remarkably different interests moral philosophers have taken in self-deception. Whether and how a thinker exercises himself about self-deception, I maintain, is evidence of his basic orientation in moral philosophy. To give some preliminary indication of what I mean by this, I must first digress a bit.

It is customary to take the central notions of ethics to be those of the good, the right, and the morally good. One way in which fundamental approaches to ethics can differ is in the way they relate these different notions, specifically, how they relate the right to the good and to the morally good, respectively.

Consider the early twentieth-century debate between Moore and Ross over "what makes right acts right," for example. Ross and Moore are best seen as disagreeing not just about whether considerations other than an act's consequences are relevant to its being right or wrong but also about the deeper question of what being a right- or wrong-making consideration or feature itself consists in. The Moore of *Principia* held the very concept of right to be derivative from the notion of good—to be right, he thought, just *is* to produce the best consequences. And while he later rejected the claim in this form, he never wavered from treating the good as fundamental. Ross, on the other hand, held the right to be independent of the good. Propositions of right were as basic and underived for him as were propositions of intrinsic goodness for Moore.

Moore and Ross represent, then, fundamentally different approaches to the question of what it is right to do. Moore treated the question as derivative, resting on the prior issue of what states of affairs are intrinsically worth bringing about (and on the empirical question of what can be done to bring them about). For Ross, though, the question of what a person ought to do was itself basic. The concept of right, he thought, does not derive from that of the good, nor do propositions regarding what is worth bringing about provide any rationale for propositions of right and wrong. There are fundamental truths about what a person ought to do that require no independent basis. So where Moore's theory was *value-* or *end-state-based,* Ross's was *duty-* or *conduct-based.* They differed fundamentally.

In addition to these two, there is a third fundamental strategy. And that is to begin with an ideal of *character,* of the morally good person, and to treat the issue of what a person ought to do as depending on that. This strategy aims to answer the question of what it is right to do by looking to an independent account of the moral person and asking, roughly, what such a person would do. It is, thus, a *character-* or *moral-worth-based* strategy.

Now this is an approach that is ordinarily associated with Aristotle and with what is called "an ethics of virtue."[9] The idea is to give some relatively specific account of the virtues, as including courage, justice, and benevolence, for example, and perhaps some master virtue such as practical wisdom, and to treat the right as depending on what a virtuous person, so characterized, would do.

There is, however, another, more formalist, or as I shall say, constitutionalist, version of the third strategy. Rather than beginning with a material ideal of character, with a view about the specific concerns and traits a good person has, constitutionalists start with a conception of the moral person as having certain "formal" virtues they hold to be necessary for integrity of moral constitution. Their ideal of character is of a person who assumes responsibility for her own moral integrity by regulating her life by her own best judgment. I call this a constitutionalist ideal of character since its central theme is that moral integrity involves self-government and because its project is to elaborate the "constitution" for such self-government—the constitution of the moral agent as such.[10]

Constitutionalist versions of the third strategy begin, then, with an ideal of the morally autonomous and integral person and seek to justify a theory of right based on this ideal. To exploit the political metaphor further, they derive their theory of policy from their constitutional theory.

The best example of this sort of view is, I believe, Kant's. While Kant's ethics are often referred to as an "ethics of duty," it is important to appreciate that the *Groundwork* begins with a discussion, not of Kant's fundamental principles of right, the formulations of the Categorical Imperative, but of the good will, the morally good person. And while the good will is defined as someone who acts on his own conception of duty, or, as Kant says, *from* duty, Kant also writes that "the concept of *duty* . . . includes that of a good will."[11] Moreover, the *Groundwork*'s first statement of the Categorical Imperative occurs at the end of a passage that begins: "But what kind of law can this be the thought of which, even without regard to the results expected from it, has to determine the will if this is to be called good absolutely and without qualification."[12] Evidently Kant thought the justification for fundamental principles of right to depend on his prior account of the good will. Principles of right must be capable of guiding the conduct of a morally good person, and to play this role they must have, so to speak, the right form. His thought seems to have been, to put it much too briefly, that since the morally good person's principled conduct is motivated by an impartial endorsement of principle, principles of right must be eligible to guide the conduct of all persons when a choice is made from a perspective that is impartial between them.

Nor is Kant the only example of the constitutional strategy. Although Butler can hardly be said to have had a theory of right in the full modern sense, he held, like Kant, that a person should be guided by principles he can reflectively ratify from a certain point of view. And he held the capacity to guide conduct by principles so ratified to be necessary for moral agency, and the exercise of that capacity both to constitute moral integrity and to be the main responsibility of the moral life.

Now I can be more specific about my thesis. Philosophers who, like Kant and Butler, pursue the constitutional strategy in ethics are more likely to take a deep interest in self-deception than are those who pursue other strategies. This does not mean that self-deception will receive no consideration within either a value- or duty-based ethical theory, only that it is apt to be less fundamental. No such theorist is likely to hold, as Mary Gregor argues Kant did, that "self-deceit . . . destroys the condition of moral action as such."[13]

The essay will have three main parts. I begin in Part I with a discussion of self-deception, especially of a particular sort of self-deception that has exercised constitutionalists. In Part II, I develop more fully the distinction between constitutional and other fundamental strategies in ethics, and explore the ways the former is elaborated in Butler and Kant. Finally, in Part III, I attempt to explain why it is that constitutionalists have been so deeply concerned about self-deception.

I

In order to understand constitutionalists' concern with self-deception we shall want to know both what it is about self-deception that concerns them and what it is about constitutionalism that makes them so concerned. In this section we shall begin to approach the former by considering what self-deception actually is. My aim here is to describe a particular sort of self-deception, a kind intimately related to conscience and judgment, that I shall later argue is particularly vexing to constitutionalists.

Almost everyone who has written on the topic, including Kant, interestingly enough, has found self-deception puzzling almost to the point of paradox. Kant put the point well: everyone agrees that self-deception occurs in some important sense; what is puzzling is how it *can* occur. "The reality of many an *internal* lie . . . is easy to set forth; yet to explain its possibility seems more difficult. Since a second person is required whom one intends to deceive, deceiving oneself deliberately seems in itself to contain a contradiction."[14] Faced with this puzzle almost all writers have held that what we call self-deception cannot be a literal copy of other-deception. Some writers, however, go so far in draining self-deception of seemingly paradoxical elements that they lose its distinctive character.[15]

It is, of course, true, and quite unparadoxical, if disconcerting, that attention, beliefs, and thoughts can be a function of desire in such a way that we simply "fail to notice or ignore what we know to be the case."[16] And even more obviously, a desire that something be the case can lead to misevaluating evidence, and consequently to the belief that it is the case.[17] But these phenomena seem, as it were, "too unparadoxical" to be self-deception, at least of the sort that has the greatest interest for ethics.

As M. R. Haight remarks, there is an element of apparent choice in the self-deceiver's benighted state, or at least in his thoughts, that need not figure in impulsive forgetting or in wishful thinking.[18] Unlike the latter, self-deception is something a person apparently *does*. Moreover, self-deception is at least like other-deception in this respect: a person can be charged with and held responsible for it. It is apparently a moral matter in a way that simply believing or thinking something as the causal result of desires may not be. Young children, after all, are notorious both for impulsive inattention to what they know and for wishful thinking, but are not apt to be characterized as self-deceived.

Another thing distinguishing self-deception from mere desire-biased belief and impulsive forgetting is that the agent's being less than fully honest with herself is partly explained by beliefs she has that are not the result of self-deception and that conflict with thoughts the deception aims to accomplish. Consider Butler's persuasive illustration:

> It is not uncommon for persons, who run out their fortunes, entirely to neglect looking into the state of their affairs, and this from a general knowledge, that the condition of them is bad. These extravagant people are perpetually ruined before they themselves expect it: and they tell you for an excuse and tell you truly, that they did not think they were so much in debt, or that their expenses

so far exceeded their income. And yet no one will take this for an excuse, who is sensible that their ignorance of their particular circumstances was owing to their general knowledge of them.[19]

Yet if self-deception is more like other-deception than "too unparadoxical" accounts would have it, but cannot be exactly like it without genuine paradox, then what does it involve? Paradox apparently arises when the self-deceiver is represented as simultaneously knowing (or believing) something, as deceiver, and as believing it not to be the case, as deceived. The problem is not just that the person has apparently contradictory beliefs, but that his having one belief plays a role in his apparently having the other. Something, it seems, must give. Either he does not really know or believe the relevant truth or he does not really believe it to be false. But in the former case he appears to lack the perversity characteristic of the self-deceiver, and in the latter his avowals lack the self-deceiver's apparent sincerity.

It is, of course, possible for a person intentionally to bring about a change in her beliefs over time. At t_1 she may know that p is the case but prefer to believe that not-p and so undertake to bring about a change in her beliefs so that at t_2 she will believe not-p and also believe that her belief that not-p is not the result of a desire to believe not-p rather than p despite the evidence. But what we call self-deception is rarely like that. Or, if it is, it is usually through an intervening process in which we think of the person as deceiver and deceived, in some sense, at the same time. Self-deception is not like taking a belief-changing pill. Even when a person's deception of herself is so far gone that she cannot recover her earlier knowledge and continues to be deceived though not to be deceiver, we still think that there was a time when the person was deceiver and deceived, surely not literally, but in some sense. But if not in the literal sense of knowing the truth and simultaneously bringing about a belief that it is false, then in what sense?

Perhaps the self-deceiver does not come literally to believe anything contrary to what he knows or what he knows he has good reason to suspect. Perhaps what his "deception" of himself accomplishes is, rather, contrary thoughts, not mere "thinkings of," but genuine "thinkings that," thinkings with the assertion stroke, as it were.[20] Such thoughts would be episodes, not the dispositional behavior-explaining states that beliefs are. An actor playing Hamlet can think to himself, "I have killed Polonius," without believing that he has. Or children playing mud pies can be thinking the pies are decorated with raisins even as they believe that they are topped with stones.[21]

Often what matters for certain purposes, especially from the first-person perspective in deliberating about what to do, is not what we believe but what we think. Consider what happens, for example, when one person is seduced by another into doing something against better judgment. The seducer need not bring about a change in the seduced's belief about what it would be best to do. It will be sufficient if he can be induced to put his belief out of mind and dwell on attractive aspects of the offered alternative.

Actually, seduction probably provides a better model than other-deception for what goes on in self-deception since it represents the lines of responsibility more accurately. The seduced bears a responsibility for his seduction that the deceived normally does not for his deception. The self-deceiver does not really put one over on his unsuspecting self and so bear responsibility for deceiving but not for being deceived. As far as responsibility goes, what he does is more like a seduction of himself.

Characteristically, then, the self-deceiver thinks thoughts that are in conflict with what he knows or, at any rate, with what he believes. Moreover, his doing so is somehow the result of his own choices: to disregard or explain away conflicting evidence, to focus on supporting evidence, or sometimes simply to indulge in the thoughts quite irrespective of evidence. Often the latter case involves a kind of fantasy or play. Haight cites the example of Polly from Mary McCarthy's *The Group,* who, when told by her lover that their affair is over, decides to go ahead and buy food for two.[22] She remarks that it would be implausible to regard Polly as literally believing that Gus was coming to dinner despite what he said. It makes more sense to think of her as acting out a fantasy, engaging in a kind of desperate play in the teeth of what she knows and believes. Since there is nothing she can do about her situation at least she can pretend and feel better.

One kind of conduct we call self-deception is largely a matter of refusing seriously to confront what one really believes, preferring to persist in playing out a fantasy. Actually, this may be sound strategy in some cases. Haight also discusses the case of an alcoholic who knows and believes the worst but persists in the fantasy (thought) that he is a moderate drinker in the hope that if he continues so to think he will at least get no worse.[23]

What brings us up short in trying to understand such cases is the apparent psychological impossibility of simultaneously thinking that one is only a moderate drinker with no serious drinking problem and that one has a serious problem that will get worse unless one continues to think of oneself as a moderate drinker. But there need be no such simultaneous thoughts. The drinker can think the latter when he honestly confronts himself and the former when he indulges his fantasy. Or he may never express the desperate hope to himself.

Often there is a social dimension to "self-deceptive" fantasies: an invitation to others to collude by reflecting the illusory presentation of self. And often it will seem more desirable to others to play along than to risk embarrassment, personal hurt, or in some cases, shaking the current social order. We are apt to think, for example, that many if not most privileged members of such cruel and oppressive societies as apartheid-ridden South Africa or Nazi Germany must be involved in some kind of self-deception about the evils of their societies and their own complicity. But that need not mean that they literally believe that nothing is rotten or that they are not complicit; they may be involved in an elaborate collusion to maintain a certain view, a certain way of *thinking* of their society. Not to think that way "aloud" is to threaten the fabric of everyday relationships. And not to do so alone is to risk a frightening alienation from others who provide a home context. Moreover, they may be true even if each individually would prefer a different order but is too frightened to take a stand, either publically or privately.[24]

I shall have more to say about the relation between self-deception, social approval, and self-esteem below when I consider the relation between self-deception and conscience or judgment. My point here is that the *activity* of deceiving oneself may not involve *believing* anything that contradicts what the self-deceiver is in a position to know and often does believe. It may, however, result in such a belief.

At this point one might wonder whether these remarks don't threaten to make self-deception "too unparadoxical" also. Mere fantasy is not self-deception. To turn an argument I used earlier back on myself: young children have fantasies, but we would hardly characterize them as self-deceived.

A significant difference between simple fantasy and self-deception is that the self-deceiver's fantasies have a serious purpose. They are not engaged in playfully, for their own sake—a diversion that can be abandoned at will. Rather their purpose is, at least, to numb the self-deceiver's ability to think clearly on some issue so that when it occurs to her, her "thinkings that" will not reflect her beliefs; or their purpose is, at most, to change her very beliefs themselves. While ordinary pretending is quite consistent with awareness of pretense, self-deception involves as well a second-order pretense that one is not pretending at a first-order level; this second-order pretense deflects cues that might return one from ordinary first-order, playful pretending to the real world.[25] It tends to corrupt, therefore, the self-deceiver's very ability to abandon the first-order pretense. Self-deception is on the way to delusion in a way that innocent play is not.

The common saying that self-deceivers fool themselves is suggestive here. Just as a king can be indulgently confirmed by a parroting jester, and hence fooled by his fool, so can one indulge oneself in one's own thoughts by failing to treat them seriously and critically as thoughts, and hence, apparently, be indulged by one's own complaisance. We seem to be able to play jester to our own king and vice versa.

To this point I have been following out the suggestion that self-deception is unparadoxical since the self-deceiver need not literally believe what he knows to be false. It is enough, on this suggestion, that he think thoughts that amount to a kind of elaborate pretense—not simply the first-order pretense involved in fantasy, but also the second-order pretense that his pretensions are real. When the self-deceiver plays the role of fool to himself, he must also pretend that he is not simply playing that role.

It may be complained against this picture, however, that self-deception must involve more than second-order pretense. Even second-order pretense, after all, is still pretense. Unless a person is *taken in* by his pretense, unless it informs what he believes, if only momentarily, he is not self-deceived. Or so it might be argued.[26]

The motivation for the suggestion that self-deception need involve no self-induced deceptive beliefs was to escape the paradox of construing self-deception as simply an internalized version of other-deception. But, it might be suggested, self-induced deceptive beliefs are paradoxical only if it is supposed that a single, unitary self is both the agent and the victim of deception. But this need not be so. The "agent" might be processes within the self of which the "deceived self" is quite unaware.

If it is objected that this removes any responsibility from the self-deceiver, it can be replied that we are often responsible for making ourselves aware of things of which we are unaware. That the self-deceiver is in fact unaware of the agents of his deception does not mean that he cannot become aware of them and thereby exercise a measure of control over them. Just as we sometimes hold ourselves responsible for being taken in by others when we should not have been—"I should have known better," we tell ourselves—so do we hold ourselves responsible for being taken in by ourselves.

Complex issues in the philosophy of mind divide these contending pictures: What is it to think an "affirmative" thought, and how does that relate to belief? Can one act on a thought without believing it? Is second-order pretense really possible? Happily, we do not need to settle these issues here. Our present concern is to describe a kind of self-deception that has been particularly vexing to constitutionalists. And we can do that without deciding between these competing views.

Whether or not a person must undergo a change in belief as a result of second-order pretense to be self-deceived, it is the second-order character of the pretense that is most significant to constitutionalists. Perhaps no harm is done by calling other sorts of self-induced cognitive mistakes self-deception. But there is something significantly different about the case in which a person represents his thought, beliefs, aims, and intentions to himself as though they were well grounded, and as though he would not have them unless they were so justified, when in fact they, as well as their representation as justified, are the result of quite different factors, and the person is in a position to know this.

Rationalization is the stock-in-trade of the second-order pretense involved in this serious sort of self-deception. Thoughts are represented to oneself as the result of rational judgment, as supported by reasons, when in fact that representation's very purpose is to defend oneself against honest criti-

cal thought. This is the sort of self-deception that has most troubled constitutionalist moral philosophers. The self-deceiver undermines her own moral
character and integrity by corrupting the very capacity for independent moral
judgment that, in their view, makes integrity possible.

Self-deception of any serious sort requires the capacity for judgment. That
is why we hesitate to characterize young children as self-deceived. Self-
deceivers are held responsible only because it is thought possible for them to
make reasonable judgments about that with respect to which they are said to
be self-deceived. If that is not possible, then they are not self-deceived; they
are deluded, perhaps, or mentally incompetent, or some such. Moreover, the
charge of self-deception is only apt to be made when some question of
responsible judgment arises. We do not ordinarily consider people who are
generous-minded towards others to be self-deceived when they look for things
to like in people in something other than a completely objective way, actively granting the benefit of the doubt, and so on. Nor is the competitor
who puts all thoughts of his (quite possible, perhaps likely) defeat out of his
mind a self-deceiver. In these instances there is no abdication of responsible
judgment.

In addition, the characteristic technique of the sort of self-deception that
vexes constitutionalists is a counterfeit of judgment. Only creatures with the
capacity for judgment can rationalize, for only they know the language in
whose terms the pretense must be carried off. If self-deception is like seduction in respect of dual responsibility of subject and object, it is a seduction
whose most serious instances require the forms of "sweet reason."

When the object of self-deception is the moral character of a person's conduct or character, then it is the forms of moral judgment that must be
observed. Self-deception of this sort involves "moral" rationalization, a characterization of conduct or character as acceptable to conscience occasioned
by the belief or suspicion that it is not. Moral rationalizing that corrupts
conscience is the sort of self-deception that concerns constitutionalists most.
To see why, we need to appreciate the role conscience and moral judgment
play in the constitutionalist view of morality.

The notion of conscience gains its sense from the theory of morals and
moral development within which it is embedded. Generally speaking, it can
be taken to refer to a capacity for and disposition to moral judgment. But
what that involves depends on what morality and moral judgment are. If
morality is simply the posited laws of society or of God, then conscience is
their internalized voice. For an intuitionistic moral realist like Ross, on the
other hand, conscience is the faculty through which an external and independent moral reality is cognized. For constitutionalists, however, conscience is
both a reflective and a constructive faculty. It is the capacity to reflect on
conduct and character in a certain way, from a certain point of view, where

this way of thinking is held to constitute moral judgment. Conscience, for constitutionalists, is not a capacity through which we cognize an independent moral reality. It is rather that through which a person constitutes morality: both her own moral integrity, through its actual exercise, and the obligations she is under, through its ideal exercise.

Parts II and III below are devoted, respectively, to a more comprehensive treatment of these aspects of constitutionalism and of why they explain constitutionalist concern with self-deception. In what remains of this section I wish to make some general remarks about the relation between self-deception and conscience.

There is another feature of conscience, at least as we ordinarily think of it: what Mill called "the internal sanction of duty"[27] and Butler "the discernment of [actions] as of good or ill desert."[28] Negative self-judgment is often connected to self-reproach, to feelings of guilt and shame; and often self-deception is a defense against these.

A person may be susceptible to self-reproach and profound feelings of guilt though the "internal judge, who threatens him and keeps him in awe"[29] is not in any authentic way the person himself, but some authoritative figure: God, perhaps, or parents. Conscience here is the "voice within" of an authoritative judge without. Constitutionalist moral philosophers have strongly resisted such a view of conscience. They have held there to be a "voice within" that is the individual's own authentic moral voice, and that moral integrity is impossible without expressing this voice.

Self-deception always involves a person's unwillingness to accept something, to *admit* it to his thoughts and mental life. Because conscience involves a judgment of onseself, it provides the occasion for self-deception if there are thoughts about oneself that one cannot, or more properly will not, bear. Unlike the person who "has no shame," the moral rationalizer has either too much, or too great a fear of, shame. And to avoid it he misrepresents himself to himself.

It is important to distinguish the person who will admit an unpleasant truth about herself, but prefers to arrange her life so that she is faced with it infrequently, from the person who simply will not admit it, who flees it whenever it raises its ugly head. The godfather whose kiss amounts to a death order and who prefers to keep himself above the dirty business is not a self-deceiver if this arrangement is not undertaken to confound his fundamental estimate of himself.

The self-deceiver's is. "The presentation of the self in everyday life," in Erving Goffman's phrase, is made as surely to oneself as to others. And the self-deceiver must present himself with an acceptable image; so he plays a self he can accept. Joan Didion gives a remarkable example of how one can be brought up short in recognizing the theatricality of one's own make-believe:

It was once suggested to me that, as an antidote to crying, I put my head in a paper bag. As it happens, there is a sound physiological reason, something to do with oxygen, for doing exactly that, but the psychological effect alone is incalculable: it is difficult in the extreme to continue fancying oneself Cathy in *Wuthering Heights* with one's head in a Food Fair bag.[30]

A "mind on the outs with itself" (Didion's phrase) is forced to choose between playing roles that present a more acceptable view and seeing itself honestly, hoping to come to terms, but risking staying "out of humour with [itself]" (Butler's phrase). The second alternative can be frightening; there simply is no assurance that one *will* accept oneself.

Conscience provides the context for moral rationalization, but, curiously enough, the fear of self-rejection that can make self-deception a path of least resistance is often related to distrust of one's own conscientious judgment and to a substitution for it of the views, demands, and expectations of others. It is related, in short, to lack of a kind of self-respect. Unable to maintain an acceptable self-image, one turns to others in the desperate hope that they can provide for one what one cannot provide acceptably for oneself—a self. Didion chronicles the process wisely.

[If we lack self-respect] we are peculiarly in thrall to everyone we see, curiously determined to live out—since our self-image is untenable—their false notions of us. We flatter ourselves by thinking this compulsion to please others an attractive trait: a gist for imaginative empathy, evidence of our willingness to give. *Of course* I will play Francesca to your Paolo, Helen Keller to anyone's Annie Sullivan: no expectation is too misplaced, no role too ludicrous. At the mercy of those we cannot but hold in contempt, we play roles doomed to failure before they are begun . . . .

It is the phenomenon sometimes called "alienation from self." In its advanced stages we no longer answer the telephone, because someone might want something; that we could say *no* without drowning in self-reproach is an idea alien to this game.[31]

The resulting alienation includes an alienation from one's own "moral voice." The self-reproach Didion describes in the last paragraph is less the authentic issue of the individual's own moral thinking than an internalization of external demands. To escape condemnation in her own eyes, or the risk of that, the self-deceiver attempts an "escape from freedom." She escapes the responsibility of making her own conscientious judgments and substitutes the voice of external demand.

Alternatively, of course, she may be escaping not her own judgments, but those of significant authoritative others—parents for example. This is especially likely if her sense of herself and her own judgment is not sufficiently developed to oppose to authorities from whom moral concepts are initially internalized, or if her acceptance as a child by parents was conditional on meeting their demands. She may even simply identify morality with these external demands.

To the extent that someone lacks any independent perspective from which critically to appropriate moral standards and simply identifies them with external demands, we are, I think, less likely to think of him as self-deceiving. There will be the same sorts of repression and evasive action as the self-deceiver takes, but the person will seem less responsible if he lacks some independent critical perspective. Serious self-deception of the sort most worrisome to constitutionalists requires a capacity for independent critical thought. It involves the pretense of such thought as a defense against what one believes or suspects would be the upshot of the genuine article.

II

Self-deception is a matter for concern on any view of ethics. That people are liable to mistake their circumstances, alternatives, and themselves in self-serving ways is disconcerting whatever one's moral philosophical approach. How disconcerting it is for value- and duty-based approaches, however, depends on complex empirical considerations. What matters ultimately for the philosophical consequentialist is how self-deception affects the total value of states of affairs that occur as a consequence. And for at least one sort of duty-based theorist, what matters is the effect self-deception has on the performance of right acts. Depending on details in theories of good and right respectively, self-deception need not be intrinsically problematic on either approach. If sufficiently compensating mechanisms exist, even large-scale self-deception can have a negligible, indeed benign, effect on the total value of consequent states of affairs or on the performance of right acts.

On the constitutionalist approach, however, self-deception is intrinsically problematic, especially when it is the sort of self-deception involving moral rationalization. In the next section I shall try to say why this is so. Before I can do that, however, I need in this section to refocus distinctions between fundamental approaches, and say a good bit more about the constitutional approach. As systematic moral philosophies, value-, duty-, and character-based approaches do not simply embody different views of the right, the good, and the morally good, taken one by one. Rather they seek to interrelate these views in such a way as to reveal a picture of what ethics is, in some sense, fundamentally about.

To recapitulate briefly: value-based approaches begin with a view of the intrinsic value of states that can occur as a consequence of acts, or of traits of character, but which value is independent, respectively, of the rightness of acts, or of the moral goodness of character traits. Then an act's being right, or a character trait's being a morally good one, is held to depend on the intrinsic value of its consequent states.[32]

Duty-based approaches are similar to those that are value-based in holding that whether an act is right is fully independent of its relation to moral character; roughly, that what a person ought to *do* is independent of how a person ought to *be*. But unlike them, they also hold that the rightness of acts does not derive from intrinsic value. The point is not that duty-based approaches cannot hold a consequentialist normative position: that it is right always to maximize welfare, or intrinsic value. There is nothing in the duty-based approach to prevent that. The point is that if it is right to maximize intrinsic value, or to do anything else for that matter, its *being* right does not derive from the intrinsic value of the relevant states; that is fundamental and underived. So duty-based approaches may or may not employ the notion of intrinsic value crucial to the value-based approach; whether they do depends on the content of fundamental duties. Finally, since duty is basic, goodness of character is also treated as derivative.

Character-based approaches reject the tenet shared by the other two. They hold that what it is right to do is not independent of goodness of character, that is, of moral goodness. They hold that what a person ought to do depends on what a person ought to be.

What characterizes the constitutionalist version of the character-based approach is that it holds the "first virtue" of moral character to be a sort of moral self-government and integrity that involves a person's being guided by his own best conscientious judgment. Constitutionalist ideals contain, therefore, two main aspects. In addition to the basic idea that a person of moral integrity is governed by his own best moral judgment, they also contain an account of what moral judgment is. Moral autonomy, according to this tradition, consists not simply in adherence to principle, indeed not even to principles an individual happens sincerely to believe to be moral. Rather, constitutionalists have had a fairly definite view of what moral judgment is.[33]

It is crucial to constitutionalism that what makes a judgment a moral one be features of its form and of the process through which it is made. If moral judgment is identified by content, for example, by its relating to the accomplishment of some specific end, or to the avoidance of certain acts as such, then the account will threaten to collapse into either a value- or duty-based approach. It is important, therefore, that constitutionalist accounts of moral judgment include only formal features, such as generality, universality, and publicity, and procedural features, such as impartiality, dispassionateness, and informedness.[34] In this way the constitutionalist ideal of the moral person incorporates analogues of political ideals of due process and the rule of law.

Now there is an important sense in which constitutionalism is properly considered an, indeed *the,* internalist strategy in ethics. First, goodness of character is held to be the excellence of features that, it is also held, a person must have to have a morally evaluable character at all. And it is thought to include, at its most fundamental level, no particular concern for anything outside the moral person, whether for any state or for any act. Second, a person is held to be bound by nothing except what would spring from his own duly constituted internal constitution. So-called "ethics of virtue" may agree with constitutionalism that what it is right to do depends on what a person of good character would do, and so be internalist in that sense. But they are apt also to hold that certain specific concerns, which may well not be generable from the inside by the excellent exercise of capacities necessary for moral character at all, are part of good character. This internalist (in the present sense) aspect of the constitutionalist approach partly explains why self-deception looms so large for it as a central problem of the moral life.[35]

As I said, there are two crucial features of the constitutionalist approach: the thesis that the morally good person is guided by his own best moral judgment and a thesis about what moral judgment is. For Butler, moral judgment consisted in a reflective assessment of "actions and characters" that aims to be dispassionate (involving "cool reflection") and disinterested ("without regard to their consequences to [oneself]"). So the faculty of judgment, what Butler called alternately conscience or the "principle of reflection," consists in the capacity to be affected by a dispassionate and disinterested reflective consideration of acts and characters.[36]

"It is by virtue of this capacity, natural to man," Butler held, "that he is a moral agent, that he is a law to himself." (p. 37) The last clause brings in the second main constitutionalist idea: the capacity that is necessary for moral agency is also sufficient to generate a moral agent's main responsibility, namely, to exercise and be guided by his own capacity for judgment. Butler states:

> the very constitution of our nature requires, that we bring our whole conduct before this superior faculty; wait its determination; enforce upon ourselves its authority, and make it the business of our lives, as it is absolutely the whole business of a moral agent, to conform ourselves to it. This is the true meaning of that ancient precept, *Reverence thyself.* (p. 17)

Butler took over the Platonic theme that a person's integrity or internal order requires regulation by a capacity for rational judgment, but he gave it a crucial "liberal" and internalist twist. Unlike Plato's *nous,* the principle of reflection does not bring us into contact with an external metaphysical realm of values, and so the motivation it gives us is not metaphysically mysterious. It simply consists in the capacity to have a responsive attitude to "acts and characters" when considered from a certain point of view; in accordance with due process, as it were. In Rawls's terms, the "principle of reflection embodies a "pure" rather than a "perfect" or "imperfect" procedure. There is no fact of the matter about what a person ought to do or be that is independent of what a person would approve of were he to reflect dispassionately and disinterestedly. Moral judgment in accordance with due process constitutes morality; it does not put one into the best position to discern independently constituted moral truths.[37]

Butler's tying the capacity for reflective judgment to a fundamental responsibility to exercise the capacity and this to the "ancient precept, Reverence thyself," anticipates the further development of these themes in Kant. Crucial to the notion of a moral agent in Kant's ethics is "the power to act in accordance with his idea of laws—that is, in accordance with principles."[38] But how are judgments of principle to be made? Kant's account echoes the procedural aspects of Butler's and adds to it the element of the rule of law. Roughly: a person should only act consistently with principles (laws) he could rationally choose all persons to be guided by were his choice to be made from a standpoint that is impartial between them.[39] Moral agency, then, involves some capacity to take up such a perspective (more or less successfully), to consider this sort of legislative question, and to guide conduct by consideration of it.

This is one part of constitutionalism: a theory of moral judgment. The other part consists in the thesis that by virtue of having a capacity for judgment, and for guiding conduct by it, an agent has a fundamental responsibility to exercise the capacity. The form this takes in Kant is his doctrine of rational nature as an end in itself. Having the capacity for critical self-legislation of the sort described gives one a dignity that demands respect for the capacity, from oneself as well as from others, as an end in itself, to be exercised for its own sake and never simply to serve other purposes.[40]

While constitutionalism thinks of the morally good person as governed by his own best judgment, it is a caricature of the view to suppose that it recommends explicit deliberation and judgment before every act. Surely no careful reader of Butler could suppose this. It is from him, after all, that English moral philosophy learned the "paradox of egoism": the commonplace that an agent's own happiness is best promoted if he is not constantly moved by a concern for his own happiness. This, of course, is no real paradox, but only a practical problem. We could point to a similar "paradox" of conscience. A person may be likelier on certain occasions, in certain areas of life, and in the long run, to act in ways he would approve of on reflection "in a cool hour" if he were not explicitly to deliberate and form a judgment before each action. This is again no paradox but a problem that can be at least partially solved because we can reflectively form and be guided by judgments about larger slices of conduct than specific acts—we can consider how best to comport ourselves in kinds of situations, areas of life, and so on, and attempt to cultivate or confirm habits accordingly. Continuing flexibility to changing and unexpected circumstances remains important, of course. But this is best handled not with continual deliberation case by case, but with the development of a moral sensitivity or watchfulness: a readiness to deliberate when circumstances call for it and a perceptiveness to the relevant circumstances. The person who is guided by his best judgment is not explicitly guided act by act.

Nor, as Arthur Kuflik points out, should the ideal of moral autonomy enshrined by constitutionalists be confused with self-sufficiency.[41] With some matters it will be proper, on reflection, to rely on the views of knowledgeable others, especially when complicated empirical issues are involved. Like the question of how much deliberation is appropriate, the issue of when and how to rely on others' views is one the agent himself confronts as morally autonomous. The crucial point for constitutionalists is not that each agent must deliberate and decide independently what to do in each case. It is rather that each agent is ultimately responsible for the way he conducts himself, and hence for relying on others or habit, or for not doing so, to the extent that he does.

III

We are finally in a position to see why self-deception is taken so seriously by constitutionalists. There are, I think, three basic reasons. Two relate to the two main aspects of constitutionalism, and a further reason relates to a vice to which the person aspiring to a constitutionalist ideal appears peculiarly susceptible.

The most profound source of constitutionalist concern about self-deception is the thesis that the fundamental responsibility of a moral agent, his "whole business," is to exercise and be guided by his moral judgment. Most obviously, the person who deceives himself about morally relevant features of his situation, about the moral character of his acts or motives, fails to be guided by his best moral judgment. He believes, or at least suspects, things that would in his own view be crucially relevant to what he should do and that he fails to take account of in his practical thinking.

So far self-deception seems only to involve a fault of omission, but it is worse than that. Self-deceptive failure to be guided by one's best judgment is not simple carelessness; it is, at the very least, motivated carelessness— "wilfulness," Butler says. Thus David, in the central example of Butler's sermon on self-deceit, can hardly just fail to notice that he has murdered Uriah; he must actively ignore it. The self-deceiver purposefully diverts herself from honestly making and confronting her best judgment. I noted above that constitutionalists are likely to hold that the morally good person will develop general habits that must be supplemented by a watchfulness of circumstances that signal the appropriateness of further reflection. When a person self-deceptively looks away from features she knows to be relevant, she subverts the moral sensitivity crucial to constitutionalist moral character.

But there is a more serious sort of self-deception still. This is self-deception that purposefully substitutes a counterfeit of moral judgment for the real thing—moral rationalization. It is one thing to fail to confront one's own sincere moral scrutiny, even purposefully, and yet another purposefully to misrepresent one's best judgment to oneself. In the first instance a person may still call himself to account if he honestly tries. He may do so by trying seriously to think things through and come to his own judgment. In the second instance, however, the person undermines even his own attempts to think things through by misrepresenting his own judgment to himself. In so doing he undermines the very capacity that constitutionalists hold to be necessary for moral integrity and character.

Since Butler centers his discussion of self-deceit around an example of willful ignorance, rather than moral rationalization, it may seem that he does not really think the latter to be especially problematic. But that is not so. At the end of the sermon, for instance, he proposes that the Golden Rule be understood as having two parts.

> One is, to substitute another for yourself, when you take a survey of any part of your behaviour, or consider what is proper and fit and reasonable for you to do upon any occasion; the other part is, that you substitute yourself in the room of another; consider yourself as the person affected by such a behaviour, or towards whom such an action is done: and then you would not only see, but likewise feel, the reasonableness or unreasonableness of such an action or behaviour.[42]

He notes, however, that, "alas," people are also able to deceive themselves in applying this rule. This must be the sort of self-deception to which he refers (just after) as "this deep and calm source of delusion; which . . . *corrupts* conscience, which is the guide of life" (emphasis added).

Moreover, Butler devotes an entire sermon ("Upon the Character of Balaam") to moral rationalization. Balaam, having told Balak that he will not defy God by cursing Israel, and being offered yet further riches by Balak to do so, "deliberates whether by some means or other he might not be able to obtain leave to curse Israel" (p. 95). Balaam's fault is not that he simply fails to consider, or even that he willfully ignores, what he is doing. On the contrary, Butler says, in his case "doubt and deliberation is itself dishonesty" (p. 100). The motive for deliberation is not an honest desire to discover what he should do since, Butler says, he already knows that full well. He deliberates "for the sake of the reward," to see whether there is not some way of representing what he wants to do as morally acceptable. "Good God," Butler writes, "what inconsistency, what perplexity is here!" (p. 97).

Self-deceptive rationalization is not only a misuse of judgment, it threatens the very capacity for judgment. Constitutionalists must regard it, therefore, as both wrong in itself and a threat to the very possibility of moral integrity. So, in the first vein, Kant held self-deception to be a violation of "man's duty to himself considered only as a moral being," since it involves treating the source of his dignity, his rational nature, not as an end in itself, but simply as a means to some further purpose.[43] And, in the second, Butler wrote that "it is a corruption of the whole moral character in its principle."[44]

Another source of concern about self-deception concerns the second aspect of constitutionalist approaches: their formal and procedural account of moral judgment. Moral judgment is not, on the constitutionalist picture, an attempt to perceive or discover independent moral facts. The truth about what one ought to do is itself constituted by the deliverances of moral judgments made in accordance with due process. For Butler, what mattered was how one would be "affected" when reflecting on an "act or character" from a dispassionate and disinterested point of view. For Kant, it concerned what principles one would rationally choose all to act on from an impartial perspective.

The procedural and internalist character of constitutionalism provides at least two reasons for concern about self-deception. One reason is relatively superficial and epistemological. The second is deeper and metaphysical. The relatively superficial, epistemological worry is that in representing moral judgment as involving *self*-reflection as well as reflection on the object of judgment, constitutionalists conceive it in a way that makes it particularly vulnerable to self-deception. We are likelier to be able to deceive ourselves about what we ought to do, if we accept a constitutionalist view of what obligation rests on, than we would be if we accepted, say, some external naturalist view. Other people, for example, may provide little check on an individual's self-deceptive moral judgment if the latter concerns what his own considered responses or choices would be under complicated hypothetical, indeed unrealizable, conditions.

The second, more profound concern stemming from constitutionalism's procedural aspect is that when persons substitute a counterfeit of moral judgment for the real thing, they are, in effect, counterfeiting morality.[45] According to constitutionalism no moral standards exist that are independent of what a person could, in principle, ratify for himself by the excellent use of his capacity for moral judgment. According to constitutionalists, then, the person who engages in moral rationalization is not simply falsely representing morality, he is attempting falsely to constitute it.

In addition to these two, there is a third reason why constitutionalists must be concerned about self-deception and prize what Kant termed the "moral self-knowledge, which tries to fathom the scarcely penetrable depths of the heart."[46] The morally good person, as represented by the constitutionalists, may be confused with the self-righteous person; the person who lives by his own moral lights may not be adequately distinguished from the person who ardently scans his life for moral light to bask in. And so people who aspire to the constitutionalist ideal may be peculiarly susceptible to that vice.

The point is not that there is no real difference between the two; there is. The morally good person's concern is to conduct himself in ways he can approve of, while the self-righteous person's is to approve of himself, to think of himself as worthy of approval. The important point is rather that since, in contrast with other views, the constitutionalist's morally good person is self-regulating and so has a conception of herself as guided by moral considerations, a person who aims at this ideal may settle for the conception and not the reality.

Moreover, the person whose primary need is to think of himself as good is especially prone to a sort of self-deception that can lead easily to cruelty, both towards others and towards himself. Unwilling to accept his own faults, a person may attempt to reassure himself of his good moral character by playing the stern moral judge and meting out stiff punishment to others, and when the jig is up from time to time, to himself. Butler writes of people who talk "with great severity against particular vices, which, if all the world be not mistaken, they themselves are notoriously guilty of."[47] And he recalls David's response to Nathan's parable of a transgression similar to David's own: "the man that hath done this thing shall die," describing it as "pronounced with the utmost indignation."[48] Because self-righteous cruelty is a potential consequence of a perversion of their ideal of moral goodness, constitutionalists have a further reason to be concerned about the self-deception that makes it possible.

For at least these reasons, then, self-deception poses an especially profound threat to the moral life as constitutionalists conceive it. Both Butler's and Kant's interest in self-deception is therefore no accident. It is a consequence of their fundamental approach to moral philosophy. Self-deception is, of course, not irrelevant on other fundamental approaches. Consequentialists, for example, often point to self-deception, among other phenomena, in recommending that societies promulgate relatively specific rules rather than leave people free to maximize the good as they see it. The point, rather, is that because only constitutionalists conceive the defining principle of moral character to be guidance by the person's own moral judgment, only they are apt to hold that self-deception is "a corruption of the whole moral character in its principle." For constitutionalists, serious self-deception is the moral analogue of subversion of constitutional order.

NOTES

For discussions of earlier drafts of this essay, I am indebted to Gregory Trianosky, Nicholas White, and, especially, David Velleman.

1. Joseph Butler, *The Works of Joseph Butler,* ed. J. H. Bernard (London: The Theological Library, 1900), 1:136.

2. Immanuel Kant, *The Metaphysical Principles of Virtue,* trans. J. Ellington (Indianapolis: Bobbs-Merrill Co., 1964), p. 103; Königliche Preussische Akademie der Wissenschaften edition (Berlin), henceforth *Ak.,* pp. 440–441.

3. Kant, *Handschrifter Nachlass,* vol. 23, *Ak.,* p. 400 (quoted in Mary J. Gregor, *Laws of Freedom* [Oxford: Basil Blackwell, 1963], p. 157).

4. Adam Smith, *The Theory of Moral Sentiments* (Oxford: Clarendon Press, 1976), pt. 3, chap. 4.

5. Pp. 100–103; *Ak.,* pp. 438–440.

6. Jeremy Bentham, *A Comment on the Commentaries,* ed. Everett (Oxford: Clarendon Press, 1928), p. 103. For J. S. Mill's critique of Bentham's denigration of conscience see his "Remarks on Bentham's Philosophy," in *Essays on Ethics, Religion, and Society,* ed. J. M. Robson (Toronto: Univ. of Toronto Press, 1969), p. 13.

7. "[A] feeling in our own mind; a pain, more or less intense, attendant on violation of duty. . . . This feeling, when disinterested and connecting itself with the pure idea of duty, and not with some particular form of it, or with any of the merely accessory circumstances, is the essence of conscience." John Stuart Mill, "Of the Ultimate Sanction of the Principle of Utility," chap. 3 in *Utilitarianism* (Indianapolis: Bobbs-Merrill Co., 1957), p. 36.

8. Jean-Paul Sartre, *Being and Nothingness,* trans. Hazel Barnes (New York: Washington Square Press, 1966), pp. 86–116.

9. It is possible to hold an "ethics of virtue" without holding any particular *theory* of right. Indeed, those who favor this approach often criticize the very idea of theories of right in the modern sense.

10. This characterization shares important aspects with what Rawls calls "constructivism," but it stresses a person's internal moral constitution and integrity. See John Rawls, "Kantian Constructivism in Moral Theory, The Dewey Lectures 1980," *Journal of Philosophy* 78 (1980):515–572.

11. Immanuel Kant, *Groundwork of the Metaphysics of Morals,* trans. H. J. Paton (New York: Harper Torchbooks, 1964), p. 65; *Ak.,* p. 397.

12. Ibid., pp. 69–70; *Ak.,* p. 402.

13. Gregor, op. cit., p. 153. Although I mentioned Smith and Sartre above as being among those philosophers who have taken self-deception seriously, I shall not discuss them directly. While neither is a constitutionalist in my sense, both have affinities with this tradition. While Sartre is disinclined to say that the person who can choose between living authentically or self-deceptively has a *moral* responsibility to do the former, or that moral integrity and character are constituted by so living, he nonetheless speaks of a genuine responsibility to live authentically, and says that "sincerity presents itself as a demand" (in *Existentialism,* ed. Robert Solomon [New York: Modern Library, 1974], pp. 198, 211).

Smith is a complex figure who resists neat classification. While he is usually classed along with Hutcheson and Hume as a proto-utilitarian, his view of conscience as authoritative in Butler's sense and as a more important motive in the moral life than benevolence marks a real departure from Hume and the early Hutcheson:

[W]hat is it which prompts the generous, upon all occasions, and the mean upon many, to sacrifice their own interests to the greater interests of others? It is not the soft power of humanity, it is not that feeble spark of benevolence which Nature has lighted up in the human heart. . . . It is reason, principle, conscience, the inhabitant of the breast, the man within, the great judge and arbiter of our conduct. (Smith, op. cit., p. 137)

The "inhabitant of the breast" for Smith was not an internalized external spectator, but the person's own imagined sense of what he would feel as a spectator. Smith also stresses the Stoic notion of self-command, which has important affinities with constitutionalism.

There are other examples of moralists who concern themselves with self-deception and for whom ethics is fundamentally concerned with authenticity or sincerity. Shaftesbury would be one. His *Soliloquy* (in *Characteristics,* ed. John M. Robertson [Indianapolis, Ind.: Bobbs-Merrill Co., 1964], vol. 1), treats of both matters. A particularly interesting instance is Daniel Dyke, whose *Mystery of Self-Deceiving* (London, 1615) apparently influenced La Rochefoucauld (see Derek Jarrett, *England in the Age of Hogarth* [New Haven: Yale Univ. Press, 1986], p. 180). This book illustrates a source of constitutionalism in the Puritan idea of scrutiny of the soul. It combines an exceedingly careful and illuminating catalogue of varieties of self-deception with the thesis that "sincerity is the highest perfection attainable in this life" (*Mystery of Self-Deceiving,* p. 362).

14. Kant, *Metaphysical Principles of Virtue,* p. 91; *Ak.,* p. 430.

15. Herbert Fingarette discusses some of these in his *Self-Deception* (London: Routledge and Kegan Paul, 1969), pp. 12–33.

16. Raphael Demos, "Lying to Oneself," *Journal of Philosophy* 57 (1960):594–595.

17. Alfred R. Mele counts this as self-deception in his "Self-Deception," *Philosophical Quarterly* 33 (1983):365–377.

18. M. R. Haight, *A Study of Self-Deception* (Sussex: Harvester Press, 1980), pp. 3f. She notes also, in regard to Demos' formulation, that ignoring involves choice in a way that failing to notice typically does not.

19. Butler, op. cit., 1:133.

20. Paul Boghossian suggested this formulation to me. For this general approach, see Kent Bach, "An Analysis of Self-Deception," *Philosophy and Phenomenological Research* 41 (1981):351–370.

21. The example comes from Kendall Walton's "Pictures and Make Believe," *Philosophical Review* 82 (1973):283–319. The children "make believe" that the mud pies are topped with raisins. Walton believes that attitudes towards fiction and towards works of art more generally can be modeled on "make believe." And Jerry Guthrie has proposed that self-deception can be modeled on this view of art: self-deception is "a form of art in which the deceiver is the author of the work, the star of the work, and an ever-constant audience for the work" ("Self-Deception and Emotional Response to Fiction," *British Journal of Aesthetics* 21 [1981]:73).

22. Haight, op. cit., pp. 112–113.

23. Ibid., p. 110.

24. For a very illuminating discussion of these and related phenomena see John

Sabini and Maury Silver, "On Destroying the Innocent with a Clear Conscience: A Sociopsychology of the Holocaust," in *Moralities of Everyday Life* (Oxford: Oxford Univ. Press, 1982), pp. 55–87.

25. I am indebted for this formulation to discussion with Greg Trianosky.

26. Here I am indebted to discussion with David Velleman.

27. Mill, *Utilitarianism*, p. 36.

28. Joseph Butler, "A Dissertation Upon the Nature of Virtue," in *Works,* 2:288. Also in *Five Sermons,* ed. S. L. Darwall (Indianapolis: Hackett, 1983), p. 70. Because the latter is more widely available, I will refer to it where possible.

29. Kant, *Metaphysical Principles of Virtue,* p. 100; *Ak.,* p. 428.

30. Joan Didion, "On Self-Respect," in *Slouching Towards Bethlehem* (New York: Farrar, Straus and Giroux, 1968), pp. 146–147.

31. Ibid., pp. 147–148.

32. Indirect consequentialist theories of right are, I think, less well motivated than act-consequentialism on a purely value-based approach. It is, of course, open to someone to hold, as Mill did in chap. V of *Utilitarianism,* that the terms 'right' and 'wrong' are best defined (indeed on grounds of utility!) through a connection to rule-governed social practices of reproach, and to advance rule-utilitarianism as a theory of right so defined. But then the further question whether a person should on any given occasion do what is right so defined can still be raised; and the natural good-based answer to this question is act-consequentialist, or so it seems to me.

33. On this point see Arthur Kuflik, "The Inalienability of Autonomy," *Philosophy and Public Affairs* 13 (1984):272f.

34. The only exceptions—and they are important—are ends that a moral agent can be presumed to have as such.

35. I discuss this aspect of Butler's and Kant's views in relation to the contemporary problem of "agent-centered restrictions" in "Agent-Centered Restrictions From the Inside Out," *Philosophical Studies* 50 (1986):291–319.

36. Butler, *Five Sermons,* pp. 16–17, 29–30, 37–40, 69–70. Further references to this work will be placed parenthetically in the text.

37. This reading of Butler stresses passages and themes that are admittedly in some tension with others, for example, his referring to the principle of reflection as a moral faculty of "perception." As evidence for the view of Butler presented here I would cite, in addition to the "law to himself" passages: (a) the fact that Butler takes it as sufficient evidence of a person's having conscience that he would not "be affected in the same way towards" two different actions considered dispassionately and disinterestedly (p. 30), and (b) his holding that "though the good of the creation be the only end of the Author of it, yet He may have laid us under particular obligations, which we may discern and feel ourselves under, quite distinct from a perception that the observance or violation of them is for the happiness or misery of our fellow creatures" (p. 66). It is plain from the context that Butler thought it sufficient for the Creator's having "laid us under particular obligations" that He have created us with certain fundamental dispositions to dispassionate and disinterested approval and disapproval, without having somehow to make changes in some independent moral reality that we can discern.

Despite the liberal and anti-intuitionist strands in Butler's thought I have emphasized, it is surely also true that Butler belonged to a tradition of divine teleology, as indeed did Kant, that saw individual lives as playing a role in a sort of "Divine corporation." On this important point see J. B. Schneewind, "The Divine Corporation and the History of Ethics," in *Philosophy in History,* ed. R. Rorty et al. (Cambridge: Cambridge Univ. Press, 1984), pp. 173–191.

38. Kant, *Groundwork,* p. 80; *Ak.,* p. 412.

39. This rendering emphasizes the "realm of ends" idea. See *Groundwork,* pp. 100f; *Ak.,* pp. 432f.

40. It is important to recognize that Kant's second formulation of the Categorical Imperative says, "Act in such a way that you always treat humanity [*Menschheit*], whether *in* your own person or in the person of any other, never simply as a means, but always at the same time as an end" (*Groundwork,* p. 96; *Ak.,* p. 429, emphasis added). As translator Paton notes on p. 138, by '*Menschheit*' Kant means to refer to rational nature as such, as the context makes clear. Thus the principle is one of respect for rational nature in oneself and others.

41. Kuflik, op. cit., p. 273.

42. Butler, *Works* 1:135–136. Further references to this in the next two paragraphs will be placed parenthetically in the text.

43. Kant, *Metaphysical Principles of Virtue,* p. 90; *Ak.,* pp. 428f.

44. Butler, *Works* 1:130. For a contemporary view along these same lines see W. D. Falk's "Morality, Self, and Others," in *Ought, Reasons, and Morality* (Ithaca, N.Y.: Cornell Univ. Press, 1986), pp. 198–231.

45. I am indebted for this formulation to David Velleman.

46. Kant, *Metaphysical Principles of Virtue,* p. 104; *Ak.,* p. 441.

47. Butler, *Works* 1:126.

48. Ibid., p. 125.

20

WHAT IS WRONG WITH
SELF-DECEPTION?

Marcia Baron

1. Most of us agree that there is something objectionable about self-deception. But despite the considerable attention that philosophers have given to the question of what self-deception is, remarkably little attempt has been made to say what is wrong with self-deception.[1] What follows is a foray into that question.

Why is it that so little attention has been paid to this question? One possibility is that self-deception is assumed to be wrong for the same reasons, and in the same way, that deception of others is wrong. Deception of others is usually held to be prima facie wrong, and self-deception is assumed to have the same status. It will be my contention that deception and self-deception are wrong in rather different ways, and that the moral status of self-deception is a bit higher than that of deception.[2]

Before elaborating, several caveats and clarifications are in order. First, I shall not be concerned with the question whether (more precisely, under what circumstances) self-deceivers are morally responsible for their self-deception. Still less will I be concerned with the conditions under which it is appropriate to attribute self-deception to others.[3] To those who think that 'X is wrong' entails that anyone who commits X or engages in X deserves to be (and, moreover, should be) blamed and perhaps also punished, it will seem strange that I do not, in asking under what conditions self-deception is wrong, address how we are to identify self-deceivers and whether they are to be regarded as morally responsible and blameworthy for their self-deception. Since I reject this view and understand 'X is wrong' more broadly, I regard questions of moral responsibility, blameworthiness, and attribution of self-deception as issues beyond the scope of this paper.

Second, with respect to some discussions it is helpful to distinguish self-deception as a *state of being deceived* from self-deception as a *process* by which one comes to be deceived (by oneself), and by which one perpetuates the state of being self-deceived. In asking what is wrong with self-deception I am focusing on self-deception as a process.[4] That is, I am asking what is wrong with inducing or sustaining self-deception.[5]

Finally, something must be said on the subject of what self-deception is. To avoid a lengthy and tedious account of self-deception, I will simply indicate the sorts of phenomena that I have in mind in speaking of self-deception.[6] In some cases there will be many who deny that what I describe counts as self-deception.[7] Whether or not all the phenomena are to be counted as self-deception does not much concern me; those who think they should not be so counted can read, in place of "self-deception" as it appears throughout this essay, "self-deception and related phenomena."[8]

The phenomena I have in mind are not only those which to many people are paradigmatic cases of self-deception, e.g., those in which the agent believes both p and not-p,[9] or in which she believes p but "avows or is disposed to avow not-p,"[10] but also those in which the propositional attitude is something weaker than belief. If in self-deception one "deep down" believes p, there is a related phenomenon in which one strongly suspects that p, or suspects it, not strongly perhaps, but with intense fear and horror. One fears that p; is afraid to investigate, lest it turn out that p is the case; flees from hints that it is; and shores up evidence that not-p. Thus (or so it appears to some viewers) Hannah in Woody Allen's film *Hannah and Her Sisters* must have some suspicion that her husband is having an affair with her sister (or at least hoping to), though she apparently never articulates her fear. We imagine that she must be telling herself a story to explain his perplexing irritability and distraction in a way that will allay any unarticulated fears, and that she must somehow keep herself from noticing the inordinate attention he pays to her sister. In another film, *Daughter Rite,* by Michelle Citron, the strategy of hiding from the evidence is made more explicit. The young woman who recounts her attempt to tell her mother that her stepfather raped her earlier that evening, while the mother was at a church supper, reports that at the first mention that something terrible had happened, her mother turned away from her and, smiling at herself in the mirror, cut her daughter short by relating what she had eaten at the church dinner. Hannah does not believe that her sister and her husband are having an affair; the mother does not believe that her husband raped her daughter. They are preventing themselves from arriving at such a view; suspecting, perhaps vaguely, that something too horrible to face is going on, they take care to avoid finding out exactly what it is.

This suffices, I hope, to indicate what I understand the subject of my inquiry to be.

2. Certain types of examples of self-deception immediately come to mind when we try to think of instances of it. I deceive myself into thinking that I am not an alcoholic, just someone who really likes to have a good time, hang loose, and enjoy a good drink and a pleasant stupor. It relaxes me, but I don't *have* to drink and could quit if I wanted to. Or I am a smoker who figures, "Sure, smoking increases my risks of getting cancer and other diseases, but

so do a lot of other things, and you can't avoid everything that's bad for you. Besides, the evidence isn't all *that* strong; who knows, maybe they'll say in ten years that it isn't really as serious a health risk as was thought." Or consider Joseph Butler's example of "extravagant people" who are "perpetually ruined before they themselves expected it." They "neglect looking into the states of their affairs, and this from a general knowledge, that the condition of them is bad."[11]

If we focus on these sorts of cases or the example from *Daughter Rite,* it is no wonder if we think that *of course* self-deception is objectionable. It seems, when we think of it in this way, to be bad in every instance of it (even if excusable sometimes, and in some instances the lesser of two evils). Like deception, it seems to be a bad thing in need of justification, a justification that recognizes that it is prima facie wrong to deceive and thus that it can only be shown to be permissible in a given instance by demonstrating that its wrongness is outweighed by countervailing considerations.

But if we look at a broader span of cases of self-deception, it is less clear that self-deception is always prima facie wrong. Consider some other cases: the AIDS victim who deceives himself into believing that his chances of recovery are at least fifty-fifty; the Salvadoran who convinces himself that his sister escaped into the mountains or fled to Mexico, and was not, despite the evidence, tortured and killed by the army's death squads. It is difficult to find these instances of self-deception objectionable.[12] The same is true of an example M. R. Haight offers of Emma, a hospitalized paralytic who can see and hear, but not move or communicate.

> Emma has a favourite daughter, Joan, who does not visit her. Others do, and she should know from what they say that Joan has no good reason not to come. But she will not accept that Joan does not care about her—perhaps even dislikes her now that she is ill. She tells herself 'Joan has such a busy life!'—but Joan's sister Lucy comes, and Lucy has a demanding job and a family and lives farther away. When Lucy's talk reminds her of this, Emma thinks how much more sensitive Joan has always been. . . . If she ever for a while thinks 'Perhaps Joan really *doesn't* care if I live or die!' she soon takes it back, calling to mind times when Joan behaved affectionately as a child, and generalizations like 'A girl can't do without her mother, even if she does sometimes seem to take her for granted!'. And so on. Juggling these thoughts . . . Emma avoids a mental life in which 'Joan does not love me' is an accepted truth.[13]

We can think of many instances in which we regard the bit of self-deception as a perfectly good way of handling a sad situation. One last case: a historian denied tenure at a second-rate school gets a job at a considerably inferior school. Imagine that he is good but not first-rate, and that he was judged by the tenure committee to be a far worse scholar and teacher than he is. In reaction to the tenure decision he exaggerates the gap between the assessment of him and what a fairer assessment would have yielded. He compares his work to that of major contemporary historians and judges his to be as good or better than most of their work.

Self-deception about one's standing in the profession need not be especially bad. Still, there is the danger of a rippling effect. Self-deception has to expand its boundaries if it is to be efficacious. To uphold my belief that p, I must reinterpret various phenomena so as to induce a belief that not-q (despite the signs that q is true). To disregard or reinterpret the evidence that q, I must believe r, and so on.

What is wrong with self-deception, I want to suggest, is best seen by examining this rippling effect. It will emerge that insofar as self-deception is wrong, it is wrong for rather different reasons than those which make deception wrong. The wrongness of deception can be ascertained by examining individual acts of deception as such, as well as by looking at the character of one who deceives. But the wrongness of self-deception comes into view only when we consider what sort of character one must have to be self-deceptive.

Before trying to figure out what is wrong with self-deception, I should emphasize that in saying that many instances of self-deception are in themselves not objectionable, I am not saying only that it is excusable. My claim is not just that the agent should not be held morally responsible and faulted for deceiving herself, but rather that in those instances it is simply not wrong (not, at least, if viewed actionally and episodically).[14]

DECEPTION AND SELF-DECEPTION

3.1 In working toward an understanding of what is wrong with self-deception, it is useful to compare it with deception. In many ways they are similar. First, both deception and self-deception involve a disregard for the truth, although in self-deception the disregard is not as openly embraced. Second, deception and self-deception are similar in that they sometimes, but not always, harm people other than the agent. If I deceive you for your own good I may, despite my intentions, harm you, but I may very well not. If I deceive you for my gain, I am more likely to do you harm, though it is of course not guaranteed that I will.

Initially self-deception seems different. It seems to have no meaningful connection with harm to others. Any connections, one might suggest, are as remote as the end points of the causal chains in Rube Goldberg's drawings. But self-deception frequently does involve fairly direct harm to others, as when I conceal from myself that I am spoiling my daughter, or deceive myself into thinking that my son is not retarded but only a little slow for his age, or that another of my children is not overweight, just healthily stocky. More generally, my self-deception may prevent me from offering assistance by hindering me from seeing a problem or from seeing it as solvable; or I may (as in the case in which I don't face up to the fact that my son is retarded) be cruel because I insist on seeing something as it isn't. I may deceive myself in such a way that I conceal from myself the damage that I am doing to someone. In other cases my self-deceit may lead into self-delusion someone who allows my opinions to shape his, and his self-delusion may blind him to a problem that he might otherwise redress.

Not that self-deception always does damage. As with deception, self-deception that harms in one set of circumstances may actually help in another. Perhaps I keep myself from being cruel to certain relatives by refusing to see the situation as it is. Knowing my penchant for righteous indignation and for expressing it caustically, thus exacerbating hostilities, I keep my gaze distracted and unfocused, or I put on my rose-hued glasses. My self-deception helps me to treat others more generously. Such a strategy wouldn't be necessary if I were a better person; but under the circumstances, it does enable me to be kinder.

3.2 Given these similarities, one might hope that we can explain what is wrong with self-deception by superimposing whatever we take to be the best account of what is wrong with deception onto self-deception, revising it slightly to improve the fit. But if we press for further details of the similarities, differences emerge which suggest that the wrongness of self-deception is quite different from that of deception. First, while disregard for the truth is part of both deception and self-deception, it is more central to the wrongness of self-deception than to deception—partly because there is much *more* wrong with deception.[15] Deception of another is wrong in roughly the way that (and for the reasons that) manipulation of another is wrong. The fact that deception, unlike manipulation, always involves leading another to believe something false (or to see things in an inaccurate way) adds only slightly to the wrongness.

Second (but closely related), there are deep differences in the nature of the harm wrought by deception and that wrought by self-deception (insofar as any is wrought). Deception, if discovered or suspected, leaves the other feeling betrayed, misled: not taken seriously, not regarded as an agent. When we speak of deception, we want immediately to shift from talk of harming to talk of *wronging* others. Not so with self-deception;[16] and there is this much truth to the idea that when self-deception harms others, the harm is less direct than the harm done to others by deception. The central harm in deception is the affront to the other's agency. The other person is treated, in deception, not as an agent but as a subject to be pushed or pulled in the direction one thinks best—all, of course, without letting her see that she is being manipulated. The deceiver arrogates to herself power over another without revealing that she is doing so. No wonder we are more inclined to speak of deception wronging the other than harming the other.

3.3 Self-deception does not harm others in the way that deception does, but this is not where most of us would try to locate an analogy anyway. The more tempting guess is that self-deception wrongs or harms the self in roughly the way that deception wrongs or harms others. Does this analogy hold up?

In one respect, at least, it seems not to. Since deception is a form of manipulation, the deceiver usurps (as far as the effects of the deception reach) a power or role that is rightfully only the agent's: the power to guide, direct, shape one's conduct. The manipulator takes the helm, doing so unbeknownst to the agent (perhaps now better termed the subject). Nothing quite like this happens in self-deception. The agent, in deceiving herself, does not usurp anything or assume a position that is not hers. This is so because it *is her place* to do all the things that it would be wrong for her to do to another adult, i.e., (for our purposes) shape her desires and her goals, steer herself away from this and toward that. It would be manipulative and invasive to do these things to another adult (though not wrong to help another who has chosen to give up smoking, develop in himself an enthusiasm for swimming, etc., in these endeavors).[17]

It is wrong to manipulate others not because "nature" should be left alone, but because it is the agent herself who should choose, to the extent that one can choose in these matters. This suggests that self-deception cannot be seen as wrong because it involves, in some sense, manipulating oneself. There is nothing wrong in trying to develop in myself a distaste for or indifference towards coffee, a deeper interest in politics, and an indifference to tawdry gossip and petty academic disputes.[18] The manipulation involved in self-transformation is not generally objectionable; manipulation of others (even to good ends) is. If there is something wrong with self-deception, it is not its manipulative aspects.[19]

3.4 Or is this so clear? I have suggested that deception is objectionable largely because it is manipulative, and that manipulation, in turn, is wrong because it undermines the other's agency. But don't I undermine my own agency when I deceive myself? With respect to the activities affected by my self-induced false beliefs or pictures, I limit my own agency. I bring it about that I operate with inadequate information (i.e., less adequate than it would have been had I not deceived myself) or a warped view of the circumstances. If I am deceived by someone else, the same thing happens; only the source is different. So, it would seem, my agency is undermined in self-deception just as it is in deception; and this suggests, contrary to the claims in the previous paragraph, that what is wrong with self-deception *can* be understood by superimposing a model of what is wrong with deception onto self-deception.

One might reply that self-deception only sometimes cripples one's agency. Whether it does depends on the content of the self-deception. It does when I dupe myself into thinking that I cannot change when in fact I can—a very pernicious and tempting form of self-deception. (E.g., I save myself the trouble of self-restraint and reform by telling myself that I'm hopelessly critical of others, but that that is just the way I am; there's nothing I can do about it and those who don't like it will just have to part company with me or put up with it.) But it doesn't, one might argue, in the case of Emma, who deceives herself about why it is that her favorite daughter never visits her in the hospital. Nor does it in the case of an academic who, knowing that he will be unable to write if he thinks that his tenure chances are fair but not good, deceives himself into believing that they are good.

This is, I think, partly right but not the whole answer. The main difference is as follows. Self-deception undermines one's agency gradually, rather than in individual instances, while deception undermines the other's agency episodically and generally noncumulatively.[20] Indeed this difference might be thought of as a symptom of deeper differences: the nature of the erosion of agency is different enough that one might object to using the same expression, "undermines our agency," for both phenomena. After all, deception undermines agency much as manipulation does: the deceiver/manipulator is deliberately controlling some of the subject's beliefs, attitudes, and decisions, while keeping the subject from recognizing that he is doing so. Self-deception does not involve this sort of duplicity. How it does erode one's agency will emerge as we see how it is that it erodes it gradually, while deception does not.

That deception undermines the other's agency in every instance of deception is, I hope, clear. That self-deception does not is evident when we consider cases in which it seems unobjectionable, as in the cases of the AIDS victim and the relative of one of the thousands of *desaparecidos* of Guatemala and El Salvador. Someone might argue that in these cases the self-deception is not entirely unobjectionable. We need not consider arguments for this position now, however,[21] for even if one believes that in the examples above self-deception is somewhat objectionable, there is, I think, no temptation at all to say that it somehow undermines one's agency. And what is at issue now is whether self-deception undermines agency as deception does.

3.5 When self-deception does undermine one's agency, it does so gradually. This happens in two ways. First, self-deception can become a habit, a strategy one falls back on too often. Second, self-deception often requires, for its efficacy, further self-deception. The need to see things a certain way, despite the evidence, becomes increasingly demanding, leading one to gaze, and to focus and interpret what one sees, in a way that supports the shaky view that one has duped oneself into taking. Self-deception is fecund. We deceive ourselves more and more lest the earlier self-deception emerge in its true colors.

In so doing we undermine our agency. The more we dupe ourselves, the less we are able to assess evidence fairly, to be open to alternative ways of seeing things, to understand ourselves, and to be in control (insofar as this is possible) of how we live our lives. The more we dupe ourselves, the less we are able to be responsible agents.[22]

Generally, I want to claim, insofar as self-deception is wrong, it is wrong because it corrupts our belief-forming processes. The effect is gradual. We allow our wishes that things be a certain way to play an increasingly dominant role in shaping how we see the world. Consider an example: someone whose financial affairs, friendships, and relationships with colleagues and family are regularly in disarray, who can't quit smoking and whose health is poor. He sees contemporaries living fairly tranquil, orderly lives. Why, he wonders, are their lives so trouble-free in comparison with mine? He might try to convince himself that their lives are really a mess, too. Or he may tell himself that they are shallow, their lives hollow; that he is deeper, more sensitive. If these explanations don't occur to him, he might take another route. Unwilling to consider the possibility that something about *him* might explain his perpetual crises, he blames them on his ex-wife or on the former marriage (though not on his contribution to its demise, for *it,* not something about him, was the problem). If he has to face the realization that he lurched from crisis to crisis long before his marriage, the self-deception fails and he needs a different explanation—his allergies. (It's him, but not his character.) They have made him irritable, unable to function well at work, and too unhappy to get his finances in order. Such a strange explanation won't seem plausible (even to him) unless buttressed. So he switches doctors until he finds one who thinks that his depression and ill health can be attributed to allergies (not allergies for which there are medical tests, of course; he has to test them himself by experimenting with his diet). He recommends to acquaintances that they see whether *they* have allergies. He clips articles from magazines linking depression with chemical imbalance. Of course he is never sure what his allergies are—if he were, he could just avoid the offending foods. (His allergies will not just be environmental; otherwise he would have no excuse except in season.) His beliefs about what allergies he has change to fill the explanatory gaps, and ultimately to sustain his picture of himself as a victim (of allergies).

Not that self-deception is always so fecund. Self-deception about matters of relatively momentary importance (or more precisely, instances in which the motivation for self-deception is short-lived), usually matters that have little to do with one's self-image and sense of self-worth, tend not to breed further self-deception. Sweltering in my disorganized vegetable garden, I have almost finished planting a row of leeks when I notice delicate sprouts in the clumps of dirt I have pushed aside. It couldn't be that I already planted this row and now, a week later, have inadvertently dug it up. Could it? No, I decide; the row I planted wasn't here, but there, to the left; these are weeds—or, if not that, I just spilled a few of the seeds when I planted last week.

This is a very different type of self-deception, self-deception motivated by my not being able *at that moment* (hot and exhausted as I am) to face the possibility that my work has been counterproductive or at least less than worthwhile. It doesn't matter at that moment, since it's too late to remedy the situation; so there is no need, really, to assess the evidence open-mindedly. Because I *can* do so later, the self-deception will not spread: it will not seek support since the motivation for it has disappeared. (It would be a different matter if being well-organized and an excellent gardener was critical to my self-esteem.)

When the motivation for the self-deception does not disappear, it frequently gains momentum. As with most "projects," from writing a paper, to quashing a popular insurgent movement in Latin America, to deceiving oneself into believing *p,* the more one invests in it, the less willing one is to abandon the project. The more one structures one's beliefs and attitudes so as to avoid believing or even seriously considering *p,* the less ready one will be to quit. But not to quit usually entails further evasion, ignoring, reinterpretation of what would otherwise be counterevidence. This is one way in which self-deception spreads. It also spreads simply by becoming a familiar and useful strategy and by eroding tendencies to open-minded reflection and to self-scrutiny. One who eschews self-criticism by telling himself that his problems are due to allergies thereby improves the climate for other self-deception, including collective self-deception, where members of a society, e.g., Nazi Germany or Reaganite U.S., deceive themselves together about a matter of common concern. Someone whose resistance to self-deception has worn down is more likely to accept convenient, self-serving jingles, rather than explore troubling complexities. Rather than risk learning something discomfiting, he adheres to a simple, unperturbing picture of things, one which preserves the images of self, country, and the world that he holds dear. Practiced at maintaining or restoring his good opinion of himself by finding a handy explanation of what would otherwise be termed his "failings," he may join in on jingoistic recitations (e.g., "The problem of poverty among Blacks in America is due to the prevalence of matriarchy in Black families"), in order to save (collective) face.[23]

3.6 My claim thus far has been that self-deception erodes agency gradually, in a way quite different from that in which deception undermines the other's agency. This is, I think, what is primarily wrong with self-deception. But there are instances in which self-deception is wrong for other (or additional) reasons. These are cases in which self-deception serves to shield the agent from the recognition of something that he really should (morally) attend to. What is shielded may be something about his own behavior, where he is doing serious harm to another yet protecting himself from seeing this. It need not be, however; it may be the conduct of another that he avoids facing up to. Even if it is not his own conduct, and even if he is not at all to blame, it may be the case that he has some responsibility to try to rectify the problem or at least alleviate the pain. (Recall, as an instance of the second type, the woman whose husband raped her daughter: in cutting off her daughter as she tries to tell her mother what happened, in refusing to hear that it happened, she withholds desperately needed comfort and reassurance.)

In both cases self-deception is a way of shirking a responsibility, and a fairly grave one. The responsibility, in these cases, is to others. But it could be otherwise. We can imagine instances in which what is cloaked by the self-deception is, in addition to being a problem *in* the agent's character and conduct, a problem primarily *to* the agent. A drug addiction; a dangerous tendency to fall in love with overbearing, dominant, and abusive people; a fear of success (really a fear of rejection if "too" successful) which leads her to quit or fail: these are all problems that the agent *ought* to recognize. If she deceives herself about them we want to say that what she does is wrong (which is of course not to say that she is blameworthy). She wrongs herself. In these cases, as in the earlier ones, self-deception is wrong because it involves a failure to face up to a serious problem, one which the agent has some hope of redressing and a responsibility to try to ameliorate.[24]

In light of the examples just presented (and the fact that there are so many others of their ilk), perhaps we should call into question my claim that the wrongness of self-deception is largely a matter of the gradual effect that self-deceptive attitudes and conduct have on one's character. I have suggested that while acts of deception (severally) are as such wrong (although sometimes justifiable), acts of self-deception are not wrong *as such,* but either as a special sort of self-deception (e.g., self-deception designed to shield the agent from an important responsibility) or collectively, as constituting a way of conducting oneself which slowly corrodes one's belief-forming processes. But perhaps there is no such difference. In the example of the woman whose husband raped her daughter, self-deception is objectionable, quite apart from its long-term, corrosive effects, because it amounts to an *evasion of something that one has no right to evade.* This suggests a strong parallel between the wrongness of deception and that of self-deception: whereas deception *always* involves concealing where there is no right (on the face of it) to conceal, self-deception *often* does. If this is right, then, it seems, deception and self-deception may be wrong in roughly the same way. There is a strong moral presumption against both, though stronger against deception. More is needed to justify deception than to justify self-deception, but both stand firmly in need of justification.

This is, I believe, the most plausible route to take in defense of the claim that the wrongness of self-deception and that of deception are analogous. But it fails, for it does not take into account something not yet discussed here: self-deception is, for most of us, virtually indispensable. And this is the case not merely because there are episodes in most lives in which we cannot bear to face the truth; it has more to do with the opacity of self-knowledge. This needs elaboration.

THE INDISPENSABILITY OF SELF-DECEPTION

4.1 Consider Lucy Honeychurch, from E. M. Forster's *A Room with a View*. She deceives herself about whether she loves Cecil, her fiancé; why (after breaking off the engagement) she wants to travel; and what her feelings are toward George, who, she knows, is in love with her.

> Lucy had hoped to return to Windy Corner when she escaped from Cecil, but she discovered that her home existed no longer. It might exist for Freddy, who still lived and thought straight, but not for one who had deliberately warped the brain. She did not acknowledge that her brain was warped, for the brain itself must assist in that acknowledgment, and she was disordering the very instrument of life. She only felt, "I do not love George; I broke off my engagement because I did not love George [Cecil?]; I must go to Greece because I do not love George; it is more important that I should look up gods in the dictionary than that I should help my mother; every one else is behaving very badly." She only felt irritable and anxious to do what she was not expected to do.[25]

By deceiving herself, or creating "muddles" (as her future father-in-law put it) to obfuscate what she does not want to own up to, Lucy causes sadness and bewilderment to herself and those close to her. So, isn't it correct to say that she acted wrongly in deceiving herself? Perhaps also that she wronged herself? (And maybe even that she did so by undermining her own agency? Although she does not corrode her belief-forming processes, she keeps herself from being able to make sensible decisions.)

The problem in taking this stand is that it supposes that it is reasonable to expect ourselves always to avoid such obfuscation of self-knowledge. It supposes that we can get it right the first time, rather than stumble along confusedly, as Lucy does, settling on *some* plan of action and *some* picture or other of what is going on, in an attempt to end the painful confusion and unease and get on with life. In fact, it is not that easy to figure out what we are about; discovering it may at times have to arise *through* self-deception, i.e., through the tension and instability of the state of self-deception.[26]

Furthermore, it is not entirely clear what it would mean to have figured out what one is about. Sometimes it is mercifully clear: Lucy sees that she really does love George. But when it is clear, the vision is typically limited. There is no sign that Lucy understands *why* she thought she didn't love George, why earlier she thought that she loved Cecil, and so on. (Nor does the reader have a "God's eye" view.)

Think of it this way: an honest (not self-deceptive) attempt to understand a complicated series of events, or a stage in one's life, or a relationship between oneself and another, will frequently have to result in choosing from various plausible interpretations. Lots of different stories can be told to explain what happened or is happening. While some accounts are clearly silly, and others only moderately plausible, there will often be, indeed will usually be, more than one plausible interpretation, and no way of adjudicating between them on the basis of their adequacy as explanations. We interpret what we see and experience, trying to make it make sense, and since there are many ways of interpreting it and usually no right way (though certainly many wrong ways), we sometimes adopt the interpretation that is the one we can best live with. In other words, we allow our desire to believe *p,* or to see things in a certain way, to shape our beliefs or the way we see things.

In self-deception, we take things further: we allow our desire to believe *p* to shape our beliefs *too* much, to the exclusion of evidence that *p* is false. So while the generally preferable way of interpreting experience rules out some possible interpretations on the grounds that they are clearly inconsistent with reality, yet allows us to pick an interpretation (among those that are not clearly ruled out by such considerations) partly on the basis of what we want to believe, self-deception allows us more interpretations from which to choose.

Self-deception is a sort of extension of something that we all do, and couldn't but do (or one might say, an "abuse"—sometimes a real abuse—of a privilege that we couldn't but have): we pick a story, though not *just* any story, to make sense out of our lives.[27] (One book on how to recover after a divorce recommends telling oneself a story, almost any story, about why it was that the marriage failed.[28] Too much attention to truth, the suggestion seems to be, would leave one dangerously agnostic; and to get on with life one has to settle on some picture of what happened.) Although it would be an exaggeration to say that we couldn't possibly get on without self-deception, it wouldn't be much of an exaggeration. Often it is just too difficult to see which are the plausible interpretations, or one may not see any plausible explanations and just have to settle on something. Or again, as appears to be Lucy Honeychurch's situation, there may be a decidedly "best" explanation, but it may be very difficult to come to see it as best until one has "created muddles" and wallowed in them for awhile.[29]

In his sermon on self-deception Butler writes: "Though a man hath the best eyes in the world, he cannot see any way but that which he turns them."[30] This appears in a section whose heading reads, "They inquire only to justify." While Butler is right to deplore the tendency to selective seeing ("Thus these persons, without passing over the least, the most minute thing, which can possibly be urged in favour of themselves, shall overlook entirely the plainest and most obvious things on the other side"), it must also be borne in mind that we can't look everywhere at once. Some turning away and most uses of blinders are objectionable, but one can't very well turn one's eyes so as to take in and attend to everything. (If it can be done at all, it is possible only at the cost of holding life at arm's length.) To make sense out of what we see, we must focus, and must interpret; and it is difficult to prevent wishful thinking or fear from affecting what we attend to and how we interpret it.

While it is not implausible to think that we could not get on without self-deception, the claim that we could not get on without deceiving each other *is* implausible. It is not difficult to imagine a world in which there was no deception; it is extremely difficult to imagine a world (with humans, and not just creatures like humans, only very shallow) with no self-deception. Similarly, it is hard to imagine how someone could set out to avoid self-deception, yet it is not hard to imagine how someone might set out to avoid deceiving (not to be confused with accidentally misleading) others.[31] The project might well be a difficult one to execute, but it is not hard to spell out how one could go about it, and partial success, anyway, would be a reasonable expectation.[32]

4.2 None of this is to say that self-deception is innocuous. To say that it would be difficult to live without ever deceiving oneself, and a peculiar project to aim to do so, is not to say that we should not worry at all about self-deception. While we need to focus, and often need to fasten onto some story despite problems of underdetermination, we needn't be rigid. We needn't refuse to call our picture or beliefs into question; indeed we should be open to doing so. In this way we will probably not avoid self-deception, but we will reduce its grip on us and, in particular, weaken its rippling effect.

While not unobjectionable, self-deception is wrong for different reasons, and in different ways, than is deception. What is wrong with self-deception is not that it deceives but that too much self-deception, or more typically, self-deception that one struggles desperately to maintain, corrodes one's belief-forming processes and often one's sense of responsibility for self.[33] This does not make every case of self-deception objectionable in itself. Some cases are, though usually not because they are instances of self-deception but because of that for which the self-deception occurs, namely, avoidance of responsibility. Generally, self-deception is objectionable because of what the agent who engages it in too routinely embraces—and gives up.

Self-deception's greatest evils do not lie in deceiving oneself in the first place, but in refusing to call into question one's beliefs (or "stories"), and in struggling to maintain those beliefs; or in refusing to engage in self-scrutiny, a refusal often conjoined with a tendency not to notice that what one does or how one lives has profound and far-reaching effects on others.[34]

What is objectionable is not so much the self-*deception* as the failure to strive to know oneself and what one is a part of, and to subject one's activities, and mode of living, to scrutiny. At the heart of the problem is the refusal to take seriously the fact that one is an agent and to take responsibility for oneself as an agent; and insofar as self-deception is wrong, usually through its rippling effects, it is this that makes it wrong. The wrongness of self-deception turns out to be closer to the wrongness of refusing to think than the wrongness of deceiving others.[35]

NOTES

1. An exception is Mike W. Martin's *Self-Deception and Morality* (Lawrence, Kans.: University Press of Kansas, 1986). Unfortunately, his book was not yet available at the time of writing.

2. By 'deception' I mean the deception of others. I say 'deception' rather than 'other-deception' because I think it is misleading to suggest that self-deception and deception of others are both instances of something broader, i.e., deception.

3. In her section on self-deception in *Secrets* (New York: Random House, 1983), Sissela Bok rightly points out the risks of misusing the concept of self-deception. "To attribute self-deception to people is to regard them as less than rational concerning the danger one takes them to be in, and makes intervention, by contrast, seem more legitimate" (p. 65). (See also her "The Self Deceived," *Social Science Information* 19 [Summer 1980]:905–22, on which her discussion in *Secrets* is based.) While the warning is appropriate, this is not an issue that bears on the question of what is wrong with self-deception. I might add that the issue is also separate from that of whether there is such a thing as self-deception and what, precisely, the familiar phenomenon is. Bok claims that there is no such thing as self-deception, but her main argument concerns the misuse of the notion of self-deception. David Kipp ("On Self-Deception," *Philosophical Quarterly* 30 (1980):305–317) arrives at the same conclusion by a route that, although different, seems also to conflate the conditions under which *we attribute* self-deception to others with the conditions under which *there is* self-deception. He thus arrives at the conclusion that what appears to be self-deception is really an attempt to deceive others about oneself, and to do so out of a concern to save face (more exactly, "spare oneself the indignity of existential defeat" [p. 317]).

4. I do not take this second caveat to be a critical one, and include it only to warn anyone who does think of self-deception as a state (and who accepts the distinction) that I am not asking 'What is wrong with the state of being deceived, where the deception was brought on by oneself?'. In his contribution to this volume (chap. 4, "Self-Deception, Rationalization, and Reasons for Acting"), Robert Audi asks: "Is [self-deception] wholly behavioral, a matter of one's actions? Is it, by contrast, a state? . . . [I]f, like most writers on the subject, one thinks there are both acts and states of self-deception, it matters greatly which of these one takes as fundamental."

Audi "takes the state of self-deception as primary and interprets acts of self-deception as deriving their character from their relation to the state." I think it somewhat misleading to speak of states of self-deception, perhaps because self-deception, unlike being deceived by others, is so very unstable. One must constantly feed one's self-deception; if it is to be called a state, it is at least very different from other cognitive states.

Cf. David Wood, "Honesty," in *Philosophy and Personal Relations,* ed. Alan Montefiore (London: Routledge and Kegan Paul, 1973), pp. 191–223, especially pp. 214ff.

5. I should note that I mean this to cover not only the usual cases but also those in which the attempts are either (a) abortive, or (b) exceptionally successful, resulting not in a state of self-deception (characterized by tension in one's beliefs) but in a state of *firm* belief in whatever it is that one desired to believe and induced oneself to believe. Both in (b) and in the ordinary cases, I don't think it much matters whether or not the self-induced belief is true or false, although of course when we speak of self-deception we usually have in mind those cases in which the belief one tries so hard to hold is false.

6. See also note 5.

7. Audi would deny that the process I spoke of in the previous paragraph counts as self-deception. He distinguishes "being deceiving toward oneself" from self-deception, the former being "behavior by which one gets into self-deception" though "it does not entail self-deception" (chap. 4 in this volume).

8. One related phenomenon that I would distinguish from self-deception is wishful thinking, understood not simply as excessive optimism (or a hope *cum* expectation that *p* will turn out to be the case), but as involving a belief that *p,* where one has very little evidence for *p* and believes it largely just because one wants it to be true. Unlike self-deception, wishful thinking need not involve tension between what one thinks, suspects, or fears, given the evidence, and what one believes wishfully; the first element need not be present. But although I would distinguish wishful thinking from self-deception, much of what I have to say in this essay concerning self-deception applies to wishful thinking. This is due to the fact that I focus on the process of inducing and maintaining self-deception, and this process overlaps with (more accurately, subsumes) that of wishful thinking. Thanks go to Brian McLaughlin for asking me to clarify this matter.

9. For an account of self-deception that has it that in self-deception one believes *p* and believes not-*p,* see Amélie Rorty, "Belief and Self-Deception," *Inquiry* 15:387–410. Rorty qualifies her account: the conditions she enumerates apply *generally*; the account does not enumerate the necessary and sufficient conditions. In a footnote she asserts that "no single list of necessary and sufficient conditions for the existence of self-deception can be formulated" (p. 408).

10. The account cited, according to which self-deception involves belief that *p* and sincere avowal (or disposition thereto) of not-*p,* is Audi's.

11. "Upon Self-Deceit," Sermon X in *The Works of Joseph Butler,* ed. W. E. Gladstone (Oxford: Clarendon Press; New York: Macmillan, 1896), 2:178.

12. Whether or not one finds these and other cases unobjectionable depends in part on one's attitude towards resignation. To those who think it important to resign oneself

and who perhaps also see a readiness to resign oneself to be a virtue, the behavior described may not seem entirely unobjectionable.

13. M. R. Haight, *A Study of Self-Deception* (Brighton: Harvester Press; Atlantic Highlands, N.J.: Humanities Press, 1980), pp. 83–84.

14. Cf. Robert Solomon, who writes that "if [Freud] gives up responsibility too easily, [Sartre] seems to deny us the possibility of sympathy and compassion" (*The Passions* [Garden City, N.Y.: Anchor Press/Doubleday, 1976], p. 401). Solomon objects to the supposition that we are always responsible for self-deception, but does not claim that self-deception is sometimes perfectly permissible, and seems instead to see self-deception as something one would not do if only one were strong enough. He writes that

> self-deception may be so central to our self-esteem . . . that . . . we "cannot" bring ourselves to face the truth. But this "cannot" is not a mechanistic *cannot,* an infliction or a disease. It is rather the sort of *cannot* that refers to the extreme *costliness* of that recognition and the *gravity* of the *investment* we have placed in our self-images. In other words, it is not really a 'cannot' at all, but another *will not.* But it is a *will not* that deserves compassion and sympathy, for it is a refusal whose overcoming can be achieved only with great courage and considerable suffering. (*The Passions,* p. 402)

15. It is, however, difficult to be sure; for one reason why deception looks to be worse than self-deception is that an agent who deceives another is more often culpable and blameworthy than is an agent who deceives herself.

16. In some cases, we do: the parent who protects himself from recognizing that his child is emotionally disturbed and in need of professional help does seem to be wronging, not merely harming, the child. This is due to the special responsibility that parents have to help their children develop into flourishing adults. In contrast, I do not (unless I am a guru of some sort, or a political leader possessed of enormous power to sway others) have a responsibility to see to it that I do not lead another adult astray through my self-delusions.

17. The case may be otherwise if the adult is in some relevant way handicapped, e.g., has had a nervous breakdown and is quite listless. Here prodding, even if manipulative, may well be in order.

18. I am not here claiming that one cannot wrong oneself, but only that manipulating oneself is not wrong.

19. Brian McLaughlin has suggested in correspondence that there is one type of self-deception whose moral aspects seem to resemble those of deception: deception of one's future self. He asks us to imagine the following sort of example. Relying on my bad memory, I tape my dishonest answers to certain questions with the aim of creating a sort of revisionist personal history. Years later I listen to the tape and am duped. I have deceived myself. Is this case of self-deception morally on a par with deception of others? I am not sure what to say about such a case; part of the problem is that it is difficult to imagine how someone could forget that his goal in making the tape was to deceive himself. The example, it seems to me, requires us to see people as more divisible in the relevant sense—and thus more subject to self-deception of a sort that strongly resembles deception—than we in fact are.

But there *are* ways of bringing it about that in the future one will hold beliefs that one now takes to be false. In "Deciding to Believe without Self-Deception," a paper presented to the 1986 Western Division meetings of the American Philosophical Association, J. Thomas Cook describes Nick, an ambitious biology major at a fundamentalist college who, recognizing that professional success is unlikely unless he accepts evolutionary theory, decides to induce in himself the relevant beliefs by placing himself in an environment conducive to such a conversion. Admitted to Harvard's graduate program in biology, Nick indeed does undergo the desired change. Now, Cook argues that Nick's self-induced (genuine) conversion does not involve deceiving himself, but let's suppose that it does. (If it makes the case more plausibly one of self-deception, suppose that Jerry Falwell is the U.S. president and Nick decides that he had better accept creationism if he wants to have a career as a biologist; although admittedly, and importantly, success in this program of belief-acquisition is very hard to envision.) If this is self-deception, is it objectionable in the way that deception is? I think that the answer is "No; and certainly not as objectionable as deception." The reason has once again to do with the inappropriateness of taking it upon oneself to alter someone else's fundamental beliefs, approach to life, or even habits; and by contrast, the permissibility (whether or not success is likely) of attempting the same vis-à-vis oneself.

20. Related to this is a difference between the motive directly associated with deception and that associated with self-deception: while I deceive another because I want her to believe p, generally I deceive myself not because I want myself to believe p, but because I want p to be true. The examples in note 19 above, if they are examples of self-deception, are exceptions to this general rule.

21. See sections 3.6 and 4.1 for a discussion of one such argument.

22. Cf. Gary Watson's introduction to his *Free Will* (Oxford: Oxford Univ. Press, 1982): "To be free is to have the capacity to effect, by unimpaired practical thought, the determinants of one's actions" (p. 8).

23. See Angela Davis's discussion of the Moynihan report, in *Women, Race and Class* (New York: Random House, 1981).

24. Redressing needn't mean solving or eradicating; that may be impossible, but its being so is not a good reason for ignoring the problem. Comforting is one way of redressing a problem; even just recognizing it, as for instance in the case of self-destructive tendencies, is an important step.

25. E. M. Forster, *A Room with a View* (New York: Random House, 1961), p. 226.

26. In saying this I am taking issue with Butler, who optimistically asserts in the sermon on self-deceit, "if it were not for that partial and fond regard to ourselves, it would certainly be no great difficulty to know our own character, what passes within, the bent and bias of our mind; much less would there be any difficulty in judging rightly of our own actions" ("Upon Self-Deceit," p. 170).

27. My thoughts owe something to Rorty's "Belief and Self-Deception" (cited in note 9) and "Self-Deception, Akrasia and Irrationality," *Social Science Information* 19:905–922. The former, in particular, brings out other respects in which self-deception is an extension of something unavoidable: motivated adherence to beliefs for which the evidence is highly debatable. See, for example, p. 390 of the former article:

A scientist may have at hand considerable evidence that goes against a half-tested, half-formulated theory. This evidence is carefully noted, but it is standard practice to leave it on the periphery of attention, unassimilated and ignored, on the grounds that until the theory is further developed, such 'evidence' cannot be interpreted or evaluated. Even after a theory is solidly formulated and widely accepted, there will generally be, on its fringes, a set of unassimilated counter-examples that are not allowed to damage it, on the expectation that a ramification of the theory will eventually account for them.

28. Morton Hunt and Bernice Hunt, *The Divorce Experience* (New York: McGraw Hill, 1977), pp. 58–59.

29. Yet a further complication: the reality to be interpreted may itself be dynamic, so that the agent's task will be not just to explain but to determine reality. Thus Forster writes: "So it was that after the gropings and the misgivings of the afternoon they pulled themselves together and settled down to a very pleasant tea-party. If they were hypocrites they did not know it, and their hypocrisy had every chance of setting and becoming true" (*A Room with a View*, p. 109).

30. Butler, "Upon Self-Deceit," p. 172.

31. I am grateful to Amélie Rorty for pointing out in correspondence the difficulty and peculiarity of a policy of avoiding self-deception.

32. Attempts to avoid self-deception involve perils that do not, I think, afflict attempts to avoid deceiving others. Deborah Lipstadt's fascinating *Beyond Belief* provides an instructive example of how attempts to avoid being duped (or engaging in collective self-deception) can backfire. Wary of being taken in as they and others had been by World War I propaganda, American journalists in the 1930s doubted the evidence of mass killings in the Third Reich.

Reports of the Germans' use of poison gas, the brutal killings of babies, and mutilations of defenseless women in Belgium all turned out to be products of the imagination. But these stories left their legacy. During World War II, even when reporters possessed proof of mass killings they doubted they had occurred because the stories seemed too similar to the false reports of the previous war. (*Beyond Belief* [New York: Free Press, 1985], p. 9)

33. I am borrowing this phrase from Charles Taylor, "Responsibility for Self," in *The Identities of Persons,* ed. Amélie Rorty (Berkeley, Los Angeles, London: Univ. of California Press, 1976).

34. Albert Speer, as he portrays himself in *Inside the Third Reich,* comes to mind in this connection: he saw himself *as an architect,* and by so viewing himself, managed to avoid taking cognizance of his contribution to the Holocaust. It is noteworthy that he feels intense remorse about his strategies of avoidance:

One day, some time in the summer of 1944, my friend Karl Hanke . . . came to see me. . . . This time . . . he seemed confused and spoke falteringly, with many breaks. He advised me never to accept an invitation to inspect a concentration camp in Upper Silesia. Never, under any circumstances. He had seen something there which he was not permitted to describe and moreover could not describe.

I did not query him, I did not query Himmler, I did not query Hitler, I did not speak with personal friends. I did not investigate—for I did not want to know what was happening there. Hanke must have been speaking of Auschwitz. . . . [F]rom that moment on, I was inescapably contaminated morally; from fear of discovering something which might have made me turn from my course, I had closed my eyes. This deliberate blindness outweighs whatever good I may have done or tried to do in the last period of the war. Those activities shrink to nothing in the face of it. Because I failed at that time, I still feel, to this day, responsible for Auschwitz in a wholly personal sense. (*Inside the Third Reich,* trans. Clara Winston and Richard Winston [New York: Macmillan, 1970], pp. 375–376)

35. I am indebted to Brian McLaughlin for his exceptionally helpful comments.

21

SELF-DECEPTION AND RESPONSIBILITY FOR THE SELF

Stephen L. White

Despite the impressive evidence of its existence, self-deception has seemed to resist coherent description. Self-deception appears to be mysterious, if not plainly paradoxical. I shall argue that this appearance is misleading. What are ostensibly puzzles about self-deception are in fact puzzles about the justification of ascriptions of responsibility.

The issues I shall raise, therefore, are not the ones ordinarily associated with self-deception. I shall argue briefly that a theory of self-deception, if it is to avoid paradox, must recognize a division of the self into interacting subsystems. And this means subsystems with their own beliefs, goals, plans, and strategies; that is to say, homunculi. But although I shall argue that a theory of self-deception must be a homuncular theory, I shall not elaborate or defend any particular version of such a theory. Homuncular theories are well understood in outline, however many difficulties their details may involve.

What makes self-deception seem paradoxical is not our inability to make sense of a divided self, but the fact that the homuncular solution is apparently unavailable. We make a distinction, where responsibility is concerned, between the person who is self-deceived and the person who is deceived by another. Given a homuncular model of the self, however, the psychology of the former does not seem relevantly different from the psychology of the latter. Thus a theory of self-deception must either provide an alternative to the homuncular model or provide an account of responsibility which makes this feature of the model intelligible.

The first and last sections, in which I discuss self-deception and the homuncular model, then, form a prologue and epilogue to the rest of the paper. The remaining sections make up the account of responsibility that I claim an adequate theory of self-deception requires. A theory of self-deception, to succeed, must make intelligible the ascription of responsibility to those who deceive themselves—despite their psychological similarities to those who are deceived by others. And it is a fundamental misconception about the constraints governing our ascriptions of responsibility, I shall argue, that has made this ascription, and hence the psychology of self-deception, seem problematic.

From Explanation to Evaluation

1. Let us understand by (full-blown) self-deception one's intentionally making oneself believe what one believes at the same time to be false or one's preventing oneself from believing what one continues to believe to be true.[1] Although it is sometimes denied that self-deception is appropriately understood on the model of other-deception,[2] these denials have never carried conviction. We say, for example, that we lie to ourselves, that we persuade ourselves of what we believe is false, or that we make it appear to ourselves that what we know is not the case. It is just this insistence on describing self-deception in terms whose intelligibility seems to presuppose the existence of distinct subjects that stands in need of explanation.

Cases that fall short of full-blown self-deception because they do not involve intentionally making oneself believe what one continues to believe is false (or preventing oneself from believing what one persists in believing is true) include the following. Suppose one believed, either truly or falsely, that one was guilty of an unforgivable offense and was tortured by the belief. One could have the belief removed by resorting to hypnosis, drugs, or brainwashing. One could instill new beliefs in similar ways. Assume that none of these methods would leave any memory of the removal of the old belief or the addition of the new ones.

None of these cases raises any of the puzzles we associate with self-deception. Nor do they exhibit any of the advantages that a self-deceptive strategy can confer. Assume the goal of self-deception is to induce or suppress a particular belief *and* to maintain the resulting state once it is acquired. Then a strategy in which the belief in the falsity of the induced belief (or in the truth of the suppressed belief) is lost has obvious drawbacks. Such a strategy is essentially a one-shot affair. As such it would leave one vulnerable to all the possible future evidence that would reintroduce the suppressed belief or destroy the belief one had intentionally induced. One-shot self-deception might be a reasonable strategy if one regarded one's actual state of belief as irrational—that is, if one were not genuinely committed to the truth of the belief to be suppressed or to the falsity of the belief to be induced. In such a case the strategy might provide the basis for useful therapy. One-shot self-deception, however, is not an optimal strategy for dealing with beliefs to which one's commitment is genuine. And it is not one that reveals the apparently paradoxical features of full-blown self-deception.

The limitations of the one-shot strategy may give the impression that the puzzle about self-deception lies in the coexistence of inconsistent beliefs.

Such an impression would be incorrect. Inconsistent beliefs do not in themselves raise interesting philosophical problems as long as they are ordinarily manifest in different contexts or if for some other reason the inconsistency does not become apparent. Nor would the one-shot strategy of inducing a later belief that one now believes is false be improved merely by retaining the belief that the belief induced is false. This would simply render the induced belief doubly vulnerable. Let us call the belief that the induced belief is false the *original belief*. In this case not only would the induced belief be vulnerable to extinction in the light of future evidence, but it would be equally vulnerable in a confrontation with the original belief.

Retaining the original belief confers a strategic advantage only if that belief allows one to insulate the induced belief from the external evidence that might disconfirm it and if the induced belief can be insulated from the original belief as well as from the role played by the original belief in insulating it from the disconfirming evidence. If this can be accomplished, it represents a significant strategic advance over the one-shot deception. One's induced belief will be far more secure if, on the basis of the original belief, one can prevent oneself from recognizing any evidence that might undermine it—including the evidence provided by one's own activity.

This feature of full-blown self-deception is spelled out clearly by Roy Schafer in his description of Freudian defenses.

> [O]ne does not know that one knows something, wishes something, considers something emotionally, or is doing or has done some other action; one keeps oneself from discovering *what* one does not know, etc., thus deceiving oneself once; and one keeps oneself from discovering *that* and *how* one is deceiving oneself in this way ("unconscious defence"), thus deceiving oneself a second time or in a second respect.[3]

It is this full-blown notion of self-deception that seems unintelligible. How can one, on the basis of one's original belief, manipulate one's ability to recognize the import of the evidence at one's disposal in such a way as to protect one's induced belief? Intentionally manipulating one's own response to the evidence seems to presuppose that one has a clear grip on the import of the evidence and thus that in the same context one both is and is not aware of its significance. It is on the basis of this kind of description that the paradoxical nature of self-deception is alleged.

The description that is paradoxical as applied to one person is, of course, nonparadoxical as applied to two. This fact suggests an approach to the problem of self-deception which is already explicit in the Freudian model. Split the self into two or more interacting subsystems, each with its own beliefs, goals, plans, and strategies. Call any model that postulates more than one such system per subject a *homuncular model*. On the basis of such a model we can describe the process of self-deception without conceptual strain. Subsystems S_1 and S_2 originally both believe that p. S_1 causes S_2 (either directly or indirectly) to lose the belief that p (and possibly to believe its negation), while itself continuing to believe that p. S_1 subsequently monitors S_2's environment for evidence that p and attempts to prevent S_2 from acquiring that evidence. S_1 also tries to prevent S_2's coming by any evidence that would reveal S_1's activity. The use of such homuncular models is by no means restricted to Freudian theory. Homuncular models are the common currency of most recent theorizing in the cognitive sciences.[4]

Natural as the homuncular approach may seem in the contemporary context, it has two drawbacks, one of which appears to be fatal. The less serious of the two is that talk of homunculi, if taken literally, raises potentially embarrassing questions. If, for example, S_1 retains the original belief that p, why is S_1 not tortured by the belief, making the strategy self-defeating? Furthermore, if S_1 is as sophisticated as the homuncular model suggests, are S_1 and S_2 both conscious? And are they both self-conscious? If so, are there two distinct persons in a single body?

Though these questions would deserve extended discussion in any systematic defense of homuncular models, I shall simply assume here what I have argued elsewhere: that talk about a multiplicity of such interacting subsystems does not commit us to a multiplicity of either self-conscious subsystems or distinct persons.[5] I shall also assume that whatever their other problems, homuncular models are sufficiently well understood that we can usefully explore the implications of a homuncular model of self-deception.[6]

Granting these assumptions, however, does nothing to stave off a seemingly conclusive objection. Regardless of whether S_1 is conscious or unconscious, S_2 must be unconscious of S_1's activities, at least as far as the induced or suppressed belief is concerned. If this were not the case, then all the puzzles that the distinction between S_1 and S_2 was intended to solve would reemerge. But given that this is the case, the following problem arises. Since we have made self-deception intelligible by assimilating it to other-deception, we can make no sense of an essential feature of the phenomenon: the fact that we hold a subject responsible for deceiving himself or herself in a way that we do not hold him or her responsible for being deceived by another. On the homuncular model there seems to be no relevant psychological difference between the subject who is deceived by another and a subject who is deceived by one of his or her subsystems of whose operation he or she is completely unconscious. The conscious experiences of the subject deceived by the operations of an unconscious subsystem and of the subject deceived by another, for example, may be exactly the same. Again we seem to have produced a model that ignores an essential aspect of self-deception: in this case the fact that deceiving oneself is something one does and something for which one can be blamed, not something that happens to one and something that entitles one to the sympathy of others.

It is the apparent inadequacy of the homuncular model to explain the pattern in our ascriptions of responsibility, I think, that explains why philosophers have not generally taken this otherwise attractive line concerning self-deception.[7] The argument for the inadequacy of a homuncular explanation, however, depends on the assumption that differences in our ascriptions of responsibility to different subjects can be justified only by reference to relevant differences in the psychologies of the subjects in question. I shall argue that on its most natural interpretation, this seemingly uncontroversial assumption is false.

I argue in section 2 that any theory that attempts to ground the ascription of responsibility in relevant features of a subject's psychology faces a dilemma. On the natural interpretation of what such a grounding involves, any subject who is a candidate for punishment or blame is psychologically either not relevantly different from the psychopath or not relevantly different from the compulsive. In neither case does there seem to be any way in which the subject could acquiesce and be justified in acquiescing in the suffering that being blamed or being punished involves. And without the possibility of such acquiescence, we do not have a practice involving responsibility, blame, and punishment, but one involving the exercise of manipulation, power, and control.

In section 3 I argue that theories that avoid this dilemma by attempting to justify our ascriptions of responsibility in terms of their contribution to social welfare fail. I examine the most sophisticated version of this kind of theory, which is due to P. F. Strawson. I conclude that his references to our characteristic reactive attitudes toward those who have injured others—attitudes such as guilt and remorse if we have caused the injury ourselves and resentment and indignation if it has been caused by another—are not sufficient to justify our practices where responsibility is concerned.

In section 4 I contrast the class of dispositions to which our reactive attitudes belong—nonmaximizing dispositions—with another class that I call self-supporting dispositions. I argue that because they are not self-supporting, nonmaximizing dispositions could not provide the foundations for an institution of social control that resembled our institution of punishment.

By reference to self-supporting dispositions, I develop in section 5 an alternative form of justification of our practices regarding responsibility, punishment, and blame. I call a form of justification which appeals to our self-supporting dispositions an internal justification. The suffering caused by a practice of ascribing responsibility and blame which has an internal justification is necessarily suffering in which we could acquiesce, even when the suffering is our own. Such a practice may have an internal justification *without* satisfying the constraint that differences in the ascription of responsibility must be grounded in relevant psychological differences, as these are ordinarily understood. Thus the major objection to the homuncular model of self-deception will have been removed.

I conclude this section by examining the limits of internal justification. I argue that it is not the case that any conceivable practice concerning responsibility, punishment, and blame would have an internal justification for some possible population of subjects. I do claim, however, that radically different practices could each have an internal justification for appropriately different populations. The view, then, entails a form of relativism where responsibility is concerned.

In section 6 I consider the kind of internal justification to which our own practices regarding responsibility in general and responsibility for self-deception in particular are susceptible. Although I give only a suggestion of what an internal justification of these practices might be like, I argue that unless there is *some* such justification, the suffering these practices entail will not be suffering in which we could acquiesce. I conclude that in such a case, the practices would require either radical revision or rejection.

A DILEMMA FOR INTRINSIC THEORIES

2. The objection to a homuncular model of self-deception depends on two assumptions. The first is that we do in fact treat self-deceivers differently from the victims of other-deception where responsibility is concerned. The second is that differences in the ascription of responsibility to different subjects can be justified only by relevant differences in their psychologies. The first assumption seems hard to avoid. I shall take it for granted in what follows. The second assumption, which I shall argue is false, requires some clarification.

Let us say that the constraint that differences in the ascription of responsibility to two subjects are justified only if there are relevant differences in the subjects' psychologies is the constraint that justification must appeal to *intrinsic properties* of the subjects in question. Call this constraint the *intrinsic property constraint*. This means, first, that the justification of an ascription of responsibility depends only on the subject of the ascription. Facts, for example, about the deterrent value of holding the subject responsible, or about any other social benefit that might accrue, are irrelevant. Second, the psychological facts on which justification depends must be independent of the subject's general values and commitments on the one hand and beliefs about responsibility on the other. This means that whether the ascription of responsibility to a subject in another culture is justified can be settled by reference to the same standards that apply in our own culture. Thus questions about responsibility are questions about which an entire culture may be mistaken.

(The relevance of this second requirement will become clear in section 5.) Finally, let us call any theory that justifies only practices satisfying the intrinsic property constraint an *intrinsic theory*.

There are two ways in which the assumption that the intrinsic property constraint governs ascriptions of responsibility could figure in an objection to a homuncular account of self-deception. It might be held that our actual practices involving responsibility satisfy the intrinsic property constraint and that they are justified. In this case a homuncular model of self-deception would be impossible to reconcile with our practice of holding self-deceivers responsible. On the homuncular model, self-deceivers have the same intrinsic properties as the victims of other-deception. And given that our practices discriminate between them, if the practices are justified, the homuncular model (which together with the intrinsic property constraint entails that they are unjustified) must be wrong. Alternatively, it might be held that although our actual practices are unjustified (either because they fail to satisfy the intrinsic property constraint or for some other reason), there is a true theory of responsibility justifying an alternative set of practices that *do* satisfy the constraint—and these practices involve ascribing responsibility to self-deceivers. Again this would rule out the homuncular model.

My argument that the intrinsic property constraint is false has three stages. I shall argue, first, that there are good reasons to believe that our actual practices where punishment, responsibility, and blame are concerned are not governed by this constraint. This is intended to lend intuitive plausibility to the claim that ascriptions of responsibility which violate the constraint may still be justified. Second, I shall argue that anyone who believes *both* that psychopaths and compulsives are inappropriate candidates for punishment and blame *and* that the intrinsic property constraint is true is faced with a dilemma. *Any* candidate for punishment and blame, I shall argue, is either not relevantly different from the psychopath or is not relevantly different from the compulsive (given the intrinsic property constraint). Finally, I shall argue that not even those who regard the psychopath as an appropriate candidate for punishment and blame are immune to the problems that the intrinsic property constraint raises. Holding that the psychopath is an appropriate candidate raises the question how the suffering that such punishment and blame would entail could be justified. And this is a question, I shall claim, that has no answer. The solution is not to suppose that punishing the psychopath is justified, but to abandon the intrinsic property constraint. In so doing we make it possible to draw a defensible distinction between psychopaths and compulsives on the one hand and genuinely appropriate candidates for punishment and blame on the other.[8]

The best argument for the claim that our practices concerning responsibility do not satisfy the intrinsic property constraint (i.e., for the first stage of the argument that the intrinsic property constraint is false) is provided by our attitudes toward our beliefs, desires, emotions, and character traits. As many philosophers have argued,[9] we seem to be held responsible for such states as unjustified anger or resentment, self-righteousness, lack of feeling or sympathy for others, racist or sexist sentiments, bitterness, jealousy, and cowardice. This is the case even when there is no reason to believe that any of the following are true: (1) such states are under our voluntary control, (2) they are the foreseeable consequences of our voluntary choices in the past, or (3) all that we are really being blamed for are our voluntary or intentional manifestations of these states. Given that these states are outside our voluntary control, there is apparently no psychological difference between such states and the states for which we are not ordinarily held responsible—for example, having caught the flu, being a certain height, or lacking musical talent—which *by itself* justifies the difference in our ascriptions of responsibility. Thus there is apparently no *relevant* psychological difference between the two sets of states.

Moreover, there are other important classes of events that are outside our control but for which we are apparently held responsible. We are blamed for the intentions we form, even though another subject who would have formed the same intention in our circumstances (say to lie rather than face embarrassment) is not blamed because he or she never encountered the same situation. And we may be blamed for the consequences of our actions (say causing a death through a minor act of negligence) even though someone with the same motives and intentions and the same degree of conscientiousness is not blamed because an accident never ensues.[10] Even philosophers who regard departures from the intrinsic property constraint as irrational generally agree that such departures are a common feature of our actual practices regarding responsibility and blame.[11]

These arguments that our actual practices fail to satisfy the intrinsic property constraint are, of course, controversial and by no means conclusive. They do, however, raise significant doubts where its validity is concerned. I shall now go on to provide the second stage of my argument that the intrinsic property constraint is false. This is the argument for the claim that those who accept both the inappropriateness of punishing or blaming psychopaths and compulsives *and* the intrinsic property constraint confront a dilemma.

In order to state the dilemma, I shall need the notion of a certain form of equilibrium with respect to one's noninstrumental or intrinsic desires.[12] Such an equilibrium has analogies with John Rawls' reflective equilibrium and depends on the fact that, like our moral convictions, our noninstrumental desires may either support or fail to support one another.[13] The relation of support among noninstrumental desires is modeled on the relation of support among beliefs to which the proponents of coherentist accounts of epistemic justification appeal. Like that relation, the relation of support is not a logical one. Nor, given that the desires are all noninstrumental, is it a means-end relation. One's desire to bring aesthetic pleasure to others may (given one's beliefs) support and be supported by one's desire to become a musician. One does not desire to become a musician as a *means* to giving pleasure to others or vice versa. Nonetheless, the two desires can be mutually reinforcing. In contrast, the desire to live a life of luxury does not support and is not supported by the desire to pursue a career of honest public service and to live entirely on one's own earnings (given any ordinary set of beliefs). As these examples suggest, support among noninstrumental desires is always relative to a set of background beliefs. I shall follow the lead of those who discuss support in the context of epistemology by treating support among desires, for the most part, as primitive.

Imagine now that we had a pill that would allow us to add and subtract noninstrumental desires at will. Such a pill would enable us to destroy noninstrumental desires that were badly supported relative to our other noninstrumental desires and to add noninstrumental desires that would be well supported. This involves no commitment, of course, to the intelligibility of our revising our set of noninstrumental desires from a point of view that is neutral with regard to all the desires simultaneously. The motivation for adding and subtracting desires must be grounded in the noninstrumental desires that remain fixed. The model here is the familiar one of Neurath's ship: repair is possible only as long as the vessel itself remains afloat.

Given the notion of such a pill, we can define a subject's *ideal reflective equilibrium* (IRE) as the most coherent extension of the subject's noninstrumental or intrinsic desires that that subject could and would produce given access to the pill (and given his or her actual beliefs): that is, the extension that that subject would produce in maximizing the degree of mutual support among his or her noninstrumental desires.[14] In the real world, many of a subject's noninstrumental desires will be out of IRE in the sense that they are unsupported or badly supported by the subject's other noninstrumental desires. Such desires would not survive the existence of the pill in terms of which the IRE is defined. As the case of drug addiction shows, however, there is no connection between the strength of a desire and its degree of support—the desire for a drug may be overwhelming, though almost entirely unsupported by other desires. We can distinguish, then, between the *motivational strength* of a desire for a subject—the tendency of the subject to act to fulfill the desire—and its *evaluational strength*—the tendency of the subject to keep the desire in his or her IRE. In the case of a normal heroin addict, the motivational strength of the desire for heroin will be extremely high and its evaluational strength will be very low. To say that a desire is *out of IRE* for some subject is to say that its evaluational strength would not be enough to make it part of that subject's IRE.

Among the noninstrumental or intrinsic desires of a subject's IRE, there is a special subset I shall call the *conative core*. These are the unconditional desires that have a bearing on decisions the subject might realistically be called upon to make. By an *unconditional desire,* I mean a desire that a state of affairs be realized regardless of whether that desire itself persists. If, for example, one has a noninstrumental desire that one drink tea rather than coffee, one will ordinarily desire that this happen only as long as the desire persists. Hence the desire is conditional. If, however, one desires that one treat others honestly or that one keep one's promises, one would normally desire that these states of affairs be realized whether one continues to desire them or not.[15]

The conative core of one's IRE, then, is the most coherent extension of those unconditional desires on which one might plausibly have to act. And given their relation to action, the pressure for coherence among these desires is even greater than among ordinary noninstrumental desires. Hence the conative core is stable in the following sense. First, (keeping one's beliefs fixed) one could not be motivated to change the desires in one's IRE in general and in one's conative core in particular. Any motivation for change would have been exhausted in the formation of the IRE and its corresponding conative core. Second, any local change in one's conative core, if brought about from outside, would be reversed if one had access to the appropriate pill. (At least this would be true on the plausible assumption that none of one's unconditional desires were unsupported in the way that a bare preference, for example for one flavor over another, might be.) Third, though a sufficiently drastic change in one's conative core would not be reversed (since it would give rise to an alternative equilibrium that would itself be stable), one's motivation would not carry *across* such a change. That is, if one knew now that such a change would occur at time *t* and that it could not be prevented, one would not be motivated to sacrifice the satisfaction of one's present desires for the satisfaction of desires after *t*. If one's desires were unconditional, one would give no weight to the fact that in the future one would no longer have those desires, or would have incompatible desires, or would even have incompatible desires that were unconditional. Suppose, for example, that one were a Nietzschean and that one's most fundamental Nietzschean desires were unconditional. If one knew that after time *t* one would have the noninstrumental desires of an orthodox Christian, one could not be rationally motivated to sacrifice one's present Nietzschean desires for the satisfaction of one's future Christian ones. Hence the conative core represents one's deepest commitments—those commitments that, to the extent that any set of commitments can, define who one is.[16]

Suppose, now, that a subject performs an antisocial act on the basis of a desire that (for that subject) is in IRE. Since the desire that motivates the action is in IRE, there is no other desire or set of desires to which we could appeal to provide the subject with a reason not to perform the action. Suppose, for example, the action involved driving after drinking. Since the action stems from a desire in IRE, one could not appeal to the subject's sympathy for accident victims or their families in attempting to demonstrate the necessity for reform. Such an appeal to the subject's other desires and sympathies makes sense only on the assumption that the desire that motivates the action is *not* in IRE.

A scenario in which an antisocial act stems from a desire in IRE would be possible if, for example, the subject in question were a rational psychopath. Such a subject lacks any sympathy for others to which we could appeal in providing that subject with a reason to refrain from the action (beyond whatever calculation he or she has made about the possibility of punishment). And it is not hard to understand why philosophers have been reluctant to hold psychopaths responsible for their antisocial actions.[17] Since there is nothing in the psychopaths' attitudes, desires, values, hopes, or concerns to which we could appeal, there is no possible means by which they could come to *acquiesce* in our condemnation of their behavior and in the justice of their punishment. They would normally experience no feelings of guilt or remorse for their actions, and if such feelings arose, they would be unsupported by the psychopaths' other noninstrumental desires. For example, any wish experienced by such a psychopath that he or she had not performed the action in question would be eliminated by the same pill that defines IRE. Similarly, any desire to make amends, secure forgiveness, or bring about self-reform would be isolated and unsupported and hence would be eliminated. Thus in the sense in which justification is necessarily connected with motivation,[18] such feelings would be completely unjustified. Therefore, such subjects would be beyond the reach of *punishment* (where genuine punishment requires the possibility that guilt and remorse should be *justified* even for the subjects themselves), though not beyond being deterred, manipulated, and controlled. Let us call subjects in this situation *unreachable*.

Although the claim that our actual practice involves a reluctance to hold psychopaths responsible for their actions is relatively uncontroversial, the stronger claim that this reluctance is in virtue of their unreachability may not be. I shall not, however, go on to make this stronger claim. What I suggest is that it is their unreachability that *justifies* this reluctance.

Imagine that one existed peacefully as an outsider in the midst of a native population whose taboos one regarded as irrational superstitions. And suppose one were in the habit of breaking the taboos whenever the chances of being discovered were slight. If one were caught and made to suffer, how could one regard the suffering as more than a piece of bad luck brought on by the unforeseen consequences of actions that under the circumstances were completely justified? Assuming one were unreachable, it is difficult to see how one could be rationally justified in feeling remorse or guilt or how one could construe such suffering as genuine punishment—regardless of how much one might regret the upshot of one's actions.

The psychopath's lack of sympathy for others, then, is not a necessary condition of his or her being outside our practice of ascribing responsibility and blame and administering punishment—being unreachable has the same effect. Nor is a lack of sympathy sufficient. A subject who lacked any sympathy for others but who could be reached by moral argument would ordinarily be subject to punishment and blame. Since our practice of ascribing responsibility, punishment, and blame requires the reachability of those to whom responsibility and blame are ascribed, not only psychopaths, but all those whose socially proscribed actions are done in IRE, and in whom remorse could find no motivational support, fall outside the practice.[19] Nonpsychopathic subjects who are nonetheless unreachable include, among others, act-utilitarian fanatics, subjects with a radically different conception of the good from ours, and subjects with a radically different conception of responsibility, whenever any of these subjects act in IRE. Among subjects acting in IRE, only those who are mistaken about the facts and who are open to a different version of them are not unreachable. And since their actions are done in ignorance, such subjects are still not appropriate candidates for the ascription of responsibility and blame.

The upshot is that subjects in IRE who are prima facie candidates for punishment or blame are either unreachable or ignorant. Thus on an intrinsic theory, which requires that ascriptions of responsibility be justified solely in terms of relevant features of the subject's psychology, a subject in IRE will be no more appropriate as a candidate for punishment or blame than a subject who is ignorant or psychopathic.

From the perspective of the intrinsic property constraint, however, the prospects for the ascription of responsibility are no better for subjects out of IRE. A subject who acts on a desire that is out of IRE is acting on a desire that he or she would, if possible, eliminate. Such a desire is cause for regret and the action it motivates may be associated with feelings of guilt or shame. This guilt or shame, however, would be no more justified for the subject acting out of IRE than it would be for the compulsive—at least if such justification had to appeal to intrinsic differences. Such feelings do not prevent the subject who is out of IRE from acting on the desire, because its motivational strength is out of proportion to its evaluational strength. And given the definition of a desire's motivational strength, there is no sense to the suggestion that the subject might have chosen not to act on the desire in spite of its motivational strength. Thus the psychology of such a subject is in relevant respects like that of the compulsive. A subject acting on a desire out of IRE may not exhibit the repetitive and identifiable behavioral patterns of the compulsive, but though this is a psychological difference, it is hard to see how it could be a relevant one. Hence the subject acting out of IRE is no better candidate for punishment or blame than the subject whose action is compelled.

The dilemma for any intrinsic theory of responsibility, then, is this. Any prima facie candidate for either punishment or blame acts either in or out of IRE. A subject who acts *in IRE* and who is not ignorant of any crucial facts is not relevantly different in psychology from the psychopath: both act in a state that makes them unreachable. A subject who acts *out of IRE* is not relevantly different from the compulsive: both act on a desire whose motivational strength is out of proportion to its evaluational strength. Hence, neither type of subject, and thus no subject, is responsible in the sense of being an appropriate candidate for punishment or blame.

It might be objected that ignorance is not always excused and may lead to actions whose motivating desires are neither like those of the compulsive nor like those of the psychopath. On the intrinsic conception of responsibility, however, this objection merely moves the problem one step back. If liability to punishment or blame is to be based on relevant features of a subject's psychology, then this basis could not consist in ignorance per se. Rather, the ignorance must have been brought about by actions for which the subject was responsible and subject to blame. And such actions must have stemmed either from a desire in IRE or from a desire out of IRE. Hence the dilemma for intrinsic theories of responsibility reappears.

This dilemma posed by stage two of the argument against the intrinsic property constraint depends on the assumption that the psychopath is an inappropriate candidate for punishment or blame. But this assumption can be justified. Punishment of the psychopath could, of course, be justified on consequentialist grounds, but as I argued (in note 19), such a justification is irrelevant to the problem of self-deception. And as I shall argue in section 3, consequentialist theories do not provide a plausible account of our actual practice regarding responsibility.

Traditional retributivist theories (those that observe the intrinsic property constraint) fare no better where punishment of the psychopath is concerned. Such theories cannot answer the following question: If there is no justification of the psychopath's suffering in terms of social utility (and the retributivist must be willing to impose the suffering even when there is no social payoff) and there is no justification from the subject's own point of view, what prevents the suffering from being gratuitous? To this line of argument it might be objected that the demand for such justification begs the question against the retributivist. In particular, the objection might be that between the fact that the subject acted on a desire from which he or she was in no way alienated and the claim that the subject is an appropriate candidate for punishment and blame there is no gap that requires justification. But this is not the case. I shall go on to show that such justification is possible. Since it is, the alleged gap exists. Thus there is an important justificatory role which is played by the alternative theory of responsibility to be proposed and for which an ordinary retributivist theory is inadequate.

Extrinsic Theories and Reactive Attitudes

3. Once the problems for intrinsic theories are clearly in focus, the alternative provided by existing extrinsic theories is unlikely to hold much appeal. If our institutions of blame and punishment cannot be justified on intrinsic grounds, then the claim that they serve as a deterrent to wrongdoing and thereby contribute to aggregate utility is likely to ring hollow. For such considerations to count as a justification of the pain and suffering necessarily inflicted by punishment and blame seems to presuppose that the recipient is blameworthy in some sense other than being the most efficient means to the production of aggregate utility or some alternative social goal. The extrinsic justification alone, when the assumption that an intrinsic justification exists has been dropped, is simply not of the right kind to justify anything like our current practices where responsibility is concerned. Such a justification of our current practices seems either to miss the point or to change the subject. The problem for the subject who is punished on the basis of this rationale is like the problem for the subject who is punished while being unreachable: although each subject can recognize in the suffering involved the intended manipulative effect and the (perhaps) efficacious exercise of power, neither subject can view the suffering in the light of any concept recognizably like that of desert.[20]

This argument against extrinsic theories has been challenged by P. F. Strawson.[21] According to Strawson, the justification of our customary practices of ascribing responsibility in terms of their efficacy in regulating behavior in socially desirable ways is to be either supplemented or replaced by another sort of justification. On Strawson's view, the justification of these practices is grounded in our reactive attitudes toward those from whom we expect and demand goodwill. Under normal circumstances we are prone to exhibit a characteristic pattern of responses toward someone who has caused an injury. If we have been injured by someone else, the characteristic response is resentment. If we are witnesses to the injury of someone else by a third party, the characteristic response is moral indignation. And if we ourselves have injured someone, the response is guilt or shame. This last case involves what Strawson calls self-reactive attitudes. On the positive side, our reactive attitudes include our feelings of gratitude and of moral approbation.

Under special circumstances these feelings are suspended. Injuries due to ignorance make such responses as resentment inappropriate with regard to that particular *action,* but they do not lead to our suspending our reactive attitudes toward the *agent* in question. We are fully prepared to respond with our normal reactive attitudes, both positive and negative, to the *other* actions in which that agent is engaged. Other circumstances do lead to such a suspension. The claim that an agent was not himself or herself, or was under great strain, or was schizophrenic, or was hopelessly compulsive leads us to withdraw our reactive attitude toward the agent either temporarily or on a permanent basis. Instead of seeing the offending agent as the appropriate target of resentment or moral indignation, we see him or her as someone to be managed or handled, cured or treated.

Strawson's analysis of our reactive attitudes provides a reply to my earlier objection to extrinsic theories. The objection was that we could not justify the imposition of suffering merely by reference to the contribution that suffering would make to social welfare. To do so would be to treat the alleged wrongdoer as a convenient instrument of social policy, but not as someone toward whom resentment or indignation (and for whom guilt or remorse) would be justified. This would be, in Strawson's terms, to take the objective attitude toward the alleged wrongdoer and to see that person as an appropriate subject for management or manipulation. Such a practice provides no place for our reactive attitudes toward those on whom suffering is imposed or whose behavior is modified. Nor does it allow any scope for the self-reactive attitudes of guilt or shame on the part of such subjects. Strawson's reply is that we can have an extrinsic justification of our practices without abandoning our reactive or participatory attitudes. Strawson claims that we suspend our reactive attitudes only under genuinely abnormal circumstances. We would not, if Strawson is right, be able to suspend them across the board on the basis of general, theoretical considerations, even supposing we had strong arguments for doing so. Thus we could not suspend such attitudes on the basis of our recognition of the dilemma for intrinsic theories. And, according to Strawson, even if we *could* choose whether or not to suspend our reactive attitudes, we could choose rationally only by weighing the gains and losses for human existence. The implication is clear that in Strawson's view, if we chose rationally we would choose to keep our reactive attitudes.

There is no question that Strawson has accurately diagnosed and eliminated an important difficulty for an extrinsic justification of our practices in ascribing responsibility. The objection to such a justification is that it alienates the participants in those practices from the practices themselves. Instead of justifying punishment and blame by reference to the subjects on whom such punishment falls, we justify it in terms of its social efficacy. The picture this suggests is that of a society forced to go through the distasteful ritual of inflicting suffering on those who are distinguished only by the fact that their suffering will maximize social utility. Punishment in such a case would amount to the self-conscious and cynical victimization of those who were made to suffer. And Strawson is correct in pointing out that we are not alienated from our own practices in this way.

For Strawson the gap between social utility and the pain and suffering of particular individuals is bridged by our tendency to feel resentment, moral indignation, guilt, and shame when an injury has been caused. As Strawson puts it, "the preparedness to acquiesce in that infliction of suffering on the offender which is an essential part of punishment is all of a piece with this whole range of [reactive] attitudes."[22] And as he goes on to add, our prepared-ness to acquiesce in our own suffering when we have caused injury to another is part and parcel of the attitudes in this same range.

My position, like Strawson's, will depend on the assumption that for a practice to be genuinely one involving responsibility, blame, and punishment, it must be possible for subjects to acquiesce in the suffering it involves—including their own. Because the difference between my view and Strawson's turns on whether reactive and self-reactive attitudes alone are sufficient for acquiescence in the suffering of others and of oneself, it is necessary to say more explicitly what I take this to entail. Acquiescence in the suffering brought on by punishment and blame requires, first, the ability to accept and support the suffering involved, where this includes the ability to respond with the appropriate reactive attitudes. Beyond this, however, one's acceptance and support must be *justified* and must be justified in a way that is conceptu-ally connected with motivation.

These requirements are more in line with our understanding of what is necessary for an institution to count as one of punishment than is Strawson's assumption that only reactive attitudes are necessary. An act of inflicting suffering that we would not count as punishment would not become punish-ment merely because its victims accepted it as a result of (say) neurotic guilt. Nor would it become punishment merely because it was accepted (as a result of neurotic guilt) and there was *some* justification of that acceptance. The fact, for example, that the acceptance had a utilitarian justification (unbe-knownst to those involved) would not make the suffering a case of punish-ment. Even if the utilitarian justification were recognized by those involved, the acceptance of the suffering would not necessarily have a rational justifica-tion for those who suffered. The subjects in question might be completely unmotivated to make such a contribution to aggregate utility. Under these circumstances acceptance of the suffering would not count as acquiescence. What acquiescence requires is that the acceptance be motivated by the justifi-cation—and not merely as a matter of contingent psychological fact. Such a fact would itself require justification in the same way that the psychological fact of our possessing certain reactive attitudes does. Hence the justification must provide its own motivation—and do so necessarily.[23]

Thus although Strawson's complaint that the usual extrinsic theories pro-vide no role for reactive attitudes is justified, he is wrong in assuming that reference to our reactive attitudes rules out all possible forms of alienation from our own practices. One of the difficulties for Strawson's position lies in the fact that he fails to recognize the problems that arise for an intrinsic justification of our practices concerning punishment and blame. And in the absence of such an intrinsic justification, Strawson has no reply to the objec-tion that we could come to see our reactive attitudes themselves as being as much in need of justification (and as difficult to justify) as our practices regarding punishment. Though we might continue to feel indignation at some of those who cause injury to others and feel no distaste in making such individuals suffer, we might also find this very lack of distaste itself a source of shame and regret.

Moreover, though Strawson is undoubtedly right to claim that eradicating such feelings is not a practical possibility, it is clearly a logical possibility. And it is certainly not irrelevant to ask whether we would be justified in doing so if we had the technology to make such a fundamental change in the structure of our interpersonal attitudes. Nothing that Strawson has said rules out the claim that we should eliminate our reactive attitudes and accept a revised conception of those who injure others along the lines suggested by contemporary psychiatry—and with it an attenuated sense of our personal responsibility. Hence, Strawson cannot plausibly claim to have filled the gap that he has correctly noted between the social efficacy of our practices and the real pain and suffering of actual individuals.

From Nonmaximizing to Self-Supporting Dispositions

4. Changing our perspective on self-deception to focus on our evaluation of the phenomenon rather than its explanation will have meant replacing one puzzle with another if there is no adequate account of our ascriptions of responsibility to self-deceivers. And as we have seen in sections 2 and 3 none of the usual accounts is adequate. In this section I shall discuss a class of dispositions—the nonmaximizing dispositions—of which, as it turns out, self-deception is a member. This will help to clarify the nature of the difficulties with our present treatments of responsibility. I shall then go on to examine a second class—the self-supporting dispositions—which provides the basis for a solution to these difficulties. In the two sections that follow I shall apply these results to the problem of ascriptions of responsibility in order to show the kind of justification to which our ascriptions in general, and our practice of ascribing responsibility for self-deception in particular, are open.

Let us say that d is a *nonmaximizing disposition* for a subject S between t and t' (where D is the set of S's desires at t and B is the set of S's beliefs at t) if and only if d prevents S's actions from maximizing the satisfaction of the desires in D (given the beliefs in B), even though D and B remain S's underlying beliefs and desires between t and t'. Such a disposition might be the result of some of S's desires or beliefs in D or B becoming temporarily inaccessible or diminished in strength. Alternatively, it might result from the temporary emergence of desires or beliefs that are not part of D or B or from the temporary increase in strength of some of those that are. Thus, although one always acts on what is motivationally one's strongest desire, that desire may be a temporary aberration relative to one's underlying desires and beliefs.

(On this definition, full-blown self-deception yields a nonmaximizing disposition. When one is self-deceived in the full-blown sense, one will maximize the satisfaction of one's desires not relative to the underlying set of beliefs which contains one's original belief, but relative to the new set that contains the induced belief. In contrast, one-shot self-deception will not yield a nonmaximizing disposition, since the original belief does not remain part of one's underlying belief set.)

There are many familiar ways in which nonmaximizing dispositions can give one a strategic advantage over others.[24] One might, for example, induce in oneself the disposition to ignore any threats made against one, come what may. One might do so by inducing a disposition to become so angry if threatened that one would temporarily lose touch with all the desires that conflict with the desire not to capitulate. One's disposition to ignore these threats whatever the consequences would effectively deter any threat whose execution would impose a significant cost on the person making it, as long as one's disposition were known to potential threat-initiators. A potential threat-initiator would calculate correctly that he or she stood to gain nothing by threatening such a perfect threat-ignorer and that he or she stood to lose either credibility or the cost of executing the threat. Of course, if for some reason a potential threat-initiator were *not* deterred, then even if it would maximize the satisfaction of one's underlying desires to capitulate, one would be disposed not to do so. Hence such a disposition is a disposition to act in a way that will not maximize the satisfaction of one's underlying desires (relative to one's underlying beliefs) *if* it is ever *manifest*. But the *acquisition* of the disposition could maximize the satisfaction of those same underlying desires (relative to the underlying beliefs), because its *possession* would keep one out of precisely those situations in which one would act on it.

With this definition of nonmaximizing dispositions in mind, we can strengthen the conclusion of section 3. That conclusion was that Strawson had not shown that our reactive attitudes were justified and so had not shown that our practices regarding responsibility were justified. The stronger claims for which I shall now argue are the following. First, our reactive attitudes are a kind of nonmaximizing disposition. Second, nonmaximizing dispositions, by their very nature, cannot themselves serve as the ultimate ground of a set of practices and institutions where responsibility is concerned. Third, in virtue of being nonmaximizing dispositions, our reactive attitudes cannot be justified (under the conditions that characterize our institutions of responsibility, punishment, and blame) by reference to their consequences. Thus they cannot play the justificatory role for which Strawson has them slated.

To see that our reactive attitudes are nonmaximizing, we need only notice that they are dispositions to cause suffering in the form of punishment or blame or to acquiesce in our own suffering, even when such suffering has no deterrent (or more generally act-consequentialist) rationale. This must be the case since in expressing our reactive attitudes, we are ignoring questions of social efficacy, the consideration of which would make our attitudes objective rather than reactive. Thus our reactive attitudes are dispositions that prevent our actions from maximizing our overriding concerns to prevent pointless and unnecessary suffering.

The reason nonmaximizing dispositions cannot themselves provide the ultimate support for practices such as those concerning responsibility is a direct consequence of their definition. A nonmaximizing disposition prevents our actions from maximizing the satisfaction of our desires, given our beliefs. Whether this is the result of our temporarily losing touch with some of our underlying beliefs or desires or of the temporary emergence of new ones, we will retain the motivational resources to criticize our nonmaximizing dispositions. Such dispositions will be open to criticism for their failure to maximize the satisfaction of those desires relative to those beliefs. Thus, however resistant to change they might turn out to be in practice, we could have good reason to regret our reactive attitudes and to hope for new therapies or drugs that would improve the prospects for their change or elimination.

Strawson must argue, then, not just that our reactive attitudes are deeply ingrained but that they are themselves in fact justified. And the claim that such dispositions are justified by the contribution they make to our human good, that is, by their consequences,[25] is very implausible. There are two reasons for the implausibility. The first is that such dispositions are unlikely to be efficacious under the conditions imposed by the fact that our practices of punishment and blame constitute our primary institution of social control. Reactive attitudes construed as nonmaximizing dispositions cannot provide the basis for institutions that are deliberately designed to function independently of the attitudes of individual participants.

The inadequacy of our reactive attitudes to support our institutions is clear in view of the following characteristics of our institutions and attitudes. Our reactive attitudes are often of shorter duration than the institutional proceedings for ascribing responsibility and blame, and they will almost certainly be of shorter duration than the punishment prescribed in the most serious cases. Our reactive attitudes may also depend on the point of view adopted, for example, whether we take the perspective of the victim or the accused, and they may shift with shifts in our perspective. There are also institutional mechanisms designed to help us suppress the reactive attitudes and to put us in touch with our underlying beliefs and desires. Examples include the arguments of defense attorneys alleging the pointlessness of the suffering their clients' punishment would entail. Our institutions of punishment and blame are also designed to deal with those cases in which the stakes are highest. And the combination of high stakes, long and impersonal proceedings and penalties, and mechanisms designed to give us access to our underlying desires virtually guarantees that nonmaximizing dispositions in general, and our reactive attitudes in particular, will not be sustained in the context of the institutions they are meant to support.

The second reason that the claim that our reactive attitudes are justified by their consequences fails is that there may well be alternatives in dealing with social deviance which do not require that we inflict pain and suffering. A social practice governed by the medical or psychiatric model of social deviance or by models derived from the social or behavioral sciences provides an obvious example.[26] Since our attitudes on these issues are open to criticism and revision, the uneasiness we might feel at such an objectivist approach is not *in itself* sufficient to support our current practices regarding responsibility, punishment, and blame.

This failure of our reactive attitudes in the role for which Strawson intended them stems from the following fact. Like all nonmaximizing dispositions, reactive attitudes cannot be *self-supporting*. That is, our motivational makeup is such that we have the resources both to criticize our pattern of emotional responses and in the long run, where it is feasible, to change it. There is, however, a class of dispositions that resemble nonmaximizing dispositions and which are self-supporting. Recall the definition of an ideal reflective equilibrium. Given a subject's actual noninstrumental desires, that subject's IRE is the set of noninstrumental desires that would result if he or she could subtract the desires that were badly supported and add desires that would be well supported. By definition, a subject's IRE is not open to criticism from inside which could motivate that subject to change it. Hence the set of desires that emerge in IRE, taken as a whole (and given the subject's beliefs), constitutes a self-supporting disposition.

But in what sense does such a disposition resemble a nonmaximizing disposition? In other words, what are the analogues in the case of a self-supporting disposition consisting in a set of desires in IRE to the two salient features of nonmaximizing dispositions: that they dispose one to act against one's own interests and that it may nevertheless be true of some that it is in one's interests to acquire them? And if there are analogues to these features of nonmaximizing dispositions, how do they coexist with that feature that makes one's desires in IRE suitable to play the role that Strawson assigns to reactive attitudes—that one cannot be motivated to replace or override one's desires in IRE?

To see the relation between a nonmaximizing and a self-supporting disposition, imagine an act-consequentialist with no noninstrumental desire to keep her promises except as this contributes to the satisfaction of her other desires. She desires various kinds of states of affairs, and her problem is to maximize the satisfaction of those desires. And suppose she faces the following situation. First, the potential benefits of cooperating with others (and hence of making and keeping contracts and promises) are very great, especially in undertakings in which the stakes are high. Second, there is a large number of others who are disposed to cooperate with those who are similarly disposed. Third, most subjects are adept at distinguishing those who are genuinely disposed to cooperate from those who are disposed to feign cooperation and to defect when it is to their advantage to do so.

As an act-consequentialist, she will be motivated, under such circumstances, to acquire a disposition to cooperate. Moreover, she will be motivated to acquire a self-supporting disposition to keep promises, even when the stakes are high and it is disadvantageous to do so. For unless the disposition is self-supporting, she will be motivated to have the disposition overridden or destroyed whenever the stakes are sufficiently high that what she gains by breaking a promise offsets any damage to her credibility. Similarly, unless the disposition to keep promises is self-supporting, she will be motivated to break them whenever she could do so undetected. If others are able to tell whether she possesses a self-supporting disposition, a disposition that was not self-supporting would not secure for her the desired benefits.

As an act-consequentialist, she can acquire such a self-supporting disposition to keep contracts and promises by acquiring a complete IRE that contains as part of its conative core the noninstrumental desire to keep her promises even at great cost to herself. Since this desire is part of the conative core of an IRE, it cannot be an isolated one. Like any other such desire, this desire must be supported by a large number of other noninstrumental desires, such as the desire to preserve her honor at great cost and desires that define the role of honor in all the significant areas of her life. In general such a disposition is not guaranteed to maximize her original act-consequentialist desires. What prevents this disposition from being nonmaximizing in the strict sense defined is that the original act-consequentialist desires do *not* persist as her underlying desires. When she acquires the disposition, there is no longer any interesting sense in which she is an act-consequentialist. Her motive, as an act-consequentialist, to acquire it rests on its contribution to the satisfaction of her original desires. But under circumstances she hopes will (partly as a result of her having the disposition) never arise, her actions would not maximize the satisfaction of *those* desires. Those desires would be sacrificed in favor of the desires that called for (say) the preservation of her honor even at great cost.[27]

The acquisition of such a self-supporting disposition is an irreversible choice. Though one may be motivated to acquire such a disposition to secure the benefits of cooperation, one cannot be motivated (as always, keeping one's beliefs fixed) to eliminate it. Thus the act of acquiring such a disposition is self-constitutive or self-defining. I shall go on to claim that it is by reference to such self-supporting and self-defining dispositions that our ascriptions of responsibility are to be justified.

INTERNAL JUSTIFICATION

5. As an act-consequentialist, one would be justified, given certain assumptions about the others in one's community, in acquiring a self-supporting disposition to keep promises even at great cost to oneself. Under similar conditions one would be justified in acquiring a self-supporting disposition to acquiesce in inflicting suffering on those who have caused injuries even when one is oneself the subject who suffers. One would, in other words, be justified in acquiring a self-supporting disposition in virtue of which one would be prepared, on particular occasions, to inflict more suffering on those who had caused injuries and less suffering on those who had not caused injuries than would an act-consequentialist. One would be prepared, for example, to acquiesce in the punishment of those who had injured others but could be spared without any loss of deterrent effect in the future, and to refrain from causing suffering to those who had injured no one but whose suffering would be far outweighed by the future benefits to others.

Though the *acquisition* of this disposition would be justified on act-consequentialist grounds, those grounds would not be what justified the *possession* of the disposition to those who, in virtue of its acquisition, were no longer act-consequentialists. For such subjects, the extrinsic, act-consequentialist considerations would no longer be relevant. And given the argument that our ascriptions of responsibility discriminate where there are no relevant psychological differences, the intrinsic theories of justification would provide no alternative.

There is, however, an alternative to either an act-consequentialist justification or an intrinsic justification of this disposition. Imagine a subject for whom this disposition is part of a self-supporting disposition and in particular part of the conative core of the subject's IRE. It follows that the desire to support our practices in ascribing responsibility is supported by a large number of other desires the subject has which are both noninstrumental and unconditional.

But what sorts of desires would support the desire to support these practices? Consider what would be lost if, on the basis of a psychological theory of deviant behavior and a medical approach to social control, we came to regard all punishment and blame—and hence our present conception of responsibility—as unjustified. Our concept of personal responsibility is intimately tied to our concepts of privacy and autonomy. Dispense with notions like responsibility, and we open ourselves to intervention aimed at preventing and not merely punishing social transgressions. Similarly, with no reason for the degree of intervention in one's affairs to reflect any actual injuries one has caused, one's sense of autonomy and privacy would be further eroded. Also, with different assumptions about responsibility go different assumptions about the rationality of one's motivations, and our notions of integrity and self-respect are likely to be lost or changed in radical and unpredictable ways. Moreover, since some social control must be internalized, if this is not accomplished through a sense of personal responsibility, it is difficult to see how it is to be accomplished except through the inculcation of false beliefs or by the direct conditioning of a significant number of desired responses. The first alternative puts even further pressure on our notions of self-respect and autonomy, whereas the second seems incompatible with the value we place on creativity and on one's right to pursue one's own possibly idiosyncratic projects, when these involve no harm to others.

Let us call a justification that appeals to our noninstrumental desires in IRE an *internal justification*. Internal justification is conceptually tied to motivation. To a subject whose conative core contains desires for self-respect, autonomy, privacy, and the possibility of nonconformity in something like our senses, the desire to support our practices regarding responsibility will be well supported. By appeal to these other desires, the desire to support these practices will be both justified and motivated.

Such a justification answers the critic who claims that an extrinsic and consequentialist justification of our practices is out of place. If one is made to suffer under our practices of ascribing responsibility or one objects to such suffering, one can be made to see that the concept of responsibility involved is an inseparable component of a set of concepts that are together constitutive both of one's deepest commitments and of one's sense of what makes one the person one is.

What I have given is merely a sketch of a certain kind of justification of our practices regarding responsibility. Such a sketch is no guarantee that a justification of this kind actually exists. My own view is that this type of strategy regarding justification is promising, but the only claim I shall defend is that unless such a justification exists, there is no way of answering the objections of a certain kind of skeptic about our current practices. In the remainder of this section I shall first clarify the notion of internal justification. I shall then go on to discuss the kinds of skeptical questions that might be raised and the limitations on the kind of justification I have proposed.

What is the relation between an internal justification of our practices and the intrinsic justification discussed in section 2? An internal justification of our practices regarding responsibility, if it exists, depends on our noninstrumental desires, such as those for autonomy, privacy, integrity, and the possibility of nonconformity. Our commitment to these values simply consists in there being the appropriate mutually supporting desires in the conative core of our IRE. Thus, given the second component of the intrinsic property constraint, which does not allow such values and commitments to count as a relevant psychological basis for the ascription of responsibility, an internal justification is necessarily extrinsic.

This result is in line with the way in which intrinsic theories are ordinarily understood. Traditional answers to the question what constitutes a relevant psychological difference between those who are held responsible and those who are not require that the actions for which we are held responsible should be intentional, not impulsive, not the result of a rage or an irresistible impulse, not due to compulsion or a drug-induced state, and not the result of low intelligence. It has ordinarily been assumed that whether one believes one is responsible or whether our practices of ascribing responsibility are supported in one's IRE are not psychological considerations relevant to the question whether one actually *is* responsible. Given the internal conception of justification, our practices would be justified for a community of subjects who had internalized personal ideals and self-conceptions like ours; for a community of subjects who had not, the possibility of acquiescing in our practices of punishment and blame might not exist. And on any ordinary understanding of intrinsic theories, the question whether a subject is responsible is not in this way relative to our beliefs and desires.

But though internal justification is extrinsic, it is unrelated to extrinsic justifications as *they* are normally understood. On the usual understanding, extrinsic justifications appeal to consequentialist considerations in order to justify the suffering that our practices concerning responsibility and punishment involve. For those for whom our practices have an internal justification, however, such an appeal is unnecessary. For such people the acceptance of the suffering will be supported by dispositions superficially similar to Strawson's reactive attitudes. Their difference lies in the fact that they will themselves be supported by noninstrumental and unconditional desires in IRE. For such people the acceptance of the suffering would remain even if the suffering were their own and even if they had the ability to change their attitudes at will. Thus an appeal to consequentialist considerations to justify our practices would be, for such people, not only unnecessary but irrelevant.

My claim, then, is that any justification of our actual ascriptions of responsibility must be either consequentialist or internal; there is no intrinsic justification of the ascriptions. But the distinction between intrinsic and internal justification suggests a serious limitation on the latter. Internal justification of our ascriptions of responsibility only works, assuming it does, for those who share our personal ideals and self-conceptions. And for those who do not, radically different practices may have an internal justification. For a community that shared our ideals, the complete medicalization of social control not only would be repugnant but would be unjustified in the internal sense. For a community that did not share these ideals, a medical paradigm might provide the ideal model for dealing with deviance.

This limitation on intrinsic justification does not trivialize the claim that such a justification is available for our practices of ascribing responsibility. That such a claim might be trivial is suggested by the following argument.

Whether a set of practices regarding responsibility is justified for a community depends on the noninstrumental desires that the members of the community have or would have in IRE. Since a group of people could be conditioned (or caused—at least in principle) to have any coherent set of desires, any scheme of social control, regardless of how outrageous, could be justified for some appropriately conditioned community.

The claim, however, that any set of institutions of social control could have an internal justification—if this means an internal justification that does not involve seriously mistaken beliefs—is almost certainly false. Imagine a society that successfully deters undesirable behavior by inflicting punishment on a certain number of people chosen at random. Assume that most people believe the gods control the process by which the victims are picked and that they believe, therefore, that the process is just. (Trial by ordeal might provide a rough approximation.)

Consider the position of the act-consequentialist deciding whether to adopt a disposition that will make her a part of the group, though she does not share the members' belief in the gods. Suppose she recognizes that membership in the group is the only alternative to the anarchy that prevails outside the group, that the advantages of group membership far outweigh the risks of being victimized, and that group membership requires a genuine self-supporting disposition to support the practices of social control even at great cost. Under these circumstances the act-consequentialist would seem to have every reason to acquire the self-supporting disposition required for membership. The acquisition of the disposition would have a consequentialist justification for her while she remained an act-consequentialist, and the social institutions would have an internalist justification for her after the nonconsequentialist disposition was acquired.

The difficulty is that even with a perfect technology for the creation of dispositions, the disposition in question may not exist. Given that the act-consequentialist believes that the victims are selected at random, what could she tell herself if she or a close friend were selected? What kind of disposition would allow her to acquiesce in such a victimization? She could, of course, acquire a disposition to feel loathing or antipathy toward the victims selected, and such a disposition might well extend to her own case. But the question is whether such a disposition could be self-supporting. Assuming a reasonable amount of sympathy in general for herself and others (and this might also be a requirement for group membership), what kinds of commitments and self-conception could override the temptation to spare one of the chosen victims if it were in her power to do so without being detected? Although the act-consequentialist might internalize a sense of repugnance at doing so, given the technology for changing one's dispositions, this is a disposition she would be motivated to override or eliminate if the relevant situation arose. But this means that given her beliefs, the act-consequentialist could not acquire the relevant self-supporting disposition. Hence for those who have no false beliefs about the machinations of the gods, the institutions in question seem to have no internal justification.[28]

Because the fact that they have an internal justification is a nontrivial fact about our practices regarding responsibility, we now have an answer to at least one skeptic (on the assumption that the sketch of an internal justification can be filled out). This is the skeptic who shares our self-conception and commitments, but who wonders how our practice of ascribing responsibility and blame can be justified in the light of the problems for intrinsic theories. Let us call this person the *sympathetic anticonsequentialist skeptic*. Such a skeptic is answered by making explicit the support that the noninstrumental desire to acquiesce in our institutions of punishment and blame derives from his or her noninstrumental desires for autonomy, privacy, integrity, creativity, and so forth. By the same token, there is a skeptic we cannot answer, namely the skeptic who does not share our set of ideals and commitments, but who has internalized some alternative set. Let us call this person the *unsympathetic anticonsequentialist skeptic*. For such a skeptic, our practices of social control do not have an internal justification, whereas some radically different practices will.

A third skeptic is the *act-consequentialist skeptic*. Since we have seen that under a set of conditions that are not completely unrealistic, an act-consequentialist would be motivated to adopt an IRE supporting our institutions of social control, we have a reply to the act-consequentialist skeptic as well. This is not to say that an act-consequentialist with no prior commitments could not adopt a self-conception that would support an alternative social practice. From the point of view of an act-consequentialist, a set of commitments supporting a medical approach to socially undesirable behavior might be equally attractive. This is simply to say that from a consequentialist point of view, there may be diverse solutions to the problem of securing social harmony.

There is a fourth skeptic, however, who, like the unsympathetic anticonsequentialist skeptic, cannot be answered. This is the skeptic who insists that only an intrinsic justification could justify our practices and despairs of finding one. Such a skeptic is like the critic of compatibilism who is aware that the distinctions in our actual ascriptions of responsibility are based on systematic psychological differences, but who does not find the differences relevant. Such a critic presses the difficulties we have seen for any intrinsic justification and claims that the psychological facts to which an internal justification appeals are equally irrelevant. This skeptic is no more impressed by external justifications and, I shall assume, is equally unimpressed by notions like agent-causation. That we have no answer to such a skeptic shows that skepticism about responsibility has a deeper source than the compatibilist generally recognizes. There is no justification of our practices which would rule out radical alternatives like those governed by the medical model. But the inference from the lack of an absolute justification to the conclusion that there is no justification at all is, as we have seen, unfounded.

RESPONSIBILITY AND SELF-DECEPTION

6. The question that remains is how the discussion of responsibility in general bears on the problem of self-deception. What the discussion of responsibility has shown is that ascriptions of responsibility which have no intrinsic justification can have both a consequentialist and an internal justification. This means that to hold a subject responsible for the operations of an unconscious subsystem is not *necessarily* unjustified. This falls obviously short of showing that it is justified in this particular instance. We do not, after all, hold people responsible for all the operations of their unconscious subsystems. What makes such a practice appropriate in the case of self-deception?

Suppose we take our discussion of responsibility in general as a guide. If there is an internal justification of our practices regarding self-deception, we should expect some special connection between avoiding self-deception and our notions of autonomy, integrity, and responsibility. And the ideal that consists in being undeceived by oneself does in fact seem tied to our concept of responsibility in a way that one's remaining immune to the deceptive strategies of others does not. The claim is, in other words, that to view ourselves as merely the victims of self-deception and not as its perpetrators would be at least partly to undermine the ideal of autonomy that is constitutive of our practices regarding responsibility.[29]

Suppose, however, that the following objection is made. Granted it is difficult to imagine a practice involving responsibility, in anything like our sense, in which punishment and blame are entirely displaced by medical intervention. And given the problems for intrinsic theories, we are bound to assign or withhold blame on grounds that, according to the intrinsic property constraint, cannot be relevant. Still, it might be objected, the ideal of being responsible oneself for remaining undeceived by oneself is not so central to our notion of responsibility that we cannot imagine a similar notion that lacks this ideal.

The answer to this objection involves recalling the central claim of the paper. That claim is that our practice of ascribing blame for self-deception could be justified for a group with beliefs and commitments not unlike ours. There is a form of justification—internal justification—which would justify our practice of blaming self-deceivers in particular and of punishment and blame in general for such a group. Since I shall leave open the question whether we are such a group, the question whether the desire to acquiesce in blaming self-deceivers would occur in *our* ideal reflective equilibria will not be settled here. Nonetheless, I shall briefly sketch two reasons for thinking that the answer is not obviously no.

The first reason is that even if we eliminated our tendency to blame self-deceivers, this would bring our practices of ascribing responsibility no closer to satisfying the intrinsic property constraint. We would continue to blame some people for actions motivated by desires out of IRE, while others whose actions were also motivated by such desires would be excused as compulsives. And we would do so despite the lack of a relevant (by the standards of the intrinsic property constraint) psychological difference between the two cases. To suppose that the desires that make up the conative core of our IRE's would not support such a distinction would be to suppose that nothing like our practice of ascribing responsibility would be supported— either because we would cease to regard any form of compulsion as an excuse, or because we would excuse everyone acting on a desire that was out of IRE. The former alternative would represent a radical tightening of the standards we apply in evaluating excuses. And the latter alternative, as we have seen, would leave only the psychopath and other unreachable subjects as legitimate objects of punishment and blame.

The second reason is that just as we blame some actions stemming from desires out of IRE and not others, so we are likely to blame some actions and not others stemming from self-deception (and some instances and not others of self-deception itself). Since it would require a lengthy discussion of the excuses we do and do not accept, I shall not try to characterize the grounds on which we distinguish some actions but not others as compulsive where they all stem from desires out of IRE. I shall, therefore, not try to work out an analogous distinction between the forms of self-deception which are likely to be excused and those which are not. It seems plausible, however, to suppose that as the desire motivating the deception becomes more remote from our conscious desires and projects, the likelihood of its being excused will increase. Furthermore, if we think of psychological operations as mechanical to the extent that they are insensitive to the influence of our conscious beliefs and desires, then the more mechanical self-deceptions seem less likely to incur blame. As self-deception becomes more closely tied to projects that we recognize as our own, however, and becomes a more flexible manifestation of our conscious beliefs and desires, our responsibility for its consequences will be more difficult to deny.

What I have shown is the intelligibility of people with beliefs and desires not unlike ours having noninstrumental desires in IRE to support the practice of punishment in spite of the dilemma for any intrinsic justification. Since the practice of ascribing responsibility and blame to self-deceivers is intelligible on the same grounds, this provides one solution to the problem of self-deception. More precisely, it removes the most serious objection by far to the homuncular solution. But to show the intelligibility of people with beliefs and desires at least *similar* to ours for whom the practice of blaming self-deception has an internal justification is one thing. To show that such a practice has an internal justification for us is another. It may not, either because our desires in IRE do not support our practices of punishment in general or because they do not support our practice of blaming self-deceivers in particular. If this is the case, then these practices are unjustified in any sense that would allow us to *acquiesce* in the suffering they involve. And this provides a second solution to the problem of self-deception. If our blaming self-deceivers is unjustified or justified only on consequentialist grounds, then the alleged implausibility of the homuncular solution is merely apparent. In either case the objection to the homuncular solution has been met.

A satisfactory treatment, then, of the problem of self-deception involves three basic revisions of the underlying assumptions with which it is ordinarily approached. First, we must come to see the problem not in terms of the explanation of self-deception, but in terms of the evaluation of our responsibility for its occurrence. The mechanism of self-deception is unmysterious given the prevalence of homuncular models in the cognitive sciences. It is the ascription of responsibility for the operation of an unconscious mechanism—that is, the ascription of responsibility in violation of the intrinsic property constraint—which raises the most serious philosophical problems.

Second, we must drop the assumption that our practice of ascribing responsibility could have a justification in which discriminations in our ascriptions to different subjects are justified by differences in the intrinsic properties of the subjects' psychologies. Furthermore, though the acquisition of a disposition to support our practices regarding responsibility might have a consequentialist justification, for those whose commitments actually *do* support our practices, no such justification is possible.

Finally, we must abandon the expectation of an absolute justification of our institutions and practices. If we do, we can explain the possibility of an internal justification of our institutions and practices by reference to the notion of a self-supporting disposition. Though the justification is not absolute, it is the only justification that can appeal to those who have internalized the ideals on which these practices depend. In this paper I have provided only the barest sketch of how such an internal justification would be completed and of how it might be applied to the specific case of self-deception. But if the completion of such a task is impossible, this would entail not just a change in our attitude toward self-deception but a wholesale revision of our conception of responsibility and of ourselves.[30]

NOTES

1. This is a stipulative definition. The question whether there are cases we would describe as self-deception (if we had access to all the facts) which do not fall under

this definition is one I shall leave open. What distinguishes this case is its theoretical simplicity, the fact that it is likely to figure in the analysis of at least some more complex cases, and the fact that it is the most difficult case. For some of the difficulties in giving necessary and sufficient conditions for our actual use of the term see Jennifer Radden, "Defining Self-Deception," *Dialogue* 23 (1984):103–120.

2. See F. A. Siegler, "Demos on Lying to Oneself," *Journal of Philosophy* 59 (1962):469–475; J. V. Canfield and D. F. Gustafson, "Self-Deception," *Analysis* 23 (1962):32–36; T. Penelhum, "Pleasure and Falsity," in *Philosophy of Mind,* ed. Stuart Hampshire (New York: Harper and Row, 1966), pp. 242–266.

3. Roy Schafer, *A New Language for Psychoanalysis* (New Haven: Yale Univ. Press, 1976), p. 234.

4. See Daniel Dennett, "Why the Law of Effect Will Not Go Away" and "Artificial Intelligence as Philosophy and as Psychology," both in his *Brainstorms* (Montgomery, Vt.: Bradford Books, 1978), pp. 71–89 and 109–126, and William Lycan, "Form, Function, and Feel," *Journal of Philosophy* 78 (1981):24–50.

5. Stephen L. White, "What Is It Like to Be an Homunculus?" (in preparation).

6. For a number of sophisticated objections to homuncular theories see Ronald de Sousa, "Rational Homunculi," in *The Identities of Persons,* ed. Amélie Rorty (Berkeley: Univ. of California Press, 1976), pp. 217–238. De Sousa's objections, however, depend on his assumption that weakness of the will provides the strongest case for homuncular analyses. I would agree that if weakness of the will provides the strongest case, then such analyses seem misguided. But I want to claim that self-deception provides a far stronger case for homuncular analyses than the one de Sousa criticizes.

7. For a discussion that emphasizes the self-deceiver's responsibility see Herbert Fingarette, *Self-Deception* (London: Routledge and Kegan Paul, 1969), chap. 2.

8. I shall not discuss determinism in what follows. However, it will make the motivation for the position I defend clearer if I make explicit my assumption that any justification of our practices of assigning punishment and blame should apply in what is, as it were, the worst-case scenario for responsibility. This may be a case in which determinism is true, a case in which some combination of determinism and indeterminism holds, or a case in which some alternative is realized. My own view is that any coherent possibility is a worst-case scenario. But to defend this would require an argument that goes beyond the scope of the paper.

9. Robert M. Adams, "Involuntary Sins," *Philosophical Review* 94 (1985):3–31; Thomas Nagel, "Moral Luck," in his *Mortal Questions* (New York: Cambridge Univ. Press, 1979), p. 28; Joel Feinberg, "Problematic Responsibility in Law and Morals," in his *Doing and Deserving* (Princeton: Princeton Univ. Press, 1970), p. 35.

10. Thomas Nagel, op. cit.; Joel Feinberg, op. cit.; Bernard Williams, "Moral Luck," in his *Moral Luck* (New York: Cambridge Univ. Press, 1981), pp. 20–39.

11. J. L. Mackie, *Ethics* (New York: Penguin Books, 1977), pp. 203–226; Holly Smith, "Culpable Ignorance," *Philosophical Review* 92 (1983):543–571.

12. I use the expressions 'intrinsic desire' and 'noninstrumental desire' interchangeably, but I avoid the term 'intrinsic desire' in order to prevent confusion. Having the intrinsic desires one has is not one of one's intrinsic properties, since it involves one's values and commitments. And it provides the basis not for an intrinsic but for an internal justification (i.e., a justification that necessarily provides motivation) for a set of practices regarding responsibility.

13. This point is also made by Stephen Darwall; see *Impartial Reason* (Ithaca: Cornell Univ. Press, 1983), p. 109. I develop the notion of an equilibrium with respect to one's noninstrumental desires in more detail in "Rawls and Ideal Reflective Equilibria" (in preparation).

14. Nothing depends on the assumption that the IRE for a particular subject at a given time will be determined uniquely (without appeal to the subject's ability to make arbitrary choices). Nonetheless, the assumption that in normal cases there will be significantly different possible equilibria is likely to stem from a misunderstanding of the concept. It should be emphasized that the addition and subtraction of desires is not motivated by an abstract commitment to coherence. What would motivate the heroin addict to eliminate the desire for heroin are competing desires, such as the desire for success in a conventional career, the desire for fulfilling relationships with nonaddicts, and the desire for a long and healthy life—desires that are systematically frustrated by the desire for heroin. Thus there would be no temptation to maximize coherence by eliminating all but one desire (and hence no necessity of choosing among the many ways of doing this). Given that one starts with a wide variety of noninstrumental desires, the desire to maximize coherence by eliminating all but one would itself be eliminated by its failure to cohere with a significant number of other desires.

Furthermore, the idea that a single desire would make up a maximally coherent set is mistaken. Though we may increase the chances that a set of beliefs is *consistent* by eliminating most of the beliefs in the set, we will not ordinarily increase its *coherence*. Though in a normal set of beliefs there is always the possibility of conflict, the various beliefs also support one another in virtue (at least in part) of the explanatory relations between them. Similarly, given a set consisting in a very small number of desires, though the potential for conflict would be minimized, the set would not be highly coherent. Such desires would be unsupported by other desires and hence arbitrary: if such a desire were to fade there would be no motivation to replace it. But desires which are mutually supporting may give one another significance that they would not have in isolation. (Gilbert Harman speaks of adopting ends in order to give significance to ends one has previously had and unity to one's life as a whole. I would not understand this, however, as Harman seems to, solely in terms of the means-end relation. See "Practical Reasoning," *Review of Metaphysics* 29 [1976]:461–463.)

Thus coherence among noninstrumental desires is maximized in a way which is motivated by the desires one already has: one eliminates those desires which are a source of serious conflict, adds desires which could help resolve existing conflicts (say by adding noninstrumental desires to do things which are required by one's other noninstrumental desires), and adjusts the strength of one's desires to maximize their joint satisfaction. The fact that this procedure still allows the possibility of a significant area of indeterminacy for particular agents will not affect the points I shall go on to make.

15. On the distinction between conditional and unconditional desires see Derek Parfit, *Reasons and Persons* (New York: Oxford Univ. Press, 1984), pp. 151–154. For related distinctions among desires see Stephen Schiffer, "A Paradox of Desire," *American Philosophical Quarterly* 13 (1976):197–199; Thomas Nagel, *The Possibility of Altruism* (New York: Oxford Univ. Press, 1970), pp. 29–30; and Bernard Williams, "The Makropulos Case; Reflections on the Tedium of Immortality," in his *Problems of the Self* (New York: Cambridge Univ. Press, 1973), pp. 85–87.

16. The desires in one's IRE are endorsed, at least to the extent that they would not be eliminated. The desires in one's conative core, however, represent commitments of a kind that it seems appropriate to identify as one's most fundamental values. Thus the notion of a conative core plays a role similar to the role played by Harry Frankfurt's notion of the first-order desires with which one identifies in virtue of one's second-order desires. (See his "Freedom of the Will and the Concept of a Person," in *Free Will,* ed. Gary Watson [New York: Oxford Univ. Press, 1982], pp. 81–95.) By switching from a foundationalist to a coherentist approach, however, I avoid the obvious problem for Frankfurt of an infinite regress to increasingly higher-order desires. More important, I avoid the problem that there is no necessary connection between a desire's being of higher order and its being a desire with which one identifies.

17. See Vinit Haksar, "Aristotle and the Punishment of Psychopaths," *Philosophy* 39 (1964):323–340; Herbert Fingarette, *On Responsibility* (New York: Basic Books, 1967), chap. 2; Joel Feinberg, "Crime, Clutchability, and Individual Treatment," in *Doing and Deserving* (Princeton: Princeton Univ. Press, 1970), pp. 252–271; J. G. Murphy, "Moral Death: A Kantian Essay on Psychopathy," *Ethics* 82 (1972): 288–294.

18. I shall be assuming throughout that justification is necessarily motivating. The assumption is defended below in this section.

19. The requirement that any justification of our practice of ascribing responsibility, punishment, and blame must show how those made to suffer could be justified in acquiescing in the suffering and in feeling guilt and remorse is not arbitrary. The requirement stems from the problem of distinguishing genuine punishment and blame from mere manipulation. As I shall argue in section 3, this distinction is firmly entrenched in our actual practices concerning responsibility, and no weaker requirement seems capable of capturing it.

There is another reason, however, for the requirement that a theory preserve this distinction. In the context of a defense of a homuncular view of self-deception, the problem is to justify, in the ascription of responsibility, a distinction between self-deception and other-deception which has no intrinsic justification. This problem only arises on the assumption that genuine punishment and blame involve more than manipulation to produce some desired result—and that there is more to justifying such distinctions in ascribing responsibility than such a consequentialist approach allows. The reason the problem only arises on this assumption is that the consequences of blaming people for self-deception and for being deceived by others clearly differ in socially significant ways. Self-deception is far more likely to work to one's own advantage and to the disadvantage of others than is one's being deceived by another. Hence there are far stronger consequentialist considerations in favor of blaming the former than the latter. Thus on a consequentialist approach to responsibility, the original problem for homuncular models of self-deception never arises.

Given the distinction between punishment and manipulation, the claim that *punishment* requires reachability does not imply, of course, that the *manipulation* of those who are unreachable is never justified. And we are surely justified in protecting ourselves against those who fall outside our practice of responsibility, punishment, and blame, just as we protect ourselves from the criminally insane. But the justification of such practices will differ from the justification of genuine punishment. For those who are unreachable, pain and suffering in excess of what is required to prevent greater pain and suffering would almost certainly be unjustified, though it would often be justified for those who are reachable. On the other hand, measures that minimize suffering but would violate the autonomy of those who are reachable might well be justified for those who are not.

20. Given that neither consequentialist nor retributivist theories can justify the punishment of psychopaths, it would be useless to appeal to hybrid theories of punishment. If social utility cannot justify such punishment and retributivist theories fail, then the claim that the punishment is justified because it is a part of an institution which maximizes social utility and that the institution provides constraints which prevent punishing the innocent is equally inadequate. If neither the utilitarian nor the retributivist justification is cogent on its own, then requiring that they both apply cannot solve the problem.

21. P. F. Strawson, "Freedom and Resentment," in Watson, *Free Will* (cited in note 16), pp. 59–80.

22. Ibid., p. 77.

23. Notice that this account reverses the normal order of justification where responsibility is concerned. On the usual account, the metaphysical and value-neutral fact that one could have done otherwise (together with other, similarly value-neutral facts) grounds the ascription of responsibility which justifies the imposition of punishment or blame. On my account, the ascription of responsibility is grounded in our acceptance of the suffering that punishment and blame involve, our possession of the appropriate reactive attitudes toward that subject, and a certain kind of justification (to be described in section 5) of that acceptance and those attitudes. If there is any sense in which one could have done anything other than one did, it is to be understood in terms of the notion of one's being responsible and not vice versa. For an argument against the idea that one's ability to have done other than one did should be analyzed in terms that are ultimately normative, see Bernard Berofsky, "The Irrelevance of Morality to Freedom," in *Action and Responsibility*, ed. Faculty of the Department of Philosophy, Bowling Green State University (Bowling Green, Ohio: The Applied Philosophy Program, Bowling Green State Univ., 1980), pp. 38–47.

24. See Parfit, *Reasons and Persons*, pp. 12–23.

25. To interpret Strawson in this way is in effect to regard his position as a species of motive utilitarianism. (See Robert M. Adams, "Motive Utilitarianism," *Journal of Philosophy* 73 [1976]:467–481.) To understand Strawson in this way is to suppose that the good to which the reactive attitudes contribute and which would justify our keeping them if we had the technology to bring about their elimination is independent of the attitudes themselves. Call this the *thin interpretation* of Strawson. On the *thick interpretation*, Strawson would deny this. On the thick interpretation, Strawson's position would be much closer to the one I outline in sections 4 and 5. Strawson, however, does not develop the conceptual apparatus necessary to clarify the distinction between the positions corresponding to the thick and thin interpretations. Nor does he discuss the relativistic implications, which I discuss in section 5, of the position corresponding to the thick interpretation.

26. See, for example, Karl Menninger, *The Crime of Punishment* (New York: Viking, 1968); B. F. Skinner, *Beyond Freedom and Dignity* (New York: Alfred A. Knopf, 1971); and Barbara Wootton, *Crime and the Criminal Law* (London: Stevens

and Sons, 1963) and *Social Science and Social Pathology* (London: Allen and Unwin, 1959), part 2.

27. These social conditions faced by the act-consequentialist will be part of the argument (in section 5) that our self-supporting dispositions where responsibility is concerned have an act-consequentialist rationale. But is it necessary, for cooperation, to require that subjects have an *internalized* disposition to keep promises even at great cost? If it is not, if some social mechanism of enforcement would secure the benefits, then the legitimacy of justifying a self-supporting disposition by reference to such a requirement is open to dispute. The question, then, is whether the requirements that motivate the acquisition of a self-supporting disposition to keep promises are realistic.

The answer, I think, is yes. The institution of a *social* mechanism for enforcing contracts and promises itself presupposes self-supporting dispositions of the sort described. Even the practices of enforcement we associate with organized criminal activity presuppose self-supporting dispositions to uphold contracts regardless of the consequences, at least on the part of the enforcers. Hence the reference to social mechanisms of enforcement postpones rather than solves the difficulties inherent in securing the benefits of cooperation.

28. The act-consequentialist might, of course, acquire an *indirect disposition* to support the institution of punishment in the lottery society. She might do so by acquiring a self-supporting disposition to keep her word and then promise to support the institution. Because the disposition is indirect, however, it would not provide the grounds for her acquiescing in the punishment of others in the sense of being justified in feeling resentment or moral indignation. Nor would it justify her feeling guilt or remorse in her own case. Moreover, her disposition to support the institution in question is clearly parasitic on her self-supporting disposition to keep her promises come what may. And this latter disposition is precisely the kind that an account of responsibility should explain. Thus this possibility is one we can ignore where the justification of punishment and blame are concerned.

There is another alternative to an indirect disposition, and that is an alienated disposition. Recall that the argument against Strawson's appeal to nonmaximizing dispositions to support our institution of punishment depended on a number of specific features of the social context in which it occurs: that judicial procedures are lengthy, impersonal, open to scrutiny, and subject to criticism and appeal and that particular decisions and not just the institutions themselves must be explained and defended. This means that there is room for a number of practices in some ways like punishment which are based on nonmaximizing rather than self-supporting dispositions.

Consider again the act-consequentialist who wants to join the society in which punishment is distributed by lottery. We have seen that given a perfect technology for acquiring and extinguishing dispositions, she cannot form the direct disposition to support the practice of punishment come what may. Suppose, however, we consider the case of imperfect technology. Let us define a *noncrisis period* as one in which a nonmaximizing disposition is supported on consequentialist grounds and a *crisis period* as one in which it is not. For the act-consequentialist, any period in which she calculates that the chances of her or a loved one's being chosen for punishment are outweighed by the advantages of living in the lottery society is a noncrisis period. In such a period it is to her advantage to join the society if she can and support its practices. And she is disposed to do so. If against all odds the act-consequentialist or a loved one is chosen as one of the people to be sacrificed, she enters a crisis period. It will then be to her advantage (and she will be disposed) to thwart the society's practices if she can and to eliminate any dispositions of hers that would prevent her doing so.

It is the possibility of such crisis periods which keeps the act-consequentialist from joining the society (or allows her to join only on the basis of an indirect disposition, the possibility of which is irrelevant for our purposes). Acquisition of a self-supporting disposition to uphold the society's practices would eliminate the possibility, since unlike nonmaximizing dispositions, self-supporting dispositions are always supported for the subject who has them. For the act-consequentialist, however, there is no direct self-supporting disposition not involving false beliefs to support the punishment lottery.

Suppose that the technology for eliminating dispositions were, however, imperfect. The act-consequentialist might then join the society on the following terms. Assume that she could induce a disposition to support the practice of punishment which, although not inextinguishable, could not (for technological reasons) be eliminated during the time span of any crisis period likely to occur. (The wheels of justice might move faster than any form of therapy or conditioning that could remove the disposition.) Such a disposition exists. All that is required is a desire whose motivational strength is great enough. In the absence of perfect technology, its lack of support among other desires is no impediment to its survival, and its strength ensures that it will be acted upon. From the point of view of the members of the lottery society, such a disposition to support the society's institutions would be a perfectly adequate alternative to one which was self-supporting.

From the point of view of the act-consequentialist, however, this disposition differs significantly from a self-supporting disposition. Let us call this disposition that is not self-supporting an *alienated disposition*. The terminology is appropriate because for the act-consequentialist to act on this disposition would be for her to act against her best judgment. Her action would be analogous to that of a drug addict succumbing to a desire that he or she would destroy if the possibility were open.

Thus an alienated disposition, like an indirect disposition, to support the institution of punishment is not a disposition to acquiesce in the punishment of oneself or others, or to recognize that punishment as appropriate, or to be justified in feeling resentment, indignation, guilt, or remorse. Hence the claim stands that unless our practice of ascribing responsibility and blame for self-deception has an internal justification, we cannot acquiesce in the suffering that such practices entail.

29. There is further support for the plausibility of this claim in Stephen Darwall's discussion of self-deception and autonomy in "Self-Deception, Autonomy, and Moral Constitution," chap. 19 in this volume.

30. I am grateful to Jonathan Adler, Robert Audi, Akeel Bilgrami, Stephen Darwall, Mark Johnston, Brian McLaughlin, and Georges Rey for their comments on earlier drafts. I have benefited especially from the discussion of these issues with Jonathan Glover and from his recent work on responsibility (presented at the University of Michigan in 1985 and included in part in "Self-Creation," *Proceedings of the British Academy* 69 [1983]:445–471).

Part VI

SELF-DECEPTION IN LITERATURE

22

LOVE'S KNOWLEDGE

MARTHA NUSSBAUM

> And if a cataleptic impression does not exist, neither will there be any assent to it, and thus there will not be any certainty either. And if there is no certainty, neither will there be a system of certainties, that is to say a science. From which it follows that there will be no science of life either.
>
> —Sextus Empiricus, *Adversus Mathematicos* vii, 182

> As we examine this view closely, it looks to us more like a prayer than like the truth.
>
> —Sextus, ibid., xi, 401

Françoise brings him the news: "Mademoiselle Albertine has gone." Only a moment before, he believed with confidence that he did not love her any longer. Now the news of her departure brings a reaction so powerful, an anguish so overwhelming, that this view of his condition simply vanishes. Marcel knows, and knows with certainty, without the least room for doubt, that he loves Albertine.[1]

We deceive ourselves about love—about who; and how; and when; and whether. We also discover and correct our self-deceptions. The forces making for both deception and unmasking here are various and powerful: the unsurpassed danger, the urgent need for protection and self-sufficiency, the opposite and equal need for joy and communication and connection. Any of these can serve either truth of falsity, as the occasion demands. The difficulty then becomes: how in the midst of this confusion (and delight and pain) do we know what view of ourselves, what parts of ourselves, to trust? Which stories about the condition of the heart are the reliable ones and which the self-deceiving fictions? We find ourselves asking where, in this plurality of discordant voices with which we address ourselves on this topic of perennial self-interest, is the criterion of truth? (And what does it mean to look for a criterion here? Could that demand itself be a tool of self-deception?)

Proust tells us that the sort of knowledge of the heart we need in this case cannot be given us by the science of psychology, or, indeed, by any sort of scientific use of intellect. Knowledge of the heart must come from the heart—

from and in its pains and longings, its emotional responses. I examine this part of Proust's view, and its relation to the "scientific" opposition. The view raises a number of troubling questions, which are only partially answered by the more elaborate account of emotion's interaction with reflection that Proust develops in his final volume. I then examine an alternative view of knowledge of love, one that opposes the scientific account in a more radical way. I find this view in a short story by Ann Beattie. Finally, I ask about the relationship between these views of love's knowledge and the styles in which they are expressed, and make some remarks about a philosophical criticism of literature.

KNOWLEDGE OF THE HEART BY INTELLECTUAL SCRUTINY

1. We need to begin with a picture of the view that Proust is opposing when he offers his account of how we come to know our own love. It is important to recognize from the beginning that this is not simply a rival alternative account of the matter, incompatible with Proust's as one belief is incompatible with another. It is also, according to Proust, a form of activity that we engage in, a commitment we make, when we wish to avoid or block the sort of knowledge that he will describe. It is a practical barrier to this knowledge as well as a theoretical rival. To believe in the theoretical rival and live accordingly is not just to be in error; it is to engage in a fundamental form of self-deception.

The rival view is this. Knowledge of whether one loves someone—knowledge of the condition of one's heart where love is concerned—can best be attained by a detached, unemotional, exact intellectual scrutiny of one's condition, conducted in the way a scientist would conduct a piece of research. We attend carefully, with subtle intellectual precision, to the vicissitudes of our passion, sorting, analyzing, classifying. This sort of scrutiny is both necessary and sufficient for the requisite self-knowledge.[2] Proust's Marcel is deeply attached to this view. Just before he receives the news of Albertine's departure, he has, accordingly, been surveying the contents of his heart in the scientific manner: "I had believed that I was leaving nothing out of account, like a rigorous analyst; I had believed that I knew the state of my own heart" (III: 426).[3] This inspection convinces him that no love for Albertine is present. He is tired of her. He desires other women.

This view of knowledge has, it hardly needs to be said, powerful roots in our entire intellectual tradition, and especially our philosophical tradition. It is also a view on which much of the thought about method and about writing in that tradition relies. The view (as it is defended by thinkers otherwise as diverse as Plato and Locke)[4] holds that our passions and our feelings are unnecessary to the search for truth about any matter whatever. What is more, feelings can easily impede that search, either by distracting the searching intellect or, still worse, by distorting its view of the world. Desire, as Plato puts it in the *Phaedo,* binds the soul to its bodily prison house and forces it to view everything from within that distorting enclosure. The result is that intellect is "bewitched," distorted in its function; a captive, it "collaborates in its own imprisonment." In short, self-deception about our condition, when it occurs, is the result of the corruption of reason by feeling and desire. Intellect "itself by itself" is never self-deceptive. Though of course it may fail to reach its goal for some external reason, it never presents a biased or one-sided view of truth. It is never internally corrupt or corrupting. Nor does it require supplementation from any other source. "Itself by itself" it reaches the truth.

This view has implications for questions of method and style. Locke has, of course, an altogether different view from Plato's about the relationship between intellect and bodily sense-perception, but he is no more charitable to the passions and their role in the search for truth. His attack on rhetorical and emotive features of style (which I have discussed further elsewhere) presupposes that the passions are never necessary to the grasp of truth, and are usually pernicious. I quote it as typical of a prejudice that runs through much of our philosophical tradition:

> But yet, if we would speak of things as they are, we must allow that all . . . the artificial and figurative application of words eloquence hath invented, are for nothing else but to insinuate wrong *ideas,* move the passions, and thereby mislead the judgment, and so indeed are perfect cheat; and therefore . . . they are certainly, in all discourses that pretend to inform or instruct, wholly to be avoided, and, where truth and knowledge are concerned, cannot but be thought a great fault either of the language or person that makes use of them. (*Essay,* bk. 3, chap. 10)[5]

Notice especially the inference: "move the passions and *thereby* mislead the judgment"; notice also the explicit claim that the emotive elements in style have no good or necessary function and that they can and should be altogether dropped. Intellect is a sufficient criterion of truth; we have no other veridical elements. Therefore a discourse that claims to search for truth and impart knowledge must speak in the language of the intellect, addressing itself to (and, as Plato might say, encouraging the separation of) the reader's own intellect. Using this view of knowledge and of discourse as our (somewhat simplified) target, we can now proceed to explore Proust's counterproposal.

THE CATALEPTIC IMPRESSION: KNOWLEDGE IN SUFFERING

2. Self-assured and complacent, carrying out his analytical scrutiny of the heart, Marcel hears the words, "Mademoiselle Albertine has gone." Im-

mediately the anguish occasioned by these words cuts away the pseudotruths of the intellect, revealing the truth of his love. "How much further does anguish penetrate in psychology," he observes, "than psychology itself" (III:425). The shock of loss and the attendant welling up of pain show him that his theories were forms of self-deceptive rationalization—not only *false* about his condition but also manifestations and accomplices of a reflex to deny and close off one's vulnerabilities that Proust finds to be very deep in all of human life. The primary and most ubiquitous form of this reflex is seen in the operations of habit, which makes the pain of our vulnerability tolerable to us by concealing need, concealing particularity (hence vulnerability to loss), concealing all the pain-inflicting features of the world—simply making us used to them, dead to their assaults. When we are used to them we do not feel them or long for them in the same way; we are no longer so painfully afflicted by our failure to control and possess them. Marcel has been able to conclude that he is not in love with Albertine, in part because he is used to her. His calm, methodical intellectual scrutiny is powerless to dislodge this "dread deity, so riveted to one's being, its insignificant face so incrusted in one's heart" (III:426). Indeed, it fails altogether to discern the all-important distinction between the face of habit and the true face of the heart.

In various ways, indeed, intellect actively aids and abets habit, concealing that true face. First, the guided tour of the heart conducted by intellect treats all landmarks as on a par, pointing out as salient and interesting many desires that are actually trivial and superficial. Like the account of social life offered in the parody journal of the Frères Goncourt (in which the color of the border on a dinner plate has the same importance as the expression in someone's eyes), intellect's account of psychology lacks all sense of proportion, of depth and importance. Accordingly, it is inclined to reckon up everything in terms of the numbers, "comparing the mediocrity of the pleasures that Albertine afforded me with the richness of the desires which she prevented me from realizing" (III:425). This cost-benefit analysis of the heart—the only comparative assessment of which intellect, by itself, is capable—is bound, Proust suggests, to miss differences of depth. Not only to miss them, but to impede their recognition. Cost-benefit analysis is a way of comforting oneself, of putting oneself in control by pretending that all losses can be made up by sufficient quantities of something else. This stratagem opposes the recognition of love—and, indeed, love itself.[6] Furthermore, we can see that not only the content of the intellectual account but the very fact of engaging in intellectual self-scrutiny is, here, a distorting source of comfort and distance. The very feeling that he is being subtle and profound, that he is "leaving nothing out of account, like a rigorous analyst," leads Marcel into complacency, deterring him from a richer or deeper inquiry, making him less likely to attend to the promptings of his own heart.

What is the antidote to these stratagems? To remove such powerful obstacles to truth, we require the instrument that is "the subtlest, most powerful, most appropriate for grasping the truth." This instrument is given to us in suffering.

> Our intelligence, however lucid, cannot perceive the elements that compose it and remain unsuspected so long as, from the volatile state in which they generally exist, a phenomenon capable of isolating them has not subjected them to the first stages of solidification. I had been mistaken in thinking that I could see clearly into my own heart. But this knowledge, which the shrewdest perceptions of the mind would not have given me, had now been brought to me, hard, glittering, strange, like a crystallised salt, by the abrupt reaction of pain. (III:426)

The Stoic philosopher Zeno argued that all our knowledge of the external world is built upon the foundation of certain special perceptual impressions: those which, by their own internal character, their own experienced quality, certify their own veracity.[7] From (or in) assent to such impressions, we get the cataleptic condition, a condition of certainty and confidence from which nothing can dislodge us. On the basis of such certainties is built all science, natural and ethical. (Science is defined as a system of *katalēpseis*.) The cataleptic impression is said to have the power, just through its own felt quality, to drag us to assent, to convince us that things could not be otherwise. It is defined as a mark or impress in the soul, "one that is imprinted and stamped upon us by reality itself and in accordance with reality, one that could not possibly come from what is not that reality."[8] The experience of having one is compared to a balance scale being weighed down by a very heavy weight— you just have to go along with it; it compels assent.[9] Again, Zeno compares its closure and certainty to a closed fist: it's that firm; there's no room for opposition.[10] It seems to me that Marcel—who elsewhere reveals his serious interest in the Hellenistic philosophers[11]—is working out a (highly non-Stoic)[12] analogue to Zeno's view for our knowledge of the inner world. Knowledge of our heart's condition is given to us in and through certain powerful impressions, impressions that come from the reality itself of our condition and could not possibly come from anything else but that reality. Indeed he uses explicitly Zenonian language of the way in which we gain self-knowledge through these experiences. He tells us that the impression is "the only criterion of truth" (III:914); that all our understanding of our life is built up on the basis of the text "that reality has dictated to us, whose impression in us has been made by reality itself" (III:914). The cataleptic impressions in this case, however, are emotional impressions: specifically impressions of anguish.

What is it about the impressions of suffering that makes them cataleptic? Why do they convince Marcel that truth is *here,* rather than in the deliverances of intellect? We are conscious, first of all, of their sheer *power.* The suffering is "hard, glittering, strange"; "an anguish such that I felt I could not endure

it much longer" (III:425); an "immense new jolt" (429); a "physical blow . . .
to the heart" (431); "like . . . a thunderbolt" (431); it makes "an open wound"
(425). The power of this impression simply overwhelms every other impression. The superficial impressions of the intellect "could no longer even begin
to compete . . . , had vanished instantaneously" (425).

These passages show us that, in addition to sheer force, there are also
surprise and passivity. The impression comes upon Marcel unbidden, unan-
nounced, uncontrolled. Because he neither predicts nor governs it, because
it simply gets stamped upon him, it seems natural to conclude that it is
authentic and not a stratagem devised by self-assuaging reason. Just as the
Stoic perceptual impressions drag the perceiving agent to assent not only by
their vividness but also by their unbidden and external character—they seem
such as could not have been made up; they must have come from reality
itself—so too with these emotional impressions. For Proust it is especially
significant that surprise, vivid particularity, and extreme qualitative intensity
are all characteristics that are systematically concealed by the workings of
habit, the primary form of self-deception and self-concealment. What has
these features must have escaped the workings of self-deception, must have
come from reality itself.

We notice, finally, that the very painfulness of these impressions is essential
to their cataleptic character. Our primary aim is to comfort ourselves, to as-
suage pain, to cover our wounds. Then what has the character of pain must
have escaped these mechanisms of comfort and concealment; must, then,
have come from the true unconcealed nature of our condition.

We now confront an ambiguity in Marcel's account.[13] He has told us that
certain self-impressions are criterial of psychological truth about ourselves.
But this picture can be understood in more than one way. On one interpretation, the impression gives us access to truths that could *in principle* (even if
not in fact) be grasped in other ways, for example, by intellect. We, perhaps,
cannot so grasp them because of certain obstacles in human psychology. But
they exist in the heart, apart from the suffering, available for knowledge.
Marcel's love is the sort of thing that some superior being—say, a god—could
see and know without pain. Pure intellectual knowledge of the heart as it is
in itself is possible in principle, apart from emotion; it is not in the very
nature of the knowledge itself that it involves suffering. On this reading,
Marcel will be taking issue with the intellectualist only about the instrumental
means to knowing; also, in some cases, about the content of the knowledge
gained. But he will not be taking issue in a fundamental way about what
knowing *is,* what activity or passivity of the person constitutes it.

There is, however, another possibility. For the Stoic the cataleptic impression is not simply a route to knowing; it *is* knowing. It doesn't point beyond
itself *to* knowledge; it goes to constitute knowledge. (Science is a system
made up of katalēpseis.) If we follow the analogy strictly, then, we find that

knowledge of our love is not the fruit of the impression of suffering, a fruit that might in principle have been had apart from the suffering. The suffering itself is a piece of self-knowing. *In* responding to a loss with anguish, we are grasping our love. The love is not some separate fact about us that is signaled by the impression; the impression reveals the love by constituting it. Love is not a structure in the heart waiting to be discovered; it is embodied in, made up out of, experiences of suffering. It is "produced" in Marcel's heart by Françoise's words (III:425).

This reading is borne out by Marcel's chemical analogy. A catalyst does not reveal chemical compounds that were there all along. It brings about a chemical reaction. It precipitates out the salt. The salt was not there before, or not in that state or form. The words, like the catalyst, both reveal a chemical structure and create something that was not there in the same way. Françoise's words are like the catalyst. They do not simply remove impediments to scientific knowledge, as if some curtains were pulled back and Marcel could now see exactly what he could have seen before had the curtains not been there. They bring about a change, which *is* the suffering; and this suffering is not so much an object of scientific knowing as an alternative to that knowing. In place of scientific knowing is substituted something that *counts as* knowing himself in a way that the scientific sort of grasping didn't—because it is not a stratagem for mastery of anything, but simply a naked case of his human incompleteness and neediness. Its relation to self-deception is not that of a rival and more accurate account of standing structures in the heart. It *is* the thing from which the deception was protecting him, namely the love, the needy, painful reaching out that is not only a specific condition of his heart now towards Albertine but also a fundamental condition of the human soul.

Marcel is brought, then, by and in the cataleptic impression, to an acknowledgment of his love. There are elements of both discovery and creation here, at both the particular and general levels. Love of Albertine is both discovered and created. It is discovered, in that habit and intellect were masking from Marcel a psychological condition that was ready for suffering, and that, like the chemicals, needed only to be affected slightly by the catalyst in order to turn itself into love. It is created, because love denied and successfully repressed is not exactly love. While he was busily denying that he loved her, he simply was not loving her. At the general level, again, Marcel both discovers and enacts a permanent underlying feature of his condition, namely his neediness, his hunger for possession and completeness. That too was there in a sense before the loss, because that's what human life is made of. But in denying and repressing it, Marcel became temporarily self-sufficient, closed, and estranged from his humanity. The pain he feels for Albertine gives him access to his permanent underlying condition by being a case of that condition, and no such case was present a moment before. Before the suffering he was indeed self-deceived—both because he was denying a general structural feature of his humanity and because he was denying the particular readiness of his soul to feel hopeless love for Albertine. He was on the verge of a precipice and thought he was safely immured in his own rationality. But his case shows us as well how the successful denial of love is the (temporary) extinction and death of love, how self-deception can aim at and nearly achieve self-change.

We now see exactly how and why Marcel's account of self-knowledge is no simple rival to the intellectual account. It tells us that the intellectual account was wrong: wrong about the content of the truth about Marcel, wrong about the methods appropriate for gaining this knowledge, wrong, as well, about what sort of experience of the person knowing is. And it tells us that to try to grasp love intellectually is a way of not suffering, not loving; a practical rival, a stratagem of flight.

CATALEPTIC IMPRESSIONS AND THE SCIENCE OF LIFE

3. Marcel's cataleptic view is a powerful alternative to its theoretical and practical rival. And most of us have had such experiences, in which the self-protective tissue of rationalization is in a moment cut through, as by a surgeon's knife. Zeno's picture seems more compelling, in fact, as a story about emotional knowing than as an account of perceptual knowledge, its intended function. And yet, as we reflect on Marcel's story, mining, as Proust urges, our own experience for similar material, we begin to feel a certain discontent.

This blind, unbidden surge of painful affect: is it really the "subtle and powerful" instrument Marcel believes it is? Can't it too be deceptive—occasioned, for example, by egocentric needs and frustrations that have little to do with love? Isn't it, moreover, in its very violence and rage—qualities that were important to its cataleptic status—a rather coarse and blunt instrument, lacking in responsiveness and discrimination?

There are several different worries here; we need to disentangle them. They fall into two groups: worries that Marcel has picked the wrong impressions to be the cataleptic ones, and more general worries about the whole cataleptic idea. First, then: if there are cataleptic feelings where love is concerned, why must they be feelings of suffering? We understand why Marcel thinks this: these are the only ones we would never fake. But still, as I consider my own experiences here, I find myself asking, Why not feelings of joy? Or some gentler passions, such as the feeling of tender concern? Why not, indeed, experiences that are more essentially relational in nature—experiences of the exchange of feeling, the mutual communication of emotion; experiences that cannot be characterized without mention of the other person's awareness and activity? If we accept Marcel's claim that our natural psychological tendency is always towards self-insulation and the blunting of intrusive stimuli, then it does seem reasonable to suppose that a feeling of intense suffering wouldn't be there if it weren't in some sense true, an emanation from depths that we usually conceal. But should we accept this story? And even if we do, does it give us reason to think that other feelings could not also have depth?

We notice, further, that if suffering is the only reliable impression where the heart is concerned, and if suffering *is* love, then the only reliable answer to the question "Do I love?" must always be "yes." We can see why Proust wishes to say this, but it seems peculiar nonetheless. Aren't there possibilities of self-deception on both sides?

This brings us to our second group of questions. Can any feeling, taken in isolation from its context, its history, its relationship to other feelings and actions, really be cataleptic? Can't we be wrong about it and what it signifies? Emotions are not, nor does Proust believe they are, simply raw feelings, individuated by their felt quality alone. Then to be sure that this pain is love—and not, for example, fear or grief or envy—we need to scrutinize the beliefs and the circumstances that go with it, and their relation to our other beliefs and circumstances. Perhaps this scrutiny will disclose that Marcel was simply ill or lacking sleep; perhaps he is really feeling discouragement about his literary career, or a fear of death—and not love at all. The impression does not seem to come reliably labeled with the name of the emotion it is. And even if it is love, can one impression inform him, beyond doubt, that it is a love of Albertine (and not longing for his grandmother, or some more general desire for comfort and attention)? Impressions, in short, require interpretation. And reliable interpretation may well be impossible if we are given only a single experience in isolation. Even an extended pattern might be wrongly understood. But to concede this much is to give up cataleptic impressions.

All this leads us to ask whether Marcel has not been too hasty in (apparently) dismissing intellect and its scrutiny from the enterprise of self-knowing. He may perhaps have shown that it is not sufficient for knowledge of love; he has not shown that it is not necessary. We shall shortly see that Proust later concedes this point—in a limited way.

But now we come upon a deeper criticism, which we borrow from Sextus Empiricus' attack on the Stoic cataleptic impression. This is that Marcel's whole project has about it an odd air of circularity. How do we know love? By a cataleptic impression. But what is this thing, love, that gets known? It is understood to be, is more or less defined as, the very thing that is revealed to us in cataleptic impressions. We privilege the impression of suffering as the criterion, and then we adopt an account of love (hardly the only possible account) according to which love is exactly what this criterion reveals to us. We suspect that Marcel will not allow love to be something that cannot be cataleptically conveyed, something toward which we cannot have the certainty

of the single and solitary impression. We suspect that at the root of his emphatic rejection from the account of love of many aspects of what we usually
call love—say, mutuality, laughter, well-wishing, tenderness—is the thought
that there is, for these things, no catalepsis. Even so, the Stoic defines
the cataleptic impression as "that which is imprinted and impressed by what
is real," etc., and then defines "what is real" as "that which produces a cataleptic impression."[14] In this way, the science of life is established on a sure
foundation.

Marcel's relation to the science of self-knowledge now begins to look more
complex than we had suspected. We said that the attempt to grasp love
intellectually was a way of avoiding loving. We said that in the cataleptic
impression there is acknowledgment of one's own vulnerability and incompleteness, an end to our flight from ourselves. But isn't the whole idea of
basing love and its knowledge on cataleptic impressions itself a form of
flight—from openness to the other, from all those things in love for which
there is in fact no certain criterion? Isn't his whole enterprise just a new and
more subtle expression of the rage for control, the need for possession and
certainty, the denial of incompleteness and neediness that characterized the
intellectual project? Isn't he still hungry for a science of life?

For consider a remarkable consequence of the project. Proustian catalepsis
is a solitary event. This is emphasized in the narrative, where true knowledge
of love arrives in Albertine's absence, indeed at a time when, although he
doesn't know it, Marcel will never see her again. The experience does not
require Albertine's participation or even awareness; it has no element of mutuality or exchange. And it certainly does not presuppose any knowledge of
or trust in the feelings of the other. It coexists here with the belief that he
does not and cannot know whether she loves him. In fact, the cataleptic
experience seems to possess even object-directed intentionality only in a very
minimal way. What Marcel feels is a gap or lack in himself, an open wound,
a blow to the heart, a hell inside himself. Is all of this really love of Albertine?
And isn't it clear that the determination to have cataleptic certainty, together
with the recognition that the separateness and independence of the other gives
no purchase in the other for such certainty, is what has led him to portray
the nature of love in this highly peculiar manner?

The result is actually more disturbing still. We said that the cataleptic impression can coexist with skepticism about the feelings of the other. In fact,
it implies this skepticism. For on the cataleptic view an emotion can be known
if and only if it can be vividly experienced. What you can't have you can't
know. But the other's will, thoughts, feelings are, for Marcel, paradigmatic
of that which cannot be had. They beckon to him out of Albertine's defiant,
silent eyes at Balbec, a secret world closed to his will, a vast space his ambitious thoughts can never cover.[15] His projects of possession, doomed before they begin, satisfied only in their own self-undercutting—as when he

guards a sleeping Albertine, who at that moment no longer eludes him, but who, in having become merely "a being that breathes," does not inspire love either—teach him that the heart and mind of another are unknowable, even unapproachable, except in fantasies and projections that are really elements of the knower's own life, not the other's. "The human being is the being who cannot depart from himself, who knows others only in himself, and, if he says the contrary, lies." Albertine can never be for him anything more than "the generating center of an immense construction that rose above the plane of my heart" (III:445). In short: "I understood that my love was less a love for her than a love in me. . . . It is the misfortune of beings to be for us nothing else but useful showcases for the contents of our own minds" (III:568).[16]

This condition is their misfortune; in a sense it is also ours. But skepticism is not just an incidental and unfortunate consequence of Marcel's epistemology. It is at the same time its underlying motivation. It is because this is a suspicious man who can be content with nothing less than full control, who cannot tolerate the other's separate life, that he demands cataleptic impressions and a certainty that the other can never give him. It is because he wishes not to be tormented by the ungovernable inner life of the other that he adopts a position that allows him to conclude that the other's inner life is nothing more than the constructive workings of his own mind. The skeptical conclusion consoles far more than it agonizes. It means that he is alone and self-sufficient in the world of knowledge. That love is not a source of dangerous openness, but a rather interesting relation with oneself.

CATALEPSIS ORDERED BY REFLECTION:
PROUST'S FINAL VIEW

4. Before we turn away from Proust, we should recognize that this is not Marcel's final word on the knowledge of love. The position he articulates in the novel's last volume complicates the cataleptic view, apparently in response to some of our criticisms. I think we shall see, however, that our deepest worries remain unaddressed.

Intellect, Marcel still insists, must begin its work from unbidden nonintellectual truths, "those which life communicates to us against our will in an impression which is material because it enters through the senses but yet has a spiritual meaning which it is possible for us to extract" (III:912). Intellect, using cataleptic impressions, and above all impressions of suffering, as its basic material, extracts from them the general "laws and ideas" to which they point. We *think* what we had "merely felt" before. Reflection achieves this generality by drawing on a number of impressions and linking them together in an artistic way. "It is our passions which draw the outlines of our books, the ensuing intervals of repose that write them" (III:945).

What truths about love does reflection deliver that would not have been perspicuous in and through feeling alone? First of all, the general form and pattern of one's loves:

> A work, even one that is directly autobiographical, is at the very least put together out of several interrelated episodes in the life of the author—earlier episodes which have inspired the work and later ones which resemble it just as much, the later loves being traced after the pattern of the earlier. For to the women whom we have loved most in our life we are not so faithful as we are to ourself, and sooner or later we forget her in order—since this is one of the characteristics of that self—to be able to begin to love again. At most our faculty of loving has received from this woman whom we so loved a particular stamp, which will cause us to be faithful to her even in our infidelity. We shall need, with the woman who succeeds her, those same morning walks or the same practice of taking her home every evening or giving her a hundred times too much money . . . These substitutions add then to our work something that is disinterested and more general. (III:145–146)

But this generalizing power does more: it shows us that love is not simply a repeated experience; it is a permanent structural feature of our soul. "If our love is not only love of a Gilberte (the one who is causing us so much suffering), it is not because it is also love of an Albertine, but because it is a portion of our soul . . . which must . . . detach itself from beings to restore its generality" (III:933). At this level of depth, love unites in itself and shows us the unity in different disappointments and sufferings that we might previously not have called forms of love at all. In reflection we see that the suffering of love and the suffering of travel, "were not different disappointments at all but the varied aspects which are assumed, according to the particular circumstances which bring it into play, by our inherent powerlessness to realize ourselves in material enjoyment or in effective action" (III:911). In other words, we know this love for Albertine as an instance of our loving, and our loving as the general form of our permanent finitude and incompleteness—in this way deriving a far more complete and correct understanding of love than we could have had in the impression alone.

Finally, reflection shows us "the intermittences of the heart"—the alternations between love and its denial, suffering and denial of suffering, that constitute the most essential and ubiquitous structural feature of the human heart. In suffering we know only suffering. We call our rationalizations false and delusive, and we do not see to what extent they express a mechanism that is regular and deep in our lives. But this means that in love itself we do not yet have full knowledge of love—for we do not grasp its limits and boundaries. Sea creatures cannot be said to know the sea in the way that a creature does who can survey and dwell in both sea and land, noticing how they bound and limit one another.[17]

This reformulation of the cataleptic view appears to answer some of our worries: for reflection permits the critical assessment of impressions, their linking into an overall pattern, their classification and reclassification. Proust now concedes that about certain impressions we can be wrong: we do not notice that the pain of travel and the pain of love are one and the same emotion. Interpretation begins to play the role we sought for it. But caution is needed here. First, we still cannot be wrong about *love*. We go wrong only in failing to pick out as love another pain that is really love. The revision that takes place consists in noticing love's ubiquity as *the* basic form of desire, not in becoming more subtle and selective concerning which experiences to count as love. Second, it is essential to notice that the cataleptic impressions of love are still the unchallenged foundations of all knowledge. Reflection and art may fill in the outline; they can never challenge or revise it. "The impression is the only criterion of truth," therefore the only source for truths of reflection (III:914). The emotional impression is to the artist, Marcel continues here, what observational data are to a Baconian scientist: although in some sense the data are not really and fully known until they are integrated into a theory, still the scientist starts from them alone, and relies on them implicitly. Thus the revised view does not really answer our questions about suffering—whether it is the best guide, whether any solitary impression is really evidence of *love*.

And it has a further consequence. The connection between self-knowledge and skepticism about the other is actually reinforced in the complex view. Built upon cataleptic data and trusting these alone, reflection can never penetrate to the thoughts and feelings of the other. And, being reflection, it turns this fact into a theoretical conclusion, an "austere lesson." The greatest courage of the artist, Marcel announces, lies in his or her willingness to acknowledge the truth of skepticism, "abrogating his most cherished illusions, ceasing to believe in the objectivity of that which one has oneself created, and, instead of cradling oneself for the hundredth time with the words, 'She was very sweet,' reading *through* them, 'I enjoyed kissing her'" (III:932). Belief in the other is a weakness, a form of consoling self-deception.

And yet, we can hardly help feeling that there is something more consoling still in the austere lesson of solipsism, certified and pinned down and made scientific by the operations of thought. Sextus seems to be right: this view looks more like a wish or a prayer for something than like a statement of truth. And isn't it perhaps a wish for the very thing the intellectualist sought: freedom from disturbance and pain?[18]

LEARNING TO FALL

5. I turn now to a view that shares Proust's criticisms of intellectualism but locates love's knowledge in an altogether different place. It says, in effect,

that knowing love is knowing how to go beyond Proustian skepticism and solitude. And how is skepticism to be overcome here? By love.

Unlike Proust's view, this view does not simply substitute for the activity of the knowing intellect some other single and simple inner attitude or state of the person, holding that knowledge consists in this. It insists that knowledge of love is not a state or function of the solitary person at all, but a complex way of being, feeling, and interacting with another person. To know one's own love is to trust it, to allow oneself to be exposed. It is, above all, to trust the other person, suspending Proustian doubts. Such knowledge is not independent of evidence. Typically it is built upon a good deal of attention over time, attention that delivers a lot of evidence about the other person, about oneself, about patterns of interaction between the two. Nor is it independent of powerful feelings that have real evidential value. But it goes beyond the evidence, and it ventures outside of the inner world.

It is in the nature of this view that it is difficult to say much about it in the abstract. Its message is that there are no necessary and sufficient conditions, that knowledge of love is a love story. The best way to explore it seems to be to turn to stories ourselves. We could find it in many places (I think above all of Henry James and Virginia Woolf). But I have chosen instead a contemporary example that exemplifies the view with a remarkable compression and intensity of focus. This is Ann Beattie's story "Learning to Fall."[19] As its title announces, it is the story of a woman who learns to know her own love and not to fear her own vulnerability. I want to let this woman's voice, whose shifting rhythms are themselves part of her emerging knowledge, tell the story as far as possible. So I shall sketch the "plot" crudely, then comment on three passages.

The narrator is a woman in her thirties, a Connecticut housewife, unhappily married to a dry and successful professional man. She had a lover named Ray, in New York. She broke up with him some time before, "when I decided that loving Ray made me as confused as disliking Arthur, and that he had too much power over me and that I could not be his lover anymore" (p. 12). Now when she goes into the city, she avoids Ray by taking with her the son of her best friend, Ruth. The boy is lonely, slightly brain-damaged third grader with a drooping mouth and unusual capacities of perception. This day she takes him to various places in the city, all the while thinking about Ray but not calling him. Then, discovering that she has (perhaps intentionally) made them late for the train back to Connecticut, she does call. He joins them for coffee. The end of this story I shall discuss in detail, but first we need the beginning.

> Ruth's house, early morning: a bowl of apples on the kitchen table, crumbs on the checkered tablecloth. "I love you," she says to Andrew. "Did you guess that I loved you?" "I know it," he says. He's annoyed that his mother is being mushy

in front of me. He is eager to seem independent, and cranky because he just woke up. I'm cranky too, even after the drive to Ruth's in the cold. I'm drinking coffee to wake up. If someone said that he loved me at this moment, I'd never believe him; I can't think straight so early in the morning, hate to make conversation, am angry at the long, cold winter. (p. 3)

Ruth is the trusting and trusted, the one most capable of love, the one whose poor messy warm house is for the narrator the antithesis of the opulent sterility of her own marriage. ("She earns hardly any money at the community college, but her half-gallons of wine taste better than the expensive bottles Arthur's friends uncork. She will reach out and touch you to let you know she is listening when you talk, instead of suggesting that you go out to see some movie for amusement" [p. 8].) We begin in Ruth's house, situated as by a stage direction, surrounded by her presence. For Ruth, asking a question about love is—can only be—a loving game, a way of saying I love you gently and playfully. "Did you guess," she can ask, because their whole life is so far beyond guessing. (The boy's father left her abruptly, shortly before the birth, and has had no contact with them since. Even at that, she's "not bitter," just "angry at myself. I don't often misjudge people that way" [p. 9].) The little boy has never thought of asking a real skeptical question. To him all the question means is that his mother's being mushy. "I know it" is the reply the game demands; but for him as for her, it has nothing to do with really seeking for knowledge. He isn't examining his (or his mother's) psychology; he isn't looking for or experiencing any cataleptic anything. He's just eating his breakfast, saying the usual things. Knowledge of love is his whole way of life with his mother. We see that he isn't sure he likes this knowledge. He wants to separate himself, learn not to say those words. He may already think of male adulthood as requiring that repudiation.[20] To repudiate it, however, would not be to discover some new facts about her heart or his. It would be simply to stop playing that game, living that life.

The narrator is a skeptic. She wouldn't believe a claim of love. She wouldn't believe it because she is angry, confused, sleepy, ill-at-ease with conversation. She doesn't have Ruth's grace at touching and being touched. She holds herself to one side, aloof, wondering. She drinks coffee a lot, and Andrew knows she doesn't eat "during the day" (p. 4). She has to control everything, her thinness, her lover, the time. Always early, hurrying for the train, fascinated with the food she refuses.

This brings me to her watch.

I look at my watch. The watch was a Christmas present from Arthur. It's almost touching that he isn't embarrassed to give me such impersonal presents as eggcups and digital watches. To see the time, you have to push in the tiny button on the side. As long as you hold it, the time stays lit, changes. Take away your hand and the watch turns clear red again. (p. 7)

The watch is impersonal time, time scrutinized, controlled, and intellectualized: the time of the skeptic. (Ruth just takes the time, feeling there's "plenty of" it, hand on your back, not on her watch.) Hand always on the time, she won't let the things happen that take time. It took eight years, she remembers, for Andrew to trust someone other than his mother.[21] Only with Andrew—because she has fun with him, because she "know[s] him so well," because he is not alarming and she pities him—does she take her hands off the watch sometimes. "I almost love him." Her whimsical fantasy of Superman launching himself from the Superman patch on Andrew's knee and flying a foot above the ground, disconcerting the passers by (p. 4)—this has a charm, an unguarded quality of enjoyment and humor, that we haven't seen in this woman before. It's possibly the first time she hasn't had a thought for herself.

It's after she has been walking down the street with Andrew, swinging hands, that she realizes that they are late. The watch is wrong and she knew it. (It wasn't even good at its impersonal job.) Andrew "thinks what I think—that if I had meant to, we could have caught the train" (p. 11). While she was relying on it to distance her from love, to keep her from that knowledge by precise knowledge, another part of her was using its untrustworthiness to work towards trust of another sort. She goes to a pay phone in Grand Central and calls Ray.

For the intellectualist view, knowledge of love is measured by the clock like everything else. It is in measured time, and it is itself a measuring, assessing activity, very like the measuring of the watch. (It weighed and measured one pleasure against another counting costs and benefits.) Proust shows us how the temporality of the heart breaks with the rhythms of measuring devices. The full story of love—its intermittences, its rhythms of pain and avoidance—can be comprehended only by a reflection that observes the specifically human temporality of desire and habit, which proceeds by its own laws of felt duration. And the blinding moment of cataleptic knowledge, like any other break in the walls of habit, has the feeling of eternity, of the whole of a life: mysterious and momentary, instantaneous yet forever, "hard, glittering, strange," with the precipitous finality of death. It is not a progress or a sequence; it is not a relation evolving over time. In fact, it's because it is not a relation at all—it has really nothing to do with the other, it's a chemical reaction in oneself—that it can have this instantaneous character. Proust moves us from clock time to human time, but to a human time that will not take time for things to happen—because they might happen, and then one would perhaps not be alone. Beattie's narrator turns from her digital watch to a different sort of human time—to a trust that evolves over time, that is learned, that must be permitted, in time, through missing a train and taking the time, to happen.[22]

What do we know about this man? More, I find, in the story's ten pages than about Albertine in three thousand. That's already a sign of something. He makes himself felt from the first, long before we see him, as an intrusive, confusing presence—with his soft voice, his laconic speech, his boots, his joy in physical objects, his beautiful hands, and his patience. His sexual power, intense yet gentle, is everywhere she goes—the Guggenheim, the loft in Soho, the station phone booth. From the beginning this is a story about two people, the story of a knowledge that resides in the other and in the space between them. "I used to sleep with him and then hold his head as if I believed in phrenology. He used to hold my hands as I held his head. Ray has the most beautiful hands I have ever seen." She's using the present tense, watching them. "Want to stay in town?" he says (p. 12).

The moment that's comparable to and so different from Proust's is precipitated by the boy, catalyst with a Superman patch on his knee—omnipotence, a foot above the ground. They are sitting in a restaurant booth. Andrew is eating as always, drinking a milkshake. More coffee for her. Ray wanted a drink, but he has to put up with coffee. The story ends this way:

> Andrew shifts in the booth, looks at me as if he wants to say something. I lean my head toward him. "What?" I say softly. He starts a rush of whispering.
>
> "His mother is learning to fall," I say.
>
> "What does that mean?" Ray says.
>
> "In her dance class," Andrew says. He looks at me again, shy. "Tell him."
>
> "I've never seen her do it," I say. "She told me about it—it's an exercise or something. She's learning to fall."
>
> Ray nods. He looks like a professor being patient with a student who has just reached an obvious conclusion. You know when Ray isn't interested. He holds his head very straight and looks you right in the eye, as though he is.
>
> "Does she just go plop?" he says to Andrew.
>
> "Not really," Andrew says, more to me than to Ray. "It's kind of slow."
>
> I imagine Ruth bringing her arms in front of her, head bent, an almost penitential position, and then a loosening in the knees, a slow folding downward.
>
> Ray reaches across the table and pulls my arms away from the front of my body, and his touch startles me so that I jump, almost upsetting my coffee.
>
> "Let's take a walk," he says. "Come on. You've got time."
>
> He puts two dollars down and pushes the money and the check to the back of the table. I hold Andrew's parka for him and he backs into it. Ray adjusts it on his shoulders. Ray bends over and feels in Andrew's pockets.
>
> "What are you doing?" Andrew says.
>
> "Sometimes disappearing mittens have a way of reappearing," Ray says. "I guess not."
>
> Ray zips his own green jacket and pulls on his hat. I walk out of the restaurant beside him, and Andrew follows.
>
> "I'm not going far," Andrew says. "It's cold."
>
> I clutch the envelope. Ray looks at me and smiles, it's so obvious that I'm holding the envelope with both hands so I don't have to hold his hand. He moves

in close and puts his hand around my shoulder. No hand-swinging like children—the proper gentleman and the lady out for a stroll. What Ruth has known all along: what will happen can't be stopped. Aim for grace. (pp. 13–14)

She knows what Ruth knew all along: what will happen can't be stopped. But what this means is that she lets herself not stop it, she decides to stop stopping it. She discovers what will happen by letting it happen. Like Ruth, slowly falling in the class exercise that teaches and manifests trust, she learns to fall. As Andrew says, she doesn't just go plop (as Marcel did, abruptly plunging); she gently, slowly yields to her own slow folding, to the folding of his arm around her. She lets that touch not startle her. Like Ruth's bodily fall and, as she sees, like prayer, it's something done yet, once you do it, fundamentally uncontrolled; no accident, yet a yielding; an aiming, but for grace. You can't aim for grace really. It has so little connection, if any, with your efforts and actions. Yet what else can you do? How else are you supposed to pray? You open yourself to that possibility.

Is this discovery or creation? Both, we have to say. A pattern is there already; it vibrates through the story. The final moment has the conviction, the power, the crazy joy it does because it is the emerging of something that has been there all along and has been repressed. We can talk of self-deception here just as we could in Marcel's case, because she has been denying the power Ray continuously exerts over her imaginings and her actions. Andrew knew about her what she denied to herself. But of course she is loving Ray now as she didn't before. Love feared and avoided is not just sitting there beneath the skin waiting to be laid bare, any more than Ruth's slow fall Platonically inhabits the narrator's stiff, thin, coffee-drinking body. It has to be created. The removal of self-deception is also a change in the self. Both discovery and creation are present on the general level too, as she both finds a vulnerable and passionate side of herself that had been denied and makes herself evolve into a more trusting woman. She decides to let those elements flourish, be actualized.[23]

The cataleptic view has its role to play inside these experiences. There's no doubt that she was missing him, that she missed the train because she was missing him. There's no doubt either of the power of her arousal, and also her fear, when he reaches across the table and takes her hand. All this has some role in her knowledge of love, and the power of those impressions is a part of what prepares her love. But that's the point: they prepare it, they aren't it. The knowing itself is a relation, a dizzy elated falling. There are powerful feelings here—sexual feelings, feelings, I think, of profound joy and nakedness and giddiness and freedom: the feelings of falling. But he's too intrinsic to it all for us to say that those feelings just *are* the falling, the loving. The loving is about him, an opening toward him, as prayer in her image, would be an opening toward God. She could also say that faith is a certain strong feeling in the region of the heart. Proust's prayer, the cataleptic prayer, is that this should be all there is to say.

Knowledge of her own condition and knowledge of him are inextricable here. Not in the sense that she has succeeded in doing phrenology, in getting a scientific account of his head that's beyond doubt. Not in the sense that she possesses his experiences or feels them herself. She could be wrong, that's clear. Evidence is not for nothing, either in her view or in ours about her. It's not for nothing that she has this history with him, that she knows how he makes jokes, that he has waited so patiently for her. But none of this puts her, or us, beyond doubt of him. Ruth misjudged someone and was betrayed. Faith is never beyond doubt; grace can never be assured. The enterprise of proving God's existence has little to do with it. You aim for it by not asking to prove it. What puts her beyond doubt is the absence of the demand for proof, the simple fact that she allows his arm to stay around her back. (We must add: in this she allows herself to be tender and attentive toward him, to notice and respond to what he is doing, in a way that she hadn't before, caught up as she was in her own anxiety.)

I find myself returning again, as I consider this pair, to their jokes, to the entire role of jokes and humor in separating this view of love from Proust's. Ray thinks it is very important to make this woman laugh. "You know what, lady?" he says, after his first success; "I do better amusing you over the phone than in person" (p. 12). He knows, as we do when she laughed then (for the first time in the story), that her laughter is a yielding, a surrender of that tight control. And at the end her yielding comes in a smile, responding to his smile. She shares with him the joke of her own tightness as she holds the envelope so she doesn't have to hold his hand. The "proper gentleman and the lady out for a stroll" are, I imagine, laughing together (as that phrase indicates, so comically inappropriate for an improper, adulterous woman and her lover with his black boots and his language so unlike Arthur's—yet so appropriate, too, to their gentleness with one another, to their relationship that goes so far beyond eggcups and digital watches)—laughing at the comedy of control and uncontrol, self-sufficiency and yielding. Laughter is something social and relational, something involving a context of trust, in a way that suffering is not. It requires exchange and conversation; it requires a real live other person—whereas Marcel's agonies go on in a lonely room and distract him from all outward attentions. To imagine love as a form of mourning is already to court solipsism; to imagine it as a form of laughter (of smiling conversation) is to insist that it presupposes, or is, a transcendence of solipsism, the achievement of community.[24] It is worth adding here: we imagine that this pair have a happy sexual life together, whereas Marcel's view implies that there is really nothing but masturbation. "The beings whom we love . . . are nothing but a vast vague space where we can externalize our own desires" (III:505). As Cary Grant once said, "Why that's no good. That's not even conversation."

And why do we trust Ray, and not wonder who he is really, with his boots and his ballet tickets, what his intentions really are? Because we follow her. For that matter, why do we trust her? Why do we suppose without doubt that she is telling us the truth? Because, like her, we have learned to fall. Reading a story is like that. Like her love, it takes time; you learn it from childhood. And if your mother asked you, "Did you guess that that character was really feeling what I said she was?" you'd be as amused, or mystified, or annoyed, or embarrassed as Andrew at the breakfast table.

Forms of Discourse and Arts of Life

6. What, then, do we make of the fact that we are dealing here with a story? Proust argues that a work that is going to represent knowledge of love must be a work capable of representing cataleptic suffering. Furthermore, if it is to convey this knowledge, not merely to represent it, it must be capable of eliciting responses of suffering in the reader. The reader of Proust's novel comes to know his or her own love by way of a very complex activity, one that involves empathetic involvement with Marcel's suffering, sympathetic responses to his suffering, and the concomitant "mining" of his or her own life experience for analogous loves. In the process of suffering, the reader is brought into contact with the reality of his or her own condition. The final Proustian view adds to this picture the activity of reflection. For even as Marcel, creating his literary work, discerns and articulates the pattern of his loves, making perspicuous the structure of their intermittence, even so the reader, comprehending the overall pattern of Proust's work (and setting her own life before her in a similarly perspicuous structure) is delivered, like Marcel, from bondage to the present experience and takes possession of the entirety of her love. The only text that could promote this sort of knowing would be a text that had the requisite combination of emotive material with reflection—that is to say, a text like the sui generis hybrid that is Proust's novel. His view concerning the truth of the human heart—what its content is and through what activities of knowing it is grasped—determines his view concerning what text or texts can serve as vehicles and sources for knowing.[25]

If we turn now to Beattie, something analogous is borne in upon us—and with even greater force. For if it is not possible to grasp the truth of the cataleptic view in isolation from texts that both show and give us cataleptic experiences, it is surely more difficult by far to show in a non-narrative text the view of love and its knowledge that I have ascribed to Beattie.[26] This knowledge is "kind of slow"; it unfolds, evolves, in human time. It is no one thing at all, but a complex way of being with another person, a deliberate yielding to uncontrollable external influences. There are no necessary and sufficient conditions, and no certainty. To show these ideas adequately in a text, we seem to require a text that shows a temporal sequence of events (that has a plot), that can represent the complexities of a concrete human relationship, that can show both denial and yielding; that gives no definitions and allows the mysterious to remain so.[27] Could any non-narrative text do all this? We can barely imagine how we (or Zeno) might describe and defend the cataleptic view of love in an article, without reference to any whole literary work—using, perhaps, schematic examples. We can imagine this because the experience in question is fundamentally self-contained and isolated. And it announces a set of necessary and sufficient conditions; it tells us what love *is*. With Beattie's view, a treatment even by schematic examples is bound to seem empty, lacking in the richness of texture that displays knowledge of love here. We seem to require no unit shorter than this actual story, with all its open-endedness. The view says that we cannot love if we try to have a science of life; its embodiment must be a text that departs, itself, from the scientific.

If we now consider *our* relation *to* the literary work, the case for its ineliminability becomes still stronger. For, as I suggested, this story not only describes falling and learning to fall; it also enlists us in just such a trusting and loving activity. We read it suspending skepticism; we allow ourselves to be touched by the text, by the characters as they converse with us over time. We could be wrong, but we allow ourselves to believe. The attitude we have before a philosophical text can look, by contrast, retentive and unloving—asking for reasons, questioning and scrutinizing each claim, wresting clarity from the obscure. Beattie knows what she's doing when she links love's knowledge with faith and not with philosophical argument (when she represents Ruth as a teacher of literature, reading the Russian novelists, and not a teacher of philosophy, reading Kant). We aren't very loving creatures, apparently, when we philosophize. "The unexamined life is not worth living"—not, perhaps, the saying of an altogether trusting man. "Did you guess that I love you?" "You use this word love all the time, Mother, applying it to many different things. But could you possibly tell me, please, what the *one* thing is that you are speaking of whenever you use that word? For I feel I lack an understanding of what these things all share, and you surely must know this, Mother, since you speak of love so often." He won't be answered. And, speaking this way, he's not her child any longer.

Before a literary work (like this story) we are humble, open, active yet porous. Before a philosophical work, in its working through, we are active, controlling, aiming to leave no flank undefended and no mystery undispelled.

This is too simple and schematic, clearly; but it says something. It's not just emotion that's lacking, although that's part of it. It's also passivity; it's trust, the acceptance of incompleteness.

But this sounds very fishy, coming at the end of a discussion like this one. For what could I mean by saying that Ann Beattie's story gives us all the knowledge we need, when I am here very obviously composing a paper *about* that story and about its relation to two other stories? Is Beattie's story really sufficient by itself to give an account of the knowledge of love and to convey this knowledge to us? Could I have ended by quoting the story and dropping my commentary on it?[28] Indeed, do we need the framework of the paper at all? Couldn't we just have the story alone, perhaps along with Proust's novel? Is there anything about the knowledge I'm describing that is essentially philosophical? Or with regard to which philosophy is not only not an adversary, but actually a friend?

Here, as often, I find myself saying Aristotelian things.[29] I believe that we have made progress in understanding when we have set these three opposed views of love and its knowledge beside one another, examining their relationships both to one another and to our experiences. In a certain sense there is nothing in this paper that is not already in the stories and in whatever it is about our experience that makes us take an interest in these stories. But it is philosophy, or philosophical criticism, that has set up the confrontation, clarified the oppositions, moved us from an unarticulated sympathy with this or that story to a reflective grasp of our own sympathies. We see more clearly what our relation to Marcel's story is when we see in what way it entails solipsism—and how that solipsism is overcome, in the opposing story, not by any trick of the intellect but by love itself. We contrasted the skeptical and mistrustful demeanor of the reader of philosophy with the openness of the reader of stories. This is in a sense correct. But we must now also acknowledge that it was philosophy, and not the story, that showed us the boundaries and limits of the stories—that returned us to Beattie's story and, so to speak, permitted us to trust it, by clarifying its relation to Proust's cataleptic solipsism. Again, it was philosophy and not a surge of emotion that articulated for us the idea that knowledge might *be* something other than intellectual grasping—might be an emotional response, or even a complex form of life. And although it is true that we must at some level have known that already, our understanding, after the reflective examination, is of a firmer order; we are less likely to be derailed from it or led into mistrusting it by the claim of specious theory. Philosophy can itself be specious theory. There is no doubt of that. But the very probing and questioning that seemed, in philosophy, unloving, can also express, properly and patiently applied, the most tender and protective care for the "appearances"—for our experiences of love and our love stories.

There is another aspect to this point. We suggested that theories about love, especially philosophical theories, fall short of what we discovered in the story because they are too simple. They want to find just one thing that love is in the soul, just one thing that its knowledge is, instead of looking to see what is there. The story could show us a complexity, a many-sidedness, a temporally evolving plurality that was not present in the explicit theories, even Proust's. We said that it was very difficult indeed to speak about this view philosophically precisely because of this complexity. All right. But, here again, wasn't it philosophy that said, "Look and see?" That wouldn't let us stop with some excessively simple idea, say Proust's? Wasn't it philosophy that directed us to the story and showed us why it was important? This is going to seem hopelessly arrogant and chauvinistic, and someone will surely say, "No no, it was the human heart itself; it was love itself. We don't need a professor of philosophy to tell us this." In one sense, the reply is just. But sometimes, I think, the human heart needs reflection as an ally. Sometimes we need explicit philosophy to return us to the truths of the heart and to permit us to trust that multiplicity, that bewildering indefiniteness. To direct us *to* the "appearances," rather than to somewhere "out there" or *beneath* or *behind* them.

What are those times? Times, perhaps, when someone is feeling the need for a science of life. And since, as Proust and Beattie in their different ways show, this need is as deep and persistent as our need for self-sufficiency and our fear of exposure, and is in fact a form of that need, this would mean that a therapeutic philosophy will always have a job to do: exposing these various self-deceptive projects, showing their underlying kinship and their strange consequences, and pointing to the parts of life that they cover or deny. A moment ago we depicted the philosopher as a skeptical and untrusting character, a character whose Socratic refusal of the unexamined brings him close to the searchers for the cataleptic. This is true of some philosophers and in some contexts. But we must also acknowledge that in certain contexts this skeptical uneasiness can lead back to and express a respect for the multiplicity of the everyday. In certain contexts it is above all the philosopher who does in fact say, "Look and see; observe the many-sidedness; observe that here there is no cataleptic certainty." Who, dismantling simplifications, knocking down certainties, clears a space in which love stories can exist and have their force.[30]

To make room for love stories, philosophy must be more literary, more closely allied to stories, and more respectful of mystery and open-endedness than it frequently is. It must draw very close to the best and most truly reasonable of nonphilosophical writing. I find this conception of a human philosophy beautifully articulated in William James's "The Moral Philosopher and the Moral Life":

In all this the philosopher is just like the rest of us non-philosophers, so far as we are just and sympathetic instinctively, and so far as we are open to the voice of complaint. His function is in fact indistinguishable from that of the best kind of statesman at the present day. His books upon ethics, therefore, so far as they truly touch the moral life, must more and more ally themselves with a literature which is confessedly tentative and suggestive rather than dogmatic,—I mean with novels and dramas of the deeper sort, with sermons, with books on statecraft and philanthropy and social and economical reform. Treated in this way ethical treatises may be voluminous and luminous as well; but they never can be *final,* except in their abstractest and vaguest features; and they must more and more abandon the old-fashioned, clear-cut, and would-be 'scientific' form.[31]

But, I think, the philosopher would be neither fully just nor fully luminous if she or he simply left the field to these other forms of writing. James asks for alliance, not surrender. It is evident that not just any type of philosophy could be the ally of literature; to be an ally it must adopt forms and procedures that do not negate the insights of literature. But our picture of an Aristotelian philosophy has indicated why it should still retain a separate critical identity— why an alliance of still separate spheres may be necessary for the justice and luminosity of both.

No form of discourse is cataleptic. None contains in its very style and methods a sure and certain criterion of truth. None is incapable of being used for self-deceptive ends. But perhaps in the attentive—or I might even (too naively?) say loving—conversation of philosophy and literature, with one another, we could hope to find, occasionally, mysterious and incomplete, in some moments not governed by the watch, some analogue of the deliberate fall, the aim for grace.[32]

NOTES

1. I have discussed this passage and its view of knowledge in "Fictions of the Soul," *Philosophy and Literature* 7 (1983):145–161. The present discussion modifies many of the views expressed in that article, and expands on others.

2. On this point there is a longer discussion in my "Fictions," with reference to Plato.

3. My references to Marcel Proust's *Remembrance of Things Past* will be to the volumes and pages of the translation by C. K. Scott Moncrieff and A. Mayor, as revised by Terence Kilmartin (New York, 1981). In several cases I have retranslated the French myself, in order to bring out more clearly some aspect of the original, but I still give the pages of the Kilmartin edition.

4. On this comparison and related issues, see my "Fictions" and my *The Fragility of Goodness: Luck and Ethics in Greek Tragedy and Philosophy* (Cambridge, 1986), especially chap. 1, Interlude 1; on Plato see chaps. 5–7.

5. On this passage, see also Paul de Man, "The Epistemology of Metaphor," *Critical Inquiry* 5 (1978):13–30.

6. On these issues, see the further discussion in my *Fragility,* chap. 10. On the modification of our emotional life by a belief in commensurability, see chap. 4, parts of which have also been published as "Plato on Commensurability and Desire," *Proceedings of the Aristotelian Society,* supp. vol. 58 (1984):55–80. In a Matchette Lecture, "The Discernment of Perception: An Aristotelian Model for Public and Private Rationality," I have discussed the relationship between Aristotle's attack on commensurability and some models of rationality in contemporary economic theory. Part of this manuscript appears under the title "The Discernment of Perception" in *Proceedings of the Boston Area Colloquium in Ancient Philosophy* I (1985):135–178, with a commentary by Dan Brock.

7. The cataleptic impression is an enormously complex historical issue. For the main ancient sources, see J. von Arnim, *Stoicorum Veterum Fragmenta* I (Stuttgart, 1905). 52–73, and II (1903). 52–70. The most important texts are: Diogenes Laertius, *Lives of the Philosophers* VII (Zeno). 45–46, 50–54; Sextus Empiricus, *Adversus Mathematicos* (hereafter *M*), VII.227ff., 236ff., 248ff., 426; Cicero, *Academica Priora* II.18, 77, 144; and Cicero, *Academica Posteriora* I.41. The view I articulate here—that the impression itself compels assent by its own intrinsic character—is the view most commonly taken by the ancient expositors (two of whom, however, are quite hostile to the view). This is surely the idea that Marcel, as a reader of Sextus and of Cicero, would have absorbed. Modern commentators have tried to find in the evidence a more complex and sophisticated position, and it has at least become clear that later Stoics modified the original simple Zenonian view. For discussions of all the evidence, see: J. Annas, "Truth and Reality," in *Doubt and Dogmatism,* ed. J. Barnes et al. (Oxford, 1980), pp. 84–104; M. Frede, "Stoics and Skeptics on Clear and Distinct Impressions," in *The Skeptical Tradition,* ed. M. Burnyeat (Berkeley, 1983), pp. 65–94; J. Rist, *Stoic Philosophy* (Cambridge, 1969), chap. 8; and F. Sandbach, *"Phantasia Katalēptikē,"* in *Problems in Stoicism,* ed. A. A. Long (London, 1971), pp. 9–21.

"Cataleptic" is the Greek *katalēptikē,* an adjective from the verb *katalambanein,* "apprehend," "grasp," "firmly grasp." It is probably active rather than passive: "apprehensive," "firmly grasping (reality)." In the epigraphs I have translated the associated noun *katalēpsis* (the condition of the person who has such an impression) as "certainty." This seems to me appropriate: it brings out the essential point that this person now has an absolutely indubitable and unshakable grasp of some part of reality, a grasp that could not have been produced by nonreality. However, it is important to note that only an orderly system (*sustēma*) of such *katalēpseis* will constitute scientific understanding or *epistēmē.*

One further point about these impressions should be borne in mind as we consider Proust's analogue: they can be, and very frequently are, propositional—i.e., impressions *that* such-and-such is the case.

8. For the definition, see Sextus, *M* VII.248, 426; Sextus, *Outlines of Pyrrhonism* II.4; Diogenes, *Lives* VII.50; and Cicero, *Acad. Pr.* II.18, 77. The point of the last clause seems to be not only that the impression couldn't come from what is altogether unreal or nonexistent but also that it couldn't come from anything else but the very reality that it claims to represent. For the definition of science (*technē*) as a "system of *katalēpseis* ordered together for some useful practical purpose," see reference in von Arnim, *SVF* I.73.

9. See Cicero, *Acad. Pr.* II.38; cf. Sextus, *M* VII.405.

10. Cicero, *Acad. Post.* I.41 and *Acad. Pr.* II.144. (*Technē* itself is like a hand grasping the closed fist.)

11. See Proust, *Remembrance,* especially I:768, where the anxiety aroused in Marcel by the sight of a beautiful girl prompts the following remark:

> and I found a certain wisdom in the philosophers who recommend us to set a limit to our desires (if, that is, they refer to our desire for people, for that is the only kind that leads to anxiety, having for its object something unknown but conscious. To suppose that philosophy could be referring to the desire for wealth would be too absurd.)

The connection between setting a limit to desire and the avoidance of anxiety is an individuating feature, prominently stressed, in Hellenistic ethical thought (both Epicurean and Stoic), and in Skepticism as well, with slight variation. (It should also be borne in mind that the Hellenistic philosophers were central in Marcel's curriculum in a way that they are not for us; were read more widely than Cicero and Plutarch above Aristotle, and the Skeptics too enjoyed continuous prominence.) Only a short time after this interesting remark, Marcel meets Albertine.

12. The true Stoic could never countenance an emotional cataleptic impression. This would come close to being a contradiction in terms, since the Stoics argued that emotions are forms of false judgment. However, as one looks into this more closely, the difference grows narrower. The false judgments with which emotions are identical for the Stoic are judgments about the value of external uncontrolled objects: thus love—*if* we understand by this an emotion involving a high valuation of the loved one, seen as a separate being—is a false emotion in their terms. But it is not at all clear that Marcel's conception of love would be objectionable to the Stoic in this way (see below).

13. This discussion closely follows the treatment of this contrast in my "Fictions," but with some significant changes, especially concerning the relationship between creation and discovery. I now say that there are both creation and discovery on both the particular and general levels, whereas before I said that the particular love was created, the general discovered.

14. See Sextus, *M* VII.426. A different and extremely interesting account of Marcel's error is in Richard Wollheim, *The Thread of Life* (Cambridge, Mass., 1984), pp. 191ff.

15. See Proust, *Remembrance* I:847ff.

16. There are many other similar statements; for only a few examples, see Proust, *Remembrance* III:656, 908–909, 950.

17. Here I am responding to criticisms of my account of Proust in "Fictions" made at the time of its first presentation, in different ways, by Peter Brooks and Richard Wollheim.

18. Here I am obviously not pursuing all the relevant aspects of Proust's account of our knowledge of others. Above all, I am not pursuing the claim of the last volume that we *can* have knowledge of the mind of another in one case: we can know the mind of the artist through reading a work of literary art. I therefore ascribe both the simple and the complex cataleptic views to the character Marcel without drawing any

official conclusions about Proust's overall view, even of our knowledge of those we love. But I do think it fair to say that the novel as a whole discourages optimism about knowledge of another within personal love and appears to endorse Marcel's solipsistic conclusion, by showing all apparently more hopeful cases of loving to be based upon some kind of self-deception.

19. Ann Beattie, "Learning to Fall," in *The Burning House* (New York, 1979), pp. 3–14.

20. It is perhaps worth mentioning that discussion with Brown University undergraduates (taking my course on Philosophy and the Novel) showed that male students overwhelmingly sympathized with the cataleptic view, while female students stressed the importance of time and a pattern of interaction. (Were they talking about the same phenomenon? Were they, like Marcel, shaping the definiendum in accordance with epistemological convictions? Does the gap between the two groups pose new epistemological problems of its own?) I do not believe at all that one view is in any deep or necessary way a male view and the other a female view. But it may be that the emphasis on autonomy and control in the education of males in this culture leads many of them in the direction of a view of love that promises such self-sufficiency. This is borne out by the portrait of Andrew here. Also see the related observations of Carol Gilligan, in *In a Different Voice* (Cambridge, Mass., 1982).

21. The story depicts love of a lover as continuous with, and yet infinitely more difficult and risky than, love of the parent. Andrew's difficulty in turning from the safe reliability of home to the outer world of children and strangers is extreme, born of his handicap. But his self-consciousness, unusual for a child, is here an image of what the narrator takes to be true for adult love in general—the difficulty of allowing oneself to be exposed, the fear of being criticized, deceived, and mocked. She doesn't feel any more at home in her body than Andrew does in his, and she too is afraid of being rejected. Also, and more, she is afraid of being accepted.

22. On the importance of time for the trust required in love and friendship, see Aristotle, *Nicomachean Ethics* 1156b25ff. See also Stanley Cavell's reading of *It Happened One Night* in *Pursuits of Happiness* (Cambridge, Mass., 1982), chap. 2. Several motifs in Cavell's discussion of this film intersect with the reading of Beattie here: see particularly the discussion of eating. Diogenes tells us that Zeno, famed in general for iron self-control, didn't like to be publicly associated with the humbler bodily functions. To cure him of this shame, the Cynic philosopher Crates

> gave him a potful of lentil-soup to carry through the Ceramicus; and when he saw that he was ashamed and tried to keep it out of sight, with a blow of his staff he broke the pot. As Zeno took to flight with the lentil-soup flowing down his legs, Crates said, 'Why run away, my little Phoenician? Nothing terrible has befallen you.'" (*Lives* VII.3, trans. Hicks, with my revisions)

Diogenes also reports that at parties Zeno liked to sit at the far end of the couch, so as not to be too near others (VII.14).

23. I have been asked whether this story and the view I find in it depend on Ray's being this sort of secure, strong, (apparently) non-neurotic person, towards whom she can safely quite simply fall. Could we talk of falling, and so forth, if he was as complex and neurotic as she? The answer, I believe, is yes; we could in that case

speak of learning to fall on both sides. But then it would have to be a much longer story.

24. Cf. Cavell, *Pursuits,* esp. chap. 2, pp. 80ff., and also the chapter on *The Philadelphia Story,* from which film the remark at the end of this paragraph is quoted.

25. On this, see the longer discussion in my "Fictions." On the general issue, see my *Fragility,* esp. chaps. 1 and 7, and Interludes 1 and 2. For further pertinent discussion of Proust's view of art, see Mary Rawlinson, "Art and Truth: Reading Proust," *Philosophy and Literature* 6 (1982):1–16, and the very illuminating discussion of Proust's narrative technique in Gerard Genette's *Narrative Discourse,* trans. Jane E. Lewin (Oxford and Ithaca, 1980).

26. This difficulty is beautifully confronted in part IV of Stanley Cavell's *The Claim of Reason,* where Cavell, in order to tell the story of our acknowledgment and avoidance of others and ourselves, tells stories, moves in and out of complex examples, takes time to let them unfold, and ends with a reading of Shakespeare's *Othello.* One difficulty that philosophers have sometimes had with this book is that there is no one place in it where Cavell gives a concise definition of acknowledgment, with necessary and sufficient conditions. But this does not mean that he has not given a philosophical account of the sort the subject matter requires.

27. On the depth of our interest in plot and the connections between structures of plot and forms of human desire, see Peter Brooks, *Reading for the Plot* (New York, 1983).

28. Richard Wollheim made this point in response to my "Flawed Crystals: James's *The Golden Bowl* and Literature as Moral Philosophy," *New Literary History* 14 (1983):25–50; Wollheim's reply is on pp. 185–191 of the same issue, and my reply to him (and to Patrick Gardiner and Hilary Putnam) is on pp. 201–208. I am now closer to Wollheim's position than I was in that reply.

29. See my "Saving Aristotle's Appearances," in *Language and Logos,* ed. M. Schofield and M. Nussbaum (Cambridge, 1982), pp. 267–293; a longer version, with reference to Wittgenstein, is chap. 8 of my *Fragility.*

30. On this image and Wittgenstein's use of it, see my *Fragility,* chap. 8. A similar account of philosophy in its relation to literature is developed in Cora Diamond's "Having a Rough Story about What Moral Philosophy Is," *New Literary History* 14 (1983):155–169.

31. William James, "The Moral Philosopher and the Moral Life," reprinted in James, *Essays on Faith and Morals,* ed. Ralph Barton Perry (New York, 1962), pp. 184–215; quotation from p. 210.

32. I am grateful to Jeffrey Cobb, who, in conversation as we taught Proust together in the fall of 1984, asked questions that provoked some of the central points of this paper. An invitation to present the paper to a philosophy department colloquium at the State University of New York at Stony Brook was a source of valuable discussion, and I am especially grateful to Mary Rawlinson, Eva Kittay, and Patricia Athay for their questions. Others who generously helped me with written comments include Sissela Bok, Arthur Danto, Cynthia Freeland, David Halperin, Brian McLaughlin, Henry Richardson, Amélie Rorty, and Gregory Vlastos. I know that I have not adequately responded to all the points they raised.

23

ERROR OR SELF-DECEPTION?
THE CASE OF EDUARD IN GOETHE'S
ELECTIVE AFFINITIES

MARGRET KOHLENBACH

Eduard, a wealthy nobleman in the prime of life, loves Ottilie, a young orphan, who has been living at his castle for a short while. In his love Ottilie for the first time finds joy and the courage to live for a happiness other than the dubious one of self-sacrifice. But Charlotte, Eduard's wife, defends her marriage: Ottilie is to leave the castle.

It is Eduard who departs hastily, however. That he wants a divorce he has not confessed to Charlotte. He has promised not to try to see Ottilie in secret, as long as she is allowed to stay with Charlotte at the castle. Eduard withdraws to one of his country estates where he wanders about in dreams of his love. He is convinced, he says, that fate has decided on his and Ottilie's happiness. Finally, he asks Mittler, a declared enemy of divorce, to obtain Charlotte's consent to theirs. As an answer he receives the news that Charlotte is expecting his child. She writes to him that he should recognize in this fact the hand of Heaven, which gives their bond new strength.

Eduard despairs. He goes to war. He survives. Meanwhile, his child is born. Back on his estate he thinks nonetheless that he has conquered Ottilie and overcome any hindrance to his love. But the longed-for happiness fails to materialize. In the last analysis, it is not Charlotte but Ottilie herself who prevents it. Ottilie is involved in the accident that takes the life of Charlotte and Eduard's child. Burdened with feelings of guilt and with the grief she suffered from Eduard's long absence, she decides to return to her old attitude of self-sacrifice.

Ottilie does not completely succeed in renouncing Eduard. She stays at the castle when Eduard returns. But Ottilie withdraws from life, implacable as orphans sometimes are who do not take permission to live as a matter of course. Ottilie ceases to eat. She dies. Desperate about the death of his beloved, Eduard follows her.

Goethe, who tells this story in his novel *Die Wahlverwandtschaften* (Elective Affinities), takes Eduard to be "quite inestimable . . . because he loves absolutely."[1] Eduard himself believes that nobody surpasses him in the art of loving (I, 18, 139).[2] I have my doubts. Eduard's "absolute" love is blind to the pain he inflicts on his beloved by his hesitation and awkwardness. He wouldn't have to act very differently from the way he does, if he wanted to *prevent* his wish of love from coming true. At first blush, however, some of the things he says do seem to betray the insight that would make his behavior appear unwise. Eduard, one is inclined to say, knows of "the uncertainties of life" (I, 18, 141); thus he knows that one shouldn't trust in fate to turn everything to a good end. Eduard seems to know that it is Charlotte's resistance to a divorce which has to be overcome. So he ought to know that dreaming on his estate and fighting in battle will not bring him happiness with Ottilie. One is inclined to say that Eduard, trusting fate and taking victory in battle to be the overcoming of what stands in the way of his love, makes himself blind to something he knows but doesn't want to know. One is inclined to say that Eduard is deceiving himself.

"Self-deception," used in this way, is a contradictory notion. If Eduard makes himself blind to something he knows, then he does not believe and hence does not know something that he does know and hence does believe. Various ways to resolve the paradox suggest themselves. The conflicting statements may receive temporal indices, so that Eduard is said to know and not to know or to believe and not to believe the same thing at different times. Alternatively, one may try to attribute knowing and not knowing or believing and not believing to different agencies in Eduard. The first proposal, however, does not seem to do justice to the phenomenon, and the second may offer only a specious solution.

The reason the temporal account does not appear satisfactory is that Eduard does not encounter situations that would shatter his faith in destiny and confront him with Charlotte's resistance. Given the number of things that tell against his optimistic fatalism, that cannot be an accident. Hence Eduard seems to proceed systematically and to avoid deliberately what could make his faith tumble. To do that, he does not have to know that what he believes is false. But he has to know that there are strong reasons against his belief in fate and, furthermore, he has to know which situations would confront him with these reasons. Accordingly, Eduard believes simultaneously both that fate determines things in his favor and that it probably does no such thing.

The assumption of different psychic agencies allows us to account for the simultaneity of Eduard's believing in fate and his knowing of reasons against it. One agency in Eduard, so the idea goes, knows the belief held by the other agency to be false. Or at least, the first agency has the sort of knowledge, the intentions, plans, and strategic ability required for systematic evasion of counterevidence to what the second takes to be true. Now theories assuming different, autonomous psychic agencies are suspected of offering specious explanations because we may just not understand what it means to talk of different agencies in a person, agencies that know this or decide that. It seems that theories of this kind harbor an inconsistent concept of "irrational" phenomena like self-deception and so fail to resolve the paradox.

I shall try to explain Eduard's case without assuming different psychic agencies. I shall argue that one can get quite far in explaining his behavior without requiring more than what we ordinarily refer to in explaining human behavior: desires, beliefs, errors, knowledge, habits, and so on. I don't think my explanation can be instantly applied to other cases of what is normally called "self-deception." (We don't even know whether the term refers to only one kind of phenomenon.) Nor is the explanation of Eduard's behavior going to be complete. But it should be sufficient to give some plausibility to the idea of explaining so-called irrationality without recourse to specific modes of explanation or to constructions of a psychic machinery with different agencies.

To call Eduard self-deceived in the paradoxical sense I have presented is not to record a given phenomenon; it is to interpret what he says and does. Nothing he says or does shows unambiguously that he knows his belief in fate is false or that he knows he has to avoid certain situations to keep his belief. We infer that he knows these things from ambiguous or unclear statements of his and from the striking regularity with which Eduard does not in fact encounter certain situations that would jeopardize his optimistic fatalism. But the inference is not compelling, for one need not attribute Eduard's statements to self-deception in the paradoxical sense. His "evasive" behavior may be due to things other than his knowledge that the belief in fate is false and his intention to avoid situations critical for it. At any rate, this is what I shall argue. The beliefs, intentions, and habits that such an interpretation attributes to Eduard do involve error, but not an "irrationality" distinct from error.

At one point in Goethe's novel, one seems to catch Eduard in the very act of deceiving himself. I am referring to Eduard's stay on the estate after his hasty separation from Charlotte and Ottilie and before his departure for the military campaign. In Eduard's view, fate has decided that he and Ottilie are going to be happy together. His conviction is put to the test through the separation from his beloved and his promise not to try to see her. But he takes a goblet bearing his and Ottilie's initials to be a sign that fate favors his love. (The glass did not break when, at the laying of a cornerstone, it was flung into the air according to custom. A bystander caught it.) On his estate Eduard corroborates and exercises his faith in destiny by drinking daily from the goblet. When Mittler, an acquaintance of Eduard's, comes to see him, he objects to the baron's superstition. Eduard replies: "In this uncertainty of life, suspended between hope and fear, leave the poor heart at least a kind of guiding star to which to turn, even if it cannot steer by it" (I, 18, 141).

Eduard is familiar with the experience of the faithful heart that takes signs, suitably interpreted, as "guiding stars" on its path. But it is not entirely out of this experience that he answers Mittler. His phrase includes a doubt about that faith. Something one cannot steer by is indeed no guiding star. Perhaps Eduard takes that into consideration by adding "a kind of" before "guiding star." But he cannot successfully reconcile his faith, expressed in his still speaking of a guiding star, with his doubt, expressed in the final clause. In considering something "a kind of guiding star" that one cannot steer by he is mistaken as well.

However, even if Eduard speaks in one breath of guiding stars and of the impossibility of steering by them, we need not conclude that he believes and doubts his belief at the same moment, let alone that he believes and knows that his belief is false. Eduard is speaking out of his conflicting experiences and has not yet achieved clarity. Doubts about his belief in fate, or at least the theoretical possibility of doubting, are not foreign to him. But that is not sufficient for judging that his belief is due to self-deception.

The impression that Eduard is deceiving himself is strengthened by the fact that he not only believes in fate and is familiar with doubt but also wants to believe in fate and employs autosuggestion to corroborate his belief. That Eduard asks Mittler to allow men their so-called guiding stars just when his own words show doubts about their power to guide indicates that the certainty of not being exposed to the "uncertainty of life" is desirable for him even independently of its truth. It is not that the truth of his belief doesn't matter to him at all. On the contrary, the certainty of being guided can appear valuable only if actual guidance seems valuable, too. But Eduard is inclined to be content with certainty and not to pursue doubts he once had or dispel other possible doubts. Eduard is inclined to believe without examining whether what he believes is true.

This inclination is visible in the way Eduard strengthens his wavering belief. To drink from a glass bearing his and Ottilie's initials is not a way to test the truth of the sentence: "Fate will lead me to the happy fulfillment of my love." For only if he takes it a priori as a sign of fate can the glass seem to have any relevance for the question about the lovers' future. Eduard's auto-suggestive ritual with the goblet is the attempt to keep up a belief he knows to be questionable, without touching on the issue of its truth.[3] The ritual shows that in some circumstances Eduard is prepared to accept the risk of error if, though doubting sometimes or knowing of possible doubts, he nevertheless wants certainty.

This description differs in an important way from the idea of self-deception. To accept the risk of error one does not have to know that the belief in question is false, nor does one need to generate or preserve a false belief in oneself with intention. But we imply such knowledge and such intention when we describe people as deceiving themselves.[4]

To say that Eduard is prepared to risk error avoids the conceptual problems of "self-deception." But two questions arise. The first is whether it is sufficient to characterize Eduard's behavior in this way. Eduard's autosuggestive practices give grounds for rejecting that description as insufficient. His case is different from one of straightforward wishful thinking.[5] Eduard not only wants to believe and does so: he also does something to preserve and strengthen the belief, without asking, as would seem natural, whether it is true. How can we make sense of that without assuming an intention on his part to maintain a belief whose falsity he at least vaguely feels? To say that he is merely prepared to accept the risk of error seems too weak. And even if it were sufficient, would not that account imply just as much irrationality as does the talk of self-deception? The paradoxes of this notion may be avoided. Still, there is nothing particularly rational about Eduard's preparedness to run the risk of error in matters vital to him. I shall return to this question.

But I shall start by considering the second question: Why is Eduard prepared to run the risk of error by believing in fate? It will take some time to answer. Unlike the standard examples of self-deception in philosophical discussion, Eduard's belief in fate is presented by Goethe as part and parcel of a way of life. Eduard's behavior in risking error belongs to a more general pattern that is independent of his exercises in autosuggestion. His belief in fate is similar to the way he deals with other matters. This is what I shall try to show first, turning in particular to Eduard's most characteristic trait, his love for Ottilie.

Still at the castle, Eduard, after Ottilie's first, though wordless, avowal of love, spends the night outdoors. Finally he is drawn back to the house, under the windows of his love. "'Walls and locks divide us,' he said to himself, 'but our hearts are not divided. If she were standing here now, she would fall into my arms, and I into hers, and what more is needed beyond this certainty!'" (I, 13, 104). What more is needed, I should think, is the real embrace of the lovers. Yet Eduard fervently kisses the copy of a contract Ottilie wrote for him (I, 13, 104). He is satisfied by the "certainty" that they would embrace under certain circumstances, so much so that he thinks he doesn't need more. In this passionate night, counterfactual love and kisses on legal documents suffice to make Eduard happy.

Similarly on the night of Ottilie's birthday. "You are mine," he tells her, and goes on to say that he has said and sworn it to her so often, but now it shall happen (I, 15, 119). What does happen, though, is that Eduard has a prepared fireworks display set off. Ottilie, frightened, leans against him, and that makes Eduard "feel to the full that she belonged to him completely" (I, 15, 119). He is happy. His happiness seems "boundless" (I, 15, 120). To an unusual degree, Eduard is capable of deriving happiness from fantasies, from experiencing his feelings, and from the conviction of being loved.

For happiness, for at least a partial satisfaction of his wishes, Eduard does not need real love, that is to say, a love lived out with Ottilie. Two desires play a role in his search for happiness. On the one hand he does want to realize his feelings and live an unencumbered life of love with Ottilie. Otherwise there would be no conflict. He could continue to join his wife at night and imagine holding "nobody but Ottilie" in his arms (I, 11, 96), or he could go on passionately kissing copies of contracts. But as Goethe says, imagination cannot assert its right over reality for very long (I, 11, 96f.). On the other hand, he desires a happiness provided by the mere idea and the feeling of love and by the certainty of being loved in turn. This I call the happiness of imagination, not because it is not really felt, but because it can be acquired by mere imagining. In the extreme case, the beloved is not needed for the happiness of imagination. It isn't necessary to live, to act, to talk with him, or to touch him. To feel this sort of happiness is not at all extraordinary. Probably every lover is familiar with the happiness that mere thinking, feeling, and imagining can give. But usually this sort of happiness only accompanies, or is the subjective aspect of, real happiness and is desired only together with the latter. Eduard, by contrast, desires happiness of imagination by itself.

He himself speaks of his desire for just the imagination of love. Having fled from the castle, Eduard first desires that Ottilie should come to him. Since that seems impossible, he imagines "that the impossible must become possible" (I, 18, 138). But now it is not Ottilie's coming that he calls "impossible," but rather, to use his own words, "the approach of her spirit."

> When I wake up at night, and the lamp flings an uncertain light about the room, her image, her spirit, a sense of her presence should float past, approach, seize me, for just a moment, so that I would have a kind of assurance that she thinks of me, that she is mine. (I, 18, 138)

Eduard says neither that Ottilie's "image, her spirit, a sense of her presence" did give him the "assurance" of her love, nor that in a moment of such "assurance" he knows or would know it to be Ottilie's image only. Nor is the point that Ottilie may in fact think of Eduard and love him. The point is that Eduard in this passage speaks of his wish for the illusion of Ottilie's presence, having spoken of his wish for her real presence just before. Her image, her spirit *should* float past and approach him.

Eduard desires a fantasy and a so-called "assurance" of her love, even if they are produced by things as unreliable as spirits in an uncertain light. The way he talks about his desire does take into account that "her image, her spirit, a sense of her presence" are not apt to provide more than a fallible feeling of certainty. He mitigates the glaring absurdity of images, of all things, giving an "assurance" by speaking of "a kind of" assurance only. The phrase recalls the way he defends his belief in fate against Mittler (see above p. 517f.). In fact, Eduard's love and his belief in fate correspond on a number of points.

Both love in real life with Ottilie and real guidance of his life are desirable to Eduard. When these appear impossible or dubious, he is content with subjective "certainty," with imaginations of love and the mere belief in fate. In both cases, certainty does not require a corresponding reality, either created or known. Certainty is to be provided by means of autosuggestion, by imagining Ottilie's spirit on the one hand and by performing the goblet ritual on the other. What Eduard chiefly wants is to feel loved by Ottilie and to believe himself guided by fate, no matter whether he actually is either. That preference for feeling and believing over a corresponding reality is another name for his willingness to accept the risk of error. To understand this willingness is our task.

Let us proceed here from Eduard's love rather than from his belief in fate. Eduard's desire for the imagination of Ottilie's love appears odd. If he is free to wish for what he himself thinks impossible, why does he wish for her spirit to appear and not for her actual presence right away? He by no means generally prefers Ottilie's spirit to herself. His conjuration in the bedroom takes place only after the desire for her real presence has remained unfulfilled and because fulfillment seems impossible. So it is not because Eduard would think the happiness of imagination greater in principle than the happiness of real love that he wishes for Ottilie's illusory rather than her actual presence.[6] If it is not the greater good, it must be the one more likely to be realized that determines him.[7] Eduard must think it more probable that Ottilie's spirit or her image should seize him and give him "a kind of assurance" of her love than that Ottilie might actually appear. This shows, first, that Eduard is in fact not convinced that the desired happiness of imaginary love is impossible. Something that is more probable than something else is not impossible. Second, it shows how great Eduard takes the obstacles to real love to be.

It may be objected that it is less likely for a mere imagination of love to be satisfying than for love itself to be realized, even under unfavorable circumstances. It would not be rational to prefer an inconsiderable good, however easily accessible, to a greater one more difficult to come by. Eduard, whose passions urge him "into the infinite" (I, 13, 105), would be the last person to be affected by such pusillanimity.

But this objection disregards Eduard's character in another way. For him happiness of imagination is not an inconsiderable good. Mere imagination and feeling can satisfy him to an uncommon degree (see above p. 519), and an uncommon number of things can set them going in him.[8] So he desires happiness of imagination *both* because it is easily accessible for him and because it is, in his view, not so very inferior in value to real happiness. Eduard's desire for imagination by itself is as understandable as any desire. Although its permanent realization would be tantamount to madness, it is a reasonable desire, if the views that make sense of his behavior are correct.[9]

So the question is: Are a shared life and real love for Eduard and Ottilie as impossible or improbable as Eduard thinks? Also, is the difference in value between real happiness and happiness of imagination as small as Eduard must assume if his persistent inclination to prefer the latter is to be understood? I shall consider the latter question first.

For Eduard, the difference in value between the happiness of imagination and real happiness is relatively small because the former can be very great in his case. But that is not the only reason. Another is that to him happiness in real love appears less desirable than to others. He feels his love for Ottilie by no means as an unequivocal good. This comes out in his dreams, whose "delightful ephemeral fantasies" (I, 18, 139) are not without pain. In his dreams, Ottilie "sometimes does something which injures the pure idea which I have of her; only then do I feel how much I love her, suffering indescribable anguish" (I, 18, 139). A most intense feeling of love and great anxiety merge in Eduard's delightful nightmares. Both are due to the fact that Ottilie does something in these dreams that does not correspond to the idea Eduard has of her. He is dreaming of Ottilie as a woman with a life of her own, beyond what she is in his idea of her. It is that woman, independent of his "idea," of his images and desires, whom he would have to face in real love.

Given that it is his "pure" idea of her she injures in his dreams, we may assume that Ottilie, the "celestial being hovering above him" (I, 7, 62), turns out in his dreams to be a young woman with sexual desires. Unlike Charlotte (I, 11, 96), Ottilie in his dreams even "does something" to fulfill such impure desires. The "pure idea" of her is Eduard's protection against the body of a woman which gives him "indescribable anguish." But Ottilie's "impurity" does not only cause him fear: it also makes him feel his love most intensely. Wishing for this feeling, he also wishes that Ottilie, the physical being, might compromise his idea of her. Thus his dreams, in which Ottilie emerges out of the veils of his idea of her, are evidence, too, of his desire for real love. At the same time, Eduard fears any love that is more than the play he puts on in his imagination. It is this fear that diminishes the value of real love in his eyes.

Eduard's fear is not well founded. It is not dangerous to love a woman who is different from what one's own "pure," incorporeal idea makes her out to be. At any rate, it is less dangerous than the company of a "celestial being" (I, 7, 62), raising herself above him (II, 17, 289). For that company is fatal to him. If it is partly because of Eduard's fear that the difference in value between real happiness and the happiness of imagination is only small in his view, and if his fear is not well founded, one of the conditions under which his desire for mere imagination could be considered reasonable (see above p. 521) is not met.

The second condition was that real love is impossible or very improbable in his case. If this is so, he has reason to desire only the happiness of imagination. If it is so, he would have such reason even in case the happiness of imagination should be inferior in value to real happiness by an amount larger than his fear allows him to perceive.

Eduard, having left the women at the castle, thinks it impossible that Ottilie would dare "to run away and throw herself into" his arms (I, 18, 138). Indeed it is not probable that the timid orphan will muster the courage to act as independently as that. Still, it is not impossible. As the narrator observes, in Ottilie's situation "a woman's heart, used to waiting and hoping" wants to "become active, to attempt and do something for its happiness, too" (I, 17, 134). Eduard, thinking her coming impossible, fails to consider that Ottilie might become active to further her wishes. He fails to see the possibility of her acting in a way he experienced as both desirable and dangerous in his ambivalent dreams. Thus his fear may be accompanied not only by an underestimation of the happiness in real love but also by the mistaken belief that it is impossible in his case.

This is not to say that his fear drives him to the mistaken belief or causes it. That would be as obscure as talk of self-deception. Nor do we need a story along these lines to account for his error. It is understandable that he does not see the possibility of real love or takes it to be very unlikely. For in desiring it he meets with resistance, Charlotte's in particular, and the idea that resistance can be overcome by action is foreign to him. He is not acquainted with such action from his own experience. The little he does to fulfill his desire for real love is ill-suited to the purpose.[10] Learning that Charlotte, contrary to what he expected, does not share his wish for a divorce, he dares not express his wish and, in panic, leaves the place (I, 16, 122–127) where he could "become active and do something for his happiness, too" (I, 17, 134). He is less familiar than others with asserting wishes incompatible with others', going through with the conflict, and overcoming resistance. "The spoiled child of wealthy parents," successful in everything, didn't have to learn that anything "in the world could obstruct his desires" (I, 2, 11f.).[11] So he didn't learn to hold to them and thinks his cause lost as soon as he comes up against obstacles.

It need not be Eduard's fear of an independently acting Ottilie which makes him mistakenly believe that real love is impossible or unlikely for him. Rather, it is his scant experience in furthering his desires against resistance that makes both the fear and the belief understandable. If I am not used to trying to realize my desires in the face of opposition, I shall find people who are acting independently overpowering and threatening; and, meeting with obstacles, I shall think the chances of success more limited than I would otherwise. Eduard's fear and his error occur together, but one need not be causing the other. They are both to be explained by reference to a third fact, i.e., that the experience of conflict has been largely lacking in Eduard's life. That the fear causes the error may appear plausible insofar as Eduard's history is not taken into consideration.

Eduard's belief that happiness in real love is impossible or improbable in his case is false, however understandable. The difficulties standing in his way are not insurmountable. Society in the novel allows divorce (I, 9, 77). Even Charlotte would, in the long run, feel the force of the argument that it is not advisable to continue a marriage against one partner's will. But Eduard, overwhelmed by panic and despair on encountering resistance, does not even enter into argument and declare his will. So he fails to see how he could find satisfaction and mistakenly thinks it is impossible or very improbable. Because this belief is mistaken, the second of the conditions under which his desire for mere imagination could be considered reasonable (see above p. 521) does not obtain.

Errors understandable in light of his experience explain Eduard's persistent attempt to find happiness in imagination. To this end he employs suitable means. For autosuggestion does serve a happiness that demands only an altering of one's mental state. His seemingly irrational behavior does not contrast with rational behavior. It is rational behavior based on error.

Now Eduard's belief in fate becomes comprehensible as well. Even the feeling of being guided by a superior power is a desirable alleviation for one who is afraid of any obstacle whatever, since any of them threatens him with the impossibility of what he wants. Eduard's drinking ritual with the goblet serves to procure that valuable feeling.

So our two initial questions can be answered. One was why Eduard is prepared to accept the risk of error. He is so because of certain mistaken beliefs due to a specifically restricted experience. Unfamiliar with achieving what he wants despite resistance, he comes to be mistaken both about the value of goods he desires and about his chances of obtaining them. Because of these errors, Eduard, when facing conflict, consistently prefers to pursue those of his desires which can be satisfied whether or not there is a reality corresponding to the feeling or belief in question. In attempting to strengthen his belief in fate, Eduard does not need to ask whether this belief is true and so runs the risk of error. Striving for happiness in fantasies of love, he does not care whether the images and the assurances they give him are correct. In both cases, he runs the risk of error because truth is immaterial to his concern.

The second question was whether it is sufficient to describe Eduard as running the risk of error or whether we must suppose him to deceive himself intentionally. There were reasons to suppose this. As we saw, Eduard does things that serve to maintain a belief he at least has doubts about and he fails to ask whether it is true. But that failure can be explained in a different way. He doesn't worry about truth because his preferred desires don't depend on knowing, and altering, real situations. He desires a happiness he can gain, to an extraordinary degree, from the feelings that arise from his fantasies, irrespective of a corresponding reality. And not only that, for this purpose, he doesn't need to ask about truth. He is less accustomed to doing so than others are, for he didn't need to know and to change things to be happy. The desires he had or was allowed to have met no resistance (I, 2, 11f.). Thus to understand his failure to ask about the truth of his belief it is not necessary to assume a self-deceptive intention to protect the cherished belief from probable defeat.

The fact that Eduard is striving for a happiness of mere imagination and feeling explains furthermore the impression that he is systematic in avoiding situations liable to destroy his belief in fate (see above p. 516) an impression that seems at first to support the diagnosis of self-deception. Even if it is not by accident that Eduard doesn't encounter such situations, this need not be because he knows that his favorite belief would meet with insuperable difficulties. Perhaps he does not encounter them because he has no reason to seek them, given that happiness of imagination is what he desires above all else. If he wants to dream of Ottilie, he would be a fool to quarrel with Charlotte.

In the picture of Eduard that emerges, his fantasies of love and his belief in fate are related features of a general pattern in his behavior which includes the willingness to accept the risk of error (see above). But this is not sufficient to understand him. There is an important difference between his belief in fate and his mere images and feelings of love. On the one hand, Eduard sometimes imagines the loving Ottilie. As he puts it, he sees her and sees her doing what gives him most pleasure (I, 18, 138). Sometimes, on the other hand, he wants to believe, and does believe, that fate has "decided" on joining them and that their relationship is therefore "indestructible" (I, 18, 141). The difference is that ideas of the first kind do not touch on how the actual train of events is going to continue or end, whereas the belief in fate does include the conviction that the separation from Ottilie cannot last. The actual future course of Eduard's life and love is referred to in one case and not in the other.

According to Eduard not only his relationship with Ottilie is "indestructible"; so are all relationships that have been decided on by fate (I, 18, 141). "Fate" means, then, an omnipotent agency whose decisions necessarily come true. But the way Eduard puts his belief shows that it is not the transcendent necessity of fate's decisions he is most concerned with. There would be no point in stressing the indestructibility of such decisions. That Eduard finds the indestructibility of relationships decided on by fate worth mentioning shows that what counts for him is the *reality* that results from fate's decisions.

The omnipotence of Eduard's "fate" explains why, in connection with his belief, he never considers the problem of how to overcome the actual separation from Ottilie. With omnipotent agencies, the decision and the realization of what is decided are, in principle, identical. With less powerful, mortal beings, fate's decision and the reality it attains may come apart. For the believer the difference is due to the different ways in which omnipotent beings and humans exist. The difference is not a practical problem; it has nothing to do with obstacles to decisions or to desires. No further action is needed to make something happen that is decided by fate. It happens automatically.

So Eduard's belief in fate, by contrast to his mere images of love, does refer to a fulfillment of his desire for love realized. Still, in the way fulfillment is conceived here the experience of his desire for happiness of imagination comes to the fore again. The idea of fulfillment without overcoming resistance is familiar to him from his love fantasies. It is familiar, too, from his history, in which virtually no desire met with hindrances of any importance. In his belief in fate, Eduard applies these experiences to a different wish, that for happiness in real love, which does encounter resistance. He treats the wish for real happiness as if it were the wish for the happiness of imagination, unobstructed by Charlotte's resistance. Turned into a decision of fate, the wish becomes part of a fantastic world without obstacles; real happiness with Ottilie seems a necessity. Eduard imagines a fulfillment of love which does not require any action, which one is just "guided" to.

The question is crucial now whether even these ideas can be considered merely erroneous or whether here finally we need to have recourse to the notion of self-deception. That Eduard indulges in fantasies of love and in a feeling of security derived from his belief in fate could be understood as rational, given certain errors on his part (see above p. 524). Can the belief in fate be regarded as a comprehensible error, too, even if its contents are taken into account; even if, that is, it is considered not just a source of the feeling of security but an anticipation of the lovers' actual future?

It is difficult to regard it as just a comprehensible error because of the glaring inconsistency in Eduard's views of the matter. He believes that real love with Ottilie is impossible or very unlikely, given the obstacles he encounters, and he also believes that it is necessary or that it at any rate suffers as little from obstructions as his imagination does. One should think this inconsistency must catch his eye and make him see that something is wrong with his optimistic fatalism. But then, in sticking to his belief, he would not only be in error. He would be holding to a belief that he knows to be false. One is all the more inclined to think Eduard self-deceived insofar as the fantastic world of his belief excludes what he has palpably experienced: Charlotte's insistence on continuing their marriage. Out of fear he would foster a belief that from his own experience he knows, but doesn't want to know, to be false, namely, that Charlotte is not opposed to his desire.

Actually, there is an explanation for Eduard's belief in fate which does not call upon the idea of self-deception. Treating the real good as if it were one of mere imagination, Eduard is mistaken in an understandable way—only mistaken. The key to this explanation is contained in a passage in which Eduard himself speaks of "self-deception."

Back on his estate after the campaign, Eduard makes up his mind to negotiate with Charlotte. He now calls the belief he had at the time of his goblet ritual "illusion" (II, 12, 251) and finds that to "give way to the hope, to the expectation that everything will turn out well by itself, that chance will guide and favour us, would be an unpardonable self-deception" (II, 12, 255). He goes on to give a strikingly enlightened analysis of the situation, culminating in a sentence that seems to fly in the face of any belief in fate: "We are no longer master of what came out of it [i.e., things done before], but we are master in counteracting the harm we have done, and to direct the situation toward our happiness" (II, 12, 255). This is the later Eduard. The agent replaces guiding fate as master of the situation. Taking himself to determine the future, he calls the expectation of automatic fulfillment of desires, which was Eduard's attitude before the war, "self-deception." The inactive believer in fate appears to have given way to the independent, enlightened rational agent.

I shall try to show that the appearance is misleading. The speciousness of Eduard's new rationality will also call into question the judgment passed in the name of that rationality, to the effect that Eduard was deceiving himself before.

Eduard's enlightened-sounding talk obscures the fact that his thinking has not overcome the belief in fate, but actually continues it. His new self-confidence originates from his military campaign, which accustomed him by "a livelier sort of existence" "to more definite decisions" (II, 12, 250). The thoughts with which he entered the campaign he describes, in hindsight, as follows:

> 'I will make myself, in lieu of the glass, a sign of whether our union is possible or not. I shall go in quest of death—not a madman, but a man who hopes to live. Ottilie shall be the prize I fight for; it shall be she whom I hope to win and conquer—in line of battle, in every entrenchment, in every besieged fortress. I will perform miracles with the wish to be spared, with the thought of winning Ottilie, not of losing her.' (II, 12, 251)

We are invited to take Eduard's going to war as the well-considered opening of a decision process, in some ways similar to an ordeal. From his fantasies of fate at the time of the goblet this conjuration differs in that now the action is meant not only to instill the conviction of destiny's favor but to procure, over and above the conviction, the thing in question, that is, Ottilie. The goblet ritual was meant to keep up the belief in an omnipotent, favorable agency in which decision and execution coincide. Now it seems to Eduard that the union of desire and its realization is given immediately. Having survived all the dangers, he finds himself as one "who has overcome every obstacle, whose way is now plain before him. Ottilie is mine; anything that still lies between this thought and its realization I can only regard as insignificant" (II, 12, 251).

Eduard's campaign is a reaction to the insufficiency of mere fantasies of fate which fail to provide the good that is desired. As Eduard presents it, the campaign actualized what the mere belief in fate viewed as a transcendent union of decision and execution. That is to say, Eduard ascribes a magical character to his military activity. For experience shows that to go to war is not a suitable means to fulfill one's desires for love and marriage.

The narrator, however, does not agree that Eduard actually set out to attain happiness in real love by exercising magic. From what he tells us we can gather that this is only Eduard's later interpretation, which in important ways distorts what happened. The distortion concerns mainly the situation in which Eduard decided to go to war. At that point, Eduard had received the news that Charlotte was pregnant, and saw his hope for her consent to a divorce defeated. The narrator continues:

> What happened after that moment in Eduard's soul would be difficult to describe. In an uproar like this, old habits and old inclinations finally come out again to kill time and fill the space of life. Hunting and wars are an ever-ready resource of this kind for a nobleman. Eduard longed for outward danger to counterbalance the inner one. He longed for death, because life threatened to become unbearable; it even comforted him to think that he would cease to be and by this could make his loved ones and his friends happy. (I, 18, 143f.)

After the war Eduard's account replaces the "uproar" in his soul—whose description eludes the narrator—with a well-formed rhetoric of thoughts which allegedly accompanied the resolve to fight in the war, interpreting it as the opening of a magical decision procedure. To make Eduard's departure plausible, the narrator mentions confusion, habit, occasion, a desire to fill time and the space of life, great inner pain, and a longing for death. All this, together with the shock of Charlotte's letter, is mitigated in Eduard's late account or entirely passed over in silence, giving way to a magical teleology of his proceeding to war which covers up the confusion and despair of that time. Eduard's story that he intended right from the start to conquer Ottilie in battle puts a new meaning on the events, the result being that in principle his wish for Ottilie is already fulfilled. So his story resembles his belief in the goblet. It is another piece of superstition. There is no difference in kind between taking the failure of a glass to break and taking one's own survival in war as a sign that one's wife must cease refusing a divorce.[12]

Just when Eduard is calling his own previous attitude "self-deception," he is caught in a very similar attitude. He used to expect "that everything will turn out well by itself." But "to regard as insignificant" any obstacle to his wishes is exactly the same thing. It is this similarity between his former and his present attitude which tells against the idea that the belief in fate he had before the war was due to self-deception. To call someone self-deceived is to credit oneself with the knowledge that the belief in question is false.

Eduard, too, calling the expectation that everything will turn out well by itself "self-deception," knows that it is false. At the same time, regarding any obstacle as insignificant, he has in effect just that expectation. So he holds what he knows to be false. One might be inclined to say that another act of self-deception would have to remove the knowledge that is shown in his critique of self-deception, so as to allow him the optimistic belief he holds.

But in fact his knowledge and his belief are compatible. For he fails to see that his present belief is an instance of the expectation he considers deceptive. He fails to see that the story he tells about the campaign, ending with the insignificance of any obstacle, only repeats the superstition whose groundless optimism he rejects. Since he fails to see this, the fact that in spite of his enlightened talk he keeps his superstitious beliefs is no ground for charging him with yet another maneuver of self-deception. To deceive someone, I have to know the falsity of just that belief I generate or confirm in the other. If I merely know that some kind of belief is false and generate a belief in the other without knowing that it is a belief of that kind, I do not deceive him. I mislead him erroneously. This is Eduard's case.

But if Eduard, while talking of his illusion and of self-deception, is still entangled in his old errors without recognizing them, it is hardly plausible to suppose that he knew the falsity of his optimistic fatalism before the war. It would be odd to credit him with this knowledge then, since he lacks it even now that he is criticizing superstitious expectations. The very fact that he fails to recognize the old illusion in the new attitude shows that its falsity is not well-known to him; one recognizes what is well-known in diverse situations. To trace back the expectation that things will turn out well by themselves to an act of self-deception, as Eduard proposes, is not a convincing diagnosis—not for his case at any rate.

To discard completely any talk of self-deception in Eduard's case requires one further step. Thus far I have argued that Eduard fails to recognize the similarity between his new optimism and his former belief in fate. But in that way he seems blind to the obvious. If the later Eduard's blindness is to tell against the earlier Eduard's self-deception, it in turn needs to be explained without recourse to self-deception.

Eduard's story of the campaign distorts what happened. But he doesn't invent it *ex nihilo*. Like any other remembrance it links together various parts of experience. When his friend, the major, points out to him the considerations against a divorce, Eduard replies: "All this has passed before my mind, in the tumult of battle, when the earth shook from the continuous roar of cannonades, when the bullets whizzed and whistled, and my comrades fell to right and left, when my horse was hit and my cap riddled" (II, 12, 253). Eduard, "courageous when necessary" (I, 2, 12), flees in panic from, as it were, civilian opposition, but stands his ground in great danger on the battlefield. In fighting, he thinks of the hindrances to his love. (Incidentally, the fact that he does not merely indulge in fantasies of Ottilie while in battle but attends to what separates them indicates how strong his desire for real love is.)

Now Eduard's construction, turning the campaign into a magical procedure for conquering Ottilie, falsely correlates simultaneous parts of his experience. Overcoming the enemy's resistance in battle becomes overcoming the resistance to his love, which resistance he was thinking of in fighting. This is how Eduard errs, and errs in inferring. "Ottilie is mine; anything that still lies between this thought and its realization I can only regard as insignificant." But he only errs. The mistake is an understandable one for Eduard, given his experience; even an easy one to make. Imaginings and thoughts "passing before the mind" can reach an unusual intensity with him (see above p. 519). And it is not an uncommon mistake. An intention to deceive oneself is not required to explain it. On the train I talk with a friend of the bright summer light in the countryside we are traversing, and I am thinking of paintings by Cézanne which I saw not long ago and have in mind quite vividly. Some days later I refer to a conversation about Cézanne which I think we had on the train. Eduard's mistake is of that kind.[13]

His error gives rise to a new self-confidence after the war. True, to regard any obstacle as insignificant is on a par with his former belief in fate. But the magical conception differs in one important point from the former idea of a transcendent union of decision and execution. The magical conception has a substratum of real struggle, suffering, overcoming of resistance. Erroneously connecting the real fighting with the obstacles to his love, Eduard finds himself as one "who has reached his goal, who has overcome every obstacle, whose way is now plain before him." At the time of the goblet ritual he kept expecting that the transcendent union of fate's decision and execution would turn real, and time and again despaired of it, too. Now he himself has acted and reached a goal in the face of opposition. As Ottilie's "conqueror," he feels so different from the former Eduard that the similarity between his present view of the situation and the one he had before the war doesn't occur to him. This is why he fails to recognize the old superstition in his new optimism.

The later Eduard's blindness can be understood without recourse to self-deception. Hence, as argued above, self-deception is not a plausible explanation of the former Eduard's belief in fate either. How can this belief be understood, then? How can Eduard take himself to be living in a world from which Charlotte's opposition, which he actually experienced, has been deleted? And how can the incoherence in thinking that happiness with Ottilie is both necessary and impossible fail to compel Eduard to renounce his optimistic fatalism?

In Eduard's belief in fate, his wish for real love becomes part of a fantastic world devoid of obstacles. But it would be misleading to say that he construes this world on purpose so as to deny Charlotte's opposition, which he is afraid of. Eduard's optimistic fatalism accords with experiences he had long before Charlotte's resistance. For a long time, Eduard's wishes have appeared to attain fulfillment automatically (I, 2, 11f.). Charlotte's opposition is a novel experience for him: a mature, strong, and important wish of his is not being consented to. But he need not be assumed to cheat himself out of this experience by believing in fate. This assumption presupposes that his experience of Charlotte's resistance is like that of a person who has had this sort of experience a number of times before; that is to say, that it is an experience of something that has to be reckoned with in the future. But Goethe tells only of anguish and confusion (I, 16, 125–127). That is convincing. In anguish and confusion we respond to things that obstruct our strongest desires and are unaccountable in the view of the world we are used to. Goethe goes on to relate how Eduard, having left the castle after the unfinished argument with Charlotte, largely continues in his habitual ways of thinking and imagining, of just assuming the automatic fulfillment of his wishes.[14] That, too, is convincing. As Goethe says in another context, in such confusion "old habits and old inclinations finally come out again" (I, 18, 143). We hardly ever change our life, or our conception of ourselves and the world, right on the spot when encountering one novel experience. That Eduard doesn't do so can be understood without a special explanation, such as self-deception. Rather, it would demand explanation if he did change.

For Eduard, the resistance he encounters means that the order of things he is accustomed to is out of joint. It is as if a man were to find one morning that the sun were not rising. He knows he can't make the sun rise. But he counts on the sun rising again the next morning, for that is what he is acquainted with. Charlotte's opposition breaks the law that was continuously supported by Eduard's experience, i.e., that desires are satisfied automatically. But since for him resistance is not something to be reckoned with in the future, he just waits for the old order of things to be restored. It is Charlotte's turn, rather, to repair her violation of the law and come back to conformity.

Eduard believes that the law of automatic satisfaction has become invalid only temporarily. That is why in spite of the inconsistency in his beliefs he fails to give up optimistic fatalism. The old order of things being still valid in principle, he considers the satisfaction of his desire for real love necessary. On the other hand, the order being invalid for the moment, satisfaction of his desire depends on what he does himself and therefore appears impossible or very improbable to him, inexperienced as he is.[15] In Eduard's view, his inconsistent opinions answer to a momentary confusion in the order of the world. So it's up to the world to set itself right, not up to him to recant his optimistic fatalism.

We can understand Eduard without supposing him to deceive himself. If so, why is that supposition so attractive? What is it that recommends a hypothesis with the rather strange implication that a person knows that what he believes is false? Which advantage can outweigh what is at least the danger of paradox and therefore of failure to understand the person?

Eduard fails to recognize the old superstition in his optimism after the campaign. To say that he must and does, but deprives himself of this knowledge by deceiving himself, is to deny that what I find a natural idea may appear outlandish to him, namely, to compare his attitudes from before and after the war. Eduard, believing in fate, doesn't take into account the experience of Charlotte's opposition. To say that he construes a fantastic world so as to deny an experience he is afraid of is to suppose that originally he shares my view of the world according to which resistance is something to be reckoned with.

Ascribing self-deception to a person, I avoid the difficult task of understanding an experience of things widely different from my own and of making sense of what seems to me a strange sort of error. I assume that the other shares my view, and what is incompatible with it I account for by means of the paradoxical notion of his deceiving himself into thinking what he knows to be false.[16]

Talk of self-deception doesn't help in understanding Eduard. I shall renounce it if I take seriously the notion that Eduard, because of his different history, is liable to other errors than I am; that he experiences things in other ways and with other results than I think "one" does, or must, experience them. Eduard does not have to know what, supposedly, one just cannot fail to know in certain situations. There may be no such thing.

NOTES

I am very grateful to Marion Faber for helping me with the English.

1. Letter of February 21, 1810, to Karl Friedrich von Reinhard, in *Goethes Briefe* (Hamburg, 1965), 3:120.

2. References to Goethe's *Die Wahlverwandtschaften* are given by part, chapter, and page number in the translation by Elizabeth Mayer and Louise Bogan (Goethe, *Elective Affinities*, [South Bend, Ind.: Gateway, 1963]). Passages from the novel are quoted from this translation, except for those I have modified to draw out features of the original which do not become apparent in the Mayer/Bogan rendering. In these cases, I have changed their text to obtain a more literal version, using also an older, anonymous translation published by Collier (New York) without date.

3. Eduard's private ritual may look more familiar, though not easier to understand, once we think of similar practices in collective religions. For instance, it may not be rare that Christians pray to God that He strengthen their belief in Him.

4. That the current idea of self-deception includes intentionality is shown by the fact that self-deception is taken as a case of irrationality, not of error.

5. I leave open the question whether there is such a thing as wishful thinking in a straightforward sense of the term. The notion that a wish "causes" a belief may be due to an abstraction from other things besides wish and belief, which come into play in the relevant cases.

6. Even if Eduard doesn't consider the happiness of imagination superior in principle to real happiness, he may still find attractions in the former which the latter lacks. See below p. 522.

7. This claim and the argument that follows can be taken as an application of Pascal's wager to Eduard's case.

8. The fireworks he arranged and the timid gesture of a young woman suffice to make him "feel to the full that she belonged to him completely" (I, 15, 119). Sometimes glasses that fail to break and the assimilation of a childlike handwriting (I, 3, 30) to his (I, 12, 100) have similar effects. Admittedly, with Ottilie away, occasions for setting off his imagination in this way are going to be sparse. Eduard may still succeed, though.

9. It is not irrational, moreover, only if happiness of mere imagination, in spite of the madness attending it in the long run, is preferred to all the goods whose attainment requires one to live "in reality," that is to say, in the same world with others.

10. By leaving the castle and promising not to try to see Ottilie, Eduard reduces himself to immobility. Furthermore, once the panic is over, he could try to obtain release from his promise or break it (which he does after the campaign [II, 13, 259f.]). Finally, it is extremely awkward to send Mittler, of all people, to ask Charlotte for her consent to a divorce, Mittler, who cannot bring himself "to mention the word 'divorce' even in passing" (I, 18, 142).

11. Eduard's inability to distinguish between his wishes and others', or "reality" (see II, 13, 258f.), need not be traced back to his parents' spoiling him, sparing him any disappointment, as the narrator suggests (I, 2, 11f.). Actually, Eduard's parents did not fulfill his every wish. They "persuaded" him to marry a woman he didn't love (ibid.) and so to renounce Charlotte, temporarily as it turned out. But to persuade someone ("*bereden*" in German) means not seriously to consider his wishes or even not to allow him to develop them. Eduard's weakness, then, may be due to his not being free to follow out or to develop wishes deviating from those of his parents.

12. Admittedly, there are differences between the two things. One I shall mention below p. 530.

13. Eduard's belief that he "conquered" Ottilie can be understood in another way still. We are all familiar with the idea of earning satisfaction of our wishes by suffering. It is a common line of reasoning for the characters in the novel, too. Charlotte, for instance, thinks that, having renounced herself, i.e., having suffered, she is entitled to others doing the same (I, 16, 122). Eduard argues similarly before the campaign (I, 16, 126).

14. He continues only "largely," since for all his optimistic fatalism he time and time again falls into despair (I, 18, 137). The experience of not having his desire fulfilled automatically, persistent as it is, does begin to affect him. Perhaps this is also why he sometimes entertains the thought that his belief in fate is doubtful, as mentioned above p. 518.

15. As long as the old order of automatic satisfaction is out of force, Eduard may deliberate about pursuing real happiness or that of imagination the way others would do (though subject to the errors mentioned above). To prefer the happiness of imagination is all the more natural for him, since he still counts on the restoration of the old order which would procure for him the happiness of real love anyway.

16. Incidentally, this is also true of Eduard's own talk of self-deception: "To give way to the hope, to the expectation that everything will turn out well by itself, that chance will guide and favor us, would be an unpardonable self-deception" (II, 12, 255). To expect that everything will turn out well by itself is to think a favorable solution will come about in any event. So it is not to believe that it will come about by chance, but necessarily. Eduard, speaking of "chance," supposes the hypothetical self-deceiver to know what he now does know, i.e., that it is an illusion to believe in guidance by an omnipotent agency's signs. The connection of incompatible perspectives stands out in Eduard's paradoxical talk of guidance by chance.

24

UNDERSTANDING A SELF-DECEIVER

Rüdiger Bittner

It was not Verena's habit either to talk or to think about her dignity, and when Olive found her taking that tone she felt more than ever that the dreadful, ominous, fatal part of the situation was simply that now, for the first time in all the history of their sacred friendship, Verena was not sincere. She was not sincere when she told her that she wanted to be helped against Mr. Ransom—when she exhorted her, that way, to keep everything that was salutary and fortifying before her eyes. Olive did not go so far as to believe that she was playing a part and putting her off with words which, glossing over her treachery, only made it more cruel; she would have admitted that that treachery was as yet unwitting, that Verena deceived herself first of all, thinking she really wished to be saved. (Henry James, *The Bostonians,* chap. 37)[1]

What is it that Olive would have admitted when admitting that Verena deceived herself first of all?

Here is the situation. Olive and Verena have become intimate friends, in common devotion to the feminist cause. Basil Ransom, admiring Verena and despising feminism, tries to persuade her to leave both Olive and the cause and to marry him. As yet it is not clear which way Verena will decide. But it is clear that he and what he is saying weigh heavily with her. In her struggle Verena asks Olive to help her by reminding her of the reasons against following this man. But she refuses to escape his attack by leaving the place, on the grounds that such a course would lack dignity. This shows, according to Olive, that Verena's request for help against Ransom is not sincere. It is due to self-deception. Verena does think, Olive concedes, that she wishes to be saved from Ransom. But in thinking this she is deceived, Olive claims; deceived by herself.

The question is what that means. Talk of deceiving oneself involves a difficulty.[2] In many cases, if you deceive someone, you bring it about that he or she believes something that you, correctly, take to be false. (In many cases only, because one may deceive someone by behaving misleadingly without intending to do so and without thinking that the belief instilled in the other person is false.) Accordingly, if Verena deceives herself, she brings it about that she believes something, namely, that she really wishes to be saved from Ransom, which she also, correctly, takes to be false. Deceived, she believes that she wants to be saved; deceiving, she believes, rightly, that she does not want it. This is a confusing description. One does not understand what a person is believing who believes something and also thinks it is false. Admittedly, it may not be a contradiction to say this about someone.[3] It is a contradiction if whoever takes something to be false does not believe that it is true. This looks like a safe thing to say, but may be disputed. No matter. What is wrong with asserting a contradiction is that one does not know what is being said. The present trouble is similar. One does not understand what is being said of a person when she is said to believe something and to take it to be false, too. At any rate, to say such a thing of a person is strange enough to make understandable the request for an explanation.

The difficulty about self-deception that is being raised here is not that people cannot be taken to be as irrational as to believe something and disbelieve it, too, so that self-deception is an incredible thing to happen. The difficulty is to make sense of what is said in calling someone self-deceived. Thus to insist that there is the phenomenon of self-deception after all misses the point. Nobody doubts that there are cases commonly called "self-deception." What this characterization means is the question.

Various ways to resolve the difficulty suggest themselves.[4] One is to introduce temporal distinctions. With ordinary deceptions, it is only generally, not invariably the case that there is a time in which both the deceiver knows the truth and the victim errs. (A letter of recommendation may arrive after the writer died.) What is sometimes true of ordinary deception may always be true of self-deception, namely, that the times of the deceiver's knowing and the victim's erring do not overlap. So construed, self-deception is easy to understand. If Verena is deceiving herself, she is bringing it about that at some time later she believes something that at some time before she rightly took to be false.

Maybe self-deception so construed looks unrealistic: how could one make oneself exchange truth for error? It is easy. I am disappointed about the few letters I receive these days and send myself an empty envelope. Mail being slow enough, I forget the maneuver, and one morning I happily think that someone wrote to me. To be sure, that is not self-deception proper. The deception does not stick. But serious self-deception may be explained along these lines.

For one thing, one may not always recall one's manipulation as easily. Perhaps the psychoanalytic theory of the unconscious can be reconstrued as claiming that under certain conditions people sometimes thoroughly forget the part they played in the story. Dreams, neurotic symptoms, lapses would be so many letters written by oneself, though not with an intention to deceive, which acquire an objective standing because one does not recognize one's own hand. A particular sort of interpretation is required to discover their source and their meaning and so to break their spell.

For another thing, the deception may even stick with one who remembers that it was he himself who made himself believe the opposite of what he used to believe.[5] Pascal, having convinced the infidel by the wager argument of the advisability of believing the Christian creed, though not of its truth, proceeds to describe how to actually come to believe: taking holy water, having masses said, doing everything as if believing already—"this will, in a natural way even, lead you to believe and make you stupid."[6] In this way, then, the infidel is to intentionally make himself accept a belief that at present he takes to be false, and rightly so, be it granted for the sake of the argument. Moreover, once he has acquired the belief, remembering how he reached it will not make him waver. In fact, Pascal notes that this way of acquiring the Christian belief is recommended by people who know it from their own case.[7]

Experience shows that Pascal's method is effective. People do come to believe things in this way. "Qui s'accoutume à la foi la croît."[8] Here, then, is a coherent, realistic, and serious account of self-deception: self-deceivers make themselves believe later what they rightly took to be false before. However, the account fails to grasp what "deceiving oneself" means in the James text quoted at the beginning. Olive is not thinking that Verena is currently engaged in an activity that will eventually render her deceived, as one could indeed say of the infidel going to church that he is busy getting himself deceived. Verena, according to Olive, is not working towards error, she is in error. She actually thinks what is not true, namely, that she wants to be saved from Ransom. Nor can Olive be understood as thinking that Verena already completed the task of instilling a false belief in herself. Olive would have admitted, we are told, that Verena's treachery was "as yet un-witting." As yet: Olive cannot be thinking that at some previous stage Verena set herself going towards the false belief. So according to Olive there has not been, nor is there presently, a process in which Verena makes herself accept a belief that she took, correctly, to be false before. When Olive speaks of Verena's self-deception, she must mean something different from what the present account suggests.

A second way to explain self-deception is to introduce a distinction in the person concerned. That is a natural idea, because many current locutions suggest an intrasubjective duality, "self-controlled," for example, and "self-effacing" or "to find oneself doing something." Given the duality, the problem is easily solved. Verena is two, one of them deceiving the other. On this account, there is strictly speaking no self-deception, if that term requires the identity of deceiver and deceived. So-called self-deception is a special case of other-deception, the case in which deceiver and deceived belong to one person.

There are two objections to this, a general and a specific one. The general objection is that it is an explanation by what is more obscure. The idea of an intrasubjective duality, such that one part is deceiving and the other is being deceived, is unclear beyond hope. Not that it is difficult to conceive one person as being two entities. A person is not one by nature, but just as well many parts, stages, or whatever.[9] The difficulty is that to ascribe deceiving and being deceived to the intrasubjective parts only makes sense if these are understood to exhibit a fairly rich array of other qualities as well. It is no use to credit a molecule in the blood with deceiving another. Such a statement is not meaningless in principle, it just does not help because it does not tie in with other things that seem to be true about molecules. To provide a suitable setting for talk of deceiver and deceived as different parts in the person, either must be understood as having beliefs, intentions, and reasons and as capable of suffering failure. That is to say, they must be understood pretty much like human beings, except that they do not have a body apart or, if they do, it is not known what its demarcation is.[10] Yet the idea of two quasi-human beings in the person itself lacks just that sort of sense that it provides for talk of one part of the person deceiving the other. It does not tie in with the world we know. It is a myth. For a myth is a story that does make sense of some particular matter by incorporating it in a broader frame, but fails to make sense of that frame in terms of the world at large. Myths are islands of sense.

The specific objection is that this account of self-deception again fails to grasp the concept Olive uses. The point is similar to the one before. That some part of Verena deceives another part of her into thinking that she really wants to be saved no more shows her treachery to be "as yet unwitting" than did the idea that a former Verena induces the deception in a later one. In fact, if one part of Verena deceived the other, the treachery was, in part at least, not unwitting. Olive must mean something different still.

A third idea for explaining self-deception is to distinguish different ways of finding out what a person believes or wants.[11] Roughly, you either ask or watch her. If you ask, you normally suppose that the person has immediate knowledge of the matter and you are requesting to have this piece of knowledge disclosed to you. So there seems to be an immediate knowledge of a person's beliefs and wants, available only to the person herself, and a mediate knowledge, available in principle to everybody, including the person in question, which is based on the person's behavior. The beliefs and wants that a person knows about immediately may be called "conscious," and those not immediately known to her, but ascribed on behavioral evidence, may be called "unconscious." Self-deception may then be explained as the case of a person who consciously believes one thing; unconsciously, and rightly, believes the opposite; unconsciously wants to keep the latter belief unconscious; and succeeds in doing so. Thus Verena consciously thinks she wants to be saved from Ransom. This is what she is immediately aware of when she asks Olive for help. However, unconsciously she knows she does not want to be saved from him. It is unconsciously that she knows this because she wants, unconsciously too, that knowledge to stay unconscious. The knowledge and the want count as unconscious because they are ascribed on behavioral grounds, namely, her refusal to depart and her unwonted reasoning in support of that decision. Maybe these grounds are not strong enough to support the claim that Verena has this knowledge and want. No matter. The present question is not whether Olive has a good case for charging Verena with self-deception, but what the charge means.

Still, it is difficult to see how the account solves the problem at hand. The proposal may be understood in two ways. According to a strong version, what is accessible in immediate knowledge and in mediate knowledge are two sorts of things. There is no such thing as the beliefs and wants a person just has, independently of whether they are grasped in immediate or in mediate knowledge or in both. There are only beliefs-in-immediate-knowledge on the one hand and beliefs-in-mediate-knowledge on the other, and similarly for wants. The ordinary terms "belief" and "want" are ambiguous, covering items from either realm. In this way, the problem of the self-deceiver's conflicting beliefs indeed disappears. Verena immediately-believes one thing and mediately-believes the opposite, but since these are different sorts of things, there is no problem here. There appeared to be a problem only because of the ambiguity of "belief." Whoever is wondering how a screw can have both a size of three inches and a size of half an inch should be told that a screw has different sorts of sizes, length and width. In the same way, whoever is wondering how people can believe something and take it to be false, too, should be told that people have different sorts of beliefs, immediate and mediate ones.

But in this version the account is unacceptable. If belief-immediately-known and belief-mediately-known are two sorts of things, then in ordinary talk what you ascribe to yourself as your belief and what I ascribe to you as your belief will often be different things. They will be different whenever you and I found out about what we both call your belief in the different ways described. In that case, what I say about what I call your belief will not conform, contradict, support, or be supported by what you say about what you call your belief. You leave the house with an umbrella; I start a conversation by asking, "You expect rain, don't you?" and you reply, "I do indeed." According to the present proposal, this is a case of people talking past each other, unless you found out that you expect rain by watching yourself carrying an umbrella. If you answer instead, "No, I am going to return the umbrella to a friend who forgot it here," you do not deny what I was saying; you change the subject. Such consequences warrant rejecting the proposal. It is no use to make sense of self-deception by making nonsense of a lot of so-far unproblematic talk of beliefs and wants.[12]

On a weaker and more natural reading, the same sort of beliefs and wants is accessible in immediate and in mediate knowledge. The different ways to discover beliefs or wants are indeed different ways, the point of this metaphor being that in different ways the same spot may be reached. You immediately know that you expect rain; I take my clue from the umbrella in your hand; but what I figure out in this way is the very thing you are aware of.

But the distinction, so construed, does not solve the problem. Conflicting statements about the same subject do not conflict any less for being supported by evidence of different kinds. If in immediate knowledge a person is found to believe one thing and in mediate knowledge to believe the opposite, the person is found to believe one thing and its opposite simply, which was the original problem. Thus it is useless to assign the self-deceiver's conflicting beliefs to the different provinces of what is known. They conflict, however known.

A fourth way of dealing with the difficulty was suggested by Mary Haight.[13] She gives up conceiving of the cases called "self-deception" on the lines indicated by this title. As the phrase is, she denies the phenomenon. Instead, she explains so-called self-deceptions as lies to other people only.[14] Applied to the present case, the solution runs like this. When Olive calls Verena self-deceived, she knows as little as we do what she means. She fails to realize the truth, which is that Verena does not deceive herself, but rather her, Olive. Verena actually knows what Olive thinks she does not know, namely, that she does not want to be saved from Ransom. She only pretends not to know it and deceives Olive into thinking that she doesn't. So she gains time. As long as Olive thinks that she, Verena, is mistaken as to what she really wants, Verena is protected from the full reproach of outright treachery: "that treachery was as yet unwitting." True, at some point the pretense is going to break down. But by that time both Olive and Verena will have become accustomed to the idea of Verena's leaving, so that the actual separation should be less painful. On the present account, then, what Olive takes to be Verena's self-deception is in fact Verena's deceiving her in order to smooth a transition that she, Verena, is perfectly aware of desiring.[15]

It is a coherent story, and it might be true. But it is not a likely story. It credits Verena with much shrewdness and luck in lying to Olive. Verena, it is said, gets Olive to believe that she, Verena, does not know what she really wants. But it is difficult to get Olive to believe that. It is difficult, but not because Olive herself knows, or thinks she knows, what Verena wants, although Olive may well know, and take herself to know, more about Verena's wishes than Verena herself. It is difficult because Olive also knows that the evidence that clearly tells her about what Verena wants, namely, her decision to stay and the unusual reasoning to support it, is before Verena's eyes as well. That is to say, Verena has to get Olive to believe that she, Verena, is blind to what the facts in front of her make obvious to Olive. It is true, this is not an absurd thing for Olive to believe. People are blind sometimes to the obvious. Indeed, that is often the reason for thinking them self-deceived.

Consequently, it is not an absurd project for Verena to get Olive to suppose such blindness in her. Only, it's tricky.

While we easily fail, for various reasons, to notice what is obvious, it is quite difficult persuasively to pretend that one fails when one doesn't. In a way, Haight's solution only shifts the problem. The conceptual difficulty about self-deception returns as the technical difficulty of making someone else hold a fairly wild opinion as to what one knows and doesn't know, an opinion wild enough to be expressed in the judgment that one suffers from self-deception. It is not impossible, it is just hard. Moreover, it is a precarious undertaking. Instead of thinking Verena to be ignorant of what she really wants, Olive may quite easily hit on the correct idea that she is deceiving her, a very undesirable outcome for Verena.

However, Haight has an answer to the objection: "But if we therefore cannot believe that A is lying, we forget that what he may dread above everything else is *having to admit* to us that p" (p. 109). Applied to the present case, the answer is: Verena knows that she wants to leave Olive and pretends not to know it. But by so pretending she does not try to deceive Olive into thinking that she does not know it. She tries, and succeeds, to avoid admitting that she knows it. It is true that for all Verena knows, Olive might not learn anything new from Verena's admitting that she knows she wants to leave her. Even so it may be highly desirable for Verena not to admit it. An explicit admission may change the situation uncomfortably. Verena's treachery would be out in the open, and Olive, though knowing of it before, would react in a different way. Figaro, when his first plot has been detected and everyone knows the truth, still refuses to admit his machination in order to deprive the Count of the extra leverage a confession would give him.[16] With another example, Verena is like the woman on the date in Sartre's story.[17] Contrary to what Sartre says, the woman does notice that the man takes her hand. But noticing something and admitting, by some voluntary and sufficient sign,[18] to have noticed it are two things; and not by actually noticing the man's advance but by admitting to have noticed it the woman becomes bound to do something about it. This is what she does not want, so she does not admit that she noticed it. She ignores it.

Actually, this is not an amendment of Haight's proposal; it is a new one, the fifth. On the first three accounts, Verena is deceived, at some time, in some part, or in some way, as to what she really wants. On the fourth account, Verena deceives Olive into thinking that she, Verena, does not know what she really wants. On the present account, Verena is neither trying to deceive nor being deceived herself. She pretends. She is double. Not in the way of the intrasubjective duality mentioned above: there is not one part in her that knows the truth and another that is in error. The duality here is that between what she appears to be and what she really is. Asking for Olive's help against

Ransom, Verena appears not to know that she really wants the opposite. But she does know it. She only makes herself appear not to. She conceals her knowledge. This she does not to deceive Olive but to avoid the unpleasant consequences of admitting it.

To conceal knowledge without trying to deceive is a familiar phenomenon. It is characteristic of many forms of play. A child playing with a doll does not lack knowledge of the difference between a human being and a piece of stuff. She withholds this piece of knowledge temporarily. It does not "come into play." Incidentally, the rule-governed character of games, their most prominent feature in recent philosophical discussion, can perhaps be understood in terms of concealed knowledge. The chess player would be described, not as following the rule "Never move a pawn backwards!" but as disregarding the fact that this is a piece of wood that could be moved in whatever way she likes. For the time being, this piece of wood is a pawn for her, and it is just a fact about pawns that they do not move backwards, in the way it is a fact about cows that they eat grass. Thus the chess player resembles the child with the doll. For the time being, she treats this piece of stuff as a child, and since it is a fact about children that they are taken to bed at the proper time, that is what she does with the doll now. In a similar way Verena is to be understood as playing. For the time being, she withholds her knowing what she wants from appearing in what she does. She acts as if she did not know it. Like other players she does not aim at deceiving people about what she knows. Unlike some other players she tries by playing to make things easier for herself and possibly for others, that is, for Olive.

But to conceal knowledge in order to get along more easily is a familiar phenomenon, too. Polite expressions are a case in point. "If you leave your name and your number, I shall be happy to return your call"—that phrase does not deceive anyone into thinking that happiness will spring from one's calling back. The message just has a nicer ring, evoking perhaps an image of shared benevolence, of people who do find happiness in serving others. However, if what Verena does is just ordinary nondeceptive pretending, why does Olive fail to perceive it as such? Why does she take recourse to the strange idea of Verena's deceiving herself?

Because she sees reason to believe that Verena is not pretending. Verena appears intense and earnest in asking her help. And Verena was never given to pretending. She was sincere "in all the history of their sacred friendship." For Olive, these are strong reasons. She has been Verena's intimate friend for a long time; they have been living together; she knows her probably as well as one comes to know any human being. So she thinks she can tell that Verena is not pretending when asking her for help; she thinks she knows that dissimulation is not in her nature. It is for these reasons that Olive, on finding Verena insincere, still does not think that she is "playing a part." She rather thinks that Verena deceived herself. In a desperate attempt to make sense of the appearances, she thinks Verena to be both dishonest and candid: dishonest, because making herself believe what she knows to be false; candid, because acting on that belief without pretense. Ordinary people, the idea is, may pretend right away; honest persons like Verena have to fool themselves first.

The attempt is desperate not just because the idea of making oneself believe what one knows to be false is so hard to understand. It is desperate also because Verena's honesty should tell as strongly against the assumption that she deceived herself as it tells against the assumption that she is pretending when asking for Olive's help. However, Olive's reasons for believing that Verena is not pretending are good. They are plausible, even if not conclusive. Verena is unlike Figaro. She does not stand aloof from the game. She is not cold-bloodedly making up the show. (This by the way points to a problem about Figaro: the opera fails to convince us that he is not just a schemer, but a lover.) Verena is serious in what she tells Olive. Or so she appears. True, appearances might deceive. Verena might be a super-Figaro, dissembling and never known to do so. Her sincerity now and before might be fake throughout. But that is unlikely. We do come to know people to some extent, and there are very few, if any, super-Figaros, whose duplicity withstands a long, close, and friendly observation. Verena might also, for all her sincerity up to now, abruptly change in the novel situation. People do suddenly change. But do they change as deeply, as suddenly as that? Olive could rightly claim that this assumption no more helps in understanding Verena than the idea of her self-deception does.

The account under discussion does not stand up, then. The proposed solution that so-called self-deceivers are pretending does not work for the case at hand. Olive's past and present experience shows that Verena is not pretending.[19] To claim that she is is to talk about a different situation, in which the problem of self-deception does not even arise. If Verena can simply be taken to be dissimulating, Olive has no reason for thinking her self-deceived. Olive does think her self-deceived because of the conflicting evidence. Verena appears honest, now as always, and she appears dishonest, insisting as she does on staying.

One may take a hard line here. There is no such thing as conflicting evidence. If the grounds for supposing Verena to be sincere are as strong as suggested, they should override those for the opposite assumption. That Verena declines to leave and defends the decision by a strange reasoning is not sufficient evidence then to establish that she is insincere. Or the other way round, this evidence seems to be stronger, so that the opposite suggestion is defeated. In that case, Verena will appear to be lying or pretending after all, her appearance of sincerity notwithstanding. Or perhaps the evidence on both sides is even, and judgment is suspended. In any event, there is no genuine conflict. The notion of self-deception is not needed.

But that is too harsh. It is like arguing that a phrase is never used ambiguously, because the evidence for one interpretation always outweighs the evidence for the other, unless they are even and no judgment is passed. But we do think that phrases are used ambiguously, because the total evidence concerning their interpretation displays patterns striking enough to deserve being accounted for. To discard nearly half the evidence as defeated by the opposite hypothesis is to be insensitive to salient features of the material. The case of self-deception is similar. To insist that the evidence, unless tied, shows Verena to be either sincere or insincere is to pass over a characteristic feature of the evidence which needs accounting for, namely, that it seems to show both. True, if the question of whether Verena is sincere or not is pressed, the total evidence, unless tied, will yield an unambiguous Yes or No. But that only shows that this is not the right question to press. The task is, rather, to describe Verena so as to make sense of her appearing both to be sincere and to be insincere.

This is not a problem specifically about self-deception. It is as much a problem about play. The reasons that tell against a pretense on Verena's part tell as strongly against taking the player to pretend not to know certain things. If Verena, intense and earnest as she is in imploring Olive, does not conceal her knowledge, neither does the child with the doll, absorbed as she is in playing. If Verena is too serious to be merely playing, players sometimes are as serious and cannot be "merely playing" either. Again, pressing the question whether the child knows that it is just a bit of stuff she is playing with, one will have grounds for an unambiguous Yes or No, unless the evidence is balanced. But again the important question is how to describe her so as to make sense of her appearing both to know and not to know this fact. For she does appear to know it; everyone does. And she appears not to know it: she talks to the doll.

It may be suggested that both Verena and the child should be described, not as pretending not to know the relevant fact, but as not using that piece of knowledge for some period of time. True, it may be said, they do not conceal their knowledge. Engrossed as each is in her "play," she cannot also be withholding that knowledge from appearing in what she does. Instead, the knowledge just became concealed from her, by whatever cause. Like a folder removed from the files, it is inaccessible temporarily. Verena, the suggestion goes, still has the knowledge that she really wants to leave Olive, but it is knowledge ineffective for the time being. Therefore she is quite honest in asking Olive to help her against Ransom. The child still has the knowledge that the doll is just a piece of stuff. But it is knowledge off duty. It does not prevent her from being perfectly serious in treating the doll as a human being.

But the suggestion does not lead far. To be sure, the distinction between knowledge in use, which finds expression in what the person thinks, says, or does, and knowledge merely had is familiar. One may know whether Fifth Avenue goes uptown or downtown while lying on the beach in France and thinking about what to have for dinner. But explanations can be given as to why someone's knowledge fails to be used on a given occasion. Irrelevance will be the most frequent one. Others will be that the person is too tired, that she is, for some reason or other, unwilling to use her knowledge, and so on. But these explanations do not fit Verena's or the child's case. The knowledge withheld there is very much to the point; there is no question of physical inabilities; an unwillingness to use their knowledge was excluded in the discussion about pretending; and another explanation, which would work, is not in sight. So it may be true enough that their knowledge is ineffective for the time being. But one wants to know why—which is the original problem. Why does Verena's and the child's knowledge fail to come into play?[20]

But this is a dangerous way of putting the matter. Talk of knowledge that is being withheld suggests that there is this piece of knowledge, subsisting independently of what is done with it. It suggests that one has knowledge in the way one has subway tokens, which may come to be used or not, and not in the way one has a good time, where there is nothing had over and above what one does and finds. It suggests that pieces of knowledge are preserved in the mind and put to work on occasion, so that the question about Verena and the child becomes why theirs are not. This is not to say that the distinction between knowledge used and knowledge had must be read this way. It may be taken as just a summary of the sentences: one may know which way Fifth Avenue goes while not driving in the area, one may know a proof when not presenting it, and so on. Still, it is a natural reading.[21]

It could be argued that this idea of knowledge as something contained and preserved in the mind does not make sense. It will not be argued here; it is too large a topic. Nor will a case be made for the positive suggestion that to know something is just to have thought, felt, said, done, encountered certain things and not others. The knowledge one has is the experience itself one went through, not its outcome. Knowing that Fifth Avenue goes downtown is not something one acquired by going through certain activities, something like an inner eye's recognizing this fact or like an apparatus's producing appropriate behavior under suitable circumstances. It is one's having gone through these activities—taking the bus downtown, getting lost on the way to the Metropolitan Museum, figuring out on the map how to get there, enjoying this kind of thing, and so on. To know something is to have had a particular sort of history, to have gone one sort of way through the world; that some knowledge comes into play in a given situation is a continuation of that thread. What I will argue is that this assumption opens up an understanding both of Verena's alleged self-deception and of the child's play.

The problem about the child was that there are good grounds to suppose her to know that the doll is not a human being, but that, lost in her play, she appears not to know it. Now there is no knowledge independently subsisting in her mind anyway. Such knowledge, to the effect that it is "merely a doll" she is playing with, would indeed be difficult to reconcile with her absorption in playing. One might expect that her inner self, seeing that she is holding not a child but just a piece of stuff, should remind her of the fact and wake her up. One wonders why the knowledge, lying ready in her mind, is not put to work, relevant as it seems. But now her knowledge is part of her history, not something beyond. So the conflict between what she does and what she knows does not arise. There is only the sequence of what she thinks, does, encounters.

And of that sequence good sense can be made. These are games children have with dolls. For example, they do not care about them sometimes and sometimes seek them urgently. When giving them a treat, they are not surprised that the food does not diminish, but are very serious about feeding them nonetheless. There is the series of things that constitutes the child's knowing that the doll is not human, and there is the series of things which constitutes treating the doll as a child. The two series are interwoven and form a pattern that is understandable because it ties in with what we know of other children playing with dolls, of other playings of children, of playing in general. To be sure, asked in earnest whether the doll is really a human being, the child may well answer in the negative.[22] But that does not show that deep in her heart she knew that it is only a doll. It shows that this is how she responds to people making serious faces, and that reaction is understandable again.

"So we are barred forever from knowing what she believes about the doll?" On the contrary. Here is what she believes: her taking care of her, neglecting her, loving her dearly, and so on. "But she really does know, doesn't she, that the doll is not a human being?" If that means that she has, over and above her care, neglect, love, and so on, an awareness of this fact, then she does not really know it, nor anything else. If it means that all in all her way with the doll should rather be taken as a case of knowing than of not knowing this fact, it may well be true, though hard to decide. And it does not particularly matter. That is just the question whether her way with the doll should be grouped together with those ways of people which are generally taken to be cases of knowing something or rather with those which are considered as cases of not knowing it. But these are just two out of a large number of comparisons that may be made, many of them certainly being more illuminating than these. What matters is that by means of such comparisons the girl's way with the doll can be made sense of in terms of what we are acquainted with in experience.

Verena's alleged self-deception can be accounted for on similar lines. The problem was that there are good grounds to suppose that she knows she really wants to leave Olive, but that, sincerely asking Olive to help her against Ransom, she appears not to know it. Now it may be true that her refusal to leave and the unwonted appeal to her dignity to support her decision actually are evidence for her wish to join Ransom. Furthermore, it is true that these facts are before her eyes. Even so, following the general assumption made above, she does not know of her wish in the sense that an awareness of it is present in her mind. Such an awareness would indeed strikingly contrast with her sincere request for Olive's help. One should expect that an inner awareness of what she really wants would not allow her sincerely to say to Olive what she does. In the face of her wish she could not but be lying or pretending. That awareness gone, there is only the series of what she thinks and feels, does, and encounters.

And of that story good sense can be made, even in various ways. In the first place, she insists on confronting Ransom because she feels that this is very important to her, for reasons she may just vaguely perceive. She does think that evading him would be beneath her dignity. Olive, in finding this an unusual thought with Verena, may be right. Perhaps this is the first time in her life that she sees reason to apply the concept of dignity to herself. Even so, the fact that she does not want to leave, allegedly because of her dignity, may well be taken as showing that she really wishes to go with Ransom. But it need not. More importantly, one can understand that this is not what Verena is thinking. First, the idea that this is what she really wants may just never strike her, unaccustomed as she is in particular, unaccustomed as she may be in general, to thinking of herself as wishing something. There are people who never do. Second, the idea may occur to her, but as a daydream only, not taken seriously. Third, she may actually begin to wonder whether living with Ransom is what she desires. But then, frightened by the idea as well, anguished at losing hold of what has been the center of her life for years, she may shy away from it. Not that she consciously bans it from consciousness: she just does not think closely about the matter, painful as it is.

Now if this or something similar is what Verena is thinking, she may well implore Olive from all her heart to help her. Bewildered by the situation, she habitually turns to Olive for guidance. Frightened by what her courage might lead her to, she thinks Olive can save her. In fact, she asks Olive for help in a situation that is so difficult just because her dependence on Olive is being challenged. This may not be wise. It is intelligible. People in trouble are like that. What Verena thinks, feels, and does is comprehensible as the story of a person who is about to grow out of what used to hold her and to change many of her ways. The inquiry about what, supposedly underlying the appearances, she does or does not know misses the point of her story.

Eventually Verena will go off with Ransom. It will seem that Olive was right in thinking that this is what Verena really wants; but it will only seem so, because even the final dénouement cannot tell definitively. But if Olive is right, it is a mistake on Verena's part to ask her for help. Not that Verena knows better: it is a mistake relative to what she wants and is going to do, a mistake in the sense of being on the wrong track.[23] This is what Verena's alleged self-deception comes to. She is neither deceiving anyone nor being deceived. She just goes wrong. Contrary to what the word suggests, her so-called self-deception is not something like putting on colored glasses. It is something like making an unnecessary detour or like getting into a rut. It is not an action or state she chose; it is a condition she got entangled in. One suffers from self-deception.

Why then does Olive think that Verena is deceiving herself? As Olive takes herself to know what Verena really wants, why doesn't she think that Verena is simply making a mistake in asking her for help against Ransom? It is a mistake, moreover, which Olive could easily make sense of on the lines indicated, as being due to fear or lack of confidence in a bewildering situation. Olive, not having read Sartre, may not see the conceptual problems about the notion of self-deception, so that she considers "being mistaken" and "deceiving oneself" as equally unproblematic locutions. Even so, why does she prefer the latter?

The reason is that Verena can be blamed for deceiving herself. It would be inappropriate to blame her for being on the wrong track. One may regret that she is, or try to help her find her way, but not blame her. True, sometimes people are blamed for being on the wrong track. But this is a mistake itself. What can be blamed is not one's being wrong, but things like lack of due attention or failure to get the relevant information in time, which led to one's being wrong. If none of this applies, blame is out of place, even though it was certainly the person's own doing, say, to take that turn that proved to be false. This is Verena's case. Not without her own doing did she get into the bewildering situation, and it is she who reacts to it in a mistaken way. But she does not choose to go wrong. Nor did she fail to take proper precautions before. She was not in a position to, not being alive to the difficulties of the situation before entering it. By contrast, the notion that Verena deceived herself does suggest that she, at some time, in some part, or in some way, had the truth and decided against it, by bringing about the deception in herself which makes her go wrong. "Self-deception" tells in secular terms a story of the fall, of man's being in the light and turning away from it, of self-imposed blindness.[24]

So the deceptions of self-deceivers can be blamed on them. According to Olive, Verena did choose, though indirectly, to go wrong. Thus it is not the case that Verena deceives herself and Olive blames her for it. It is the other way round: Olive takes Verena to be deceiving herself in order to blame her. Admittedly, Olive considers Verena's self-deception as a less grave fault than conscious lying. "Olive did not go so far as to believe that she was playing a part." Presumably she did not go so far because that belief seemed to her incompatible with what she knew about Verena's character. But if taking Verena to be deceiving herself is not to go so far as to accuse her of outright dishonesty, it is to go nonetheless in that direction. It is to go far enough to accuse her.

And why is Olive bent on blaming Verena? Why does she fail to understand the anxiety and confusion that make Verena liable to go wrong? Because Olive is hurt. She anticipates that Verena is going to leave her. That bears hard on her. Suffering at Verena's hands, she finds fault with her.[25] Actually, what she finds fault with, Verena's alleged self-deception, is not the cause of her suffering, Verena's imminent leaving. But that is usual in resentment. We tend to blame, or to blame more severely, what people did who annoyed us by doing something quite different. Olive is understandable enough in blaming Verena. Yet like Verena she is mistaken. Blaming Verena will not help Olive. Resentment only festers the wound.

NOTES

1. London: Penguin, 1984.

2. J. P. Sartre was the first to point it out (*L'Être et le Néant* [Paris, 1943], pp. 84f.). Actually Sartre speaks of "mauvaise foi," which is not equivalent to "self-deception." However, he does accept the rendering of "mauvaise foi" by "mensonge à soi," "lying to oneself" (p. 83), which indicates that the difference between "mauvaise foi" and "self-deception" may be neglected.

3. J. Canfield and P. McNally, "Paradoxes of Self-Deception," *Analysis* 21, (1961):141f.

4. I shall discuss only those that have not been sufficiently treated in the literature. So I shall not return to R. Demos' proposal to distinguish between simple awareness and awareness together with noticing ("Lying to Oneself," *Journal of Philosophy* 57 [1960]:593. See F. Siegler, "Demos on Lying to Oneself," *Journal of Philosophy* 59 [1962]:472, and D. Pugmire, "'Strong' Self-Deception," *Inquiry* 12 [1969]:344). Nor shall I consider the suggestion of Canfield and D. Gustafson to understand self-deception as believing something under belief-adverse circumstances ("Self-Deception," *Analysis* 23 [1962]:35f. See P. Gardiner, "Error, Faith and Self-Deception," *Proceedings of the Aristotelian Society* 70 [1969/70]:228–232).

5. Bernard Williams disagrees: "With regard to no belief could I know—or, if all this is to be done in full consciousness, even suspect—that I had acquired it at will." But it is not clear why this should be so. In fact, Williams goes on to distinguish between acquiring a belief at will "just like that" and acquiring it at will "by more roundabout routes," like hypnosis, drugs, and similar things. He claims that the latter idea "does not seem evidently incoherent," whereas the former does. But whether it makes sense to speak of someone's acquiring a belief at will should not depend on whether one tries to do it by means of drugs or directly. (Williams, "Deciding to Believe," in *Problems of the Self* [Cambridge, 1973], pp. 148–150.)

6. "Naturellement même çela vous fera croîre et vous abêtira" (B. Pascal, *Pensées*, ed. Lafuma, fragment 418; ed. Brunschvicg, fragment 233.)

7. Jon Elster reads Pascal as requiring, under the title of "*abêtissement*," "stupidification," that the person forget the process of acquiring the belief. He is led to this reading because he agrees with Williams (see note 5 above) that one cannot know of a belief that one acquired it at will. But that point is doubtful, and Elster's reading

conflicts with Pascal's remark mentioned above. (Elster, *Ulysses and the Sirens* [Cambridge, 1979], pp. 50f.)

8. Pascal, *Pensées,* ed. Lafuma, fragment 419; ed. Brunschvicg, fragment 89.

9. A point repeatedly emphasized by Nelson Goodman, e.g., in "The Way the World Is," in *Problems and Projects* [Indianapolis, 1972], pp. 24–32.

10. Donald Davidson, advocating a division of the mind into parts independent of each other to some extent, furnishes them with a "supporting structure of reasons, of interlocking beliefs, expectations, assumptions, attitudes and desires." But he claims that no little agents in the parts are called for. Actually, however, the parts basically are little agents. (Davidson, "Paradoxes of Irrationality," in *Philosophical Essays on Freud,* ed. R. Wollheim and J. Hopkins [Cambridge, 1982], pp. 300, 304. David Pears offers a similar account; see his paper "Motivated Irrationality, Freudian Theory and Cognitive Dissonance," in the Wollheim/Hopkins volume just cited, and his book *Motivated Irrationality* [Oxford, 1984].)

11. Ernst Tugendhat, in discussion, and Jens Kulenkampff, in an unpublished paper, suggested this idea, Tugendhat in turn referring to Alasdair MacIntyre's treatment of unconscious intentions (*The Unconscious* [London and New York, 1958], pp. 54–60). But my statement may not adequately represent their idea.

12. MacIntyre apparently rejects the strong version (*The Unconscious,* p. 54). Tugendhat argues against assuming an ambiguity between the first- and third-person uses of terms like "belief" and "want" (*Selbstbewußtsein und Selbstbestimmung* [Frankfurt, 1979]).

13. M. R. Haight, *A Study of Self-Deception* (Brighton, 1980). The argument of the book is not easy to discern, so what follows may not truly represent Haight's idea.

14. Ibid., p. 108.

15. This is perhaps an interpersonal variant of Elster's idea to reinterpret apparent cases of self-deception as "successful or unsuccessful attempts at self-modification" (*Ulysses and the Sirens,* p. 176).

16. Mozart, *Le Nozze di Figaro,* finale of the second act.

17. Sartre, *L'Être et le Néant,* pp. 91f.

18. Hobbes' phrase, *Leviathan,* chap. 14.

19. Criticism on these lines is probably what is intended when accounts like the present or the previous one are charged with "denying the phenomenon." One cannot deny phenomena. What one can deny are statements well supported by experience, and this is the case here.

20. Haight uses the notion of "buried knowledge" to explain self-deception, knowledge being buried "if it is not recalled when recollection is to be expected" (p. 13). But that notion merely reiterates the problem; it does not solve it. Why then does a person fail to recall, in a given case, a piece of knowledge that she has and which is relevant? In a similar way, Hans Georg Gadamer says of the player that "he knows that what he is doing 'is only play,' but he does not know what it is that he 'knows' there." ("Er weiss nicht, was er da 'weiss'," *Wahrheit und Methode* [Tübingen, 1975], pp. 97f.) Since normally people do know what it is they know, one wonders how it is that the player doesn't.

21. It may be called the Augustinian reading, Augustine's conception of memory as a treasure house in the soul (*Confessions* X, 12–37) being applied here to knowledge in general.

22. Ludwig Wittgenstein, *Philosophische Untersuchungen,* trans. E. Anscombe (Oxford, 1967), § 187: "Your 'I Knew already then . . . ' means something like this: 'If I had been asked then which number he should write down after 1000, I should have answered "1002".' And that I do not doubt."

23. In playing with the doll, the child is not making a mistake, even though she will give up that play before long.

24. There is a similar idea in the opening statement of Kant's essay on enlightenment. "Enlightenment is man's emergence from his self-incurred immaturity" ("An Answer to the Question: 'What Is Enlightenment?'" *Kant's Political Writings,* ed. H. Riess, trans. H. Nisbet [Cambridge, 1970], p. 54). The idea is inconsistent unless it is assumed that man's infancy, oddly enough, was preceded by a state of majority (since infancy excludes responsibility), and that is essentially the story of the fall.

25. This is basically what Nietzsche called "resentment"; see his descriptions in the chapter "Von den Verächtern des Leibes" in pt. 1 of *Also sprach Zarathustra* and in secs. 13–28 in the third essay of *Zur Genealogie der Moral.*

BIBLIOGRAPHY

UMA NARAYAN

Books

Dyke, Daniel. *The Mystery of Selfe-Deceiving; or, Discourse and Discovery of the Deceitfulness of Mans Heart.* Printed by Richard Bishop, 1642.

Elster, Jon. *Sour Grapes: Studies in the Subversion of Rationality.* Cambridge: Cambridge University Press, 1983.

―――. *Ulysses and the Sirens.* Cambridge: Cambridge University Press, 1979.

―――, ed. *The Multiple Self.* Cambridge: Cambridge University Press, 1985.

Faber, Frederick. *Self-Deceit.* Wallingford, Pa.: Pendle Hill, 1983.

Fingarette, Herbert. *Self-Deception.* London: Routledge and Kegan Paul; New York: Humanities Press, 1969.

Haight, M. R. *A Study of Self-Deception.* Sussex: Harvester Press, 1980.

MacIntyre, Alasdair. *The Unconscious.* New York: Humanities Press, 1958.

Martin, Michael, ed. *Self-Deception and Self-Understanding: New Essays in Philosophy and Psychology.* Lawrence: University Press of Kansas, 1985.

Mele, Alfred R. *Irrationality: An Essay on Akrasia, Self-Deception, and Self-Control.* New York: Oxford University Press, 1987.

Wilshire, Bruce. *Role Playing and Identity: The Limits of Theatre as Metaphor.* Bloomington: Indiana University Press, 1982.

Articles

Alexander, Peter, "Wishes, Symptoms and Actions," *Proceedings of the Aristotelian Society* 48 (1974):119–134.

Anscombe, G. E. M. "Pretending." In *Philosophy of Mind,* edited by Stuart Hampshire. New York: Harper and Row, 1966.

Audi, Robert. "The Epistemic Authority of the First Person," *The Personalist* 56 (1975):5–15.

―――. "Epistemic Disavowals and Self-Deception," *The Personalist* 57 (1976):378–385.

―――. "The Limits of Self-Knowledge," *Canadian Journal of Philosophy* 4 (1974):253–267.

―――. "Self-Deception, Action, and Will," *Erkenntnis* 18 (1982):133–158.

―――. "Self-Deception and Rationality." In *Self-Deception and Self-Understanding,* edited by Michael Martin. Lawrence: University Press of Kansas, 1985.

Bach, Kent. "An Analysis of Self-Deception," *Philosophy and Phenomenological Research* 41 (1981):351–370.

Bell, Linda. "Sartre, Dialectic, and the Problem of Overcoming Bad Faith," *Man and World* 10 (1977):292–302.

Bergoffen, Debra. "Sartre and the Myth of Natural Scarcity," *Journal of British Social Phenomenology* 13 (1982):15–25.

Bok, Sissela. "The Self Deceived," *Social Science Information* 19 (1980):905–922.

Boyers, Robert. "Observations on Lying and Liars," *Review of Existential Psychiatry* 13 (1974):150–168.

Burrell, David, and Stanley Hauerwas. "Self-Deception and Autobiography: Theological and Ethical Reflections on Speer's *Inside the Third Reich*," *Journal of Religious Ethics* 2 (1974):99–117.

Butler, Joseph. "Upon Self-Deceit." In *The Works of Joseph Butler*, edited by W. E. Gladstone. Oxford: Clarendon Press, 1896.

Canfield, John V., and Don F. Gustafson. "Self-Deception," *Analysis* 23 (1962):32–36.

Canfield, John V., and Patrick McNally. "Paradoxes of Self-Deception," *Analysis* 21 (1961):140–144.

Champlin, T. S. "Double Deception," *Mind* 85 (1976):100–102.

———. "Self-Deception: A Problem About Autobiography," *Proceedings of the Aristotelian Society*, supp. vol. 53 (1979):77–94.

———. "Self-Deception—A Reflexive Dilemma," *Philosophy* 52 (1977):281–299.

Chisholm, Roderick M., and Thomas Feehan. "The Intent to Deceive," *Journal of Philosophy* 74 (1977):143–159.

Cioffi, Frank, and Peter Alexander. "Symposium: Wishes, Symptoms and Actions," *Proceedings of the Aristotelian Society* 48 (1974):97–134.

Collins, Arthur W. "Unconscious Belief," *Journal of Philosophy* 66 (1969):667–680.

Cosentino, Dante A. "Self-Deception without Paradox," *Philosophy Research Archives* 6 (1980):443–465.

Daniels, Charles B. "Self-Deception and Inter-personal Deception," *The Personalist* 55 (1974):244–252.

Davidson, Donald. "Deception and Division." In *Actions and Events*, edited by E. LePore and B. McLaughlin. New York: Basil Blackwell, 1985.

———. "Paradoxes of Irrationality." In *Philosophical Essays on Freud*, edited by R. Wollheim and J. Hopkins. Cambridge: Cambridge University Press, 1982.

Demos, Raphael. "Lying to Oneself," *Journal of Philosophy* 57 (1960):588–595.

———. "What Is It that I Want?" *Ethics* 55 (1945):182–195.

de Sousa, Ronald B. "Rational Homunculi." In *The Identities of Persons*, edited by A. O. Rorty. Berkeley, Los Angeles, London: University of California Press, 1976.

———. "Self-Deceptive Emotions," *Journal of Philosophy* 75 (1978):684–697. Reprinted in *Explaining Emotions*, edited by A. O. Rorty. Berkeley, Los Angeles, London: University of California Press, 1980.

Deutsche, Eliot. "Personhood and Self-Deception." Chapter 1 in *Personhood, Creativity and Freedom*. Honolulu: University of Hawaii Press, 1982.

Douglas, W., and K. Gibbins. "Inadequacy of Voice Recognition as a Demonstration of Self-Deception," *Journal of Personality and Social Psychology* 44 (1983):589–592.

Evans, Donald. "Moral Weakness," *Philosophy* 50 (1975):295–310.

Exdell, John, and James R. Hamilton. "The Incorrigibility of First-Person Disavowals," *The Personalist* 56 (1975):389–394.

Factor, R. Lance. "Self-Deception and the Functionalist Theory of Mental Processes," *The Personalist* 58 (1977):115–123.

Foss, Jeffrey. "Rethinking Self-Deception," *American Philosophical Quarterly* 17 (1980):237–243.

Fox, Michael. "On Unconscious Emotions," *Philosophy and Phenomenological Research* 34 (1973):151–170.

———. "Unconscious Emotions: A Reply to Professor Mullane's 'Unconscious and Disguised Emotions'," *Philosophy and Phenomenological Research* 36 (1976):412–414.

Frenkel-Brunswik, Else. "Mechanisms of Self-Deception," *Journal of Social Psychology* 10 (1939):409–420.

Fuller, Gary. "Other Deception," *Southwestern Journal of Philosophy* 7 (1976):21–31.

Gardiner, Patrick. "Error, Faith and Self-Deception," *Proceedings of the Aristotelian Society* 70 (1969/70):221–243.

Gilligan, S., and G. Bower. "Cognitive Consequences of Emotional Arousal." In *Emotions, Cognition and Behaviour,* edited by C. Izard, J. Kagan, and R. Zajonc. Cambridge: Cambridge University Press, 1984.

Gollwitzer, P., W. Earle, and W. Stephan. "Affect as a Determinant of Egotism: Residual Excitation and Performance Attributions," *Journal of Personality and Social Psychology* 43 (1982):702–709.

Gur, Ruben C., and Harold A. Sackheim. "Self-Deception: A Concept in Search of a Phenomenon," *Journal of Personality and Social Psychology* 37 (1979):147–169.

Guthrie, Jerry L. "Self-Deception and Emotional Response to Fiction," *British Journal of Aesthetics* 21 (1981):65–75.

Hamlyn, D. W. "Self-Deception," *Proceedings of the Aristotelian Society* 45 (1971):45–60.

Harvey, J., and G. Weary. "Current Issues in Attribution Theory and Research," *Annual Review of Psychology* 35 (1984):427–459.

Hausman, Carl R. "Creativity and Self-Deception," *Journal of Existentialism* 7 (1967):295–308.

Heil, J. "Doxastic Incontinence," *Mind* 93 (1984):56–70.

Hellman, Nathan. "Bach on Self-Deception," *Philosophy and Phenomenological Research* 44 (1983):113–120.

Jordan, James N. "On Comprehending Free-will," *Southern Journal of Philosophy* 11 (1973):184–201.

Joseph, R. "Awareness, the Origin of Thought, and the Role of Conscious Self-Deception in Resistance and Repression," *Psychological Reports* 46 (1980):767–781.

Keen, Ernest. "Suicide and Self-Deception," *Psychoanalytic Review* 60 (1973/74):575–585.

Ketchum, Sara Ann. "Moral Re-description and Political Self-Deception." In *Sexist Language,* edited by Mary Vetterling-Braggin. Totowa, N.J.: Littlefield, 1981.

King-Farlow, John. "Akrasia, Mastery and the Master-Self," *Pacific Philosophical Quarterly* 62 (1981):47–60.

————. "Deceptions? Assertions? or Second-String Verbiage?" *Philosophy* 56 (1981):100–105.

————. "Philosophical Nationalism: Self-Deception and Self-Direction," *Dialogue* 17 (1978):591–615.

————. "Self-Deceivers and Sartrian Seducers," *Analysis* 23 (1963):131–136.

Kipp, David. "On Self-Deception," *Philosophical Quarterly* 30 (1980):305–317.

Kovar, Leo. "The Pursuit of Self-Deception," *Review of Existential Psychology and Psychiatry* 13 (1974):136–149.

Lemmon, E. J. "Moral Dilemmas," *Philosophical Review* 71 (1962):139–158.

Linehan, Elizabeth A. "Ignorance, Self-Deception and Moral Accountability," *Journal of Value Inquiry* 16 (1982):101–115.

Martin, Mike W. "Demystifying Doublethink: Self-Deception, Truth and Freedom in *1984*," *Social Theory and Practice* 10 (1984):319–331.

————. "Factor's Functionalist Account of Self-Deception," *The Personalist* 60 (1979):336–342.

————. "Immorality and Self-Deception," *Dialogue* 16 (1977):274–280.

————. "Morality and Self-Deception: Paradox, Ambiguity or Vagueness?" *Man and World* 12 (1979):47–60.

————. "Sartre on Lying to Oneself," *Philosophy Research Archives* 4 (1978):1–26.

————. "Self-Deception, Self-Pretence, and Emotional Detachment," *Mind* 88 (1979):441–446.

Mele, Alfred R. "Incontinent Believing," *Philosophical Quarterly* 36 (1986):212–222.

————. "Self-Deception," *Philosophical Quarterly* 33 (1983):365–377.

————. "Self-Deception, Action and Will: Comments," *Erkenntnis* 18 (1982):159–164.

Miri, Mrinal. "Self-Deception," *Philosophy and Phenomenological Research* 34 (1974):576–585.

Monts, Kenneth J., A. Louis, and Rudy Nydegger. "Interpersonal Self-Deception and Personality Co-relates," *Journal of Social Psychology* 103 (1977):91–99.

Morris, Phyllis Sutton. "Self-Deception: Sartre's Resolution of the Paradox." In *Jean-Paul Sartre,* edited by Hugh J. Silverman and Frederick A. Elliston. Pittsburgh: Duquesne University Press, 1980.

Mounce, H. O. "Self-Deception," *Proceedings of the Aristotelean Society* 45 (1971):61–72.

Murphy, Gardner. "Experiments in Over-coming Self-Deception," *Psychophysiology* 6 (1970):790–799.

Murphy, Gardner, and Wendell M. Swenson, "Outgrowing Self-Deception," *American Journal of Psychiatry* 133 (1976):115–128.

Nisbett, Richard E., and Timothy D. Wilson. "The Halo Effect: Evidence for Unconscious Alteration of Judgements," *Journal of Personality and Social Psychology* 35 (1977):250–256.

Palmer, Anthony. "Characterizing Self-Deception," *Mind* 88 (1979):45–58.

————. "Self-Deception: A Problem About Autobiography," *Proceedings of the Aristotelian Society,* supp. vol. 53 (1979):61–76.

Paluch, Stanley. "Self-Deception," *Inquiry* 10 (1967):268–278.

Paskow, Alan. "Towards a Theory of Self-Deception," *Man and World* 12 (1979): 178–191.

Pears, David. "Freud, Sartre and Self-Deception." In *Freud,* edited by R. Wollheim. Garden City, N.Y.: Anchor Books, 1974.

———. "Motivated Irrationality, Freudian Theory and Cognitive Dissonance." In *Philosophical Essays on Freud,* edited by R. Wollheim and J. Hopkins. Cambridge: Cambridge University Press, 1982.

Penelhum, Terence, W. E. Kennick, and Arnold Isenberg. "Symposium: Pleasure and Falsity," *American Philosophical Quarterly* 1 (1964):81–91.

Peterman, James. "Self-Deception and the Problem of Avoidance," *Southern Journal of Philosophy* 21 (1983):565–574.

Phillips, D. Z. "Bad Faith and Sartre's Waiter," *Philosophy* 56 (1981):23–31.

Pole, David. "The Socratic Injunction," *Journal of the British Society for Phenomenology* 2 (1971):31–40.

Pugmire, David. "'Strong' Self-Deception," *Inquiry* 12 (1969):339–346.

Quattrone, George, and Amos Tversky. "Causal versus Diagnostic Contingencies: On Self-Deception and the Voter's Illusion," *Journal of Personality and Social Psychology* 46 (1984):237–248.

Reilly, Richard. "Self-Deception: Resolving the Epistemological Paradox," *The Personalist* 57 (1976):391–394.

Rorty, Amélie Oksenberg. "Akratic Believers," *American Philosophical Quarterly* 20 (1983):175–183.

———. "Belief and Self-Deception," *Inquiry* 15 (1972):387–410.

———. "Self-Deception, Akrasia and Irrationality," *Social Science Information* 19 (1980):905–922.

Russell, J. Michael. "Reflection and Self-Deception," *Journal for Research in Phenomenology* 11 (1981):62–74.

———. "Saying, Feeling, and Self-Deception," *Behaviorism* 6 (1978):27–43.

Sackheim, Harold A., and Ruben C. Gur. "Self-Deception, Other-Deception, and Self-Reported Psychopathology," *Journal of Consulting and Clinical Psychology* 47 (1979):213–215.

———. "Self-Deception, Self-Confrontation, and Consciousness." In *Consciousness and Self-Regulation: Advances in Research and Theory,* edited by Gary E. Schwartz and David Shapiro. New York: Plenum Press, 1978.

Santoni, Ronald E. "Bad Faith and 'Lying to Oneself'," *Philosophy and Phenomenological Research* 38 (1978):384–398.

———. "Sartre on 'Sincerity': Bad Faith? or Equivocation?" *The Personalist* 53 (1972):150–160.

Saunders, John Turk. "The Paradox of Self-Deception," *Philosophy and Phenomenological Research* 35 (1975):559–570.

Scott-Taggart, M. J. "Socratic Irony and Self Deceit," *Ratio* 14 (1972):1–15.

Shapiro, Gary. "Choice and Universality in Sartre's Ethics," *Man and World* 7 (1974):20–36.

Siegler, Frederick A. "An Analysis of Self-Deception," *Nous* 2 (1968):147–164.

———. "Demos on Lying to Oneself," *Journal of Philosophy* 59 (1962):469–475.

———. "Self-Deception," *Australian Journal of Philosophy* 41 (1963):29–43.

———. "Self-Deception and Other Deception," *Journal of Philosophy* 60 (1963):759–764.

———. "Unconscious Intentions," *Inquiry* 10 (1967):251–267.

Smith, Adam. "Of the Nature of Self-Deceit." In *The Theory of Moral Sentiments*. New York: Kelley, 1966.

Snyder, C. "Collaborative Companions: The Relationship of Self-Deception and Excuse Making." In *Self-Deception and Self-Understanding,* edited by M. W. Martin. Lawrence: University Press of Kansas, 1985.

Sorensen, R. "Self-Deception and Scattered Events," *Mind* 94 (1985):64–69.

Stern, Laurent. "On Make-Believe," *Philosophy and Phenomenological Research* 28 (1967/68):24–38.

Stone, Robert V. "Sartre on Bad Faith and Authenticity." In *The Philosophy of Jean-Paul Sartre,* edited by P. A. Schilpp. La Salle, Ill.: Open Court, 1981.

Swann, William J., and Stephen J. Read. "Self-Verification Processes: How We Sustain Our Self-Conceptions," *Journal of Experimental Social Psychology* 17 (1981):351–372.

Szabados, Béla. "Fingarette on Self-Deception," *Philosophical Papers* 6 (1977):21–30.

———. "The Morality of Self-Deception," *Dialogue* 13 (1974):25–34.

———. "Rorty on Belief and Self-Deception," *Inquiry* 17 (1974):464–473.

———. "Self-Deception," *Canadian Journal of Philosophy* 4 (1974):51–68.

———. "Wishful Thinking and Self-Deception," *Analysis* 33 (1973):201–205.

Tversky, Amos. "Self-Deception and Self-Perception." In *The Multiple Self,* edited by Jon Elster. Cambridge: Cambridge University Press, 1985.

Warner, Richard. "Deception and Self-Deception in Shamanism and Psychiatry," *International Journal of Social Psychiatry* 26 (1980):41–52.

Welles, Jim. "The Socio-biology of Self-Deception," *Human Ethology Newsletter* 3 (1981):14–19.

Wilshire, Bruce. "Self, Body and Self-Deception," *Man and World* 5 (1972):422–451.

Wilson, Catherine. "Self-Deception and Psychological Realism," *Philosophical Investigations* 3 (1980):47–60.

Reviews

de Sousa, Ronald B. Review of *Self-Deception,* by Herbert Fingarette, *Inquiry* 13 (1970):308–321.

Drengson, Alan. Critical Notice of H. Fingarette, *Self-Deception, Canadian Journal of Philosophy* 3 (1974):475–484.

King-Farlow, John. Critical Notice of Herbert Fingarette's *Self-Deception, Metaphilosophy* 4 (1973):76–84.

Szabados, Béla. "Review of M. R. Haight's *A Study of Self-Deception,*" *Canadian Philosophical Review* 1 (1982):259–263.

CONTRIBUTORS

Amélie Oksenberg Rorty is a professor of philosophy at Rutgers University.

Brian P. McLaughlin is an associate professor of philosophy at Rutgers University.

Mark Johnston is an associate professor of philosophy at Princeton University.

Robert Audi is a professor of philosophy at the University of Nebraska.

Bas C. van Fraassen is a professor of philosophy at Princeton University.

David H. Sanford is a professor of philosophy at Duke University.

Adam Morton is a professor of philosophy at the University of Bristol.

Frederick F. Schmitt is an associate professor of philosophy at the University of Illinois, Urbana-Champaign.

Allen W. Wood is a professor of philosophy at the Sage School of Philosophy, Cornell University.

Edward Erwin is a professor of philosophy at the University of Miami.

Leila Tov-Ruach is an Israeli Psychiatrist, who writes and lectures on philosophical psychology.

Georges Rey is an associate professor of philosophy at the University of Maryland.

Adrian M. S. Piper is an associate professor of philosophy at Georgetown University.

Ronald B. de Sousa is a professor of philosophy at the University of Toronto.

Rom Harré is a professor of philosophy at Oxford University.

William Ruddick is a professor of philosophy at New York University.

Bruce Wilshire is a professor of philosophy at Rutgers University.

Stephen L. Darwall is a professor of philosophy at the University of Michigan.

Marcia Baron is an assistant professor of philosophy at the University of Illinois, Urbana-Champaign.

Stephen L. White is an assistant professor of philosophy at Tufts University.

Martha Nussbaum is a professor of philosophy at Brown University.

Margret Kohlenbach is a lecturer of German at the University of Sussex.

Rüdiger Bittner is professor of philosophy at the Hochschule Hildesheim, West Germany.

Designer: U.C. Press Staff
Compositor: Prestige Typography
Text: 10/12 Times Roman
Display: Times Roman
Printer: Vail-Ballou
Binder: Vail-Ballou